The shotgun would have been no use without its cartridges. Much has already been written about the histories of shotguns but very little about the cartridges. This book should help in rectifying this situation.

Alphabetically recorded are many firms and their cartridges of the British Isles, which also includes the Republic of Ireland. These range in time from the first years in breech loadings up until the mid 1950s. It covers the time when most shotgun cartridges were closed by rolled-turnover and an over-shot wad.

It is a history of the cartridge and is well illustrated, bringing back nostalgia to many older shooting folk. It is also a history of the loading activities that once were common place in many towns and cities across the British Isles.

No shooter should be without this book on his bookshelf and to the collector of old cartridges it is a must.

Cartridges of the British Isles

Great Great Granfer's Shotgun Fodder

by

Ken J. Rutterford

Published 2006 by arima publishing

www.arimapublishing.com

ISBN 1-84549-111-4

© Ken J. Rutterford 2006

All rights reserved

This book is copyright. Subject to statutory exception and to provisions of relevant collective licensing agreements, no part of this publication may be reproduced, stored in a retrieval system, or transmitted in any form or by any means, without the prior written permission of the author.

Printed and bound in the United Kingdom

This book is sold subject to the conditions that it shall not, by way of trade or otherwise, be lent, re-sold, hired out, or otherwise circulated without the publisher's prior consent in any form of binding or cover other than that which it is published and without a similar condition including this condition being imposed on the subsequent purchaser.

arima publishing
ASK House, Northgate Avenue
Bury St Edmunds, Suffolk IP32 6BB
t: (+44) 01284 700321

www.arimapublishing.com

Dedication

This book is dedicated to my wife, Daphne, for the support she has given me. Also for the patience and endurance she has shown in allowing me to follow my hobby of searching out cartridges and drawing the many illustrations.

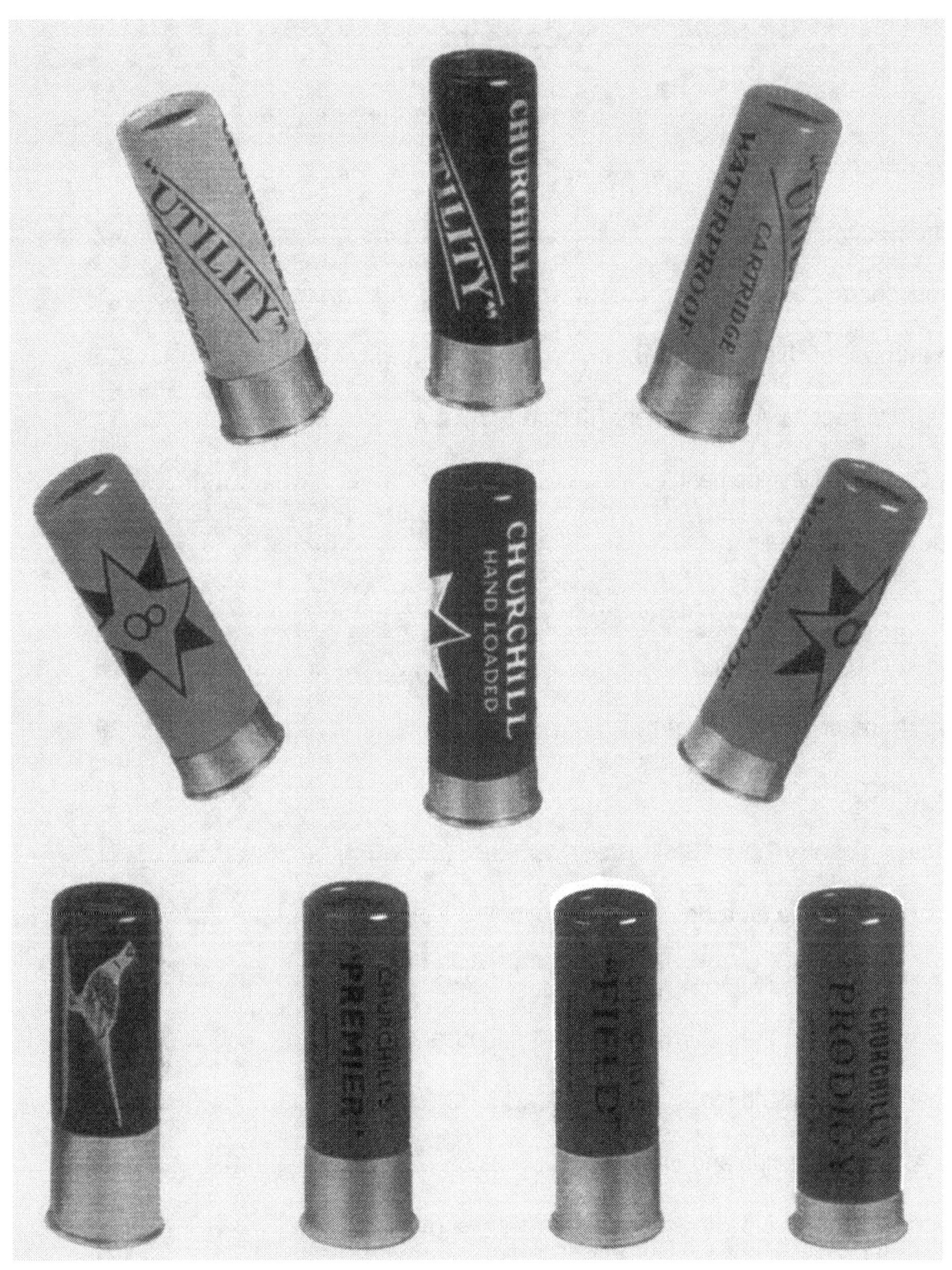

Churchill's Cartridges.
Cartridges of a London gunmaker, circa 1933.

Contents

Dedication 3

Churchill's Cartridges 5

Acknowledgments 7

Introduction 8

The Purpose of this Book 10

Letter (Harrods) & Advertisement (Kent & Son) 11

The Cartridge Development 12

Made in Great Britain 15

Letterhead (James & Co.) 17

Loaded in the British Isles 18

Advertisement (W. J. George) 19

Eley Wire Cartridge Leaflets & Two Cartridges From Hampshire 20

A Typical Country Town (Basingstoke) 21

Explanation of the Cartridge List and Illustrated Plates 23

Captain Robert Scott's Cartridges 25

Known Firms and Their Cartridges (In Alphabetical Order) 27

A Few of the Unidentified 151

The A. & E. (Addenda and Erratum) 152

Advertisement for Eley Rocket Tracer Cartridges (circa 1934)
& Typical Cartridge Box Label (Thos. Turner & Sons Ltd, "Fillbag") 154

Typical Gauge (Bore) Sizes 155

The Illustrated Plates (A1 to T2) 157

Index of Firms 333

Acknowledgments

This book has been compiled with thanks to the help of so many individual persons over very many years. There were those kind people that have taken the time to stop what they were doing and relate to me about what their firms had done many years ago. Then there are librarians that have assisted me in gleaning the enormous amount of information on these many old has-been firms. These librarians were from many parts of the country. Not forgetting the numerous collectors who over the years have kindly let me have access to their prized collections. This to make many notes and to take sets of photographs. About five or six photographs to each set. Most of the drawings in this book could not have been made if it had not been for the photographs. A few of these collectors have taken photographs for me and then sent them to me through the post from places as far away as Australia.

There has been so many people that have helped me enormously in bringing this work to fruition that I am no longer able to remember them all by name. Now that I am in my middle seventies, regretfully my memory is now fast failing me. Because of this, I had at first decided not to mention any names. Since then, I have now had second thoughts. Several people have given me so much help that it is only right that I should mention their names. In so doing, then I must also mention others that spring to mind. I know that many kind people may have got left out. If you are one of these persons that I have failed to mention, then I here apologize to you. I here thank each and every one of you whether I have named you or not for the contributions that you have made towards this book.

Contributors remembered

G. Barrell; J. Blunt; J. Buchanan; R. C. Cameron; I. L. Carter; T. J. Carvell; B. Charlton; G. Crouch; D. Cullum; J. Gant; J. Glossop; C. Goodchild; F. R. Gordon; T. Grange; C. Hart; J. Haydock; E. Hughes; R. Jenkins; B. C. Johnson; B. Kemp; G. Klinect; J. F. Kuntz; C. Lewis; R. P. Long; J. Luttrell; P. F. McGowan; T. Matthews; K. Mitchell; A. J. Morris; M. O'Brien; E. Pinkney; W. Polden; G. Purslow; A. Richardson; J. R. Russell; R. A. Rutterford; N. Sharp; G. Shawcross; M. Snell; I. D. Southgate; R. W. Stadt; R. Thorne; M. Trapaud; J. Van-Vliet; G. Vella; D. J. Walrond; T. Warnock; R. Wastie; M. Woolhead; R. Wright; A. Yeates; D. G. Yelland; W. Young.

Known contributors who are no longer with us

D. Andrew; G. Boothroyd; T. Claridge; D. Fleet; A. Francis; P. Harvey; D. J. Hedlund; G. Parker; D. Stegall; C. Twyman; E. Wastie.

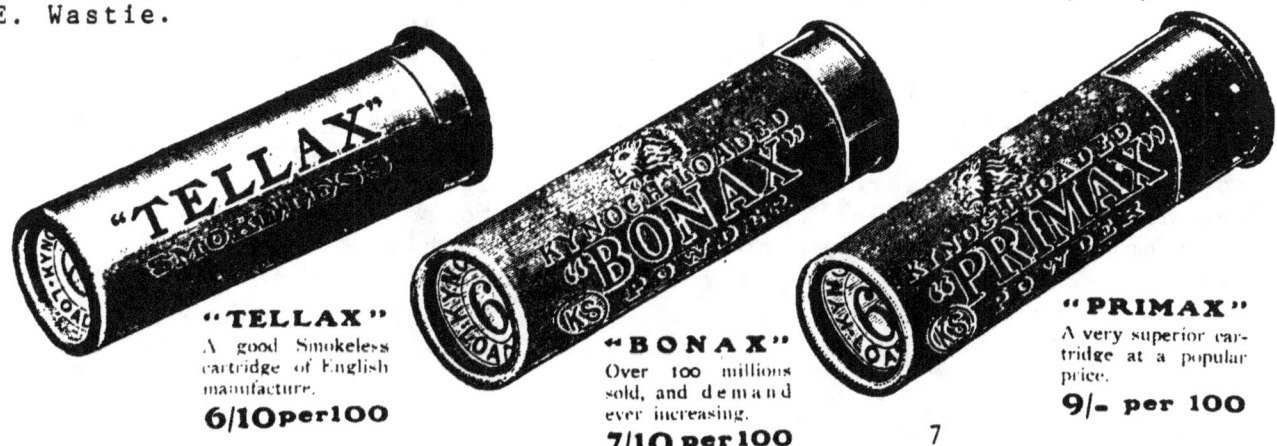

"TELLAX" A good Smokeless cartridge of English manufacture. **6/10 per 100**

"BONAX" Over 100 millions sold, and demand ever increasing. **7/10 per 100**

"PRIMAX" A very superior cartridge at a popular price. **9/- per 100**

Introduction

Ever since I was a child I have been attracted to shotgun cartridges. Throughout the many years that have come and gone, I had built up for myself several small collections of them. Now that I am in my seventies, my interests in these old cartridges and those firms that sold them is still as strong as ever. Once a person has been bitten by the cartridge collecting bug there is no known cure. Well if there is, I have yet still to find it. All the same, it is a most interesting and rewarding hobby. Through this hobby, I have made many friends in far off countries and have travelled to Australia and the U.S.A. where I got to meet some of them. I have also had overseas collectors visit me at home in England. Yes, it is a world-wide hobby and I hold no regrets from having acquired this interest in shotgun cartridges.

I was born deep down in some Hampshire woodlands and I am the eldest of two sons from a gamekeeping family. I did say acquired this interest, as spent cartridge cases became my toy building blocks. Oh yes, I was given those wooden squared building blocks with coloured paper pictures stuck on their sides, but these I soon discarded for my old cardboard shoe box that held those colourful brass and paper cartridge cases. Many of which still contained that fine aroma from the residue of the burnt gunpowders. As a toddler, and later when a schoolboy, it was then that I made my very first small collections of them. These collections of used cases were eventually disposed of by my parents. I just wish that I still had some of them today.

The first six years of my life were spent in that Hampshire dwelling down in Sarson Wood where the general public seldom ventured. The woodland tracks that led to the keepers bungalow were often so mudded which made it almost impossible for the local tradesmen to be able to deliver items to our home. During the winter months one needed wellies' in order to reach the graveled lane which then led to the metalled highway. Of course one could wear galoshes over one's shoes providing you were careful not to sink in below ankle depth. Once on the highway, there was a bus service into Andover. My memories of shopping in Andover were climbing up the high steps into Mr Chamberlain's corner gunshop where my mother would buy my father cartridges for his pigeon shooting. Just inside the entrance to the woodlands was a wooden box cupboard that stood on four stakes. Once every week my mother wood push, or rather drag the pram to that boxed cupboard to collect the groceries. Conditions like this would not be tolerated today. In the 1920's and the 1930's the crime rate was low. A keeper could safely keep his guns in the corner of the living room and have no need to keep his home locked.

For those first few years in my life I had no playmates. All the same, I was quite happy. I grew up to love the solitude and the beauty of these woodlands with the primroses and the constant bird songs. Come each shooting season, the gentry would stand to the front of our home with their pairs of guns and their loaders. Often with royalty amoung them. The general public would not venture down there, but the well-to-do did. After the shooting was over, the ground would be littered with spent cartridge cases. As soon as the guns had moved on, I was then allowed out to replenish my box with fresh cartridge cases. My parents left Hampshire to live in Berkshire when I was just six years old and it was then that I started my schooling.

I broke the chain by not becoming a gamekeeper. My schooling ended when I reached the age of fourteen. This was during the early war years when England had it's back to the wall. Keepering was discontinued and my parents persuaded me to take up factory work and help in the manufacturing of war materials. I had left a village school that had been absolutely swamped out with many London evacuees. In those days there were no such things as 'O' levels, but I did receive a very good education although it was only at a village school. At the age of eighteen, I did my stint in the R.A.F. where I ended up working on Merlin engined Spitfires. After this it was back to factory life, but I failed to settle down. I yearned for an outdoor life. I eventually found this with G.P.O. Telephones.

For the next thirty years I climbed telephone poles and most of this work took me out into the countryside. From the tops of these poles and with my head often up among the leaves on the trees I would be belted up so that I could work by using both hands. It was from these lofty perches that I could enjoy the wildlife and all that the countryside had to offer. Come weekends when I was not required to work on the telephones, and depending on the time of the year, much of my leisure time was used in pigeon shooting. During the shooting seasons it would be beating up pheasants. Beating gave me the opportunitys to enjoy lots of beautiful woodlands over several large country estates. I had got to know my area from the roads, now I got to know it from the private paths. Wrapped up warm and on the move was far more healthy than being belted up a pole catching the freezing winds. Hands got frozen as one could not work with wire with gloves on. Nevertheless, the springs, summers and autumns well and truly made up for the winters.

I will end this with an interesting little story. I was working on my own up a pole changing broken insulators when I spotted a row of gun-pegs. I walked this row of pegs to see how much shooting had taken place and to see if I could find any cartridge cases that were new to me. I picked up one paper tubed case that had got soaked through. In those days we were issued with Primus stoves. Lunch time, I made myself a warm cuppa' and in the back of my travelling tool store, I placed a flattend-out galvanized metal pole roof over the top of the lit Primus stove. This way it spread the heat out into the rear of my vehicle. I then placed my wet cartridge case on the corner of this metal plate to dry out. Huddled up close to the stove for warmth, I had my head deep in a book when there was an almighty bang. My first thought was that the sove had exploded. No, it was still burning away giving out it's heat. Steam pressure had built up below the paper base-wad in that sodden cartridge case. It had blown the tube complete with base-wad out of the metal head. And that is how you can get a second bang out of a used cartridge case.

The Purpose of this Book

It was towards the end of 1984 that I was forced to take my retirement from British Telecom, or BT for short, which my employer had now become. My wife and I started this retirement with a vacation to Australia where we stayed at the home of a pen-friend and his wife. I had got to know our hosts through exchanging cartridge cases over many years. Having returned home to Pomyland, I looked around for something to occupy my continuous leisure time. It was then that I decided to write a book. This I had published. It's title was, 'Collecting Shotgun Cartridges'. My book became the first of it's kind on this subject. At that time I was most overjoyed in getting it published, but I was never to be happy with the final end product. Much of what I had written had been left out and the publishers had stayed strictly to the collecting side only. The result of this was that the book became only half as thick as what they said it would be when we first sat around a table. I myself considered it to have been well over priced. Worst still, it contained many mistakes with vital references left out. Yes, some of the mistakes were of my own making, but not all. Like this book, I had relied heavily on what many people had told me. Some of these had been very elderly gentlemen who had kindly given me some of their precious time. I was later to find out that some of their facts were not as correct as what I had taken them to be. Much to my surprise, this book is still very much sought after and it's price has since doubled.

Since that book I have longed to do better. I tried, but then came a world recession and that put a stopper on it. I have since come to realize that those people that collect old shotgun cartridges like to know what the printings were that decorated the case walls. This then got me making drawings of cartridges. So far, I have now drawn over two and a half thousand of them. The majority of them have been British, or have had British connections. I now included all the information of these cartridges within the frames of the drawings. This line of thinking was, any mistakes made would be entirely my own.

Drawing these became another hobby of mine. I was offered a good price and so I parted with my fine collection of old cartridges, though I later came to regret in doing so. It was adding fresh drawings to my growing collection of drawings that then became my present hobby. These drawings are now a history of the shotgun cartridge in their own right. So the purpose of this book is to place many of my drawings on record. Within this book I have used only those of the British Isles for I have made far too many drawings than to be able to use them all in one book. By publishing this book it should give many people the chance to enjoy them and so help in retaining a little bit more of our past.

By placing all of the information within the frames of the drawings had not been without problems. One of these was that I was often left with a lack of space. In making these drawings I have had to use photocopying machines. These have not always been precisely true with each other. Often things have gone a little out of square and some circles have developed a small amount of ovality. These problems I could not do much about. In this book I have done away with the squared frames and information that they contained. By doing this I have now been able to show many more of my drawings, Infact, nearly twice as many.

HARRODS
HARRODS LTD
KNIGHTSBRIDGE
LONDON SW1

Telephone Sloane 1234   Telegrams "Harrods London Telex"

21 Feb 63

K Rutherford Esq
11 White Gates
Wickham

Dear Sir

Thank you for your enquiry but unfortunately we do not have our own cartridge now. We only deal with Three Crowns and Grand Prix, and Remington in the future. The ones we used to stock were as follows:-

Hurlingham, Eley G. Tight Pegamoid, Primax, Curtis & Harvey's, Nobels Sporting Ballistite, Neonite "Red Star" Felixite. These were the cartridge we sold during 1914 and about that time.

Yours faithfully
Harrods Ltd.

MOE: 65.

One of many letters from which I gleaned information on old shotgun cartridges.

A typical ironmongers shop that once loaded cartridges.
Kent & Son sold The Cheap Cartridge and The Wantage Cartridge.

The Cartridge Development

Breech-loading guns date back to the mid-nineteenth century. Shotgun ammunition was developed along side and on similar lines as the metallic rifle, pistol and machinegun ammunition. In this book it is only the ammunition relating to shotguns that is being dealt with. Not in their ballistics, but by their brand names and those firms that produced them.

All present day cartridges are what are classified as centre fire cartridges. These cartridges can trace their roots back to the begining of breech-loading. Also stemming from those early beginings were the pinfire cartridges. Over a period of time which lasted about fifty years, the pinfire guns gradually declined and the centre-fire became the excepted for all sporting purposes. The last of the British pinfire cartridges were manufactured only in 16 and 12 gauge during the 1930's. Apart from the two methods of fire just mentioned, there were two other odd kinds of detonation. They were the needle-fire and the battery-electric-fire, but neither of these were developed into fruition. That is as far as the shotgun was concerned.

The first major step towards the developing of breech-loading was the invention of the percussion cap. The Reverant J. Forsyth, a Scotsman, paved the way by using fulminate in cupped copper caps. These being used by placing over nipples on muzzle-loading guns. By the 1820's, sporting guns of this type were well established in Britain, although it took the government another twenty years before they decided to use this method of detonation in the armed services. Most of the credit in the developing of breech-loading must go to France. It was a Frenchman, Mr Lefaucheux who invented the pinfire gun and it's cartridge. This had drop down barrels from the breech. This cartridge was similar to the cartridges of today in as much as, when fired, the metal head expanded so sealing the breech of the gun from gas escapement. This system then became the one that has been adhered to ever since.

The pinfire cartridge is also a centrally fired cartridge because it's percussion cap is centrally placed. It differs from the known centre-fire by having a protruding hard brass pin which acted the same job as the striker pin in a modern gun. In a pinfire cartridge case, the centrally placed cap lays on it's side and inline with the striker pin. Nearly all shotgun pinfire cartridges had wound paper tubes. There were the few exceptions where a case was constructed entirely of brass. In the days when pinfire cartridges were first marketed it was very rare to find a customers name printed on the paper tube. The going method then was to stamp into the base of the brass head the customers name and place of business. Often in such a way as to apply the stamping as raised wording. The gauge size of the cartridge was usually placed in the centre of the stamping. If the customers name was not shown on the brass, then it could be printed on the over-shot wad. This top wad was also known as the over-shot card, or shot size card. You may call it what you will.

Pinfire guns and their cartridges were never that popular as they were somewhat clumsy. For the manufacturer they took longer to box up. For the user they posed some positive dangers. They were not recommended to have been carried in jacket pockets. A fall or a blow may have caused an explosion too close to the body for comfort. Not only that, but the protruding pins would play havoc with the pocket linings. Also much more care had to be taken when inserting the cartridge into the gun chamber. The pin on the cartridge had to be positioned into a slot on the end of the barrel prior to closing the gun. While loading, this could cause one to remove one's eyes from an advancing target. I was once told about one of these cartridges that had been accidentally dropped and exploded. Having landed on it's pin it had spun like a catherine wheel. As it was not in an enclosed chamber, no person was hurt.

Near on fifty years ago I was given a wooden box that contained fifty Eley-Kynoch I.C.I. 16 gauge pinfire cartridges. Like all pinfire cartridges that I have seen they were black powder loaded. This full box of cartridges were all loaded with number six shot. They were of the last of the British type made and having straw-white paper tubes with no printings. These Eleys' listed as being light brown and they were a product of the 1930's. Many a person has said to me that they had considered pinfire cartridges to have been very dangerous. On going back a few decades, I would send these old cartridges by rail. They had to be in a wooden box and marked, 'Not liable to explode in bulk'. I once received a wooden box of old rare cartridges from a collector who owned a gunshop. It had one of it's sides off showing a line of nails. Half of it's contents had been squashed and the outer layer of cartridges looked like a closed concertina. After that, when ever I sent a box of cartridges by rail I always added the extra wording, 'If handled with care'. I did not share many other peoples views on the dangers of pinfire cartridges and so I decided to find out for myself just how dangerous these cartridges could be. I then experimented with two of them from out of my box of fifty. I withdrew their factory loadings and then reloaded them again. This time I replaced the black powder with dry sand and so making them harmless. I then re-rolled their turnovers on a closing machine. I carried these two cartridges around with me for ages. They were shown to many shooters who had never seen a pinfire cartridge. On many occasions I purposely dropped them and threw them at the ground. In doing so it did upset some people. Their pins never shifted and their caps never exploded. Finally, through wear and tear, and with doing no good for my pockets, they fell to pieces on their own accord. It is true that they were the youngest of their species, but my little experiment gave me a lot more confidence when handling these kind of cartridges.

Many of the last of these being made were loaded up as black powder blanks. These were used in alarm guns. A gamekeeper once gave me one of these guns. I was given it as it still contained a row of very old swollen cartridges. Although it was called an alarm gun, it had no barrels. It was a large and heavy galvanized metal box. It was worked by winding up a clockwork motor. This allowed metal rods to be dropped down at set intervals on to the pins of a row of these cartridges. A metal boxed cover then enclosed all the works and the cartridges thus protecting the inside from the weather. This cover was fitted with a carrying handle. Infact, it was more of a bird scarer than a gun.

Returning back to the subject in question, once again credit must be given to another Frenchman. It was in 1853 that Mr Bellford took out a patent for a central fired cartridge. Then Mr Lancaster in England took up his patent, but made little success from it. Then two years later, Mr Pottet who was another Frenchman, took out further patents and so made modifications to this same cartridge. Mr George H. Daw of London, England, also patented a central fire cartridge on what we might now call, modern lines. It was while this cartridge was undergoing it's final development that a lengthy and most complicated lawsuit took place between Mr Daw and Messrs Eley Brothers who were also in London. It was Messrs Eley Brothers who came out on top, but how different British cartridge manufacture might have become had this case had swung in the other direction.

Another kind of cartridge which was first produced for use in muzzle loading guns and then later was adapted for loading into shotgun cartridges were the Eley Wire Cartridges. Marketed by Messrs Eley Brothers, Ltd, they were constructed from a thin wire mesh which formed a wire cage that held the shot load. The whole caged cartridge then being covered by a thin printed paper outer skin. They were made in several sizes and contained no explosives but soft bone dust was packed between the shot. These cartridges for loading into cartridge cases were known as The Royal Cartridge, The Green Cartridge and The Universal Cartridge which did not contain any wire. Each finnished cartridge was then given an outer white paper wrapper. Their purpose was to increase the range and hitting power.

When ejecting guns were introduced on the market, gunmakers recommended that the best quality half brass and full length brass cartridges be used in them. These full length brass cartridges then became commonly known as Ejectors. Most of them had wound inner paper tubes and having outer brass extensions. Some others such as Kynoch Patent were constructed with no inner paper tubes. A few of the first of these high brass cartridge cases had their upper extensions constructed from diagonally wrapped thin brass. These were refered to as of Boxer construction. This name being derived from a Colonel Boxer.

With the introduction of breech-loading, it took several years before barrel sizes became standardised. In other words, the gauge or bore of a gun. In the early days there were some very odd sizes. Numbers 11 and 15 to name just two. These did not last all that long. Due to this, cartridges of these sizes are now very rare and can fetch very high prices. Later on, Cogswell & Harrison, Ltd, tried to be clever and they marketed a $14\frac{3}{4}$ bore gun, but it did them no good at all. Of the few of these guns that were made, most of them had to be returned to have their gauges altered. Apart from three very small garden gun sizes, the early gauge sizes went as follows: .360, .410, 32, 28, 24, 20, 18 being rare, 16, 14, 12, 10, 8, 4 and 2 which was also rare. There were also several very large sizes that were made for punt guns and pyrotechnic flares etc. Later on, many of these sizes were to gradually disappear from the market. Eventually the range of sizes got whittled down to; .410, 28, 20, 16, 12, 10 and 8. The next to go was 8 with the most popular sizes becoming .410, 20 and 12.

Except for the .360 and the .410, the bore sizes of guns are arrived at as follows. To give an example we will discuss the 12 bore or 12 gauge. A mould that can cast twelve exact spherical lead balls to the pound was known as a twelve mould. The barrel of a gun that just one of these balls would exactly fit would then be known as a 12 bore or 12 gauge. The word 'gauge' being actually determined by the size of the cartridge case. All the same, those three words,'bore', 'gauge' and 'calibre' (caliber) have been indiscriminately used in describing the sizes of guns and their ammunition.

One word of warning, when out shooting never mix 20 and 12 gauge cartridges. A 20 cartridge slipped into a 12 barrel by mistake and then followed by a 12 cartridge would cause a most disastrous explosion.

Made in Great Britain

The first successful manufacturer of sporting cartridges in Great Britain were Eley Brothers, Ltd. They were a London firm and they manufactured their own cartridge cases. It is not now known when this large firm was first founded, but the firm of Eley was known to have been active as early as 1828. They obviously never made cartridge cases then as breech loading never came in until the middle of the 1850's. It's founder William Eley was tragically killed in his own laboratory by an explosion of mercury fulminate. It was his three sons that then carried on the family business which eventually became Eley Brothers, Ltd. They then had their premises in Gray's Inn Road, London WC. The first cartridge cases that they made were pinfires. This was then soon followed by centre-fire cartridges. Apart from making the cases, they also loaded them. They sold empty ready capped cases and also loaded cartridges. The cartridges were made in the following gauge sizes: .360, .410, 32, 28, 24, 20, 16, 14, 12, 10, 8, 4 and 2. Their early made cases had raised headstampings. From 1896 and onwards, their paper tubed cartridges were then wound with the same coloured paper throughout. Previous to this, most of their tubes had been wound with a brown paper and having just a coloured paper on the outer layers. Knowing this also helps one in dating old cartridges.

Eley Brothers were soon to receive some competition. One small firm, The Arms & Ammunition Manufacturing Co, Ltd that had addresses in London and Birmingham were known to have been in business in 1891. This firm was never much of a threat to Eley as they did not reign for long. Another early cartridge and cartridge case manufacturer was Frederick Joyce & Co, Ltd. They did find a share in the markets. Their cartridge cases were made to a high quality. During 1907, the Nobel Explosives Co, Ltd then gained complete control over their London factory for their own supply of cartridge cases.

Eley Brothers largest rival was to be the firm owned by George Kynoch. Later to become, G. Kynoch & Co, Ltd. Their history has been well documented in the book 'Kynoch' by Dale J. Hedlund and produced by Armory Publications. George first started working in the explosives trade when he took up employment with Pursall & Phillips who were manufacturing percussion caps for use with muzzle loading guns. Their factory was in Whittal Street in the heart of Birmingham's gunmaking trade area. In the October of 1859, this factory had a disastrous explosion that destroyed the firms premises and killed nineteen of their workforce. The good citizens of Birmingham were not too hapy at having this explosives firm in their midst and so it was that Pursall was granted permission to erect a powder magazine and build a percussion cap factory at Whitton which at that time was way outside the city's built up suburbia. Although very small, this new factory then started it's operations under the supervision of George Kynoch.

Eventually George took over this factory and it's business which was then situated on a four acre site. George soon had the business manufacturing both military and sporting ammunition. He made a lion's head his trade mark and called his factory 'The Lion Works'. These works kept on expanding and many other commoditys were produced. Some of these were soap, candles, bicycles and town gas engines.

By 1882, solid drawn brass bottle-necked cartridges were being made for the British Government. Come 1884, and George had converted his business into a limited company as, G. Kynoch & Co, Ltd. After this, things did not go well for George on the board of directors. In 1887, George was asked to resign from his own company. The firm of Kynoch then continued up and until the ending of the Great War, the war to end all wars and later to be known as World War One.

Many other large firms also sold their own brands of shotgun cartridges. Of these there were the gunpowder manufacturers who loaded cases while using their own powders. The Schultze Gunpowder Co, Ltd was just one such firm. Schultze were eventually acquired by Messrs Eley Brothers, Ltd in 1911. The town of Stowmarket in suffolk was home to The Explosives Company. This firm soon decided to change it's name to the E.C. Powder Co, Ltd. This because there had been so much confusion between them and other explosives type firms. They then marketed their E.C. brand gunpowder which they also loaded into their own brand cartridges. Later they changed their name again to the New Explosives Co, Ltd. They then sold cartridges that had brand names after their powders such as, Felixite, Primrose, Red Star, Shotgun Neonite and Stowmarket. The majority of these being loaded into Eley Brothers cases.

The Halls Powder Co sold their own cartridges. These were loaded with Cannonite. The firm of Curtis's & Harvey who were then famous for their Smokeless Diamond also marketed their own branded cartridges. Another firm that was active at around this time was Lucks Explosives, Ltd. They also were Stowmarket based and later had mills at Dartford in Kent. They also sold cartridges that were loaded by using their own gunpowders. Those that I have seen had yellow imported paper tubed cases that were made in Bavaria, now a part of Germany.

It was in 1909 that the Schultze Company formed an alliance with the gun and cartridge case manufacturers, Cogswell & Harrison, Ltd. In that October the name Cogschultze was registered to them. Cartridges were loaded using Schultze powders into Cogswell & Harrison's cases, but the coming world war soon put a stop to what had become an interesting enterprise.

During the 1914-18 war the many explosives trades firms had been working flat-out keeping our military forces supplied with ammunition. With the signing of the armistice, very large cuts would have had to have been made in their workforces. Prior to this, several of the explosives trades had joined forces with each other. To give an instance, Curtis's & Harvey, Ltd had already amalgamated with John Hall of Faversham in 1898. To avoid the severe competition with each other, these firms had held discussions. The result from all of this was one large merger. In November 1918, a brand new firm came into being called, Explosives Trades, Ltd. 'E.T.L.' for short. Seventeen firms then all joined forces. Some of their first shotgun cartridges that they produced carried the initials E.T.L. added to their headstampings.

This name, Explosives Trades caused some confusion with a few other firms and so a name change took place in 1920. The firm was then renamed, Nobel Industries, Ltd. This name not to be confused with the old explosives manufacturers, Nobel Explosives, Ltd. The initials N.I. were sometimes added to the headstampings. By this time, some forty firms had been engulfed into this large merger. The outcome was that all shotgun cartridges would then be manufactured from the Witton Factory. Altogether with all the powder mills and the shot manufacturing plants both here in the U.K. and abroad, Nobel Industries then owned over ninety factories.

After a while the manufacture of all sporting gunpowders was concentrated at the Scottish Ardeer Factory. Schultze being transfered in 1920, E.C. Powder in 1923 and Smokeless Diamond in 1934. Prior to this, most of the gunpowder mills had been quite small and situated way out from the built-up areas and in the countryside.

Many of the older firms names were to be seen right up until the Second World War printed on cartridge cases. Of the many brand names that were still retained were: Acme, Bonax, Clyde, Eley, Gastight, Grand Prix, Kynoch, Nobel, Noneka, Pegamoid (Name of the paper maker), Primax, Schultze and Zenith. A trade mark was registered to the firm of an active volcano. By knowing such items as this can be a help in dating some of the older cartridges. Headstampings were often ELEY NOBEL or KYNOCH NOBEL so honouring those names, Eley, Kynoch and Nobel.

In this world nothing ever seems to stay the same for long. In 1926, the large firm, Imperial Chemical Industries, Ltd gained the controling interest at Witton and from then on, most shotgun cartridges carried that famous wording, Made in Great Britain. If only this could be so today. I am still not sure as to which year that it was that the I.C.I. circle first made it's appearance on the headstampings. After the Second World war, the war that failed to end all wars, the production of shotgun cartridges returned to normality. Then in 1962 the Metal Division of I.C.I. was hived off into a separate public company. The Witton Factory then became, Imperial Metal Industries (Kynoch), Ltd. From then on the I.C.I. circle was removed from all the headstampings. In 1973 the Witton Factory was blasted by the big bang. It was it's worst explosion of it's long history. Six employees were killed and the whole factory was thrown out of action. After this the name Kynoch was dropped and all cartridges were just known as Eley. Later on still the firm became known as, Eley Hawk, but all of this later history is beyond the scope of this book.

A letter heading from James & Co, of Hungerford.
They sold cartridges called, Kennett Smokeless and Marlborough.

Loaded in the British Isles

Unloaded ready capped and printed cartridge cases were sold in their thousands here in England and abroad. These by the cartridge case manufacturers. They were purchased country wide by other smaller firms who then loaded them up and boxed them. They then sold their own brands of cartridges. The British cartridge case manufacturing firms have always had to endure strong competition from the many overseas case manufacturers. Those firms that loaded their own brands of cartridges were always looking for new ways of improving their profit margins. It was a tough old world. One of the ways that they could do this was to import less well made cases and their components from overseas markets. In the early days of breech loading, many cartridge cases of both pinfire and centre-fire got imported into the British Isles.

From around 1890 onwards, and up into the 1930's, was the heyday of town and city cartridge loadings. These loadings taking place in large citys and many of our country towns. Occasionally in a few villages as well. The kind of firms that sold their own cartridges were mostly in the gunmaking, gunsmithing and ironmonger trades. It was not unknown for garages and cycle dealers to do likewise. Especially if the owner of the firm was a keen shot. Many of these trades people had their fingers in more than one pie. Often in some of the small towns there would have been more than one firm that loaded up their own cartridges. Each firm then selling their own celebrated cartridge brands in strong competition. Not only with each other, but also with the competition that came from the large explosives firms who were also marketing their own brands that were being advertised and sold on a country wide basis.

Due to all of this competition, it is not that surprising that many a firm named a cartridge 'The Challenge'. This competition induced many a small firm to import some nasty cheap cartridge cases and components. At one time, things got that bad that Kynoch & Co when advertising their bottom of the range cartridges wrote in a 1910 advertisment, 'Tellax' Cartridges. Introduced to meet the competition of cheap foreign rubbish that has been sold in this country. The shooter who buys a cartridge at the lower price than this does so at the risk of losing his eye or fingers. To be fair to the overseas manufacturers, although rubbish had been imported into the British Isles, many of the cartridge cases and components were of superb quality. In a few cases, even better than some British. What one has to remember is that one usually got what one payed for. Remember, all of these firms were in business solely to make profits. While some firms only bought British made cases, others often dabbled in both British and foreign.

Apart from those firms which I have just mentioned, there were some firms that loaded up shotgun ammunition to sell to other country-wide spread firms that wished to sell their own cartridge brands. It was not every firm that decided to load their own. Prior to World War Two, Frank Dyke & Co, Ltd loaded cartridges for many. He imported German cartridge cases and components. Jas R. Watson & Co did likewise, only they obtained many of their cases and components from Belgium. Chas Hellis & Sons also loaded for the many and they used both foreign and British cases. Three other of these inbetween the wars firms were: The Midland Gun Co, The Mullerite Cartridge Works and the Trent Gun & Cartridge works. Having just mention these few, it is only fair to say that there were also a few other smaller firms that did likewise.

By the coming of Hitler's war, nearly all of these town loadings had fizzled out. Many shopkeepers were not that keen on knowing that their neighbours were using gunpowder on just the other side of their walls. I also expect that the insurance companies also took a hand in the ceasing of these town loadings. From then on, and by the late 1940's in the post war years, those firms that sold their own branded cartridges would obtain them ready loaded. This would have been done for them by the explosives manufacturing firms. Although nearly all of these shop loadings had ceased, there were still the odd one or two who still enjoyed selling their own loadings.

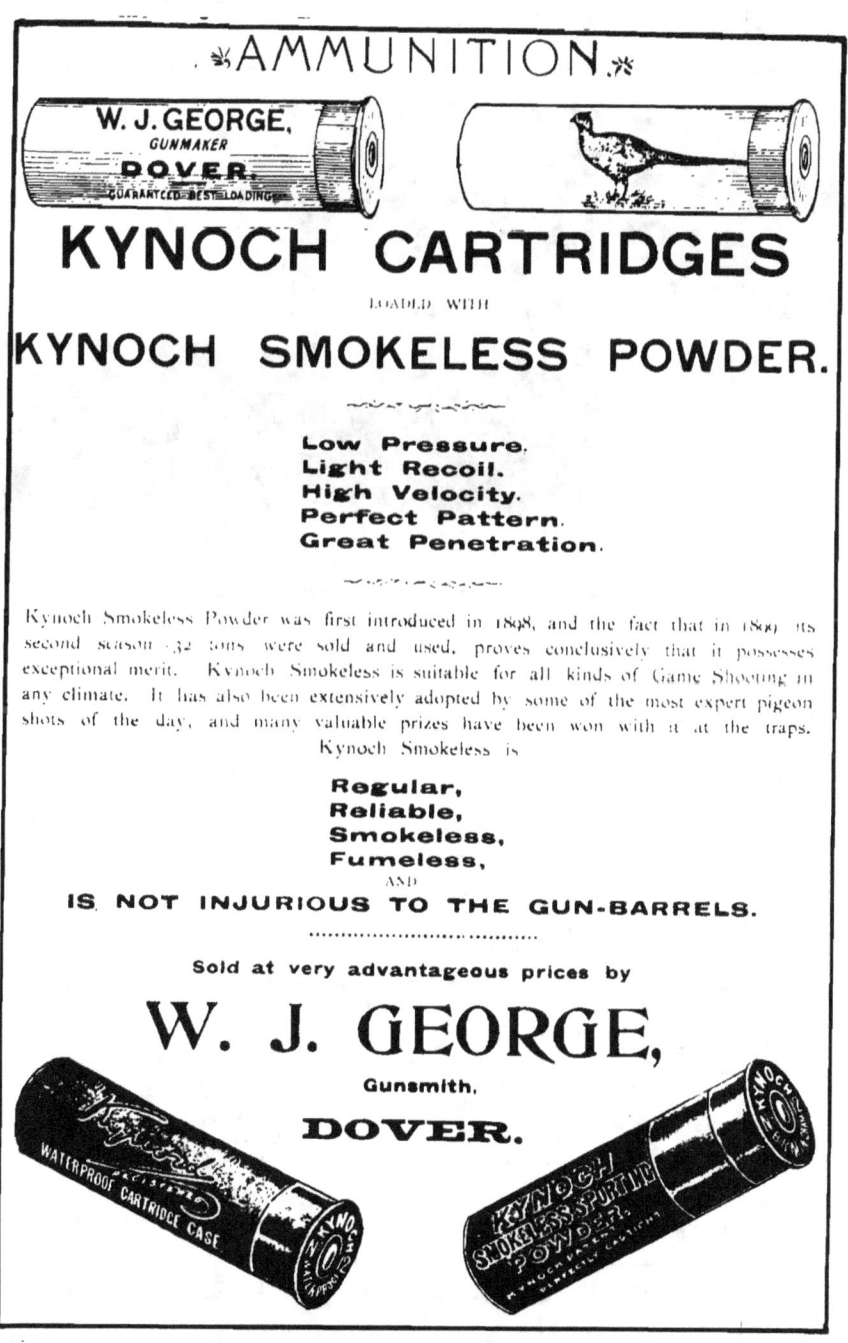

Note that the word GUNMAKER is printed on the cartridge while GUNSMITH is on the advert.

DIRECTIONS FOR USING
ELEY'S IMPROVED PATENT WIRE CARTRIDGES, and UNIVERSAL SHOT CARTRIDGES.

Charge with powder; then tear the outside case by means of the tape; place the cartridge in the barrel with its wadding uppermost, and ram it down smartly. It is not requisite to place a wadding between it and the powder.

To Draw the Cartridge. — Screw a wadding upon the worm of the ramrod to keep the rod in the centre of the barrel, and then screw firmly into the cartridge. If the wadding of the cartridge should tear off in the barrel, shake out the shot, and the empty case may be drawn or fired out.

The wadding attached to the cartridge is intended to fit the barrel tight; but the lower end of the cartridge should be quite easy in the barrel until expanded by the blow of the ramrod.

Should the cartridge be too loose, a wadding may be put upon it without injuring the shooting.

Should the cartridge be left in the second barrel during several discharges of the first, the same precaution is necessary as with a loose charge, namely, occasionally to try if the charge has risen while loading the other barrel.

The Outside White Case, which envelopes each cartridge, is intended to protect the cartridge from being broken or damaged when carried loose in the pocket. It should be stripped off before placing the cartridge in Eley's Patent Cartridge Case.

TWO CARTRIDGES FROM HAMPSHIRE

The above cartridge was from the gunshop where I was often taken when I was a mere toddler.

Below is a cartridge from one of the many firms which traded out of Basingstoke. Punter's phone number was Basingstoke 31. They were established in 1904.

The *ROYAL CARTRIDGE* is for general shooting, being equally adapted for long or moderate distances. It will be found an effective charge 15 yards from the gun, and continues to disperse its shot, strong and close, 30 yards further than a loose charge. It is intended for the second barrel at the commencement of the season.

The *GREEN CARTRIDGE* is only for very long shots, and should not be used except in open places.

The *UNIVERSAL SHOT CARTRIDGE* is intended for general use, or entirely to supersede the shot-pouch. It consists of shot packed between layers of soft bone-dust, without containing any wire. It will be found to cover as large a surface as the loose charge at the distance of five yards from the gun, and will put 25 per cent. more shot in a target at 40 yards, and with great additional force, possessing all the advantages and conveniences of the Wire Cartridge. — Made up in packets containing 6 doz. charges, price 4s., which will be found very little to exceed the price of the loose charge.

ELEY BROS. beg to inform Sportsmen that they have invented a perfectly *WATER-PROOF PERCUSSION CAP*, which they warrant to stand immersion in sea water for several days, and remain uninjured by change of climate for any period.

ELEY BROS., London.
MANUFACTURERS of every description of SPORTING AMMUNITION
(Gunpowder excepted).

Above and below, leaflets of wire cartridges.

A Typical Country Town

Over the years covered by this book, the amount of cartridge sales by the many firms of the British Isles has been extensive. In order to portray a little of the activitys that once took place I am now going to describe just one country town. For this I have chosen the small Hampshire town of Basingstoke. I have several reasons for choosing this town. The first one is because it was in my own locality. The second is that over the years it has had many more firms than most that sold shotgun cartridges. The third reason was being local, I have been able to give it considerably more research.

The Municipal Borough of Basingstoke maybe more well known by most people by it's two well known transport manufacturing firms. These were Thornycroft and Wallis & Steevens. The Thornycroft Steam Wagon Company enjoyed quite a success with their early wagons and in later years they became known as, John I. Thornycroft & Co. They vastly contributed to the many buses and lorries that served our transport needs during the times of war and peace. Wallis & Steevens also built steam engines. They supplied the British Empire, now Commonwealth, with many of their traction engines, steam wagons and road rollers. They also supplied to the home market. While these two firms were active in business, the town had other firms who were also very active. The ones that I will be discussing here are the ones which sold their own cartridges and often in strong competition with each other. In the mid 1950's, the period in time in which this book goes up to, Basingstoke then had a population of nineteen and a half thousand people. The period of which I am covering here is when it was a grand old market town with plenty of character. Since then, most of it has been knocked down and rebuilt as an overspill for Londoners. I now visualize it as just one more of these modern concrete jungles.

In the years leading up to the 1914-18 war, the town had several firms that bought in their cartridge cases and the components and then loaded up shotgun cartridges. These loading activitys were nearly always carried out in an upstair room above the main shop. These shops were often situated within the main shopping area of the town such as a market place. After the Great War, these town loadings gradually dwindled out. Firms would still continue to sell their own brands of cartridges, but these would then have been factory loaded for them by the larger manufacturers.

Through my research which includes collecting and metal detecting, I now know that there has been at least ten firms in Basingstoke that have had their names carried on shotgun cartridges. This has been extremely good going for such a small town. So now we will take a look at these firms in an alphabetical order.

Edwin Chamberlain occupied the gunmakers shop at 35 Wote Street. He also had his other shop at, 1 Bridge Street in Andover. J. C. Cording & Company were in later years to use these same premises as a field sports store. They then had their other shop at 86 Northbrook Street in Newbury. This firm also sold their own cartridges but they were crimped closed.

H. M. Julian, later as, Julian & Sons, had a hardware and cycle business in the town. I have been told that gunsmithing was also undertaken. They traded from premises at 3 and 4 Church Street. I did once own in my collection a cartridge from them. This I would date to have been circa, 1890.

T. M. Kingdon & Company who's address was 5 The Market Place was another ironmongers shop. I also once owned one of his cartridges, but his name was only on the headstamping.

At one time there was a gentleman trading in the town who was known as Ted Lewis. I have only ever seen one cartridge case of his that was printed, Lewis Basingstoke. Since then I have been told that there had been others. The one that I saw had a black paper tube which portrayed a running rabbit printed in silver. This unused cartridge case was last seen in a Cornish collection. Ted was known to have done gunsmithing in the town.

Another ironmonger was Chas Pinders and in 1898 he was trading from a shop in the Market Place. I have never seen a complete cartridge of his, but old brass heads have been metal detected that had his name stamped on them.

Arthur F. Punter was another ironmonger who ran his business from 46 Wote Street. In later years the proprietor of this firm was J. M. Emberton. In the late 1930's they sold a cartridge that was loaded for them called The Minimax. There had been previous versions of this cartridge. They also had their own version of Frank Dyke's Shamrock. This cartridge also had their name on it's case wall along with the wording, The Farmers Friend. I was once shown one of their old catalogues printed on yellow pages. It pictured a cartridge with a standing cock pheasant on it's tube. The stamping on the head was Punter.Basingstoke. Since then, old cartridge remains have been unearthed through metal detecting which carried this same stamping.

Temple & Co, Basingstoke. This was the stamping on a 12 gauge pinfire head that has recently been found by a metal detectorist. Information of this old firm I have found precisely nothing.

Thomas Turner & Sons, Ltd, this a firm which had started it's gunmaking business in Reading. It's shop was 35 Wote Street. Prior to being in Basingstoke, it had branched out to Newbury where they had taken over the gunmaking shop from a Mr Walker at 86 Northbrook Street. They then continued branching out by coming to Basingstoke. Here in August 1922, they took over the gunmakers shop from Edwin Chamberlain. This then left Edwin with only his Andover premises. They then traded in Basingstoke for many years in competition with others. One brand of cartridge that sold well from 35 Wote Street was their Grey Rapid. J. C. Cording & Company moved west from Piccadilly in London after the Second World war. They followed in Turner's footsteps by first taking over their Newbury shop and then branching south to Basingstoke by taking over their Wote Street shop.

Finally there was the large ironmongers firm of R. H. Wagstaff & Company. They had their premises at 16 New Street and at 22 Winchester Street. Wagstaff & Co are known to have been in business in 1898. They were to loose their Winchester Street premises when they were burnt down in The Great Fire of Basingstoke that had started in another shop on April 17th 1905. Due to too small sized water mains and ineficient horse drawn steam fire appliances, the fire soon got well out of hand by burning down and gutting other premises. In Wagstaff & Co, firemen had to manhandle kegs of gunpowder while bullets were exploding around them. One fire appliance was sent from Andover on a special train and another arrived at 8pm from Alton running on only half it's horse power, litterally. I have only seen the one cartridge case by Wagstaff & Co. It was called, A.1., and it now resides in a Hampshire collection.

Explanation of the Cartridge List and Illustrated Plates

Each entry in this list has been given a separate number. Placed below some of these entry numbers will be found two digit letter-numbers ie, A2. When these letter-numbers are shown, they refer to the numbering of the illustrated plates which can be found towards the rear of this book. Having then located the plates with the corresponding letter-numbers, all one needs to do then is to look for the entry numbers on the plates. If no letter-numbers are shown below an entry number, then no illustration has been drawn for that entry.

On researching this book, information has come in from many sources. When ever iv'e toured the country, I have often made for the reference libraries in the various counties. Old trade directories have given me access to dates and addresses. Most of these libraries do not hold complete sets of these old books and so I have only been able to arrive at potted histories. Another problem has been that these books are usually only kept in the large towns and citys. On tour, I use a camper van with a fitted high top. These large towns seldom cater for high top vehicles. I have had no chance in parking in a multi-storey car park and open car parks are often fitted at their entrance with height restriction barriers. Goal posts, but as I have not been able to score, I have had to drive back out of these towns with no chance of visiting their libraries. There has been times when I have followed parking signs only to arrive at them and find that they have restricted me. Often a row of cars following have made it very difficult in retracing my way back out. When will these councils ever learn ?

In those ages of long past, there was no such thing as a trades description act. Many so called gunmakers had never made a gun in their lives. They may have bought some in for resale and then stamped their names on them. Likewise, where I have shown under the heading Business the word Ironmonger, these firms were as stated. All the same, some of them could quite well have had more than one string to their bow. Additional trades such as gunsmith or sadler etc. In this book I have tried to show the firms by the way that they have described them-selves. Often I have taken the description from the printings on their cartridges. A gunmaker may also have made rifles and pistols, but on his cartridges he may just have refered to him-self as a gunmaker and so gunmaker I have shown.

Amoung the addresses that I have shown you will notice that those on the other side of the Irish Sea I have located them as being in Ireland. You may well ask, why not show England, Scotland and Wales. My reason for so doing is because the majority of road atlases do not show Ireland. It could save a person from searching through an atlas and not being able to find what he or she was looking for.

By listing information under the title Remarks can often help in the dating of old cartridges and it also gives a little history. It can be very difficult to date all old cartridges. A cartridge of say 1890, if it has been kept in good condition may look more recent than a cartridge of 1955 that has been kept in a poor condition. By studying some of the information given will help in narrowing down the age of a cartridge to a decade or so over this lengthy span of time.

You will see that on the drawings of the illustrated plates that I have wrote in colours. These colours that I have given are there for a rough guide only. To give an instance, I may have shown blue, then this colour would have been used. Not in all cases but in some, the cartridge shown may also have been produced in red or another colour. The lack of space has stopped me from showing more than the one colour. The colour shown refers only to the outer layer of the paper tube. Some cartridge tubes may have been wound from brown or white papers with the colours only on the outer layers. Others may have been wound with the same colour paper all the way through. Lack of space has not allowed me to show these tube constructions and there is no way that I can dabble into the ballistics of these old cartridges. They are far too precious than to pull to pieces in order to see what their innards were like.

Likewise I have not had the room to show the colours of the inks that were used in the printings. The majority of the printings were in black, but reds and blues have been used on some. Many dark cases such as purple or black had printings of gold, silver, yellow or white. Many people describe colours differently. Colours that have been given by some of the cartridge manufacturers are often nothing like those illustrated in brochures of the paint manufacturers. If they could not get it together, then what chance have I got. Most paper tube colours are what I would describe as dirty. This is due to the waterproofing which they had been given either by wax impregnation or coated with clear lacquered varnish.

Just a few notes on the colours that I have used on my drawings. In the early days, many cartridges had their tubes wound from a rough textured brown paper. This colour brown has always reminded me of a dried-out cowpat. Hence my use of the word, Cowpat. Nut brown is a brown with a reddish tinge as on a hazel nut. Many of the cartridge cases described by their makers as Eau-de-nil have often ranged from a blue-greenish-white to a dark greyish-green. What I have refered to as Spring green was circa 1938-9 when used with the headstamping ELEY-KYNOCH 12 I.C.I. 12. This then decided me to refer to the dark green as Winter green and a more middle green as a Summer green. As I have stated, these colours shown are just for a rough guide only.

All that I have written is what I have taken to be correct. Having relied heavily on so many other peoples information I will except that mistakes can or have been made. One purpose of this book was to place on record what is known before it all becomes lost to us for ever. Many of the firms that are listed would have produced more than the few brand names that are shown. New information will forever keep on filtering through. Metal detecting will continue to unearth more of our past. In fact, what has been placed in this book could well be only the tip of what was a very large iceberg.

This cartridge list has been compiled from many notes that I have made. These notes had been filed and some of them may have been recorded near on fifty years ago. Unfortunately in those early days of making my notes I did not always write down the brand names. This is the reason that in some instances I have used the wording, Unnamed or name not recorded. Where a cartridge has been seen that carried no brand name I have used the word, Unnamed. High brass cartridges whether with an inner paper tube or not were the best quality in their day and were recommended for using in ejecting guns. These are shown in this cartridge list by the word, Ejector.

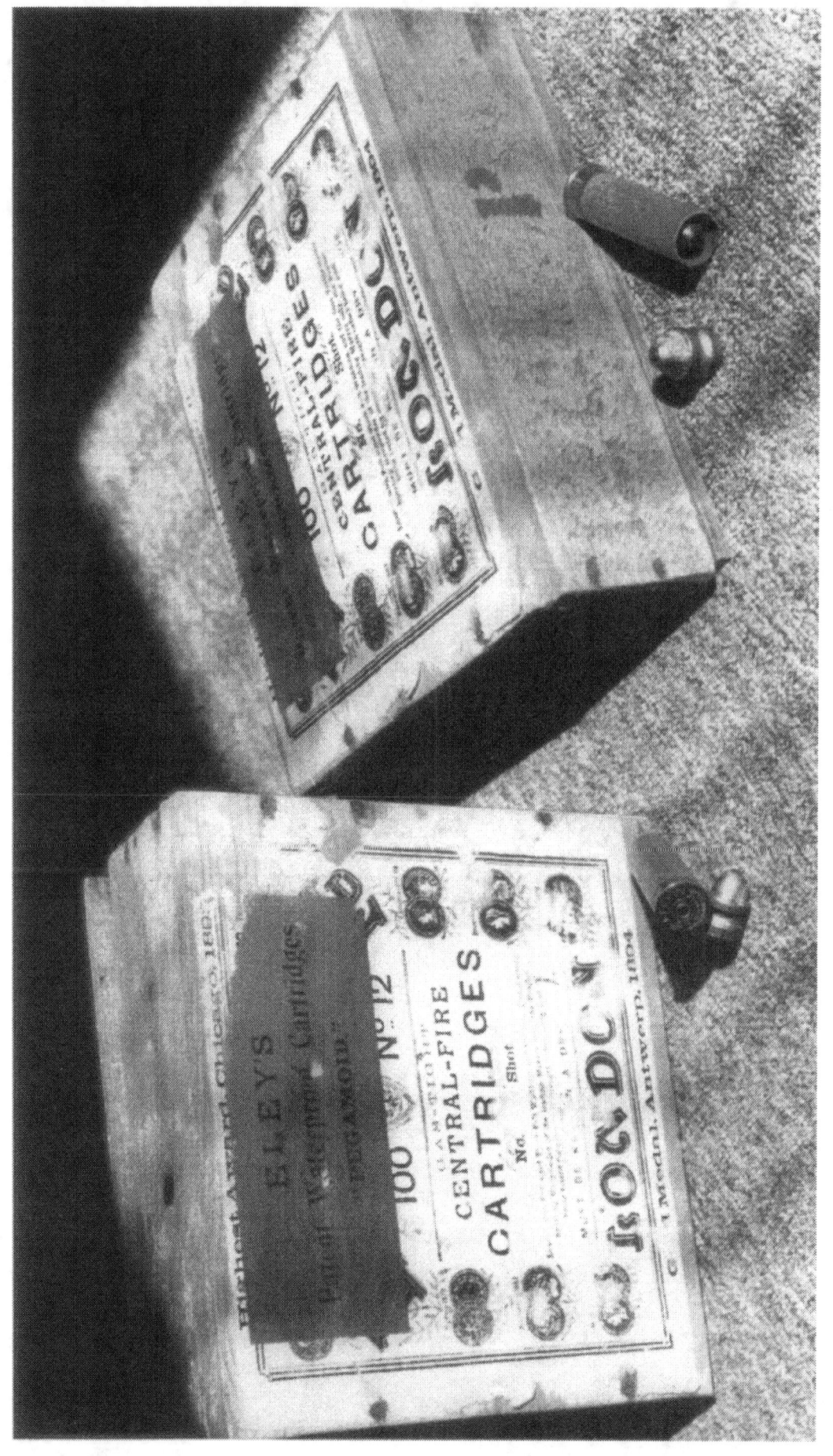

Actually one box of cartridges. Two photographs superimposed.
A box of cartridges left at the South Pole in 1912 by Captain Robert Scott, which he found no use for.

Known Firms and Their Cartridges (In Alphabetical Order)

1. **ACCLES ARMS, AMMUNITION & MANUFACTURING CO:** Perry Bar,
A3 Birmingham, Warwicks (W. Midlands).
Business: Gun and cartridge makers.
Cartridges: Unnamed.
Remarks: This firm was founded at the time that Grenfell & Accles was terminated. The firm was active between 1896 and 1899. Their name has been seen on headstampings only. See number 403, Grenfell & Accles in this cartridge list.

2. **HENRY R. ADAMS:** 120 High Street, Crediton, Devon.
A2 **Business:** Ironmonger.
Cartridges: Yeo Vale.

3. **J. H. ADAMS & SONS:** Littleport, Cambs.
A1 **Business:** Ironmongers.
Cartridges: Eley Gas-tight Cartridge Case.

4. **ADAMS & CO:** Finsbury, Islington, London N4.
A1 **Remarks:** Their name has been seen on a headstamping from found cartridge remains.

5. **R. J. ADGEY:** 99 Peter's Hill, Belfast, Northern Ireland.
Cartridges: De Luxe; De Luxe Special; Favourite, Universal Metal Lined.

6. **ADGEY & MURPHY:** Belfast Northern Ireland.
A1 **Remarks:** Their name has been seen on a headstamping on old cartridge remains.

7. **HENRY ADKIN.** Later as, **H. ADKIN & SONS:** 57 High Street. Also
A1 at, Castle Road, Bedford, Beds.
A3 **Business:** Gunmakers.
Cartridges: 20 Gauge; Ajax; Demon; Reliance; Special Loading.

8. **T. ADSETT & SON:** 101 High Street. Later at, 90 High Street,
A1 Guildford, Surrey.
Business: Gunmakers.
Cartridges: Smokeless Cartridge.

9. **J. AGNEW:** 118 High Street, Colchester, Essex.
A3 **Cartridges:** Special Smokeless Gastight.

10. **AGNEW & SON:** 79 South Street, Exeter, Devon.
A1 **Business:** Gunmakers.
A3 **Cartridges:** The Devonia; Ejector; Exon Smokeless; ISCA; Special Smokeless.

11. **AGRICULTURAL EXECUTIVE COMMITTEE (A.E.C.):**
H7 **Remarks:** See number 488, H. M. Government of Great Britain in this cartridge list.

12. **M. AITKEN & SONS:** Crieff, Perthshire.
A1 **Cartridges:** Kynoch's Ejector.

13. **H. ESAU AKRILL:** 18 Market Place, Beverley, Yorks (Humberside).
A3   **Business:** Gunmaker.
    Cartridges: The Collector; The County; The Holderness; Pegamoid; The Special; The Universal.

14. **J. P. ALBRIGHT:** Crown Street, Diss, Norfolk.
    Cartridges: Kynoch's Ejector.

15. **E. ALDRIDGE:** Hyde Park Corner, Ipswich, Suffolk.
A3   **Cartridges:** The Anglian; The Crown; The Hyde Park.
A5

16. **ALEXANDER BROTHERS:** High Street, Fordingbridge, Hants.
A1   **Business:** Ironmongers and general stores.
A3   **Cartridges:** The Fordingbridge.

17. **ALEXANDER & DUNCAN:** The Lion Works, Leominster. Also at,
A3   Hereford, Herefs (H & W).
    Business: Constructional and agricultural engineers.
    Cartridges: Unnamed.

18. **ALEX ALLAN:** Dufftown, Banffs (Grampian).
    Cartridges: Unnamed.

19. **ARTHUR ALLAN, LTD:** 144 Trongate. Later at, 3 West Nile
A1   Street, Glasgow, Lanarks (Stathclyde).
A2   **Business:** First as ironmonger. Then as cutler. Later as
A4   gunmaker.
    Cartridges: Empire; Famous A.A.; The Imperial; Super A.A.; Three Star.
    Remarks: Allans' were established in 1863. They ceased trading in Trongate in 1925.

20. **ALPASS & BAKER:** Wiveliscombe, Somerset.
    Business: Ironmongers.
    Cartridges: Unnamed.
    Remarks: Their over-shot wad of white card with red printing has been seen loaded into an Eley Brothers plain case.

21. **ALTHAM & SON:** Penrith, Cumberland (Cumbria).
A2   **Cartridges:** Eley's Pegamoid.
A4

22. **JOHN ANDERSON & SON:** 52 Market Place, Malton, Yorks.
A2   **Business:** Gun and cartridge manufacturers and sports dealers.
    Cartridges: The Derwent; The Eclipse; The Malton .410; The Rabbit.

23. **C. W. ANDREWS:** London. (Rest of the address is not known).
    Remarks: The name has been seen on a headstamping only.

24. **THOMAS WILLIAM ANNS:** London Street, Faringdon, Berks (Oxon).
A2   **Business:** Ironmonger.
    Cartridges: Eley's Gas-tight Case for Schultze Powder.

25. **APPS & SON:** East Cross, Tenterden, Kent.
    Business: Ironmongers.
    Remarks: An advertisment referred to their cartridges, etc.

26. **ARMS & AMMUNITION MANUFACTURING CO, LTD:** 140 Southwark Street, SE. Also at, 143 Queen Victoria Street, London EC.
    Business: Manufacturers.
    Remarks: Details of their cartridges are not known. The firm was incorporated into that of Jas R. Watson & Co, in 1904.

27. **ARMSTRONGS (SPORTING GUN DEPOT).** Also as, **ARMSTRONG & CO:**
    A5 10 Neville Street, Newcastle-upon-Tyne, Northumberland (Tyne &
    A7 Wear).
    Business: Sports stores.
    Cartridges: The A.C.C.; The 'C' Cartridge; Gastight; Preasure Reducing Case.
    Remarks: This firm may have had contacts with a firm called, The Breakable Wad Co.

28. **ARMY & NAVY CO-OPERATIVE SOCIETY, LTD.** Later changed to,
    A2 **ARMY & NAVY STORES, LTD:** 8 Howick Place, Westminster. Also
    A4 at, 105 Victoria Street, Westminster, London SW1.
    A7 **Business:** Department stores and gunmakers.
    Cartridges: The Coronation Cartridge; The Every Day Cartridge; The Every Day Nitro; Pegamoid; The Reliable; The Victoria.
    Remarks: They also had a branch in Bombay, India. Like many other large firms they listed and sold many other firms cartridges as well as their own.

29. **S. R. ARNOLD:** Louth, Lincs.
    A2 **Business:** Gunsmith.
    Cartridges: Express Special.

30. **HENRY ATKIN:** 18 Oxendon Street West. Was also at, 2 Jermyn
    A5 Street. Later at, 41 Jermyn Street. Later still at, 88 Jermyn
    A7 Street, London SW1.
    Business: Gunmaker.
    Cartridges: The Covert; Ejector; The Ever Ready; The Gem; The Jermyn; Pegamoid; The Raleigh.
    Remarks: The firms final business was conducted from, 27 St. James's Street, London. Now in the days of paper crimped closed cartridges it then joined forces with Grant & Lang. They then became, Atkin, Grant & Lang. See the next entry.

31. **ATKIN, GRANT & LANG:** 7 Bury Street, St. James's, London SW1.
    Business: Gunmakers.
    Cartridges: The Raleigh. (Other brands were closed by crimping).

32. **ATKINSON:** 31 Oxford Street, Swansea, Glamorgan.
    A5 **Business:** Gun dealers.
    Cartridges: The Grand Finale.

33. **T. ATKINSON.** Later became, **T. ATKINSON & SONS:** 19A Strickland
    A5 Gate, Kendal, Westmorland (Cumbria).
    A7 **Cartridges:** The Ajax; The Kendal Castle; The Kent; The Kentdal; The Reliable.

34. **WILLIAM ATKINSON.** Later as, **W. ATKINSON & SONS:** 20 Market
    A8 Street, Lancaster. Also at, Morcambe, Lancs and Kendal, Westmorland (Cumbria).
    Business: Gun and fishing tackle makers.

34. **WILLIAM ATKINSON:** Continued.
    Cartridges: Eley Grand Prix Case; Lancaster Castle Brand (Paradox slug or shot); Utility Smokeless.
    Remarks: This firm was known to have been at, 20 Market Street during 1886/87.

35. **ATKINSON & GRIFFIN:** Kendal, Westmorland (Cumbria).
    Cartridges: The Reliable.

36. **K. ATTRILL:** Pyle Street, Newport, Isle of Wight.
    Remarks: I was once informed that cartridges had been loaded at their premises.

37. **T. C. AUSTIN:** Ashford, Kent.
A6 **Business:** Gunmaker.
A8 **Cartridges:** Eley Case.
    Remarks: Several cartridges have been seen with Eley Brothers case wall printings plus extra printings. These in 12 and 16 gauge sizes.

38. **AUTOMATIC SHRAPNELL CO:** 36 George Street, Edinburgh, Lothian.
A6 **Business:** Manufacturer of John's Patent Shrapnell Shells.
    Remarks: These were made in several sizes and sold to other firms for loading into cartridge cases in place of the normal shot loads.

39. **AVERILL & SON:** Evesham, Worcs (H & W).
A6 **Cartridges:** Averill's Express.

40. **BACON & CURTIS, LTD:** 44 & 180 High Street, Poole, Dorset.
A6 Also at, 106 Christchurch Road, Bournemouth, Hants (Dorset).
    Business: Ironmongers, wholesale and retail.
    Remarks: Their name has been seen on over-shot wads. They were known to have been in business between 1907 and 1939 and could have been for much longer.

41. **BAGNALL & KIRKWOOD:** 31 Westgate Road, Newcastle-upon-Tyne,
A6 Northumberland (Tyne & Wear).
    Business: Gunmakers and fishing tackle experts.
    Cartridges: The Pointer; The Setter; The Tyne.

42. **E. BAILDHAM & SON:** Stratford-upon-Avon, Warwickshire.
    Business: Ironmonger.
    Cartridges: The Duck Fowler; The Extra; The Standard.

43. **CHARLES STUART BAILEY:** 8 Barnards Inn, Holborn, Middlesex (Great London). Also at, Waltham Abbey, Essex.
    Business: Inventor and possibly a cartridge manufacturer.
    Cartridges: Unnamed (F. Joyce case).
    Remarks: In 1882 he patented a gas-check for a central fire shotgun cartridge. An extra thin layer of brass covered over the primer cap. This patent was used by Frederick Joyce of F Joyce & Co, Ltd.

44. **W. R. BAILEY:** Congresbury, Somerset.
A6 **Business:** Ironmonger and agricultural dealer.
    Cartridges: The Somerset Velocity.

45. **C.T. BAKER, LTD:** Market Place & Norwich Road, Holt. Also at, Sheringham, Norfolk.
   Business: Ironmonger.
   Remarks: They once loaded and sold their own cartridges in strong competition with Joseph Baker & Son who were just along the road at Fakenham. There was no family connection between these two firms. As far as it is known, no cartridges by them have entered a collection. All of their remaining unloaded cartridge cases were handed into the police and were destroyed.

46. **F. T. BAKER:** 29 Glasshouse Street, Piccadilly Circus. Later
A9 at, 64 Haymarket Street, London SW.
   Business: Gun and rifle makers.
   Cartridges: Baker's Bakerite; Baker's Best; Ejector; Fred T. Baker's Vermin Smokeless.
   Remarks: Fred was known to have been active in Glasshouse Street in 1905 and in Haymarket Street in 1913.

47. **J. C. BAKER:** 48 Foregate Street, Worcester, Worcs (H & W).
A9 **Business:** Ironmonger.
   Cartridges: Baker's Special Bull's Eye Cartridge.

48. **JOSEPH BAKER & SON:** Market Place & Norwich Street, Fakenham,
A8 Norfolk.
A9 **Business:** Ironmongers and gunsmiths.
   Cartridges: Baker's Special; Union Jack; West Norfolk.

49. **J. T. BAKER:** 103 Victoria Road, Darlington, County Durham.
A9 **Business:** Gun and fishing tackle dealer.
   Cartridges: Sipe Smokeless.
   Remarks: The above cartridge was by L. E. Personne and it's Italian made case had the wordings, Baker Darlington on the case wall.

50. **SYDNEY W. BAKER.** Crowcombe Station, Somerset.
   Business: General merchant.
   Cartridges: S. W. Baker's Deadsure Special Smokeless Cartridge.

51. **W. E. BAKER.** Later as, **W. E. BAKER & CO:** 2 Bedford Square.
A8 Also at, North Street, Tavistock, Devon.
A9 **Business:** Ironmongers.
   Cartridges: Unnamed (Witton Brand case with W.E.BAKER on the headstamping).

52. **JAMES BALDWIN & SONS:** Morville Street, Birmingham. Also in Glasgow and London.
   Business: An 1896 advertisement illustrated their own name on a printed over-shot wad.

53. **FRANK A. BALES.** Later became, **GEORGE WILLIAM BALES:**
A8 15 Cornhill, Ipswich, Suffolk.
A9 **Business:** Gunmakers.
   Remarks: Pinfire cartridge heads have been found stamped F.A.BALES and G.W.BALES.

54. **BALLS:** Bungay, Suffolk.
   Remarks: Many years ago I was told that shotgun cartridges had been loaded on their premises.

55. **BALLS BROTHERS:** 64 Queen Street, Newton Abbot, Devon.
A9   **Business:** Ironmongers.
    Cartridges: Smokeless Cartridge.

56. **J. J. BALMFORTH:** Aughton Street, Ormskirk, Lancs.
    Business: Engineer and ironmonger.
    Cartridges: Balmforth's Special.

57. **HENRY BAMFORD & SONS:** Market Place, Uttoxeter, Staffs.
    Business: Ironmongers and agricultural dealers.
    Cartridges: Mow-em-down; The Plough.

58. **JAS GAY BANFIELD & SONS, LTD:** Tenbury Wells, Worcs (H & W).
A9   **Business:** Ironmongers.
    Cartridges: Unitro Cartridge Case.

59. **BAPTY & CO, LTD:** 703 Harrow Road, London E11.
A9   **Business:** Arms Retailers.
    Cartridges: Unnamed (American case, name on over-shot wad only).

60. **H. W. BARFORD & CO, LTD:** 14-16 Bishop Street, Coventry,
B1   Warwicks (W. Midlands).
    Cartridges: Special Imperial.

61. **H. BARHAM.** Later as, **C. H. BARHAM:** 95 Tilehouse Street,
B1   Hitchin, Herts.
    Business: Gunmakers.
    Cartridges: The Challenge; The Comet Cartridge; The Hert's Cartridge.

62. **BARKERS:** Corner House, Huddersfield, Yorks.
B1   **Cartridges:** The De Luxe.

63. **BARKER BROTHERS:** Grantham, Lincs.
B1   **Cartridges:** Mullerite Smokeless (Extra tube printing).

64. **BARNARD & LEVET:** Bird Street, Lichfield, Staffs.
B1   **Business:** Ironmongers.
B4   **Cartridges:** Unnamed.

65. **ALBERT BARNES:** Ulverston, Lancs (Cumbria).
B1   **Business:** Gunmaker.
    Cartridges: The Lonsdale; The Referendum.

66. **GEORGE JAS BARNES.** Later became, **G. J. BARNES & SON:**
A8   29 Church Street, Calne, Wilts.
B1   **Business:** Ironmongers.
    Cartridges: Kynoch's Perfectly Gas-tight Cartridge (Barnes name on headstamping only).
    Remarks: Trade directories have shown, G. J. Barnes in 1920. G. J. Barnes & Son in 1927.

67. **JOHN BARNES:** Burn's Statue Square, Ayr, Ayrs.
A8   **Business:** Gunmaker.
    Cartridges; The Challenger; The Chieftain.

68. **WILLIAM BARNES:** Market Place, Ashbourne, Derbys.
A8 **Business:** Ironmonger.
    Cartridges: Special Red.

69. **THOMAS WILLIAM BARNETT:** Sturminster Newton, Dorset.
    Business: Ironmonger.
    Cartridges: The Crown.

70. **BARNITT & CO:** Colliergate, York, Yorks.
B1 **Cartridges:** Barnitt's Special.

71. **H. BARNWELL & SONS, LTD:** Hartley Wintney, Hants.
B1 **Business:** Cartridge loader, cycle manufacturer and motor garage.
    Cartridges: The Hartley Special Smokeless.

72. **BARRATT:** Burton-upon-Trent, Staffs.
    Cartridges: Unnamed (Name on over-shot wad only).

73. **GEORGE T. BARTRAM:** 35 & 44 Bank Street, Braintree, Essex.
    Business: Gunmaker.
    Cartridges: Bartram's Hard Hitters.

74. **GEORGE JAS BASSETT:** 4 Swan Street, Petersfield, Hants.
B1 **Business:** Ironmonger.
    Cartridges: The Champion.
    Remarks: This firm was founded in 1927.

75. **GEORGE BATE (GUNMAKERS), LTD:** 132 Steelhouse Lane, Birmingham,
B1 Warwicks (W. Midlands).
    Business: Gunmakers.
    Cartridges: The Game; The Imperial; The Leader.
    Remarks: This firm was known to have been at the above address in 1908.

76. **A. BATES:** 22 Sun Street, Canterbury. Also at, Sturry &
B2 Whitstable, Kent.
B4 **Business:** Gunmaker.
    Cartridges: The Challenge; The Imperial Cartridge; The Rabbit.
    Remarks: A. Bates was known to have been active in 1910.

77. **A. T. BATES:** 3 St. George's Gate, Canterbury. Also at,
B2 Whitstable, Kent.
B4 **Business:** Gunmaker.
    Cartridges: The Canterbury; The Challenge.
    Remarks: There is obviously a connection between this and the last entry. As I do not know it, I have shown them separately. Another address that I have for them is 3 St. George's Street, Canterbury.

78. **E. R. BATES & SONS:** 3 George Gate. Also at, 71 Burgate Street, Canterbury, Kent.
    Cartridges: The Challenge.
    Remarks: It is almost certain that numbers 76, 77 and 78 in this list must have had some family connections.

79. **GEORGE BATES:** 126 Seaside Road, Eastbourne, Sussex.
B2 **Business:** Gunsmith.
Cartridges: The Eastbourne; The Mallard Gastight; The Reliable.

80. **EDWARD BAYS & CO:** 22 Wood Street, Swindon (Old Town), Wilts.
B2 **Business:** Ironmongers and general furnishing.
Cartridges: Unnamed.
Remarks: E. Bays was in business as an ironmonger in 1903. He was also at, Faringdon Street, Swindon. He was not shown there at that address in the trade directories for 1899.

81. **H. & S. BEARE:** 80 Queen Street, Newton Abbot, Devon.
B2 **Business:** Ironmongers.
Cartridges: The Sharpshooter; Smokeless Sharpshooters.

82. **BECK.** Later as, **BECK & CO:** 21 Angel Hill, Tiverton, Devon.
Business: Ironmongers.
Remarks: They were known to have loaded cartridges at the turn of the century (1899-1900).

83. **H. BECKWITH:** London. (Rest of the address is not known).
Remarks: A cartridge collector told me of a 15 gauge pinfire with the stamping, H. BECKWITH LONDON. An 1838 list of London gunmakers listed, Beckwith, W. Andrews at 58 Skinner Street, Snow Hill EC1.

84. **F. BEESLEY:** 2 St. James's Street, London SW.
B2 **Business:** Gunmaker.
B4 **Cartridges:** Kynoch's Grouse Ejector; Unnamed.

85. **A. J. BELCHER:** Market Place, Wantage, Berks (Oxon).
Business: Ironmonger.
Remarks: I have been told in their shop that many years ago cartridges were loaded on their premises.

86. **AUGUSTE EDOUARD LORADOUX BELLFORD:** 16 Castle Street, Holborn, London E6.
Business: Firearms inventor.
Remarks: It is just possible that he may at some time have had his name on shotgun cartridges.

87. **BELLOW & SON:** Leominster, Hereford & Bromyard, Herefs (H & W). Also at, Tenbury Wells, Worcs (H & W).
Cartridges: Mullerite Smokeless (Extra case wall printing); Special Cartridge.

88. **A. BENIGNO:** 12-14 High Street, Peebles, Peebleshire (Borders).
B2 **Business:** Retailer in guns and ammunition.
Cartridges: Unnamed.

89. **G. W. BENNETT:** Market Place, Bideford, Devon.
Business: Ironmonger.
Cartridges: The West Country.

90. **G. W. BENNETT:** Blackpool, Lancs.
B2 **Business:** Gunsmith.
Cartridges: Mullerite Red Seal; Mullerite Yellow Seal.
Remarks: The above cartridges had extra case wall printings.

91. **JOSEPH BENTLEY:** 309 Halifax Road, Liversedge, Yorks.
B4   **Business:** Cartridge loader and sales.
     Cartridges: The Croft.
     Remarks: Joe used Greenbat Powder loaded into Greenwood & Batley orange or crimson paper tubed cases. The closures were either rolled top or by crimping.

92. **S. W. BERRY:** Woodbridge, Suffolk.
     Cartridges: Unnamed.

93. **BEVAN:** (Address is not known).
     Cartridges: The Dreadnought.

94. **BEVAN & EVANS:** Abergavenny, Monmouthshire (Gwent).
     Cartridges: The Abergavenny Ace.

95. **BEVAN & PRITCHARD:** Abergavenny, Monmouthshire (Gwent).
     Cartridges: The Abergavenny Ace.
     Remarks: Obviously, the listing numbers 94 and 95 were of the same firm with a name change.

96. **G. & G. BISSET:** London. (Rest of the address is not known).
B4   **Cartridges:** Unnamed (Pinfire with the firm's name on the headstamping).

97. **J. BLACK:** Bollington, Near Macclesfield, Cheshire.
B4   **Business:** Gun dealer.
     Cartridges: The Bollin.

98. **C. G. BLACKADDER:** Castle Douglas, Kirkcudbright (D & G).
B4   **Cartridges:** The Black Douglas.

99. **J. BLAIN:** Carlisle, Cumberland (Cumbria).
     Business: Ironmonger.
     Cartridges: Unnamed or name not recorded.

100. **BLAKE BROTHERS:** Ross-on-Wye, Herefs (H & W).
     Business: Ironmongers.
     Cartridges: The Wye Valley.

101. **JAMES BLAKE:** 12 The Square, Kelso, Roxburghs (Borders).
B3   **Cartridges:** The Roxburgh; Roxburgh Special Smokeless.
B4

102. **J. BLANCH & SON:** 29 Gracechurch Street. Also at,
B3   4 Bishopgate Churchyard, London EC2.
     Business: Gunmakers.
     Cartridges: Ejector; Improved Gas-tight Cartridge charged with E.C. Powder.
     Remarks: Their business was later incorporated into the business of Alfred Davis. See number 247 in this cartridge list.

103. **THOMAS BLAND & SONS:** 430 West Strand. Later at, King
B3   William Street, London EC4.
B5   **Business:** Gunmakers.
     Cartridges: The 'B'; The 'Bee'; Pegamoid; Unnamed.

104. **RICHARD BLANTON:** Market Place; Ringwood, Hants.
B3   **Business:** Gunmaker.
B5   **Cartridges:** The Competitor; The Imperial.

105. **BLYTHE & WRIGHT:** Station Road, Sheringham, Norfolk.
Business: Ironmongers.
Remarks: This firm was known to have loaded cartridges many years ago.

106. **H. W. BOLE:** Kyrle Street, Hereford, Herefs (H & W).
B3   **Cartridges:** The Kyrle Cartridge.

107. **EDWARD BOND:** 25 White Hart Street, Thetford, Norfolk.
Business: Gun and rifle maker.
Remarks: It is most likely that he had his name on cartridges, circa 1925. Edward was known to have been trading from the above address between 1925 and 1929. As the old trade directories were not complete, this period of time could be stretched either way.

108. **G. E. BOND & SON:** 2 Castle Street, Thetford, Norfolk.
B3   **Business:** Gunmakers and cartridge loaders.
B4   **Cartridges:** Eley's Ejector; Gastight .410; The Invincible.
B5   **Remarks:** Trade directories have shown them to have been active at the above address between 1904 and 1916. This period of time could have been for much longer.

109. **J. S. BOREHAM:** Colchester, Essex.
B3   **Business:** Field sports dealer.
Cartridges: Excel Cartridge; Kynoch Witton Brand case (Boreham's name on the headstamping only).
Remarks: This firm terminated it's business in the late 1890's. The business was taken over by Radcliffe. See number 840 in this cartridge list.

110. **BOSS & CO, LTD:** 13 Dover Street. Later at, 41 Albemarle
B5   Street. Then at, 13-14 Cork Street, London W1.
B6   **Business:** Gunmakers and cartridge loaders.
B8   **Cartridges:** Ejector; High Velocity; Pegamoid; Regent; Special; Special High Velocity; Unnamed.
Remarks: Some of the unnamed were catalogued by their paper tube colours, ie, Brown Brand, Green Brand and Orange Brand. Post World War Two cartridges were a dark varnished pink. This firm turned a full circle by going back to 13 Dover Street and selling some paper tubed rolled top cartridges.

111. **CHARLES BOSWELL:** 126 The Strand. Later at, 15 Mill Street,
B6   Hanover Square, London W1.
B8   **Business:** Gun and rifle maker.
Cartridges: Kynoch's Grouse Ejector; Special Express; Unnamed.

112. **C. BOTWELL:** Bungay, Suffolk.
Cartridges: Unnamed.

113. **BOWDEN:** Chagford, Dartmoor, Devon.
Cartridges: Unnamed.

114. **JOHN BOWEN:** Carmarthen, Carm (Dyfed).
Cartridges: Myrddin.

115. **BOWERBANKS:** Penrith, Cumberland (Cumbria). Also at, Kirkby
B6 Stephen, Westmorland (Cumbria).
Cartridges: Sure Killer; Unnamed.

116. **BOZARD:** Later as, **BOZARD & CO:** 33 New Bond Street. Also at,
B6 4 Panton Street, Haymarket, London SW.
Remarks: Their name has been seen on over-shot wads.

117. **JOSEPH BRADDELL & SON, LTD:** Mayfair, Arthur Square, Belfast 1,
B6 Northern Ireland.
B8 **Business:** Gunmakers.
Cartridges: The Castle; De Luxe Special; Ejector; Eley Ejector;
The Empire; The J.B.; The Meteor; The Mors; The Special;
Special Gastight; The Victory.
Remarks: This firm was first established in 1811. A mid 1930's
catalogue listed their cartridges and also, F.N. All-Metal
HV, Nobel's Sporting Ballistite and a full range of the Eley
I.C.I. brands including pinfires.

118. **BRAND:** Edinburgh, Midlothian. Also at, Broxburn, West
Lothian.
Business: Cartridge loading with patent waddings.
Cartridges: Unnamed or name not recorded.

119. **BRIND GILLINGHAM:** Ock Street, Abingdon, Berks (Oxon).
Business: Ironmongers.
Remarks: I was once informed that they had loaded their own
cartridges.

120. **WILLIAM BRITT & SONS:** 21 South Street, Chesterfield, Derbys.
B9 **Business:** ironmongers.
Cartridges: The Sydenham Cartridge.
Remarks: The above cartridge was named after a large glass
dome. This firm was known to have been active as early as
1881. It fially closed it's doors during the mid-1980's.

121. **R. BROADHURST:** Smithford Street, Coventry, Warwicks
(W. Midlands).
Business: General ironmongery and furnishings.
Cartridges: Eley's Special Smokeless.

122. **S.BROADWAY & CO:** 84 Bridge Street, Worksop, Notts.
Cartridges; The Dukeries Smokeless.

123. **BROCKS EXPLOSIVES:** Hemel Hempstead, Herts.
Business: Pyrotechnic manufacturers.
Cartridges: Bird Scaring Cartridge (Ejected a humming star).

124. **JOHN BROMLEY & CO:** Bridgnorth, Newport, Shifnal & Wellington,
Salop.
Business: Ironmongers.
Cartridges: The Rabbit Special; Unnamed.

125. **BROOKER:** Hitchin, Herts.
B9 **Cartridges:** Unnamed (Name on over-shot wad only).

126. **E. J. BROWN & CO:** Rotherham, Yorks.
B6 **Cartridges:** Kynoch Perfectly Gas-tight.

127. **J. BROWN:** Morpeth, Northumberland.
B6 **Cartridges:** Smokeless Cartridge; Special Cartridge.
B9

128. **BROWN & MURRY:** Haddington, East Lothian.
Remarks: This firm has been seen on a headstamping on some cartridge remains found by metal detecting.

129. **F. BUCK:** Wincanton, Somerset.
B6 **Cartridges:** Eley Gastight Quality Case (Name on wad only).

130. **BUCK & CO:** 11-12 St. Andrew's Hill, London EC.
B7 **Business:** Arms and ammunition dealers.
Cartridges: Shamrock Brand.

131. **J. BUCKLAND.** Later as, **J. BUCKLAND & SONS:** Taunton, Somerset.
B7 **Cartridges:** Special Smokeless Cartridge.

132. **BUCKMASTER & WOOD:** 5 Market Place, Wokingham, Berks.
B9 **Business:** Ironmongers.
Cartridges: Unnamed.
Remarks: They were entered in trade directories for 1899 and 1903. A 1907 entery was shown as just Joseph Buckmaster at 5 and 7 Market Place.

133. **BUDGE:** Fore Street, Callington, Cornwall.
Business: Clockmakers and gun dealers.
Remarks: I was informed that it was quite possible that in the past they could have sold their own cartridges.

134. **JOHN BUDGEN & CO:** 49 & 51 High Street, Maidenhead, Berks.
B7 **Business:** Ironmongers.
Cartridges: Sudden Death Smokeless.

135. **J. U. BUGLER:** Ashford, Kent.
Business: Ironmonger and gunsmith.
Cartridges: The National.

136. **J. BULCOCK:** Burnley, Lancs.
Cartridges: Kynoch Ejector.

137. **BULLEN BROTHERS:** 32-33 Boscawen Street, Truro, Cornwall.
Business: Ironmongers.
Cartridges: Unnamed.

138. **GEORGE G. BULLMORE:** 1 St. George Road, Newquay. Also at, St.
B7 Columb, Cornwall.
Business: Ironmonger and agricultural merchant.
Cartridges: Unnamed.

139. **A. C. BULPIN:** Newton Abbot, Devon.
B7 **Cartridges:** Bulpin's Straight Shot Cartridge.

140. **R. H. BUNNER:** Montgomery, Montgomeryshire (Powys).
Business: Ironmonger.
Remarks: An old loading machine was at one time installed on their premises.

141. **W. BUNTING:** Cromford, Near Wirksworth, Derbys.
B7 **Cartridges:** Mullerite Green Seal (Extra tube printing);
B9 Mullerite Yellow Seal (Extra tube printing).

142. **FREDERICK H. BURGESS, LTD:** Eccleshall, Newcastle &
B7 Wolverhampton, Staffs. Also at, Newport & Shrewsbury, Salop.
Cartridges: Champion.

143. **WILLIAM BURGESS:** Malvern Wells, Worcs (H & W).
Business: Dealer in guns and game.
Cartridges: Unnamed pinfire (16 gauge with Burgess's name on the headstamping).

144. **JAMES BURROW:** 116 Fishergate, Preston, Lancs. Also at, 46
B9 Lowther Street, Carlisle, Cumberland (Cumbria).
C1 **Cartridges:** The Economic; The Challenge; Eley's Gastight Case (Extra case wall printing); The Field; The Paragon.

145. **BUSSEMS & PARKIN, LTD:** Mildehal, Suffolk.
C1 **Business:** Ironmongers.
Cartridges: Unnamed.

146. **GEORGE G. BUSSEY & CO:** London (Rest of the address is not
B9 known).
C1 **Cartridges:** Ejector.

147. **BUTCHER:** Watton, Norfolk.
Remarks: BUTCHER.WATTON. has been seen printed in red on a white over-shot wad.

148. **A. R. BUTLER:** Fore Street, Bampton. Also at, Tiverton, Devon.
Business: Cycle agent and ironmonger.
Cartridges: Butler's Japs; The Special; The Wensledale.

149. **BUYERS ASSOCIATION:** 72 Wigmore Street, London W.
Cartridges: Unnamed (Name on the headstamping).

150. **E. CALDER:** 67 King Street, Aberdeen, Aberdeenshire (Grampian).
Business: Gunmaker.
Cartridges: County Favourite.

151. **J. CALVERT:** Walsden, Near Todmorden, Yorks.
Cartridges: Eley Ejector (J.CALVERT.WALSDEN. on the headstamping).

152. **CAMBRIDGE & CO:** Carrickfergus, Northern Ireland.
S9? **Business:** Ironmongers and gun dealers.
Cartridges: The Antrim; The County Down; The Ulster.
Remarks: Their Antrim cartridge might just be the one illustrated on Plate S9.

153. **WILLIAM CAMERON.** Later as, **W. CAMERON & CO:** Ballymena, County Antrim, Northern Ireland.
Business: Gun and ammunition merchants.
Cartridges: The Cameronia; Cameron's Special.

154. **R. CAMPBELL & SONS:** Leyburn, Yorks.
B9
C1 **Cartridges:** The Special Cartridge; The Wensledale.

155. **RICHARD LOVAT CAPELL:** 47 Gold Street. Also at, The Cattle
C1 Market, Northampton, Northants.
Business: ironmonger.
Cartridges: The Capella.
Remarks: Capell was known to have been active between 1894 and 1924.

156. **CARR BROTHERS:** Cloth Hall Street, Huddersfield, Yorks.
C1 **Business:** Gunmakers.
Cartridges: Eley Ejector (Carr Bros on the headstamping).

157. **E. P. CARR & CO:** 4 Lower Parliament Street, Nottingham,
C1 Notts.
Business: Ironmongers and dealers in guns, revolvers and general arms.
Cartridges: Ejector; Unnamed.
Remarks: Established in 1828, this firm was known to have still been active in 1912.

158. **W. C. CARSWELL:** 4A Chapel Street, Liverpool, Lancs
B9 (Merseyside).
C2 **Business:** gunmaker.
Cartridges: The Banshee; Carswell's Special.

159. **CARTRIDGE SYNDICATE, LTD:** 20-23 Holborn, London EC1.
C2 **Business:** Cartridge sales.
C3 **Cartridges:** The London; Spartan; Spartan Deep Shell.
Remarks: Their cartridges were loaded by Trent Gun & Cartridge at Grimsby, Lincs. See number 1009 in this cartridge list. It is possible that these two firms were linked. Their name was not printed on the cartridges or their boxes. My information has been taken from some 1930's advertisments.

160. **F. G. CASSWELL:** Midsomer Norton, Radstock & Bath, Somerset (Avon).
Business: Ironmonger.
Cartridges: Unnamed.

161. **CAVERHILL:** Berwick (Believed to have been Berwick-upon-Tweed, Northumberland.
Remarks: The wording, CAVERHILL.BERWICK. has been seen printed on an over-shot wad.

162. **HERBERT CAWDRON:** The Butlands, Wells-Next-The-Sea, Norfolk.
C2 **Business:** Ammunition dealer.
Cartridges: The Holkham Cartridge.

163. **ARTHUR CHAMBERLAIN:** 18 Queen Street, Salisbury, Wilts.
C2   Was also at, Shepton Mallet, Somerset.
C3   **Business:** Gunmaker and cartridge loader.
Cartridges: The A.C. County; The A.C. Wiltshire; The Command; Ejector; Pegamoid; The Sarum; Smokeless .410; The Stonehenge; Unnamed; The Wessex.
Remarks: Arthur was known to have been active at 18 Queen Street way into the 1930's.

164. **EDWIN CHAMBERLAIN:** 1 Bridge Street, Andover. Also at, 35
C2   Wote Street, Basingstoke, Hants.
C3   **Business:** Gunmaker and cartridge loader.
C4   **Cartridges:** The Smokeless; The Universal; Unnamed.
Remarks: Many different cartridges by him were not given brand names. His Basingstoke premises were taken over by Thomas Turner & Sons in August 1922. See number 1021 in this cartridge list. From then on Edwin conducted all of his business from his Andover shop. Therefore any cartridge with Basingstoke marked on it must be prior to 1923.

165. **J. CHAMBERS & SON:** High Street (North), Dunstable, Beds.
C5   **Business:** Ironmongers.
Remarks: An old cartridge head of theirs has been found through metal detecting.

166. **R. CHAMBERS:** Bath, Somerset (Avon).
Remarks: This name has been seen printed on an over-shot wad.

167. **SEPTIMUS CHAMBERS:** 63 Broad Street, Bristol, Glos (Avon).
B9   Also at, 21 Castle Street, Cardiff, Glamorgan. And also at,
C5   Shepton Mallet, Somerset.
Business: Gunmaker.
Cartridges: Patent No, 15848 (Two coloured printings); Special Smokeless Kynoch Perfectly Gas-tight.

168. **B. E. CHAPLIN:** 6 Southgate Street, Winchester, Hants.
Business: Gunmaker.
Cartridges: Ideal; The Winton.
Remarks: Both H. A. Davis and Hammond Bros also loaded a cartridge called, The Winton. See numbers 245 and 420 in this cartridge list.

169. **W. CHAPPELL:** 57 Queen Street, Newton Abbot, Devon.
Business: Ironmonger.
Remarks: I was given information that this firm once sold their own cartridges.

170. **Mrs S. CHARLES:** 46 High Street, Stourport, Worcs (H & W).
Business: Ironmonger.
Cartridges: Unnamed or name not recorded (Headstamping was CHARLES No 12 WORCESTER.

171. **R. S. CHITTY:** 6 Lion Street, Chichester, Sussex.
C5   **Cartridges:** The Chichester Cross; The Pheasant; The Wonder.

172. **EDWIN J. CHURCHILL:** 8 Agar Street, The Strand. Later at,
C4 39-42 Leicester Square, London WC2.
C5 **Business:** Gunmaker and cartridge loader.
C7 **Cartridges:** 8-Points Cartridge; 8-Star; A.G. (Accuracy Guaranteed); Ejector; Express XXV; Churchill's 1935 Cartridge; The Field; The Imperial; Olympic Trapshooting Cartridge; The Pheasant; The Premier; The Prodigy; Special; Special Trapshooting Cartridge; Unnamed; Utility; The Waterproof Metal Lined.
Remarks: Churchill moved from Agar Street to Leicester Square in May 1925. Their premises were later shared with The Hercules Arms Co, Ltd. See number 471 in this cartridge list.

173. **CLAPHAM:** Wigton, Cumberland (Cumbria).
C6 **Remarks:** Several over-shot wads turned up with the printings CLAPHAM.WIGTON.

174. **CHARLES CLARKE:** 17 Winchester Street, Salisbury, Wilts.
C6 **Business:** Gunsmith.
Cartridges: The Original J.W.G.
Remarks: On some of his cartridges it was stated that he also had a premises in London.

175. **FRANK CLARKE:** Castle Street, Thetford, Norfolk.
C6 **Business:** Ironmonger, cycle agent and pram maker.
Cartridges: The Grafton; The Invincible.
Remarks: Frank was in business between 1904 and 1965. The gunmakers Bond in Thetford also loaded a cartridge called The Invincible. See number 108 in this cartridge list.

176. **HENRY CLARKE.** Later as, **H. CLARKE & SONS:** 37½ Gallowtree
C6 Gate. Also at, 20 Humberstone Gate, Leicester, Leics.
C7 **Business:** Gunmakers.
Cartridges: The Alma; The Express Cartridge; The Express Special Loading; The Midland Cartridge; Unnamed.
Remarks: This firm was established in 1832. The above addresses were taken from an 1881 trade directory.

177. **P. J. CLARKE:** Market Place & South Street, Bourne, Lincs.
C6 **Remarks:** Their name has been seen on a headstamping.

178. **CLARKE & DYKE:** Salisbury, Wilts. Also in, Southampton,
C6 Hants, and in London. (Addresses not known).
C7 **Business:** Gunsmiths.
C8 **Cartridges:** The J.W.G.; The Salisbury.

179. **CLATWORTHY.** Later as, **CLATWORTHY COOKE & CO:** Taunton,
C6 Somerset.
Business: Ironmongers.
Cartridges: Ejector; The Pheasant Cartridge.

180. **CLAYTON & SON:** Huntingdon & St. Neots, Hunts (Cambs).
C6 **Business:** Sports outfitters.
Cartridges: Special British Loaded Smokeless.

181. **CLEMENT:** Abingdon, Berks (Oxon).
Remarks: This name was given to me as a possible for having sold their own cartridges.

182. **THOMAS CLEMITSON:** Haydon Bridge, Northumberland.
Business: Ironmonger.
Cartridges: The Langley Castle.

183. **R. CLIMIE & SON:** Greenock, Renfrews (South Clyde).
C6 **Business:** Gunmakers.
Cartridges: Smokeless Cartridge; Special Cartridge.

184. **F. K. CLISBY:** Marlow, Bucks.
Business: Gunmaker and cartridge loading expert.
Cartridges: Special Loading.

185. **R. H. CLOUGH:** 14 Church Street, West Hartlepool, County
c9 Durham (Cleveland).
Cartridges: Unnamed.

186. **THOMAS CLOUGH.** Later as, **THOS CLOUGH & SON:** 52 High Street,
C6 King's Lynn, Norfolk.
Business: gunmakers.
Cartridges: The Sandringham; Unnamed.

187. **THE CLUB CARTRIDGE CO, LTD:** 2 Pickering Place, London SW.
C9 **Business:** Ammunition sales.
Cartridges: Clubs are Trumps.

188. **BELL GAVIN CLYDE:** Clyde House, 46 Windsor Terrace, Glasgow, Lanarkshire.
Remarks: He was known to have sold cartridges by Frank Dyke & Co and also Mullerite. It is possible that he may have had his name printed on some of them.

189. **J. H. COCK & CO:** Market Place, Cirencester, Gloucestershire.
C9 **Business:** Ironmongers and gunsmiths.
Cartridges: Unnamed.

190. **COGSCHULTZE AMMUNITION & POWDER CO, LTD:** London. (Rest of
C9 the address is not known).
Business: Cartridge loadings and sales.
Cartridges: The Bono; The Farmo; Gastight; The Molto; The Pluvoid; The Ranger; The Westro.
Remarks: This firm was founded in August 1911 with a capital of £10,000. It used for it's products, Cogswell & Harrison's cartridge cases and the Schultze Gunpowder Co's powders. See number 905 and number 191 below. This firm ran in business for atleast two years and it may have continued on into the 1914-18 War.

191. **COGSWELL & HARRISON, LTD:** 141 New Bond Street. Also at, The
C8 Strand. Later at, 168 Piccadilly, London W1. At one time it
C9 was also at, 94 Queen Street, Exeter, Devon. It also had a
D2 branch in Paris, France.
Business; Gun and cartridge makers.
Cartridges: The Ardit; The Avant-tout; The Blagdon; The Blagdonette; The Certus; Ejector; Exceltor; Gastight Cartridge Case; Kynoch's Grouse Ejector; The Huntic; The Kelor; The Konor; The Markor; The Markoride; The Midget; The New 14¾ Bore (Circa 1912); Nitro; Pegamoid; The Stelor; Swiftsure; Unnamed; The Victor; The Victor Universal; The Victoroid.

191. **COGSWELL & HARRISON, LTD:** Continued.
Remarks: This firm was founded by Benjamin Cogswell in 1770. The partnership with Edwin Harrison came in 1837. By 1877, the firm was known to have been in residence at 223-4 The Strand, London. In 1932 the firm became liquidated, but a new firm emerged in 1933. It then continued in business until 1982. Their zig-zag trade markings were registered to them in 1887. The firm was known to have been at, 141-2 New Bond Street during 1889.

192. **JOHN COLBY EVANS:** 4-5 Dark Gate, Carmarthen, Carmarthenshire (Dyfed).
Business: Ironmonger.
Cartridges: Unnamed.

193. **F. J. COLE, LTD:** 171 Cricklade Street. Later at, 26 Castle
D1 Street, Cirencester, Gloucestershire.
Business: Gunmaker.
Cartridges: The Castle; The Champion; The County Favourite.
Remarks: Circa 1910-14, Fraser J. Cole was listed in the local directories as being at, 171 Cricklade Street. As Cole Fraser Jnr, this firm was still in business at the start of the Second World War.

194. **COLE & SON:** Devizes & Chippenham, Wilts. Also at,
B9 Portsmouth, Hants. For a short period they were also at,
D1 Windsor, Berkshire.
Business: Gunmakers.
Cartridges: The Crown; The Crown Favourite; The Globe Cartridge; The King Cole; The Signature.
Remarks: Cartridges have been seen with the wordings, Devizes, Portsmouth & Chippenham. Also worded, Devizes, Portsmouth & Windsor. Due to this, I am not sure if the Chippenham and the Windsor branches may have been active at the same time. It has been listed that a Mr Frank Cole was trading in 1899 from 14 Market Place, Devizes. By 1903, it was Frank Cole & Son and they were then at 33 Market Place, Devizes. Also in 1903, a Mr John Cole was trading from the Market Place in Chippenham.

195. **JOHN COLLINS, LTD:** Drogheda, County Louth, Republic of Ireland.
Business: Caterers.
Remarks: I have been told that a cartridge has been seen by this firm.

196. **J. COLLIS, LTD:** Strood, Rochester & Gravesend, Kent.
D1 **Cartridges:** The All Round; The Famous Nullisecundus (also spelt as, Nulli Secundus).

197. **COLTMAN & CO:** The Cattle Market. Later at, 49 Station Street,
D1 Burton-upon-Trent, Staffs. Was also at, Uttoxeter, Staffs,
D3 and Ashbourne and Derby, Derbys.
Business: Gunmakers and cartridge loaders.
Cartridges: The Burton; Ejector; The Field; The K.C. (Keepers Cartridge) (Was also known as, The Staffordshire Knot); The Marvel .410; The Partridge; Pegamoid; The Pheasant; The Rabbit.

197. **COLTMAN & CO:** Continued.
Remarks: Two special brands that Coltman loaded for a Wolverhampton firm were, The Governor and The Victor.

198. **COLTMAN & SON:** Stafford Street (The rest of the address is not known).
Remarks: A photograph of one of their cartridges would not divulge any more information.

199. **ROY CONWAY:** Grimsby, Lincolnshire (Humberside).
D1 **Cartridges:** Kynoch's Patent Ejector (14 gauge); Humber Duck & Goose Cartridge.

200. **ARTHUR CONYERS:** 3 West Street, Blandford Forum, Dorset.
D2 **Business:** Gunmaker and cartridge loader.
D4 **Cartridges:** The Dorset County; Ejector; The Express; The Express DeLuxe; The Marvel .410; Unnamed; Water Resisting Case.
Remarks: Arthur was one of the sons from the firm, H. Conyers & Sons. This, the next firm entered in this cartridge list. He started his Blandford business in the late 1880's. Both pin and centre fire cartridges were loaded. Many of his early cartridges carried no names.

201. **H. CONYERS & SONS:** 71 Middle Street, Great Driffield. Also
D4 at, Pocklington, Yorks. At one time at, 59 East Street, Blandford Forum, Dorset.
Business: Gunmakers.
Cartridges: The Express; Unnamed.
Remarks: Conyers & Sons, one of whom was named Frank, were known to have loaded black powder cartridges without brand names.

202. **C. COOK & CO:** Bazaar, Leigh (Rest of the address is not known).
Cartridges: Smokeless Cartridge.

203. **THOMAS COOK:** Shepton Mallet, Somerset. Also at, Midsomer Norton & Bath, Somerset (Avon).
Remarks: Were known to have sold their own cartridges.

204. **J. E. COOKE:** Bromyard, Herefs (H & W).
D4 **Cartridges:** Unnamed.

205. **J. COOMBES:** Wheddon Cross, Somerset.
Cartridges: Unnamed.

206. **WILLIAMS COOMBS:** Frome, Somerset.
D4 **Cartridges:** The Eclipse Cartridge (kynoch's Perfectly Gas-tight).

207. **GEORGE COONEY:** Cross Street - John Street Corner, Kells,
D3 County Meath, Republic of Ireland.
D4 **Business:** Hardware merchant.
Cartridges: Kynoch's Perfectly Gas-tight; Unnamed.
Remarks: This business terminated circa, 1932-33.

208. **GEO COOPER & SONS (PICKERING), LTD:** Market Place, Pickering. Also at, Kirbymoorside, Yorks.
Cartridges: The Noted Ryedale.

209. **SIDNEY LANCELOT CORDEN.** Later as, **S. L. CORDEN & SONS:**
D3 37 High Street, Warminster, Wilts.
D4 **Business:** Ironmongers, furnishings, gun and cartridge makers.
Cartridges: Quickfire; Special Smokeless; Unnamed.
Remarks: Still in business but the firm no longer loads cartridges.

210. **JOHN CORNISH:** 17-18 Fore Street, Oakhampton, Devon.
D4 **Business:** Ironmonger.
Cartridges: The Noted Dartmoor; The Okement.

211. **THE CORNWALL CARTRIDGE WORKS:** Liskeard, Cornwall.
D3 **Business:** Cartridge loading and sales.
D5 **Cartridges:** The British Challenge; The Cornubia; The Cornwall; The Enterprise; The Tamar; The Trelawney.

212. **A. C. CORY:** Diss, Norfolk.
Business: Gun and ammunition dealer.
Cartridges: The Champion.

213. **GEORGE COSTER & SON:** 145 West Nile Street, Glasgow, Lanarks (Strathclyde).
Business: Gunmaker.
Cartridges: G. C. & S.

214. **WALTER COTON:** 153 Foleshill Road, Coventry, Warwickshire
D3 (W. Midlands).
D5 **Business:** Gunsmith and cartridge expert.
Cartridges: Special Keeper's Cartridge; Unnamed.
Remarks: Walter sold many yellow paper tubed cartridges with standing cock-pheasants printed on them. These carried no brand names. In his time he was a crack clay shooter. I have been told that his was one of the many premises that got blitzed during the big Coventry raid on November 14th 1940.

215. **THE COTTAGE GUNSHOP:** Dunnet, Caithness (Highlands).
H4 **Business:** Gunsmiths and cartridge loaders.
Cartridges: Economax.
Remarks: Post World War Two, Colin Haygarth founded this business. He produced his Economax cartridges with paper tubes and rolled over closures. Later brands are not listed here as they were closed by crimping. See number 452 in this cartridge list.

216. **ADAM COTTAM:** Dalton (Rest of the address is not known).
Cartridges: Kynoch's Perfectly Gas-tight.
Remarks: A cartridge head has been found with the stamping, COTTAM No 12 DALTON.

217. **COTTIS & SON:** Epping, Essex.
Cartridges: Champion Smokeless.

218. **COULSON:** Bellingham, Northumberland.
D5 **Cartridges:** The Border Cartridge; Special Smokeless.

219. **B. & J. V. COULTAS:** 91-92 Westgate, Grantham, Lincs.
Remarks: Cartridge remains have been found with headstamping, B.& J.V.COULTAS No 12 GRANTHAM.

220. **W. COULTS:** Grantham, Lincs.
Remarks: I have been told of a cartridge head that was found that carried this name. I have decided to include the firm here, but I expect that a mistake could well have been made. I believe that Coultas in entry number 219 was most likely an ironmonger.

221. **THE COUNTRY GENTLEMENS ASSOCIATION:** Icknield Way, Letchworth,
D3 Hertfordshire.
D5 **Business:** Sporting association.
Cartridges: The C.G.A. Improved Gastight; The C.G.A. Improved Waterproof Cartridge; The C.G.A. Keepers Cartridge.

222. **COX & SON, LTD:** 28 High Street. Also at, 7 Bernard Street,
D3 Southampton, Hants.
D6 **Business:** Gunmakers.
Cartridges: J.W.G.; The Popular; The Southampton Cartridge; Special Cartridge.
Remarks: For interest, see the following in this cartridge list: Clarke & Dyke; Cox & Clarke; Cox & Macpherson; John Patstone & Son; Patstone & Cox. Their cartridge list numbers are: 178; 223; 224; 789; 790.

223. **COX & CLARKE:** 28 High Street, Southampton, Hampshire.
D6 **Business:** gunmakers.
Cartridges: Fourten; Southampton Cartridge.

224. **COX & MACPHERSON:** 62 High Street, Southampton, Hampshire.
Business: Gunmakers.
Cartridges: Special.
Remarks: This firm is known to have been active at the above address in 1907 while at the same time Cox & Son were trading from number 28 in the same street.

225. **COZENS & SHAW, LTD:** 11 Dudley Street, Wolverhampton, Staffs.
D6 (W. Midlands).
Business: Ironmongers.
Cartridges: The Reliable.
Remarks: The above address was taken from an 1896 directory.

226. **THOMAS CRADDOCK.** Later as, **THOS CRADDOCK & SON:** Leyburn, Yorkshire.
Business: Ironmongers.
Remarks: Their name has been seen printed on an old style over-shot wad.

227. **ALFRED GEORGE CREBER:** Torcot, Menheniot, Liskeard, Cornwall.
Business: Cartridge loading and sales.
Remarks: Alfred later founded The Cornwall Cartridge Works. See number 211 in this cartridge list.

228. **G. CREIGHTON:** 8 Warwick Road, Carlisle, Cumberland (Cumbria).
D5 **Business:** Gunmaker.
Cartridges: Unnamed.

229. **D. B. CROCKART:** 33-35 County Place, Perth, Perthshire
D5 (Tayside).
Business: Gun and fishing tackle maker.
Cartridges: The Perth Cartridge; The Spotfinder; The True Line.

230. **D. CROCKART & SONS.** Later as, **D. CROCKART & CO:** 35 King
D6 Street, Stirling, Stirlingshire (Central).
Business: Gun, rifle and fishing tackle makers.
Cartridges: The Crockart; Ejector; The Grampion; The Stirling; Unnamed.

231. **J. CROCKART & SON:** Blairgowrie, Perthshire (Tayside).
Business: Gun, rifle and fishing tackle makers.
Cartridges: J. C. & S.
Remarks: This firm was established in 1852.

232. **CROSS BROTHERS, LTD:** 3-4 St. Mary's Street. Also at, Church
D6 Street, Cardiff, Glamorgan.
Business: Sports outfitters.
Cartridges: The Cardiff.

233. **S. B. CROSS:** 183 Price Street. Also at, Chester Street,
D6 Birkenhead, Cheshire (Merseyside).
Business: Explosives dealers.
Cartridges: Unnamed.

234. **C. G. CRUDGINGTON:** Bath, Somerset (Avon).
Business: Gunsmith and field sports.
Cartridges: The Spa.

235. **CURTIS'S & HARVEY, LTD:** 3 Gracechurch Street. Also at, Cannon
D6 Street House, London EC.
E1 **Business:** Gunpowder and cartridge manufacturers.
Cartridges: Amberite; Ejector; Feather Weight; Gastight; Lined Nitro; The Marvel; Ruby; Smokeless Diamond; Unlined Nitro.
Remarks: Many of their cartridges took their names from the powders that they contained. Most paper tube colours were either blue, brown or grey. C. & H. eventually amalgamated with their rivals, John Hall & Son who owned mills at Faversham, Kent. See number 415 in this cartridge list. In the November of 1918, they were then absorbed into a large new firm called, Explosives Trades, Ltd. See number 308 in this cartridge list.

236. **H. & J. CUTLACK:** 11 High Street, Eley, Cambridgeshire.
Business: ironmongers.
Remarks: Information that I was given is that at one time they sold their own cartridges.

237. **J. H. CUTTS:** Macclesfield, Cheshire.
Cartridges: The Special.

238. **T. A. DADLEY:** Stowmarket, Suffolk.
Business: Gunmaker.
Cartridges: The Hard Hitting Cartridge.

239. **T. DAINTITH:** Bridge Street, Warrington, Lancs (Ches).
D7 **Business:** Gunmaker.
Cartridges: Ejector; Eley Pegamoid; Special; Unnamed.

240. **N. S. DALL:** Chichester, Sussex.
Remarks: A cartridge remains has been found that had Dall's name on the headstamping.

241. **WALTER DARLOW, LTD.** Later as, **W. DARLOW & CO:** 27 Midland
D7 Road, Bedford, Bedfordshire. Later at, 8 Orford Hill,
E1 Norwich, Norfolk.
Business: Ironmongers and gunmakers.
Cartridges: 20 Gauge; The Big Bag; The Castle; The Lightning; The Orford; The Special; Special Gastight.
Remarks: There was an entry for this firm in an 1894 directory that listed them as both ironmongers and gunmakers.

242. **DATE BROTHERS:** Frome, Somerset.
Business: Sports depot.
Cartridges: The County Cartridge for Fur and Feather.

243. **JAMES A. DAVIDSON:** Wells-next-the-Sea, Norfolk.
D7 **Business:** Wine and spirit merchant. Also a cartridge loader.
Cartridges: Joyce's Long Brass Smokeless; The New Era.

244. **FRANCIS DAVIE:** 153 High Street, Elgin, Morayshire (Grampian).
D7 **Business:** Gunmaker.
Cartridges: The Moray Cartridge; Unnamed.

245. **HOWARD A. DAVIES:** 6 Southgate Street, Winchester, Hampshire.
D7 **Business:** gunmaker.
E1 **Cartridges:** The Flight; The Winton.
Remarks: His business was taken over by B. E. Chaplin who continued to market a cartridge called The Winton. Winton being a shortend name for Winchester. See number 168 in this cartridge list.

246. **T. DAVIES:** Llandyssul, Cardiganshire (Dyfed).
D7 **Cartridges:** The Instanto Cartridge; Kynoch's Perfectly Gastight.

247. **ALFRED DAVIS:** 4 Bishopgate Churchyard, Old Broad Street,
D8 London EC2.
Business: Gunmaker.
Cartridges: The Bishopgate.
Remarks: From J. Blanch & Son. See number 102 in this cartridge list.

248. **M. H. DAVIS & SONS:** Aberystwyth, Cardiganshire (Dyfed).
Business: Ironmongers.
Remarks: I collected this firms name and address, but I failed to record their cartridge information.

249. **GEORGE H. DAW:** 67 St. James's Street. Also at, 57
D8 Threadneedle Street, London EC.
Business: Central fire cartridge developer.
Cartridges: Unnamed (As such, became known as, The Daw Cartridge).

249. **GEORGE H. DAW:** Continued.
Remarks; Mr Daw's cartridges date from 1861. It was in 1866, that George took Colonel Boxer and Messrs Eley Brothers to court as he considered that between them, they had both made infringements on his patents. George lost his case while Eley Brothers came out of it the better. Had he had won, then British made cartridges could well have taken on another line.

250. **A. DAWE:** Oakhampton, Devonshire.
Business: Ironmonger.
Cartridges: Eley's Gastight Cartridge Case for Schultze Sporting Powder.

251. **F. DAWSON:** Altringham, Cheshire (Gt. Manchester).
D8   **Cartridges:** Kleenkiller; Eley Gastight Cartridge Case for Schultze Powder.

252. **J. G. DEABILL:** Carlton, Nottingham, Nottinghamshire.
Cartridges: The Partridge.

253. **ARTHUR DENNIS:** Great Dunmow, Essex.
D8   **Cartridges:** The Demon.

254. **DESBOROUGH & SON:** Derby, Derbyshire.
D8   **Cartridges:** The Dovedale Cartridge.

255. **DEVON & SOMERSET STORES:** 245-246 High Street, Exeter, Devon.
D8   **Business:** Department stores and ironmongers.
Cartridges: The Red Deer.

256. **P. DICKER:** Odiham, Hampshire.
Cartridges: The Lightning Cartridge.

257. **JOHN T. DICKINS:** 69 Bridge Street, Northampton, Northants.
D8   **Business:** Ironmonger.
Cartridges: Kynoch 5/8" Brass (Name on over-shot wad); Nobel Gas-tight Cartridge Case (Name on over-shot wad).

258. **JOHN DICKSON & SON, LTD:** 20 Royal Exchange. Also at, 21
D9   Frederick Street, Edinburgh, Midlothian. Was also in Glasgow
E2   and Kelso-on-Tweed, Roxburgh.
Business: Gunmakers.
Cartridges: The Capital; Ejector; Dickson's Favourite; The Jubilee; Dickson's Pegamoid; The Special Blue Shell; Rabbit Cartridge; Unnamed.
Remarks: John Dickson & Son incorporated the businesses of Alex Henry; Alex Martin and Mortimer & Son. See numbers 467, 689 and 725 in this cartridge list.

259. **SIDNEY WILLIAM DIGBY:** 35 High Street, Shaftesbury, Dorset.
Business: Ironmonger.
Cartridges: The Demon.

260. **DINWOODIE & NICHOLSON:** Thornhill, Dumfries (Dumfries &
D9   Galloway).
Cartridges: Eley Best Gas-tight Case.

261. **FREDERICK M. DISS:** Colchester, Essex.
     Cartridges: Kynoch Gastight (Name on over-shot wad).

262. **E. DISTIN & SON:** 39 High Street, Totnes, Devonshire.
D9   **Business:** Ironmongers.
     Cartridges: Demon Cartridge.

263. **DIXON & CO:** Aston Common, Birmingham, Warwicks (W. Midlands).
D9   **Cartridges:** Special Hand-Loaded (Kynoch Perfectly Gas-tight); Special Hand-Loaded Pigeon Cartridge.

264. **DOBSON & ROSSON:** 4 Market Head, Derby, Derbyshire.
D9   **Business:** Gunmakers.
     Cartridges: Unnamed.
     Remarks: Their above address was taken from an 1884 directory. Also see Charles Rosson number 879 in this cartridge list.

265. **G. DODD:** Perry Bar, Birmingham, Warwickshire (W. Midlands).
D9   **Cartridges:** Dodd's Calthorpe Cartridge.

266. **W. G. DONALDSON:** Grantown-on-Spey, Morayshire (Highland).
E1   **Cartridges:** The Triumph.

267. **R. DOTT THOMSON:** 1-2 Cross, Cupar, Fifeshire.
E2   **Business:** Ironmonger and cycle agent.
     Cartridges: Special Smokeless Cartridge.

268. **J. D. DOUGALL & SONS:** Glasgow, Lanarkshire (Strathclyde).
E2   Also in London (Address not known).
     Business: Gun and rifle makers.
     Cartridges: Ejector; Pegamoid Special Loading; Unnamed.
     Remarks: Their Glasgow addresses were: 52 Argyle Arcade Street; 88 Trongate; 177 Trongate; 23 Gordon Street; 39 Gordon Street; 3 West Nile Street; 18A-18B Renfield Street; 4 Bothwell Street; 10 Waterloo Street. These addresses were used between 1830 and 1927.

269. **DOWNING:** Southwell, Nottinghamshire.
E3   **Cartridges:** Schultze Co's Westminster (Downing's name only on the pink over-shot wad).

270. **R. L. DUGDALE, LTD:** 18 Friar Gate, Preston, Lancashire.
     Cartridges: Champion Smokeless; Mullerite Yellow Seal (Extra tube printing).

271. **A. J. DUKES:** Rugby, Warwickshire.
E3   **Remarks:** Cartridge remains have been found with their headstamping.

272. **A. H. DUNCALFE:** 5 Merridale Road, Wolverhampton, Staffs
E3   (W. Midlands).
     Business: Ironmongers and sanitary ware manufacturers.
     Cartridges: Mullerite Yellow Seal (Extra tube printing).
     Remarks: The above address was taken from a 1932 directory.

273. **STANLEY DUNCAN & SONS:** 62 Anlaby Road, Hull, Yorks
E3   (Humberside).
     Business: Gunmakers.
     Cartridges: Duncan's Special Load.

274. **THOMAS SMITH DUNCOMB:** 5 High Street, Stamford, Lincolnshire.
Business: Ironmonger.
Remarks: A cartridge seen had the name spelt on it as, T. S. Duncomb.

275. **DYER & ROBSON:** London (Rest of the address is not known).
E2 **Cartridges:** Superior; Very's Patent Signal Cartridge.
E3

276. **FRANK DYKE & CO, LTD:** 10 Union Street, London SE1. Also at,
E2 1-7 Ernest Avenue, West Norwood, London SE.
E3 **Business:** Cartridge loader and merchant.
Cartridges: Frank Dyke's Supreme; Rabbit Cartridge; Shamrock; Shamrock .410; Special; Special Gastight; Unnamed; Yellow Wizard; Yellow Wizard Rustless.
Remarks: Frank Dyke & Co, Ltd, loaded very many cartridges for lots of other firms country-wide. They used many German made cases and components. The majority of his own brands did not carry his name and these included The Shamrock and The Yellow Wizard. Infact, his very first Yellow Wizards had no case wall printings. This firm was one of the many that lost their premises due to German bombing during the Second World War.

277. **A. H. DYKES:** Stowmarket, Suffolk.
Cartridges: Unnamed.

278. **MARTIN DYMON:** Callington, Cornwall.
S8 **Cartridges:** The Kit-Hill.

279. **G. A. EARLE:** Bridgnorth, Shropshire.
E3 **Business:** Ironmonger.
Cartridges: Earle's Special Cartridge.

280. **EASTMOND.** Later as, **EASTMOND & SON:** 10 Fore Street, Great Torrington, Devonshire.
Business: Ironmongers.
Cartridges: Mullerite Smokeless (Extra tube printing).
Remarks: They were known to have sold Eley Brothers and Curtis's & Harvey's brands as well as their own.

281. **THE E. C. POWDER CO, LTD:** 20 Bucklersbury. Also at, 40 New
E4 Broad Street, London EC.
Business: Gunpowder manufacturers.
Cartridges: E.C.; E.C. Pegamoid; Eley Ejector.
Remarks: Known as, The Explosives Company, it got easily confused by name with the other gunpowder manufacturers. The Nobel Explosives Company, just to give an example. So as to avoid this, the initials to the company's name were used and this is how they arrived at using the letters 'E.C'. It is believed that the cartridge loading side of this firm became, The New Explosives Company, Ltd. See number 742 in this cartridge list. Anyhow, both of these firms were eventually wound up when they merged into the large new firm of, Explosives Trades, Ltd. This was in the November of 1918. See number 308 in this cartridge list.

282. **R. E. EDMONDS:** Stalham, Norfolk.
Business: Ironmonger.
Cartridges: The Stalham; The Stalham Superior.

283. **EDMONDS & WELLDON:** Rugby, Warwickshire.
E4 **Remarks:** Cartridge remains have been found with headstamping, EDMONDS & WELLDON No 12 RUGBY.

284. **EDNIE & KININMONTH:** Forfar, Angus (Tayside).
E4 **Business:** Ironmongers and seed merchants.
Cartridges: Unnamed.

285. **EDWARDS, LTD:** Newport, Monmouthshire (Gwent).
E4 **Business:** Gunsmiths and cartridge makers.
E5 **Cartridges:** The Champion; The Newport.

286. **AUBREY EDWARDS & CO, LTD:** 32 Oxford Street, Swansea, West
E4 Glamorgan.
E5 **Cartridges:** The Eclipse; The Gower.

287. **C. G. EDWARDS & SON:** 2 George Street. Also at, Frankfort
E4 Lane, Plymouth, Devonshire.
Business: Gunmakers.
Cartridges: The Eddystone; The Smeaton.

288. **EDWARDS & MELUISH:** Harborne, Birmingham, Warwickshire
E4 (W. Midlands).
E5 **Cartridges:** The Edmel Smokeless.

289. **ELDERKIN & SON:** Spalding, Lincolnshire.
E4 **Business:** Gun repair specialists.
Cartridges: The Premier.

290. **ELEY BROTHERS, LTD:** 254 Gray's Inn Road, London WC4. Works
E5 at, Angel Road, Edmonton, London N18.
E6 **Business:** Ammunition and explosives manufacturers. Apart from
E7 large military, rifle and pistol, sporting cartridges were
E8 made. These included needle-gun, Patent wire for both breech
E9 and muzzle loading, Pinfire, Centre-fire, Special militar and
F1 Punt gun.
F2 **Depots**
   (British Isles): Birmingham: 29-30 Whittal Street, Warwicks (W. Midlands). 'Eley Bros, Ltd'.
   Dublin: 9 Dawson Street, Republic of Ireland. 'Eley Bros, Ltd'.
   Exeter: Fore Street, Devonshire. 'Evans Gadd & Co'.
   Glasgow: 68 Mitchell Street, Lanarks. 'James Ferrier & Son'.
Depots
(Overseas): Belgium, Canada, United States of America, Italy with representatives in London, Australia, Cuba, Scandinavia, South Africa, South America and British North America.
Cartridges (Patent Wire):
Muzzle Loading: Colour blue. For use in muzzle loading guns.
The Green: Colour green. Made for long distance shooting.
The Royal: Colour red. For the second barrel but could be used in either.
The Universal: Colour yellow. For use in first barrel. It contained no wire.

290. **ELEY BROTHERS, LTD:** Continued.
   Cartridges (Pinfire): Details taken mostly from a 1902 Price List.
   BLUE, BEST QUALITY: (Not listed in 1902). Gauges 12, 14, 16.
   BROWN QUALITY: Gauges 10, 12, 14, 16 20, 24, 28.
   GREEN, EXTRA QUALITY: Gauges 8, 10, 12, 14, 16, 20, 24, 28, 32. A .410 has been seen but it was not listed in 1902.
   RED QUALITY: (Not listed in 1902). A 14 gauge has been seen.

   Cartridges (Early Centre-fire): Details taken mostly from a 1902 Price List.
   BLUE, BEST QUAlity: (Not listed in 1902). Gauges seen, 12, 16.
   BROWN QUALITY: Gauges 10, 12, 14, 16, 20, 24, 28.
   GREEN, EXTRA QUALITY: Case walls printed in black with the wordings, ELEY'S Gas-tight Cartridge Case. Gauges 4, 8, 10, 12, 14, 16, 20, 24, 28, 32; .410, .360. Not shown in their 1902 Price List, Gauges 2 has been seen. Possibly there may have been a gauge 18.
   Remarks: Similar cartridges to the above have been seen with brown paper tubes with black case wall printings. (Not listed in the 1902 Price List).

   Cartridges (Early Brands): Paper tubed with extended seamless brass and loaded with many brands of gunpowders.
   EJECTOR (Extended Brass):
   (Extended Brass): Gauges 4, 8, 10, 12, 14, 16, 20, 24, 28, 32. .410 not shown in 1902.
   The E.B. NITRO CASE: Loaded with many powder brands. Gauges 12, 16, 20.
   IMPROVED GAS-TIGHT: Also known as, The E.B.L. With double brass heads and long shells having several paper tube colours. Gauges 8, 10, 12, 16, 20, 24, 28, 32, .410.
   PEGAMOID: Pegamoid was a patented brand of waterproof paper. Gauges 10, 12, 16, 20, 24, 28.
   Remarks: All Pegamoid cartridges in this list were made having this Pegamoid brand paper.
   SOLID DRAWN BRASS: Gauges 8, 10, 12, 14, 16, 20, 24, 28, 32.
   THIN BRASS: Gauge .410.
   Cartridges (Individual Powders Cases for):
   Hall's Smokeless Cannonite: Colour red. Gauges 12, 16, 20.
   Amberite: Colour grey. Gauges 10, 12, 16, 20, 24.
   Cooppal Smokeless Game: Colour red. Gauges 12, 16, 20.
   Cooppal No, 2: Colour maroon. Gauges 12, 16, 20.
   'E.C.' Colour red. Gauges 10, 12, 16, 20, 24.
   Shot Gun Rifleite: Colour red. Gauges 12, 16, 20.

290. **ELEY BROTHERS, LTD:**   Continued.
   Sporting Ballistite: Colour ceam-yellow. Gauges 12, 16, 20.
   'S,S.' Smokeless: Colour grey. Gauges 12, 16, 20.
   Cartridges
   (Short Smokeless):
   LANCASTER'S PYGMIES: Advertised in Eley Bros, Ltd price
                          lists. Case length 56 mm (2¼ inch).
                          Gauge 12. See number 597 in this
                          cartridge list.
   THE PARVO: Loaded with Sporting Ballistite Powder.
                          Case length 50 mm (2 inch). Gauge 12.
   TOM THUMB: Loaded with Curtis's & Harvey's Powder.
                          Case length 50 mm (2 inch). Gauge 12.
   THE MIDGET: Loaded with Cooppal No, 2 Powder.
                          Case length 56 mm (2¼ inch). Gauge 12.

Cartridges (Later Brands):
The 3/8" Shell Gastight; Achilles; Aquoid; Beacon Cartridge; Blacktwenty (20 Gauge); Comet; Coralite Smokeless (For Australian market); Damp Proof (Two piece half-rolled brass); 'D.S.'; 'E,B,L.'; E.B. Nitro; E.B. Nitro Case; Ecar; Ejector; Eleite; Eley Smokeless; Eloid; Erin-Go-Bragh; Express; Fourlong .410; Fourten .410; Gastight; Gastight Deep Shell Unlined; Grand Prix; Improved Gastight; Juno; Lab Case (Proofhouse only); Lightmode; Lined Nitro Case; Mars; Neptune; Pardo Smokeless: Pegamoid; Pigeon Cartridge; Pluto; Quail (Sold in Australia); Rocket; 'S.A.'; Thor; Titan; Universal; Unnamed; 'V.C.'; Vulcan: Zenith.

General Remarks:
At the time when the above brands were on the market, special cases were also supplied to many smaller firms with case walls ready printed. A few other firms were purchasing their cartridges ready loaded from Eley Brothers, Ltd. The Express I have only seen in 10 and 12 gauges and with the name only on the headstampings. The short range Quail may have only been produced for the Australian market. The Universal was made in 12, 16 and 20 gauge sizes. Eley Brothers were known at one time to make rather odd rounds such as Skin Cartridges, Eley-Boxer Bottle Shaped Cartridges, Ball Cartridges, Bulleted Breech Caps, Waterproof Rim-fires and various metalics. Puntgun Cartridges were also made. One of these that was shown to me had the name 'Lightmode' on it's case wall. The name Lightmode was registered to Messrs Eley Bros in 1904 and it was generally used on lightly loaded cartridges that were specially made in order to protect shooters from gun headaches. A cartridge box label that was printed, Eley JOB Cartridges has come to light. This was marked for 12 Gauge with number 5 shot. They were rated as 3rd quality and it is more than likely that the contents had over-printings of some brands that the firm was not able to sell in the normal way. This could have been due to various reasons. Many such cases got shipped out to the U.S.A. and were loaded up out there.

History:
The founding of the firm of Eley Brothers is now lost in to obscuity. We know that it's first two proprietors were brothers. These two chaps were Charles and William Eley and they were known to have been in business togeter in 1828. A major setback befell the firm when William was tragically

290. **ELEY BROTHERS, LTD:** Continued.
blown to pieces by exploding fulminating powder while working in their factory in 1841. At the time of the accident he was only forty-six. It was Charles who kept the wheels of industry turning by introducing his three sons into the family business. They were, William Thomas, Charles and Henry. Together they ran the firm for thirty more years.

Cartridge manufacture was started in 1828. The first cartridges made were the Patent Wire Cartridges. These held no explosives materials. The main component was made from thin wire mesh so forming a cage. This wire cage contained the shot load and the whole cartridge was then covered with a paper skin. These cartridges were then given paper outer wrappers for their protection. These wrappers had to be peeled off before using the cartridges. These Patent Wire Cartridges were first designed for ramming into muzzle loaders and were claimed to have several advantages over normal loadings. These advantages were, that the shot did not have to be measured when loading. They also contributed to the stopping of a lot of the lead foulings which occurred in the barrels. But their best claim to fame was that their hitting range was extended. The shot load through being caged, was held together over a longer distance whilst in flight. This then provided the shooter with a greater range and having tighter patterns. Eley's had bought the patents for making these cartridges from a Frenchman named Jenour in 1827. Messrs Eley Brothers also claimed another first when they introduced on the market their very first waterproofed percussion caps.

As the years rolled on, the firm exhibited many of their products in oversea exhibitions. They entered in the Great Exhibition of 1851 and also in the exhibition in Vienna in 1873 where they were awarded prize medals for their excelence of manufacture and materials. They continued to exhibit their wares in many different countries throughout the world so gaining more medals. They obtained the highest award in Chicago in 1893 and they pulled off a gold at Antwerp in the following year. In 1889 at Paris, and again in 1900, they won the Grand Prix. This name they then gave to one of their most successful cartridges. This then dates their Grand Prix Cartridges to the beginning of the 20th Century. Having won all of these medals, they then proudly depicted them on their larger cartridge boxes. If one knew the dates that each medal was won, then this could quite well help one in dating the cartridges in the boxes.

Not only did they market world-wide their own brands of cartridges, but they also sold ready capped cases for loadings. This can clearly be seen by studying this cartridge list. Very many firms world-wide purchased their cartridge cases and the internal components from Eley Bros, Ltd. Firms nearly always bought their cases with the case walls (paper tubes) readily printed. For a little extra cash they could also have their names stamped on the bases of the brass heads. I am not one-hundred percent sure, but I think that the stamping of the heads preceded the printings of the paper tubes. Also, readily printed over-shot wads could also be purchased.

Due to a need to introduce more capital into the business, Eley Bros took a bold step and became public in March 1874. Things then improved again for them and they successfully

290. **ELEY BROTHERS, LTD:** Continued.
held their place in the world market. One of their largest rivals was George Kynoch who also went public about ten years later. See number 589 in this cartridge list.
  With the ending of World War One (The 1914-18 Great War) in the November of 1918, the need for manufacturing explosives items was considerably reduced. This then brought about a large merger of the largest explosives firms. Gradually a lot of the smaller firms then joined in with the merger. It was the start of what large firms have been doing ever since. The new large firm that was formed became known as Explosives Trades, Ltd and often used their initials, E.T.L. See number 308 in this cartridge list. Eley Brothers, Ltd being one of the largest of these merged firms now found themselves no longer rivals with G. Kynoch & Co and the others. From then on, all shotgun ammunition was manufactured in the what was, Kynoch Lion Works at Witton. See number 589 in this cartridge list. Although they were merged, they were not officially liquidated until ten years later in 1928.
  William Thomas was the first of the three brothers to die. Henry resigned in 1902 shortly after the death of his brother Charles. It is good to know that even in this day, one can still purchase first rate cartridges that still carry on them the name of Eley.

291. **ELLICOTT:** Cardiff, South Glamorgan.
F4 **Cartridges:** The Ellicott Cartridge (Gastight Cartridge Case for Schultze Gunpowder. Cone based case. Patent No, 14814).

292. **WILLIAM ELLICOTT:** Broad Street, Launceston, Cornwall.
F4 **Business:** Cartridge loading.
Cartridges: The Ellicott Cartridge (Kynoch's Perfectly Gas-tight).
Remarks: An advertisement for Ellicott, Launceston, was placed on the front of the very first "Shooting Times" publication dated, 9th September 1882.

293. **H. C. ELLIOTT:** Lowfield Street, Dartford, Kent.
F4 **Business:** Gunmaker.
Cartridges: The Smasher.

294. **J. ELLIS:** Regal Sports Store, Oswestry, Shropshire.
Business: Sports store.
Cartridges: The Regal Special Smokeless.
Remarks: This firm stopped having their name on cartridges in 1947.

295. **ELTON STORES, LTD:** 140 Coniscliffe Road, Darlington, County
F2 Durham.
F4 **Business:** Department Stores.
Cartridges: Competition; Pest Control; Standard; Trapshooting.
Remarks: Their cartridges were closed by rolled turnover and by crimp closure.

296. **ELVEDEN ESTATE:** Elveden Hall, Near Thetford, Suffolk.
F4 **Business:** Private estate.
Cartridges: Elveden Estate.

297. **DAVID EMSLIE:** Elgin, Morayshire (Grampian).
F4   **Cartridges:** The Glen Moray; The Sniper.

298. **S. ENTWHISTLE:** 151 Church Street, Blackpool, Lancashire.
F4   **Business:** Gunsmith.
      Cartridges: Unnamed.

299. **ERSKINE:** Newton Stewart, Wigtownshire (Dumfries & Galloway).
      Business: Gunmaker.
      Remarks: Information gleaned was that they made their own cartridge cases during the 1890's. They closed down at around the time of the 1914-18 war.

300. **EVANS & SON:** 39 Market Place, Warminster, Wiltshire.
      Business: Ironmongers and gun and cartridge dealers.
      Cartridges: Unnamed or name not recorded.

301. **BEN EVANS & CO:** Swansea, South Glamorgan.
      Cartridges: The Special.

302. **CHARLES ALEX EVANS:** 134 High Street, Burford, Oxfordshire.
F4   **Business:** Ironmonger.
      Cartridges: The Cotswold Special Smokeless.

303. **DAN EVANS:** Dursley House, Whitland, Carmarthen (Dyfed).
      Business: Ironmonger.
      Cartridges: Ty-Gwyn.

304. **T. EVANS & SON:** Ashbourne, Derbyshire.
      Cartridges: The Moorland.

305. **THOMAS J. EVANS:** Welshpool, Montgomeryshire (Powys).
F4   **Cartridges:** Unnamed.

306. **WILLIAM EVANS:** 63 Pall Mall, London EC.
F2   **Business:** Gunmaker.
F5   **Cartridges:** 20 Bore; 16 Bore; Ejector; Gastight; High Velocity; Mark Over; Marlboro; Pall Mall; Pegamoid; Sky High.
      Remarks: This firm was known to have been trading from the above address as early as 1908.

307. **J. W. EWEN:** 45 The Green, Aberdeen, Aberdeens (Grampian).
      Cartridges: The Ewen Special.

308. **EXPLOSIVES TRADES, LTD:** Witton, Birmingham, Warwickshire
F2   (W. Midlands).
F3   **Business:** Ammunition and explosives manufacturers.
F4   **Cartridges:** For cartridge details, see Nobel Industries, Ltd. Number 756 in this cartridge list.
      Remarks: Explosives Trades, Ltd was the outcome of many merging firms. Some were large while others were small. These firms had been manufacturing explosives items and their components. The result of all these firms merging was one brand new large firm which became, Explosives Trades, Ltd. This all came into being in the November of 1918. Some of the first shotgun cartridges that they produced were stamped the initials E.T.L. to their headstampings. For more information, see number 756 in this list, Nobel Industries, Ltd. This was the name that the firm became just two years later.

309. **FAIRBURN:** Guisborough, Yorkshire (Cleveland).
    Cartridges: Unnamed or name not recorded.

310. **R. FARMER:** 12 North Street, Leighton Buzzard, Bedfordshire.
F3 **Business:** Gunmaker.
F5 **Cartridges:** The Ecel; Farmer's Challenge; Gastight.

311. **G. F. FARRELL & SONS:** 23 High Street, Chippenham, Wiltshire.
F5 **Cartridges:** The Champion Special Smokeless.

312. **BRYAN FARRELLY & SONS:** Castle Street, Kells, County Antrim,
F5 Northern Ireland.
    Cartridges: Kenlis.

313. **FAWCETT:** Kirby Lonsdale, Westmorland (Cumbria).
    Cartridges: The Lunesdale Cartridge.

314. **FAWCETT:** Laxfield, Suffolk.
    Cartridges: Unnamed or name not recorded.

315. **FENWICK & SON:** Stanhope, County Durham.
    Remarks: Their name has been seen printed in red on a white over-shot wad.

316. **FERNIE:** Aberfeldy, Perthshire (Tayside).
    Business: Shooters supplies.
    Cartridges: The Hand Loaded.

317. **FERRULES:** The Arcade, Belfast, Northern Ireland.
    Cartridges: Unnamed or name not recorded.

318. **SAMUEL FIDDIAN:** Stourbridge, Worcestershire (H & W).
    Cartridges: The Enville Smokeless Cartridge.

319. **C. F. FIELD:** Pershore, Worcestershire (H & W).
    Cartridges: The Eclipse Cartridge.

320. **B. FINCH & SONS:** 35 Bell Street, Reigate, Surrey.
F3 **Cartridges:** The Lone Flyer.

321. **FISCHER BROTHERS:** Taunton, Somerset.
    Cartridges: Unnamed or name not recorded.

322. **HERBERT J. FISHER:** Bank Street, Melksham, Wiltshire.
    Business: Ironmonger.
    Cartridges: Mullerite Smokeless.

323. **A. T. FITCHEW:** Ramsgate, Kent.
F3 **Cartridges:** Ecel.
F6

324. **C. FLETCHER:** Leeds, Yorks (Rest of the address is not known).
F5 **Cartridges:** Kynoch's Perfectly Gas-tight.

325. **Mrs E. FLETCHER.** Later as, **E. FLETCHER & SON.** Still later,
F3 **FLETCHERS (SPORTS):** Westgate Street, Gloucester, Glos.
F5 **Business:** Gunmakers.
    Cartridges: The Gloucester; The Pheasant; Unnamed.

325. **Mrs E. FLETCHER:** Continued.
Remarks: While at 158 Westgate Street, Between 1885 and 1889 and possibly for longer, the firm was then under the name of Mrs Elizabeth Fletcher. When World War One broke out, this firm was then under the name of Mrs Rose Fletcher. Another address of theirs was, 18 Westgate Street. When as Fletchers (Sports), they moved to 20-24 King's Square, Gloucester. At one time they had premises at, 92 Winchcombe Street, Cheltenham, Gloucestershire.

326. **FLINT:** Uckfield, East Sussex.
Business: Ironmonger.
Cartridges: Unnamed (Name on over-shot wad only).

327. **H. & A. FLINT:** Hemel Hempstead, Hertfordshire.
F5   **Cartridges:** Primrose Smokeless Cartridge.

328. **G. FODEN:** Openshaw, Manchester, Lancs (Gt. Manchester).
F6   **Cartridges:** Eley's Gastight Case for Curtis's & Harvey's Smokeless Diamond.

329. **FOLLETT:** Colyton & Seaton, Devonshire.
Cartridges: Eley Brown Quality Case (Name on over-shot wad only).

330. **RALPH FOORT.** Later as, **R. FOORT & SON:** 19 Queen Street. Later at, 47 Cornmarket Street, Oxford, Oxfordshire.
Business: Ironmongers.
Cartridges: The Dead Shot (In the name of, R. Foort & Son).

331. **WILLIAM FORD:** Eclipse Works, 15 St. Mary's Row. Also at,
F6   4 Price Street. And also at, 96 Potters Hill, Aston, Birmingham, Warwickshire (W. Midlands).
Business: Gunmaker.
Cartridges: The Eclipse; The Fleet; Patent Ignition Tube.

332. **FORREST & SONS:** Kelso-on-Tweed, Roxburghshire (Borders).
F3   **Business:** Gunmakers.
Cartridges: The Border Smokeless; The County; The Tweed.

333. **A. J. FOSTER:** Sheffield House, 16 The Bull Ring,
F3   Kidderminster, Worcestershire (H & W).
F6   **Business:** Gunsmith.
Cartridges: The Field Cartridge; The Quick Hit; Unnamed.

334. **FOSTER BROTHERS:** Church Street, Ashbourne, Derbyshire.
F6   **Remarks:** It is known that they once sold their own cartridges.

335. **FOSTER LOTT & CO:** The Ammunition Stores, Dorchester, Dorset.
Business: Ammunition dealers.
Cartridges: Special Schultze Smokeless Cartridge.

336. **ISAAC FOX.** Later as, **CECIL FOX:** 4 Upper Bridge Street,
F7   Canterbury, Kent.
Business: Gun and rifle makers.
Cartridges: The County Cartridge; Kynoch Gastight; Unnamed.

336. **ISAAC FOX:** Continued.
Remarks: Both Isaac and Cecil sold The County Cartridges. This business later changed hands. It was then run by H. S. Greenfield. Later they became H. S. Greenfield & Son. They both continued to market The County Cartridge. See number 399 in this cartridge list.

337. **E. J. FOY:** Minehead, Somerset.
Remarks: Their name has been seen printed on an over-shot wad.

338. **FOYS:** Athlone, Roscommon, Republic of Ireland.
Cartridges: Smokeless Cartridge.

339. **CHARLES FRANCIS.** Later as, **C. FRANCIS & SONS.** Later still as,
F3 **C. FRANCIS & SON:** Long Causeway, Peterborough,
F7 Northamptonshire (Cambridgeshire).
F8 **Business:** Gunmakers.
Cartridges: The Demon; The Reliable; The Reliance; Schultze.

340. **FRANCIS & DEAN:** 8 St. Mary's Hill, Stamford, Lincolnshire.
F6 **Business:** Gunsmiths.
Cartridges: Hy-Bird (Overprint on an imported Baikal).

341. **J. W. FRANKS:** Guisborough, Yorkshire (Cleveland).
Cartridges: Unnamed.

342. **DANIEL FRASER & CO:** 4 Leith Street, Edinburgh, Midlothian.
Business: Gunmakers.
Cartridges: Pegamoid; Unnamed.

343. **JOHN FRASER:** Edinburgh, Midlothian.
F7 **Cartridges:** Eley's Gastight Cartridge Case for S.S. Powder.

344. **NORMAN FRASER:** Station Road, Churchdown, Gloucestershire.
F7 **Business:** Gunsmith.
Cartridges: Chosen.
Remarks: The name Chosen was the abbreviated name for Churchdown. Only a small quantity of these 12 gauge cartridges were produced. Norman was not related to any of the other Frasers in this cartridge list.

345. **FREENEY:** High Street, Galway, County Galway, Republic of Ireland.
Cartridges: The Atom.

346. **W. H. FRENCH.** Later as, **FRENCH & SON:** 8 Market Square,
F7 Buckingham, Buckinghamshire.
Business: Ironmongers.
Cartridges: Nobel Explosives Co's Ejector (French's name only on the over-shot wad).

347. **E. FROST:** 6 Cowick Street, St. Thomas, Exeter, Devonshire.
F7 **Cartridges:** The Devon Special Smokeless.

348. **EDWARD FROST:** Bridlington, Yorkshire (Humberside).
F7 **Cartridges:** Unnamed.

349. **JOHN FRY:** 17 Saddlegate, Derby, Derbyshire.
G1 **Business:** Gunmaker.
Cartridges: The Derby Cartridge.

350. **S. C. FULLER:** South Street, Dorking, Surrey.
Business: Gun, cycle and sports dealer.
Cartridges: The Long Shot.
Remarks: This firm was established in 1897.

351. **FURLONG:** Saffron Walden, Essex.
Remarks: The name Furlong has been seen on a 12 gauge headstamping.

352. **FUSSELL'S, LTD:** 118-119 Cheap Side, London EC2. Also at,
G1 Abergavenny, Monmouthshire (Gwent). Also at, Port Talbot, West Glamorgan & Newport, Monmouthshire (Gwent).
Business: Gunmakers.
Cartridges: The Club.

353. **W. GALBRAITH:** 22 St. Nicholas Street, Lancaster, Lancs.
G1 **Business:** Ironmonger, general furnishing and steel merchant.
Cartridges: Smokeless Cartridge (Loaded by The New Explosives Co, Ltd). See number 742 in this cartridge list.

354. **J. & J. M. GALDING:** Monaghan, County Monaghan, Republic of Ireland.
Cartridges: Surekill.

355. **A. GALE:** Barnstaple, Devonshire.
Business: Gunmaker.
Cartridges: The Eclipse.

356. **EDWARD GALE.** Later as, **E. GALE & SONS, LTD:** 20 Joy Street,
F8 Barnstaple. Also at, 2-3 Mill Street, Bideford, Devonshire.
G1 **Business:** Gunmakers.
Cartridges: Castle; County; Farm Cartridge; The Field; The Flag; The Hawk .410; Pegamoid; Unlined Nitro; The X.L.

357. **GALLYON & SONS, LTD:** 66 Bridge Street, Cambridge, Cambs.
F8 Also at, 52 High Street, King's Lynn, Norfolk. Later at,
G1 5 Cowgate, Peterborough, Northants (Cambs). And also at, 9-11 Bedford Street, Norwich, Norfolk.
Business: Gunmakers.
Cartridges: Camroid; The Club Cartridge; The Cooppal Express; Granton; Kilham; Lynton; Newgun; Sandringham; Super Vanguard; Unnamed; The Vanguard.

358. **A. W. GAMAGE, LTD:** Holborn, London EC1.
F8 **Business:** Department stores.
G1 **Cartridges:** The A.W.G.; The Corona; The Holborn; The Referee.

359. **JOHN G. GAMBLE:** Magherafelt, Northern Ireland.
Business: Ammunition merchants.
Cartridges: Swift.

360. **WILLIAM GARDEN:** 122½ Union Street, Aberdeen, Aberdeenshire
G2 (Grampian).
Business: Gunmaker.
Cartridges: The Eclipse; Gastight; The Granite City; Special Brown.

361. **T. M. GARDINER, LTD:** Hoddeson, Hertfordshire.
G2   **Business:** Ammunition dealer.
     Cartridges: Unnamed.

362. **WILLIAM GARDNER:** 6 High Street, Chippenham, Wiltshire.
G2   **Business:** Gunmaker.
     Cartridges: Warranted Gas-tight Cartridge Case.

363. **M. GARNETT.** Later as, **M. GARNETT & SON:** Crampton Court.
G2   Later at, 31 Parliament Street, Dublin, Republic of Ireland.
     Cartridges: The Kilquick; The Pheasant; The Retriever; The Suredeath.
     Remarks: This firm later became, Garnett & Keegan at the same address.

364. **FRANK GARRETT:** Ilmington, Near Stratford-upon-Avon, Warwicks.
F8   Later at, Evesham, Worcestershire (H & W).
G2   **Business:** Cartridge loading expert.
     Cartridges: Blue Flash Pigeon Cartridge; Crimson Flash; The D.B.H. (Deadly but humane); Flash Junior .410; Golden Flash; Tempest.

365. **ARTHUR GARRICK:** Sunderland, County Durham (Tyne & Wear).
     Cartridges: The Sportsman.

366. **FREDERICK WILLIAM GEORGE:** 3-4 Queen's Square, High Wycombe,
G3   Buckinghamshire.
     Business: Ironmonger.
     Cartridges: Eley Grand Prix Case.
     Remarks: The above address was taken from a 1915 directory.

367. **W. GEORGE:** Ripon, Yorkshire.
     Business: Ironmonger.
     Cartridges: Unnamed or name not known.

368. **W. J. GEORGE:** Dover, Kent (Rest of the address is not known).
G3   **Business:** Gunmaker.
     Cartridges: Unnamed.
     Remarks: W. J. George was known to have been active in 1908.

369. **GERMANS:** Dulverton, Somerset.
     Business: Ironmongers.
     Cartridges: Unnamed.

370. **GEVELOT & CO (LONDON):** Queen Victoria Street, London EC4.
G3   **Business:** French ammunition and explosives manufacturers.
     Cartridges: Ejector (Solid drawn brass).

371. **GEORGE GIBBS, LTD:** 37 Baldwin Street. Also at, 39 Corn
F8   Street. And also at, St. John's Bridge, Bristol, Glos (Avon).
F9   Also at, 35 Savile Row, London W1.
G2   **Cartridges:** The Bristol; The County; The Covert; The Farm Cartridge; The Field; The Gibbs; The Intermediate; Kynoch 5/8" Brass.

372. **GILL & CO:** 5 High Street, Oxford, Oxfordshire.
     Business: ironmongers.
     Cartridges: The Dead Shot.
     Remarks: They were known to have been in business in 1877.

373. **JOHN H. GILL:** Danby, Yorkshire.
    Cartridges: The Tyke (Mullerite).

374. **JOHN H. GILL & SONS:** Leeming Bar, London.
    Cartridges: The Sproxton.

375. **C. GILLMAN & SONS:** Black Jack Street, Cirencester, Glos.
    Business: Ironmongers.
    Remarks: Years ago, cartridges were sold by them that carried their own name. These were produced for them by Page-Wood of Bristol.

376. **J. GILMAN & SONS, LTD:** The Corner, Stratford Street &
F9   Corporation Street, Birmingham, Warwicks (W. Midlands).
G3   **Cartridges:** Unnamed (Registered No, 28596).

377. **R. W. GLANVILLE:** 6 Wellington Street, Woolwich, London SE.
    Remarks: Their name and address has been seen printed on a Kynoch's C.B. cartridge box. Their name has also been seen printed on an over-shot wad that was loaded into a Luck's Explosives, Ltd Henrite Pigeon Cartridge.

378. **J. GLIDDON & SONS:** Willington & Minehead, Somerset.
G3   **Business:** Hardware and agricultural merchants.
    Cartridges: The Exmoor Cartridge.
    Remarks: Gliddons' took over the business from William Tarr in 1913. Tarr had also marketed an Exmoor Cartridge. See numbers 782 and 978 in this cartridge list.

379. **GLOBEMASTER ARMS & AMMUNITION:** 79 Oldstead Avenue, Hull,
G3   Yorkshire (Humberside).
    Cartridges: Gamemaster.

380. **W. GODFREY & SONS:** Yeovil, Somerset.
G3   **Cartridges:** Special Smokeless.

381. **G. E. GOLD:** 9 Castle Mill Street, Bristol, Glos (Avon).
    Business: Gunmaker.
    Cartridges: The Popular.
    Remarks: This firm was known to have been active at the above address in 1910.

382. **CHARLES GOLDEN:** Bradford, Yorkshire.
    Business: Gunmaker.
    Cartridges: Unnamed.

383. **WILLIAM GOLDEN:** 8-10 Cross Church Street, Huddersfield,
G3   Yorkshire.
    Business: Ironmonger.
    Cartridges: Ejector; Kynoch Waterproof Cartridge Case.

384. **C. E. GOLDING:** Watton, Norfolk.
F9   **Business:** Ironmonger.
    Cartridges: The Wayland.
    Remarks: Their Wayland Cartridge took it's name from the local Wayland Wood. This wood is legendary of the child's story, The Babes in the Wood.

385. **JOHN R. GOW & SONS:** 12 Union Street, Dundee, Angus (Tayside).
G3 **Business:** Gunmakers.
Cartridges: The Tayside; Unnamed.

386. **G. GRACE & SON:** 66-68 High Street, Tring, Hertfordshire.
Business: Ironmongers and pistol makers.
Cartridges: Unnamed.

387. **G. P. GRAHAM:** Cockermouth, Cumberland (Cumbria).
G4 **Business:** Gunmaker.
Cartridges: The Cumberland; The Skiddaw.

388. **J. GRAHAM & CO, LTD:** 27 Union Street, Inverness,
F9 Inverness-shire (Highland).
G4 **Business:** Gunmakers.
Cartridges: Bon-ton; Eley Ejector; The Highland; Pegamoid; The Primo; Special.

389. **J. J. GRAHAM:** Longtown, Cumberland (Cumbria).
Business: Gunsmith or gunmaker.
Cartridges: Unnamed.

390. **J. & J. GRAHAM:** Sligo, County Sligo, Republic of Ireland.
Cartridges: Unnamed or name not recorded.

391. **GRANDISONS:** London (Rest of the address is not known).
Remarks: Cartridge remains have been found with the headstamping, GRANDISONS. LONDON.

392. **STEPHEN GRANT.** Later as, **S. GRANT & SONS:** 67A St. James's
G4 Street. Later at, 7 Bury Street, St. James, London SW1.
Business: Gunmakers.
Cartridges: Instanter; Patent Gas-tight Cartridge; The R.P.
Remarks: See Grant & Lang, number 393 below.

393. **GRANT & LANG:** 7 Bury Street, St. James, London SW1.
F9 **Business:** Gunmakers.
G4 **Cartridges:** The Briton; The Curzon; The Grantbury; The Instanter; Pegamoid; Rocketer; The Velogrant.
Remarks: This business was founded by Stephen Grant in 1866. Stephen and his sons joined forces with Joseph Lang & Son, Ltd in 1925. See number 603 in this cartridge list. They also incorporated the business of Charles Lancaster & Co, Ltd and that of Watson Brothers. These two firms being numbers 597 and 1069 in this list. Grant & Lang were active up until 1960 when they then joined forces with Henry Atkin. The firm then became Atkin, Grant & Lang. See numbers 30 and 31 in this list.

394. **D. GRAY & CO:** 30 Union Street. Later at, 14 Union Street,
G4 Inverness, Inverness-shire (Highland).
Business: Gunmakers.
Cartridges: Autokill; Bas Cinteach; Gastight; Pegamoid; Waterproof.

395. **REGINALD GRAY:** Doncaster, Yorkshire.
G4 **Business:** Sports dealer.
Cartridges: The Don.

396. **EDWINSON C. GREEN.** Later as, **EDWINSON GREEN & SONS:**
F9   4 Northgate Street, Gloucester. Also at, 87 High Street,
G5   Cheltenham, Gloucestershire.
     Business: Gunmakers.
     Cartridges: The Cotswold; Fur & Feather; Maxim; S.P.Special Smokeless; Velox.

397. **W. W. GREENER.** Later as, **W. W. GREENER, LTD:** St. Mary's
F9   Square, Birmingham, Warwicks (W. Midlands). Also at, 68
G5   Haymarket, London SW1. And also at, Trinity House Lane, Hull,
G7   Yorkshire (Humberside).
G8   **Business:** Gun and rifle maker.
     Cartridges: Dead Shot; Ejector; Greener's Dwarf; Paragon; Police Gun E-K; Punt Gun; Sporting Life; Unnamed.
     Remarks: William Wellington Greener was in business between 1860 and 1966 if not in person. His firm became W. W. Greener, Ltd after 1920. The firms overseas addresses were: 8 Avenue de'Opera, Paris, France; 38 Bolshaya, Morskaya, Petersburg, U.S.A.; 176 Broadway, New York, U.S.A.

398. **GREENFIELD:** Storrington, Sussex.
G5   **Cartridges:** Eley Ejector.

399. **H. S. GREENFIELD & SON:** 4 Upper Bridge Street, Canterbury.
G5   Later at, 5 Dover Street, Canterbury, Kent.
G8   **Business:** Gun and rifle makers.
     Cartridges: The County Cartridge.
     Remarks: See number 336 Isaac Fox in this cartridge list.

400. **GREENWOOD & BATLEY:** The Albion Works, Leeds. Also at,
G6   Farnham, Yorkshire.
     Business: Cartridge manufacturers and merchants.
     Cartridges: A.E.C. Grey Squirel; A.E.C. Pest Control; The Greenwood; The Skyrack; Standard Load; Trapshooting Cartridge; Trap Shooting Load.
     Remarks: Cartridge cases were made only in 12 gauge with either crimson or orange paper tubes. Both loaded and ready capped cases were supplied to other firms. Rolled top and star crimp closures were used with their loadings. The A.E.C. cartridges were for the Agricultural Executive Committee. See number 488, H. M. Government of Great Britain in this cartridge list.

401. **GREGSON:** Blackburn, Lancashire.
G5   **Cartridges:** Eley's Ejector.

402. **G. GREIGHTON:** 8 Warwick Road; Carlisle, Cumberland (Cumbria).
     Cartridges: Unnamed.

403. **GRENFELL & ACCLES:** Perry Bar, Birmingham, Warwickshire
G6   (W. Midlands).
     Business: Cartridge case manufacturers.
     Cartridges: Unnamed.
     Remarks: This firm was disolved in 1896. For other details, see Accles Arms, Ammunition & Manufacturing Co, Ltd. This being number 1 at the start of this cartridge list.

404. **W. GRIFFITHS:** Manchester, Lancashire (Gt. Manchester).
 Cartridges: Eley's Gastight Case for E.C. Powder; Eley's Pegamoid.

405. **WILLIAM GRIFFITHS:** Bridge Street, Worcester, Worcs (H & W).
 Business: Gunmaker.
 Cartridges: Unnamed; The Worcestershire Cartridge.

406. **S. J. GRIMES:** Stamford, Lincolnshire.
G6 **Business:** Gun and ammunition depot.
 Cartridges: The Champion Special; The Stamford Cartridge.

407. **THE GUN SHOP:** Grantham, Lincolnshire.
 Business: Gun shop.
 Cartridges: Eley's Ejector (Name on over-shot wad only).

408. **GYE & MONCRIEFF:** London (Rest of the address is not known).
 Business: Gunmakers.
 Cartridges: Unnamed.

409. **J. B. HADDON:** Penzance, Cornwall.
G6 **Business:** Ironmonger.
 Cartridges: Unnamed.

410. **HAGENS:** Rugby, Warwickshire.
 Remarks: This name has been seen printed on an over-shot wad.

411. **C. HALL.** Later as, **C. HALL & CO:** Knaresborough, Yorkshire.
G8 **Business:** Gunmaker.
 Cartridges: Hall's Smokeless Castle; Unnamed.

412. **FRANK HALL:** 9 Beetwell Street, Chesterfield, Derbyshire.
G6 **Business:** Gunsmith.
G8 **Cartridges:** Hallrite Special.

413. **HUGH HALL:** Wetherby, Yorkshire.
 Business: Gunmaker and stores.
 Cartridges: The Farmers Stores.
 Remarks: Hugh was also known to have sold Kynoch & Co's brand cartridges, circa 1908-9.

414. **J. HALL:** Station Road, Wigton, Cumberland (Cumbria).
G6 **Remarks:** Cartridge remains of a 16 gauge pinfire have been found.

415. **JOHN HALL & SON:** 79 Cannon Street, London EC4.
G6 **Business:** Gunpowder manufacturers.
G8 **Cartridges:** Hall's Cannonite; Hall's Field B; Southern Cross.
 Remarks: Cartridges took their names from their firms powders. Metal detecting has unearthed a brass cartridge head with the stamping, JOHN HALL & SON LTD No 12 LONDON.

416. **T. HALL:** South Bank (Rest of the address is not known).
 Remarks: The above was seen printed on an over-shot wad that was loaded into an Eley Gastight Case for Curtis's & Harvey's Smokeless Diamond Powder.

417. **B. HALLIDAY & CO, LTD:** 63 Cannon Street, London EC4.
G6   **Business:** Gunmakers.
G8   **Cartridges:** The City; The Express; High Velocity; Pheasant; Stopem.
    Remarks: This firm first started trading in London in 1922 from, 60 Queen Victoria Street EC4.

418. **HAM & HUDDY:** 19 Fore Street, Liskeard, Cornwall.
    Business: Jewlers, but once dealt in game, guns and cartridges.
    Remarks: Their name has been seen printed on over-shot wads and on stampings of old cartridge remains.

419. **HAMEYER & CO:** 4 Market Street, Mansfield, Nottinghamshire.
    Business: Ironmongers.
    Cartridges: Kynoch Nitrone (Name on over-shot wad only).

420. **HAMMOND BROTHERS:** 40 Jewry Street, Winchester, Hampshire.
G8   **Business:** Gunmakers.
G9   **Cartridges:** Ejector; The Reliance; Trusty Servant; Winton;
H2   Yellow Seal Mullerite.
    Remarks: This firm made a move from Winchester to 48 Bridge Street, Andover, Hants during the mid 1960's. Shortly after this, they then moved into a brand new shop in Andover and they stopped trading in guns, ammunition and field sports. All they traded in then was general sports.

421. **W. T. HANCOCK:** 308 High Holborn, London WC1.
G9   **Business:** Gunmaker.
    Cartridges: Kynoch's Perfectly Gas-tight.

422. **HAND BROTHERS:** High Street, Odiham, Hampshire.
G9   **Business:** Ironmongers.
    Cartridges: The Pheasant Smokeless.

423. **F. G. HANDSCOMBE:** Bishops Stortford, Hertfordshire. Also at, Stansted, Essex.
    Business: Ironmonger.
    Cartridges: Yellow Seal Mullerite (Extra tube printing).

424. **JOHN R. HANSON:** 244 High Bridge Street. Also at, Hungate
G9   Passage, Lincoln, Lincolnshire.
    Business: Gun and cycle maker.
    Remarks: This firms name has been seen on an Eley Brothers pinfire headstamping. The above address was taken from an 1892 trade directory.

425. **L. HANSON:** 1 Cornhill, Lincoln, Lincolnshire.
G9   **Business:** Gunmaker.
    Cartridges: Kynoch Grouse Ejector.

426. **HARDING BROTHERS, LTD:** Commercial Street, Hereford, Herefordshire (H & W).
    Cartridges: The Rabbit Brand.

427. **J. HARDING:** Benfleet, Thames Estuary, Essex.
G9   **Cartridges:** Eley Brothers Blue Quality (Name on over-shot wad only).

428. **T. HARDING:** Wiveliscombe, Somerset.
Business: Ironmonger.
Cartridges: Unnamed (Name on over-shot wad only).

429. **HARDY BROTHERS, LTD:** Alnwick, Northumberland. Other branches
G9 at: 69 George Street, Edinburgh; 117 West George Street,
H2 Glasgow; 61 Pall Mall, London SW; 12 Moult Street, Manchester.
Business: gunmakers.
Cartridges: Hardy's Hotspur; Hardy's Northern; Hardy's
Northern High Velocity; Hardy's Reliance.

430. **HAREN:** London (Rest of the address is not known).
G9 **Remarks:** Their name has been seen on a headstamping.

431. **JOSEPH HARKOM & SON.** Later as, **J. HARKOM & SONS, LTD:**
H2 50 George Street, Edinburgh, Midlothian.
Business: Gunmakers.
Cartridges: Ejector.

432. **J. HARPER:** Fosseway Garage, Cropwell Bishop, Nottinghamshire.
Business: Motor garage.
Cartridges: Yellow Seal Mullerite (Extra tube printing).

433. **PERCY J. HARPER:** 59 Market Street. Also at, 44 Nantwich
G9 Road, Crewe, Cheshire.
Business: Ironmonger.
Cartridges: Harper's Invincible Smokeless.

434. **HARPUR BROTHERS:** Waterford, County Waterford, Republic of
H1 Ireland.
Cartridges: Sure Shot Brand Cartridge.

435. **GEORGE & A. HARRIS:** Market Place, Uttoxeter, Staffordshire.
H1 **Business:** Ironmongers.
Cartridges: Unnamed; Yew-Tox.

436. **H. HARRIS:** Leicester, Leics (Rest of the address is not
known).
Cartridges: Unnamed (Name on over-shot wad only).

437. **W. H. HARRIS & SON:** Totnes, Devonshire.
Business: Ironmongers.
Cartridges: Harris's Lightning.

438. **HARRISON BROTHERS:** Carlisle, Cumberland (Cumbria).
Remarks: Their name has been seen printed on an over-shot wad.

439. **T. & W. HARRISON:** Carlisle, Cumberland (Cumbria).
Cartridges: Unnamed.
Remarks: Their name has also been seen on over-shot wads and
on headstampings. There could well be connections with number
438 above in this list.

440. **HARRISON & HUSSEY, LTD:** 41 Albemarle Street, London W1.
H1 **Business:** Gunmakers.
Cartridges: The Albemarle; The Grafton; Stafford Deep Shell.

441. **HARRODS, LTD:** Brompton Road, Knightsbridge, London SW1.
H1   **Business:** Department stores.
H2   **Cartridges:** The Beaufort; The British Pioneer; Hurlingham; The Kill-Sure; The Pioneer.
    Remarks: In 1914 they were known to have sold Eley Gas-tight, Pegamoid, Primax, Curtis's & Harvey's, Nobel's Sporting Ballistite, Neonite, Red Star and Felixite. In 1963 they only sold, Hull Cartridge Co's Three Crowns, Eley Grand Prix and Remington.

442. **ERNEST FREDERICK HART:** Clare, Suffolk.
H1   **Business:** Ironmonger.
    Cartridges: Unnamed.

443. **FRED W. HART:** King Street. Also at, 39 Queen Street,
H1   Scarborough, Yorkshire.
    Business: Gunmaker.
    Cartridges: The Crackshot; The Eclipse; The Express; The Marvel .410; The Rocket.

444. **HARTFORTH:** (The name of place and address is not known).
    Remarks: Old cartridge remains with the name Hartforth on an Eley Brothers headstamping has been found.

445. **J. T. HARTWELL:** 5 West Chapel Street, Mayfair, London W1.
    Cartridges: The Mayfair Cartridge.

446. **A. B. HARVEY:** Falmouth, Cornwall.
    Cartridges: Unnamed.

447. **HARVEY GUNS:** Great Yarmouth, Norfolk.
    Business: Gun dealer.
    Remarks: A cartridge has been seen which carried their name.

448. **JOHN THOMAS HARWOOD:** St. James's Square, Yarmouth, Isle of Wight.
    Business: Ironmonger.
    Remarks: information that I was given was that in the past they had loaded shotgun cartridges.

449. **HASTE:** Chelmsford, Essex.
    Cartridges: Unnamed.

450. **G. HAWKE & SON:** 37 Fore Street, St. Austell. Also at,
H4   Trafalgar Square, Fowey, Cornwall.
    Business: Ironmongers.
    Cartridges: Mullerite Smokeless (Extra tube printing).

451. **HAWKES & SONS, LTD:** 32 East Street, Taunton. Also at,
H4   Wiveliscombe, Somerset.
    Business: Ironmongers.
    Cartridges: Hawk Brand.

452. **COLIN HAYGARTH:** The Cottage Gunshop, Dunnet, Caithness.
H4   **Business:** Gunsmith and cartridge loader.
    Cartridges: Economax.
    Remarks: Also listed as number 215 The Cottage Gunshop in this cartridge list.

453. **WILLIAM HAYNES:** 19 Duke Street. Also at, High Bridge Wharf,
H4 King's Road, Reading, Berkshire.
Business: Ironmonger.
Remarks: At one time I owned a cartridge head with Haynes name on the headstamping William was known to have been in business in 1903 and he was still active into the early 1920's.

454. **S. E. HAYWARD & CO, LTD:** Tunbridge Wells, Kent. Also at,
H4 Crowborough, Sussex.
Cartridges: The New Special Smokeless.

455. **R. HAZEL:** 15 High West Street, Dorchester, Dorset.
H4 **Business:** Ironmonger.
Cartridges: Unnamed pinfire.

456. **WALTER ERNEST HEAL.** Later as, **W. E. HEAL, LTD:** Bampton
H4 Street, Tiverton, Devonshire.
Business: Ironmonger.
Cartridges: The Special Rabbit Cartridge; The Supa Tivvy; The Tivvy; Tivvy Super.

457. **T. HEATHMAN, LTD:** 137 High Street, Crediton, Devon.
H4 **Business:** Believed to have been a gunmaker.
Cartridges: Unnamed (Kynoch Witton Brand. Heathman's name on the headstamping).

458. **CHARLES HELLIS.** Later as, **CHAS HELLIS & SONS, LTD:** 119
H2 Edgware Road. Later at, 121-3 Edgware Road, Hyde Park West,
H3 London W2.
H5 **Business:** Cartridge experts.
Cartridges: 12 X 2 inch; 12 X 2 inch Deep Shell; The Championship Cartridge; The Economist; The Edgware; The Falcon; The G.A. (Guaranteed Accuracy); The Kestrel; Kynoch Grouse Ejector; The Merlin; Pegamoid; The Service; The Standard; Unnamed.
Remarks: Two other brand names that have been seen loaded by Hellis were, Aladix Astral and Aladix Ventura. It is more than likely that they were loaded for a firm called Aladix. Charles E. Hellis founded the firm in 1884. His two sons, Charles and Clifford came into his family business in 1902. This then dates any cartridge with the wording Sons added as being from 1902 onwards. Many of their loadings carried the wording, Guaranteed Accuracy on their over-shot wads. Hellis loaded cartridges in the gauges 12, 16 and 20.
   Special loads were produced to customers orders. The Earl of Carnarvon at Highclere Castle was just one such customer. Several of these privately ordered cartridges had a family crest printed on the over-shot wad. The higher quality cartridges from Hellis had large primer caps. To start with, imported cases were used. Later on, the Eley-Kynoch I.C.I. best quality cases were loaded. Like many other firms, not all of their cartridges had brand names printed on them, but some of them may have carried a brand name on their boxes.
   Hellis's Economist cartridges were also sold by Henry Atkin from his 27 St. James's Street London premises. This was also printed on some of the box labels. Chas Hellis & Sons, Ltd finally closed their doors in 1956. It was then that they

458. **CHARLES HELLIS:** Continued.
merged with Charles Rosson of Norwich. See number 879 in this cartridge list. Together they then became Hellis-Rosson, Ltd and they continued to sell an Economist cartridge. See the next entry in this list.

459. **HELLIS-ROSSON, LTD:** 7 Bedford Street, Norwich, Norfolk.
H4　**Business:** Gunmakers and cartridge loaders.
H6　**Cartridges:** Economist; Kuvert.
Remarks: The majority of their cartridges were closed by crimping.

460. **J. HELSON:** 84 Fore Street, Exeter, Devonshire.
H4　**Cartridges:** The Demon; The Invincible; Victor.

461. **HELY:** Dublin, Republic of Ireland (Rest of the address is not known).
Cartridges: Hely's Rlymax.

462. **HELYAR:** Yeovil, Somerset.
Cartridges: Unnamed pinfire (Helyar on the headstamping).

463. **HELYER:** Ixworth, Suffolk.
Cartridges: Metalic.

464. **WALTER HEMING:** High Street, Wickham. Also at, Fareham,
H4　Hampshire.
Business: Ironmonger.
Cartridges: The Meon Valley Special Smokeless.

465. **HENDERSON:** Dundee, Angus (Tayside).
H8　**Cartridges:** Kynoch Perfectly Gas-tight Cartridge for E.C. Powder.

466. **HENRITE EXPLOSIVES:** Office at, 97 Wilton Road, London SW.
H4　Factory and powder mills at, Dartford, Kent.
H8　**Business:** Gunpowder and cartridge manufacturers.
Cartridges: Ejector; The Henrite; Pigeon Cartridge.
Remarks: The name Henrite was registered in 1899 by Luck's Explosives, Ltd. This firm was active up until 1906. See number 652 in this cartridge list. Henrite cartridges were advertised in gauges 12 and 16 in the 1907 Army & Navy Co-operative Society, Ltd's catalogue. For A.N.C.S.Ltd see number 28 in this list.

467. **ALEXANDER HENRY.** Later as, **ALEXANDER HENRY & CO:** 18
H4　Frederick Street. Also at, 12 Andrew Street, Edinbugh, Midlothian. Was also at, 23 Pall Mall, London SW1.
Business: Gunmakers.
Cartridges: unnamed.
Remarks: Of all of their cartridges that I have seen, I have never seen one of them that carried a brand name. This firm was purchased in 1902 and it traded in the name of Henry until 1939. It finally merged with the firm, Alex Martin, Ltd. See number 689 in this cartridge list.

468. **W. HENSMAN:** Boston, Lincolnshire.
Business: Gunmaker.
Cartridges: The Whirlwind.

469. **W. G. HENTON.** Later as, **W. G. HENTON & SONS:** 204 High Street, Lincoln, Lincolnshire.
Business: Ironmongers.
Cartridges: Special Loading.

470. **T. HEPPLESTONE:** 25 Shudehill, Manchester, Lancashire (Gt. Manchester).
H8
Business: Gunmaker.
Cartridges: Kynoch Grouse Ejector; Unnamed.

471. **HERCULES ARMS CO, LTD:** 8 St. Martin's Street, Leicester Square, London WC2.
H8
Business: Gun and cartridge dealers.
Cartridges: The Farm Cartridge; The Hercules; Waterproof.
Remarks: This firm shared premises with E. J. Churchill. See number 172 in this cartridge list. It was a corner building with the joining of two streets. Each firm used a different street for it's address.

472. **W. HERRING:** Street, Somerset.
H8 **Cartridges:** Special Smokeless.

473. **CHARLES M. HESFORD & CO, LTD:** Ormskirk, Lancashire.
H8 **Business:** Impliment dealers.
Cartridges: The Hesford Special.

474. **Mrs EMILY HEWEN:** 12 Market Street. Also at, Sheep Street, Wellingborough, Northamptonshire.
Business: Ironmonger.
Cartridges: Unnamed.

475. **HEWETT & SON:** Alton, Hampshire.
Cartridges: The Express.

476. **HEYWOOD & HODGE:** Torrington, Devonshire.
H8 **Cartridges:** The Reliable.

477. **HICK FERNS & CO:** 32 Kirkgate, Otley, Yorkshire.
Cartridges: The Stoppum.

478. **HICKLEY:** Farnham, Surrey.
Business: Ironmonger.
Cartridges: Unnamed or name not recorded.

479. **FREDERICK HICKS:** 67 High Street, Haverhill, Suffolk.
Business: Gun and cycle agent.
Cartridges: Special Loading.

480. **HARRY HIGGINS:** 46-48 Theme Street, Tenbury Wells, Worcestershire (H & W).
H8
Cartridges: The Dead Shot; Harry Higgins Special.

481. **E. & G. HIGHAM:** 4 Chapel Street, Liverpool, Lancashire (Merseyside).
H9
Business: Gunmakers.
Cartridges: Gastight & Metal Lined; Patent Gastight Cartridge.

482. **GEORGE G. HIGHAM:** 3 Bailey Street, Oswestry, Shropshire.
H9 Also at, Welshpool, Montgomeryshire (Powys).
Business: Gun and fishing tackle maker, cycle agent and sports dealer.
Cartridges: The Eclipse; Eley Ejector; Hios; Pegamoid; Velox.
Remarks: This firm was established in 1825, long before the invention of shotgun cartridges.

483. **HIGHCLERE CASTLE ESTATE:** Highclere Park, Hampshire.
H9 **Business:** Private country estate.
Cartridges: unnamed.
Remarks: They were a private customer to Chas Hellis & Sons, Ltd. See number 458 in this cartridge list.

484. **ARTHUR HILL.** Later as, **HILL & SON:** 9 Market Place,
H6 Horncastle, Lincolnshire.
H9 **Business:** Gunmakers.
Cartridges: The Champion; The County Cartridge; The Ideal; The Reliable.
Remarks: Arthur took over the premises in 1902 from G. H. Wilson who had also loaded a Champion Cartridge. See number 1124 in this cartridge list.

485. **RUSSELL HILLSDON:** Chichester, Horsham & Worthing, Sussex.
H9 Also in, Birmingham, Warwicks (W. Midlands) & Farnham, Surrey.
Business: Gun and field sports stores.
Cartridges: The Combat; The Goodwood; The Revenge; The Sussex Champion; Unnamed.
Remarks: I have no idea how long that this firm did business in Birmingham. Their Farnham shop opened in 1921.

486. **W. R. HINDE:** Whitehaven, Cumberland (Cumbria).
Cartridges: Special Smokeless.

487. **GEORGE HINTON & SONS, LTD:** 5 Fore Street, Taunton, Somerset.
H6 **Business:** Gunmakers.
H9 **Cartridges:** Hinton's Eclipse Gamekeepers; Special I.X.L.; The Standard; The Taunton; Unnamed.
Remarks: Established in 1815. The Standard was a Hinton name at least since 1918. The business changed hands in 1947.

488. **H. M. GOVERNMENT OF GREAT BRITAIN:** The Houses of Parliament,
H6 Westminster, London SW1.
H7 **Business:** The armed services and other military and civil
I1 depatments.
I5 **Cartridges & Remarks:** Very many shotgun type cartridges have been produced for the crown use. Eley Trapshooting for training purposes with the armed services. Shotgun cartridges were also produced for the L.D.V. Later known as The Home Guard. The Agricultural Executive Committee and the Forestry Commision both had their own pest control cartridges. The R.A.F. also had cartridges. These for bird scaring to clear airfields and aircraft signal duties. Aircraft have used engine starter cartridges and barage balloon cable cutting cartridges. Other uses have been for riot control and for use in the nations proof houses. Depending on their need, cases have been loaded as blank, powder, shot, rubber or just signal pyrotechnics.

489. **J. HOBSON:** Leamington Spa, Warwickshire.
I1   **Business:** Gunmaker.
    Cartridges: The Challenge; The Dead Shot; Hobson's Choise; Hobson's Full Stop; Kynoch Grouse Ejector.

490. **HOCKEY:** Brigg, Lincolnshire (Humberside).
    Cartridges: Hockey's Woodcraft.

491. **A. S. HOCKNELL:** Eccleshall, Staffordshire.
I1   **Business:** Ironmonger.
    Cartridges: Unnamed.

492. **A. A. HODGSON:** 27-29 Mercer Row, Louth, Lincolnshire.
I1   **Cartridges:** The Luda Cartridge.

493. **HENRY HODGSON:** 4 The Traverse, Bury St. Edmunds. Also at,
I1   6 Northgate Street, Ipswich, Suffolk.
    Business: Gunmaker.
    Cartridges: The County De-Luxe; The Eclipse; The Express; Pegamoid; The Perfect; The Special; The Suffolk; Waterproof Cartridge.

494. **J. HODGSON:** Lancaster, Lancashire.
    Cartridges: The Lancaster.

495. **JESSE P. HODGSON:** Mercer Row, Louth, Lincolnshire. Also at,
I1   Bridlington, Yorkshire (Humberside).
    Business: Gunmaker.
    Remarks: Jesse was known to have been in business in Louth between 1892 and 1904. By 1913, this Louth shop was in the name of A. A. Hodgson. Obviously family connections. See number 492 in this cartridge list. The town of Bridlington has been seen stamped into a Kynoch brass head and also printed on an over-shot wad.

496. **R. C. HODGSON:** 7 Queen Street, Ripon, Yorkshire.
I5   **Business:** Gunsmith and fishing tackle specialist.
    Cartridges: The Rapido.

497. **R. T. HODGSON:** Station Bridge, Harrogate, Yorkshire.
I1   **Business:** Ironmonger and gunsmith.
I5   **Cartridges:** The Harrogate.

498. **WILLIAM HODGSON:** 8 Middle Street, Ripon, Yorkshire.
I1   **Business:** Gunmaker.
I5   **Cartridges:** Eley Blue Quality Case; The Rapido; Special
I6   Smokeless.
    Remarks: Obviously there were family connections between R. C. Hodgson and William as they were both based in Ripon and sold Rapido cartridges.

499. **JOHN HOLDRON:** Market Street, Also in Bath Street,
    Asby-de-la-Zouch, Leicestershire.
    Business: Ironmonger.
    Cartridges: The Rabbit.

500. **CHARLES R. HOLLAND:** 43 Dollar Street, Cirencester, Glos.
I1   **Business:** Gunmaker.

500. **CHARLES R. HOLLAND:** Continued.
Cartridges: The Nonsuch Smokeless Cartridge (Kynoch Perfectly Gas-tight.
Remarks: In 1870 there was a David Holland at the above address. It is believed that Charles took over the business from him. Charles was known to have been active from 43 Dollar Street between 1885 and 1889 and perhaps for much longer.

501. **HOLLAND & HOLLAND, LTD:** 98 New Bond Street, London W1.
I2
I6
Business: Gun and rifle makers.
Cartridges: The Badminton; The Badminton High Velocity Large Cap; The Centenery Cartridge; The Dominion; Ejector; High Velocity; Nitro Ball; Nitro Paradox; Pegamoid; Recoilite; The Royal; The Twelve-Two; Two Gauge; Unnamed.
Remarks: Their Two Gauge was one of the largest paper tubed cartridges that carried a gunmakers name. Upwards in size was only the Punt Gun. The Royal was a top quality cartridge having a metal inner sleave which was crimped closed at the mouth. It also had an outer gastight brick red case wall which was printed and lacquered. It was circa 1938-39. The Recoilite Cartridge had it's name printed on the over-shot wad only. This being RECOILITE-REGD. The only box of these cartridges that I have seen were loaded with number 6 shot. The name Holland & Holland was not printed on the cartridges, only on the box. This was also the same with their Centenery Cartridges.

502. **ISAAC HOLLIS:** Weaman Row, Lench Street, Birmingham, Warwickshire (W. Midlands).
I3
Cartridges: Hollis' Special Blue Cartridge (By Royal Warrant); Hollis' Special Green Cartridge (By Royal warrant).

503. **HOLME & ASH:** 3 Scarsdale Place, Buxton, Derbyshire.
Business: Ironmongers.
Cartridges: The Peak Cartridge.
Remarks: They were known to have been in business between 1904 and 1932. They were not listed in an 1881 trade directory and it is not known the year when they closed down.

504. **HOLTOM'S:** 243 London Road (South), Lowestoft, Suffolk.
I3 **Cartridges:** Unnamed.

505. **HOME'S:** 43 Friar Street, Reading, Berkshire.
I3 **Cartridges:** Home's Special Loading.

506. **T. J. HOOKE.** Later as, **T. J. HOOKE & SONS:** 38-39 The Pavement, Coppergate, York, Yorkshire.
I3
Business: Gunmakers.
Cartridges: Ebor Cartridge .410; Eclipse Cartridge; The Gimcrack; Hooke's Imperial.
Remarks: Some other addresses for this firm were: 28-30 Coppergate, York; 20 Clarance Street, York. During 1904 the gunmaker at the above address was J. A. Hooke.

507. **HOOTON & JONES:** 60 Dale Street, Liverpool, Lancs (Merseyside).
I3
I6
Business: Gunmakers.
Cartridges: Hooton & Jones's Special; The Smokeless Cartridge.

508. **WILLIAM M. HOOTON:** Southgate, Sleaford, Lincolnshire.
Business: Gunmaker.
Cartridges: Eley E.B. Nitro Case (Name on over-shot wad only).
Remarks: The above address was taken from out of an 1892 trade directory.

509. **J, J, HOPKINS, LTD:** 2-4 Lake Street, Leighton Buzzard, Beds.
I3 **Business:** Ironmonger.
Cartridges: The Golden Pheasant Special Smokeless.

510. **ERNEST ALFRED HOPPING:** 5 Monmouth Street, Lostwithiel, Cornwall.
I3 **Business:** Ironmonger.
Cartridges: The Rabbit Cartridge.

511. **HORRELL & SON:** 19 High Street, Crediton, Devonshire.
I3 **Business:** Ironmongers.
Cartridges: Electric Smokeless Cartridge.

512. **THOMAS HORSLEY.** Later as, **T. HORSLEY & SONS, LTD:** 10 Coney
I3 Street. Later at, Micklegate, York, Yorkshire.
Business: Gunmakers.
Cartridges: Smokeless Rabbit Cartridge; Unnamed.

513. **W. HORTON:** 98 Buchanan Street. Also at, 119 Buchanan Street,
I3 Glasgow, Lanarkshire (Strathclyde).
Business: Gun, rifle and fishing tackle makers.
Cartridges: Eley's Ejector; The Extra; The Horton Cartridge; Waterproof.
Remarks: William Horton was established in 1855. He ran his business until he retired when he handed the reins over to a son. A little information on their Glasgow addresses may help in dating some of their cartridges. 1863-1877 they were at 29 Union Street. From 1878-1893 their address was, 11 Royal Exchange Square. The firm then moved to, 98 Buchanan Street where it was active up until 1912. It then made a move to 199 in the same street. During the firms lifetime, their factory works were at, 11 Prince's Square. A move was made to Osborne Street where it has been recorded that it was there in 1903. There were also branches in Oban, Argyllshire and at Stirling, Stirlingshire. These being recorded in 1896. Their business finally came to an end at some date in the late 1920's.

514. **HOWARD BROTHERS:** 240 St. Ann's Road, Tottenham, London W1.
I4 **Cartridge:** Unnamed.

515. **WILLIAM HOWE & SONS, LTD:** Shrewsbury, Shropshire.
I4 **Business:** Ironmongers.
Cartridges: Unnamed (May have been called The Plough).

516. **HOWES & SON:** Wymondham, Norfolk.
I4 **Business:** Ironmongers.
Cartridges: The Champion Smokeless Cartridge.

517. **C. S. HUDSON:** Great Underbank, Stockport, Cheshire (Gt. Manchester).
Business: Ironmonger.
Cartridges: Unnamed.

518. **HUISH:** Porlock, Somerset.
Business: Ironmongers.
Remarks: Information given was that cartridges were once loaded on their premises.

519. **HULL CARTRIDGE CO, LTD:** 58 De Grey Street, Hull, Yorkshir
I4 (Humberside).
Business: Cartridge loading and wholesales.
Cartridges: The Standard; Three Crowns; Unnamed.
Remarks: In 1947, the firm of Turners Carbides, Ltd. See number 1022 in this cartridge list. They then decided to enter into the business of loading shotgun cartridges. As the firms name was not appropriate for their new venture, the name, Hull Cartridge Company (Division of Turners Carbides, Ltd) was initiated. This name was retained until 1948 when the companies became separated from each other. The Hull Cartridge Co, Ltd was now born. From here on it was to become a thriving business.
   The original firm of Turners Carbides, Ltd was sold to, Hoechst U.K. shortly after the death of Mr Bontoft Snr who was a founder of that firm. The Hull Cartridge Co, Ltd was then retained in the ownership of the late Mr Bontoft's two sons, Kenneth and Peter.
   In the late 1950's, the Hull Cartridge Company was appointed as the sole U.K. distributors to the large American firm, Remington Arms Co, Inc. In pre World War Two days, Remington had established a branch in England. See number 848 Remington U.M.C. (England) in this cartridge list. When Remingtons changed over from paper to plastic tubed shotshells in 1962 and 1963, Hull Cartridge then excepted all of their stock of remaining paper tubed cases that were held by Remington on behalf of their associated company, Peters. These excellent paper tubed cases were wax impregnated and Hull Cartridge loaded several thousands of them during the years of 1964 and 1965. Many of these blue American cases were to be seen on our market around about that time.
   As far as it is known, the Hull gunmaker Robert Robinson was the first person to market a Hull cartridge which carried three crowns. These in a crest on the case wall printings. It was three separate crowns within a shield. The crowns were in the vertical being one below each other. Being very similar, the Hull Cartridge Co's Three Crowns cartridges were to become the most popular of their range. The company loaded very many versions of them in the gauges 12, 16 and 20. At first, English cases were used and later on imported cases which were both paper and plastic tubed. For details on the gunmaker R. Robinson, see number 875 in this list.
   Many of the firms early loads were in Eley-Kynoch cases, but such was the demand, plus the fact that the Witton Factory had a disastrous explosion that Hull Cartridge were forced to look elswhere for their supply of cartridge cases. This was the reason why Italian Fiocchi cases were imported into England in their millions. As well as producing their own branded cartridges, the firm ventured out and succeeded in capturing a large slice of the market in loading customers brands of cartridges. Today the firm resides at, Bontoft Avenue on the National Avenue Estate. This still being at Kingston Hull. Nowadays the majority loaded are plastic tubed, crimped closed.

520. **T. L. HULL & CO:** 33 High Street, Shaftesbury, Dorset.
I4   **Business:** Ironmongers.
    Cartridges: The Shaston Special Smokeless.

521. **GEORGE HUME:** Dumfries, Dumfriesshire (Dumfries & Galloway).
    Business: Gunmaker.
    Cartridges: Kynoch's Perfectly Gas-tight.

522. **HUNTER & MADDIL:** 58 Royal Avenue, Belfast, Northeren Ireland.
    Business: Gunmakers.
    Cartridges: Unnamed,
    Remarks: They were together in business circa 1890 to 1920.

523. **HUNTER & SON:** 61-62 Royal Avenue, Belfast, Northern Ireland.
I4   **Business:** Gunmakers.
    Cartridges: De Luxe; The Eclipse; Express Cartridge; The Favourite; The Ideal; The Invictus; The Long Shot; The Reliable; The Royal Cartridge; The Universal.

524. **HUNTER & VAUGHAN:** Broad Street, Bristol, Gloucestershire (Avon).
    Cartridges: Special Smokeless.
    Remarks: This firm incorporated that of Septimus Chamber & Co, Ltd. See number 167 in this cartridge list. The above address was taken from a 1914 trade directory.

525. **WILLIAM HURLSTONE:** 50 Market Place, Warminster, Wiltshire.
I4   **Business:** Ironmonger.
    Remarks: Several of his cartridge headstampings have been found on old cartridge remains, but I have never seen a complete cartridge by him. In one old directory they had spelt his name as Hurlestone. Number 50 in the Market Place got renumbered to 49. He was not listed in an 1889 directory.

526. **H. J. HUSSEY.** Later as, **H. J. HUSSEY, LTD** (Late of **LANG &**
I4   **HUSSEY, LTD**): 88 Jermyn Street. Also at, 81 New Bond Street,
I6   London SW1.
    Business: Gunmakers.
    Cartridges: Eley's Ejector; Joyce's Ejector; The Times.

527. **J. HUTCHINGS:** Aberystwith, Cardiganshire (Dyfed).
    Business: Gunmaker.
    Cartridges: Kynoch Perfectly Gas-tight;

528. **HUTCHINSON:** Kendal, Westmorland (Cumbria).
    Business: Gunmaker.
    Cartridges: Nobel's Sporting Ballistite Special Cartridge.

530. **W. H. ICKE:** Smithford Street, Coventry, Warwickshire (W. Midlands).
    Business: Ironmonger and general furnishings.
    Cartridges: Kynoch Perfectly Gas-tight.

531. **ISLEY:** Salisbury, Wiltshire.
J5   **Cartridges:** Unnamed pinfire (Plain Eley Bros 12 gauge case with a headstamping of reversed wording. The white over-shot wad had the wording ISLEY.SALISBURY. printed in red.

532. **IMPERIAL CHEMICAL INDUSTRIES (I.C.I.) METALS DIVISION (ELEY-KYNOCH), LTD:** Offices at, Millbank, London SW.
Works at, Witton, Birmingham, Warwickshire (W. Midlands).
Business: Ammunition manufacturers and merchants.
Cartridges: 2 inch Deep Shell; 4 Gauge; 8 Gauge; 10 Gauge; 20 Gauge Cartridge; 20 Gauge Case; 20th Century; 20th Century Deep Shell; Acme; Almac (Brass .410); Alphamax; Alphamax High Velocity; Alphamax Neoflak; Blank; Blanks; Bonax; British Smokeless Cartridge (Also known as the E.D.N. 'Eau-de-nil' Cartridge); British Smokeless Case (E.D.N.); Buffalo; Bull's Eye; Cable Cutter (Not shotgun but 12 gauge); Coronation; Deep Shell; D.S.C.; Ejector; Ejector Thin Brass; Empire; Empress; Extra Long (3 inch .410); Fourlong (2½ inch .410); Fourten (2 inch .410); Gastight Cartridge; Gastight Case; Gastight Quality Cartridge; Gastight Quality Case; G.P. (General Purpose, not Grand Prix); Grand Prix Cartridge; Grand Prix High Velocity Cartridge; Grand Prix Case; Grand Prix Quality Case; Hollandia; Hymax; Impax; Juno; Maximum High Velocity; Maximum Neoflak; Mettax; Nitro Case; Nitron; Noneka; Parvo; Pegamoid Cartridge; Pegamoid Case; Practice Cartridge; Primax; Quail Smokeless; Red Flash Smokeless; Rocket; Saluting Blank; Saluting Blanks; Scarebird (Removal of birds from airfields and orchards etc); Smokeless Cartridge; Sporting Ballistite Cartridge; Sporting Ballistite Case; Trapshooting; Two-Inch; Universal (Kyblack); Unlined Nitro Case; Unnamed pinfire; Velocity; Westminster; Wildfowling; Winchester Cannon (For starting guns etc); Yeoman; Zenith.
Remarks: This very large company took over from Nobel Industries, Ltd in 1926. From the begining of their control, all of the manufacturing of ammunition was undertaken from the old Kynoch Lion Works at Witton, Birmingham. You may like to refer to numbers 589 and 756, George Kynoch and Nobel Industries, Ltd in this cartridge list. Although we are here only concerned with sporting shotgun cartridges, this company also produced rifle, pistol and many other kinds of ammunition for military and civil purposes which inclued exports.

In the shotgun line, pinfire cartridges in 16 and 12 gauge were made. These had no case wall printings and were referred to as having brown paper tube. This colour was more like a straw white. These were often sold with blank loads for alarm guns, or given black powder and shot loads for the many people that still enjoyed shooting with the old pifire guns.

Some other brand cartridges that were made by them are as follows: A.E.C. Grey Squirrel; A.E.C. Pest Control; A.E.C. Rook; Agricultural Departments Reserve; Forestry Pest Control; W.A.E.C. Grey Squirrel. Many cartridges were especially loaded for the British Government during World War Two. The letters W.A.E.C. stood for, War Agricultural Executive Committee. See number 488, H.M. Government of Great Britain in this cartridge list.

The L.D.V. (Local Defence Volunteers), later renamed The Home Guard were supplied with cartridges with various coloured paper tubes with the broad arrow printed on the case walls in black. These had very heavy loads and some of them were of lethal ball. Special Trapshooting was a cartridge which was supplied to the services in 12 gauge. Their paper tube colours were straw white (Brown) and also orange. Their case

532. **IMPERIAL CHEMICAL INDUSTRIES (I.C.I.) METALS DIVISION (ELEY-KYNOCH), LTD:** Continued.
wall printings were in black and they also carried the broad arrow. One of their uses was in training the R.A.F's airgunners. Our services also used the Eley Rocket 12 gauge cartridges. These wartime cartridges had the straw white (Eley brown) cases with red case wall printings. They also carried the government broad arrow markings. Also made for military and civil use were engine starter cartridges which used shotgun type cartridge cases. Military engine starter paper tubed cases were purple.
   As can be seen by this cartridge list, I.C.I. (Eley-Kynoch) also sold cases and loaded cartridges to order to many firms within the British Isles. They also exported over-seas. All shotgun cartridge cases carried the I.C.I. Trade Mark on their headstampings, except for .410 and under. The only exceptions to this were some that were made to special orders. These included some overseas shipments. The stamping ELEY-KYNOCH I.C.I. was also used in Victoria, Australia. It eventually was discontinued when I.C.I. were taken over by Imperial Metal Industries (I.M.I.) around about 1962. Although I am briefly mentioning this later division in this list, I will not dwell on it to any degree as most of it's cartridges that were produced were closed by crimped closures. See number 533, the next entry in this cartridge list.
   At a glance of the many cartridge names listed here, one can see how I.C.I. honoured the names of the many extinct firms that had been absorbed into this large cocern. Many of these were names that had been used by Messrs Eley Brothers, G. Kynoch & Co, Nobels' and Schultze. They had found that the brand names from some of these now extinct firms still returned good sales to the present company. For comparison, see numbers 290, 308, 536, 589, 755, 756 and 905 in this cartridge list.
   Of all the names here listed under 'Cartridges', several of them may have been experimental as they were not listed in the annual price lists. Others may have been special brand names for certain overseas markets. Not all of them may have entered into full production. For the interest sake, I have illustrated a few of the rarely known brands. There could quite well have been others than those that I have listed. Please remember that those cartridges that I am able to mention in this cartridge list is only the tip of a very large iceberg.

533. **IMPERIAL METAL INDUSTRIES (I.M.I) (KYNOCH), LTD. ELEY**
J3 **AMMUNITION DIVISION:** Witton, Birmingham, West Midlands.
J4 **Business:** Ammunition manufacturers and merchants.
   Cartridges: 8 Gauge; 10 Gauge; Alphamax; Extra Long .410; Fourlong .410; Fourten .410; Gastight; Grand Prix; Grand Prix H.V.; Saluting Blank; Winchester Cannon.
   Remarks: Where should I draw the line ? I have mentioned some of the brands that were closed by rolled turnovers that were constructed with paper tubes. There may well be others like the Eley Two-Inch, but it is not my intention here to dwell on brands that were closed by crimping. This firm was the follow on from number 532 above.

534. **CHARLES INGRAM:** 18 Renfield Street. Later at, 4 Bothwell
J4   Street. Later still at, 10 Waterloo Street, Glasgow,
     Lanarkshire (Strathclyde).
     Business: Gunmaker.
     Cartridges: The C.I.; The Ingram; Unnamed.
     Remarks: This firm had some connections with John D. Dougall &
     Sons, number 268 in this cartridge list.

535. **INMAN MORROW & CO:** 27 Queen Victoria Street, Leeds, Yorkshire.
J4   **Business:** Gunmakers.
     Cartridges: Unnamed or name not recorded.

536. **IRISH METAL INDUSTRIES, LTD:** 12 Dawson Street, Dublin. Also
J5   at, Earles Island, Galway, Republic of Ireland.
     Business: Ammunition manufacturers.
     Cartridges: Acme; Alphamax; Blackthorn Cartridge; Bonax; Nobel
     Clyde; Empire; Grand Prix; Klymax; Lia-Fail; Maximum; Mettax
     Cartridge; Noneka; Pegamoid; Primax; Special Trapshooting;
     Nobel's Sporting Ballistite; Westminster; Yeoman; Zenith.
     Remarks: This Irish firm was started by I.C.I Metals Division
     Eley-Kynoch in the late 1920's or early 1930's. Most of their
     shotgun cartridges that they produced were in 12 gauge. A few
     16 and 20 gauge were also produced. This firm was in business
     up until 1971.

537. **DAVID IRONS & SONS:** Forfar, Angus (Tayside).
     Business: Ironmongers.
     Cartridges: Unnamed.

538. **GEORGE IRVIN:** Penrith, Cumberland (Cumbria).
     Business: Ironmonger and ammunition dealer.
     Cartridges: Unnamed or name not recorded.

539. **JACKSON & SONS:** Frome, Somerset.
     Remarks: A green cartridge by them had the name, The Selwood
     or Elwood or something similar.

540. **ALFRED JACKSON:** Abergavenny, Monmouthshire (Gwent).
J3   **Business:** Ironmonger.
J5   **Cartridges:** Unnamed.

541. **H. G. JACKSON:** Bungay & Halesworth, Suffolk.
     Business: Ironmonger and gunsmith.
     Cartridges: Unnamed.

542. **SAMUEL JACKSON:** 7 Church Gate, Pepper Street, Nottingham,
J5   Nottinghamshire.
     Business: Gunmaker.
     Cartridges: The Nottingham Cartridge.
     Remarks: Sam was known to have been in business between 1881
     and 1912.

543. **THOMAS JACKSON & SON:** London (Rest of the address is not
J5   known).
     Remarks: An old brass cartridge head was found and it is
     believed to have been of this firm. It had raised writing
     (Reversed stamping) and although it was 12 gauge it carried no
     gauge size. See the illustrations.

544. **WILLIAM JACKSON.** Later as, **JACKSON & SON:** 41 Silver Street,
J5   Gainsborough, Lincolnshire.
     Business: Ironmongers.
     Cartridges: Best Gastight Woodcock Brand; Jackson's Dead Shot;
     The Pheasant Loading.

545. **JAMES & CO:** Great Western Mills, Church Street, Hungerford,
J6   Berkshire.
     Business: Millers, game food manufacturers and agricultural
     merchants.
     Cartridges: The Kennett Smokeless; Marlborough.
     Remarks: Their cartridge brands were pre-World War Two. Their
     last Kennett cartridges had no tube printings. In the post-
     war years their mills were gutted by fire and the firm went
     out of business.

546. **M. JAMES & SONS:** Newcastle Emlyn, Carmarthen (Dyfed).
J6   **Business:** Ironmongers.
     Cartridges: The Gwalia.

547. **JAMES & TATTON:** 14 Market Street, Longton. Also at, Hanley,
J6   Stoke-on-Trent, Staffordshire.
     Business: Ironmongers.
     Cartridges: Special Smokeless.

548. **WILLIAM HENRY JANE:** Fore Street, Bodmin, Cornwall.
     Business: Ironmonger and practice gunmaker.
     Cartridges: The Bodmin.

549. **A. R. & H. V. JEFFERY, LTD:** 100 Old Town Street, Plymouth,
J3   Devonshire.
J6   **Business:** Gunmakers.
     Cartridges: .410; The Eddystone; The Empire; The Empire
     Cartridge.

550. **CHARLES JEFFERY.** Later as, **C. JEFFERY & SONS:** 29 High East
J3   Street, Dorchester, Dorset.
J6   **Business:** Gunmakers.
     Cartridges: The Ejector; The Empire; The Rabbit; The Royal
     Game; The Twenty.
     Remarks: Charles was known to have been in business in 1898.

551. **SAMUEL R. JEFFERY.** Later as, **S. R. JEFFERY & SON, LTD:** 134
J3   High Street, Guildford, Surrey. Was at one time also in,
J6   Salisbury, Wiltshire.
     Business: Gunmakers.
     Cartridges: Eley's Gastight Cartridge Case (Pinfire); .410
     Short; .410 Long; The Champion; The Club; Smokeless Powder;
     Special Smokeless.

552. **W. JEFFERY & SON:** 3 Russell Street, Plymouth, Devonshire.
J7   **Business:** Gunmakers.
K1   **Cartridges:** The Eddystone; The Flag; The Pegamoid; The Rabbit
     Special; The Sky High; The Smeaton; Unnamed.
     Remarks: There must have been some family connections between
     this firm and number 549 in this cartridge list.

553. **W. J. JEFFERY & CO.** Later as, **W. J. JEFFERY & CO, LTD:**
J7 St. James's, London. (For the rest of addresses, see Remarks).
K1 **Business:** Gunmakers.
    Cartridges: The Champion; The Club Smokeless; The Ejector;
    High Velocity Cartridge; The Jeffery Cartridge; Jeffery's
    XXX Cartridge; The Sharpshooter; The Sharpshooters.
    Remarks: I have four different addresses for this firm, and
    they are all in London. I do not know for sure in which order
    that they ran. Several of them may have been in use at the
    same time. The addresses are as follows: 13 King Street, St.
    James's; 60 Queen Victoria Street, EC; 26 Bury Street, St.
    James's; 9 Golden Sqare, Regent Street, W1. This last
    mentioned I believe was their final address. I also have a
    note in my files which says that they closed their premises at
    60 Queen Victoria Street in October 1921, but retaind the 26
    Bury Street shop in St. James's. I think that the firm was at
    Victoria and King Streets, circa 1905-11.

554. **JENVEY & CO.** Later as, **JENVEY & TITE:** Grantham, Lincs.
J6 **Remarks:** Some 20 gauge cartridges came to light that were
    loaded with Jenvey & Tite over-shot wads. One of these
    cartridges was stripped down and it was found to contain in
    it's loading a wad which was printed, Jenvey & Co. This
    suggests to me that this firm was named Jenvey & Co prior to
    it becoming, Jenvey & Tite. It also suggests that they most
    likely loaded their own cartridges. A 12 gauge cartridge
    remains has also been found which had their name on the
    headstamping. See the illustrations.

555. **A. J. JEWSON:** 1 Westgate, Halifax, Yorkshire.
J7 **Business:** Gun and cartridge maker and sportsman's outfitter.
K1 **Cartridges:** The Champion; The Crown; The Leader Cartridge;
    Unnamed; The Westgate.

556. **G. JOBSON:** Milford, Surrey.
J8 **Cartridges:** The Milford Special Smokeless.

557. **ROBERT BRINDLY JOHNSON:** High Street, March, Cambridgeshire.
J8 **Business:** Iron merchant and ironmonger.
    Cartridges: Unnamed.

558. **THOMAS JOHNSON & SON:** Market Place, Swaffham, Norfolk.
J8 **Business:** Gunmakers.
K2 **Cartridges:** Ejector; Johnson's Celebrated Ne-Plus-Ultra;
    The Reliable; Unnamed.
    Remarks: They were known to have loaded pinfire cartridges.

559. **JOHNSON & REID:** Darlington, Yorkshire (County Durham).
J8 **Cartridges:** Eley's Gastight Cartridge Case (Johnson & Reid's
    name on the headstamping).

560. **JOHNSON & WRIGHT:** 23A Gold Street. Also at, Woolmonger
J8 Street, Northampton, Northamptonshire.
K2 **Business:** Ironmongers.
    Cartridges: The County; Kynoch's Perfectly Gas-tight Cartridge
    Case for E.C. Gunpowder.
    Remarks: They were known to have been active between 1894 and
    1924.

561. **JONES & SON:** Oxford Street. Also at, Gloucester Street.
J8 Later at, 17 High Street, Malmesbury, Wiltshire.
Business: Ironmongers.
Cartridges: The Abbey.

562. **F. JONES:** Ilfracombe, Devonshire.
Business: Ironmonger.
Cartridges: The Champion.

563. **H. JONES:** Wrexham, Denbighshire (Clwyd).
J8 **Business:** Gunmaker.
Cartridges: Smokeless Cartridge.
Remarks: This business closed down in 1927.

564. **ROBERT JONES:** Monarch Gun Works, Manchester Street,
J8 Liverpool, Lancashire (Merseyside).
K5 **Business:** Gunmaker.
Cartridges: The Liver Cartridge; The Liver Smokeless.

565. **THOMAS JONES:** Nott Square, Carmarthen, Carm (Dyfed).
Business: Ironmonger.
Cartridges: The Majestic.

566. **W. P. JONES.** Later as, **W. PALMER JONES (GUNS), LTD:** 25
J8 Whittal Street, Birmingham, Warwickshire (W. Midlands).
Cartridges: The Accuratus; The Priority Cartridge.
Remarks: This firm was established in 1826.

567. **WILLIAM JOWETT:** 3 Kingsbury, Aylesbury, Buckinghamshire.
Business: Ironmonger.
Cartridges: The Kingsway.
Remarks: At the ending of shop loading, all unused cases were given to a museum. I myself have never seen a cartridge or cartridge case by them.

568. It is very much regretted, that due to a filing error in the initial listings, this number cannot be used.

569. **FREDERICK JOYCE & CO, LTD:** 57 Upper Thames Street. Also at,
J9 7 Suffolk Lane, London EC.
K2 **Business:** Cartridge case manufacturers and loadings.
K5 **Cartridges:** Bailey's Gastight Cartridge; The Bonnaud; Cannonite Powder; Ejector; Ejector solid drawn case; F.J. Gastight; Ideal Smokeless; Improved Gastight for Amberite Smokeless; Improved Gastight for Schultze; Joyce's Gastight Cartridge Case for Walsrode; Improved Gastight for S.S.; Improved Gastight for Walsrode; Joyce's D.B. Cartridge; Joyce's Long Brass; Joyce's National Cartridge Case; Joyce's Royalty Cartridge; Special Nitro; Special Smokeless; Unnamed; The Waltham; Waterproof Gastight.
Remarks: F. Joyce & Co, Ltd were cartridge case manufacturers and they manufactured very strong cases. Both pin and central fire cases were made in numerous gauge sizes. They sold many of their cases to other firms that loaded their own. They also exported cases. Many of these being shipped to members of The British Empire (Now, Commonwealth). Early made cases did not carry any case wall printings. During 1907, The Nobel Explosives Co, Ltd took over complete control of the Joyce company. They then used this firms plant for their own supply

569. **F. JOYCE & CO, LTD:** Continued,
of cartridge cases. A few years ago in the Oxford area some rare cartridge remains were found. These carried the headstampings, NOBEL No 12 LONDON and would date back to 1907. Since then I have only been shown one complete cartridge that carried this stamping. Obviously the Nobel Explosives firm wished to retain their origin of Glasgow on their headstampings. If you examine any late Nobel Explosives cases and Joyce cases together you will see that they are of the same pattern. To see Nobel Explosives Co, Ltd look for number 755 in this cartridge list.

570. **H. JULIAN & SONS, LTD:** 3-4 Church Street, Basingstoke, Hants.
J8 **Business:** Gunsmiths and ironmongers.
Cartridges: Eley's Gas-tight Cartridge Case for E.C. Powder (Julian's name on the headstamping).

571. **WILLIAM KAVANAGH & SON:** 12 Dame Street, Dublin, Republic of
K3 Ireland.
K5 **Business:** Gun and rifle makers.
Cartridges: Curtis's & Harvey's Amberite; The Clay pigeon; The Ideal; The Mirus; Nobel's Sporting Ballistite; The Schultze Cartridge.

572. **L. KEEGAN:** 3 Inns Quay, Dublin, Republic of Ireland.
K3 **Business:** Gunmaker.
Cartridges: The Bomb Shell; The Emerald Isle; The Faugh-A-Ballagh; The Lepracaun.

573. **KELLY & SON:** Dublin, Republic of Ireland (Rest of the address is not known).
Remarks: This firms name has been seen on an Eley headstamp.

574. **H. KEMPTON:** Bloomfield Road, Woolwich, London SE18.
K3 **Cartridges:** Rottweil Express (Kempton's name was only on the over-shot wad.

575. **ALFRED KENT.** Later as, **KENT & SON:** Market Place, Wantage,
K3 Berkshire (Oxfordshire).
K5 **Business:** Ironmongers, general furnishing, gunsmithing and coach hire.
Cartridges: Cheap Cartridge; Kynoch Perfectly Gas-tight for E.C. powder (Extra tube printings); Kynoch Perfectly Gas-tight The Wantage Cartridge; Unnamed.
Remarks: In 1877, this firm was listed in the trade directories as Alfred Kent. Most of their old cartridges that I have seen have been marked as Kent & Son. During a part of their time in business they loaded their own. These in both pin and central fire. The firm also went into the coach hire business. Come the ending of the 1914-18 war (The Great War), the firm purchased two small Fiat coaches and in the 1920's a Cheverolet was added to the fleet. During the 1930's they sold an unnamed cartridge with a pheasant printed on the case wall. After the 1939-45 (Second World War), the son, John Kent continued to market a Wantage Cartridge that was loaded for him into an Eley case. It is quite possible that his first cartridges may have been closed by a rolled turn-over, but all of them that I had seen were closed by crimping.

576. **KENYON & TROTT:** Cattle Market, Ipswich, Suffolk.
K3   **Business:** Not known at the time of selling cartridges. Later it became a plating business.
Cartridges: Unnamed (Name on over-shot wad only).

577. **HON G. KEPPEL:** (Address not known).
K9   **Business:** Not known but listed was a private cartridge.
Cartridges: Kynoch Grouse Ejector (12 gauge with Keppel's name on the headstamping).

578. **CHARLES KERR:** Stranraer, Wigtownshire (Dumfries & Galloway).
K3   **Business:** Gunmaker.
Cartridges: The Royal.

579. **HENRY ENGLISH KERRIDGE:** 184-5 King Street, Great Yarmouth,
K3   Norfolk.
Business: Gunsmith and ironmonger.
Cartridges: The Champion; The East Anglian; Unnamed.

580. **T. M. KINGDON & CO, LTD:** 5 Market Place, Basingstoke, Hants.
K9   **Business:** Ironmonger and cycle agent.
Cartridges: Eley's Gas-tight Cartridge Case (Kingdon's name on the headstamping; The Hampshire.

581. **KING'S NORTON METAL CO:** King's Norton, Birmingham, Warwicks (W. Midlands).
Remarks: The name 'Palma' was registered to them in 1904 as, King's Norton Palma Cartridges. I myself have never seen one.

582. **JAMES KIRK:** 36 Union Buildings, Ayr, Ayrshire (Strathclyde).
K9   **Business:** Gunmaker.
Cartridges: Ayr Special; The Champion; Gastight Blue Roc Pigeon Cartridge; The High Velocity; The Land of Burns; The Marksman; The Retriever; Special; Special Pegamoid; The Grouse.
Remarks: This business finally incorporated in with Arthur Allan, Ltd. See number 19 in this cartridge list.

583. **THOMAS KIRKER:** Belfast, Northern Ireland (Rest of the address is not known).
Business: Gunmaker.
Cartridges: Unnamed or name not recorded.

584. **H. KIRMAN:** Scunthorpe, Lincolnshire (Humberside).
Business: Ironmonger.
Cartridges: Farmers Special.

585. **KITHER:** Seven Oaks, West Kent.
K9   **Cartridges:** Eley's Gastight Cartridge Case for Schultze powder (The Kitther name on the over-shot wad only).

586. **J. N. KNIGHT:** Wells, Somerset.
K9   **Business:** Ironmonger.
Cartridges: Unnamed.

587. **PETER KNIGHT:** 22 Carrington Street. Also at, Clinton
K5   Street, Nottingham, Nottinghamshire.
K9   **Business:** Gunmaker.

587. **PETER KNIGHT:** Continued.
Cartridges: The Castle; The Invincible; The Thurland.
Remarks: In 1881 the address of this firm was 39 Canal Street (North). By 1904 he had moved his business to Carrington Street. Come 1932, he was at 12 Clinton Street (East). All of these addresses being in Nottingham.

588. **KYNASTON BROTHERS:** Wem. Also at, Ellesmere, Shropshire.
Business: Ironmongers.
Cartridges: Unnamed.

589. **GEORGE KYNOCH.** Later as, **G. KYNOCH & CO.** Still later as,
K4 **KYNOCH, LTD:** The Lion Works, Witton, Birmingham, Warwickshire
K5 (W. Midlands).
K6 **Business:** Ammunition and explosives manufacturers. Also
K7 manufacturers of cycles, soap, candles and town gas engines.
N9 **Cartridges:** .410; 5/16" Brass; 5/8" Brass; Absolutely Gastight; Amberite Gunpowder Cartridge; Amberite Smokeless Cartridge; Beryl; Kynoch Big Bang; Blue First Quality; The Bonax; Brown Quality; C.B. Cartridge Case; Deep-Head Gastight; Deep Shell; E.C. Gunpowder; Elax; Eureka (Old Greek for, I Have Found It); Gastight Waterproof; G.K. Special Smokeless; Green Extra Quality; Haylex; The Kardax; The K.B.; The Kyblack; The Kynoid; Light Green Cartridge Case (Nitro Powders); Magic Shell; Maroon Quality; The Nitro Ball; The Nitrone; The Opex; The Overlander (For Australian market); The Paradox 'Bullet Cartridge' (Really well-founded); Patent No, 2090 Grouse Ejector; Patent Perfect Metalic; Perfectly Gastight; The Primax; The Quail Smokeless (Mainly for overseas markets); The Sallinoid (Ball cartridge); The Snipax; The Swift (Sold in Australia and seen advertised on Kynoch advertising mirrors); The Tellax (Cheap cartridge); Triumph 'Ballistite'; Triumph 'Mullerite'; Triumph 'Smokeless Diamond'; Triumph 'Walsrode'; Unlined Nitro Case; Use Berdan Primer; Warranted Gastight; Waterproof Case; The Witton; Witton Brand; Zulu.

Also made were 4 Gauge Flare cartridges and Punt Gun cartridges etc. Along side shotgun ammunition, rifle and pistol metalics were produced for both military and civil purposes. Not forgetting railway fog detonators.
Remarks: An early address that I have for Kynoch & Co is taken from the rear cover of a Baily's Monthly Magazine dated January 1874. This address is, 48 Hampton Street, Birmingham with a London office at, 8 Cullum Street, EC. George Kynoch first entered the cartridge business in 1862 at Witton. He used a small wooden hut which later took on the name, The Cap Priming Shed. It was the very first building to have been errected on the Witton factory site. From this humble beginning, Kynoch & Co were able to grow large enough to be able to challenge Messrs Eley Brothers, Ltd and so they obtained for themselves a large cut in the market

Kynoch manufactured shotgun ammunition in many gauge sizes. These ranged from the small saloon (Garden gun) in the sizes 1, 2 and 3. These were produced in both short and long. Their cartridges then ranged up through all the gauge (Bore) sizes of the time and were produced in various chamber lengths.. Punt Gun sizes were made and one oddity that turned up was an all brass Patent Perfect Metalic Ejector in 18 gauge.

589. **GEORGE KYNOCH:** Continued.
   Also seen have been all brass ejector type pinfires in various gauge sizes. Their early pinfires had very coarse dark brown paper tubes. In my illustrations I have referred to this brown paper as Cowpat brown. This because the colour and paper texture reminds me of a dried out cowpat. The firm then progressed onwards and made other coloured paper tubes such as Green Quality and Blue Quality. Cartridge tubes were then wound from a brown paper and then given a fresh coloured paper on the outer windings.
   A variety of gastight (Often spelt Gas-tight) quality cases were specially made and printed to suit the many gunpowders that flooded the market around that time. These were made for both black and nitro powders and their primer caps designed to match the powder that the case was made. Some gunpowders were: Amberite; Cannonite; E.C.; K.S.S. (Kynoch's Smokeless Sporting); Nonpreil; Normal; Schultze; Shotgun Rifleite; Nobel's Sporting Ballistite; S.S.; T.S. and Walsrode.
   Many of the firms brand names continued through the years and lasting up until the large merger of the many explosives firms in the November of 1918. With the forming of the new large firm, Explosives Trades, Ltd, all shotgun ammunition was then manufactured from the Lion Works factory at Witton. To refer to Explosives Trades, Ltd (E.T.L.), see number 308 in this cartridge list.

590. **LACE:** Market Place, Wigan, Lancashire (Gt. Manchester).
K9 **Cartridges:** Lace's Smokeless Cartridge.

591. **ARTHUR LACEY.** Later as, **LACEY & SON:** Bridge Street, Stratford-upon-Avon, Warwickshire.
   Business: Ironmongers.
   Cartridges: The Welcome Cartridge.

592. **J. & H. LACEY:** Long Eaton, Derbyshire.
K9 **Business:** Ironmongers.
   Cartridges: Imperial Special Smokeless.

593. **E. LAKER:** Montague Street. Also at, 2 Buckingham Road,
K8 Worthing, Sussex.
K9 **Business:** Ironmonger.
   Remarks: This firms name has been seen printed on an over-shot wad.

594. **HENRY LAKER & SON:** Billinghurst, Sussex.
   Business: Sports depot.
   Cartridges: The X.L. Special.

595. **T. LAMBERT, LTD:** Parliament Street, York, Yorkshire.
L1 **Business:** Gunsmith and ironmongers.
   Cartridges: Lambert's Special Smokeless Cartridge.

596. **ROGER STANLEY LANAWAY:** Church Road, Burgess Hill, Sussex.
   Business: Ironmonger.
   Cartridges: Unnamed.

597. **CHARLES LANCASTER.** Later as, **C. LANCASTER & CO, LTD**: 151 New
K7   Bond Street. Also at, 99 Mount Street, London W.
K8   **Business**: Gunmaker and cartridge developer.
L1   **Cartridges**: Ejector; Generally Usefull; The Leicester; Medium
     Game Cartridges; The Norfolk; Patent Gastight Cartridge;
     Lancaster's Pygmies; The Twelve-Twenty; Shoot Lancaster's
     Pygmies; Special Waterproof Cartridge.
     Remarks: Charles has been looked upon as being one of the
     pioneers in the development of cartridge cases. He patented
     his own cartridge case in order to try and stop blow-backs
     which became a common occurrence in those early days of breech
     loaders. His cartridge had it's primer built in from sight.
     It must have looked much like a pinfire without a pin even
     though it was a central-fired cartridge.
     The London addresses for Lancaster were as follows: 151 New
     Bond Street. He was known to have been here in 1889; 11
     Panton Street. This address dates circa, 1925-32; Then my
     researched notes show a move back to 151 New Bond Street. Now
     this may not be so, perhaps the firm had held on to both
     premises all of the time; Likewise, my notes also have shown
     him as being at, 2 Little Bruton Street, and also in 1889. I
     just do not know the whole truth about all of these addresses
     and their dates. When one is absolutely sure of the dates
     that firms premises were in use, then this helps in dating old
     cartridges that have the addresses printed on them. C.
     Lancaster & Co, Ltd were finally incorporated into the London
     gunmaking firm, Grant & Lang. Also incorporated into Grant &
     Lang was another old London based firm, Watson Brothers. See
     numbers 393 and 1069 in this cartridge list.

598. **LANE BROTHERS**: Marlborough Street, Faringdon, Berkshire
L1   (Oxfordshire).
     Business: Ironmongers.
     Cartridges: The Eclipse; The O.B.H.

599. **CHARLES E. LANE**: Peterchurch, Golden Valley, Herefordshire
K8   (Hereford & Worcester).
L1   **Business**: Ironmonger and universal provider.
     Cartridges: Improved Gas-tight Case for Schultze Powder;
     Unnamed.

600. **CHARLES L. LANE**: 19-20 Cornhill, Bridgwater, Somerset.
K8   **Business**: Ironmonger.
L1   **Cartridges**: Lane's Champion Smokeless Cartridge.
     Remarks: Trade directories have listed them as being active
     between 1914 and 1923. They did not list them in 1910 or in
     1927.

601. **FRANK LANE & CO**: Marlborough Street, Faringdon, Berkshire
L1   (Oxfordshire).
     Business: Ironmongers.
     Cartridges: Unnamed (Pink paper tubes).
     Remarks: This firm was a continuation from Lane Brothers. See
     number 598 in this cartridge list. I have decided to list
     them both separately so that I can show the cartridges of each
     generation. This business later became Vale Ironmongers in
     Faringdon. The agricultural side was, Vale Agricultural and

601. **FRANK LANE & CO:** Continued.
they were based at Clanfield, Oxon. As Vale, they marketed a paper tube crimped closed cartridge called, The Vale. This was loaded for them by the Hull Cartridge Co, Ltd. The name Vale being taken from The Vale of the White Horse.

602. **LANES:** Cheddar, Somerset.
Business: Agricultural dealers.
Cartridges: The Cheddar Vale.

603. **JOSEPH H. LANG.** Later as, **J. LANG & SON.** Still later as,
L1 **J. LANG & SON, LTD:** 22 Cockspur Street. Later at, 10 Pall Mall & 102 New Bond Street, London W1.
Business: Gunmakers.
Cartridges: Kynoch Grouse Ejector; Lang's Special; Unnamed; The Ventracta; Lang's Waterproof Pegamoid.
Remarks: The firm of Lang eventually joined forces with the gunmaker, Stephen Grant in the May of 1925. Together they then traded from 7 Bury Street, St. James's, London as, Grant & Lang. Much later still the firm was to become, Atkin Grant & Lang. See numbers 31 and 393 in this cartridge list.

604. **JOHN LANGDON:** 20 St. Mary Street, Truro, Cornwall.
L1 **Business:** Gunsmith and cycle shop.
Cartridges: The Langdon Non Rusting Special Smokeless.

605. **JAMES JOHN LANGLEY:** Guildford Street. Also at, 68 Bute
L2 Street, Luton, Bedfordshire. Was also at, Hitchin, Herts.
Business: Gun and cartridge maker.
Cartridges: Blue Rock; Kynoch Grouse Ejector; The Prize Winner.
Remarks: Langley's cartridges were loaded into many makes of cases. For reasons best known to him he was always having to seek fresh sources for his supply of cartridge cases. Well that is how it was once told to me. He later joined forces with Aubrey Lewis at Luton. Together they then became, Langley & Lewis. Langley then pulled out and took up farming in Berkshire. His Luton premises was destroyed by fire in 1914.

606. **LANGLEY & LEWIS:** Park Square, Luton, Bedfordshire. Also at,
L2 Malden, Essex.
Business: Gunmakers.
Cartridges: Blue Rock; British Smokeless; Prize Winner.
Remarks: See the previous entry number 605 in this list.

607. **R. G. F. LAST:** Layer-de-la-Haye, Near Colchester, Essex.
Cartridges: unnamed.

608. **THOMAS LAW.** Also, **THOMAS LAW (JUNIOR):** Castle Douglas,
L2 Kirkudbrightshire (Dumfries & Galloway).
Business: Gunmakers.
Cartridges: Galloway Cartridge; Kynoch's Perfectly Gastight; Unnamed.

609. **LAWN & ALDER:** Brackley Street, London EC.
L2 **Business:** Colonial outfitters.
Cartridges: L. & A. Half Brass; L. & A. Waterproof.

610. **LAWRENCE:** Durham, County Durham.
Remarks: Lawrence's name has been seen on a headstamping on some old cartridge remains.

611. **J. F. LAYCOCK:** Wiseton, Nottinghamshire.
L2 **Cartridges:** Eley Ejector.

612. **R. LEACH:** Oldham, Lancashire (Gt. Manchester).
L2 **Cartridges:** British Smokeless Case (Leach's name was only on the over-shot wad).

613. **LEATHAM:** Durham, County Durham.
L2 **Cartridges:** Unnamed.

614. **LEAVER:** Weston-Super-Mare, Somerset (Avon).
Remarks: This name has been seen on a headstamping.

615. **LEE:** Bishop's Stortford, Hertfordshire.
Cartridges: Unnamed or name not recorded.

616. **W. LEECH.** Later as, **W. LEECH & SONS:** Conduit Street,
L3 Chelmsford, Essex.
Business: Gunmakers.
Cartridges: The Chelmsford Cartridge; The Club Smokeless; Essex County; Kynoch's Grouse Ejector; Leech's Special Load; Pigeon Cartridge; The Standard Cartridge; Unnamed; The X.L.

617. **W. R. LEESON:** Ashford, Kent. Also in London (Address not known).
Cartridges: The Invicta.
Remarks: Leeson was known to have been active in 1896.

618. **HERBERT E. LEGGETT:** Broad Street, Eye, Suffolk.
L3 **Business:** Ironmonger.
Cartridges: British Loaded Smokeless.

619. **LEIGH & JACKSON:** Market Place, Witney, Oxfordshire.
Business: Ironmongers.
Remarks: A 12 gauge brass cartridge head has been found which bore their name.

620. **CHARLES LEONARD:** Market Place, Brigg, Lincolnshire
L3 (Humberside).
Cartridges: The Glanford Cartridge.

621. **L. LePERSONNE & CO:** 7-8 Old Bailey, London EC4.
Business: Ammunition wholesalers.
Remarks: It is quite possible that they may have had their name on a cartridge, but of that I am not sure. They did market the following cartridges: Clermonite; F.N.(Fabrique Nationale d'Armes de Guerre); Lepco and Mullerite. There was an alloy outer covered cartridge called The Metalode which had a Belgium appearance about it. It could well have been marketed by them.

622. **LEVER BROTHERS:** Weston-Super-Mare, Somerset (Avon).
Cartridges: Unnamed or name not recorded.

623. **LEWIS:** Wells, Somerset.
L3 **Business:** Ironmongers.
Cartridges: The Sunset.

624. **AUBREY LEWIS:** 19 Church Street, Luton, Bedfordshire.
L3 **Business:** Gunmaker.
Cartridges: Blue Rock; The Chelt; Fourten; Eley G.P. (Extra tube printing); High Velocity; The Severn (16 Bore); The Special; Unnamed.
Remarks: Aubrey was at one time in partnership with James Langley. See numbers 605 and 606 in this cartridge list. Aubrey eventually took over complete control of the business continuing in gunmaking. He finally closed his doors in 1969.

625. **EDWIN GEORGE LEWIS:** London Street, Basingstoke, Hampshire.
L3 **Business:** Gunsmith, wireless engineer and cycle dealer.
Cartridges: The Lewis Cartridge.
Remarks: This firm was active up until 1939 and perhaps later. A 1911 Basingstoke directory showed a cycle agent in Reading Road and also in May Street. This firm was called, Lewis & Moss. There may well have been family connections between them.

626. **F. LEWIS & SONS:** Great Dunmow, Essex.
Cartridges: Unnamed.

627. **G. E. LEWIS & SONS:** 32-33 Lower Loveday Street, Birmingham, Warwickshire (W. Midlands).
Business: Gunmakers.
Cartridges: The Express; The Keepers Cartridge; Pegamoid Case; The Premier.

628. **J. D. LEWIS:** Narberth, Pembrokeshire (Dyfed).
Business: Ironmonger.
Remarks: It is known that they once loaded cartridges.

629. **RICHARD LEWIS:** 5 Lower Street, Kettering, Northamptoshire.
Business: Ironmonger.
Cartridges: Unnamed (Pinfire, name on over-shot wad only).

630. **LICHFIELD AGRICULTURAL CO:** Market Street, Lichfield, Staffs.
Business: Agricultural merchants.
Cartridges: Unnamed (Case by Eley Bros, Ltd).

631. **LIDDELL & SONS:** Haltwhistle, Northumberland.
L4 **Cartridges:** Unnamed.

632. **LIGHTWOOD:** Bournmouth, Hampshire (Dorset).
Cartridges: Unnamed.
Remarks: The unnamed cartridge listed was of old blue quality with the headstamping, LIGHTWOOD No 12 BOURNMOUTH. It was loaded with an Eley Patent Wire Cartridge.

633. **LIGHTWOOD & SON:** Price Street, Birmingham, Warwickshire (W. Midlands).
Cartridges: The Ecel.

634. **FRANK W. LIGHTWOOD:** 122A Cleethorpe Road. Later at, 172 Market Place, Brigg, Linconshire (Humberside). And also at, 14 Market Place, Market Rasen, Lincolnshire.
Business: Gunsmith.
Cartridges: The Four Best; Woodcraft.
Remarks: They were known to have been trading from the 122A Cleethorpe Road address in 1913. The production of Lightwood cartridges ceased in 1923. These had the headstampings, BRIGG, GRIMSBY & MARKET RASEN. No more cartridges were loaded by them, but in December 1972 they then commenced to market a brand of their own called, The Hy Vel Express.

635. **S. J. LIMMEX & CO:** Corner shop, Wood Street & High Street,
L4   Old Town, Swindon, Wiltshire.
Business: Ironmongers and gunsmiths.
Cartridges: The Pheasant Non Rusting Special Smokeless.
Remarks: Now recently closed down, their shop was in the old town area of Swindon. Apart from the High Street address, at one time they also had a premises at 23 Faringdon Street.

636. **LINCOLN JEFFERIES.** Later as, **LINCOLN JEFFERIES & CO:** 121
K8   Steelhouse Lane. Also at, 140 Steelhouse Lane, Birmingham, Warwickshire (W. Midlands).
Business: Gunmakers.
Cartridges: The Lincoln Smokeless; Unnamed.
Remarks: Their address printed on a Lincoln Smokeless was 140 Steelhouse Lane. On an unnamed it was 121 Steelhouse Lane.

637. **G. LINES:** Stevenage, Hertfordshire.
Cartridges: Unnamed.

638. **JAMES H. LINNINGTON:** 107A St. James's Square. Also at, 24
L4   Union Street, Newport, Isle of Wight.
Business: Ironmonger and gunsmith.
Cartridges: Extra Special; Unnamed (Pinfire).

639. **LINSCOTT:** Exeter, Devonshire.
Cartridges: Linscott's Champion.

640. **LINSLEY BROTHERS:** Lands Lane. Also at, 97 Albion Street,
L4   Leeds. Also in Bradford, Yorkshire.
M5   **Business:** Gunmakers.
Cartridges: Eley Ejector; High Velocity; Kynoch Grouse Ejector; Nomis; Standard; Steel Lined Nitro; The Swift.
Remarks: The firm of Linsley was established in 1780. At one time they made a change of address to 137 Albion Street, Leeds.

641. **ROBERT LISLE:** Queen's Hall Buildings, Derby, Derbyshire.
L5   **Business:** Gunmaker.
Cartridges: Lisle's Field Cartridge; Tiger Brand; The Victa Cartridge.
Remarks: Other Derby addresses that I have for Robert are, 5 Arcade, Sadler Gate and 25 Derwent Street.

642. **H. C. LITTLE & SON:** 14 Silver Street, Yeovil, Somerset.
L5   **Business:** Gunmakers.
Cartridges: The Blackmoor Vale; The Sparkford Vale; Unnamed.

643. **A. T. LITTLEFORD:** 2 Market Place, Cirencester, Glos.
L4   **Business:** Ironmonger and gunsmith.
    Cartridges: Specially Loaded By Improved Machinery.

644. **CHARLES F. LIVERSIDGE:** 29 Market Street, Gainsborough, Lincs.
K8   **Business:** Gunmaker.
    Cartridges: Ejector; Special Smokeless Cartridge.
    Remarks: Charles was known to have been active in 1913.

645. **LLOYD & SONS:** Station Street, Lewes, Sussex.
L5   **Business:** Gunmakers.
    Cartridges: Champion; Champion Ejector; County Cartridge; Imperial Crown; Improved Imps; Special Imperial Champion; Standard.

646. **C. H. LOCK:** 111 Long Street, Atherstone, Warwickshire.
L5   **Cartridges:** Lock's Special.

647. **LONDON SPORTING PARK, LTD:** 60 New Bond Street, London W1.
K8   **Cartridges:** Ejector; Eley Patent Gas-tight Case for Pegamoid Brand Paper (Their name was only on the headstamping).

648. **HENRY LONG & SONS:** Witney, Oxfordshire.
    Business: Ironmongers.
    Cartridges: The Witney.

649. **C. T. LOOK:** Ely, Cambridgeshire.
    Business: Ironmonger.
    Remarks: Information given to me that this firm once sold their own brand of cartridges.

650. **LOVERIDGE & CO:** 1-2 King's Street, Reading, Berkshire.
L5   **Business:** General ironmongers, furnishings and hot water
M5   engineers.
    Cartridges: The Royal County Cartridge.
    Remarks: This firm was known to have been operating in 1903. I once had in my possession an empty cartridge box that had held Kynoch Nitrones. It had been given Loveridge's name printed by a rubber stamp on it's side. Obviously they had sold other cartridges as well as their own. This was typical of the many large ironmongers stores during that era.

651. **S. LUCKES:** Bridge Street. Also in, Castle Street, Taunton, Devonshire.
    Business: Gun and ammunition dealer.
    Cartridges: Taunton Demon.
    Remarks: He also had branches at, Langport, Washford, Wiveliscombe and St. James Foundry.

652. **LUCK'S EXPLOSIVES, LTD:** Leadenhall Buildings, London EC.
L6   **Business:** Explosives manufacturers.
M5   **Cartridges:** See number 466 Henrite Explosives in this cartridge list.
    Remarks: Their works were at Stowmarket, Suffolk. Later also at Dartford, Kent. They were established in 1898 and were liquidated in 1906. Founded by A. Luck and L. Henry, they then became, Henrite Explosives. They had the name Henrite registered to them in 1899.

653. **LYNSCOTT** Exter, Devonshire.
Cartridges: unnamed or name not recorded.

MAC-Mc. These are both treated here as Mac. The next letter in the name determines the entry position.

654. **ROBERT McBEAN:** Stafford, Staffordshire.
Business: Gunmaker.
Cartridges: The Challenge Cartridge.

655 **WILLIAM McCALL & CO.** Later became, **McCALL & SONS, LTD:** 21
L6 Castle Street, Dumfries, Dumfries (Dumfries & Galloway).
M5 Business: Gunmakers.
Cartridges: All British Popular Cartridge; Eley Bros, Ltd E.B.L. cartridge with McCall's name on; The Border Cartridge; K.C.. (Keepers Cartridge); Tally Ho (The Signature).

656. **McCOLL & FRASER:** Dunfirmline, Fifeshire.
L6 Business: Gunmakers.
Cartridges: Unnamed.

657. **McCRIRICK & SONS:** 38 John Finnie Street, Kilmarnock, Ayrshire.
Business: Gunmakers.
Cartridges: Unnamed.

658. **J. McCRIRICK & SONS:** Ayr, Ayrshire (Strathclyde).
L6 Business: Gunmakers.
Remarks: A headstamping with their name on has been found through metal detecting.

659. **MACDOUGALL & CO:** Grantown-on-Spey, Morayshire (Highland).
Cartridges: The Strathspey Challenge.

660. **DUNCAN McDOUGALL:** Oban, Argyllshire (Strathclyde).
Cartridges: The Lorne.

661. **J. & J. McGALDING:** Monaghan, Republic of Ireland.
L6 Cartridges: Sure Kill.

662. **CHARLES MACGREGOR:** Kirkwall, Orkney, Orkney Islands.
Cartridges: Kynoch C.B. Cartridge Case (Extra tube printing).

663. **McILWRAITH & CO:** Elgin, Morayshire (Grampian).
Cartridges: Unnamed.

664. **ALEXANDER MACINTOSH & SONS, LTD:** 14 Market Hill, Cambridge, Cambridgeshire.
Business: Ironmongers.
Cartridges: Special Smokeless Cartridge.

665. **ALEX MACKAY & SON:** Barmore Street, Tarbert, Argyllshire.
Business: Ironmongers.
Cartridges: The Argyll.
Remarks: Mackays' started in business in 1919 by taking over the ironmonger business from John M. Macleod. John had first started the business by purchasing the Old Coaching Inn in Barmore Street in 1874.

666. **MACKENZIE & DUNCAN:** Brechin, Angus (Tayside).
L6   **Cartridges:** The Dunmax.

667. **CHARLES McLOUGHLIN.** Later as, **C. McLOUGHLIN & SON:** 89 High Street, Cheltenham, Gloucestershire.
Business: Gun and rifle makers.
Remarks: Cartridge remains with McLoughlin on the headstamping has been found. In 1870, Charles was trading on his own. Between 1895 and 1902 it is known that the son's name had been added to the business. This firm was first established in 1815.

668. **MACNAUGHTON & SONS:** 26 Hanover Street, Edinburgh, Midlothian.
L6   Also in, Perth, Perthshire (Tayside).
Business: Gunmakers.
Cartridges: Club Cartridge; Ejector; Unnamed.

669. **W. McMORRAN:** Lanark, Lanarkshire (Strathclyde).
L6   **Cartridges:** Special Smokeless.

670. **JOHN MACPHERSON.** Later as, **J. MACPHERSON & SONS:** Inverness,
L7   Inverness-shire (Highland).
Business: Gunmakers.
Cartridges: The Bargate; Barrage Cartridge; The Clack; The Killer; The Royal; Unnamed.

671. **ROBERT MACPHERSON:** Kingussie, Inverness-shire (Highland).
Cartridges: The Badenoch.

672. **JOHN McSORLEY:** Omagh, County Tyrone, Northern Ireland.
L7   **Business:** Motor agent.
Cartridges: Abercorn.

673. **McVERY BROTHERS:** Cookstown, Northern Ireland.
Cartridges: The Kill Quick.

674. **J. MALCOMSON.** Later as, **J. MALCOMSON & CO:** Lurgan, Northern
L7   Ireland.
Business: Auctioneers.
Cartridges: Unnamed.

675. **CHARLES HENRY MALEHAM.** Later as, **CHAS H. MALEHAM & CO:** 5
L7   West Bar, Sheffield, Yorkshire. Also at, 20 Regent Street, London W1.
Business: Gunmaker.
Cartridges: The Clay Bird; The Double Wing; The Regent; The Steeltown; The Wing Cartridge.
Remarks: It is known that Chas was in business at the start of the 1914-18 war, but for how long before this I do not know. In 1920, Arthur Turner took over this business and retained some of the existing cartridge brands in his own name. See number 1018 in this cartridge list. All Maleham cartridges are therefore pre-1920.

676. **MALLETT & SON:** 3, 4 and 6 Victoria Place, Truro, Cornwall.
Business: Ironmongers.
Cartridges: Unnamed or name not known.

676. **MALLETT & SON:** Continued.
Remarks: In 1935 there was also an ironmongers shop at 6 Molesworth Street, Wadebridge, Cornwall which was trading as Mallett & Son. It could have been the same firm.

677. **MALLINSONS:** Great Driffield, Yorkshire (Humberside).
L8 **Cartridges:** Mallinson's Shamrock; The Pheasant Cartridge.

678. **P. D. MALLOCH:** 34 Scott Street, Perth, Perthshire (Tayside).
L8 **Cartridges:** The Matchless; The Red Grouse; The Standard; The
M5 Triumph.

679. **ALLAN MANBY:** 69 High Street, Southwold, Suffolk.
L8 **Business:** Ironmonger.
Cartridges: The Suffolk Champion.
Remarks: He was known to have been active in 1925.

680. **F. MANBY & BROTHER:** 62 High Street, Skipton, Yorkshire.
L8 **Business:** Ironmongers.
Cartridges: Manby's Special.

681. **MANNING:** Charmanton, Somerset.
Cartridges: Unnamed or name not recorded.

682. **THOMAS GEORGE MANNING:** The Square, North Tawton, Devonshire.
Business: Ironmonger.
Remarks: I was once told of a cartridge by him.

683. **MANTON & CO:** Calcutta & New Delhi, India. They also had an
L8 office in London (Address not known).
M5 **Business:** Gun and rifle makers.
Cartridges: Manton's Contractile; Manton's Express Cartridge; Manton's For India; Manton's Special; Standard Smokeless; Manton's Tiger Brand Cartridge; Unnamed.
Remarks: I know little of this firm. All that I know is that they were more Asian than British. I have shown them here because they had a London office. In a London gunmakers list for 1838 there was a Manton & Hudson at 6 Dover Street, Piccadilly. There may well have been a connection.

684. **G. MARFELL:** Colwyn Bay, Denbighshire (Clwyd).
Cartridges: Nobel's Clyde (Extra tube printing).

685. **J. STEWART MARK:** 114 South Street, St. Andrews, Fifeshire.
Cartridges: The Markmore.

686. **MARSHALL, SONS & CO:** Britannia Iron Works, Gainsborough,
L8 Lincolnshire.
Business: Steam and oil engine and tractor manufacturers.
Cartridges: 12 gauge tractor engine start (Not shotgun).
Remarks: These engine starter cartridges are often included in cartridge collections.

687. **MARSHALL & PEARSON:** Fort-William, Inverness-shire (Highland).
L8 **Cartridges:** The Lochaber Cartridge Neonite Smokeless Powder).

688. **A. H. MARTIN:** Cross Ash, Abergavenny, Monmouths (Gwent).
L9 **Cartridges:** Trent Best Smokeless (Extra tube printing).

689. **ALEX MARTIN, LTD:** 20 Royal Exchange Square, Glasgow. Also
L9 at, 25 Bridge Street, Aberdeen, Aberdeenshire (Grampian). Was also in Stirling, Stirlingshire (Grampian).
Business: Gunmakers.
Cartridges: The AGE; The Calendonia; The Club; Hand Loaded; High Velocity; The Scotia; The Stirling; The Thistle; The Thistle High Velocity; Unnamed; The Velm.
Remarks: This firm incorporated with Alexander Henry & Co in the late 1930's. See number 467 in this cartridge list. Established in 1778. A Club Cartridge with the headstamping KYNOCH 12 12 NOBEL had printed on it's case wall, Established over 100 years ago. Later cartridges with the headstampings ELEY-KYNOCH I.C.I. have had the wording, Established over 130 years. There was nowhere near on thirty years between these two headstampings. Some of the addresses for this firm were as follows: 20-22 Royal Exchange Square. Also, 128 Union Street, Aberdeen. They were also at, 18 Frederick Street, Edinburgh and also at, Friar Street in Stirling. This firm eventually became a part of John Dickson & Son, Ltd in the 1950's. See number 258 in this list.

690. **J. F. MASON:** Eynsham Hall, Eynsham, Oxfordshire.
L9 **Business:** Private country estate.
Cartridges: Eley Ejector (Mason's name on the headstamping).

691. **J. MATHER & CO:** Castle Gate, Kirkgate & Bargate. Works at,
L9 Lombard Street, Newark. Also in, King Street, Southwell and Market Place, Bingham, Nottinghamshire.
Business: Ironmongers, automobile and agricultural engineers.
Cartridges: Jas R. Watson & Co's, The Britannia Cartridge with extra tube printing.

692. **MATTERSON, HUXLEY & WATSON:** Bishop Street, Coventry, Warwickshire (W. Midlands).
Cartridges: Unnamed or name not recorded.

693. **MATTHEWS BROTHERS:** High Street, Honiton. Also at, Lyme Street, Axminster, Devonshire.
Business: Ironmongers.
Cartridges: The Excelsior.
Remarks: Their name has also been seen on some Eley Brothers headstampings.

694. **JAMES MATTHEWS:** Ballymoney Street, Ballymena, County Antrim, Northern Ireland.
Business: Dealer in hardware, guns and ammunition.
Cartridges: Hawk; The Kingfisher; The Swift; The Wizard.
Remarks: This firm was founded in 1906. I am not sure of the shop numbering in Ballymoney Street. In my files I had, 42 and 71-72. Some details that I have been given are as follows: Hawk, a brown foreign case; Kingfisher, a light red or blue case; Swift, a yellow case with a large primer cap; Wizard, a green case. All of their cartridges that I have seen have had the headstampings, SPECIAL SMOKELESS.

695. **W. MAWBY & SON:** Birkenhead, Cheshire (Merseyside).
L9 **Cartridges:** Nobel's Clyde (Extra tube printing).

696. **MAWER & SAUNDERS:** The Square, Market Harborough, Leics.
L9   **Business:** Ironmongers.
    Cartridges: The Demon Smokeless.

697. **MAYES BROTHERS:** Wickford, Essex.
    Business: Agricultural dealers and ironmongers.
    Cartridges: The Farmer's Favourite (Has the wording, A Rabbit With Every Cartridge).

698. **W. MELLARD:** Denbigh, Denbighshire (Clwyd).
M1   **Business:** Ironmonger.
    Cartridges: Unnamed (Pinfire).

699. **A. MELVILLE & SONS:** Dunbar, East Lothian.
    Cartridges: Unnamed.

700. **H. L. MEREDITH:** 18 High Street, Bideford, Devonshire.
    Cartridges: Meredith's Special.

701. **G. F. METCALF:** 90 High Street, Burton-on-Trent, Staffs.
M1   **Cartridges:** The Champion.

702. **R. METCALFE:** 5 Market Place, Richmond, Yorkshire.
M1   **Business:** Gunmaker.
    Cartridges: The Richmond; The Swaledale; Special Smokeless.

703. **W. METCALFE:** 5 Market Place, Richmond. Also at, Shute Road,
M1   Catterick Camp, Yorkshire.
    Business: Gunsmith or gunmaker.
    Cartridges: Metcalfe's Special; Unnamed.
    Remarks: W. Metcalfe followed on from R. Metcalfe being entry number 702 in this list. I have shown them separated because of an additional address and a change of cartridge names.

704. **G. M. MICHIE & CO:** Stirling, Stirlingshire (Grampian).
M1   **Cartridges:** Michie's Unequalled.
    Remarks: All cartridges marked, 'Michie Stirling' are pre 1894.

705. **G. A. MIDGLEY:** Market Place, Winslow, Buckinghamshire.
    Business: Ironmonger.
    Cartridges: Special Loading.

706. **MIDLAND GUN CO:** The Demon Gun Works, Bath Street, Birmingham,
M2   Warwickshire (W. Midlands). Was also in, Brigg, Lincolnshire
M5   (Humberside).
M6   **Business:** Gun and cartridge makers.
S8   **Cartridges:** .410 Long; .410 Short; Best of All; Demon Cartridge; Demon Waterproof; The Double Demon; The Edward; Ejector; Gastight Steel Lined; The Imp; The Jubilee; The Keeper; The Keeper High Velocity; Perfect Smokeless; Perfection Smokeless; The Rabbit Smokeless Cartridge; The Rabbit Special Smokeless; The Record; Smokeless Gastight Perfection; Smokeless Hand Loaded; Special Smokeless Cartridge; Sudden Death; Unnamed.
    Remarks: This firm was founded in 1888 at 77 Bath Street. It moved to Vesey Street, Birmingham in 1902. They also sold pinfire cartridges and one of their early catalogues had 15 gauge cartridges added in by an inked pen. Cartridges were

706. **MIDLAND GUN CO:** Continued.
loaded to order by them for many other firms. Their telegraphic address was, 'Rifles Birmingham' and their telephone number was, 1254 Central. During the December of 1956 they were absorbed in with Parker Hale, Ltd of Golden Hillock Road, Birmingham.

707. **W. MILBURN.** Later as, **MILBURN & SON:** 5-7 High Cross Street,
M1 Brampton, Cumberland (Cumbria).
M6 **Business:** Gunsmiths and cartridge loaders.
Cartridges: The Don; Kynoch's Grouse Ejector; The Milburn; M.S.B. (Milburn & Son, Brampton); The Noxall; The Rex; Unnamed.
Remarks: The firm of Milburn was established in 1776.

708. **R. MILLETT:** Ilminster, Somerset.
Remarks: Their name has been seen printed in black on a white over-shot wad.

709. **MILLS BROTHERS:** 137 High Street, Crediton, Devonshire.
M1 **Business:** Ironmongers.
Cartridges: Kynoch C.B. Cartridge (Extra tube printing).

710. **MINTO:** Wigton, Cumberland (Cumbria).
Remarks: All though this name has been given to me as a firm that sold cartridges, I have no other information of it.

711. **MODERN ARMS CO, LTD:** 58 Southwark Ridge Road, London SE1.
M1 **Business:** Ammuniton dealers.
Cartridges: Star Standard Special Smokeless.
Remarks: I do not know if they ever had their name printed on a cartridge, but they did market the above listed cartridge in the gauges, 12, 16, 20 and 28.

712. **B. D. MOGG & SON:** Wells, Somerset.
M1 **Cartridges:** The Mendip.

713. **MONARCH GUN WORKS:** Liverpool, Lancashire (Merseyside).
M3 **Business:** Gunmakers.
Cartridges: Eley Ejector (Monarch Gunworks on the Headstamp).

714. **W. H. MONK.** Also known as, **HENRY MONK:** 77 Foregate Street,
M3 Chester, Cheshire.
Business: Gunmaker.
Cartridges: The Imperial; Pegamoid; The Popular; The Royal; The Straight; Unnamed.
Remarks: Henry sold many unnamed cartridges in the gauges 12, 16 and 20. Many depicted his rabbit and shock of corn trade mark. He was also known to have sold a two-inch Lilliput with a Jas R. Watson & Co headstamping.

715. **CHARLES MOODY:** 13 Church Street, Romsey, Hampshire.
M3 **Business:** Gunmaker.
Cartridges: Kynoch Perfectly Gas-tight (Moody's name on the over-shot wad only); Unnamed (Early blue quality case).
Remarks: Charles was known to have been active at the above address in 1901.

716. **W. F. MOODY:** 13 Church Street, Romsey, Hampshire.
M3   **Business:** Gunmaker and cutler.
Cartridges: The Ranger Special Smokeless; Moody's Special Waterproof Non Corrosive Cartridge.
Remarks: W.F. followed on after Charles. I have listed them here separated in order to show the different cartridges and the added trade of cutler. Though I have searched through several old trade directories I have not been able to find any traces of him.

717. **THOMAS HENRY MOOR:** 23 Broad Street, South Molton, Devonshire.
M3   Also at, Exford, Somerset.
Cartridges: The Molton; The Molton Special; The Rabbit; Special Rabbit Cartridge.

718. **WILLAM MOORE.** Later became, **MOORE & GREY:** 11 The Arcade,
M3   Aldershot, Hampshire. Also at, 156 Piccadilly, London W1.
Business: Gunmakers.
Cartridges: Kynoch Grouse Ejector; Unnamed (Pinfire).

719. **S. MORELAND:** Northwich, Cheshire.
Business: Gun and ammunition dealer.
Cartridges: Special Smokeless Cartridge.

720. **MORGAN:** Wem. Also at, Whitchurch, Shropshire.
Business: Gun and ammunition dealer.
Cartridges: Special Smokeless Cartridge.

721. **MORREYS:** Holmes Chapel, Near Middlewich, Cheshire.
M3   **Cartridges:** Morreys Special.

722. **H. M. MORRIS:** Rescent Road, Burgess Hill, West Sussex.
M3   **Cartridges:** Specially hand-loaded in England.

723. **P. MORRIS & SON:** Hereford, Herefordshire (H & W).
M6   **Business:** Gunsmiths and ironmongers.
M7   **Cartridges:** Hereford; The Imperial; The Lightning Cartridge.

724. **MORROW & CO (W. R. WEDGWOOD):** 4 Horton Street, Halifax. Also
M7   at, Harrowgate, Yorkshire.
Business: Gunmakers.
Cartridges: The Challenge Cartridge.

725. **MORTIMER.** Later as, **MORTIMER & SON:** 86 George Street,
M6   Edinburgh, Midlothian.
M7   **Business:** Gunmakers.
Cartridges: Eley's Patent Gas-tight Cartridge Case; Unnamed.
Remarks: This firm was established in 1720. Later they were to sell many unnamed cartridges. As, Mortimer & Son, Ltd they incorporated the business of Joseph Harkom & Sons, Ltd. See number 431 in this cartridge list. Then in 1938, they themselves were incorporated into the business of John Dickson & Son, Ltd. See number 258 in this list.

726. **H. MORTIMER:** 50 Boutport Street, Barnstaple, Devonshire.
Business: Ironmonger.
Cartridges: The Club.

102

727. **GEORGE PERCY MORTON & SON:** 22 High-Causeway, Whittlesey, Cambridgeshire.
Business: Ironmonger.
Cartridges: The Killer.

728. **C. MOTTERM:** Uttoxeter, Staffordshire.
Business: Ironmonger.
Cartridges: Unnamed or name not recorded.

729. **MOULTON & BENNETT:** Eye (Location not known. Possibly in
M7   Suffolk).
Cartridges: Unnamed (Eley Blue Quality Case. Name on over-shot wad only).

730. **MULLER & CO:** Horseshoe Yard, Mount Street, London W1. Also at, Winchmore Hill, Middlesex.
Business: Cartridge agents.
Cartridges: Clermonite; Mullerite; Negro.
Remarks: This firm set up in business in Mount Street in 1901 to market Mullerite cartridges in England. They made a move to Winchmore Hill in 1903, only to close down in 1905. The firm, Martin Pulvermann & Co, Ltd then took over the Mullerite agency. For further details see the next entry number 731 and number 834 in this cartridge list.

731. **MULLERITE CARTRIDGE WORKS.** Also known as, **BRITISH MULLERITE**
M4   **(Proprietors MARTIN PULVERMANN & CO, LTD):** 59 Bath Street.
M6   Also at, St. Mary's Row, Birmingham, Warwicks (W. Midlands).
S9   **Business:** Cartridge manufacturers and merchants.
Cartridges: The Ace; The Ace Long Range; The Black Prince; The British Champion; The Champion Smokeless; The Champion Smokeless Heavy Load; Fourtenner Long; Fourtenner Short; General Service; Green Seal; Grey Seal; Heyman Smokeless; Red Seal; Silver Ray; Smokeless; Special Clayking; Unnamed; Yellow Seal.
Remarks: The Mullerite Cartridge Works were established in Birmingham in 1922. From there they were to load cartridges for themselves and also for many other firms. Often used were the familiar yellow tubed cases with some extra printings added to the case walls. The Ace and Black Prince were loaded by Mullerite as were several others that did not carry the name of Mullerite on them. A few of their cartridges carried two of the above listed names. The Silver Ray was one such cartridge. Many of their cartridges also carried the $_{MPL}$td. monogram of Martin Pulvermann & Co, Ltd. Prior to the founding of these cartridge works, they had held the agency for all Mullerite cartridges in Great Britain. I do not know for sure, but this suggests to me that Pulvermanns' may have been absorbed into this new firm.

The name, Heyman Smokeless Cartridge was seen printed on a label wrap that was stuck around an empty Mullerite cartridge box. On this wrap was pictured a peacock with it's tail fanned out. A cartridge illustration is shown on Plate S9. It could well have been a cartridge for a Mullerite customer. On the other hand, it could have been a brand of cartridge that was produced for an overseas order.

732. **R. C. MUMFORD:** 66 High Street, Southwold, Suffolk.
Cartridges: The Stopper.

733. **W. H. MURCH:** Glastonbury, Somerset.
Cartridges: Unnamed or name not recorded.

734. **D. MURRAY & SON:** Brechin, Angus (Tayside).
Business: Gunmakers.
Cartridges: The Reliable.

735. **T. W. MURRAY & CO, LTD:** The Munster Armoury, 87 Patrick
M7 Street, Cork, County Cork, Republic of Ireland.
Business: Gun and fishing tackle makers.
Cartridges: Kynoch Extra Quality Cartridge Case; Murray's Reliable (Also known as the TWM); The Special Cartridge; Special Loading; The Speedwell Smokeless; The Wildfowler.

736. **NATIONAL ARMS & AMMUNITION CO. (N. A. & A. CO.):** Perry Bar, Birmingham, Warwickshire (W. Midlands).
Business: Gun, ammunition and cartridge case manufacturers.
Cartridges: Ejector; Express; Unnamed.
Remarks: This firm was in business between 1872 and 1882. During these ten years, this firm had two other addresses. They were: 77 Bath Street and Montgomery Street, Sparkbrook. It is most likely that these addresses were a part of the Birmingham complex. Also made by this firm were one piece thin walled brass cases. I have seen these in the gauges 14 and 16.

737. **T. NAUGHTON & SONS, LTD:** Shop Street, Galway, County Galway, Republic of Ireland.
Business: Sports dealers, ironmongers and house-hold furnishings.
Cartridges: The Blazer; The Connaught.
Remarks: This firm was established in 1891. Cartridges that I have seen were of later years being the poducts of Irish Metal Industries, Ltd. Their case walls shown the telephone number 63.

738. **C. NAYLOR, LTD:** Bridge Street, Near Snighill, Sheffield,
M7 Yorkshire.
Business: Gunmaker.
Cartridges: Naylor's Cannot Be Beaten.

739. **J. V. NEEDHAM:** 20A Temple Street. Also at, Damascus Works,
M7 Loveday Street, Birmingham, Warwickshire (W. Midlands).
Business: Gunmaker.
Cartridges: Shoot Needham Guns & Cartridges; Uneedem Smokeless Cartridges.

740. **FRANCIS NELSON.** Later as, **F. NELSON & SONS, LTD:** Sligo, County Sligo, Republic of Ireland.
Cartridges: The Favourite; The Reliable.

741. **A. NESTOR:** Limerick, County Limerick, Republic of Ireland.
M7 **Cartridges:** Kynoch Grouse Ejector (Nestor's name only on the over-shot wad).

742. **THE NEW EXPLOSIVES CO, LTD:** 62 London Wall, London EC2.
M6   Works and mills at Stowmarket, Suffolk.
M8   **Business:** Gunpowder and ammunition manufacturers.
M9   **Cartridges:** Felixite; Fourten; The Go Lightly Cartridge; The Green Rival; The Neco; The N.E. Powder; The Premier (Neonite); The Primrose Smokeless; The Red Rival; Red Star Smokeless Powder; Sixteen Bore; Twenty Bore; Unnamed.
      Remarks: Most cartridge brand names were taken from their names of gunpowders. Eley Brothers, Ltd cases were nearly always used. Their cartridge manufacture was between 1907 and 1920 when they ceased loading. See also in this cartridge list number 281, The E.C. Powder Co, Ltd.

743. **NEWLAND & STIDOLPH:** Stratford-upon-Avon, Warwickshire.
M7   **Business:** Ironmongers.
      Cartridges: Unnamed.

744. **WILLIAM NEWMAN & SON:** High Street, Haverhill, Suffolk.
N2   **Remarks:** Their name has been seen on a headstamping on old cartridge remains.

745. **GEORGE NEWNHAM.** Later as, **NEWNHAM & CO:** 29 Commercial Road,
N2   Landport. Also at, 8 Queens Road, Buckland, Portsmouth, Hampshire.
      Business: Gunmakers.
      Cartridges: The Champion; The Keepers Cartridge; Kynoch's Deep Shell Cartridge Case; The Special Game.

746. **NEW NORMAL AMMUNITION CO, LTD:** Clutterhouse Lane, Hendon,
M9   London NW4.
N2   **Business:** Cartridge loading merchants.
O1   **Cartridges:** Gastight; The Hendon; The Nimrod; The Normalis; Special Twenty.
      Remarks: In 1911-12 their address was Clutterhouse Lane, Hendon. This is now called Clutterhouse Road. The firm was listed between 1926 and 1939 as being at 37 John's Avenue, Church End, Hendon. See also number 758 the Normal Powder & Ammunition Co, Ltd in this cartridge list.

747. **T. NEWTON:** 48 King Street (West). Manchester, Lancashire
M9   (Gt. Manchester).
N2   **Business:** Gunmaker.
      Cartridges: The Lightning; Eley's Gas-tight Cartridge Case for Schultze Gunpowder; Newton's G.P.; Pegamoid Brand Paper; The Smokeless Cartridge.

748. **J. H. NICHOLAS:** Thirsk, Yorkshire.
      Business: Ironmonger.
      Cartridges: The Express.

749. **NICHOLS:** Porlock, Somerset.
      Business: Ironmongers.
      Remarks: I was told that cartridges were once loaded on their premises.

750. **J. O. & R. W. NICOLL:** Aberfeldy, Perthshire (Tayside).
      Business: Country outfitters.
      Cartridges: Unnamed or name not recorded.

750. **J. O. & R. W. NICOLL:** Continued
Remarks: Printed on some of their cartridges were the wording, 'Shooters best hand made waterproof tights made to measure'.

751. **A. P. NIGHTINGALE & SON, LTD:** 47 Canal, Salisbury, Wiltshire.
N2 **Business:** Ironmongers and agricultural merchants.
Cartridges: The Avon; The Moonraker Smokeless.

752. **NITROKOL POWDER CO:** London (Rest of the address is not known).
M9 **Cartridges:** The Redskin; The Rover.
N2 **Remarks:** The two named above were seen as unused cases.

753. **NIXON & NAUGHTON:** Newark, Nottinghamshire.
Business: Gunmakers.
Cartridges: Unnamed or name not recorded.

754. **SYDNEY A. NOBBS:** 2 Norman Street, Lincoln, Lincolnshire.
N2 **Business:** Fishing tackle dealer and taxidermist and ironmonger.
Cartridges: The Sureshot (Jas R. Watson & Co loading).

755. **NOBEL EXPLOSIVES CO, LTD:** 149 & 195 West George Street,
M9 Glasgow, Lanarkshire (Strathclyde). Also at, College Hall
N1 Chambers, Cannon Street. And also at, 1 Arundel Street, The
N2 Strand, London WC.
N3 **Business:** Explosives and ammunition manufacturers.
N4 **Cartridges '1'. Most names listed here started off with the**
N9 **word NOBEL'S:** 'A' Cartridge Case; Ajax; Challenge; Clyde; Ejector; Empire; Gas-tight Cartridge Case; Gas-tight Cartridge Case UL (Unlined); Gas-tight Waterproof Cartridge Case; Kardax; Kingsway; National; New Era; Nile; Nitro Cartridge Case; Noneka; Orion; Parvo; Pegamoid; Primrose Ballistite; Regent; Special Primrose; Sporting Ballistite (Smokeless Special Cartridge); Target; Unitro Cartridge Case; Unnamed; Valeka.
Cartridges '2'. Thought to have been for Australia and other overseas markets: Corio; Coronet; Don Smokeless; Emerite Smokeless; Excelsior; Fox; Gas-tight Waterproof Belloid Paper; Red Indian; Rex; Ringer; Starling; Sun.
Remarks: This famous firm was first founded in 1871 as The British Dynamite Co. It's purpose being to manufacture Dynamite in the British Isles under the patents held by Alfred Nobel. A factory was built at Ardeer on the banks of the River Garnock in Ayrshire. Later on, another factory was built at Waltham, Essex. The firm had it's registered offices in Glasgow and London. Many of their cartridge names referred to the powders used. Empire and Sporting Ballistite being two of the better known.
   In 1907, the Nobel Explosives Co, Ltd acquired the controlling interest of the business of F. Joyce & Co, Ltd. See number 569 in this cartridge list. They then used the patents and that plant for the manufacture of their own cartridge cases. By examining both Joyce and some Nobel brass cases side by side, the similarity can be clearly seen. By 1909, the final shares in Joyce's company were purchased and this then gave Nobel Explosives the full control of that London firm. A very rare headstamping is NOBEL No 12 LONDON. By recognizing the construction of these cases can help in dating some of the Nobel Explosives Co, Ltd cartridges.

755. **NOBEL EXPLOSIVES CO, LTD:** Continued.
An article written in the old British Cartridge Collectors Club Journal No, 42 gave details of a trade mark. It stated that in December 1909, a smoking volcano trade mark was registered to them. The wording in the encirclement being, Nobel Explosives, Ltd. Glasgow. I myself am unable to recollect ever seeing this trade mark portrayed on a shotgun cartridge. However, it was extensively used on cartridges at a later date but having the wording, Nobel Industries, Ltd. This being a completely different firm into which the Nobel Explosives Co, Ltd had then been absorbed into by the large explosives trades merger in November 1918. See the next entry in this list.

756. **NOBEL INDUSTRIES, LTD:** Works at, Witton, Birmingham, Warwicks
N4 (W. Midlands). Registered offices at, Nobel House, Buckingham
N5 Gate, London SW1.
N6 **Business:** Ammunition manufacturers and merchants.
N7 **Cartridges:** Acme; Albion; Amberite; Bonax; British Smokeless;
N8 Clyde; Deep Shell; Deep Shell Case; Ejector; Eley Extra Long;
N9 Fourlong; Fourten; Gastight; Gastight Quality Case; Grand Prix; Grand Prix Quality Case; Hollandia; Juno; Kardax; Lethal Ball; Magic Shell; Majestic; Nitro Case; Nitrone; Parvo; Pegamoid; Primax; Smokeless Cartridge; Standard Unlined; Sure Shot (South African market); Trapshooting; Twenty Gauge; Two-Inch; Unnamed (Pinfire); Velocity; Westminster; Winchester Cannon; Yeoman; Zenith; Kynoch 5/16" Brass; Kynoch 5/8" Brass.
Remarks: I have to admit that I am not one hundred percent sure of all of the names which I have listed, but I have written those that I think was most likely. A few of those listed could well have been produced for the export market.
The name of this firm came into being at the later end of 1920. It was in November 1918 that the large mergers of explosives type firms developed into Explosives Trades, Ltd. See number 308 in this cartridge list. Their name was changed to Nobel Industries, Ltd just two years later. It was then in this name that the firm continued to manufacture and market it's ammunition for the next five to six years. After this, the name was changed yet again to Imperial Chemical Industries (I.C.I.) Metals Devision (Eley-Kynoch), Ltd. See number 532 in this list. This was when Imperial Chemical Industries took over the controlling interests of the firm. It was circa 1926 to 1930 that the headstamps ELEY 12 12 NOBEL and KYNOCH 12 12 NOBEL gave way to the long running headstamp ELEY-KYNOCH 12 I.C.I. 12. and also in other gauges.
As well as loading it's own brands, the firm continued to keep it's inland and overseas markets by loading cartridges to the ordes of many other firms. Cartridge cases were still being supplied to gunsmithing and ironmonger firms for their individual loadings, but this practice in town shops was fast becoming frowned upon. Although some firms were still doing so, like the decline of the steam wagon, those times were fast changing.. Other shops were not so keen on knowing that large quantitys of explosive powders were being handled the other side of their walls.
Although many explosives type firms had been absorbed into this extra large organisation, five of the larger and more

756. **NOBEL INDUSTRIES, LTD:** Continued.
important can be singled out. These were, Eley Brothers, Ltd; Kynoch & Co, Ltd; Nobel Explosives Co, Ltd; Curtis's & Harvey, Ltd and the Schultze Gunpowder Co, Ltd. For interest refer to numbers 235, 290, 755 and 905 in this list. It was because of their importance that many of these firms original brand names were retained either on the cartridges or their components. The manufacture of the various gunpowders were gradually undertaken by the Ardeer Factory near Irvine, Ayrshire. Curtis's & Harvey's famous Smokeless Diamond commenced manufacture from there in 1934. Down under in Australia, many of the cartridge brand names which were being produced for our home market were being mingled with a few special Australian brand names. Here in England, F. Joyce & Co, Ltd were being remembered in name with the percussion caps.

At the time of the merger, many cartridges and cases that were in stock would have been sold off by the new firm. I would expect that the firms names would have been changed on the factory boards almost over night. Many other things would only have changed in a gradual process. To start with, the small initials N.I. were added to some of the headstampings. This being a follow on from the small initials, E.T.L. Eventually the headstampings settled down to the ELEY NOBEL and KYNOCH NOBEL so honouring the names of Eley, Kynoch and Nobel respectively. Many of the shops in the British Isles that were selling their own celebrated brands of cartridges that had been produced for them by the Witton Factory would often stock a few of the parent firm's brands as well.

757. **NORMAL IMPROVED AMMUNITION CO:** Hendon, London NW4.
01 **Business:** Ammunition manufacturers.
Cartridges: .410 Cartridge; Hendon; Keepers Normal; Light Blue; Normal; Normal Midget; Pegamoid; Pigeon Cases; Super Nimrod.
Remarks: This firm seems to be that of the Normal Powder Co. See the next entry in this list. It could have been in an intermediate period prior to becoming the New Normal Ammunition Co, Ltd. See number 746 in this cartridge list. I have listed the above brand names to the best of my knowledge.

758. **NORMAL POWDER CO.** Later known as, **NORMAL POWDER & AMMUNITION**
N9 **CO, LTD:** 2 Bank Buildings, Cricklewood. Also at, Hendon,
01 London NW4.
Business: Gunpowder manufacturers and cartridge loaders.
Cartridges: Possibly some of those listed under number 757 plus: Ejector; Nimrod; Unnamed; Wasters; Waterproof.
Remarks: I am still very much in the dark relating to this old firms history. They obviously became the New Normal Ammunition Co, Ltd at some later date. The questions that I would like answers to are, when and why. This their periods of activity and the addresses used when they were in business?

Many of their cartridges which are still in private collections carry the wording, 'No blow-backs, No Gun-Headaches'. Of the cartridge cases used, several that I have seen were made by the W. R. A. Co (Winchester Repeating Arms Company) of New Haven, Connecticut in the U.S.A. It is not known when this firm produced it's first shot shells as the

758. **NORMAL POWDER & AMMUNITION CO, LTD:** Continued.
Americans term them, but they were known to have been waterproofing them by 1884. The letters W.R.A.Co were used a lot on their early headstampings and certainly this was prior to using the word, Winchester. Frank H. Stewart has illustrated in his book, Shotgun Shells' (An American publication) a similar type of cartridge head. This being stamped, WINCHESTER No 12 NORMAL. This has got me wondering if our firm had started off as an off-spring of the W. R. A. Co which was later to become Winchester and much later, Winchester Western.

759. **NORMAL POWDER SYNDICATE, LTD:** 38-39 Parliament Street, London SW.
Remarks: They sold the Normal Powder Co's goods. It is not known if their name had ever been placed on a cartridge.

760. **B. NORMAN.** Later as, **NORMAN & SONS:** Woodbridge &
01 Framlingham, Suffolk.
Business: Gunmakers.
Cartridges: The Gastight; The Service; The Special; The Standard.
Remarks: This firm was established in 1870.

761. **NORRINGTON:** Chard, Somerset.
Cartridges: Norrington's Special Chardian.

762. **J. H. B. NORTH & SON:** Stamford, Lincolnshire. Also at, Broadway, Peterborough, Northamptonshire (Cambridgeshire).
Business: Agricultural merchants.
Cartridges: North's Universal.
Remarks: Cartridges were loaded for North & Son by G. L. Woods of Ovington, Norfolk. Cartridges may have been crimp closed or rolled turn over.

763. **C. W. NORTON:** Newtown, Montgomeryshire (Powys).
01 **Business:** Ironmonger.
Cartridges: Unnamed.

764. **J. E. NOTT & CO:** Brecon. Also at, Llandridod Wells,
01 Radnorshire (Powys).
Cartridges: Unnamed.

765. **JAMES ODELL:** High Street, Stoney Stratford, Buckinghamshire.
01 **Business:** Ironmonger.
Cartridges: Smokeless Cartridge.

766. **JOHN ODELL.** Later as, **ODELL BROTHERS:** 13 High Street, Newport Pagnell, Buckinghamshire (Milton Keynes).
Business: Ironmongers.
Remarks: This firm was established well over 200 years ago. in an 1877 directory the firm was listed as John Odell. Years ago I would call in their shop. I was told by the two brothers who both must have been in their eightys that they had once loaded and sold their own cartridges. These two grand old gentlemen never failed to find me a cartridge for my collection, but they never managed to find me one of their own. They possibly loaded for other ironmongers.

767. **OLBYS, LTD:** Ashford, Canterbury, Folkstone, Margate &
02 Ramsgate, Kent.
Cartridges: Olbys Cantium.

768. **HERBERT O'LEE:** Bishop's Stortford, Hertfordshire.
Cartridges: The Sharpshooter.

769. **OLIVER & CO:** Hull, Yorkshire (Humberside).
Business: Gunmakers.
Cartridges: The Estate.

770. **O'RIORDAN & FORREST:** Midleton, County Cork, Republic of
01 Ireland.
Cartridges: Unnamed.

771. **JOSEPH PHILLIP OSBORN:** The Golden Padlock, Daventry,
01 Northamptonshire.
Business: Ammunition and cartridge sales.
Cartridges: The Danetre Cartridge.

772. **CHARLES OSBORNE & CO, LTD:** 12 & 14 Whittal Street,
02 Birmingham, Warwickshire (W. Midlands).
Business: Gunmaker including maker of punt guns.
Cartridges: Unnamed; One and three quarter inch diam punt gun cartridge.

773. **WALTER OTTON.** Later as, **W. OTTON & SONS:** Exeter, Devonshire.
Business: Ironmongers.
Cartridges: The Devon; The Express; The Long Tom.

774. **OVERSEAS BUYING AGENCY:** Carmelite House, London (Rest of the address is not known).
Business: Overseas buying agency.
Cartridges: The Overseas Cartridge; Daily Mail (Printed like the newspaper heading on the case wall).
Remarks: The headstamping on the Daily Mail was WILKINSON No 12 PALL MALL.

775. **A. PAGE WOOD:** Baldwin Street, Bristol, Gloucestershire
02 (Avon).
Business: Gunmaker.
Cartridges: I Defy All To Approach It, Lion Brand Unapproachable.

776. **PAGE WOOD & CO:** 39-40 Walcot Street, Bath, Somerset (Avon).
02 **Business:** Gunmakers.
Cartridges: Unnamed.
Remarks: The illustrated cartridge was drawn from a used case. It appears that the firm was not too sure as to what it should call it's self during it's infancy. I have seen a reference to it as being A. Page Wood. It is with thanks to Mrs M. Joyce, a Bath reference librarian that I have the following information that has been taken from the Bath directories. 1890-1891 under the title, Gunmakers. Wood Page & Co. 39 & 40 Walcot Street. While listed under Walcot Street, Wood Alfred, gun manufacturers. There was no mention of a Mr Page. In the directories 1892-1893 the firm was listed as, Wood Page & Co

776. **PAGE WOOD & CO:** Continued.
and T. Page Wood & Co. Prior to 1890 and after 1893, no more listings existed of this firm although 40 Walcot Street was occupied either side of this period. This then dates the illustrated cartridge to circa, 1892.

777. **T. PAGE WOOD:** 17 Nicholas Street. Later at, 18 Pipe Lane,
N9   Bristol, Gloucestershire (Avon).
02   **Business:** Gunmaker.
03   **Cartridges:** Anti-Recoil Cartridge; Anti-Recoil Economic
Q7   Cartridge; The Bristol; The Climax Cartridge; The Double Crimp; First Quality; The Imperial Crown; The National Choke Cartridge; The Page-Wood No, 2; The Page-Wood D.S.; The Page-Wood's Shield Cartridge; The Park Row; Second Quality; Special .410; The Wildfowler.

778. **JAMES PAIN & SONS:** Salisbury, Wiltshire. Also at, Mitcham, London.
Business: Pyrotechnics and signal cartridge manufacturers.
Cartridges: Bird Scaring Cartridge (Not for shotgun); Ejector.

779. **PALMER SON & CO:** Barnet, Hertfordshire (Gt. London).
03   **Cartridges:** Eley Ejector; Rocketer.

780. **W. G. PALMER:** 29 High Street, Sittingbourne, Kent.
03   **Business:** Gunmaker.
Cartridges: The Champion Cartridge.

781. **W. & H. E. PALMER:** Rochester, Kent.
03   **Business:** Gunmakers.
Cartridges: The Century.

566. **W. P. JONES.** Was also known as, **W. PALMER JONES (GUNS):**
J8   **Remarks:** This firm is listed previously as number 566 in this cartridge list.

782. **PALMER & TARR:** Minehead, Somerset.
Cartridges: Unnamed.
Remarks: See number 378 J. Gliddon & Sons and number 978 William Tarr & Sons in this cartridge list.

783. **WILLIAM ROCHESTER PAPE:** 21 Collingwood Street, Newcastle-
03   upon-Tyne, Northumberland. Also at, Sunderland, County Durham
04   (Tyne & Wear).
Q7   **Business:** Gunmaker.
Cartridges: The Beryl; The Heather; The Pointer; The Ranger Smokeless; The Setter; The Tyne; Unnamed.
Remarks: During his time in activity, William Pape marketed many colourful and decorative cartridges. Many of them did not carry a brand name. On one of them which I have illustrated it pictures his complete gunshop and works. This was at 36 Westgate Road, Newcastle-upon-Tyne. The Beryl cartridge he named after his wife.

784. **PARAGON GUN SPECIALISTS:** 43 Ann Street, Belfast. Northern Ireland.
Business: Gun specialists.
Cartridges: The Crown; The Invincible; Paragon Special; Special.

785. **J. PARKINSON:** Dublin. Republic of Ireland.
Cartridges: Unnamed.

786. **TOM PARKINSON;** Ulverston, Lancashire (Cumberia).
04 **Cartridges:** Unnamed.

787. **C. PARSONS.** Later as, **PARSONS SHERWIN & CO, LTD:** Nuneaton &
04 Coventry, Warwickshire (W. Midlands).
Business: Agricultural and hardware merchants.
Cartridges: Special Loading; Unnamed.
Remarks: Several decades ago when their old premises at Nuneaton were being demolished, a small room at the rear revealed it's long gone cartridge loadings. It looked as though it had been kept lock shut ever since World War One. Covered in thick black dust from the ages was a loading machine and hundreds of unused printed ready capped cases. The printings on the case walls were for C. Parsons and also for Parsons Sherwin & Co, Ltd. I do not know when it was that these two people joined forces and decided to go public. It is quite possible that cartridges may have been loaded for them after the decision had been made to stop producing their own loadings.

788. **F. PARSONS:** Littlehampton Road, Worthing, West Sussex.
Business: Ironmonger.
Cartridges: The High Down.

789. **JOHN PATSTONE & SON:** 25 High Street. Later at, 28 High
04 Street, Southampton. Was at one time also in, Winchester,
Q7 Hampshire.
Business: Gunmakers.
Cartridges: The Precision; The Reliable; The Renown; Unnamed.
Remarks: Back in my early days of cartridge collecting I was given the histories of those Southampton gunshops. Alas, I never wrote them down. There was once a firm called Clarke & Dyke that did business in Southampton and Salisbury. I also have on record that there was a Chas Clarke in Salisbury. At one time there was a Cox & Clarke in Southampton. After this, Clarke seems to have dropped out of the picture. Did he then go to Salisbury, or had he come from Salisbury ?, but we did have a Cox & Macpherson in Southampton High Street. I have not seen many of their cartridges and so it makes me think that Macpherson may not have lasted in business for very long. It then looks as though a son of Cox may have entered the business, hence, Cox & Son. I now make another guess. Patstone then came on the scene and joined forces with Cox. This could have resulted in the firm Patstone & Cox. Did the wheel then turn a full circle with Cox dropping out and a son of Patstone joining the business. Mind you, all of this is just my speculation. How shall I get to know now, for number 28 the High Street, Southampton, is no longer a gunshop. I do expect that once this has been published in print, some kind person will write and tell me how wrong I have been.

790. **PATSTONE & COX:** 28 High Street, Southampton. Was once also
04 in, Winchester, Hampshire.
Q7 **Business:** Gunmakers.
Cartridges: The Pheasant; Pheasant Cartridges; The Precision.
Remarks: See the last entry, number 789 in this list.

791. **J. C. PATTERSON:** The Corner House, Market Square, Lisburn, Northern Ireland.
Business: Ironmonger.
Cartridges: The Nailer; Smokeless Cartridge.

792. **S. PAXTON & CO:** High Street, Stokesley, Yorkshire.
05 **Cartridges:** Eley Deep Shell (Eley-Kynoch I.C.I. case with the name on the over-shot wad only).
Remarks: Was known to have been active in 1937.

793. **JOSEPH PEACE, LTD:** Darlington, County Durham.
05 **Business:** Gunmaker and sports outfitter.
Cartridges: Eley G.P. Case (Name on over-shot wad only).

794. **PEARSON & CO:** Grimsby, Lincolnshire (Humberside).
05 **Cartridges:** Nobel's Sporting Ballistite (Extra tube printing).

795. **G. & J. PECK, LTD:** 43 High Street, Ely, Cambridgeshire.
Cartridges: Unnamed or name not known.
Remarks: The cartridge seen had an Eley Brothers, Ltd maroon coloured paper tube. This firm was known to have been active in 1929. Pecks' were ironmongers.

796. **CAPTAIN E. PELLIER-JOHNSON:** (Address not known).
05 **Business:** Not known. Listed below was a private cartridge.
Cartridges: Special Loading by Eley Brothers, Ltd.

797. **PENNY & SON:** Frome, Somerset.
05 **Cartridges:** The Times Cartridge.

798. **PERRINS & SON:** Worcester, Worcestershire (Hereford & Worcester).
Cartridges: Eley's Ejector (Perrin's name on the headstamping).

799. **S. PERROTT:** Kingsbridge, Devonshire.
05 **Business:** Sadler and ironmonger.
Cartridges: Patent Gastight Cartridge (Overprint on a 14 gauge Eley Brothers cartridge case for Schultze gunpowder).

800. **PHILLIPS BROTHERS:** 141 High Street, Marlborough, Wiltshire.
05 **Business:** Ironmongers.
Remarks: Their name has turned up found on headstampings on cartridge remains found through metal detecting.

801. **PHILLIPS & POWIS:** 34 & 37 West Street, Reading, Berkshire.
05 **Business:** Cycle agents.
Cartridges: The Pheasant.
Remarks: The Reading Borough Library gave a different address for this firm. They also referred to them as motocar and aviation agents. In later years they went into business at Woodley Aerodrome with Miles Aircraft. The firm then became well known for their civil range of Hawk aeroplanes in which they had several successes in the King's Cup Air Races. Also for their contribution of training aircraft in the Second World War. These were, Magisters, Mentors, Masters and Martinets.

802. **CHARLES PINDER.** Later as, **C. PINDER & CO:** Market Place,
05   Basingstoke, Hampshire.
     Business: Ironmongers.
     Remarks: Cartridge remains have been found by metal detecting. Chas is known to have been in business in 1911. He was not listed in a directory for 1907 or for 1915. It is not known if there were any family connections with the Pinder in Salisbury.

803. **J. E. PINDER:** 1 Winchester Street, Market Place, Salisbury,
05   Wiltshire.
     Business: Ironmonger.
     Cartridges: Pinder's Dead Shot Smokeless Cartridge.
     Remarks: This firm was not listed in a 1907 directory but it was listed in a 1920 directory. They were in business at least up to the start of the Second World War.

804. **HERBERT B. PITT:** 7 Silver Street, Trowbridge, Wiltshire.
06   **Business:** Ironmonger.
     Cartridges: H. B. Pitt's Premier.
     Remarks: Herbert was not listed in the 1899 trade directories. He was listed in 1903 and in 1907 where he was at 37 Roundstone Street, Trowbridge. In 1920 he was listed as being at 7 Silver Street. He was also listed as still being at this address in 1939.

805. **C. PLAYFAIR & CO:** Aberdeen, Aberdeenshire (Grampian).
05   **Cartridges:** Ejector.

806. **S. PLUMBERS, LTD:** Great Yarmouth, Norfolk.
06   **Business:** Dealers in guns and ammunition.
     Cartridges: Norfolk High Velocity Load; The Original Norfolk.
     Remarks: Plumbers may have taken over the business from West & Son who also marketed a Norfolk High Velocity Load. See number 1087 in this cartridge list.

807. **PNEUMATIC CARTRIDGE CO, LTD:** 61-67 Albert Street, Edinburgh,
06   Midlothian.
     Business: Cartridge loaders and merchants.
     Cartridges: Pneumatic No, 1; Pneumatic No, 2.

808. **PNEUMATIC CARTRIDGE CO, LTD:** 96-98 Holyrood Road; Edinburgh 8,
06   Midlothian.
Q7   **Business:** Cartridge loaders and merchants.
     Cartridges: Ejector; Pneuma; Pneumatic No, 1; Pneumatic No, 2; Pneumatic No, 3; Pneumatic .410; Pneumatic Cartridge; Pneumatic Pegamoid; Pneumatic Trapshooting Cartridge; Pneumatic Twenty Gauge.

809. **PNEUMATIC CARTRIDGE CO, LTD:** Bristol, Gloucestershire (Avon).
06   **Business:** Cartridge loaders and merchants.
     Cartridges: Pneumatic Cartridge.
     Remarks: See the previous entrys numbers 807 and 808 in this cartridge list. By showing this company in three separate sections has enabled me to show the cartridge brand names to their appropriate addresses. Pneumatics' were in business in Edinburgh between 1904 and 1954. They then made a move south to Bristol where they continued in business until around 1968.

809. **PNEUMATIC CARTRIDGE CO, LTD:** Continued.
The first patent for their Pneumatic wadding was taken out in 1904. Another patent was taken out in 1910. The wad in question was the compression wad. This was cut from solid cork with a cork plugged hole in the centre. The 12 gauge wad was about 11 mm thick with it's centre hole being about 8 mm in diameter. This hole was plugged with a cork plug about 8 mm thick.

810. **HERBERT E. POLLARD & CO:** 62 Broad Street, Worcester,
07 Worcestershire (Hereford & Worcester).
Business: Gunmakers.
Cartridges: Gas-tight; The Keepers Smokeless; The Long Shot; Our Game; Unnamed.

811. **W. H. POLLARD:** London (Rest of the address is not known).
07 **Remarks:** A headstamping has been found of this firm.

812. **POND & SON:** Market Place, Blandford Forum, Dorset.
07 **Business:** Ironmongers and agricultural merchants.
Cartridges: Unnamed (Pinfire with Pond & Son on the headstamping).
Remarks: Their telephone number was, Blandford 1.

813. **JOHN EDWARD PONTING:** 43, 44 & 46 High Street. Also at, Garsdon, Malmesbury, Wiltshire.
Business: Ironmonger.
Remarks: Many years ago I was told in their shop that in the past they had loaded their own cartridges.

814. **POOLE BROTHERS:** Taunton, Somerset.
Cartridges: Mullerite Yellow Seal (Extra tube printing).
Remarks: This firm was an agent for Mullerite cartridges.

815. **WILLIAM POOLE:** Market Hill, Haverhill, Suffolk.
Business: Ironmonger.
Remarks: It is not one hundred percent certain that they sold their own cartridges. What is certain is that they sold the products of the New Explosives Co, Ltd in those years leading up to the Great War (1914-18 World War One). See number 742 in this cartridge list.

816. **S. E. PORTER & CO:** 16-18-20 High Street, Whitchurch, Salop.
07 **Cartridges:** Gyttorp (Name only on the over-shot wad); Unnamed.

817. **J. M. POSTANS:** Walton-on-Naze, Essex.
07 **Cartridges:** Unnamed.

818. **J. Y. POTTER:** King's Lynn, Norfolk.
Cartridges: Eley's Gas-tight Cartridge Case for E.C. Powder (Name only on the over-shot wad).

819. **R. C. POTTER.** Later as, **POTTER & CO:** 1 Cornmarket, High
07 Wycombe, Buckinghamshire.
Business: Gunsmiths.
Cartridges: Unnamed (Centre and pinfire).
Remarks: They were known to have been in business in 1915.

820. **ROBERT & ERNEST POTTER:** 3 High Street, Thame, Oxfordshire.
07 **Business:** Gunsmiths and ironmongers.
    Cartridges: Unnamed.

821. **POWELL:** Tunbridge Wells, Kent.
    Cartridges: Powell's Special.

822. **T. POWELL & CO, LTD:** Bemberton, Salisbury, Wiltshire.
07 **Business:** Explosives merchants and shooting ground.
    Cartridges: Eley's Gas-tight Cartridge Case for Walsrode Powder (Powell's name on the headstamping).

823. **WILLIAM POWELL & SON (GUNMAKERS), LTD:** 35 Carrs Lane,
08 Birmingham, Warwickshire (W. Midlands).
09 **Business:** Gunmakers.
    Cartridges: Admiral; Clay Bird; Gastight Metal Lined; General; Knockout; Kynoch's Ejector; Marshal; Pegamoid; Powell's Ejector; Specially Hand Loaded; The Steel Lined; Super Velocity; Unnamed.

824. **W. J. POWELL:** Leiston, Suffolk.
08 **Business:** Gunmaker.
    Cartridges: The Lightning Smokeless.

825. **ALBERT PRATT:** 27 High Street, Knaresborough, Yorkshire.
08 **Business:** Ironmonger and ammunition dealer.
    Cartridges: The Fysche.

826. **THOMAS PRENTICE & CO:** Stowmarket, Suffolk.
08 **Cartridges:** Patent Gun Cotton Cartridge (Pinfire).

827. **PRESTON & DISTRICT FARMERS TRADING SOCIETY, LTD:** Preston,
09 Lancashire.
    Business: Agricultural trading society.
    Cartridges: Farmers General Purpose.

828. **PRESTWICH & SONS:** Longridge, Lancashire.
09 **Cartridges:** Eley's E.B. Nitro Cartridge Case (the Prestwich name on the over-shot wad only).

829. **W. H. PRICE:** Chester Street, Hold (See Remarks).
    Cartridges: The Champion.
    Remarks: I do not know of any place called Hold. Perhaps it was an abbreviation for a place. It is also possible that when the information was given to me that a mistake may have been made. Or perhaps some other letters may have been missing from off of the cartridge.

830. **PROGRESSIVE CARTRIDGE CO:** Chandlersford, Hampshire.
08 **Cartridges:** Unnamed.

831. **W. PROUT:** Launceston, Cornwall.
    Business: Dealer in motors, cycles and cartridges.
    Cartridges: Unnamed.

832. **C. F. PUGH:** Knighton, Radnorshire (Powys).
09 **Business:** Ironmonger.
    Cartridges: The Rabbit.

116

833. **HENRY PULLAN:** Linden Cycle & Gun Works, Castle Street,
08 Cirencester, Gloucestershire.
Business: Cycle and gunmaker.
Cartridges: The V.W.H. (Vale of the White Horse).

834. **MARTIN PULVERMANN & CO:** 31 Minories, London E.
Business: Wholesaler in cartridges.
Remarks: For information, see number 731 Mullerite Cartridge Works in this cartridge list.

835. **ARTHUR F. PUNTER.** Later as, **A. F. PUNTER. Proprietor, J. M.**
09 **EMBERTON:** 46 Wote Street, Basingstoke, Hampshire.
Business: Ironmongers.
Cartridges: The Minimax; Shamrock, The Farmers Friend (A Frank Dyke's cartridge with extra tube printing).
Remarks: Established in 1904, this firm had their name on cartridges up until the Second World War. The proprietor then being, J. M. Emberton. An engraved illustration in one of their yellow paged old catalogues portrayed a cartridge with a cock pheasant on the case wall and Punter's name on the headstamping.

836. **C. PURCELL:** 10 Worcester Street, Gloucester, Gloucestershire.
09 **Cartridges:** Special High Velocity Cartridge.

837. **JAMES PURDEY.** Later as, **J. PURDEY & SON, LTD.** Still later,
P1 **J. PURDEY & SONS, LTD:** 57-60 Audley House, Audley Street,
Q7 London W1.
Business: Gunmakers.
Cartridges: 2-Inch; Eley's Ejector; Pegamoid; Purdey's Deep Shell; Purdey's Large Cap; Purdey's Special; Unnamed.
Remarks: An early address that I have for James Purdey is, 314½ Oxford Street, London W1. This well known London firm of gunmakers at one time loade their own cartridges. Like many of the other large firms, they later had their cartridges loaded for them by the case manufacturers. In their early years, pinfires were sold with the Purdey name on the headstampings either in normal or raised lettering. Their cartridges were also loaded for the British Royalty. Some of these loadings had a white over-shot wad with just a crown displayed on it in either black or red print. No shot size being shown. At one time their famous Purdey Special Cartridges were sold in the gauges 12, 16 and 20.

838. **R. S. PURDEY:** Thirsk, Yorkshire.
09 **Business:** Ironmonger.
Cartridges: Warranted Gas-tight Cartridge Case.
Remarks: A cartridge box that once held 50 safety cartridges with size 5 in shot has been seen. On the box it stated that the cartridges were made by R. S. Purdey, Thirsk. The box was manufactured by W. A. Stubbs of Cobridge, Staffordshire. It was a light brown with dark brown printings.

839. **PURVIS & CO:** Alnwick, Northumberland.
P2 **Cartridges:** Sure Shot.

840. **K. D. RADCLIFFE:** 150 High Street, Colchester, Essex.
P2 **Business:** Gunsmith or gunmaker.

840. **K. D. RADCLIFFE:** Continued.
Cartridges: A true Fit; Unnamed; Warranted Gastight.
Remarks: This firm took over the Colchester based business of J. S. Boreham in November 1899. See number 109 in this cartridge list. You may note from this that all cartridges by J. S. Boreham belong to the 19th Century.

841. **ROBERT RAINE.** Later as, **RAINE BROTHERS:** Carlisle, Cumberland
P2 (Cumbria).
Business: Gunmakers.
Cartridges: The Border Cartridge; The Irresistable; Raine's Special.

842. **R. RAMSBOTTOM:** Sports Depot, Manchester, Lancashire (Gt.
P2 Manchester).
Business: Sports store.
Cartridges: Schultze; The Sudden Death Smokeless Cartridge Mk II.

843. **RANDALL WRIGHT:** Spalding, Lincolnshire.
Business: Gunsmith.
Cartridges: Amberite Cartridge.

844. **F. RANDELL, LTD:** Market Place, North Walsham. Also at,
P2 Cromer, Norfolk.
Business: Ironmonger.
Cartridges: Special Smokeless.

845. **M. RAY:** Dartford, Kent.
P2 **Business:** Gunmaker.
Cartridges: Unnamed.

846. **REDMAYNE & TODD:** Nottingham, Nottinghamshire.
Cartridges: Unnamed.

847. **E. M. REILLY & CO:** 277 Oxford Street. Also at, 16 New
P2 Oxford Street, London WC.
Business: Gunmakers.
Cartridges: Eley's Gas-tight Cartridge Case for Schultze Sporting Powder (Reilly's name on the headstamping). The Harewood; Unnamed.
Remarks: A unique 15 gauge pinfire cartridge has been seen with Reilly's name on the headstamping. Two Oxford Street addresses that I have for them are, 295 and the other dated 1890 is 277. At one time they were also at, 16 New Oxford Street, London WC1. All cartridges by E. M. Reilly & Co are prior to 1900.

848. **REMINGTON ARMS, UNION METALIC CARTRIDGE CO, LTD.** Known as,
P3 **REMINGTON U.M.C. (ENGLAND):** Offices at, Bush House, Aldwych, London WC2. Factory at, UMC Works, Brimsdown, Enfield, Middlesex (Gt London).
Business: American arms and ammunition manufacturers.
Cartridges: Arrow; Economy; Remington .410; Remington Kleanbore; Remington Nitro Club; Remilion Geranium; Unnamed.
Remarks: Kleanbore cartridges were first introduced in America in 1926. The name Kleanbore being a registered name to Remington U.M.C. James E. Burns, a chemist invented a non-

848. **REMINGTON U.M.C. (ENGLAND):** Continued.
corrosive primer. He then left his employment with the United States Cartridge Co and sold his invention to Remington. The new primer used lead styphnate, not only did it not leave any harmful residue in the bore, but it also spread a protective coating. Remington then held a public contest to choose a new name for their cartridges. Two men both came up with the name Kleanbore. They both lived in different parts of the States of America and both were given prizes.
   I do not know when this firm first became active in England, but it is known that they were a going concern in July 1913.

849. **E. G. E. REYNOLDS:** Saxmundham, Suffolk.
P3 **Business:** Sports depot.
Cartridges: The Champion Smokeless.

850. **J. REYNOLDS:** Cullompton, Devonshire.
Q7 **Cartridges:** Unnamed.

851. **RHODES:** Scarborough, Yorkshire.
Cartridges: Eley Ejector (Rhodes name on over-shot wad only).

852. **RHODES & PAGET:** Cook Lane, Keighley, Yorkshire.
Business: Ironmongers.
Cartridges: Unnamed (Firms name on the over-shot wad only).
Remarks: Their name was listed in a 1913 trade directory. Unfortunately other directories were not available, but they were not listed in 1936.

853. **C. C. RICHARDS:** Wiveliscombe, Somerset.
P3 **Business:** Ironmonger.
Cartridges: The Wivey Special Smokeless.

854. **F. J. RICHARDS:** Taunton, Somerset.
Cartridges: Kynoch's Patent Perfectly Gas-tight.
Remarks: This firm ceased trading in 1866.

855. **WILLIAM RICHARDS.** Later as, **W. RICHARDS (LIVERPOOL), LTD:**
P4 27 Old Hall Street, Liverpool, Lancashire (Merseyside). Also at, 44 Fisher Gate, Preston, Lancashire.
Business: Gunmakers.
Cartridges: The Castle; The Express; Grand Prix; The Killwell; Kynoch Grouse Ejector; The Mark Down; The R.P. Cartridge; The R.P. Gastight Smokeless Cartridge.

856. **G. B. RICHARDSON:** 18 Bridge Street, Cardiff, Glamorgan. Also at, Barnard Castle, County Durham.
Cartridges: Nulli Secundus.

857. **G. M. RICHARDSON:** Dumfries, Dumfries-shire (Dumfries &
P4 Galloway).
Cartridges: Buccleuch; Criffel; Ideal.

858. **WILLIAM G. RICHARDSON, LTD:** Barnard Castle, County Durham.
P4 **Business:** Cartridge and fishing tackle experts.
Cartridges: The Baliol; The Barnite; The Barnoid.

859. **RICKARBY & PARTNER. (A. G. RICKARBY):** 37A Finsbury Square, London EC2.
Remarks: It is not known if they ever had their name on cartridges. They were the agents in the U.K. for the American United States Cartridge Co's U.S. Defiance.

860. **JOHN RIGBY.** Later as, **J. RIGBY & CO (GUNMAKERS), LTD:** 24
P5 Suffolk Street, Dublin, Republic of Ireland. Also at, 72 St. James's Street, London SW1. Later at, 43 Sackville Street, London SW1. Later still at, 32 King Street, St. James's, London SW1.
Business: Gun and rifle makers.
Cartridges: Ejector; Rigby's Record Cartridge; Unnamed.
Remarks: This firm was founded in Dublin in 1770. This being nearly a century before cartridges were invented. Many of their cartridges never carried a brand name. They were known to have been at 43 Sackville Street in 1927.

861. **C. RIGGS & CO, LTD:** Ye Bishop's Gate Sport House, 107
P5 Bishopsgate, London EC.
Business: Gunsmiths or gunmakers.
Cartridges: The Bishop; The Gate; The Mitre.

862. **A. E. RINGWOOD:** Banbury, Oxfordshire.
P5 **Business:** Gunmaker.
Cartridges: The Dreadnought; The Ideal; The Special.

863. **R. L. AMMUNITION CO:** 27 Upper Marylebone Street, London W1.
Cartridges: Unnamed (1½ inch shell 'Powder carrier').

864. **H. E. ROBERSON:** High Street, Towcester, Northamptonshire.
Business: Ironmonger and gun and ammunition dealer.
Cartridges: The Towcester.

865. **ANGUSTUS J. ROBERTS:** 55 Broad Street, Ludlow, Shropshire.
P5 **Business:** Ironmonger.
Cartridges: The Roberts Special Smokeless.

866. **E. ROBERTS:** 141 Steelhouse Lane, Birmingham, Warwickshire (W. Midlands).
Business: Gunmaker.
Cartridges: The Forward Cartridge; The Reliance.

867. **H. P. ROBERTS:** Ottery St. Mary, Devonshire.
P5 **Business:** Ironmonger.
Cartridges: Eley Yeoman (Extra tube printing); Ottervale.

868. **H. W. ROBERTS & CO:** Rhyl, Flintshire (Clwyd).
P5 **Cartridges:** Kynoch Patent Grouse Ejector; Special Blend.

869. **T. H. ROBERTS & SON:** Parliament House, Dolgelley, Merionethshire (Dolgellau, Gwynedd).
Business: Ironmonger.
Cartridges: Unnamed.
Remarks: This firm once loaded their own cartridges. Many of their loads were in heavy gauges, shot sizes between 4 and BB.

870. **ROBERTSON:** Peebles, Peebles-shire (Borders).
Cartridges: Unnamed or name not recorded.
Remarks: The cartridge seen had a KYNOCH BIRMINGHAM headstamp.

871. **ALEXANDER ROBERTSON & SON:** Wick, Caithness (Highland).
P6 **Business:** Ironmongers.
Cartridges: Eley Gas-tight Case; The Expert; Special Smokeless.

872. **ROBINSON BROTHERS:** Loftus, Yorkshire (Cleveland).
Business: Ironmongers.
Cartridges: Unnamed.

873. **H. ROBINSON:** 102 St. John's Street, Bridlington, Yorkshire (Humberside).
Cartridges: The Burlington Express.

874. **H. ROBINSON & CO:** Bridgnorth, Shropshire.
P6 **Business:** Ironmongers, gunsmiths and cycle makers.
Cartridges: The Castle; Special Smokeless.

875. **ROBERT ROBINSON.** Later as, **R. ROBINSON (GUNMAKERS), LTD:**
P6 7 Queen Street, Kingston upon Hull, Yorkshire (Humberside).
Business: Gunmakers.
Cartridges: The Champion; Ejector; The Humber; The Kingston Smokeless; The Magnet; Sporting Ballistite.
Remarks: Robert marketed a cartridge with a shield crest on the case wall. Portrayed within this shield were three crowns in a vertical formation. His cartridges were sold long before some similar marked cartridges that became a well liked brand that were sold by the Hull Cartridge Co, Ltd. See number 519 in this cartridge list. The Robinson business was taken over, post World War Two years by Joe Wheater who continued to market a Humber Cartridge. See number 1097 in this list.

876. **R. B. RODDA & CO:** Callcutta, India. Was also in Birmingham,
P6 Warwickshire (W. Midlands).
Business: Dealers in guns and ammunition.
Cartridges: 3 inch Long Range; Champion Smokeless; Crown Smokeless; Mullerite Paragon; Rotax Ball Cartridge; The Wellesley.
Remarks: It appears that this firm had stronger connections with India than what it did with Great Britain. Several of their Rotax Cartridges have come to light in the U.K. They had the word 'Ball' printed on their case walls. These cartridges were not shot loaded and may have been loaded during the First World War.

877. **R. ROPER, SON & CO:** 8 South Street. Also at, 9 Exchange Street, Sheffield, Yorkshire.
Business: Gunmakers.
Cartridges: Eley's Gas-tight Cartridge Case; The Hallamshire Cartridge; Kynoch's Patent Perfectly Gas-tight.

878. **B. L. ROSKELLEY:** 20 Queen Street, Lostwithiel, Near St. Austell, Cornwall.
Business: Ironmonger, optician and diamond merchant.
Cartridges: Unnamed.
Remarks: His name has also been found on cartridge remains.

879. **CHARLES ROSSON.** Later as, **ROSSON & SON:** 4 Market Head. Also
P6   at, 12 Market Place, Derby, Derbyshire.
P7   **Business:** Gunmakers.
Q8   **Cartridges:** Eclipse; Kuvert; Monvill; Roedich; Unnamed; Vipax.
    Remarks: Charles later branched out to Norwich. See the next entry number 880 in this cartridge list.

880. **C. S. ROSSON & CO, LTD:** 13 Rampant Horse Street. Later at, 7
P7   Bedford Street, Norwich, Norfolk.
    Business: Gunmakers and cartridge loaders.
    Cartridges: The Crown; The Ejector; The Ektor long .410; The Kuvert; The Lowrecoil; The Monvill; The Roedich; The Sixteen Cartridge; Smokeless; Star .410; The Twenty Cartridge; Unnamed; The Vipax; Waveney.
    Remarks: This firm eventually left Derby and set up their business in Norwich. They were known to have been in Rampant Horse Street in 1916. At one time they advertised in their brochure Blue Rival cartridges, but these were closed by crimping. In 1953 a new company was formed when Charles Hellis & Sons, Ltd and C. S. Rosson & Co, Ltd, made a joint undertaking to produce shotgun cartridges with high reputations and as the firm put it, first-class specifications. Cartridges were loaded in the Norwich area and they used the old Hellis offices at 121-3 Edgware Road, London W2. Not all, but most of these cartridges were closed by star crimpings. See numbers 458 and 459 in this cartridge list.

881. **R. ROUS:** Beyton, Suffolk.
    Business: Motor garage.
    Cartridges: Unnamed.

882. **ROWE & CO:** Aylesbury, Buckinghamshire.
P7   **Cartridges:** Hall's Cannonite (Coarse Grain).

883. **W. W. ROWE:** 62 High Street, Barnstaple. Also at, 63 Winner Street, Paignton, Devonshire.
    Business: Gunmaker.
    Remarks: I have been told of a cartridge by them.

884. **ROBERT ROWELL & SON:** 7 High Street, Chipping Norton, Oxon.
P7   **Business:** Ironmongers, engineers and brass founders.
    Cartridges: Sure Killer.

885. **R. H. ROWLAND:** Thoroughfare, Woodbridge, Suffolk.
    Business: Ironmonger.
    Cartridges: Special Loading.

886. **JOHN ROWLATT:** 16 Silver Street. Also at, 23 Wellingborough
P8   Road, Finedon, Wellingborough, Northamptonshire.
    Business: Gunsmiths or gunmakers.
    Cartridges: Special Smokeless Cartridge.
    Remarks: In my notes it states that this firm was established in 1751. In an 1894 trade directory it listed this firm then as ironmongers at 16 Silver Street.

887. **ROYS:** Wroxham, Norfolk.
P8   **Business:** Ironmongers.
    Cartridges: Roys De Luxe; Roys Rabbit Cartridge.

888. **ARTHUR J. RUDD:** 54 London Street, Norwich. Also at, 17
P8   Regent Street, Great Yarmouth, Norfolk.
      Business: Gunmaker.
      Cartridges: The Norfolk; Rudd's Standard; Rudd's X.L.
      Cartridge; Star Cartridge.

889. **A. J. RUSSELL.** Later as, **A. J. RUSSELL & SONS:** 32 High
P8   Street, Maidstone, Kent.
      Business: Gunmakers.
      Cartridges: The Reliance Smokeless; S̶u̶ssell's Special.

890. **ALEX RUTHERFORD, LTD:** Sportsmans Repository, Blackwellgate,
      Darlington, County Durham.
      Business: Sports store.
      Cartridges: The Champion;

891. **W. M. E. E. RUTHERFORD:** 9 & 11 Walkergate, Berwick-upon-
      Tweed, Northumberland.
      Cartridges: Unnamed.

892. **RUTT & CO:** 13 Bridge Street, Northampton, Northamptonshire.
      Remarks: Many years ago I had entered this name in my files
      but had failed to have entered cartridge details. It is most
      likely that there were family connections with number 893 the
      next entry in this cartridge list.

893. **ALFRED H. RUTT:** Cattle Market. Also at, 9 George Row,
      Northampton, Northamptonshire.
      Business: Gunmaker.
      Cartridges: Unnamed.

894. **R. D. RYDER:** Rhayder, Radnorshire (Powys).
      Business: Ironmonger.
      Cartridges; Ryder's True Blue.

895. **H. F. SALE & SON:** Shipston-on-Stour, Warwickshire.
Q1   **Cartridges:** Champion; Rover; The Saleson.

896. **W. SAMPLE:** Amble, Northumberland.
Q1   **Business:** Gun and ammunition dealer.
      Cartridges: Unnamed.

897. **SANDBROOK & DAWE:** Crane Street, Pontypool, Monmouthshire
      (Gwent).
      Business: Ironmongers.
      Remarks: Cartridges had been loaded on their premises.

898. **SANDERS:** Plymtree, Ford Moor, Devonshire.
      Business: Private shoot.
      Remarks: I was given this name and address but with no
      cartridge details.

899. **A. SANDERS:** 79 Bank Street, Maidstone, Kent.
Q1   **Business:** Gunmaker.
      Cartridges: The Allington; Eley's Gas-tight Cartridge Case;
      Fourten; Invicta Special; Long Tom; The Medway; Unnamed.

899. **A. SANDERS:** Continued.
Remarks: This firm was established in 1838. They also at a much later date took over the gunmaking business of Swinfen. See number 975 in this cartridge list. In later years still they incorporated the Scottish business of John Fraser of Edinburgh. See number 343 in this list. At one time I had in my collection by them a 12 gauge unnamed pinfire, It was an imported R.W.S.case (Rheinische Westfalische Springstoff of Germany). Sander's name was on the over-shot wad only.

900. **JOHN HENRY SANDERS:** Combe Martin, Devonshire.
Business: Ironmonger.
Cartridges: The Mighty Atom Cartridge.

901. **SANDLEFORD PRIORY ESTATE:** Near Newbury, Berkshire.
Business: Private estate.
Remarks: Over-shot wads were purchased being specially printed with the Sandleford name. After a shoot, the best of the used cases were collected up by the head keeper who then reloaded them for the estate use. He had his own ideas on these loads and their loading method was very much non standard. The Sandleford wads were used to close the cases.

902. **G. E. SAUL:** Lymington, Hampshire.
Remarks: This name has been seen on some over-shot wads.

903. **E. F. SAUNDERS:** 53 South Street, Chichester, Sussex.
Business: Ironmonger.
Cartridges: The Golden pheasant.

904. **SAYER:** Watton, Norfolk.
Q8 **Cartridges:** Sayer's Bulzi Hard Hitting Smokeless Cartridge.

905. **SCHULTZE CO.** Also known as, **SCHULTZE GUNPOWDER CO, LTD:**
P8 3 Bucklersbury. Also at, 28 & 32 Gresham Street, London EC.
P9 **Business:** Gunpowder and cartridge manufacturers.
Cartridges: The Albion; The Bomo; The Captain (This took it's name from Captain E. Schultze); The Caro; The Conqueror; Cube Powder Cartridge; Deep Brass Gastight; Ejector; The Eyeworth; Grand Prix; Nitro; The Pickaxe; Rainproof; The Rufus Smokeless Cartridge; Schultze Smokeless Powder; The Toro; Waterproof; The Westminster; The Yeoman.
Remarks: Schultze, the smokeless gunpowder acquired it's name from it's eventor, Captain E. Schultze. He was a serving officer in the Prusian Services. The cartridge called The Captain is honouring this famous gentleman. The Schultze Gunpowder Co, Ltd was formed in Great Britain in 1868 and they had their gunpowder mill at Eyeworth Lodge, Hampshire. This was in the New Forest area. Looking through all of my gazetteers, the only Eyeworth that I can find any reference to is in Bedfordshire. I would therefore guess that the powder mill had taken it's name from a house in the country rather than from a place name. The cartridge called The Eyeworth being named after their mills.
   I am very sceptical over the various dates when the Schultze Gunpowder Co, Ltd finally merged in with Messrs Eley Bros, Ltd. My thoughts are that it all started around 1911, and that they

905. **SCULLTZE CO:** Continues.
still produced their brands of cartridges under their own name unti about 1923. Another of my notes stated that Schultze own cartridges dated from 1899 until 1923 when the company was finally liquidated. If my note was true, then it brings the period of time when the Nobel Industries, Ltd had the full control of the firm. I don't know about you, but I have found this all very confusing. Also I have read that the same time the company had joined forces with Eleys' in 1911, it was stated that it then changed it's name to The Schultze Co, Ltd. I also read that later on in 1916 when the Great War was getting very bloody, a very strong anti-German feeling which was running through the country made them decide to revert back to being known as, The Schultze Gunpowder CO, Ltd. If this is so, then all cartridges marked The Schultze Co, Ltd can be dated as being between 1911 and 1916.

In 1909, a separate company was formed. To give them their full title they were, Cogschultze Ammunition & Powder Co, Ltd. See number 190 in this cartridge list. An arrangement was made where Cogswell & Harrison, Ltd provided the cartridge cases and Schultze provided the powders. In an article that I once read it said that this concern pobably went on until the start of the 1914-18 war. Now thinking about it, the chances was that it oly ran for two years. Being as Eley Brothers, Ltd had always supplied Schultze with their cartridge cases until 1909, and as it had been reported that they had then merged with them in 1911, this could quite well have been the reason that brought it all about.

When the various firme joined the combine of Messrs Eley Brothers, Ltd it was common practice at that time to retain some of their cartridge brand names. Two Schultze names were Westminster and Yeoman and these were continued within the production right up to 1939 when the coming war put a stopper on it.

Gunpowders manufactured by the Schultze Gunpowder Co, Ltd, apart from Original Schultze, I am listing here along with their year of introduction. The powders: Imperial Schultze 1902; Cube Schultze 1908; Popular Schultze, approximately 1912; Schultze Lightning 1913; This little bit of information can be made useful when dating some old cartridges. To give an instance. Their Popular Powder dated from 1912, The merger with Eley Brothers was recorded as being 1911. Now the Grand Prix being a name of Eley origin places this cartridge as being somewhere between 1912 and 1923.

The address of 3 Bucklersbury, London was taken from an old advertisment for the wholesale of their various powders. It gave this as being the address for their company offices. It is known that in July 1896 they then used an address at. 32 Gresham Street, London EC.

906. **JOHN A. SCOTCHER.** Later as, **J. A. SCOTCHER & SON:** 4 The
P9 Traverse, Bury St. Edmunds, Suffolk.
Business: Gunsmths or gunmakers.
Cartridges: Eley's Gas-tight Cartridge Case for Schultze Gunpowders; The Invincible; Special Smokeless Cartridge.
Remarks: This business was taken over in 1913 by Henry Hodgson. Therefore all Scotcher cartridges are prio to 1913. See number 493 in this cartridge list.

907. **SCOTT & SARGEANT:** 26 East Street, Horsham, Sussex.
Business: Ironmongers.
Cartridges: The Horsham Special; The Ironmonger.

908. **SERCOMBE:** Bovey Tracey, Devonshire.
Cartridges: Unnamed (Pinfire, Sercombe on the over-shot wad only).

909. **F. A. SHARP & SON:** 69 High Street, Poole, Dorsetshire.
Business: Ironmongers.
Cartridges: Sharp's Express.

910. **J. S. SHARPE:** 35 Belmont Street, Aberdeen, Aberdeenshire
P9 (Grampian).
Business: Gun and fishing tackle dealer.
Cartridges: The Buchan; The Scottie.

911. **SHARPLAND BROTHERS:** Wellington (Rest of the address is not known).
Cartridges: The Wellington Cartridge.

912. **SHAW & CO:** West Meath, Mullingar, Republic of Ireland.
P9 **Business:** Gunmakers and stores.
Cartridges: Nobel's Sporting Ballistite (Extra tube printing).

913. **EDWARD LEADER SHEPHERD:** High Street. Also in, Lombard
P9 Street, Abingdon, Berkshire (Oxfordshire).
Business: Gunmaker and ironmonger.
Cartridges: Ejector (Name on over-shot wad only).

914. **FRANCIS B. SHUFFERY.** Later as, **SHUFFERYS, LTD:** 245 Stafford
P9 Street. Also at, 20 Caldmore, Walsall, Staffordshire
(W. Midlands).
Business: Ironmongers.
Cartridges: The Beacon.
Remarks: Many of their Beacon cartridges were found under floor boards when an old shop was stripped out.

915. **S. W. SILVER & CO:** London (Rest of the address is not known).
Remarks: Cartridge remains were found in India that had the headstamping, S.W.SILVER & Co No 12 LONDON.

916. **SIMPSON:** Piccadilly, London W1.
Cartridges: Unnamed or name not recorded.

917. **S. & J. PIPEWORK, LTD:** High Wycombe, Buckinghamshire.
Cartridges: Unnamed or name not recorded.

918. **SKELTONS, LTD:** Warrington, Lancashire (Cheshire).
P9 **Remarks:** Their name has been seen on a headstamping.

919. **SKEMPTON:** Bovey Tracey, Devonshire.
Remarks: Their name has been seen printed on an over-shot wad.

920. **SKINNER & CO:** 62 Denby Street. Also at, 63 Haywood Street,
P9 Leek, Staffordshire.
Cartridges: Champion Smokeless Cartridge; Unnamed.

921. **SLATER:** Warwick Street, Leamington Spa, Warwickshire.
   Cartridges: Unnamed or name not known.

922. **SLINGSBY:** Leeds, Yorkshire.
   Cartridges: Unnamed (Name on headstamping and over-shot wad).

923. **SLINGSBY BROTHERS.** Later as, **SLINGSBY GUNS:** 10 High Street,
P9 Boston. Also at, Sleaford, Lincolnshire.
   Business: Gunmakers.
   Cartridges: Slingsby's Champion; Slingsby's Fen; Slingsby's Special; Slingsby's Stump.

924. **JOHN SMAIL & SONS:** Morpeth, Northumberland.
   Business: Ironmongers.
   Cartridges: The Lightning Killer.

925. **P. SMALL:** 28 Pilgrim Street, Newcastle-upon-Tyne,
P9 Northumberland (Tyne & Wear).
   Cartridges: The Burnand; Kynoch's Grouse Ejector.

926. **SAMUEL SMALLWOOD:** 12 High Street. Also at, Milk Street,
Q1 Shrewsbury, Shropshire.
   Business: Gunmaker.
   Cartridges: Smallwood's Challenge; Smallwood's Kleankiller; The Nitrone Cartridge.

927. **R. B. SMART:** Atherstone, Warwickshire.
   Cartridges: Yellow Seal Mullerite (Extra tube printing).

928. **A. FISHER SMITH:** High Street, Hailsham. Also at, High
Q1 Street, Heathfield, Sussex.
   Cartridges: The Hailsham Special; Yellow Boy.

929. **BARTON SMITH:** Sligo, County Sligo, Republic of Ireland.
   Cartridges; Nulla Nisi Aroua The Unicorn; Nulla Nisi Aroua The Vogue.
   Remarks: This firm was founded by Mr Barton Smith in 1788. Irish Metal Industries, Ltd at Galway loaded two cartridges. The earlier was the Vogue which was named after the Garravogue River. The second was the Unicorn. Barton Smith were general ironmongers and traders in farm impliments. All items made for them were stamped or printed with a Unicorn. This to denote that they were made for and sold by Barton Smith. The wording 'Nulla Nisi Ardua' translated, Nothing except by hard work.

930. **C. H. SMITH & SONS:** 123 Steelhouse Lane, Birmingham,
Q2 Warwickshire (W. Midlands).
   Business: Gunmakers.
   Cartridges: The Abbey; The Invincible.

931. **CHARLES SMITH.** Later as, **CHAS SMITH & SONS:** 47 Market Place,
Q2 Newark. Also at, 28 Milton Street, Nottingham, Notts.
   Business: Gunmakers.
   Cartridges: All British Extra Special; The Castle; The Clinton; Extra Special Cartridge; Kynoch's Grouse Ejector; The Newark Cartridge; The Rufford; Schultze Load; Unnamed; The Universal.
   Remarks: Charles started his business at 37 Market Street, Newark.

932. **E. H. SMITH:** Northallerton, Yorkshire.
Cartridges: Unnamed (Woodcock portrayed on case wall).

933. **EDWARD H. SMITH & SONS:** 2 Market Place, Brigg, Lincolshire.
Business: Ironmongers.
Cartridges: The Lightning.

934. **STEVE SMITH:** 42 High Friar Street, Newcastle-under-Lyme,
Q2   Staffordshire.
Business: Gunsmith.
Cartridges: Trap and Game.
Remarks: Produced by Greenwood & Batley. Later cartridges were closed by crimping.

935. **DUNCOMB SMITH:** 5 High Street, Stamford, Lincolnshire.
Business: Ironmonger.
Cartridges: Unnamed or name not recorded.
Remarks: The spelling was as T. S. Duncomb on the seen cartridge.

936. **SMITH MIDGLEY:** Bradford, Yorkshire.
Q2   **Business:** Gunmakers.
Cartridges: The Bradford Cartridge; Pegamoid; Unnamed.

937. **G. J. SMITHSON:** Doncaster, Yorkshire.
Cartridges: Unnamed.

938. **SMOKELESS POWDER CO, LTD:** Dashwood House, New Broad Street, London EC. Works at, Barwick, Hertfordshire.
Business: Gunpowder manufacturers.
Cartridges: Smokeless S.S. Sporting.
Remarks: They were known to have been active in 1896.

939. **SMOKELESS POWDER & AMMUNITION CO. (S.P. & A. CO):** 28 Gresham
Q2   Street, London EC.
Business: Gunpowder and ammunition manufacturers.
Cartridges: Ejector; Unnamed.
Remarks: You may have noticed that their address was the same as the Schultze Gunpowder Co, Ltd. See number 905 in this cartridge list.
   The Smokeless Powder Co, Ltd was formed in 1887 to market it's S.S. gunpowder. See entry 938 above. A decade later in 1898 this firm was terminated. At the same time, a new firm came into being. It was the Smokeless Powder & Ammunition Co, Ltd with it's address at 28 Gresham Street. It is worth noting the logo similarities of the Smokeless Powder Co, Ltd to those of the Explosives Company E.C. and that of the New Explosives Co, Ltd. See numbers 281 and 742 in this cartridge list.

940. **J. F. SMYTHE, LTD:** The Sportsman's Repository, Darlington.
Q3   Also at, Dovecot Street, Stockton-on-Tees, County Durham (Cleveland).
Business: Gunmaker and cartridge loader.
Cartridges: Durham Ranger; Eley Ejector; The Field Cartridge; Gastight; Smythe's Champion; Smythe's Express; Smythe's Special Load.

941. **H. & R. SNEEZUM:** 14, 16, 18, 20 Fore Street, Ipswich,
Q2   Suffolk.
Business: Gunmakers.
Cartridges: Sneezum's Anglia; Sneezum's Special High Velocity Load.

942. **SNELLING:** Ongar, Essex.
Remarks: The wording SNELLING.ONGAR. has been seen printed on some over-shot wads.

943. **SOUTHERN COUNTIES AGRICULTURAL TRADING SOCIETY. (S.C.A.T.S.):**
Q3   Salisbury, Wiltshire.
Business: Agricultural traders.
Cartridges: Unnamed (12 gauge with S.C.A.T.S. crest).

944. **SOUTHERN COUNTIES AGRICULTURAL TRADING SOCIETY. (S.C.A.T.S.):**
Q3   Winchester, Hampshire.
Business: Agricultural traders.
Cartridges: The Challenger Smokeless.
Remarks: This firm's name was often abbreviated as S.C.A.T.S. being pronounced as 'Scatts'. I have shown these two branches as two separate listings in order to show the cartridges that were sold from each branch.

945. **SOUTHERN REMEDIAL SERVICES:** 627 Oxford Road, Reading, Berks.
Q3   **Business:** Treatments in risen damp and woodworm.
Cartridges: Unnamed.

946. **JOHN WILLIAM & EDWIN SOWMAN, LTD:** Olney, Buckinghamshire.
Q3   **Business:** Ironmongers, seed merchants, general furnishing and cycle agents.
Cartridges: The Hare; The Keeper; The Pheasant; The Sureshot Smokeless.
Remarks: in 1877, this business was in the name of Thomas Cooper.

947. **ALFRED L. SPENCER:** Finkle Street, Richmond, Yorkshire.
Q3   **Business:** Gunmaker.
Cartridges: Unnamed.
Remarks: An over-shot wad has been seen loaded into a cartridge case with an ELEY-KYNOCH I.C.I. headstamping. This wad was printed A.A.SPENCER.RICHMOND. There was also a gunmaker named Chas Spencer at 5 Finkle Street, Richmond in 1913.

948. **FREDERICK P. SPENCER:** 44 Lugley Street, Newport, Isle of
Q3   Wight.
Business: Ironmonger.
Cartridges: F.P.S. Vectis Special Loading; Spencer's Vectis Bunnie; Spencer's Vectis Special.
Remarks: He was shown as active in a 1907 trade directory. I could not find any trace of him in a 1911 directory.

949. **GEORGE SPILLER:** Sherborne, Dorsetshire.
Business: Ironmonger.
Cartridges: The Blackmoor Vale Special Cartridge.

950. **SPORTING GUN & CARTRIDGE CO:** Derwent Street, Derby, Derbys.
    Cartridges: Unnamed or name not recorded.
    Remarks: They were known to have been operating in 1910.

951. **SPORTING PARK:** 60 New Bond Street, London W1.
Q3 **Cartridges:** Eley Ejector.
    Remarks: See London Sporting Park, Ltd number 647 in this cartridge list.

952. **SPORTRIDGE (G.B.), LTD:** Address not known.
Q3 **Cartridges:** The Sportridge.

953. **STACEY:** Dulverton, Somerset.
    Remarks: Cartridge remains have been found with the headstamping, STACEY No 12 DULVERTON.

954. **PERCY STANBURY:** Mid Devon Cartridge Works, Exeter, Devon.
Q4 **Business:** Gun and cartridge expert.
    Cartridges: The Standby; Unnamed.

955. **STANBURY & STEVENS:** 14 Alphington Street, St. Thomas, Exeter.
Q4 Devonshire.
    Business: Gun and cartridge experts.
    Cartridges: The Devonia; The Game; The Ideal; The Monocle; The Red Flash; The Standby; The Swift.

956. **STANGER:** Hull, Yorkshire (Humberside).
    Remarks: Their name has been seen on an Eley headstamping.

957. **STEBBINGS & SON:** Attleborough, Norfolk.
    Business: Gun and ammunition dealers.
    Cartridges: Special Smokeless (Pheasant on tube).

958. **THOMAS STENSBY.** Later as, **T. STENSBY & CO:** Hanging Ditch.
Q4 Later at, Withy Grove, Manchester, Lancashire (Gt. Manchester).
    Business: Gun, rifle and cartridge makers.
    Cartridges: The All British; The Champion Cartridge; The Champion Gastight; The Club All British; Pegamoid; Unnamed; The Victory.
    Remarks: This firm was first established in 1810. It was then located at 20 Hanging Ditch. In 1906, the firm moved to 12 Withy Grove from 6 Withy Grove. Although I had had it written down in my notes as a move, it may well have been a numbers change within Withy Grove. Due to city development, another move was made to 1 Shudehill in the June of 1986. Both Withy Grove and Shudehill are in the same area in Manchester.

959. **CHARLES STEPHENS:** Ledbury, Herefordshire (H & W).
    Cartridges: Warranted Gas-tight Cartridge Case (Pinfire).

960. **H. STEPHENS:** 35 West Street, Horsham, Sussex.
Q4 **Business:** Ironmonger.
    Remarks: A brass cartridge heads has been found with Stephen's name on the headstamping.

961. **STERLING:** London (Rest of the address is not known).
Q4 **Cartridges:** Sterling Extra Prima Smokeless Cartridge; Unnamed.

962. **MARK J. STEWART:** 114 South Street, St. Andrews, Fifeshire.
Cartridges: The Markmore; Special Smokeless Cartridge.

963. **STILES BROTHERS:** 39 High Street. Later at, 51 Market Place, Warminster, Wiltshire.
Business: Ironmongers.
Cartridges: The Kill Quick.
Remarks: In 1895, Walter Lanning owned the ironmongers business at 39 High Street. By 1903 the owners were Evans & Son. In 1907, Stiles Brothers were in residence at number 39 and continued there up until 1915 and perhaps for longer. By 1920, the Stiles Brothers were trading from 51 Market Place. All the time, Sidney Lancelot Corden was occupying 37 High Street where he had stayed a near neighbour ever since Stiles Brothers had been in business. See number 209 in this cartridge list. Stiles Brothers closed their 51 Market Place shop in April 1987. S. L. Corden & Sons continued to trade on in name but in the hands of the Norris family.

964. **A. STOAKES:** Hastings, Sussex.
Cartridges: Nobel's Sporting Ballistite (Name on over-shot wad).
Remarks: It is not known if or what the family connections would have been. There was a gunmakers, K. Stoakes & Co at 8 George Street, Hastings in 1907.

965. **STOCKDALE:** Daybrook (The rest of the address is not known).
Cartridges: Unnamed (Name on over-shot wad only).
Remarks: The only reference that I can find to Daybrook is a road in London.

966. **A. J. STOCKER & SON.** Was also as, **C. & E. STOCKER:** Fore
Q5 Street, Chulmleigh, Devonshire.
Business: Ironmongers.
Cartridges: The Chulmleigh Cartridge; Stocker's Special Load.
Remarks: This firm was listed in a 1935 trade directory as Stocker A. J. There was no mention of a son.

967. **F. E. STOCKER:** 5 Church Street, St. Austell, Cornwall.
Business: Ironmonger.
Cartridges: Unnamed (Stocker's name was on the headstamping only on an Eley case).

968. **WILLIAM STOVIN:** 4 Westgate, Grantham, Lincolnshire.
Business: Gunmaker.
Cartridges: Unnamed.
Remarks: Cira 1892.

969. **STOWIE:** Inverness, Inverness-shire (Highland).
Remarks: An old pinfire head with raised writing has been found which bore their name.

970. **JOHN STREET & SONS:** Castle Street, Christchurch. Also at,
Q5 95 Christchurch Road, Boscombe, Hampshire.
Business: Ironmongers.
Cartridges: Unnamed.

971. **ROBERT STREET:** Long Street, Tetbury, Gloucestershire.
Business: Ironmonger.
Remarks: An Eley headstamping has been found which carried his name.

972. **J. STRONG & SON:** 65 Castle Street. Also at, 8 Warwick Road,
Q5 Carlisle, Cumberland (Cumbria).
Business: Gun and ammunition dealers.
Cartridges: Unnamed.

973. **STUCHBERY'S STORES (THOMPSON P. & S. LTD):** 63, 65 & 67 High
Q5 Street, Maidenhead, Berkshire.
Business: Ironmongery, grocery and provisions merchants.
Cartridges: Unnamed.
Remarks: The only cartridge that I have seen by them was a dummy display round, more commonly known as a window cartridge. This firm was listed in the Kelly's Directories for the years 1907 and 1920. They were not shown in the directories for 1899 and 1903.

974. **STUDLEY:** Uffculme, Devonshire.
Q5 **Cartridges:** Unnamed.
Remarks: Their name is printed on an over-shot wad that is loaded into a cartridge which is in the Tiverton Museum.

975. **J. SWINFEN:** 79 Bank Street, Maidstone, Kent.
Q5 **Business:** Gunmaker.
Cartridges: Eley's Gas-tight Cartridge Case (Swinfen's name on the headstamping); Swinfen's Special.

976. **SYKES BROTHERS:** Ossett, Yorkshire.
Q5 **Cartridges:** Eley Ejector.

977. **ROBERT SYKES & SONS, LTD:** Oldham. Also in, Stalybridge,
Q5 Lancashire (Gt. Manchester).
Cartridges: Smokeless Cartridge.

978. **WILLIAM TARR.** Later as, **WILLIAM TARR & SON:** Minehead,
Q6 Somerset.
Business: Believed to have been hardware and agricultural merchants.
Cartridges: The Exmoor.
Remarks: At one time this business was owned by Palmer & Tarr. In 1913, J. Gliddon purchased the business from Tarr & Son and they continued to market a cartridge called, The Exmoor. For your interest, see numbers 378 and 782 in this cartridge list.

979. **ELIJAH TARRANT:** 16 Sussex Street, Cambridge, Cambridgeshire.
Q6 **Remarks:** His name has been seen on cartridge remains that have been dug-up through metal detecting.

980. **TAYLOR:** Wilmslow, Cheshire.
Remarks: Some over-shot wads have been seen printed TAYLOR. WILMSLOW.

981. **ALBERT VICTOR TAYLOR:** 49 Bartholomew Street, Newbury, Berks.
Q6 **Business:** Barber, gunsmith and fishing tackle dealer.
Cartridges: Mullerite Smokeless (Extra tube printing).

981. **ALBERT VICTOR TAYLOR:** Continued.
Remarks: He was known to have been in business as a hairdresser in 1900. He started his gunsmithing a few years later and was listed as such in a 1910 directory. Mr Taylor died in the late 1940's and the family continued to run the business until about 1968.

982. **C. H. TAYLOR & SON, LTD:** 18 Market Place, Great Driffield, Yorkshire.
Business: Ironmongers.
Cartridges: Unnamed.

983. **JOHN T. TAYLOR.** Later as, **J. T. TAYLOR & SON:** 90 High
Q8 Street, Bromsgrove, Worcestershire (Hereford & Worcester).
Business: Ironmongers.
Cartridges: The Lightning Cartridge; Unnamed.

984. **S. R. TAYLOR & SONS, LTD:** Penzance. Also at, St. Ives,
Q6 Cornwall.
Cartridges: Unnamed (Taylor's name was on the headstamping but the over-shot wad was French).

985. **TAYLOR & JONES:** Monmouth, Monmouthshire (Gwent). Also at,
Q6 Ross-on-Wye, Herefordshire (Hereford & Worcester).
Cartridges: The Monno Cartridge.

986. **TEMPLE & CO:** Church Street, Basingstoke, Hampshire.
Q6 **Business:** Ironmongers.
Remarks: Cartridge remains have been found from which I have made a provisional drawing. In 1878 the firm was known as, Temple & Portsmouth. By 1880 they were listed in the directories as, Temple & Co. They were not listed in a 1907 directory.

987. **H. G. TETT:** Coventry, Warwickshire (W. Midlands).
Business: Gunsmith.
Cartridges: Unnamed.

988. **THACKER & CO:** Worcester, Worcestershire (Hereford &
Q8 Worcester).
Business: Gunmakers and fishing tackle dealers.
Cartridges: Eley Gastight Quality; Long Shot Smokeless.

989. **E. W. & R. THAIN:** Bramfield, Halesworth, Suffolk.
Cartridges: Unnamed.

990. **THOMPSON BROTHERS:** Bridgwater, Somerset.
Business: Ironmongers.
Cartridges: New Special Smokeless; Ruby; The Special; Thompson's Special.

991. **H. THOMPSON:** Boston, Lincolnshire.
Business: Gunmaker.
Cartridges: Unnamed or name not recorded.

992. **THORN & SON:** Heavitree, Exeter, Devonshire.
Business: Believed to have been an ironmongers shop.
Cartridges: Unnamed or name not recorded.

993. **THORNE BROTHERS:** Tiverton, Devonshire.
Cartridges: Smokeless Cartridge.

994. **WILLIAM THORNE:** 2 Gold Street, Tiverton, Devonshire.
Business: Ironmonger.
Cartridges: Smokeless Cartridge.
Remarks: It is obvious that there were family connections with entry number 993 as both sold a Smokeless Cartridge.

995. **S. THORNLEY, LTD:** Snow Hill. Also at, 166 Deritend, Gosta Green, Birmingham, Warwickshire (W. Midlands).
Business: Ammunition dealers.
Cartridges: Unnamed or name not recorded.

996. **F. THRASHER:** 49 Coventry Road, Birmingham, Warwickshire (W. Midlands).
Cartridges: Unnamed (Name on over-shot wad).

997. **R. THRIPLAND & SON:** Galashiels, Selkirkshire (Borders).
Q6 **Cartridges:** Eley Grand Prix Case (Name on over-shot wad); Special Smokeless; Unnamed.

998. **WILLIAM JAMES TICKNER:** High Street, Bishop's Waltham, Hants.
Q6 **Business:** Ironmonger.
Cartridges: The Sportsman.
Remarks: William was known to have been active between 1898 and 1931.

999. **G. S. TILBURY & F. A. JEFFRIES:** Parson's Garage, Littlehampton Road, Worthing, Sussex.
Bussiness: Believed to have been garage proprietors.
Cartridges: The Highdown.

1000. **WILLIAM C. TILL, LTD:** 18 High Street, Battle, Sussex.
Q6 **Business:** Ironmonger.
Cartridges: Unnamed.

1001. **R. TILNEY & SON:** Beccles, Suffolk.
Q6 **Business:** Gunsmiths.
Cartridges: Eley Pegamoid Patent (Name on over-shot wad only); Tilney's Special.

1002. **TILY & BROWN, LTD:** Guildford & Farnham, Surrey. Also at, Farnborough, Hampshire.
Q6 **Cartridges:** Farnford.

1003. **FREDERICK H. TIMS:** 5 Cathedral Lane, Truro, Cornwall.
Q8 **Business:** Gunmaker.
Cartridges: Unnamed.
Remarks: He was known to have been in business in 1902.

1004. **JOHN TINNING:** Longtown, Cumberland (Cumbria). Also at, Newcastleton, Roxburghshire.
Q8 **Cartridges:** Unnamed.

1005. **JOHN TISDALL:** 8 South Street, Chichester. Also at, Arundel, West Sussex.
Q8 **Business:** Gunmaker.
Cartridges: The Chichester Cartridge.

1006. **P. TOVEY:** Midsomer Norton, Somerset (Avon).
Remarks: I was given this name but I do not have any details on business or cartridges.

1007. **TOWT-TIVY-FARMERS:** Llanwrda, Carmarthenshire (Powys). Also at, Llansawel, Cardiganshire. And also at, Pumsaint, Lampeter, Cardiganshire (Dyfed).
Cartridges: Reyward; The T.T. Super.

1008. **E. TOZER:** Post Office Stores, Trevellas, Cornwall.
Cartridges: Unnamed.

1009. **TRENT GUN & CARTRIDGE WORKS:** Wellholme Road, Grimsby, Lincolnshire (Humberside).
Q8
Q9 **Business:** Gun and cartridge manufacturers and merchants.
Cartridges: A.E.C. Rook; Best Smokeless; Deep Shell; Favourite; London; Smokeless Air Lord; Spartan; Spartan Deep Shell; Super Range; Unnamed.
Remarks: Known to many as, Trents' Shot Tower Grimsby. The Trent factory also produced brands for many smaller firms. Their cartridge loading factory was built in 1929. Back in the 1930's, many small shops were introduced in stocking Trent cartridges including some village stores. These cartridges were cheaper than many others and they were much liked by the working class.

During the firms run in business it did quite well, but it finally went into liquidation in 1953 and closed it's doors in the April. Sad to say, but in it's later days the loadings were not quite so consistent. At the end, batches of their cartridges were sold off in lots. One chap that I knew bought some of these for resale. It was then found that a few of these contained only shot. Worst still, some others contained far more powder than they should have done. These cartridges were then quickly retrieved by the gent which was selling them.

I remember when I was a young lad my father used them and so did my father-in-law. Both of them liked them as a good cheap killing cartridge. I also remember during the early years of the Second World War beating on a pheasant shoot. A walking gun next to me was using Trent's Deep Shell. Every time that he fired off his gun there was a collosal bang and a large sheet of red flame spouted from his barrel. This was followed by a thick pall of black smoke which went drifting between the trees. I do not remember what his kills were like, but his used cartridge cases all had their mouths charred away. The first time that he shot, one of the keepers had thought that his gun had burst, and that is how I came to remember Trent cartridges.

I have included under 'Cartridges' in this listing, the A.E.C. Rook which was produced for H.M. Government of Great Britain. Also the London and Spartan range of cartridges which can be found under the Cartridge Syndicate, Ltd. See numbers 159 and 488 in this cartridge list.

1010. **S. TROUGHTON:** 24 Caunce Street, Blackpool, Lancashire.
Q9 **Business:** Gunmaker.
Cartridges: Unnamed (Pheasant printed on the tube).

1011. **TRULOCK BROTHERS:** Dublin, Republic of Ireland.
Business: Gunmakers.
Cartridges: Eley's Gas-tight Cartridge.

1012. **TRULOCK & HARRISS:** 9 Dawson Street, Dublin, Republic of
Q9 Ireland.
Business: Gunmakers.
Cartridges: E.C. Powder Cartridge; Kynoch Grouse Ejector; Nobel's Empire (Crossed flags on tube); Unnamed.

1013. **TRULOCK & HARRISS:** Pickering Place, St. James's Street, London W1.
Business: Gunmakers.
Cartridges: The Tru-iss.
Remarks: I am not sure, but it may have been the Dublin firm with a London branch. See the above entry number 1012 in this cartridge list.

1014. **J. TUCKER:** 25 Bailey Street, Oswestry, Shropshire.
R1 **Business:** Gunsmith and sports outfitter.
Cartridges: The Oswestrian.

1015. **S. TUDGE:** Bewdley, Worcestershire (Hereford & Worcester).
Business: Gun shop.
Remarks: The wording, S.TUDGE.BEWDLEY. has been seen on an over-shot wad that was loaded into a cartridge by H. W. Roberts & Co of Rhyl.

1016. **W. TULLOCH & CO:** Bishopsgate Churchyard, London EC.
Cartridges: The Special.

1017. **TURNBULL:** Bridgnorth, Shropshire.
Cartridges: Unnamed.

1018. **ARTHUR TURNER.** Later as, **ARTHUR TURNER (SHEFFIELD), LTD:**
R1 5 West Bar, Sheffield, Yorkshire.
Business: Gunmakers.
Cartridges: The Alliance; The Clay Bird; The Double Wing; The Steeltown; The Wing; The Wizard.
Remarks: Arthur took over this business in 1920 from Maleham & Co. He also retained several of the Maleham cartridge brand names. See number 675 in this cartridge list.

1019. **HENRY A. TURNER.** Later as, **H. A. TURNER, LTD:** 142 High
R1 Street. Also at, Bath Road, Marlborough, Wiltshire.
Business: Gunmaker.
Cartridges: The Kennett; Unnamed.
Remarks: Henry had both of his shops active in the late 1890's.

1020. **J. TURNER:** Penrith, Cumberland (Cumbria).
R1 **Cartridges:** Unnamed.

1021. **THOMAS TURNER & SONS.** Later as, **THOS TURNER & SONS, LTD:**
R1 8 Butter Market, Reading. Later and also at, 86 Northbrook
R2 Street, Newbury. Was also for a very short time in, High
R3 Street, Hungerford, Berkshire. Also later at, 35 Wote
R4 Street, Basingstoke, Hampshire.

1021. **THOMAS TURNER & SONS:** Continued.
Business: Gun and legging makers. Also cartridge loaders.
Cartridges: British Wonders; The Craven; The Fillbag; The Grey Rapid; Kynoch Grouse Ejector; Midget .410 Long; Midget .410 Short; The Penwood; The Renowned; Special Loading; Turner's Smokeless Wonder; Unnamed.
Remarks: As this was the local firm to my home, it is here receiving that little bit extra coverage. I believe that Thomas first set up his business at some date in the 1830's. The earliest knowledge that I have of his cartridges was when some cartridge remains were located by a metal detectorist. That found had a very narrow pinfire brass head with the raised writing, T.TURNER READING and a large 12 to the centre. Tom first started up his business in Reading and eventually his sons joined him in the business. They then extended by branching out west when they took over a shop in Newbury, a market town in the centre of good shooting country. Again I do not have a date for this, but in 1869 that shop in Northbrook Street was then being used by Mr G. E. Walker who was also a gunmaker. I have never seen a cartridge in the name of G. E. Walker, but this does not necessarily mean that there never was any. In August 1922 they then bought the gun shop off of Edwin Chamberlain in Basingstoke. See number 164 in this cartridge list. Previous to this in 1895, they had held a premises in the High Street in Hungerford. I have only seen just one entry in a trade directory and so the Hungerford shop was short lived. Their Newbury shop was run by a Mr E. Turner while another son, Mr E. B. Turner ran the Basingstoke shop. Dad then kept charge in Reading.

After the Second World War, the business was gradually run down. The Reading shop was sold and the new owners bought it with the goodwill and traded on as, Thomas Turner & Sons (Reading), Ltd. Shortly after, the Newbury shop was sold to J. C. Cording & Co, Ltd. They had moved west from Piccadilly, London. Then the Basingstoke shop was also sold to Cordings'. This old London firm continued to market some cartridges that carried the old Turner brand names. I have not shown this firm in this list as all of their cartridges were closed by crimping.

Throughout their years in business, some of their branded cartridges became associated to the various shops. Reading sold The Smokeless Wonder and The Renowned. They may also have sold the fourten Midget. At Newbury a cartridge was sold that portrayed the old Newbury Castle Gate-house. An example of this is in a large showcase which resides in the main offices of the Witton Factory. I have seen this cartridge in both 12 and 20 gauge and both in cream-yellow. No thought was then given on accidentally poking a 20 gauge cartridge in a 12 gauge gun. This show case was illustrated in my other book, 'Collecting Shotgun Cartridges'. In their later years, Turners' re-used this gate-house by placing it in an oval and portraying it on the last of their Fillbags. The Newbury shop sold The Fillbag and The Craven. Craven being the name of a large local private estate and also the name of the local hunt. The Grey Rapid was a very popular cartridge from the Basingstoke shop. During 1938-39, the firm set up it's shooting school in the north of Penwood. This about three miles to the south of Newbury just off of the Andover road.

1021. **THOMAS TURNER & SONS:** Continued.
Here they used a cartridge called The Penwood. This school was short lived due to the coming war.

Many of Turner's cartridges often displayed a crest which portrayed five male heads in a semi-oval frame. This was the Common Seal of Reading. The Reading coat of arms is very similar, but this portrays five maidens heads. I have never been able to find out who the people were that owned all of those heads. Thomas Turner & Sons (Reading), Ltd continued to display this old seal on their cartridges.

An advertisment in the Newbury Weekly News dated Thursday March 3rd 1910 listed as follows-, Nitrones at 9/- per 100; Bonax at 7/10 per 100; Fillbags at 7/6 per 100; Cravens at 10/- per 100.

1022. **TURNERS CARBIDES, LTD:** 58 De Grey Street, Hull, Yorkshire
R4 (Humberside).
Business: Cartridge dealers and merchants.
Cartridges: The .410; The Killer; The Standard; The Super; Turners' Super Cartridges.
Remarks: Turners Carbides, Ltd was formed in 1924 by the father of two sons who were directors of the Hull Cartridge Co, Ltd. See number 519 in this cartridge list. It's purpose was the selling of calcium carbide which at that time was used for lighting in some country dwellings and on many of the road transport vehicles. In 1947 the Hull Cartridge was formed at the above address.

1023. **F. TURVEY.** Later as, **F. TURVEY & SONS:** 2 Woolhall Street, Bury St. Edmunds, Suffolk.
Business: Sports store and gun and ammunition dealers.
Cartridges: Deadcert.
Remarks: Was known to have been trading in the early 1930's and at least up until 1933.

1024. **J. A. TWYBLE:** Potadown. County Down, Northern Ireland.
Business: Ironmonger.
Cartridges: The Invincible; Long Range; Surekiller.

1025. **JOHN TYLER.** Later as, **J. TYLER (HIGHBRIDGE), LTD:**
R4 Highbridge, Somerset.
Business: Gun and ammunition dealer.
Cartridges: The Falcon; The Special.

1026. **JOHN UGLOW:** Bullen Street, Thorverton, Devonshire.
R4 **Business:** See Remarks below.
Cartridges: The Demon.
Remarks: His cartridges have been known to have shown the wordings, Gunsmith and Gunmaker. An old bill head showed his firm as being a cycle agent and a gun dealer. Like many other small firms, he had had his fingers in several pies.

1027. **UNDERHILL:** Newport. Also at, Eccleshall, Staffordshire.
Cartridges: Unnamed (Pinfire).

1028. **UNITED KINGDOM CARTRIDGE CLUB (U.K.C.C.):** England.
R4 **Business:** Collectors Club.
Cartridges: First Anniversary Cartridge.

1028. **UNITED KINGDOM CARTRIDGE CLUB (U.K.C.C.):** Continued.
   Remarks: The U.K.C.C. was founded at Boxford, Berkshire on the 6th May 1990 by the amalgamation of the British Cartridge Collectors Club (B.C.C.C.) and KRUKCL. I had been the founder of KRUKCL pronounced as Cruckle. These letters stood for Ken Rutterford's United Kingdom Cartridge List.
   This is the only intentionally modern crimp closed paper tubed cartridge shown in this book. As artist and author, I here consider that I have the artistic licence to portray this cartridge being as I myself founded KRUKCL and was also a founder member of the U.K.C.C.

1029. **C. & J. URQUHART:** Dingwall, Ross & Cromarty (Highland).
R4   **Business:** Gun dealers and ironmongers.
   Cartridges: The Ardross Cartridge.

1030. **WILLIAM URTON, LTD:** Glunmangate. Later at, 7 West Bars and
R4   Park Road, Chesterfield, Derbyshire.
   Business: Ironmonger. May also have been a gunsmith.
   Cartridges: Unnamed (May have been known as The Spire).
   Remarks: William was listed in an 1881 trades directory as being at Glunmangate. A 1932 directory showed him as being at the other addresses.

1031. **UTTING & BUCKENHAM:** East Dereham, Norfolk.
   Business: Ironmongers and gun dealers.
   Remarks: I have been given details of this firm but I have failed to log any cartridge details for it.

1032. **WILLIAM VARLEY:** 3 Midland Street, Hull, Yorkshire (Humberside).
   Business: Gunmaker.
   Cartridges: Unnamed.

1033. **J. C. VAUX:** Hanwell, Ealing, London.
R4   **Cartridges:** Unnamed (Name on over-shot wad only).

1034. **J. VENABLES & SON:** 99 St. Aldate's Street, Oxford, Oxon.
R4   **Business:** Gun and rifle makers.
R5   **Cartridges:** .410 Long; .410 Short; The County; The Gastight; The Oxford; The Sixteen; Special Smokeless Metal Lined; Special Cartridge; Unnamed (Including centre and pinfire).

1035. **VERSEY:** Bristol, Gloucestershire (Avon).
   Remarks: I have been told of a grey coloured 16 gauge cartridge but I do not know if it carried a brand name. All of my searchings have not managed to find a full address for this firm.

1036. **F. VICKERY:** Luxborough, Somerset.
   Remarks: This name has been seen printed on an over-shot wad.

1037. **VINCENT BROTHERS:** Ottery St. Mary, Devonshire.
   Cartridges: The Invincible Cartridge.

1038. **J. H. WADDON:** Wedmore, Somerset.
R5   **Cartridges:** Special Smokeless Cartridge.

1039. **JOHN WADDON & SONS:** Bridgnorth, Shropshire.
Business: Ironmongers.
Cartridges: Unnamed.

1040. **JOHN WADDON & SONS:** Bridgwater, Somerset.
Cartridges: The Quantock.
Remarks: Many people have kindly provided me with names of firms and their cartridge brands. All of these I have filed over many years. Mistakes may have occurred. Having two John Waddon & Sons with a Bridgnorth and a Bridgwater may just have been a coincidence. They may both be correct, but if one of them is wrong, I would take it to have been number 1039.

1041. **WAGER & SONS:** Honiton, Devonshire.
Remarks: Their name has been seen printed on an over-shot wad.

1042. **R. H. WAGSTAFF & CO:** 16 New Street. Also at, 22 Winchester
R5 Street, Basingstoke, Hampshire.
Business: Ironmongers and ammunition dealers.
Cartridges: A 1.
Remarks: This firm was known to have been trading in 1898. Their main premises were burnt down in the great fire of Basingstoke on April 17th 1905.

1043. **WAKEFIELD:** Taunton, Somerset.
Remarks: A headstamping has been found with the stamping, WAKEFIELD 12 TAUNTON.

1044. **DERRIAN WALES:** 16 Regent Street, Great Yarmouth, Norfolk.
R5 **Business:** Gunmaker and ironmonger.
Cartridges: Unnamed.

1045. **A. E. & A. WALKER:** Tenbury Wells, Worcestershire (H & W).
Business: Ironmongers.
Cartridges: Unnamed.

1046. **F. E. WALKER:** 11 Cheap Street, Newbury, Berkshire.
R5 **Business:** Gunmaker.
Cartridges: Unnamed or name not known.
Remarks: There was also a gunmaker, G. E. Walker at 86 Northbrook Street, Newbury. There could well have been family connections. See Thomas Turner & Sons, number 1021 in this cartridge list who took over the business.

1047. **JAMES B. WALKER:** 63 Newgate Street, Newcastle-on-Tyne,
R5 Northumberland.
Business: Gun and fishing tackle dealer.
Cartridges: The Newgate.

1048. **R. WALKER:** Address not known.
Remarks: Had patents for metal over-shot wads. I would think that he would have bound to have placed his name on some of his created wads.

1049. **WALKER & COOKE:** Bromyard, Herefordshire (H & W).
Cartridges: Unnamed or name not recorded.

1050. **H. WALKINGTON:** Bridlington, Yorkshire (Humberside).
R5   **Business:** Dealer in guns and ammunition.
     Cartridges: The Reliable.

1051. **D. H. WALLAS:** Wigton & Carlisle, Cumberland (Cumbria).
R5   **Business:** Gunmaker and cartridge loader.
R6   **Cartridges:** Unnamed.

1052. **WILLIAM WALLAS:** King Street, Wigton, Cumberland (Cumbria).
R6   **Business:** Gunmaker.
     Cartridges: Eley Pegamoid; Unnamed.

1053. **WALLIS BROTHERS:** 156 High Street. Also at, 364 High Street
R6   & 1 Cornhill, Lincoln, Lincolnshire.
     Business: See Remarks below.
     Cartridges: The Big Tom of Lincoln; Gastight Cartridge Case; Smokeless Cartridge; Walbro Special.
     Remarks: Wallis Brothers appear to have started trading in Lincoln in 1885 from 364 High Street. They also had premises at 1 Cornhill. It is known that one of the brothers had a gunsmithing business at Spalding in his own right. The trades of these brothers have been listed as: Gunmakers; Gunsmiths; Electrical engineers; Cycle agents; Locksmiths; Contractors; Bell hangers and fitters. By 1892 the firm was at 156 High Street and by 1903 they also had premises in Corporation Street. By 1937 the firms Lincoln address was, 4 St. Mary's Street. It was in 1939 that Wallis Brothers joined forces with Skemptons. See number 1054 the next entry in this cartridge list.

1054. **WALLIS BROTHERS & SKEMPTONS:** Lincoln, Lincolnshire.
     Business: Gunmakers etc.
     Cartridges: The Big Tom of Lincoln; The Licoln Imp.
     Remarks: The Big Tom of Lincoln took it's name from a large bell named The Big Tom of Lincoln. This bell hangs in the tower of Lincoln Cathedral. Wallis Brothers & Skemptons ceased trading in 1959.

1055. **WANLESS & CO:** South Shields, County Durham (Tyne & Wear).
     Business: Gun and rifle makers.
     Cartridges: The Long Range.

1056. **WANLESS BROTHERS:** South Shields & Sunderland. Also at,
R6   Stockton-on-Tees, County Durham (Tyne & Wear).
     Business: Gun and rifle makers.
     Cartridges: Kynoch's Perfectly Gas-tight; The Long Range; The Waterloo; The W.B.S.

1057. **W. WANLESS:** 29 Norfolk Street. Later at, 20 Norfolk Street,
R6   Sunderland, County Durham (Tyne & Wear).
     Business: Gun and rifle maker.
     Cartridges: Kynoch's Perfectly Gas-tight; The Long Range.
     Remarks: I would think that all of the Wanless firms listed had some family connections. As I did not know their order for listing, each has been listed separately.

1058. **J. WARD & SON:** 21 Broad Street. Also at, 89 High Street,
R6   Worcester, Worcestershire (Hereford & Worcester).
     Business: Domestic engineers, ironmongers and furnishings.
     Cartridges: Kynoch Patent Grouse Ejector.

1059. **WARD & TAYLOR:** Leominster, Herefordshire (H & W).
   Business: Ironmongers.
   Cartridges: Unnamed.

1060. **A. WARD THOMPSON.** 99 Corporation Road, Middlesborough.
R6   Later as, **WARD THOMPSON BROTHERS:** 87 Borough Road,
R7   Middlesborough, Yorkshire (Cleveland).
   Business: Gunmakers.
   Cartridges: Unnamed.

1061. **EDWIN WARING:** High Street, Leamington Spa, Warwickshire.
R7   **Business:** Ironmonger and gunsmith.
   Cartridges: Unnamed.

1062. **HENRY P. WARNER & SON:** 11 Bank Street, Newton Abbot, Devon.
R7   **Business:** ironmongers.
   Cartridges: General Service Cartridge (Mullerite with extra tube printing); High Velocity Special Smokeless.

1063. **WARNERS:** Barrack Street, Bantry, County Cork, Republic of
R7   Ireland.
   Business: General stores.
   Cartridges: Unnamed.

1064. **A. E. WARREN:** 116 Peascot Street, Windsor, Berkshire.
R7   **Business:** Gunmaker.
   Cartridges: The Windsor Special.
   Remarks: There has also been found an old headstamping which was, B.WARREN No 12 WINDSOR/KYNOCH.

1065. **GEORGE ANTHONY WARREN:** 7 North Street, Horncastle. Also at, Spilsby, Lincolnshire.
   Business: Ironmonger.
   Cartridges: The Warren.

1066. **JOHN WARRICK:** 34 St. Mary's Butts. Also at, Monarch
R7   Works, Caversham Road, Reading, Berkshire.
   Business: Manufacturer of cycles and motorized tradesmans tricycles.
   Cartridges: Unnamed.

1067. **JAMES BAKEWELL WARRILOW:** Factory Lane, Chippenham, Wilts.
R7   **Business:** Gunsmith.
   Cartridges: Badminton; Ejector; Electric Long Shot Cartridge; The Good Sport; Sudden Death.
   Remarks: Jas Warrilow was in the gunsmithing business at Chippenham circa, 1886-1913.

1068. **THOMAS J. WATKINS.** Later as, **WATKINS & CO:** High Street,
R7   Banbury, Oxfordshire.
   Business: Gunmaker.
   Cartridges: Unnamed.

1069. **WATSON BROTHERS:** 29 Old Bond Street. Also at, Pall Mall,
R7   London SW1.
R8   **Business:** Gunmakers.

1069. **WATSON BROTHERS:** Continued.
Cartridges: Hi-Speed Cartridge; Non-Recoil Smokeless. Reliance.
Remarks: This firm was known to have been in business in 1901. Watson Brothers were later absorbed into Grant & Lang. See number 393 in this cartridge list.

1070. **JAMES WATSON & SON:** 24 Guild Street, Aberdeen, Aberdeenshire (Grampian).
Business: Gunmakers.
Cartridges: The Dead Shot.
Remarks: James was the successor to William Calder of the same address.

1071. **JAS R. WATSON & CO:** 35 Queen Victoria Street, London EC4.
R8 **Business:** gun and cartridge dealers.
R9 **Cartridges:** The Albion; The Britannia; The Challenge; Ejector; The Enterprise; The Lilliput; The Sureshot; The Warrior; The Wetteren.
Remarks: This firm was established in 1889. Most of their brand cartridges had Belgium made cases and used Cooppal powders. These powders were-, Black powders: Treble Strong and F. The smokeless sporting powders were: No 1 and Emerald, both of these being granular. No 2 and Excelsior being both leaflet. Customers who ordered cartridges in quantities of 10,000 and upwards could have their own names printed on the case walls if they so wished.

1072. **R. WATSON:** 19 Whittal Street, Birmingham, Warwickshire (W. Midlands).
Business: Cartridge manufacturers and gunmakers.
Cartridges: Eley Blue Case; Eley Brown Case; Joyce Red Case; Royal Green Case; Royal Red Case.
Remarks: Gunmaking was at the Rose & Crown Yard, Whittal Street. He was known to have been active in 1897.

1073. **WATSON BRACEWELL:** Peebles, Peebles-shire, (Borders).
R9 **Cartridges:** Mullerite Yellow Seal (Extra tube printing).
Remarks: This firm was an agent for Mullerite.

1074. **WEBB:** Hull, Yorkshire (Humberside).
Remarks: Cartridge remains have been found with the headstamping, WEBB.HULL. ELEY 12 LONDON.

1075. **J. WEBBER & SONS:** Exeter, Torquay & Newton Abbot, Devon
R9 **Business:** Sports depot.
Cartridges: Webber's ISCA.

1076. **WEBBER & SAUNDERS:** Tiverton, Devonshire.
R9 **Business:** Ironmongers.
Cartridges: The Pheasant; Sure Shot.

1077. **WEBBERS:** New Street, Honiton, Devonshire.
R9 **Cartridges:** The Ottervale Special Smokeless.

1078. **WEBLEY & SCOTT, LTD:** 81-91 Weaman Street, Birmingham, Warwickshire (W. Midlands).
Business: gun and rifle makers.
Remarks: They may have had their name on cartridges.

1079. **G. R. WEBSTER:** 30A Wide Bargate, Boston, Lincolnshire.
R9   **Cartridges:** The Favourite; The Field; The Snipe.

1080. **WEBSTERS:** Axminster, Devonshire.
    Business: Ironmongers.
    Cartridges: The Axe Valley.

1081. **W. R. WEDGWOOD:** See number 724, Morrow & Co in this cartridge list.

1082. **C. WEEKES & CO:** Dublin, Republic of Ireland.
    Business: Gunsmith.
    Cartridges: Weekes Patent (Brass 8 gauge).

1083. **F. WEEKS:** Lymington, Hampshire.
R9   **Cartridges:** Unnamed.
    Remarks: Was most likely loaded for them by Patstone of Sothampton, Hants.

1084. **W. A. WELCH:** 90-92 Southampton Road. Also at, 2E High Street, Eastleigh, Hampshire.
    Business: Saddler and pathletic outfitter.
    Cartridges: The Pheasant Cartridge.
    Remarks: It is not known if the name, W. A. Welch was printed on shotgun cartridges. It is known that it was printed on the sides of some cartridge boxes that contained Pheasant Cartridges by Patstone & Cox of Southampton. See number 790 in this cartridge list.

1085. **H. WELLS & SON:** Ware, Hertfordshire.
R9   **Business:** Dealer in guns and ammunition.
    Cartridges: Unnamed.

1086. **WILLIAM WELSH:** Dumfries, Dumfries-shire (Dumfries &
S1   Galloway). Also at, Castle Douglas, Kirkudbrightshire (D & G).
    Cartridges: Queen of the South.

1087. **WEST & SON:** Great Yarmouth, Norfolk.
S1   **Business:** Gunsmiths.
    Cartridges: Norfolk High Velocity Load.

1088. **Mrs ELIZA WEST:** 3 Grove Street, East Retford, Notts.
S1   **Business:** Gunmaker.
    Cartridges: Unnamed.
    Remarks: It is known that this firm was trading as E. West between 1881 and 1894.

1089. **WEST & SON:** 26 Market Square. Also at, 10 Bridge Gate
S1   Street, Retford, Nottinghamshire.
    Business: Gunmakers.
    Cartridges: The County; Deep Shell; Ejector; Fourten; The Grand National; The Sherwood; Unnamed; Waterproof Pegamoid.
    Remarks: It is known that the firm was trading as West & Son between 1912 and 1932. It could possibly have been trading for very much longer.

1090. **EDWARD WEST:** Tetbury, Gloucestershire.
Remarks: I have been given information that Ted West once sold cartridges that carried his name.

1091. **WESTGATE ESTATE:** Address not known.
S1 **Business:** Possibly a private country estate.
Cartridges: Westgate Estate.

1092. **WESTLEY RICHARDS & CO, LTD:** 12 Corporation Street. Later
S1 at, 24 Bennett's Hill, Birmingham, Warwicks (W. Midlands).
S2 Also at, New Bond Street W1. Later at, 23 Conduit Street, London W1.
Business: Gunmakers.
Cartridges: The A.L.P. Cartridge; The Aquatite; The Carlton; The Explora (Hollow slug cartridge); The Fauneta (Ball loaded cartridge); Pegamoid; The Regent (An ejector metal covered cartridge); The Right & Left; The Special; Super Magnum Explora; Westley Richards Special Accelerated L.P. Loading; The Wizard.
Remarks: This firm moved from Corporation Street to Bennett's Hill in November 1910. They moved from New Bond Street to Conduit Street in September 1917. From here they ran their own shooting school with their ground at West Hendon. A special version of their Wizard Cartridge was sold at the shooting school.

1093. **WEST LONDON SHOOTING SCHOOL:** Perivale, Ealing, London W.
S3 **Business:** Shooting School.
Cartridges: Empire; Unnamed.

1094. **CHARLES & HERBERT WESTON.** The Colonade & 7 New Road,
S3 Brighton. Also at, Hailsham, East Sussex. Later the firm became, **C. & A. WESTON:** At the Colonade, Brighton, Sussex.
Business: Gunmakers.
Cartridges: Brighton; Colonade; Ejector; National Smokeless; Smokeless Cartridge; Special Smokeless; Unnamed.
Remarks: Charles and Herbert were trading in the gunmaking business on the Colonade at Brighton since the days of the commencement of breach loading guns. Their cartridges were printed, C. & H. Weston. The business terminated during the 1970's.

1095. **J. WESTON:** Northwich, Cheshire.
Cartridges: Kynoch Nitrone (Name on over-shot wad only).

1096. **T. WHALEY & SON:** Bridge Street, St. Ives, Cambridgeshire.
S3 **Business:** Ironmongers and agricultural equipment dealers.
Cartridges: Eley Bros Grand Prix (Name on over-shot wad only); Mullerite Smokeless (Extra tube printing); Unnamed.
Remarks: This firm also sold Kynoch brand cartridges.

1097. **J. WHEATER:** 7 Queen Street. Also at, 27-29 Anlaby Road, Hull, Yorkshire (Humberside).
Business: Gunmaker.
Cartridges: The Humber.
Remarks: Joe Wheater took over the business of R. Robinson who had also marketed a Humber Cartridge. See number 875 in this cartridge list.

1098. **WHITE:** Northampton, Northants. Also in, Paris, France.
S3   **Remarks:** Old cartridge remains have been found which had the headstamping, WHITE.NORTHAMPTON & PARIS. No12.

1099. **JOHN EDWARD WHITEHOUSE.** Later as, **J. E. WHITEHOUSE & SONS:**
S4   High Street, Oakham, Rutland (Leicestershire).
Business: Gunmakers.
Cartridges: The Quorn; The Rutland.

1101. **FRANK SIDNEY WHITEMAN:** 20-21 Market Place, Wallingford,
S4   Berksire (Oxfordshire).
Business: Ironmonger and gunsmith.
Cartridges: The Fordian.
Remarks: Kelly's directories show that Frank was in business in Wallingford between 1928 and 1939 and maybe for longer. The firms telephone number was 76 and this was later changed to 3276.

1102. **H. H. WHITNEY:** Newtown (Rest of the address is not known).
Cartridges: Unnamed (Name on the over-shot wad only).

1103. **WHOLESALE ARMS & AMMUNITION TRADING CO:** 40 St. Andrew's Hill, Queen Victoria Street, London EC.
Business: Dealers in guns and ammunition.
Cartridges: Unnamed.

1104. **WILDER:** Birmingham, Warwickshire (W. Midlands). Rest of the
S4   address is not known.
Cartridges: Parachute Cartridge (A very large cartridge).

1105. **H. W. WILDMAN:** High Street, Ledbury, Herefordshire (H & W).
S4   **Business:** Ironmonger and gunsmith.
Cartridges: Unnamed.

1106. **JOHN WILKES:** 79 Beak Street, London W1.
S4   **Business:** gun and sports shop.
Cartridges: Tom-Tom.
Remarks: This firm first stated in business in Birmingham. In 1879 they moved to London where they joined forces with James Dalziel Dougal & Son at 59 St. James's Street. This business was sold in 1893 and they then moved to 1 Lower Street, St. James's Street, Piccadilly Circus. Their move to Beak Street was in 1924 where they then resided.

1107. **WILKINSON:** Durham, County Durham.
S4   **Business:** Ironmongers.
Cartridges: Unnamed.

1108. **JAMES WILKINSON & SON:** 27 Pall Mall, London SW1.
S4   **Business:** Gun and sword makers etc.
Cartridges: Ejector; Regal; Special; Wilkinson Waterproof.

1109. **WILKINSONS:** Sports Depot, Penrith, Cumberland (Cumbria).
S4   **Business:** Sports store.
Cartridges: The Beacon; The Eden.

1110. **JOSEPH WILLIAM WILLCOCKS:** 14 St. Mary's Street. Also at, 2
S4 Ironmonger Street, Stamford, Lincolnshire.
Business: Ironmonger.
Cartridges: Eley's Gas-tight Cartridge Case for E.C. Gunpowder.

1111. **C. D. WILLIAMS:** 86 Ann Street. Later at, 71-73 Victoria
S4 Street, Belfast, Northern Ireland,
Cartridges: Kynoch Patent Perfectly Gastight (Williams name on the headstamping).

1112. **E. WILLIAMS:** Aberystwyth, Cardiganshire (Dyfed).
Business: Gunsmith.
Cartridges: The Regent.

1113. **HARRY WILLIAMS:** 49 Pyle Street, Newport, Isle of Wight.
S5 **Business:** Ironmonger.
Cartridges: The Express; Unnamed.

1114. **J. S. WILLIAMS:** Pontypridd, Mid Glamorgan.
S5 **Business:** Ironmonger and explosives merchant.
Cartridges: Unnamed.

1115. **T. M. WILLIAMS:** Llandilo, Carmarthenshire (Dyfed).
Business: Ironmonger.
Cartridges: The Rabbit.

1116. **WILLIAMS & POWELL:** 27 South Castle Street, Liverpool,
S5 Lancashire (Merseyside).
Business: Gun, rifle and pistol makers.
Cartridges: The Castle; Kynoch Patent Grouse Ejector (Williams & Powell's name on the headstamping).

1117. **WILLIAMSON.** Later as, **WILLIAMSON & SON:** 34 Bull Ring,
S5 Ludlow, Shropshire.
Cartridges: Unnamed (Name on over-shot wad only).

1118. **C. WILLIAMSON:** Bridge Road, Stockton-on-Tees, County Durham (Cleveland).
Business: Gunmaker.
Cartridges: Unnamed.

1119. **D. WILLIAMSON:** George Street, Kettering, Northhamptonshire.
Business: Gunsmith.
Cartridges: Special Smokeless Cartridge.

1120. **D. WILLIAMSON:** 5 Waterloo Bridge Road, London WC2.
S5 **Business:** Gunmaker.
Cartridges: Ejector; Unnamed.

1121. **EDWIN WILSON:** Rampant Horse Street, Norwich, Norfolk.
Business: Gun, pistol and rifle maker.
Cartridges: Unnamed.

1122. **F. K. WILSON & CO:** Stokesley, Yorkshire.
S5 **Business:** Ironmongers.
Cartridges: Eley Bros EBL Shield Cartridge (Wilson's name added).

1123. **GEOFFREY WILSON:** 15 Belmont Bridge; Skipton, Yorkshire.
S5 **Business:** Gunmaker.
Cartridges: Wilkill Smokeless Cartridge.

1124. **GEOFFREY H. WILSON:** 9 Market Place, Horncastle, Lincs.
Business: Gunmaker.
Cartridges: The Champion.
Remarks: Arthur Hill took over this firm at the same address in 1902. See number 484 in this cartridge list.

1125. **J. WILSON & SONS:** 169-171 South Street, St. Andrews,
S5 Fifeshire (Fife).
Business: Ironmongers.
Cartridges: High Velocity.

1126. **JAMES WILSON.** Later as, **J. WILSON & SONS:** 47 Goodramgate,
S5 York, Yorkshire.
Business: Gunmakers.
Cartridges: Eley's Ejector; Own Loading.

1127. **THEO WILSON & SONS, LTD:** Clitheroe, Lancashire.
Business: Ironmongers.
Cartridges: Champion Smokeless.

1128. **WILTON & NICHOLLS:** 18 Market Jew Street, Penzance, Cornwall.
Business: Ironmongers.
Cartridges: Riviera.

1129. **RICHARD WISE:** 10 The Bull Ring, Kidderminster,
S5 Worcestershire (Hereford & Worcester).
Business: Ironmonger.
Cartridges: The Lightning Cartridge.

1130. **WILLIAM WITCHELL:** Church Street, Tetbury, Gloucestershire.
Business: Ironmonger.
Cartridges: Unnamed or name not recorded.

1131. **WOOD:** Bristol, Gloucestershire (Avon). Also in, Cardiff, Glamorgan.
Remarks: A cartridge has been seen with the name Wood on the over-shot wad. It was loaded into a Joyce case that had Bailey's Patent Gas-check. The printing on the case wall included the wording, Patent Machinery.

1132. **ARTHUR WOOD (NEWPORT I.W.):** 114 Pyle Street, Newport, Isle
S6 of Wight.
Business: Gunsmith and ironmonger.
Cartridges: Demon; Unnamed.
Remarks: Arthur Wood ceased trading in the 1960's.

1133. **F. WOOD:** Salisbury, Wiltshire.
S6 **Cartridges:** Unnamed (Pinfire).

1134. **GEORGE WOOD & CO:** Sheffield, Yorkshire.
Business: Gunsmiths.
Cartridges: Unnamed or name not recorded.
Remarks: This firm was absorbed into H. B. Suggs of Nottingham.

1135. **J. L. WOOD:** St. Mary's Street, Stamford, Lincolnshire.
S6   **Business:** Gunmaker.
      Cartridges: Unnamed.

1136. **WOOD & HORSPOOL:** 114 Pyle Street, Newport, Isle of Wight.
S6   **Business:** Ironmongers.
      Cartridges: Unnamed (Seen in pin and centre fire).
      Remarks: The following is information gleaned from old trade directories on Newport ironmongers. In 1880 there was a W. F. Wood at 41 High Street. In 1907, Arthur Wood was active at 114 Pyle Street. In 1911, Wood & Horspool were in business at 114 Pyle Street. By 1915, Arthur was shown as being active at 114 Pyle Street. From then on the shop was in the name of Arthur Wood. He then continued trading right up into the 1960's. The partnership with Horspool could not have lasted long. See Arthur Wood, number 1132 in this cartridge list.

1137. **T. P. WOOD & CO:** Bristol, Gloucestershire (Avon). Also at,
S6   Cardiff, Glamorgan.
      Remarks; Old cartridge remains have been found through metal detecting that carried their name on the headstamping.

1138. **WOOD PAGE & CO:** 39-40 Walcot Street, Bath, Somerset (Avon).
      Cartridges: Unnamed.
      Remarks: See Page Wood & Co, number 776 in this cartridge list.

1139. **WOODDISSE & DESBOROUGH:** Market Place, Ashbourne, Derbyshire.
      Business: Ironmongers.
      Cartridges: The Premier.
      Remarks: This firm was listed in a 1932 trade directory as just Wooddisse & Co.

1140. **R. J. WOODROW:** High Street, Brandon, Suffolk.
S6   **Business:** Ironmonger.
      Cartridges: The Champion Smokeless Cartridge.
      Remarks: Their telephone number was Brandon 2.

1141. **WOODROW & CO, LTD:** Castle Street, Salisbury, Wiltshire.
      Business: Ironmongers.
      Remarks: Cartridges were once loaded on their premises.

1142. **EDMUND WOODS:** 36 Bow Street, London.
S6   **Business:** Gunmaker.
      Cartridges: Unnamed (Headstamping, E.WOODS No 12 LONDON).
      Remarks: Edmund was active between 1864 and 1891.

1143. **GEORGE L. WOODS.** Later as, **G. L. WOODS & SONS:** Ovington,
S6   Norfolk.
      Business: Gunmakers and cartridge loaders.
      Cartridges: Castle Forbes; Norfolk Universal; Unnamed; Woods Special; Woods Supreme.
      Remarks: The cartridges listed here have been closed by rolled turnovers. This firm loaded many other brands that were closed by star crimpings. They also loaded to private orders. Many of these have been for country estates and rabbit clearance societys.

1144. **JAMES WOODWARD & SONS:** 64 St. James's Street, Pall Mall.
S7 Also at, 29 Bury Street, St. James's, London SW1.
Business: Gunmakers.
Cartridges: The Automatic; Eley Ejector; Kynoch Patent Grouse Ejector; Special Smokeless; Unnamed.

1145. **RALPH WOOLISCROFT:** 12 Derby Street, Leek, Staffordshire.
S7 **Business:** Ironmonger.
Cartridges: Eley's E.B. Nitro Cartridge Case (Wooliscroft's name on the headstamping).

1146. **GEORGE WREN:** High Street, Hungerford, Berkshire. Also in,
S7 Ramsbury, Wiltshire.
Business: Ironmonger and saddler.
Cartridges: Hungerford.
Remarks: He is known to have loaded in his Hungerford premises, 12 gauge pin and centre fire cartridges. Trade directories for the years 1869 and 1877 showed this firm as, Wren & Matthews. George Wren's business was sold out to another firm in 1925. I could be wrong, but I think that all cartridge loading ceased when George sold out.

1147. **JAMES WRIGHT:** Oakhampton, Devonshire.
Business: Ironmonger.
Cartridges: Special Load.

1148. **RANDALL WRIGHT:** Spalding, Lincolnshire.
S7 **Business:** Gunsmith.
Cartridges: Amberite Cartridge.

1149. **WRIGHTS:** Maldon. Also at, Southend-on-Sea, Essex.
S7 **Cartridges:** What Ho!!! Smokeless.

1150. **WRIGHT & CURREY:** Spalding, Lincolnshire.
S7 **Cartridges:** Amberite Cartridge.
Remarks: At one time there was a John Wright who was an ironmonger. He traded from 1 Churchgate, Spalding. Two firms with the name Wright at Spalding both sold Amberite cartridges. This makes me think that there were family connections between Randall Wright number 1148 in this list and Wright & Currey. I would also guess that John Wright was also related. If so, then their main business would have been ironmongering.

1151. **A. B. WYLIE:** 64-66 Market Place. Also at, Theatre Street,
S7 Warwick, Warwickshire.
Business: Ironmonger.
Cartridges: The Killklean.
Remarks: I was once taken upstairs and shown their old loading machine. Alas, there was not a cartridge or a cartridge case left in the place.

1152. **S. YOUNG & SONS:** Misterton, Somerset.
Cartridges: Frank Dyke's Yellow Wizard (Extra tube printing).
Remarks: See Frank Dyke & Co, Ltd number 276 in this cartridge list.

END OF CARTRIDGE LIST.

A few of the Unidentified

The majority of shotgun cartridges when purchased from shops were used in the localitys in which they had been sold. Printing their cases would have cost money, and the less money spent in their outlay would have meant a larger turn-over. This was one reason why some of the old cartridges carried so little information. In some instances, all that they carried was the firms name and place location as this was considered sufficient. As our country has many place names the same, take Newcastle and Whitchurch for examples, it is not an easy matter to be able to establish for certain from which town a cartridge may have come from.

More than often the firms would have their names printed on the case walls or paper tubes, call them which you like. This was not always the case though. Some would only have their names and perhaps their town locations carried on the over-shot wads or the headstampings, or on both. The majority of cartridges were boxed up and sold in lots of twenty-five. Many has been the time that I have seen an old and full box of cartridges that had carried a brand name. When the box had been opened, to the dismay of it's new owner, no printings at all were to be seen on the cartridges. This kind of practice was quite a common occurrence during the periods of the two world wars.

In many instances it has been anything but easy to establish where some of the old remaining cartridges had come from. If only they could talk. Also a few of these old firms may still be operative. What was once ironmongers may now be D.I.Y. stores. Likewise, old cycle agents may now being selling motorcars and often with a change of names over their doors. It is no use going in and asking them about them-selves over the counter. A person may have worked in the building for over thirty years and had never got to have known that they once loaded and sold their own brands of cartridges.

Below are just a few of the many shotgun cartridges which still defeat an identification. I have taken these to have been from the British Isles, but of this I cannot be certain. What I can be certain of is that there would have been many more of them.

20 Gauge 20. Smokeless Gastight.
The Black Thistle Special Smokeless.
De Luxe Water Resisting Loaded in Ireland.
English Pioneer Cartridge.
The Express Special Cartridge.
Gastight Metal Lined.
M. & C. CA. (On the headstamping).
Metalode Metal Lined Cartridge.
The Rabbit Special.
Smokeless Cartridge.
Smokeless Metal Lined Cartridge.
Special British.
The Supreme.
Tiger Brand.
The Trojan.
The Union Jack Brand Cartridge.
The Windsor Cartridge.

The A. & E.

Known to many as the Accident and Emergency. Yes this could apply here as I may have made a few mistakes. If so, then it has not been intentional. Should any be found at a later date, then at the end of this A & E would be the space in which to scibble in any corrections.

Since compiling the Cartridge List, two firms got accidentally left out. Due to the numbering along with the alphabetical order, they could not then be inserted. Also having completed this work, I have since been told of a few more old firms and their cartridges. Rather than leave them all out, I am including them here and giving each one a continued number.

I therefore refer to this as, The Addendum & Erratum.

Addenda

299. **ERSKINE:** Newton Stewart, Wigtownshire (D & G).
   Extra information.
   Cartridges: Unnamed.

1153. **COLTMAN:** Lutterworth, Leicestershire.
   Remarks: A stripped down cartridge revealed the use of an over-shot wad with the printing, COLTMAN.LUTTERWORTH.

1154. **WILLIAM DAWSON:** Market Place, Settle. Also at, Bentham, Yorkshire.
   Business: Ironmonger and implement dealer.
   Cartridges: The Pheasant Cartridge.

1155. **EBRALL:** Hereford, Herfordshire (Hereford & Worcester).
S4   **Remarks:** This name has been seen printed on an over-shot wad. See Plate S4, number 1105, H. W. Wildman.

1156. **GEORGE FARMILOE & SONS, LTD:** 34 St. John Street, West Smithfield, London EC.
   Remarks: Just may have had his name on cartridges. He was known to have sold F. Joyce & CO, Ltd's cartridges and was an agent for T. Sopwith & Co, Ltd's lead shot. They also dealt in household hardware.

1157. **EDWARD GIBBS:** Reepham, Norfolk.
   Business: Ironmonger.
   Cartridges; Unnamed.

1158. **HORNE:** Reading, Berkshire.
   Remarks: Metal detection has unearthed cartridge remains with what looks like, HORNE No 12 READING on the headstamping in raised lettering. My records on Berkshire though not compete go back to 1887. I have not been able to trace this firm, but it may have been before then. The remains had been centre-fire.

1159. **G. HUNT:** Aston Hill Garage, Near Lewknor, Oxfordshire.
   Business: Motor garage.
   Cartridges: The Lewknor Cartridge.

1160. **LINDSAY:** Perth, Perthshire (Tayside).
   Business: Ironmongers.
   Cartridges: The Match Clayking Cartridge.

1161. **STARSMORE:** Stanford, Lincolnshire.
   Business: Ironmongers.
   Cartridges: Unnamed.

Erratum

In the Cartridge List. Number 1100 has accidentally been left out.

Linscott number 639 and Lynscott number 653. One of these must be wrong, but which one ? Or did this firm have two ways of spelling their name.

Waddon J. & Sons. Numbers 1039 and 1040. I think one of these to be wrong, but which one.

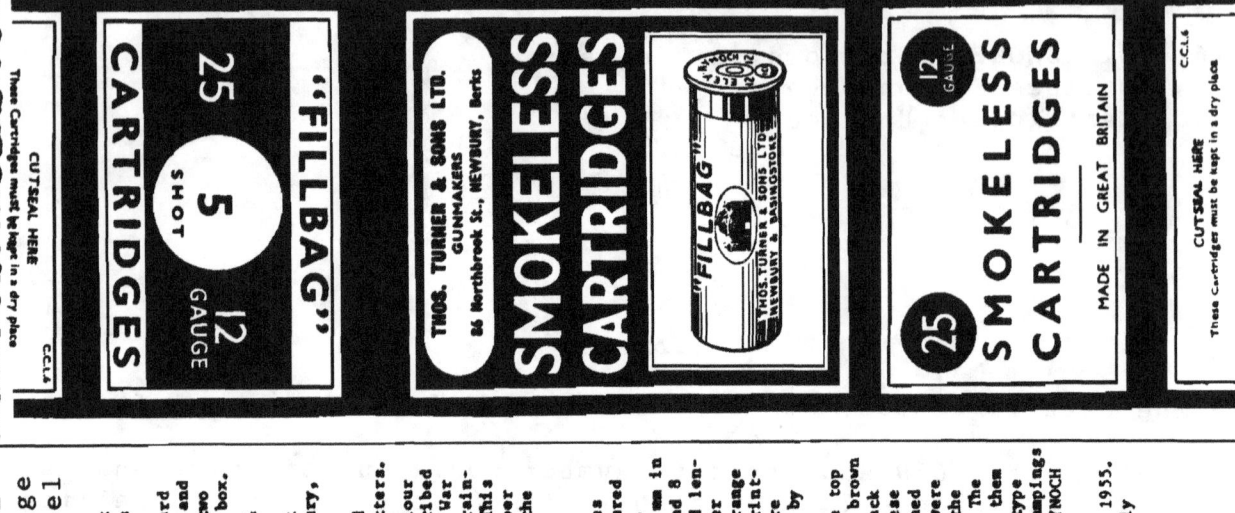

Typical cartridge box label

Cartridge box label. It has been seen on brown cardboard folding type and also on the two piece lidded box.

THOS TURNER & SONS LTD.
86 Northbrook Street, Newbury, Berkshire.

Gunmakers and sports outfitters.

The label colour is best described as the World War Two R.A.F. training yellow. This being the paper colour. All the printing was black.

The cartridges were as pictured on the label. They were 64 mm in height and had 8 mm brass head length. The paper tubes were orange with black printing. They were waterproofed by varnish. The Turner's type top wads were of brown card with black printing. These being varnished over. These were the last of the "Fillbag's". The very last of them had cluster type wads. Headstampings being ELEY-KYNOCH I.C.I.

Circa 1947 – 1955. Dates are only approximate.

'ROCKET' (TRACER) CARTRIDGES

● 5.16 in. brass, milled head, loaded with Smokeless Diamond (12 gauge) or Schultze (16 and 20 gauge). Colour: Grey. The Improved Rocket cartridge contains a tracer pellet that marks out the path of the shot charge by the emission of a bright spot of light, so that errors of aim can be detected and corrected. A box of five cartridges should always be carried. A change in the tracer mixture has enabled the original warning as to the table use of birds struck by the tracer pellet to be entirely withdrawn; game killed with a Rocket Cartridge can now be put in the bag and brought to table without question.

NOTE ON FORWARD ALLOWANCE

The use of a 'fast' cartridge cannot so lessen the time interval during which the shot charge is in the air as to affect for practical purposes of sport the amount of forward allowance required. Loading manipulations in fact, though they greatly affect penetration, pattern and recoil cannot appreciably affect forward allowance.

ELEY=KYNOCH
IMPERIAL CHEMICAL INDUSTRIES LIMITED, LONDON, S.W.1

Advertisment circa 1934.

Typical Guage (Bore) Sizes
Top row, left to right:- 4, 8, 10, 14, 16, 20, 24, 28, 32, .410, .360.
Bottom row, left to right:- 4 guage aircraft start, Punt Gun, 12 guage tractor start, 12 guage aircraft start.

The Illustrated Plates

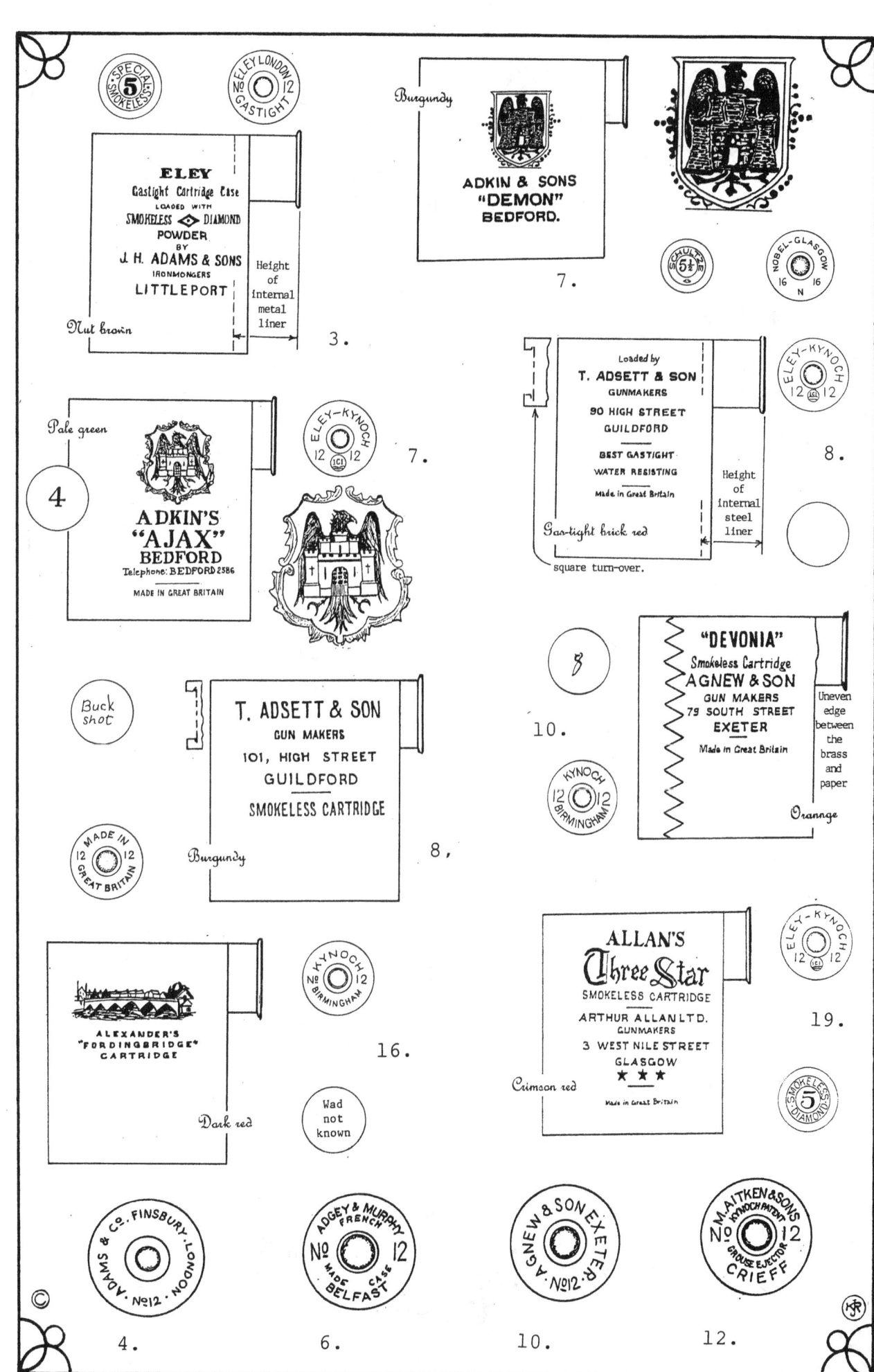

PLATE A1

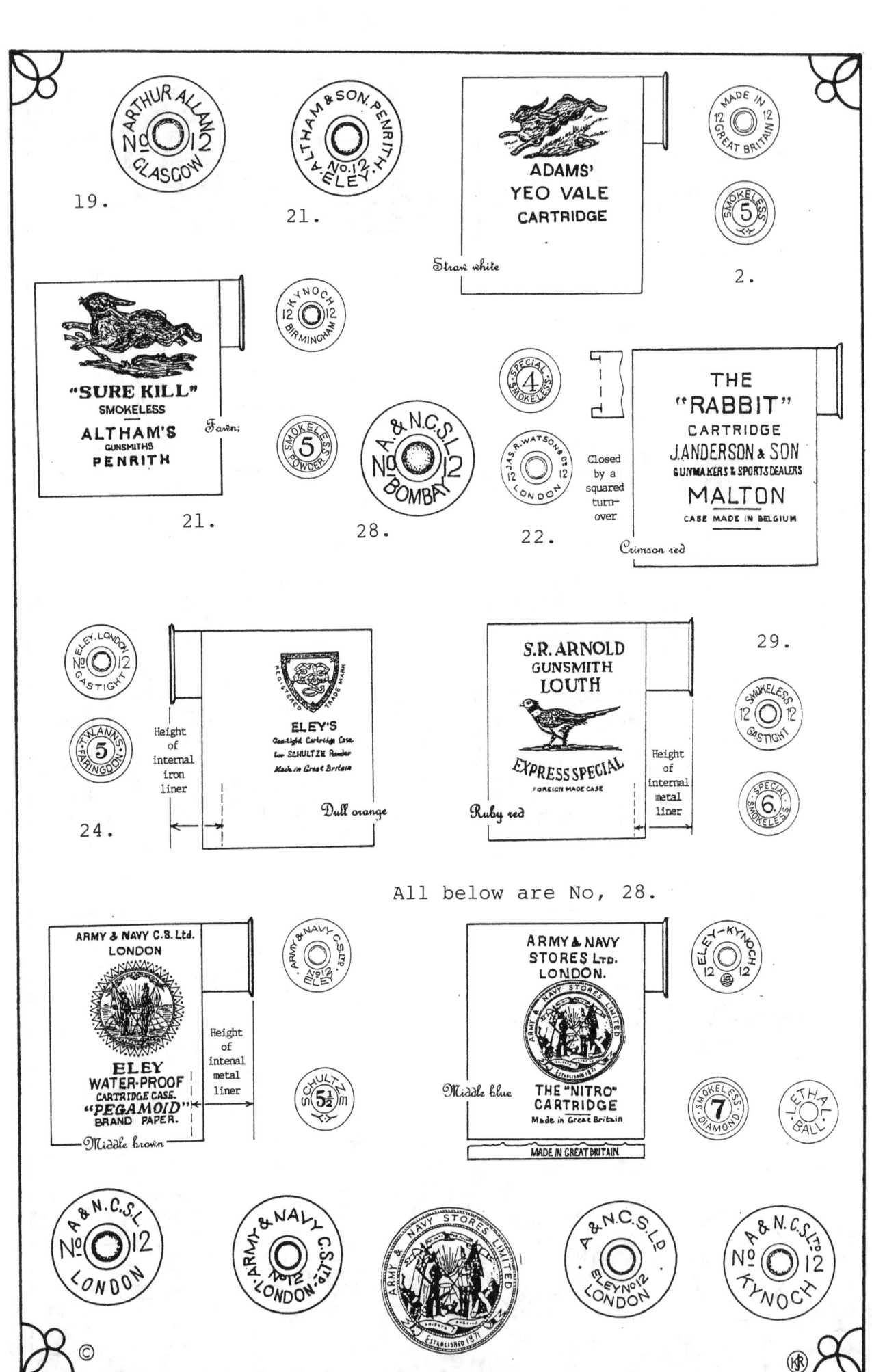

PLATE A2

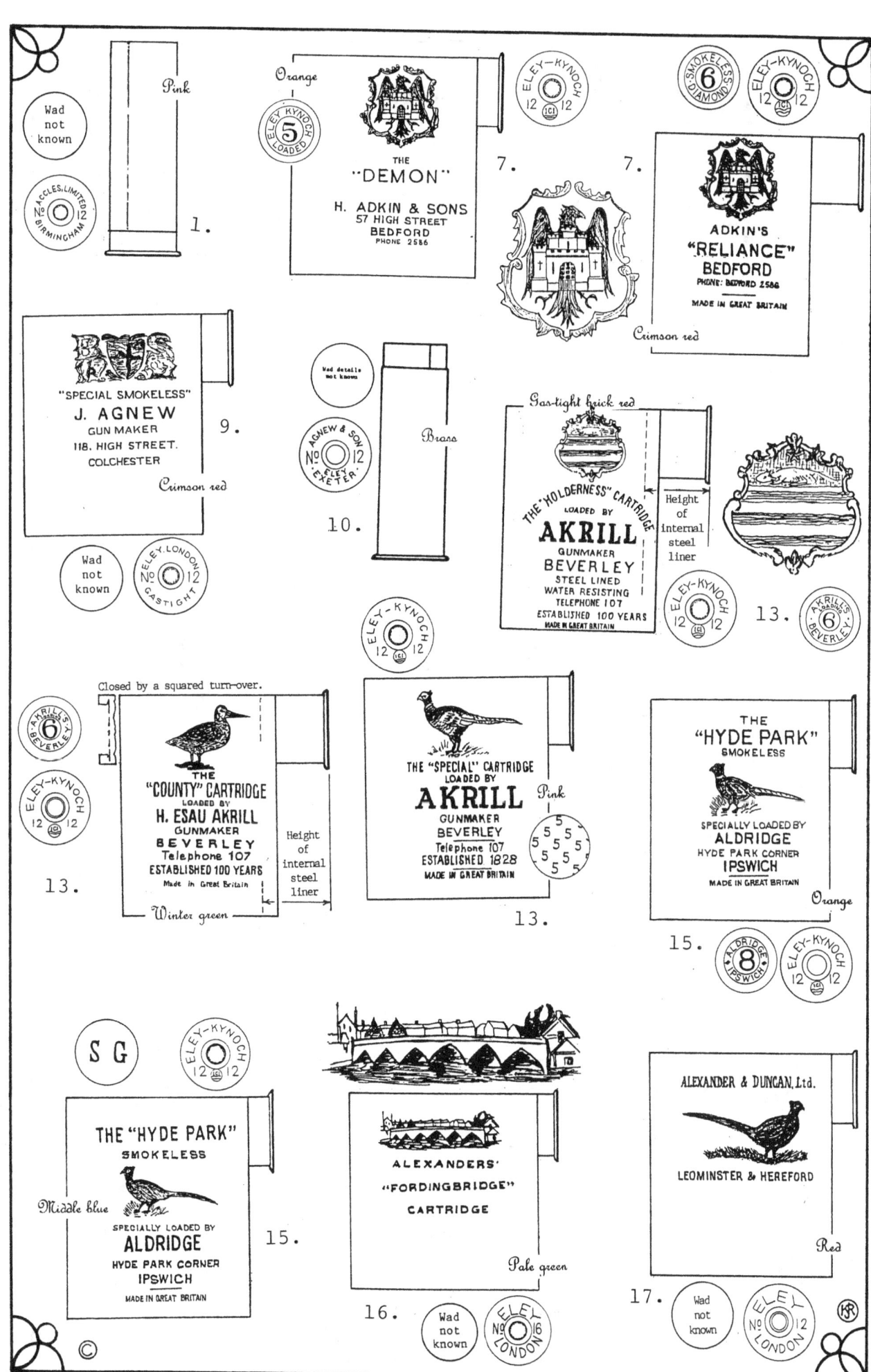

PLATE A3

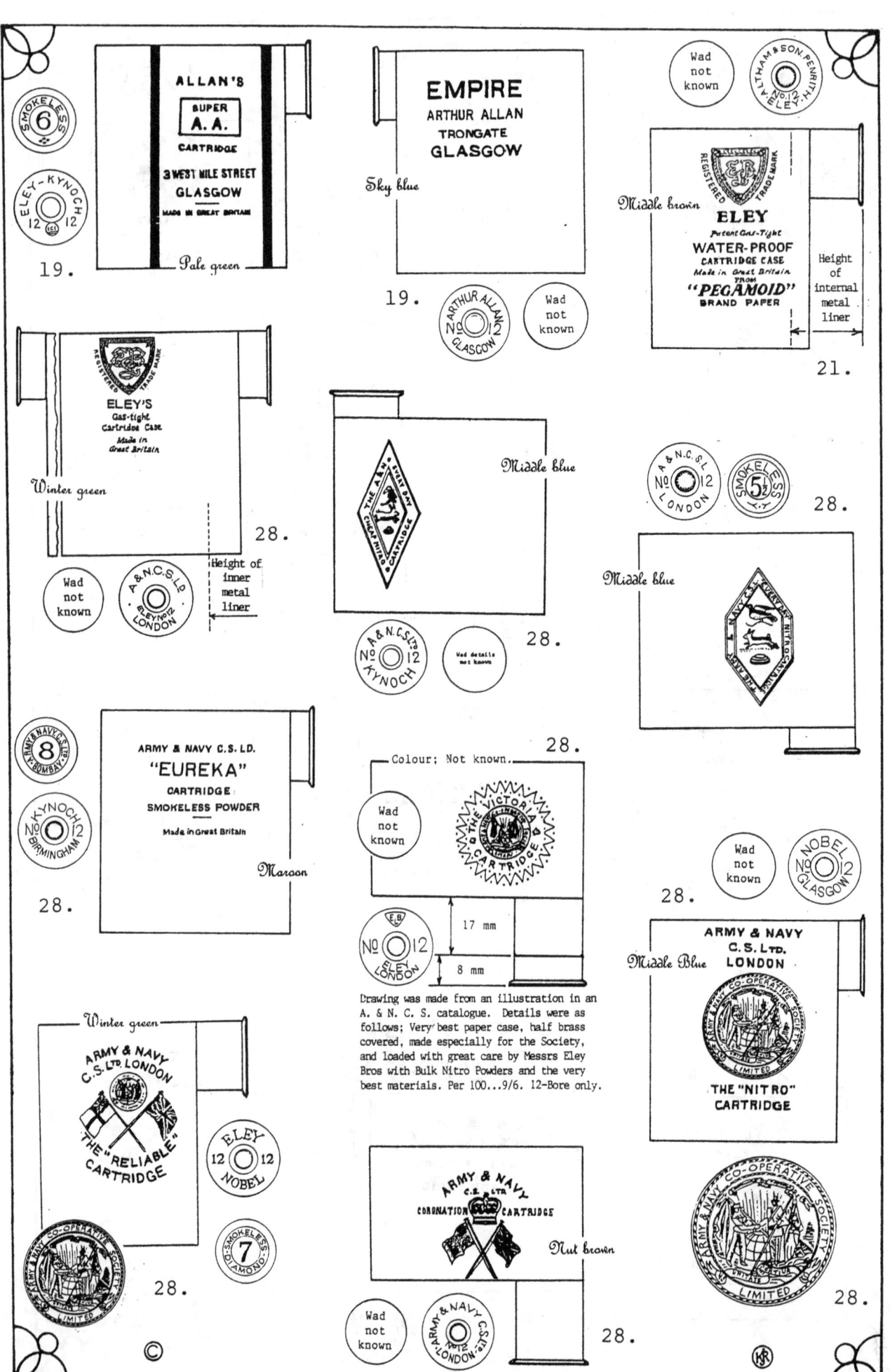

PLATE A4

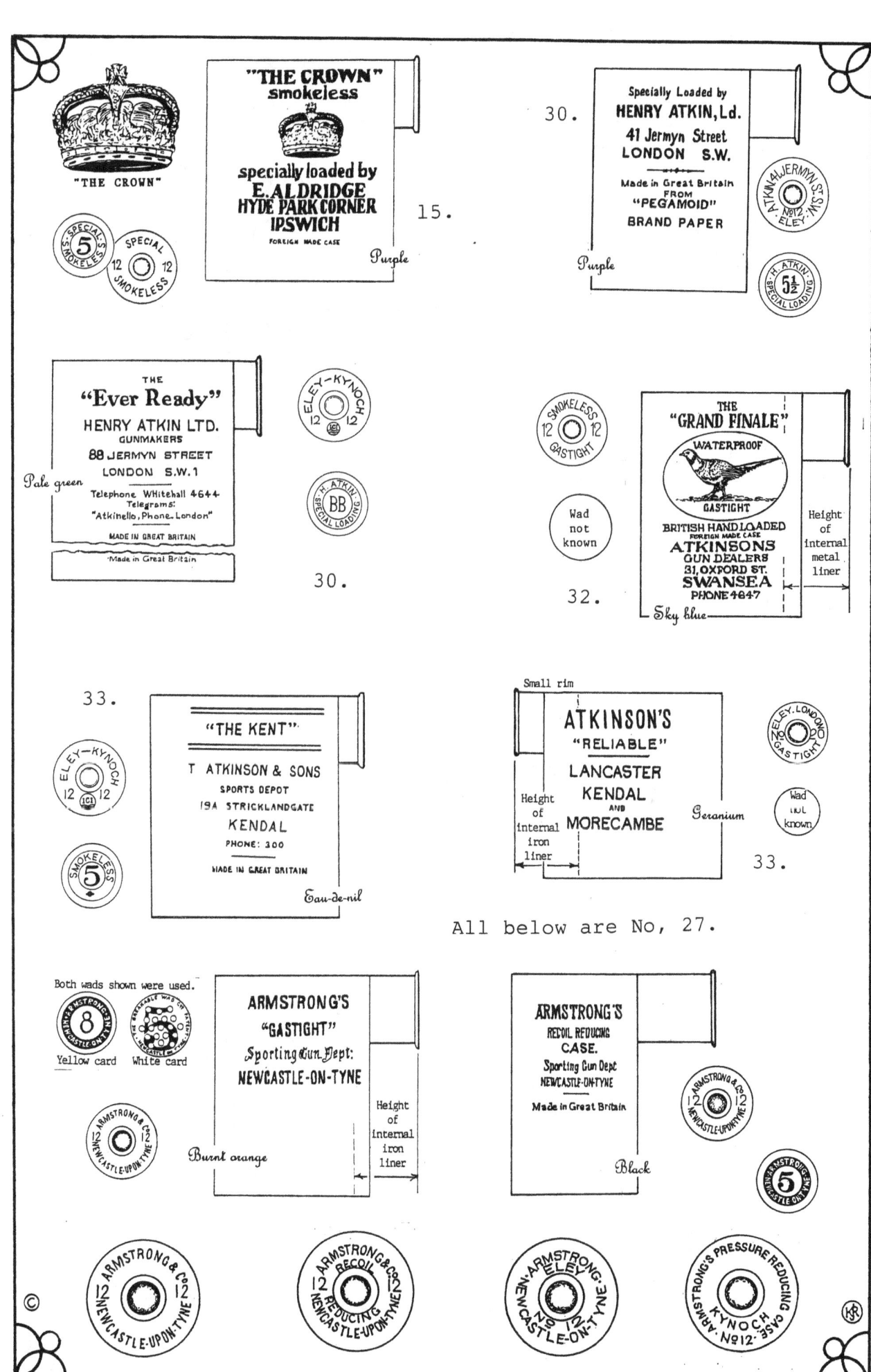

PLATE A5

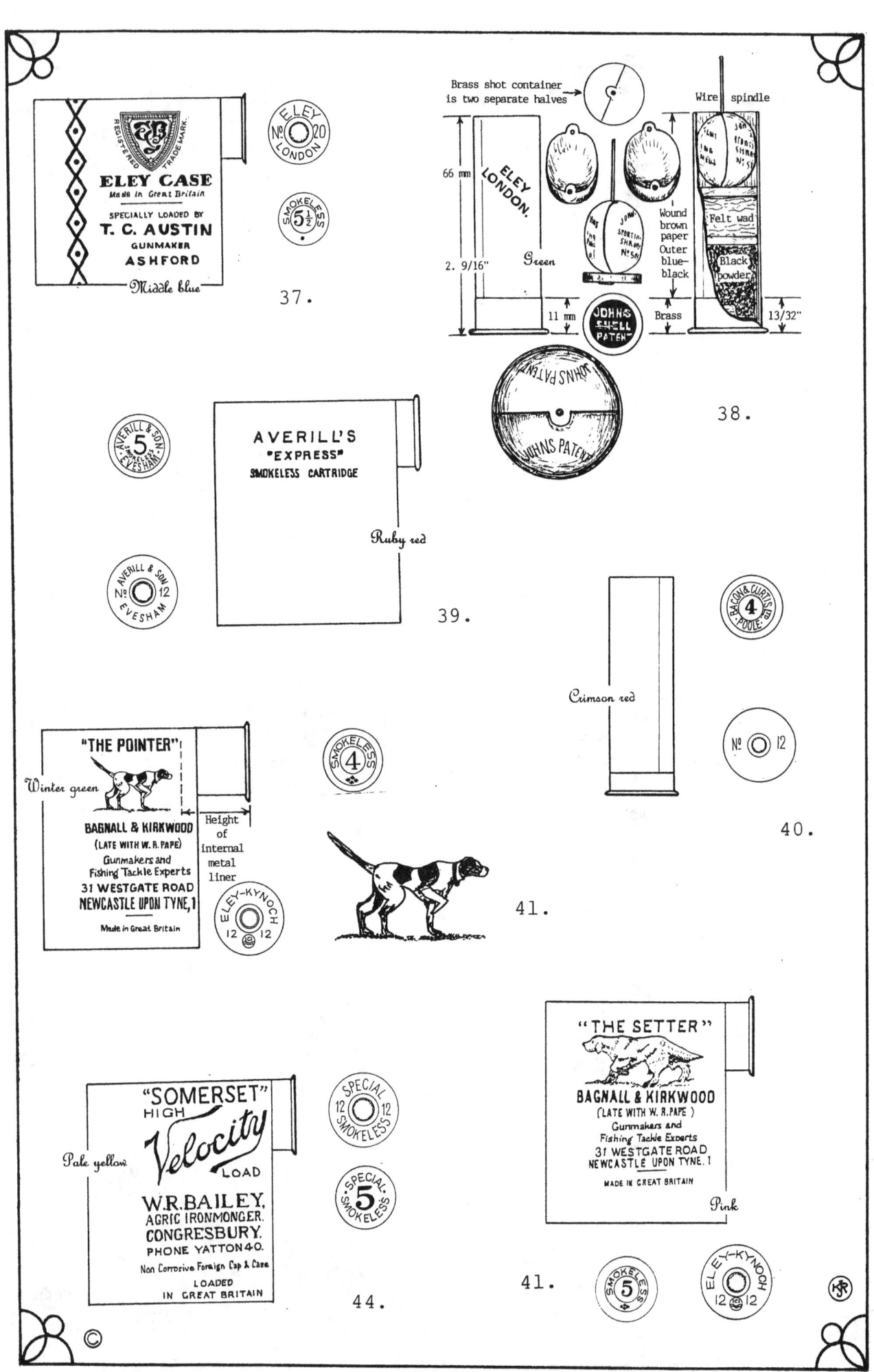

PLATE A6

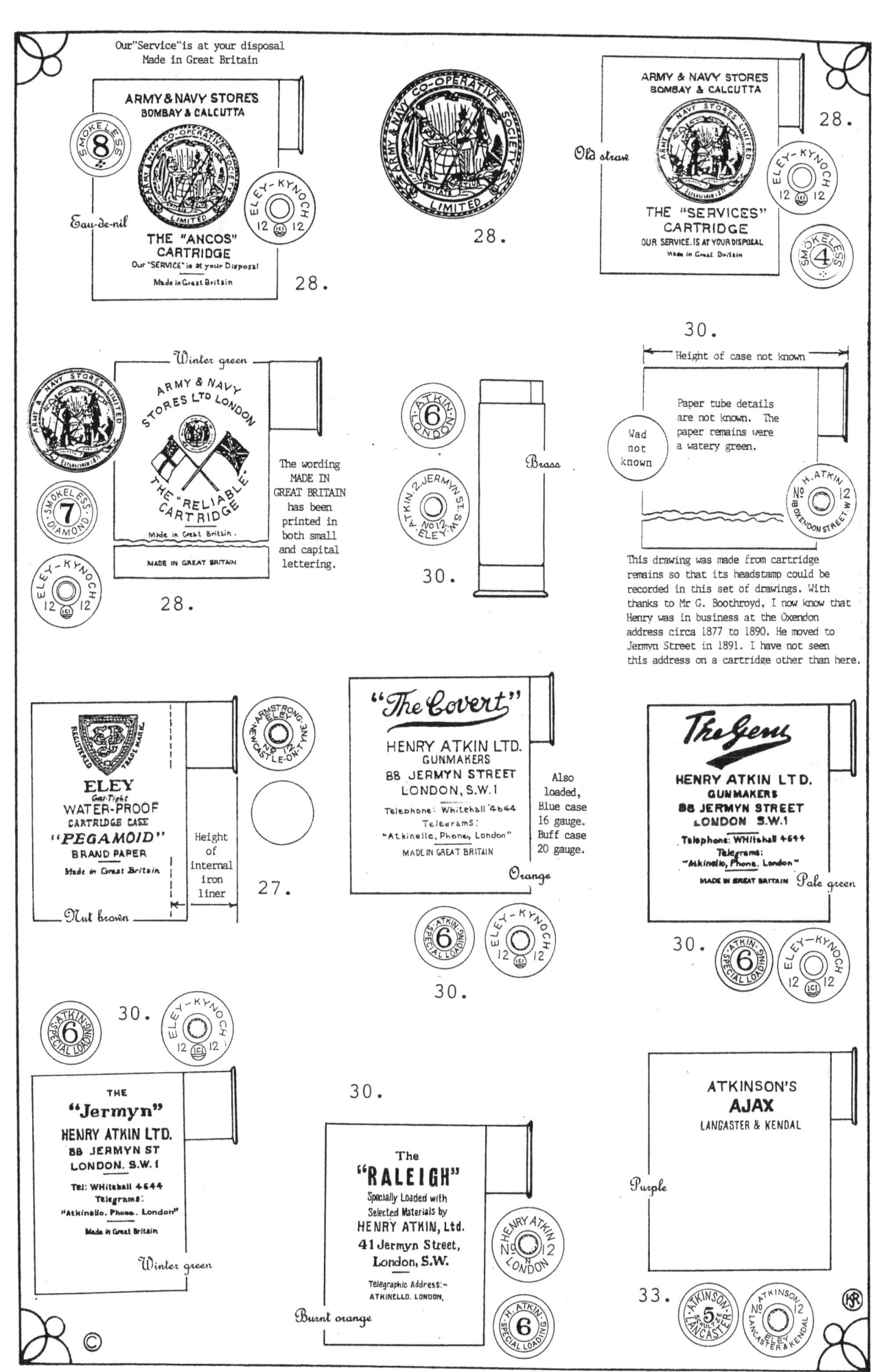

PLATE A7

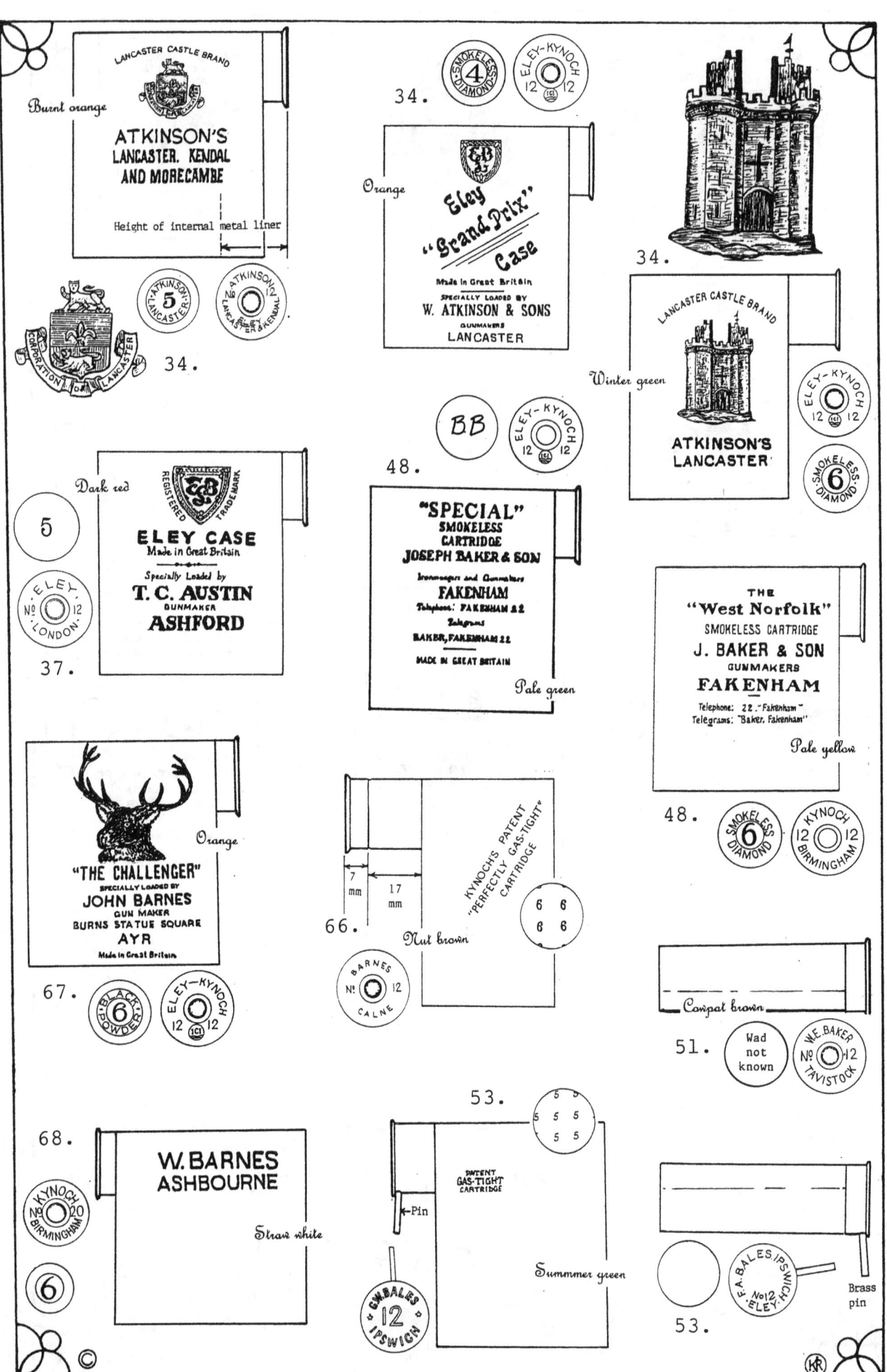

PLATE A8

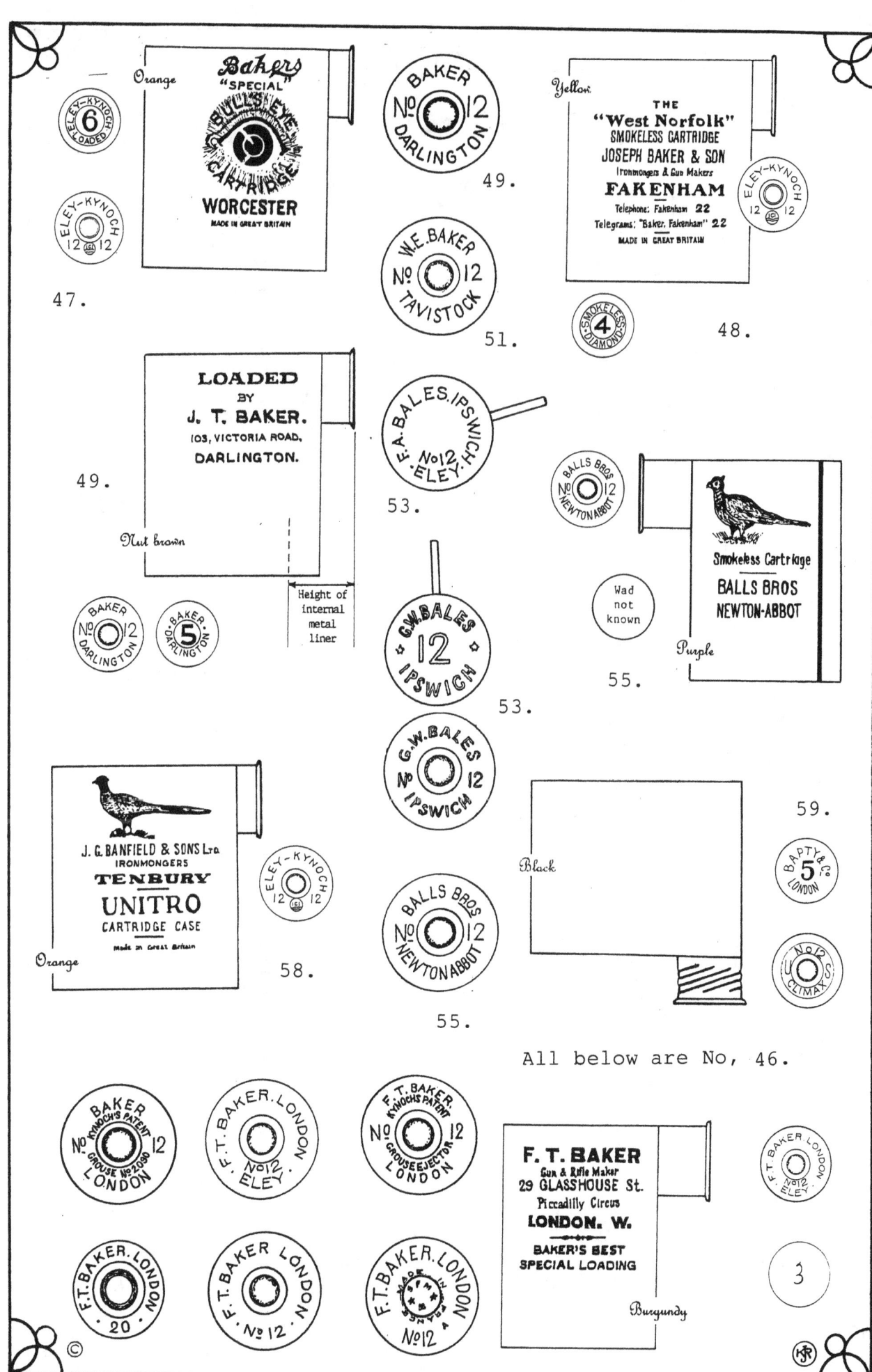

PLATE A9

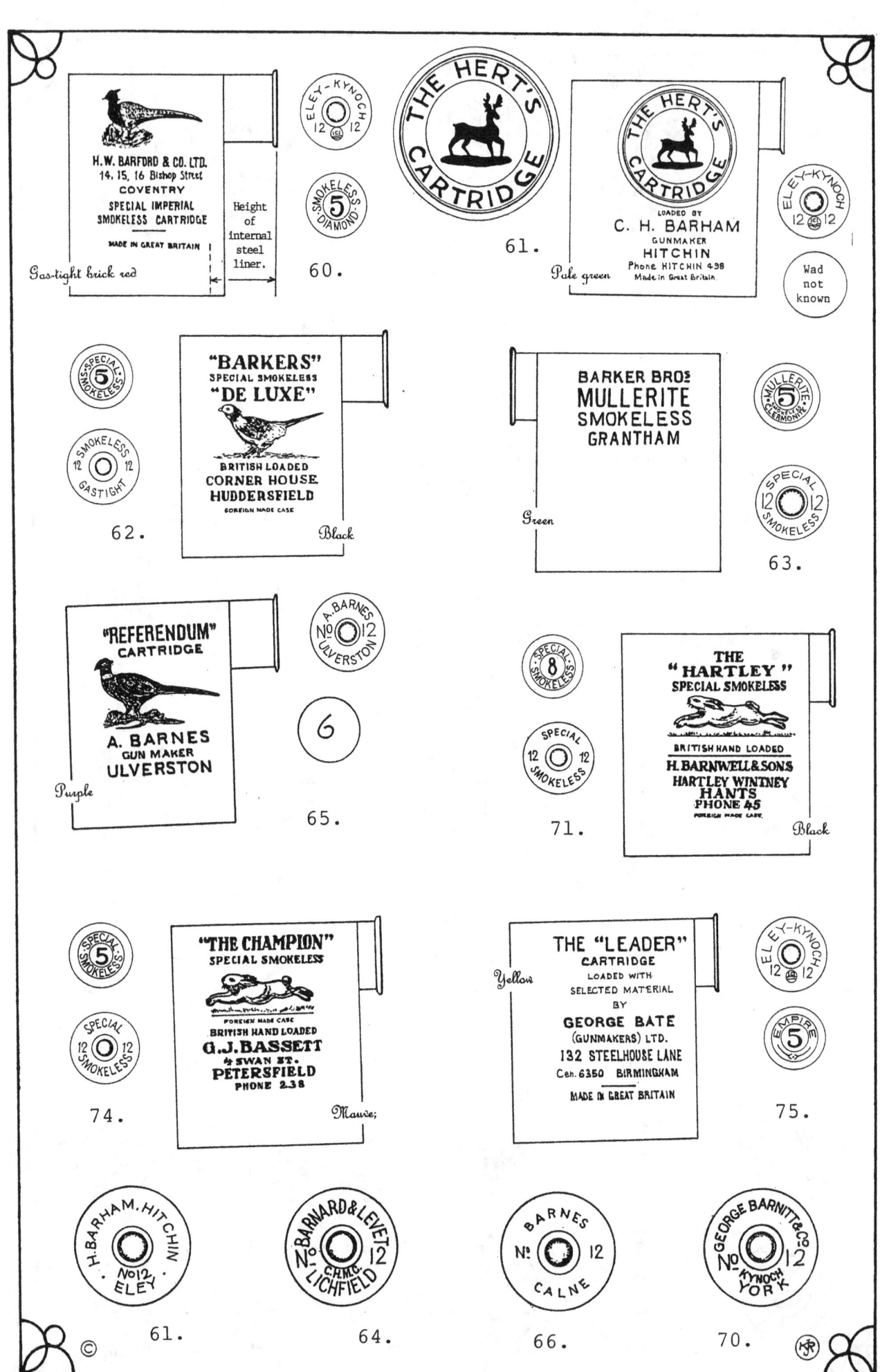

PLATE B1

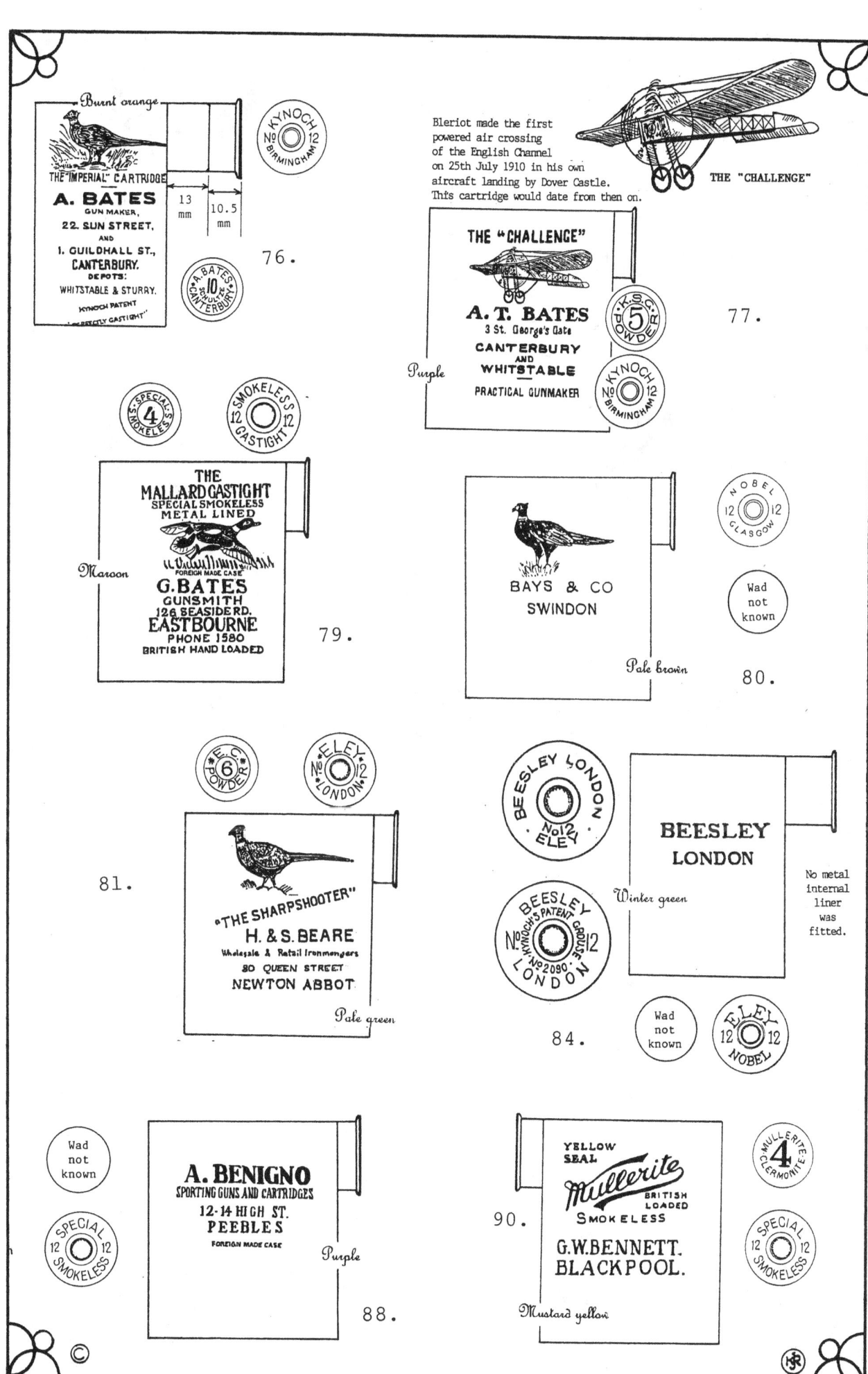

PLATE B2

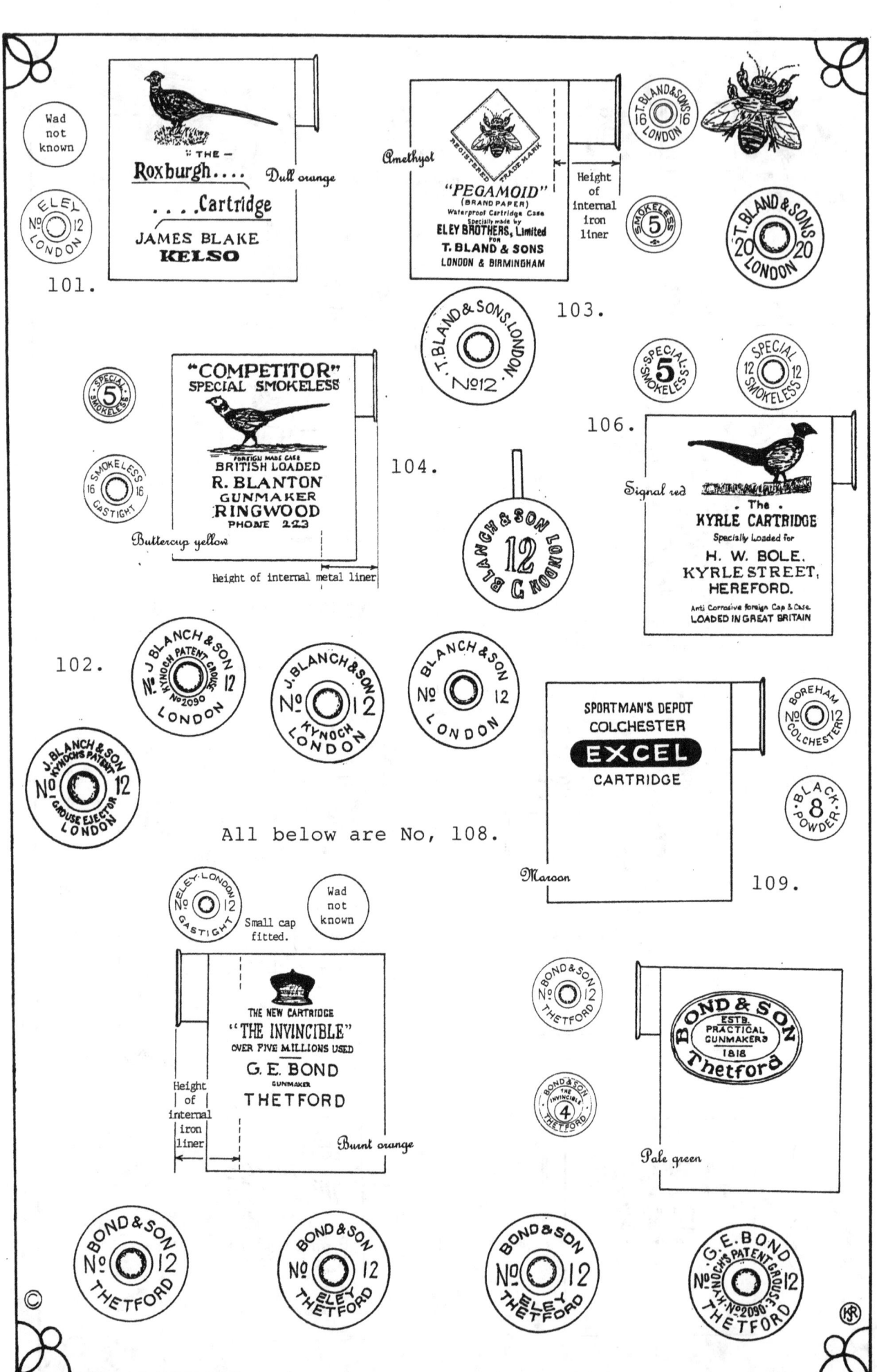

PLATE B3

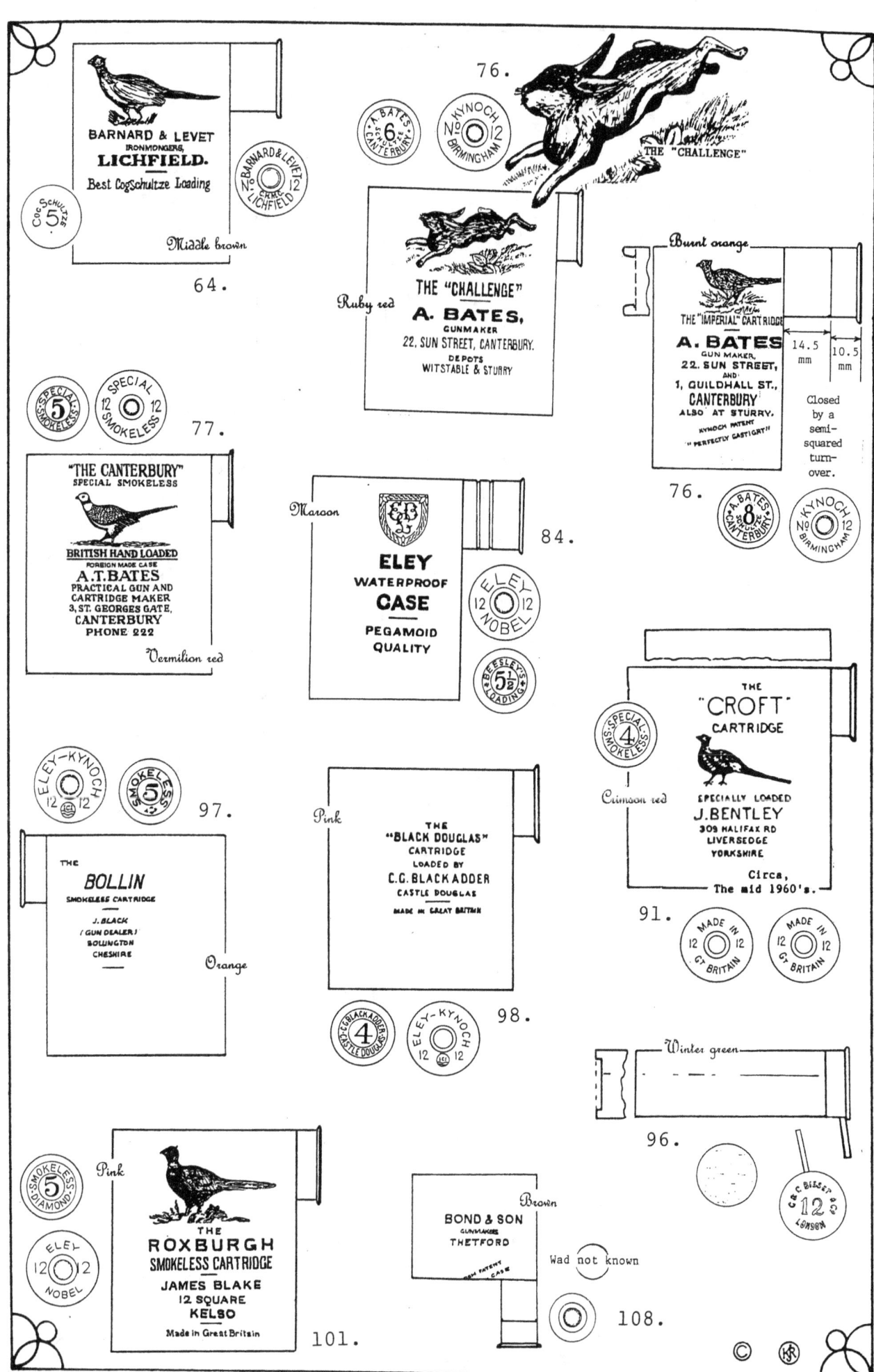

PLATE B4

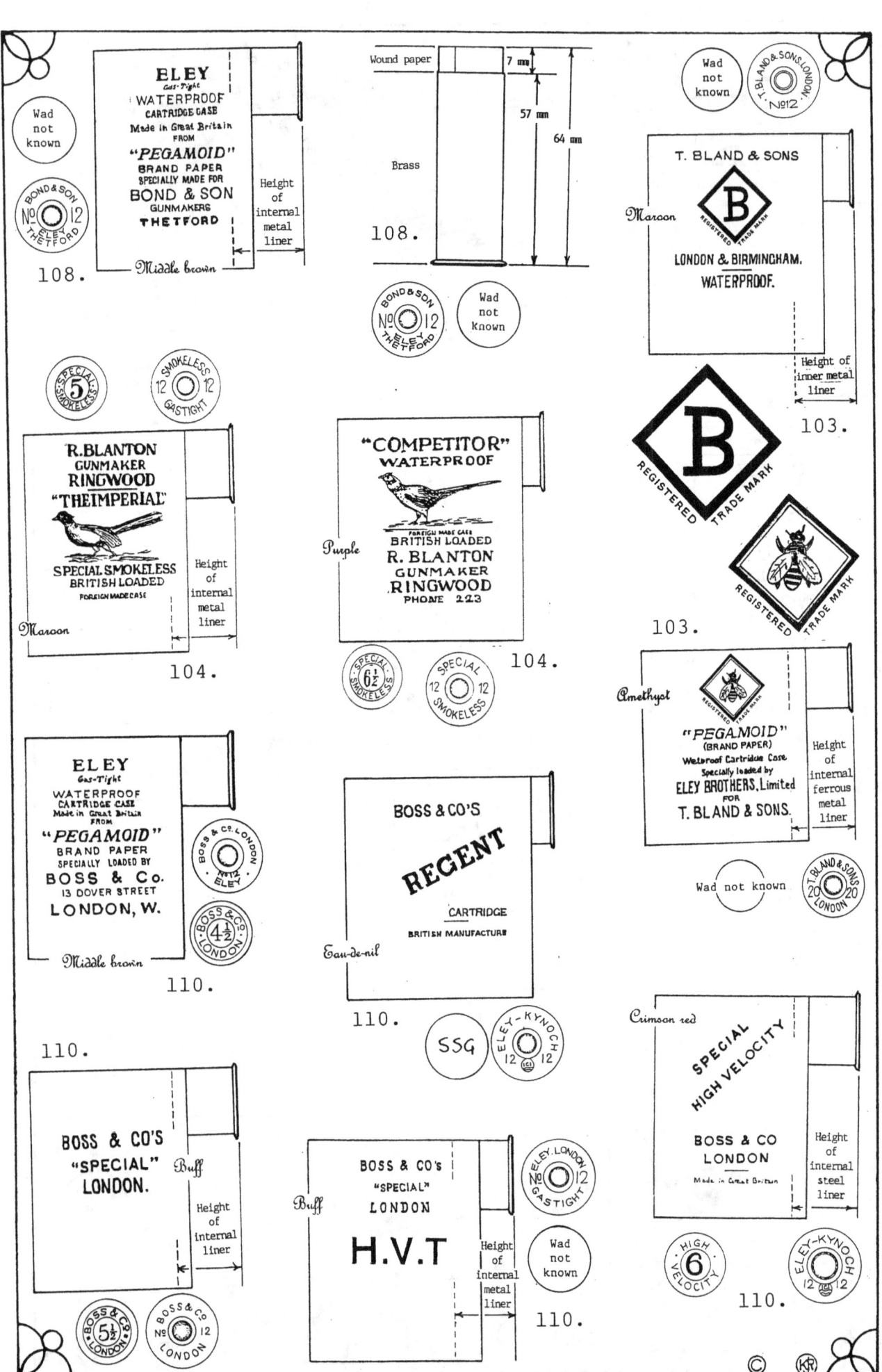

PLATE B5

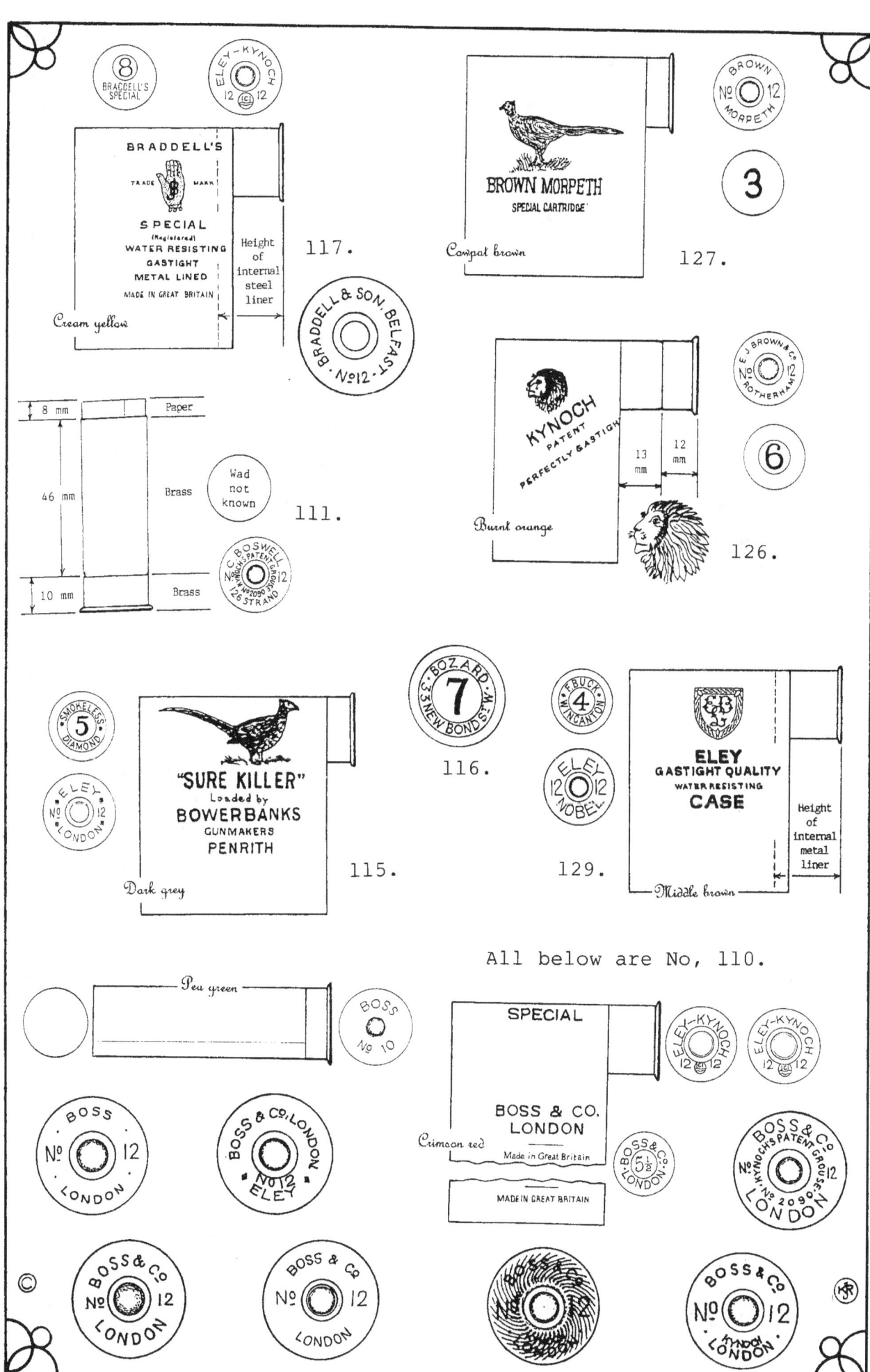

PLATE B6

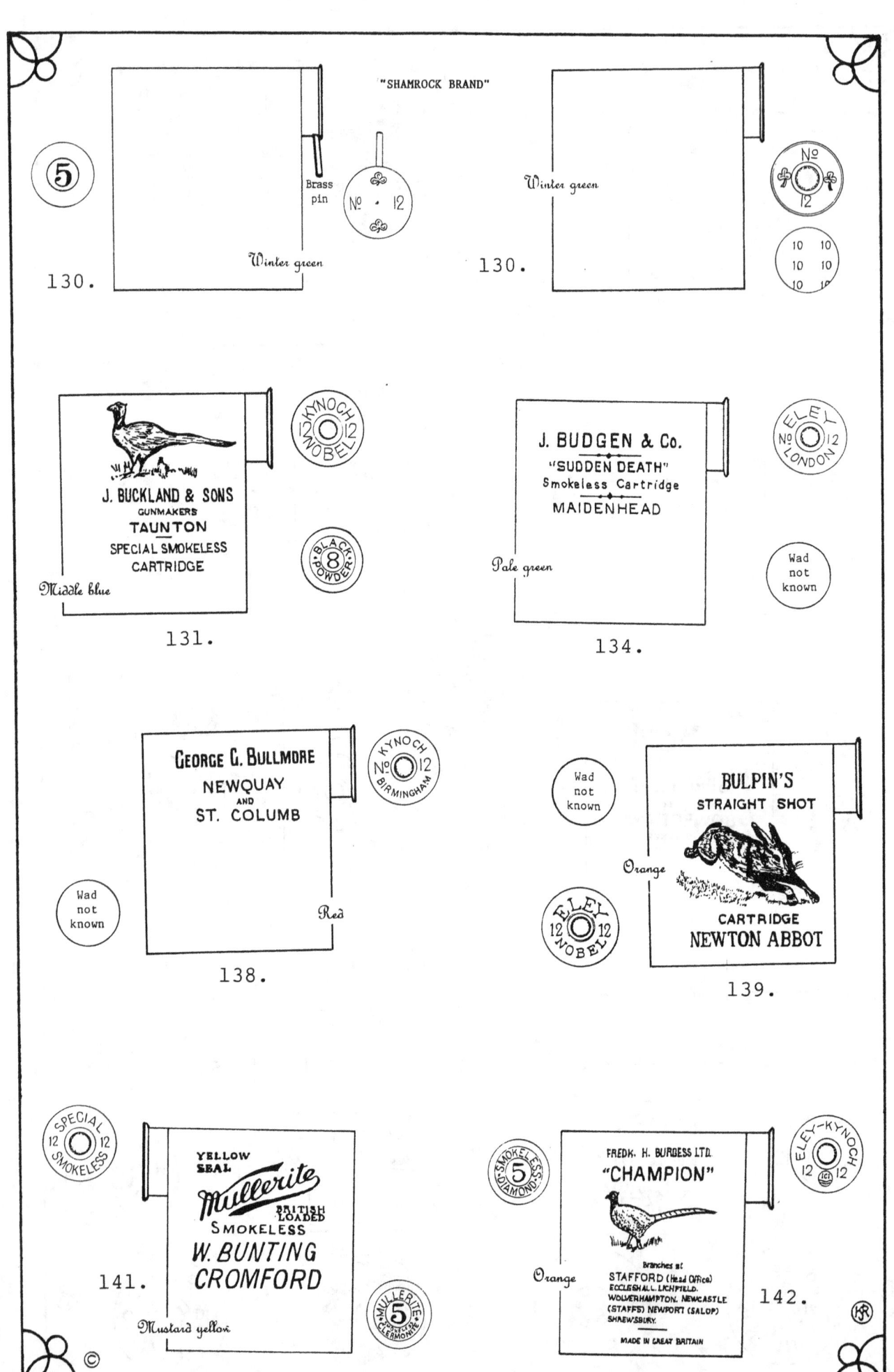

PLATE B7

PLATE B8

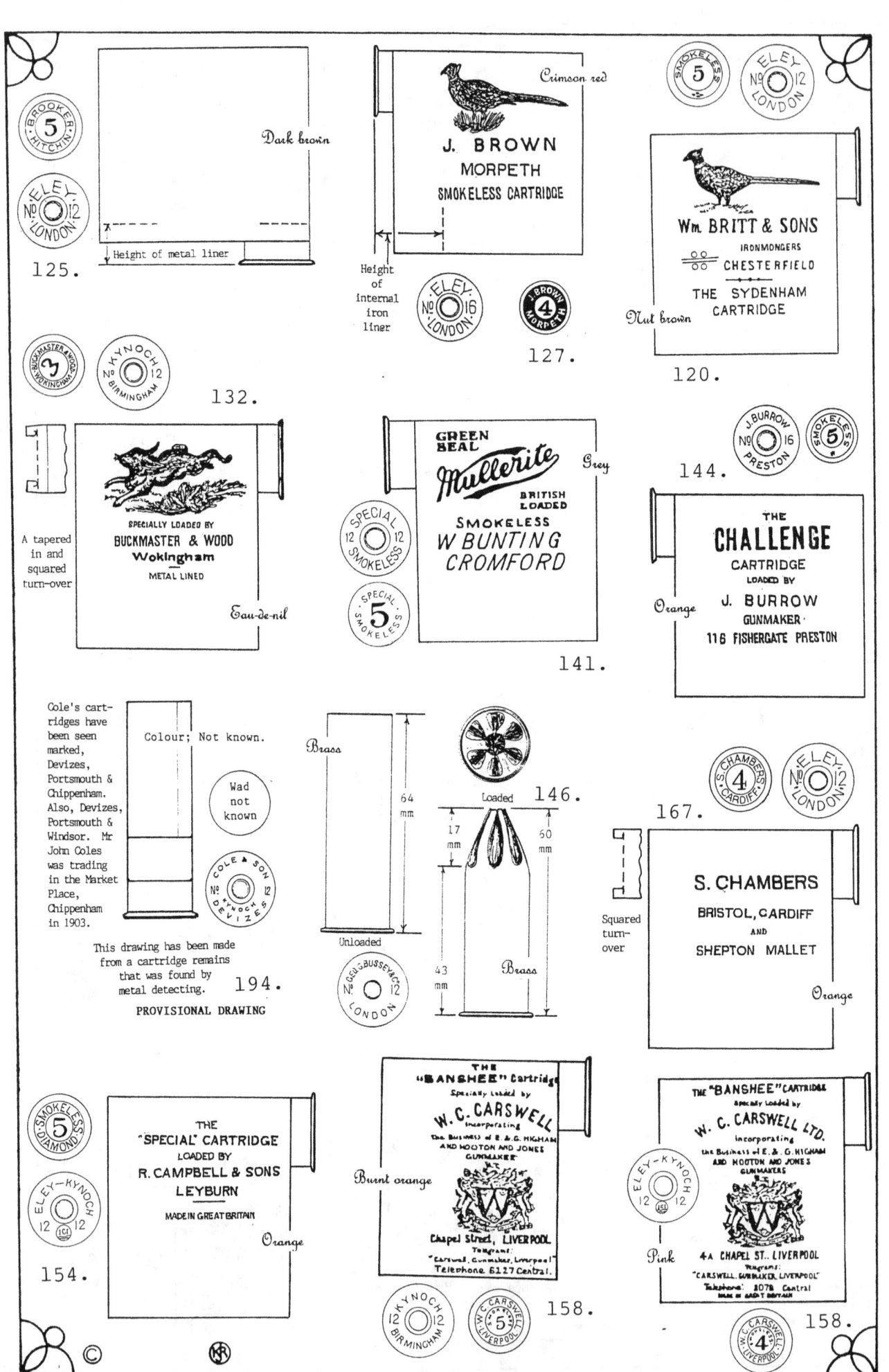

PLATE B9

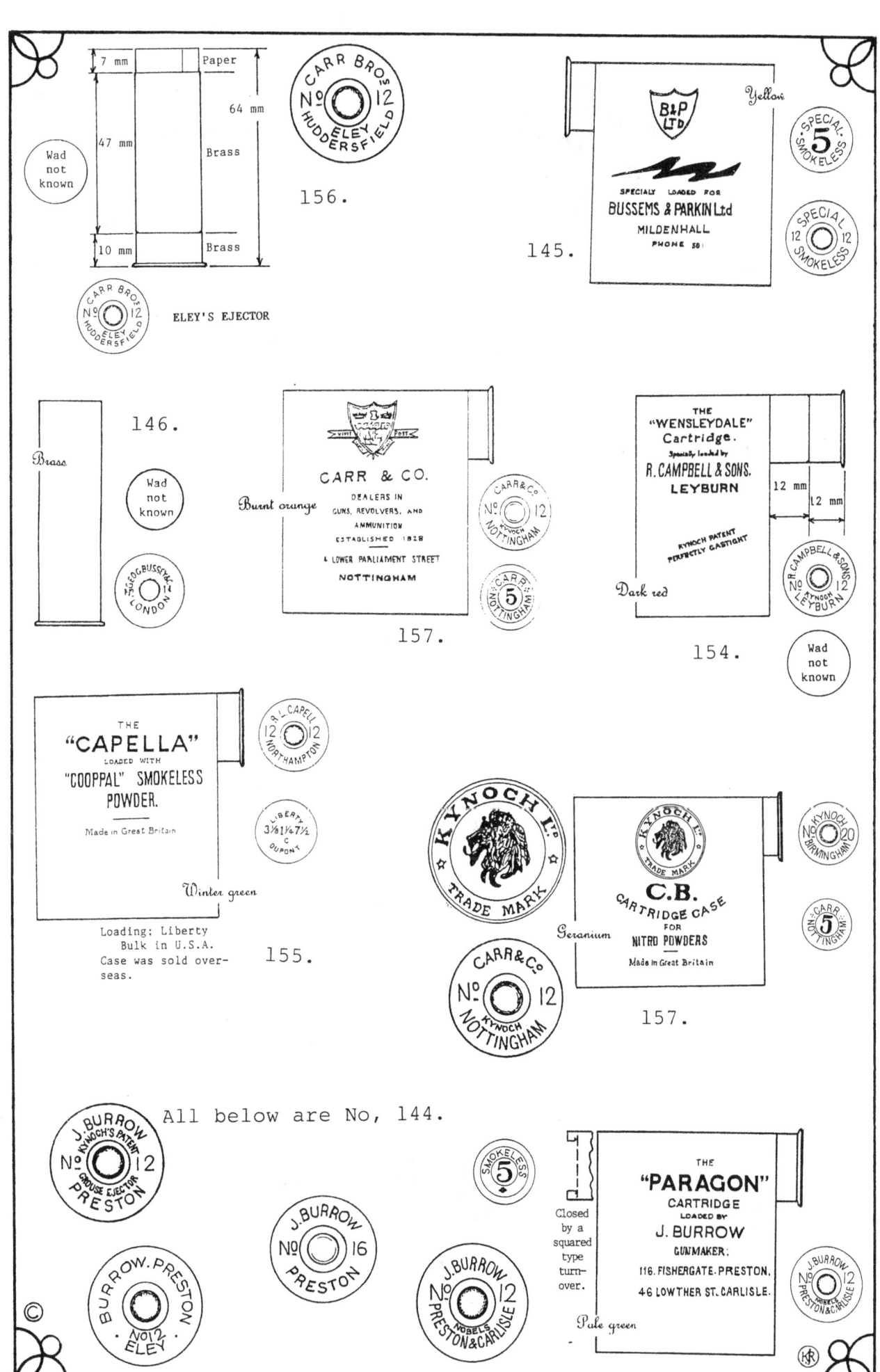

PLATE C1

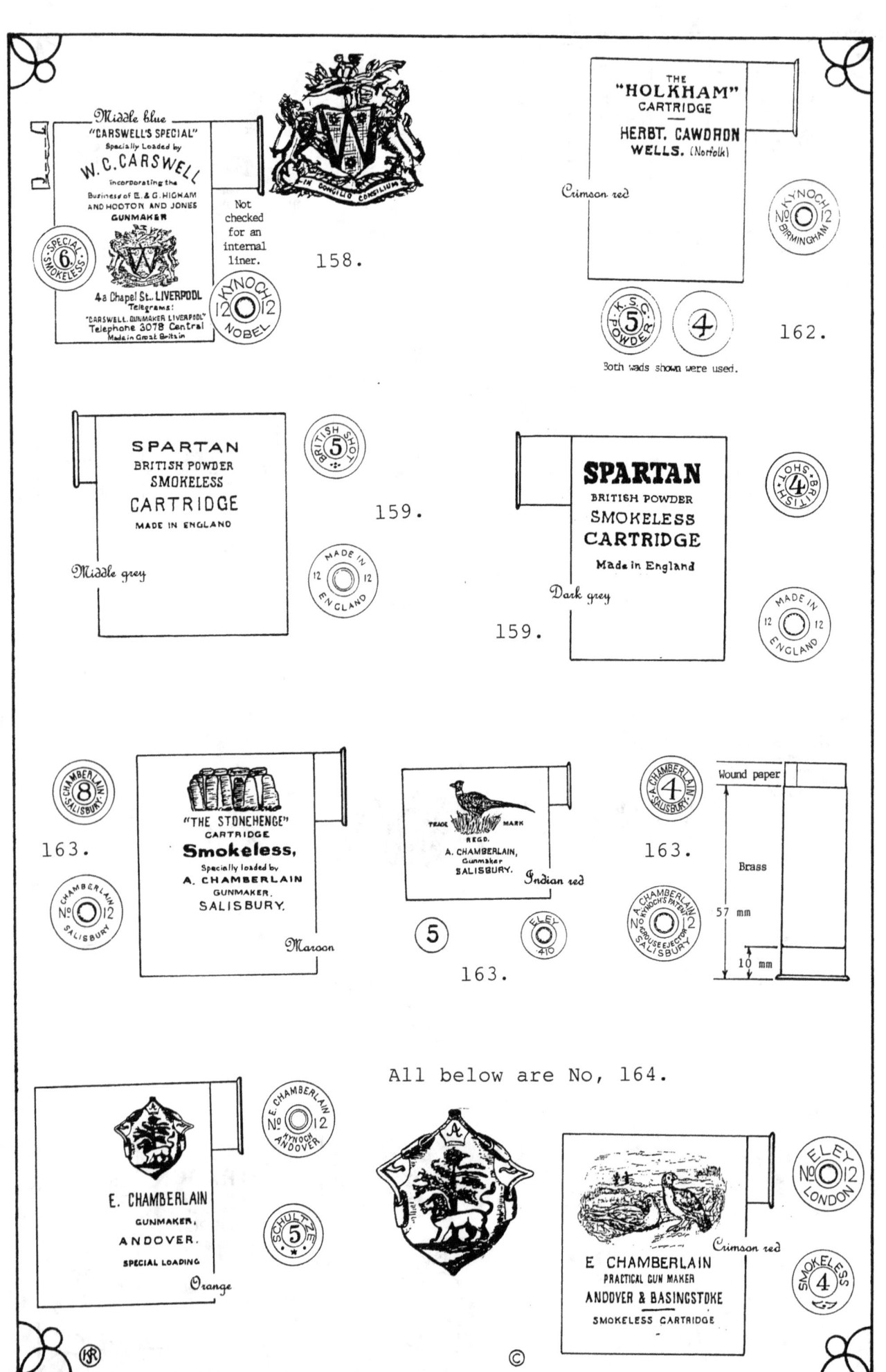

PLATE C2

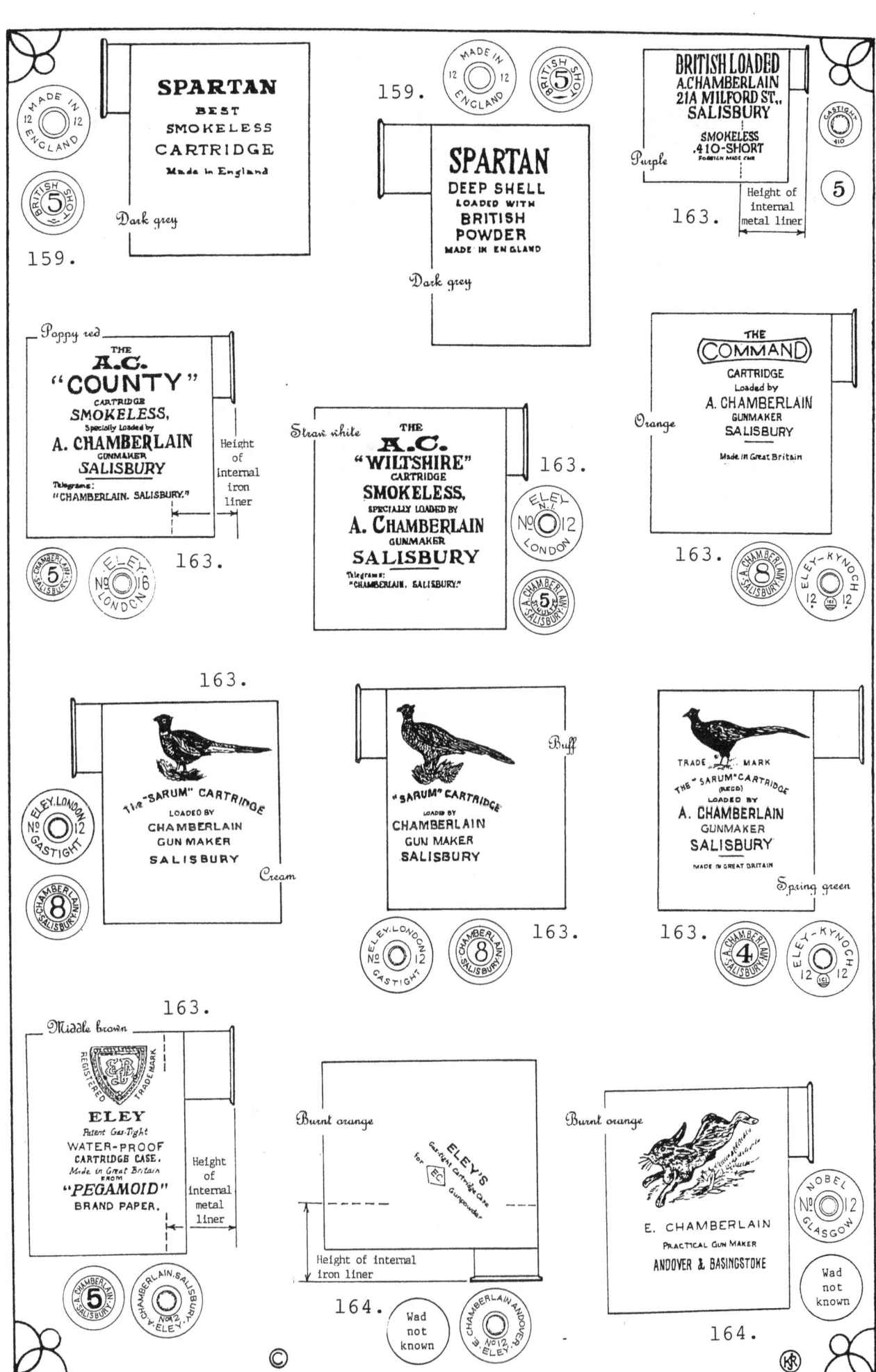

PLATE C3

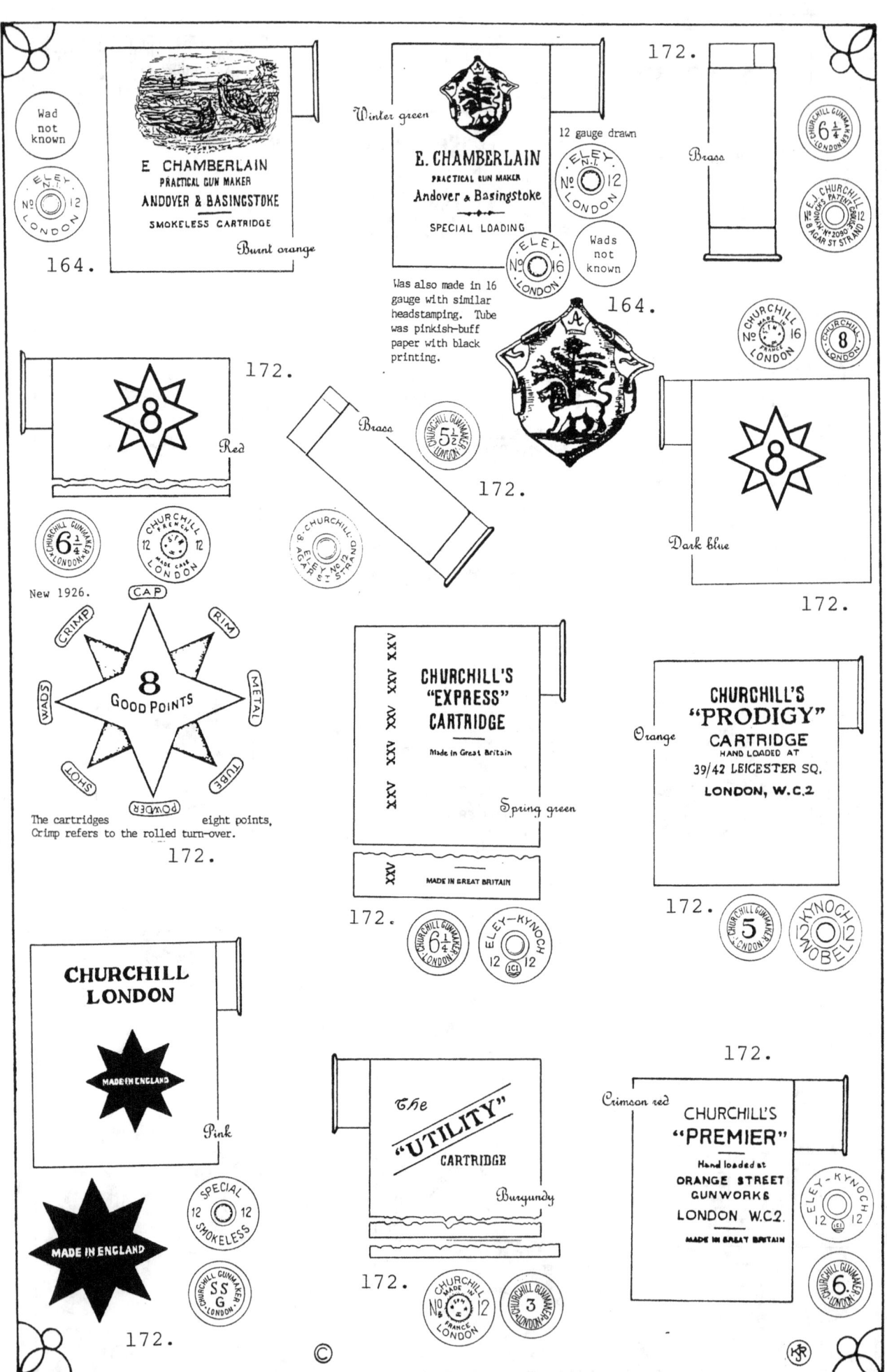

PLATE C4

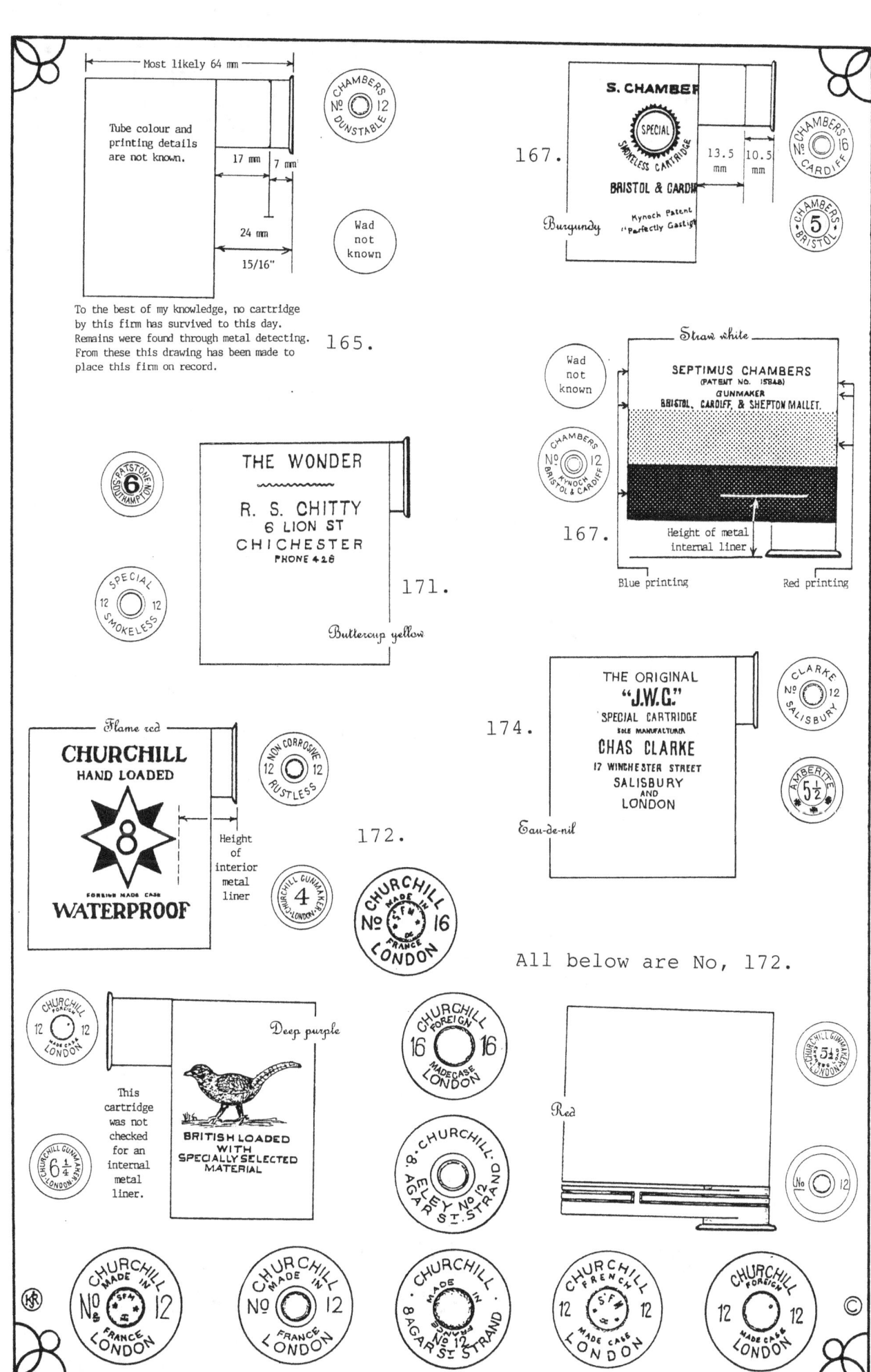

PLATE C5

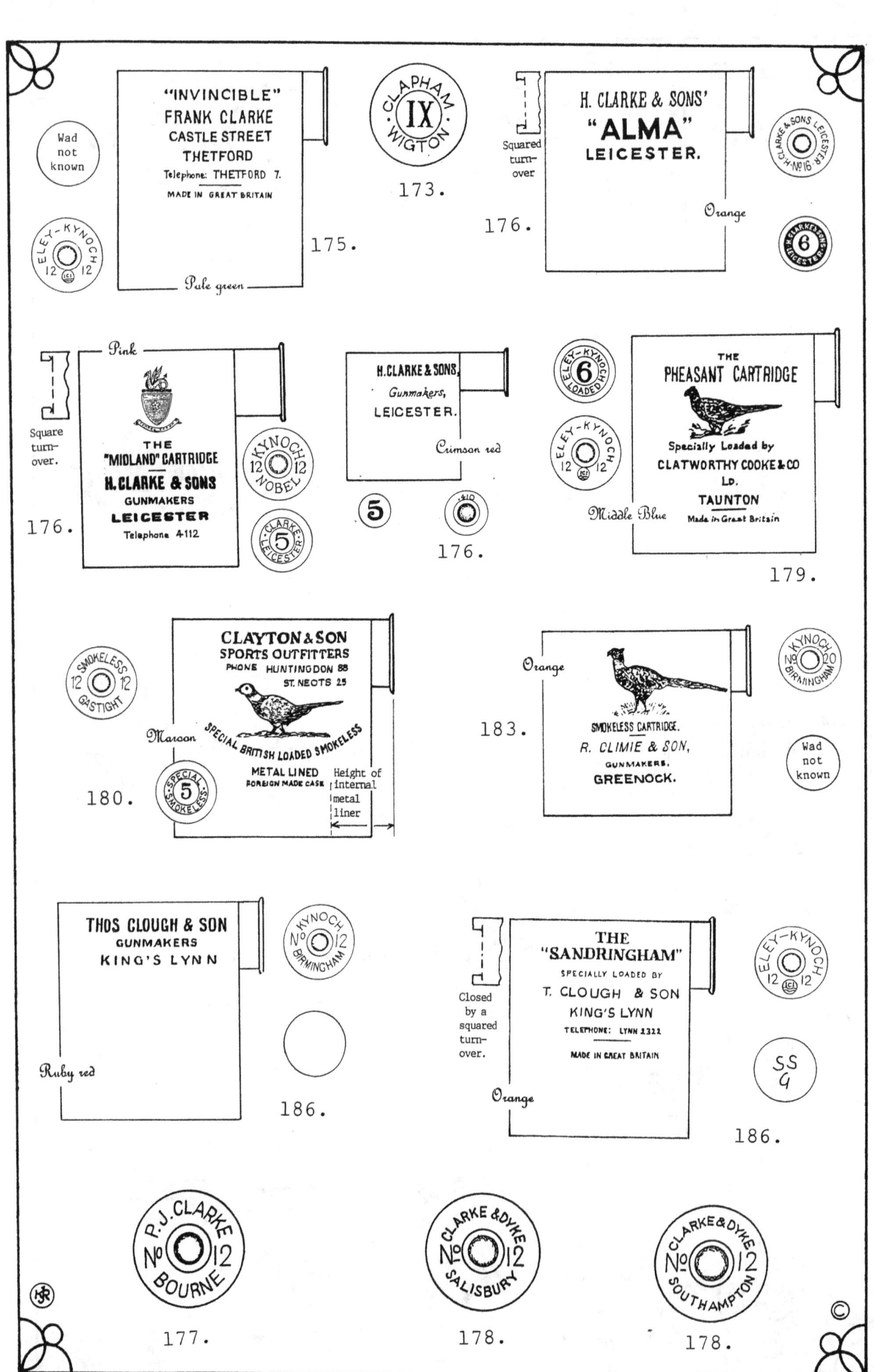

PLATE C6

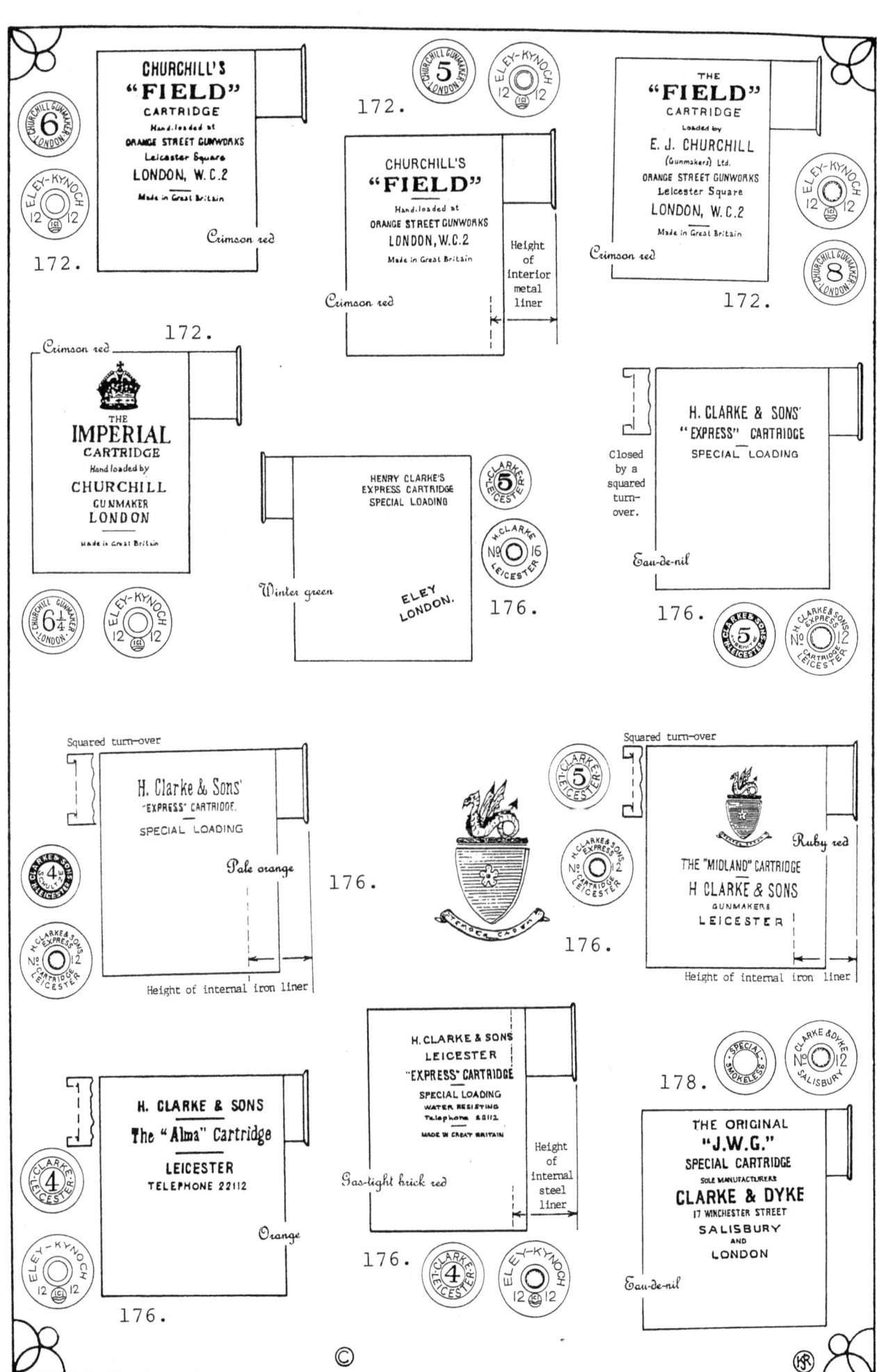

PLATE C7

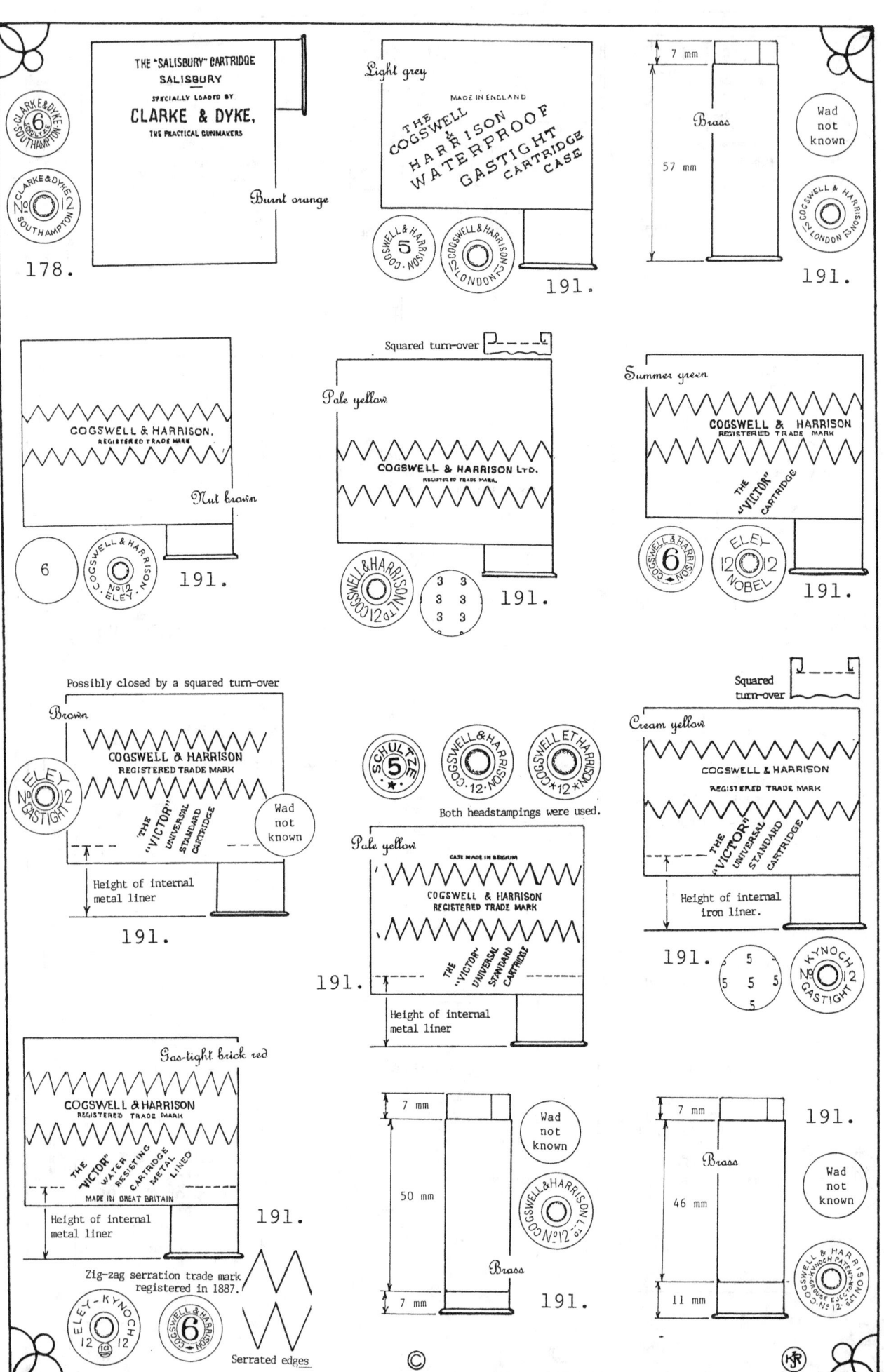

PLATE C8

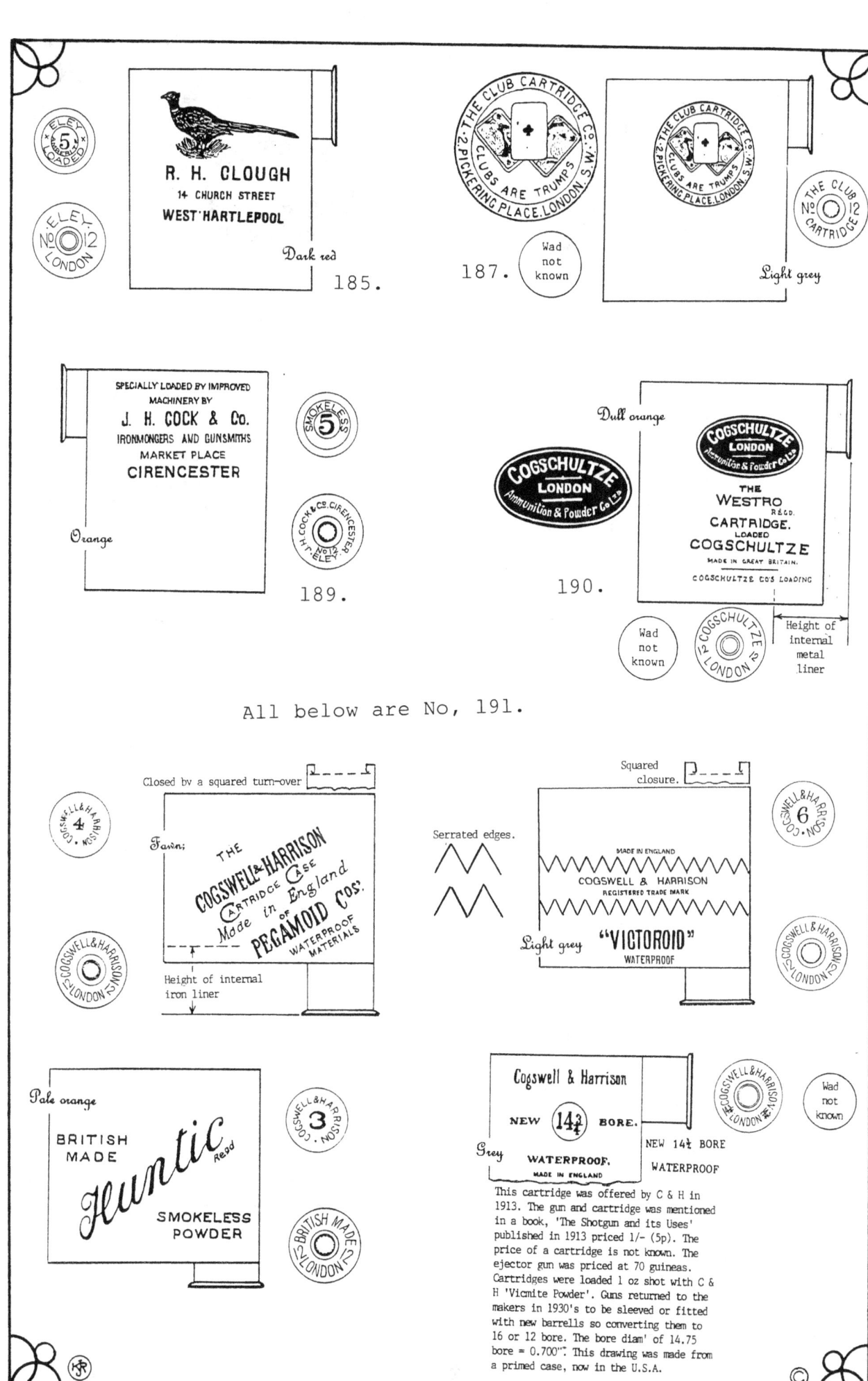

PLATE C9

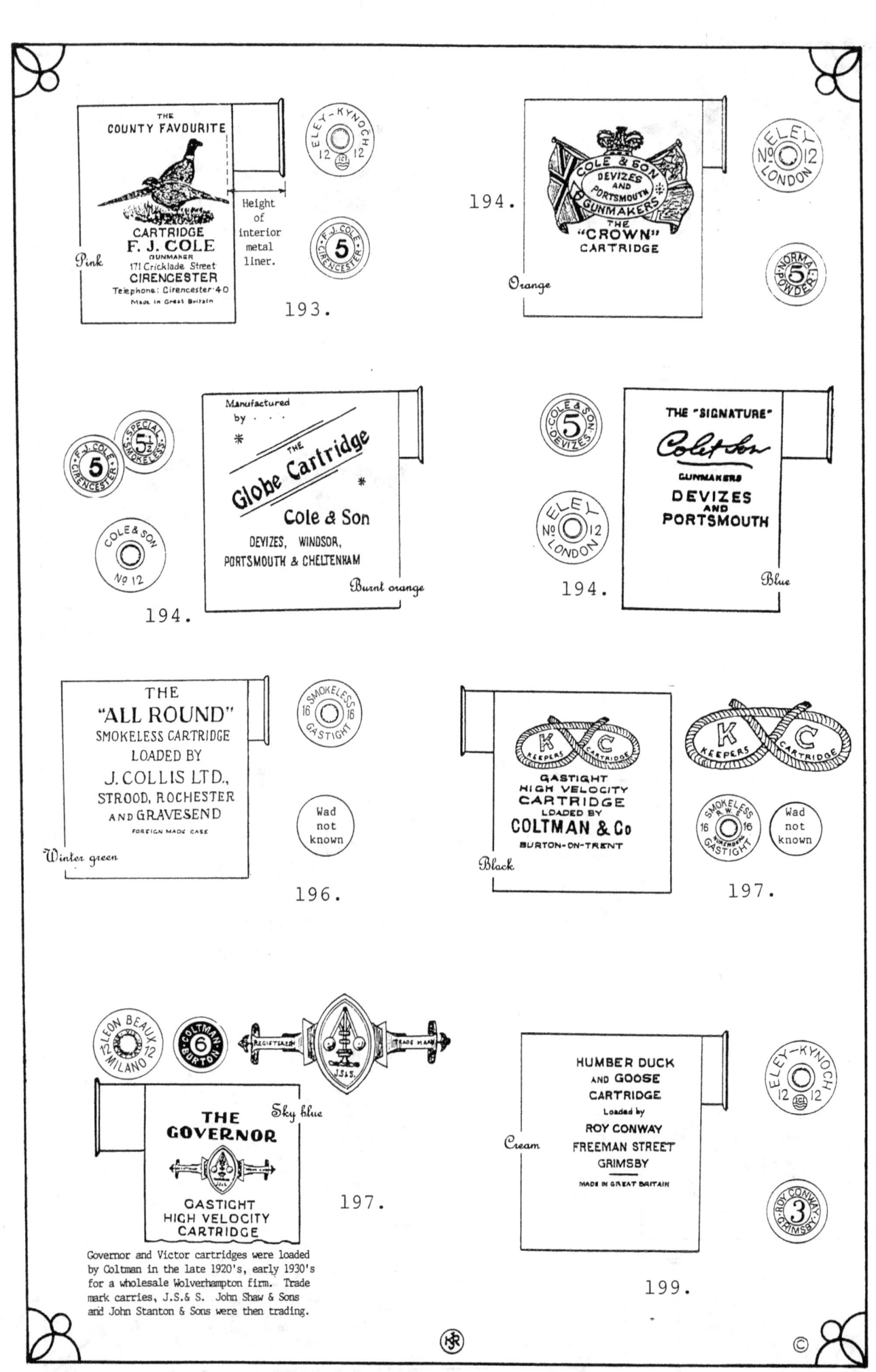

PLATE D1

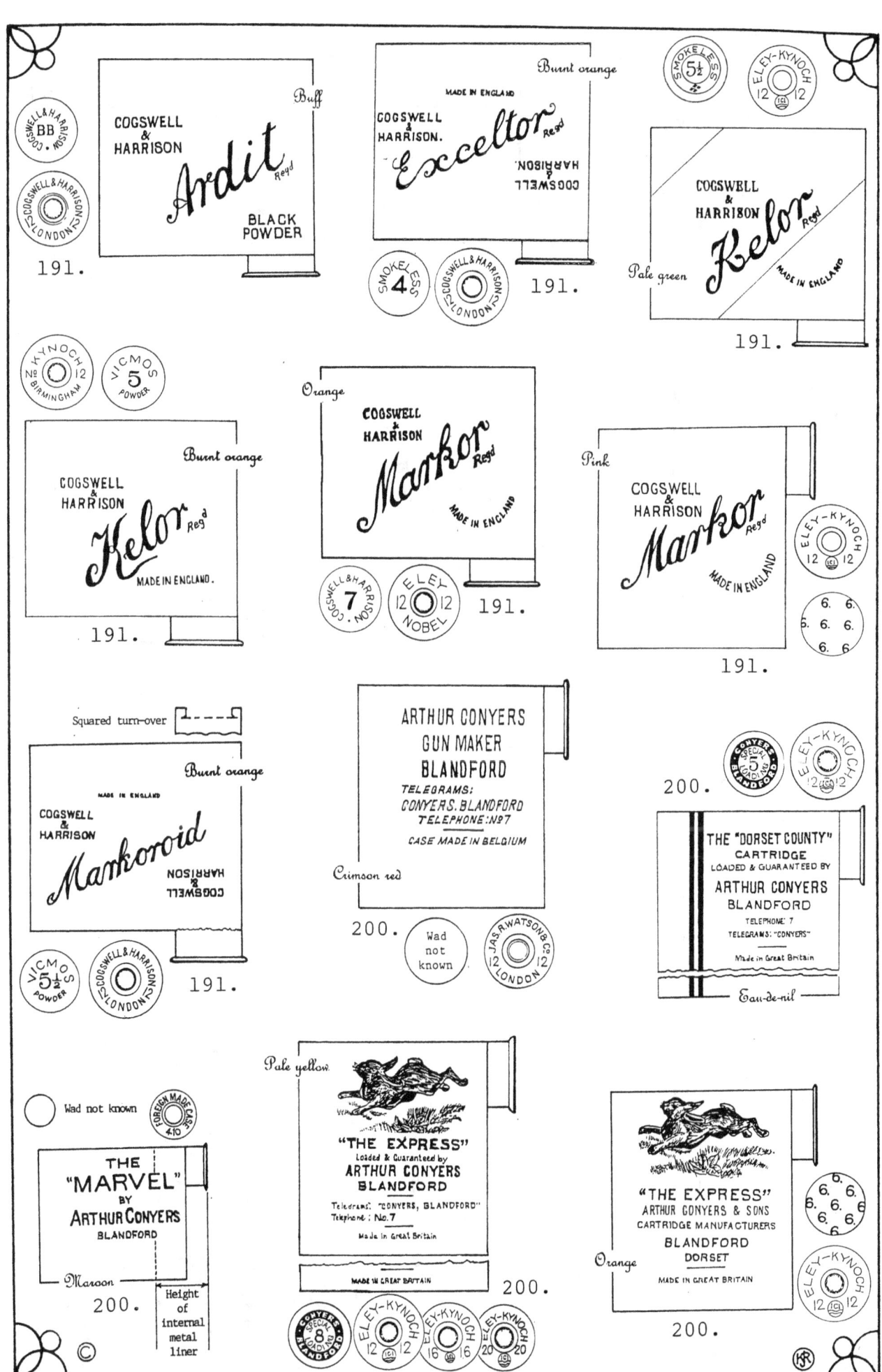

PLATE D2

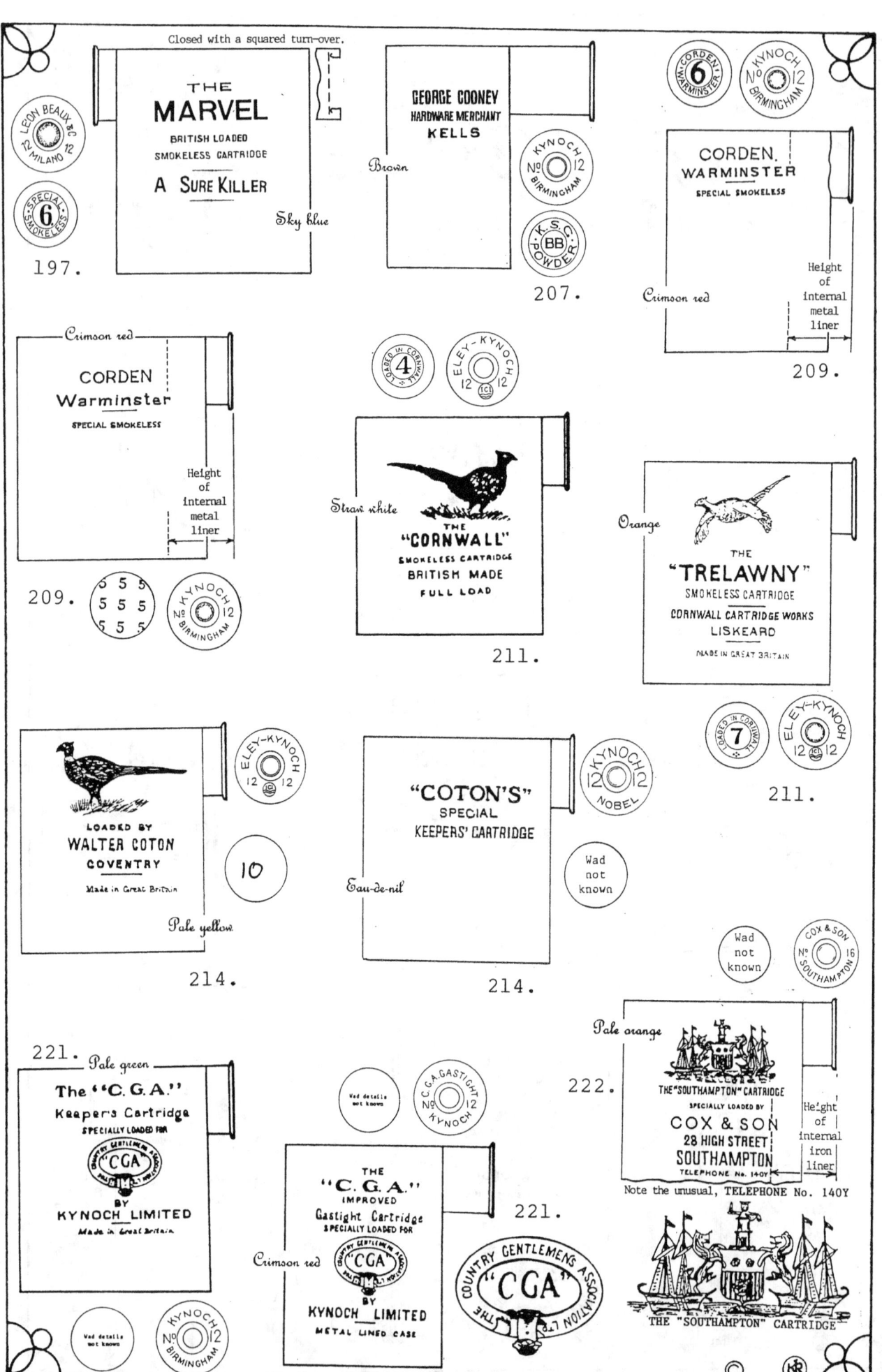

PLATE D3

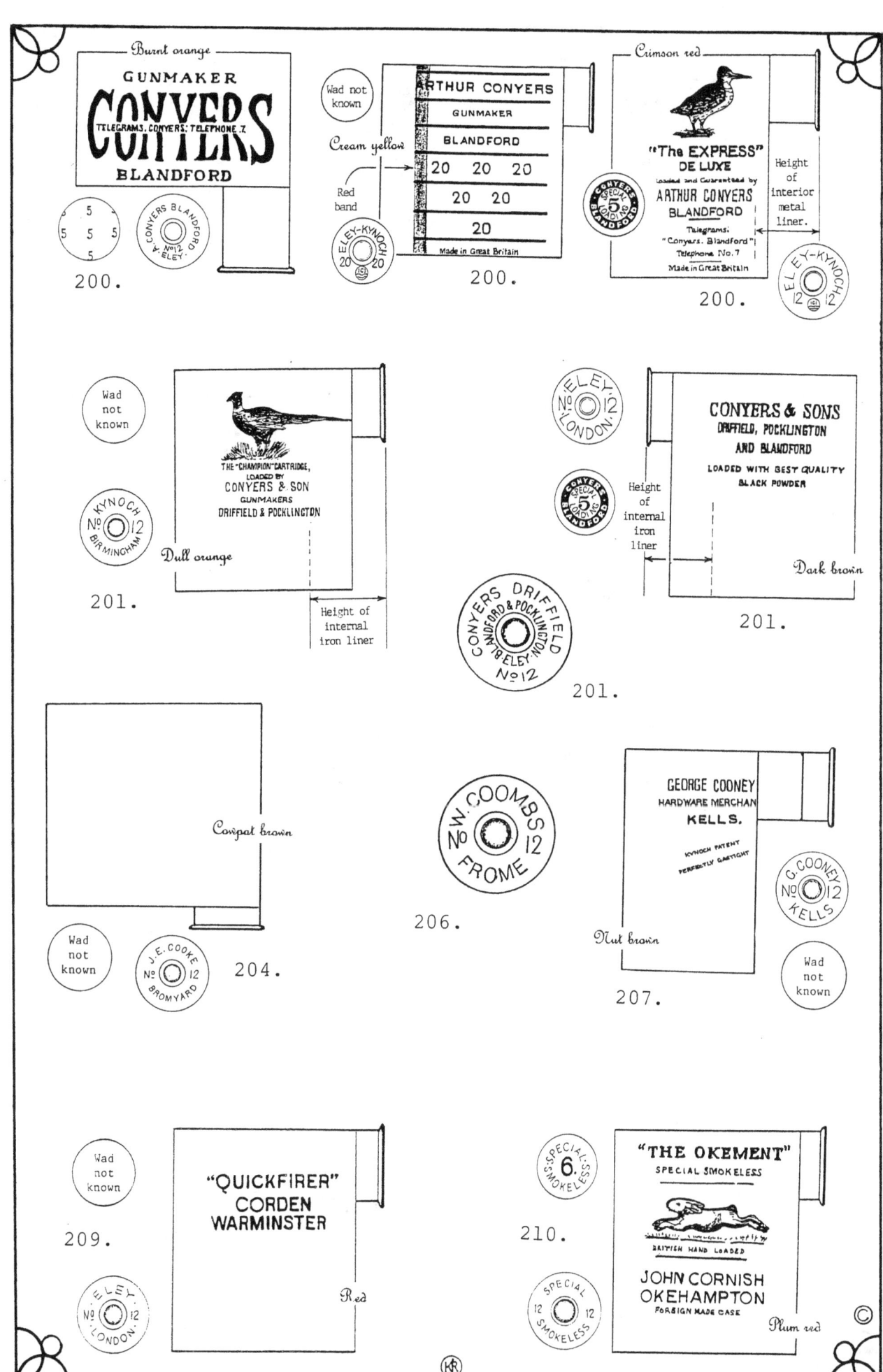

PLATE D4

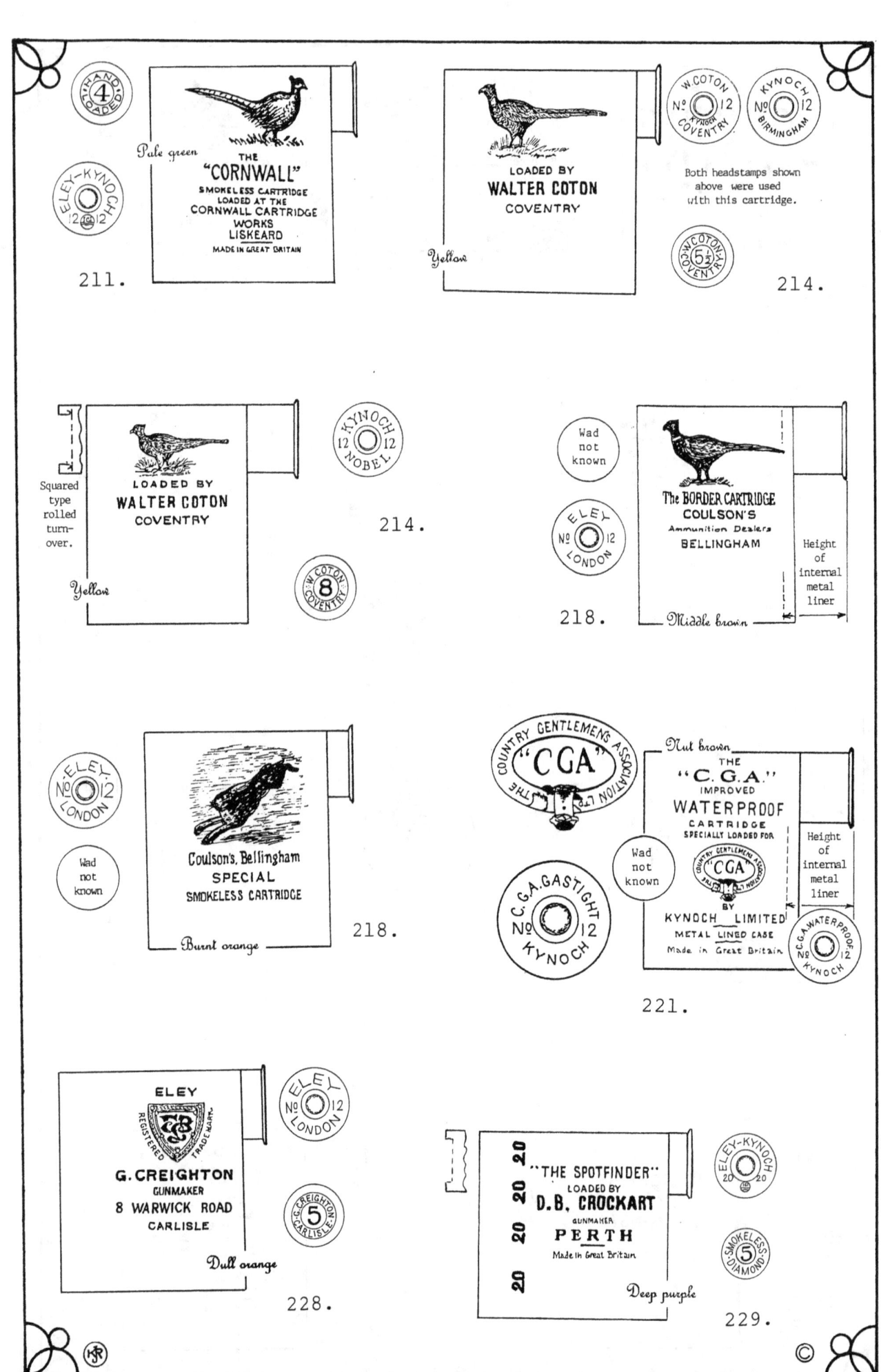

PLATE D5

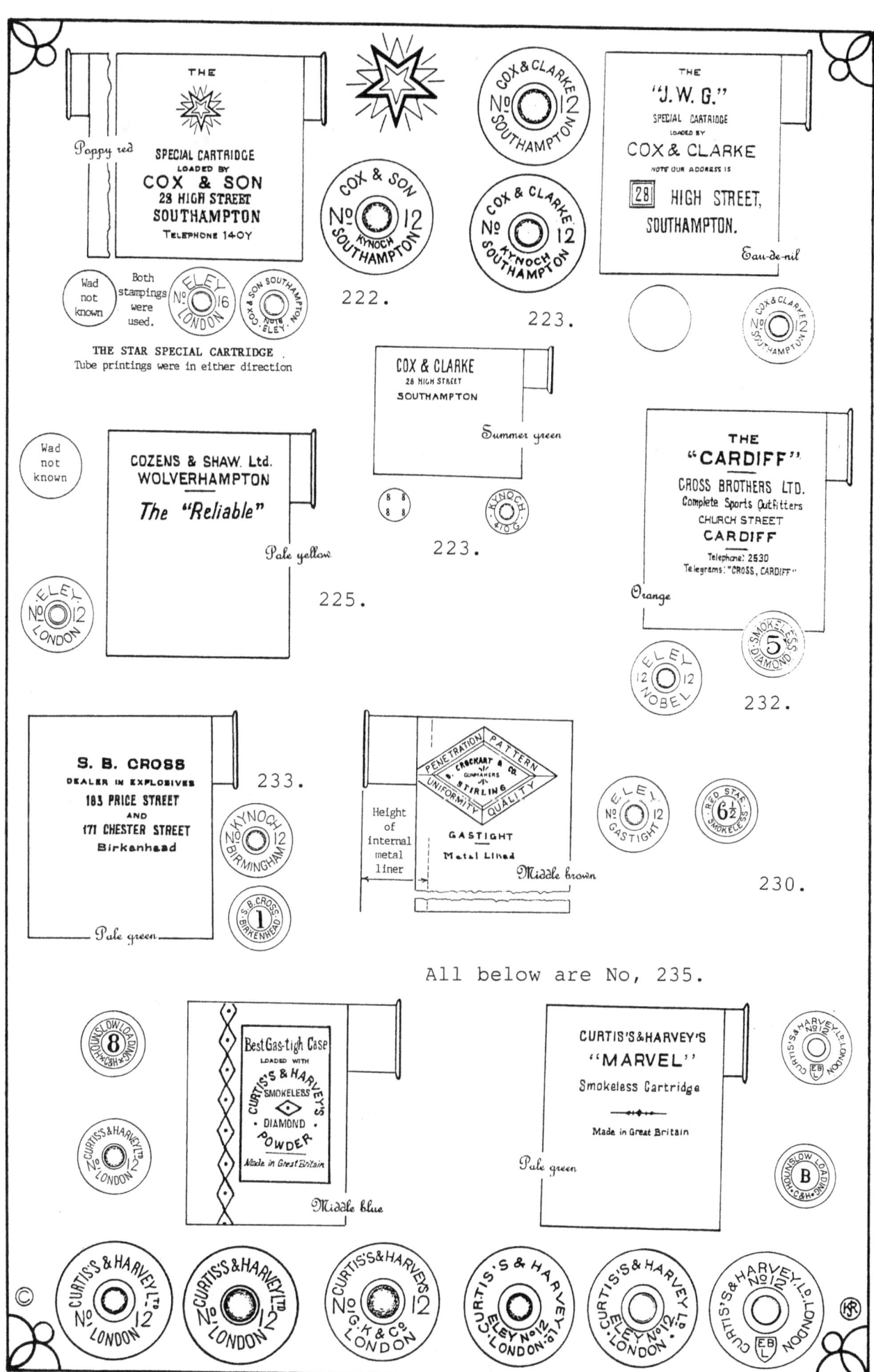

PLATE D6

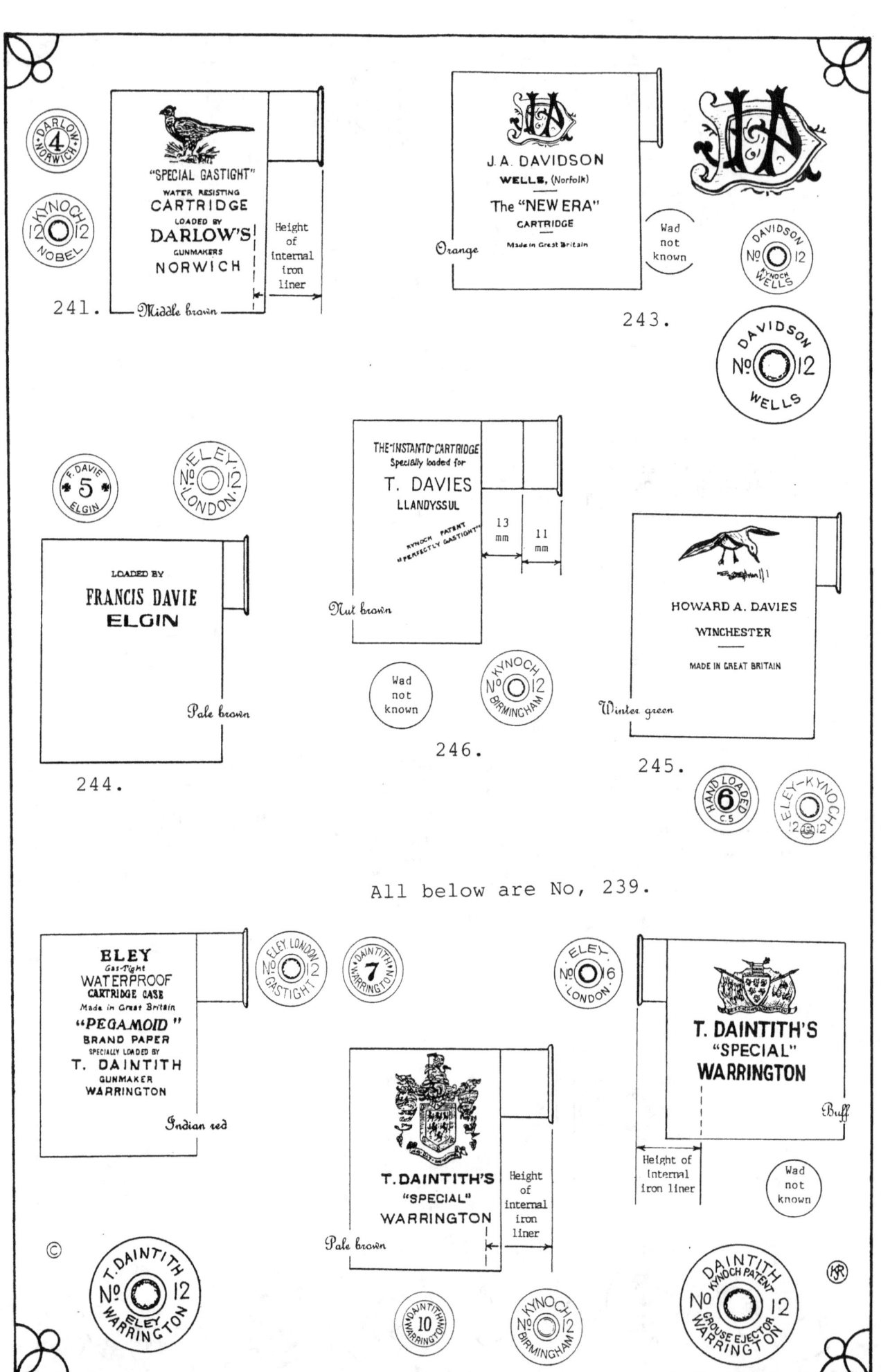

PLATE D7

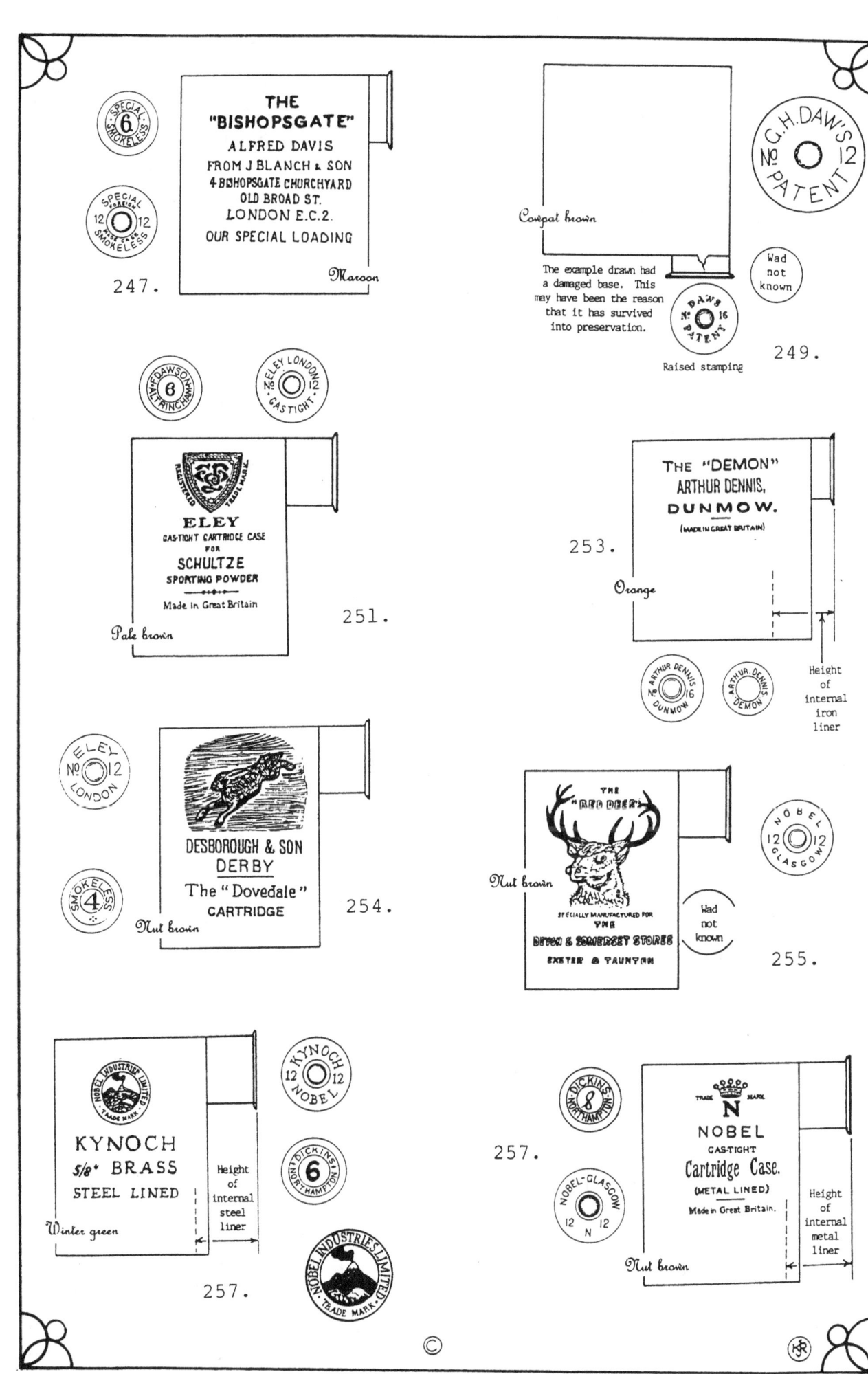

PLATE D8

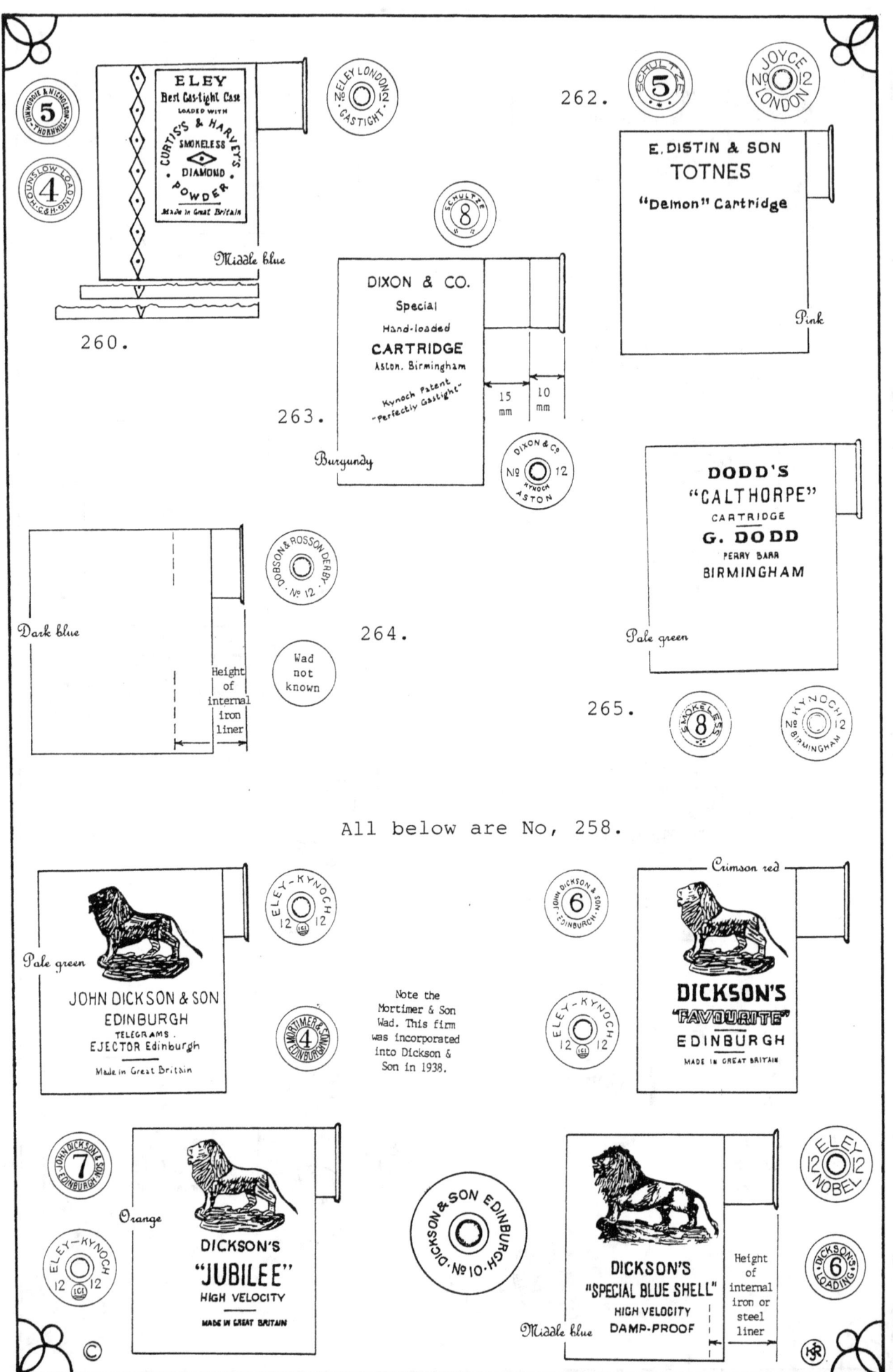

PLATE D9

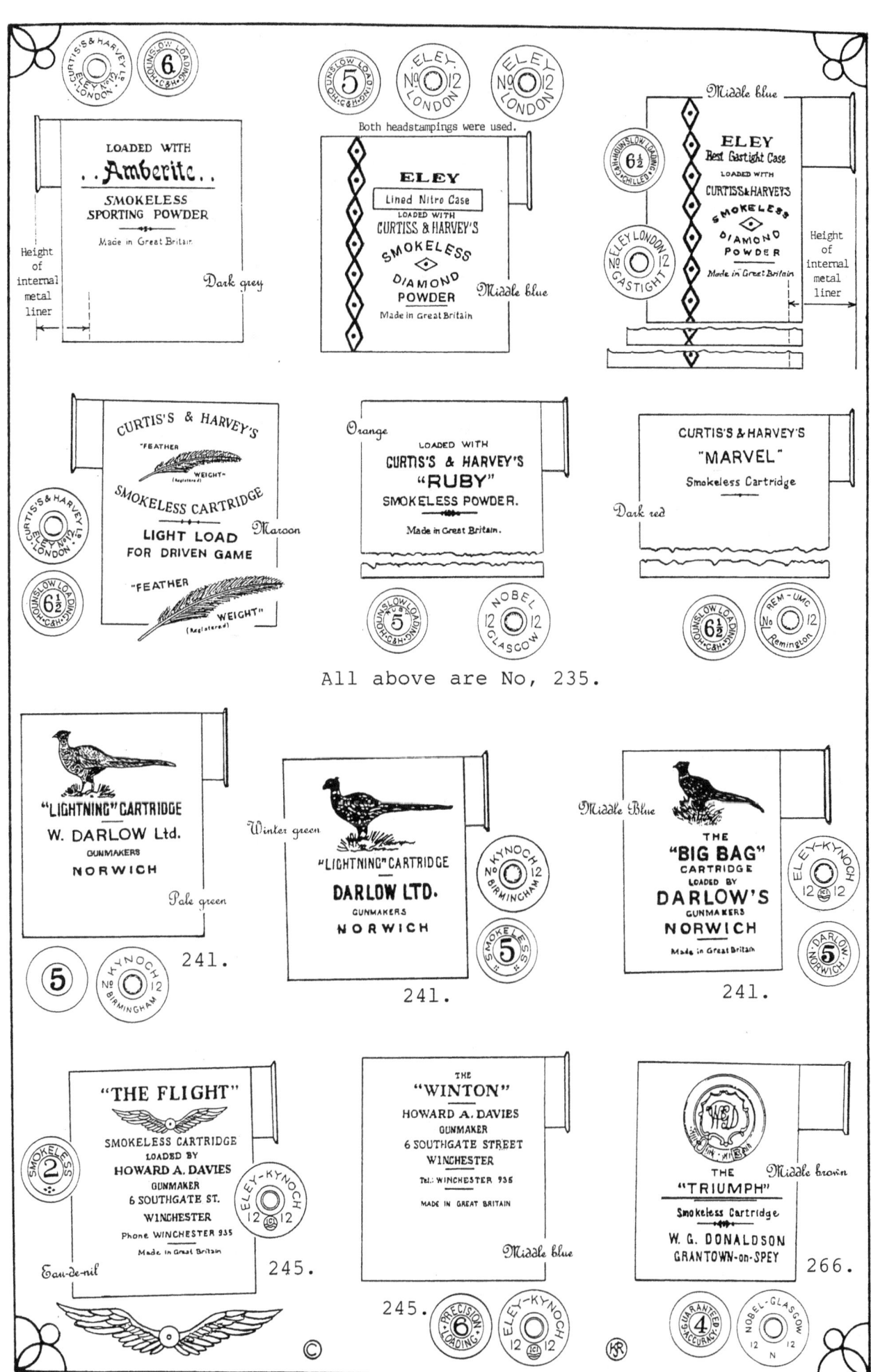

PLATE E1

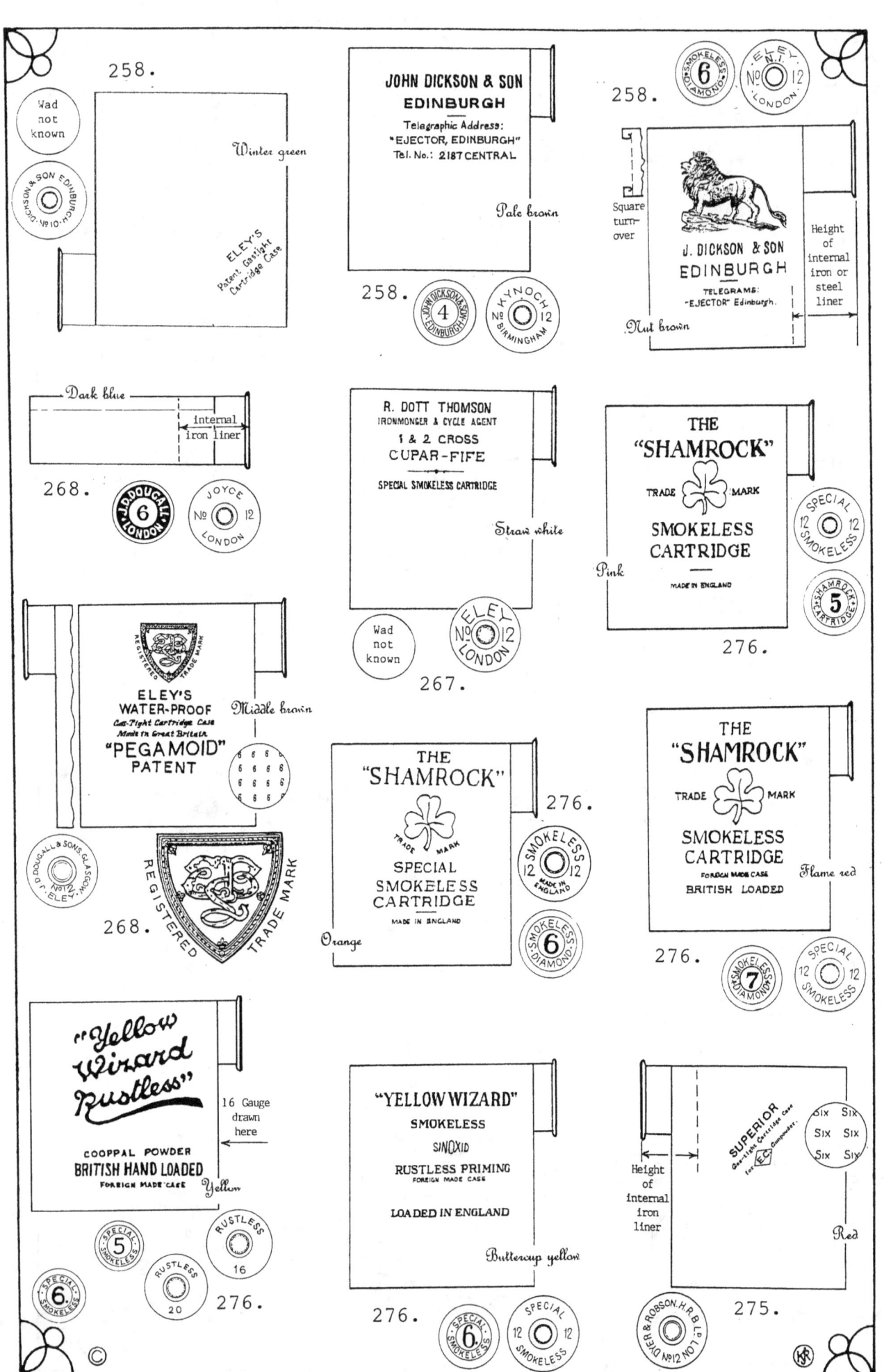

PLATE E2

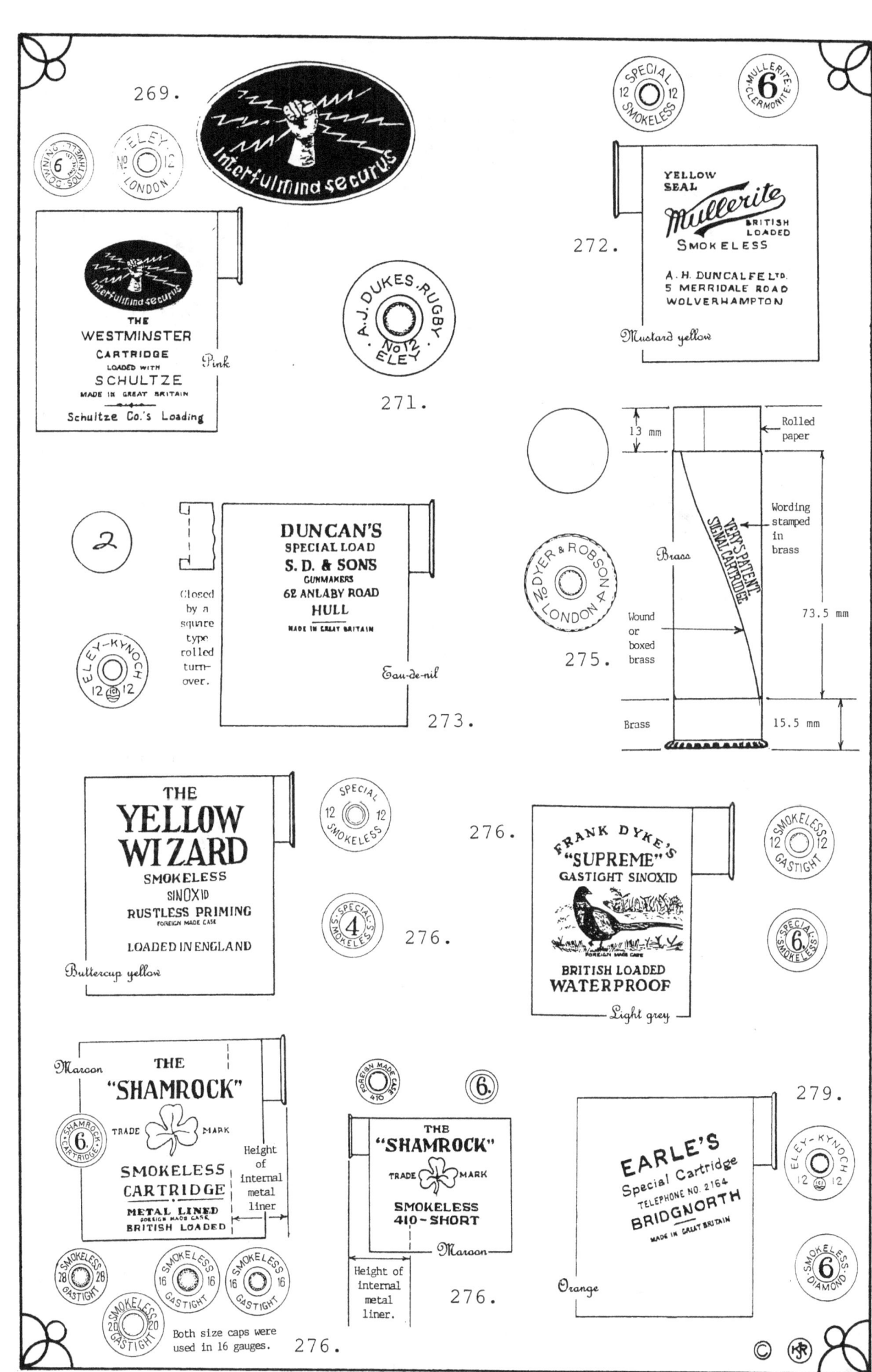

PLATE E3

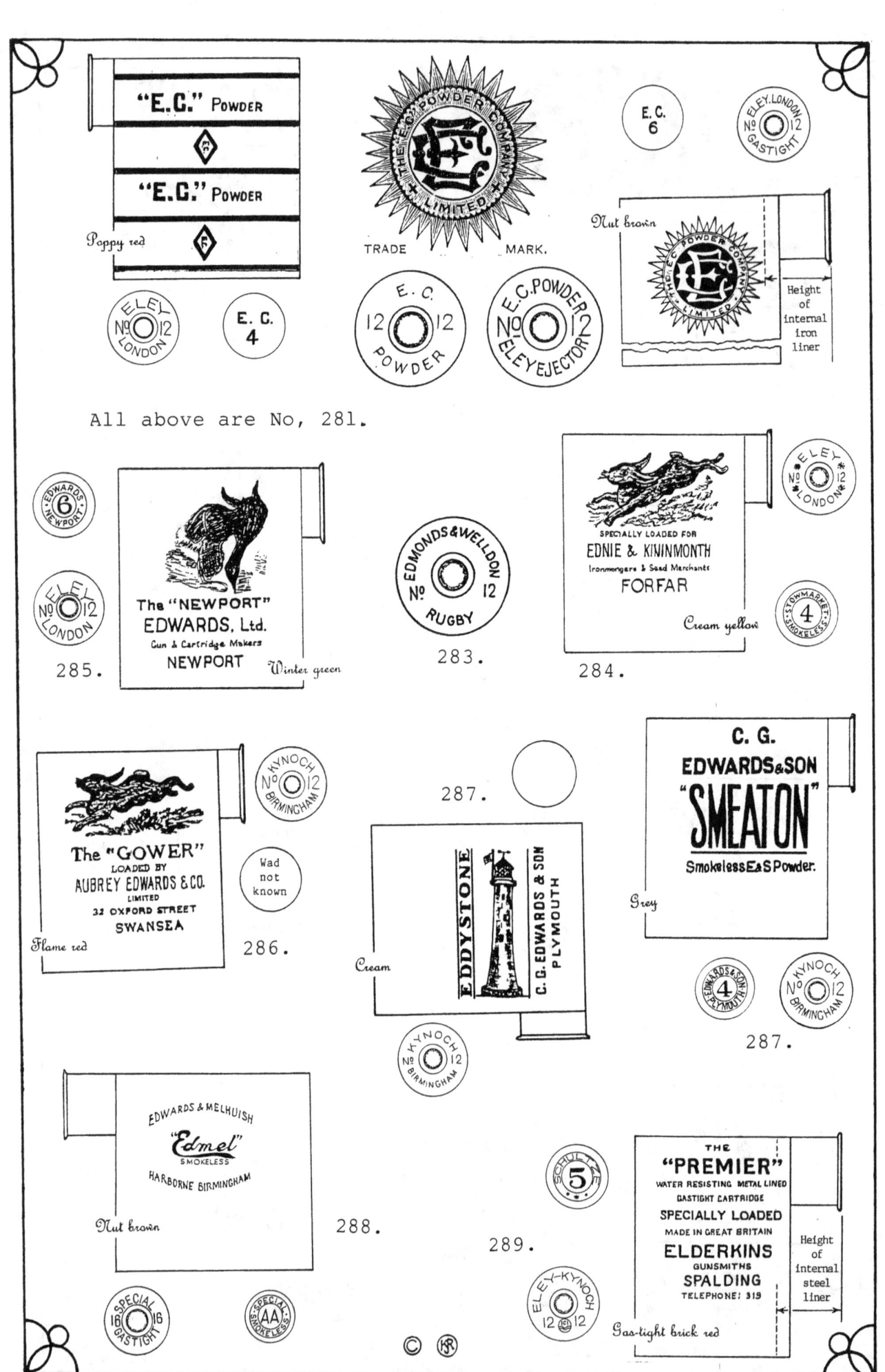

PLATE E4

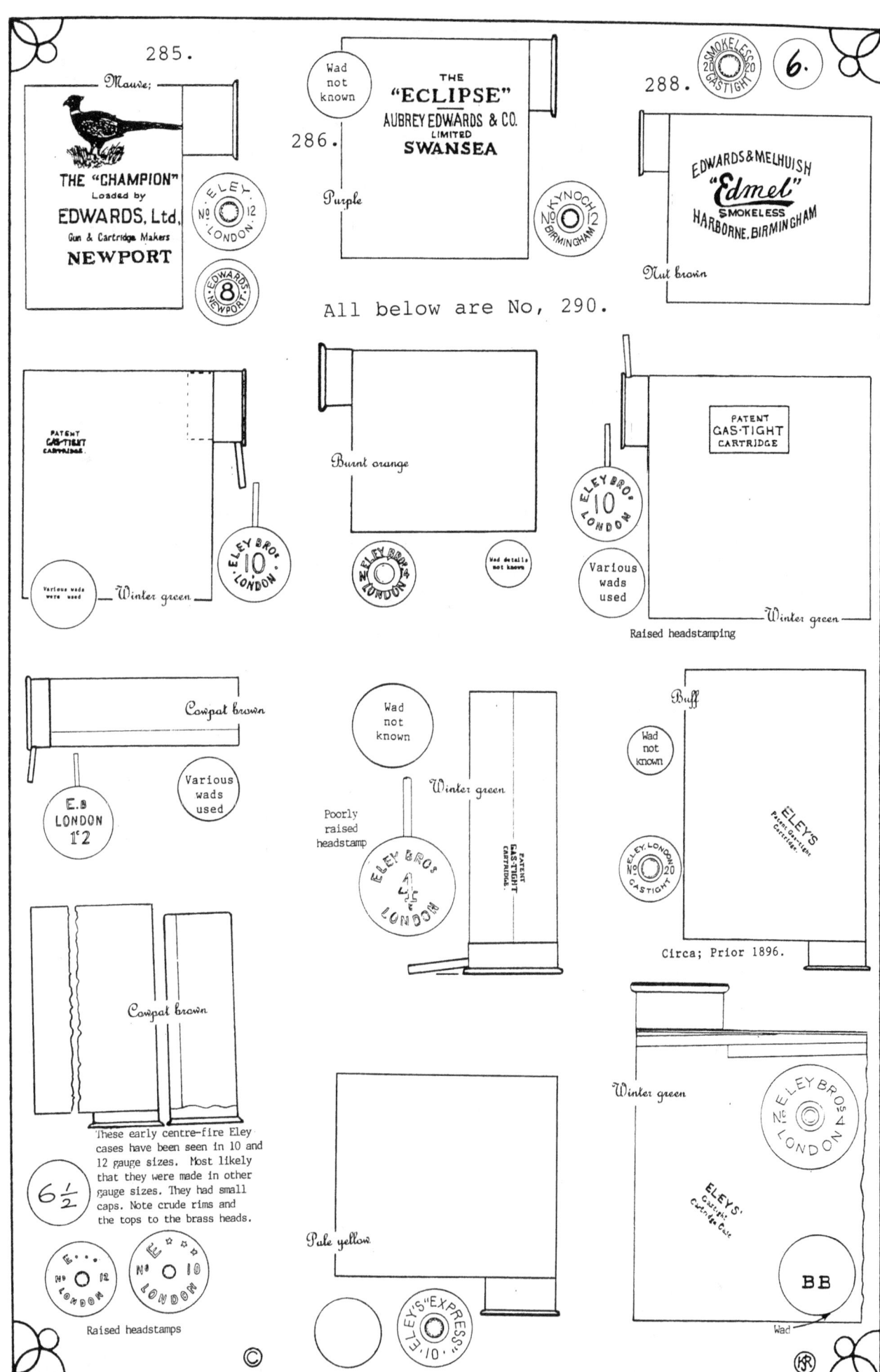

PLATE E5

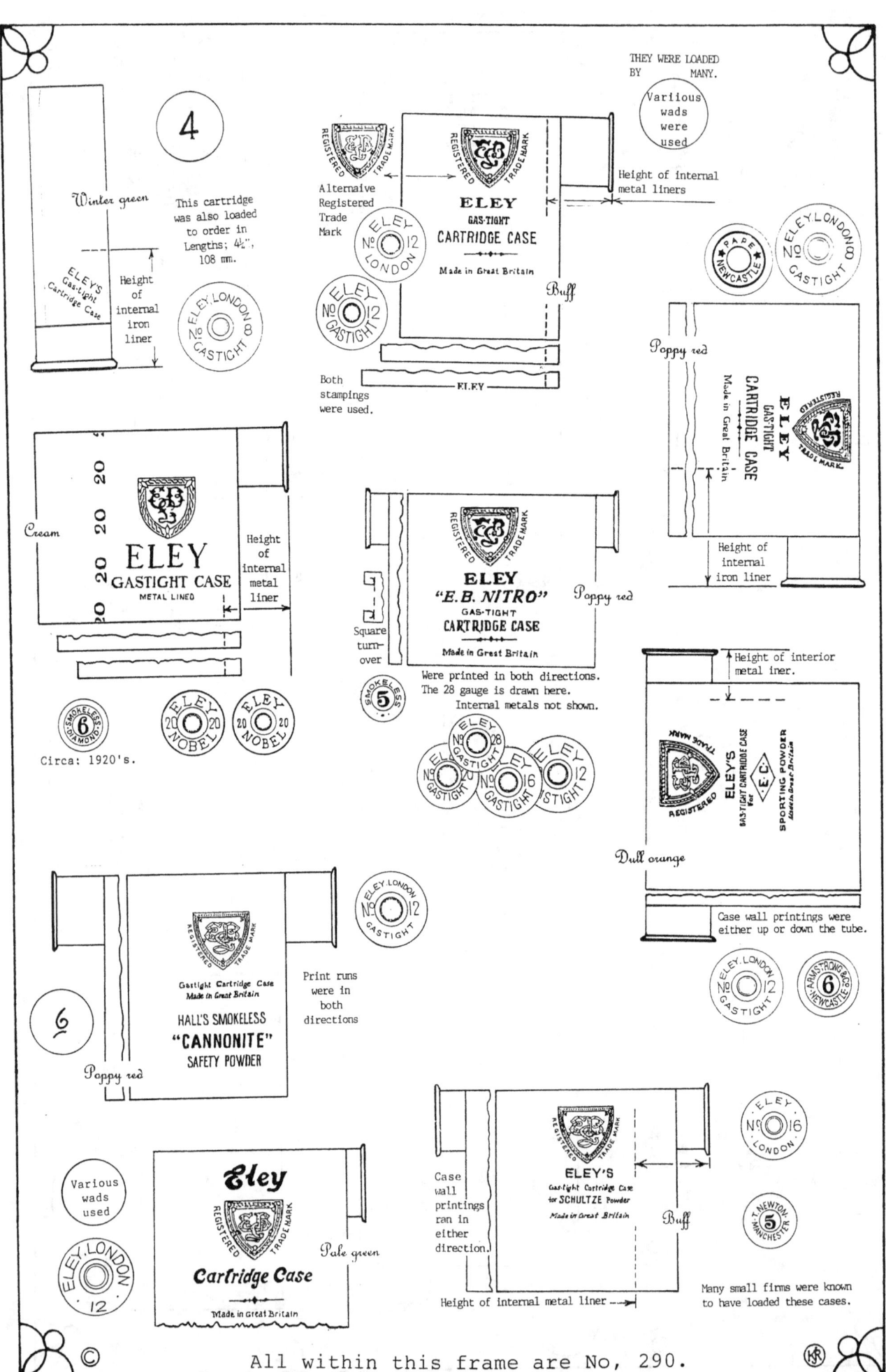

PLATE E6

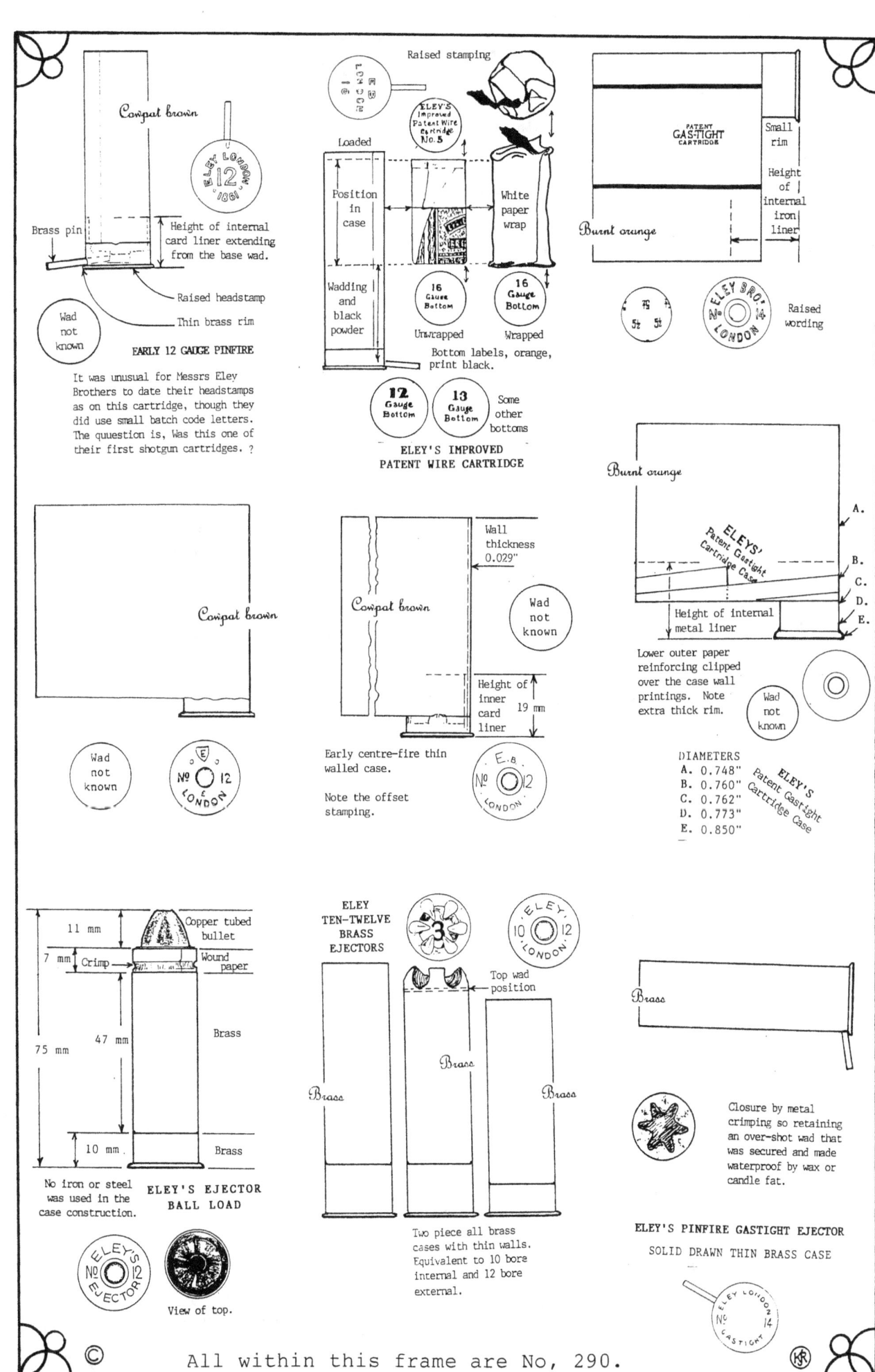

PLATE E7

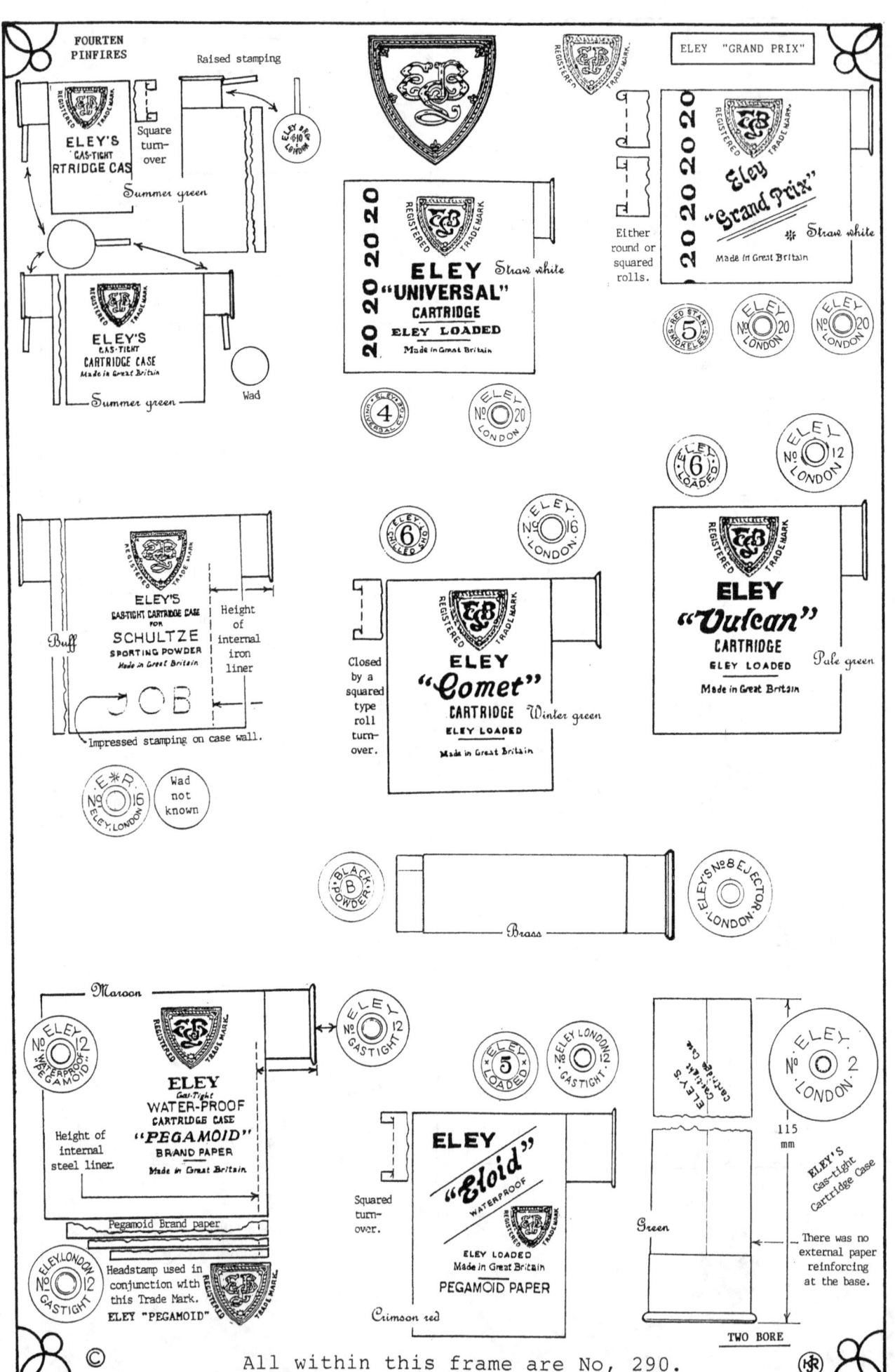

PLATE E8

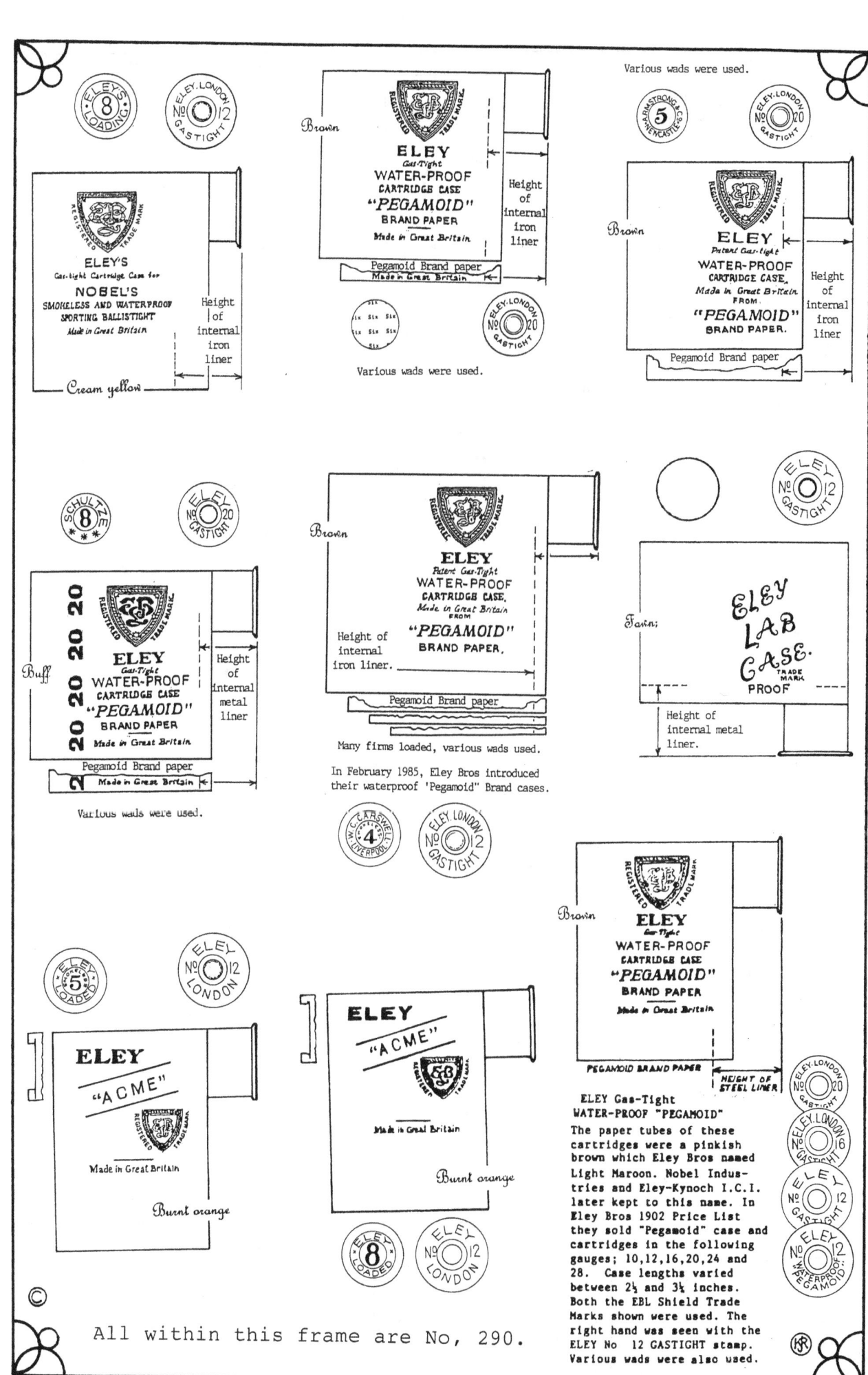

PLATE E9

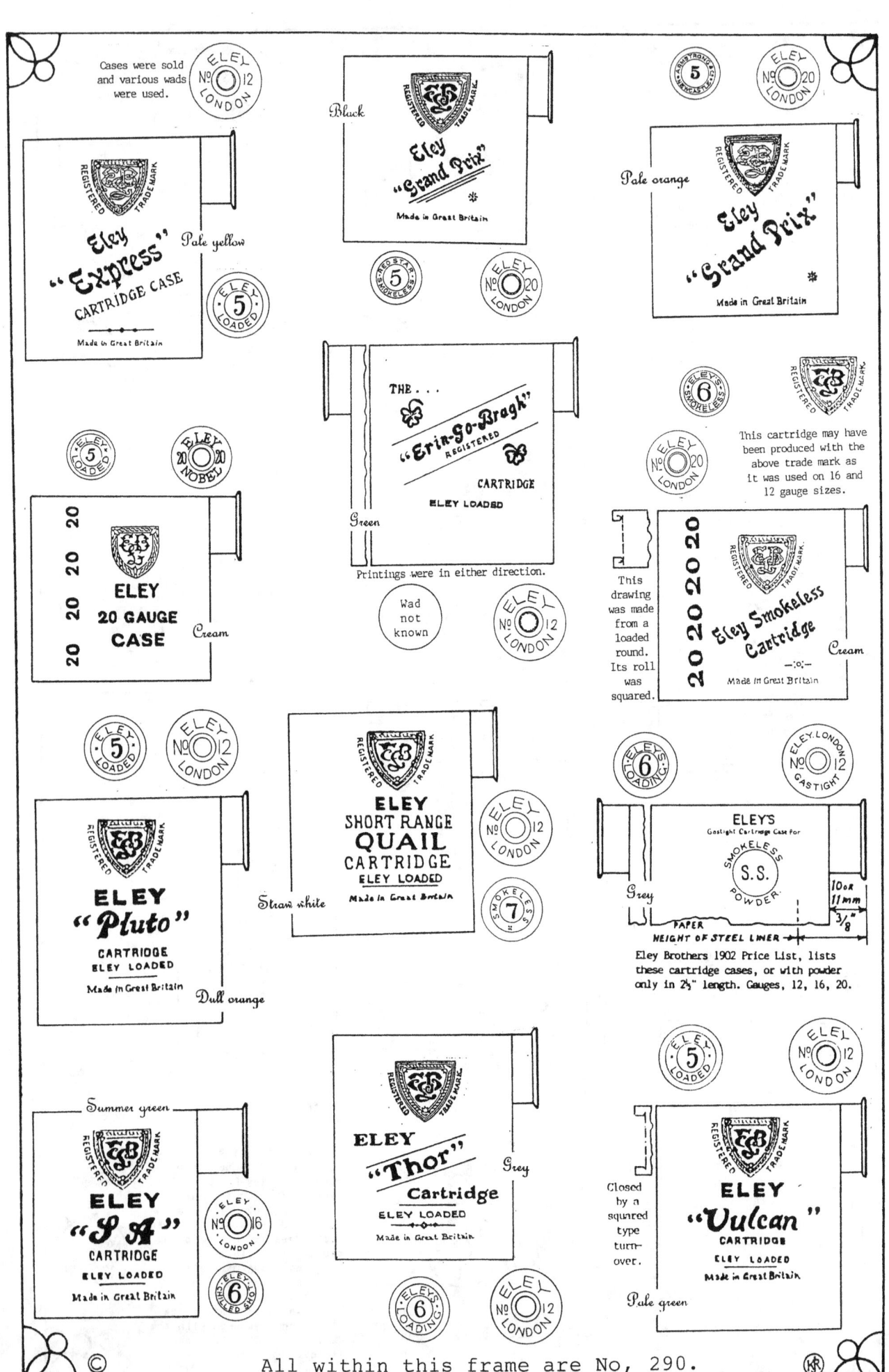

PLATE F1

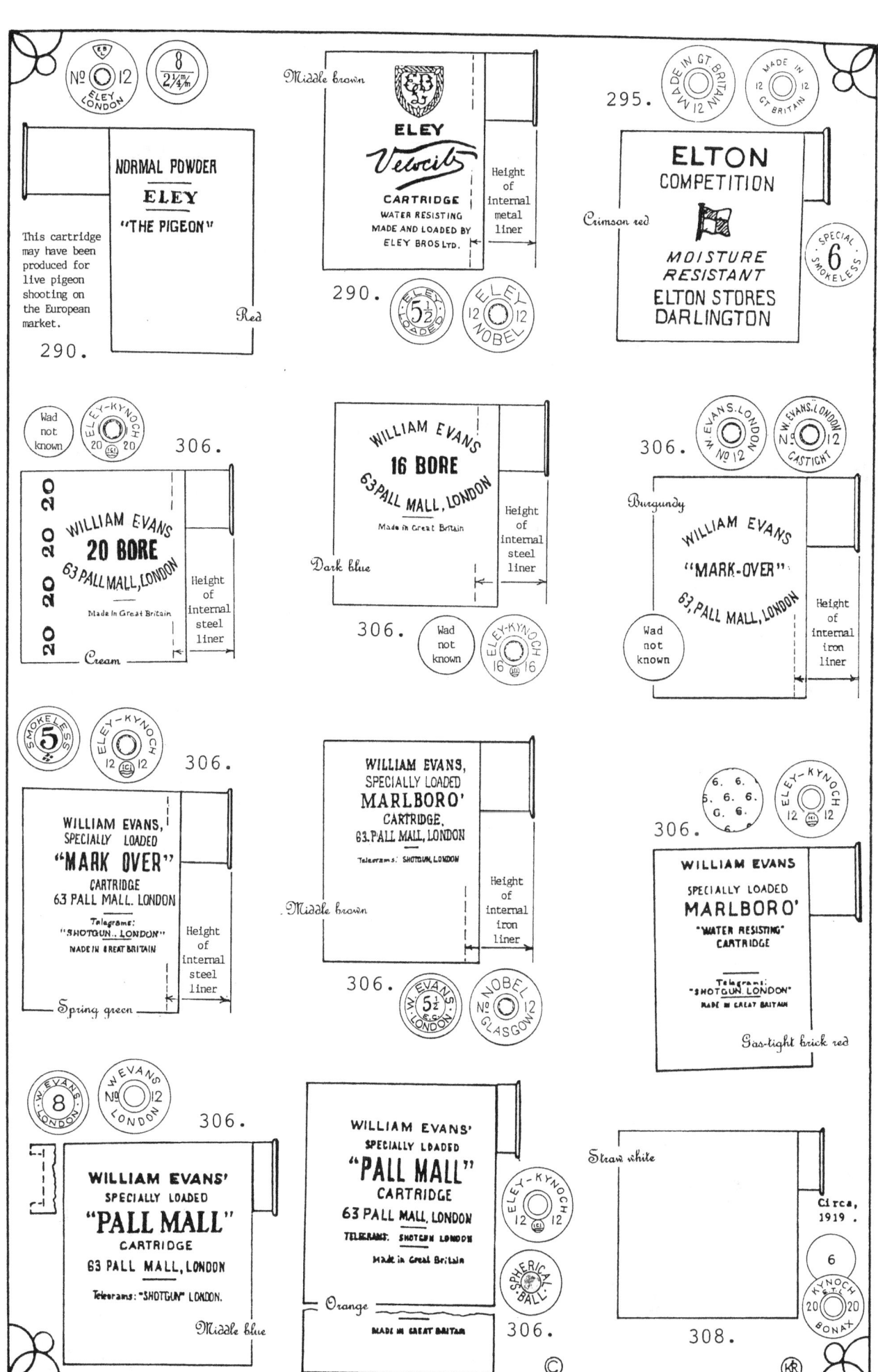

PLATE F2

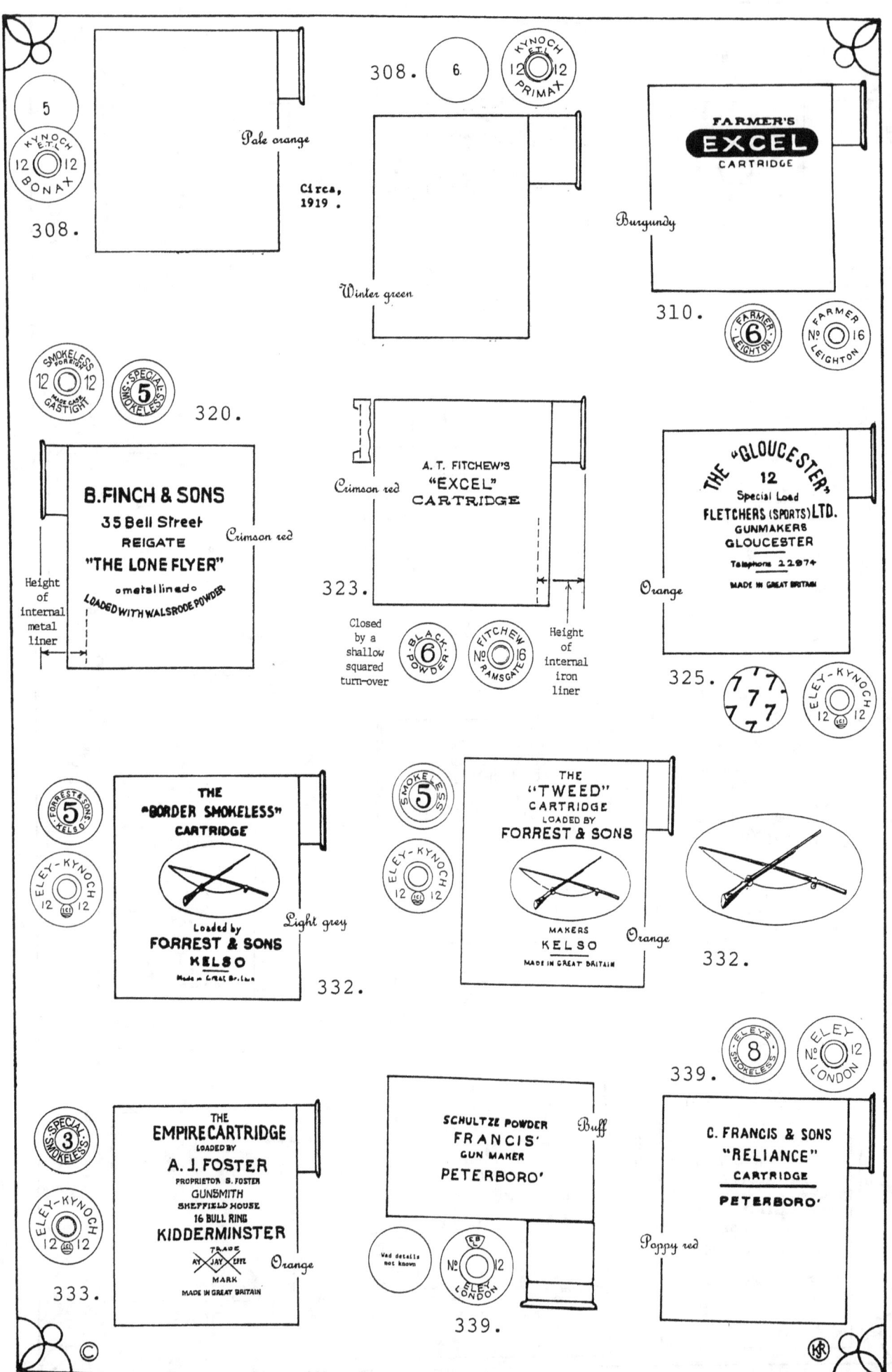

PLATE F3

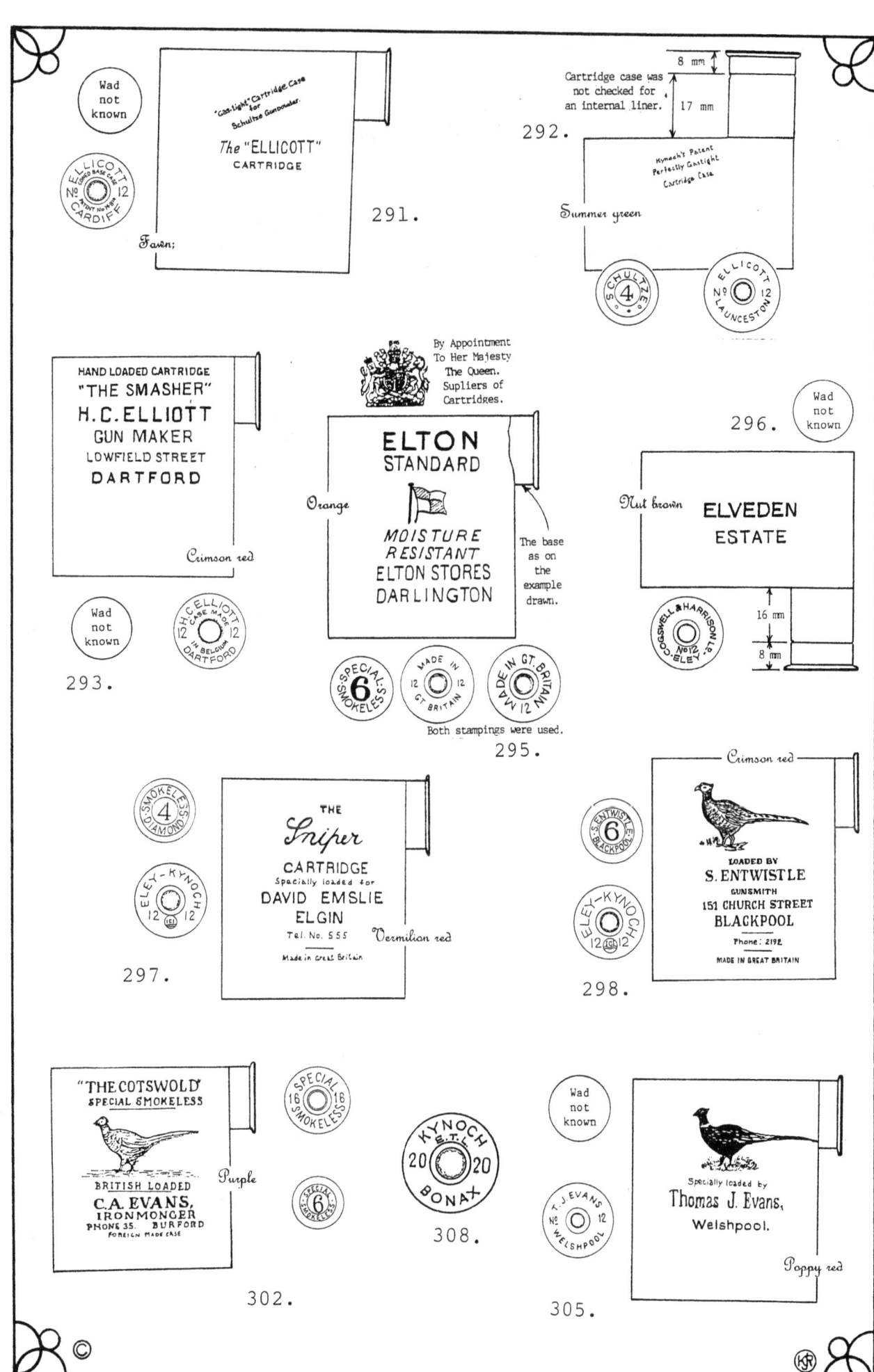

PLATE F4

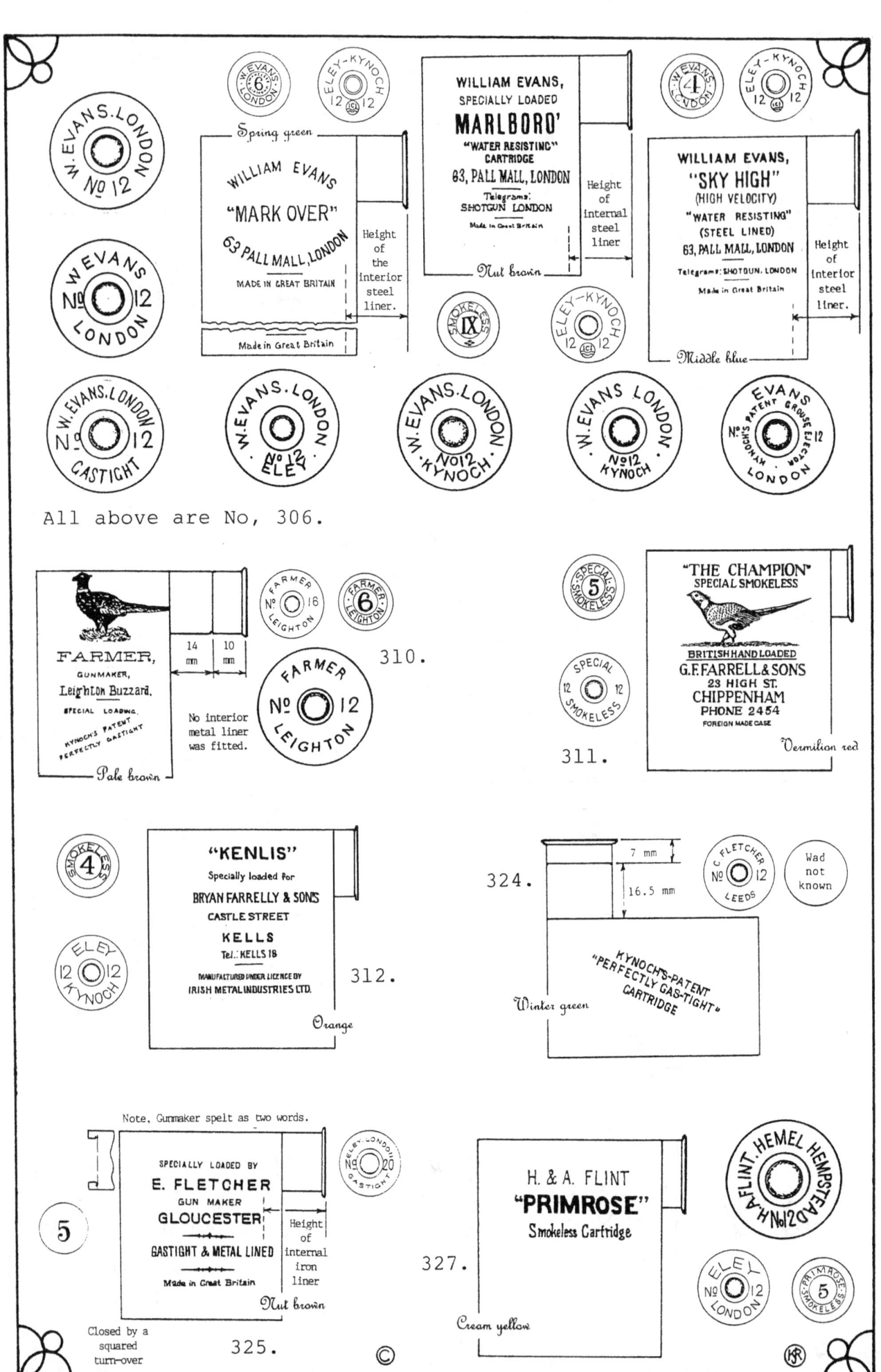

PLATE F5

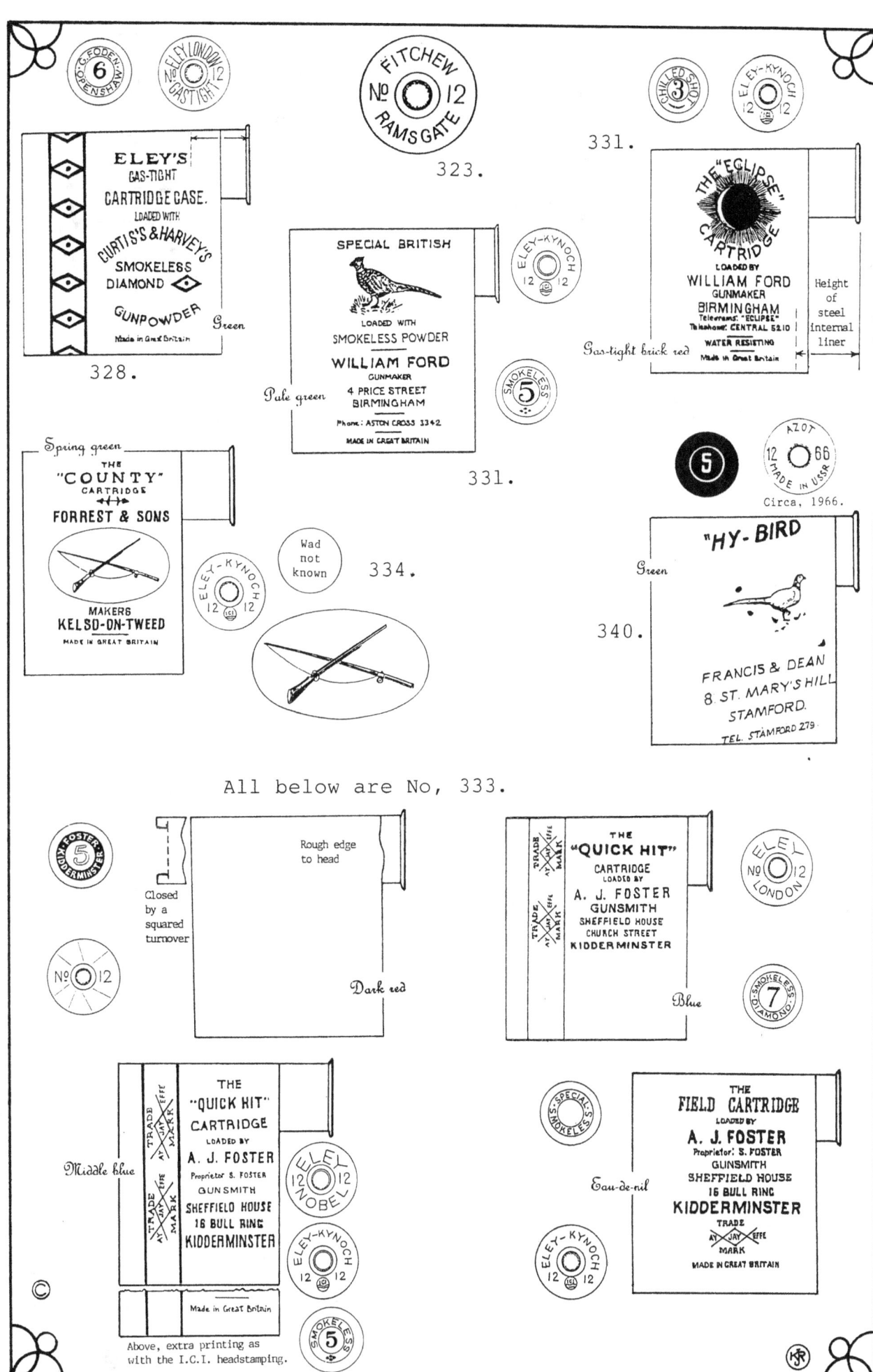

PLATE F6

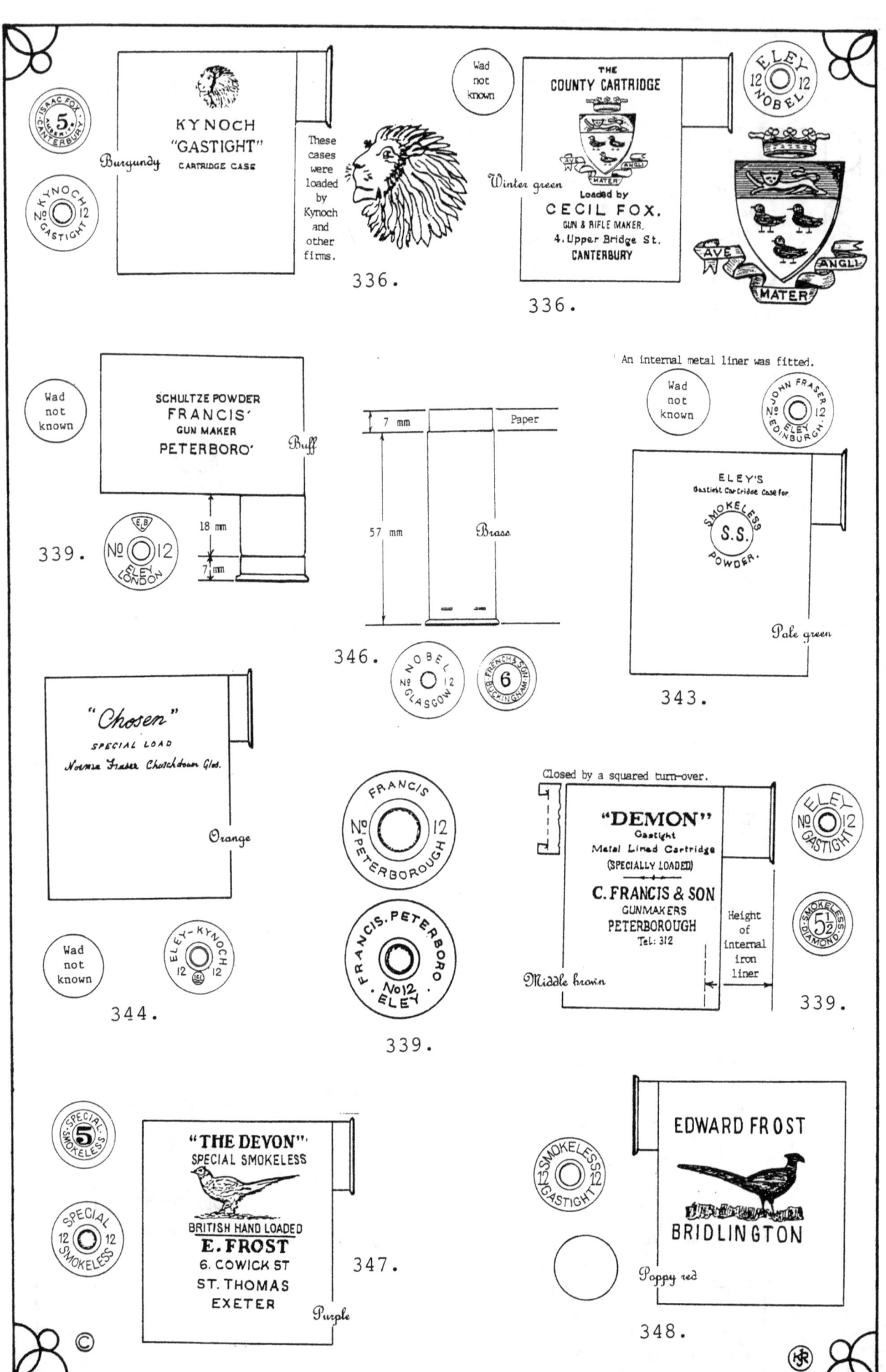

PLATE F7

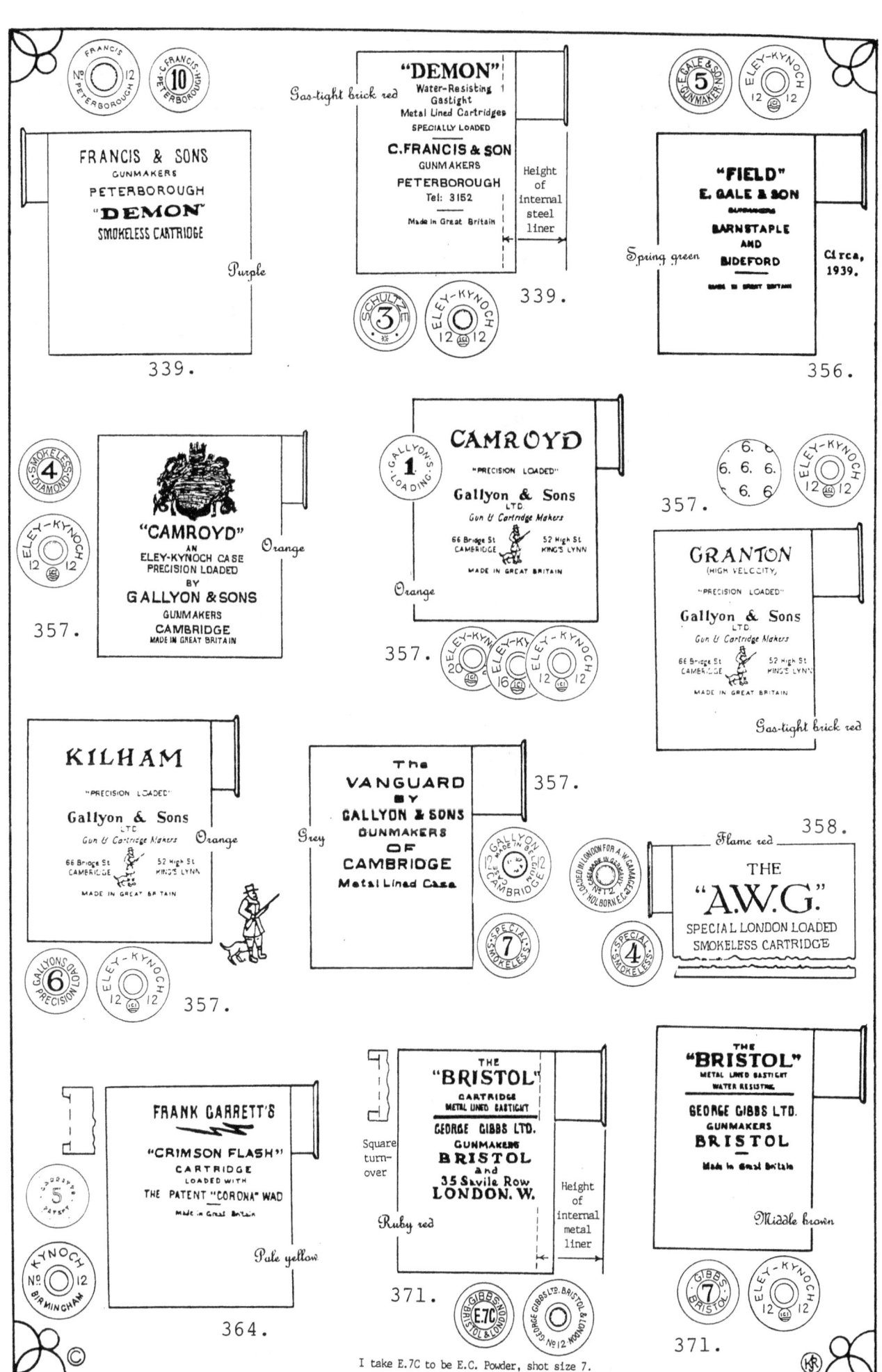

PLATE F8

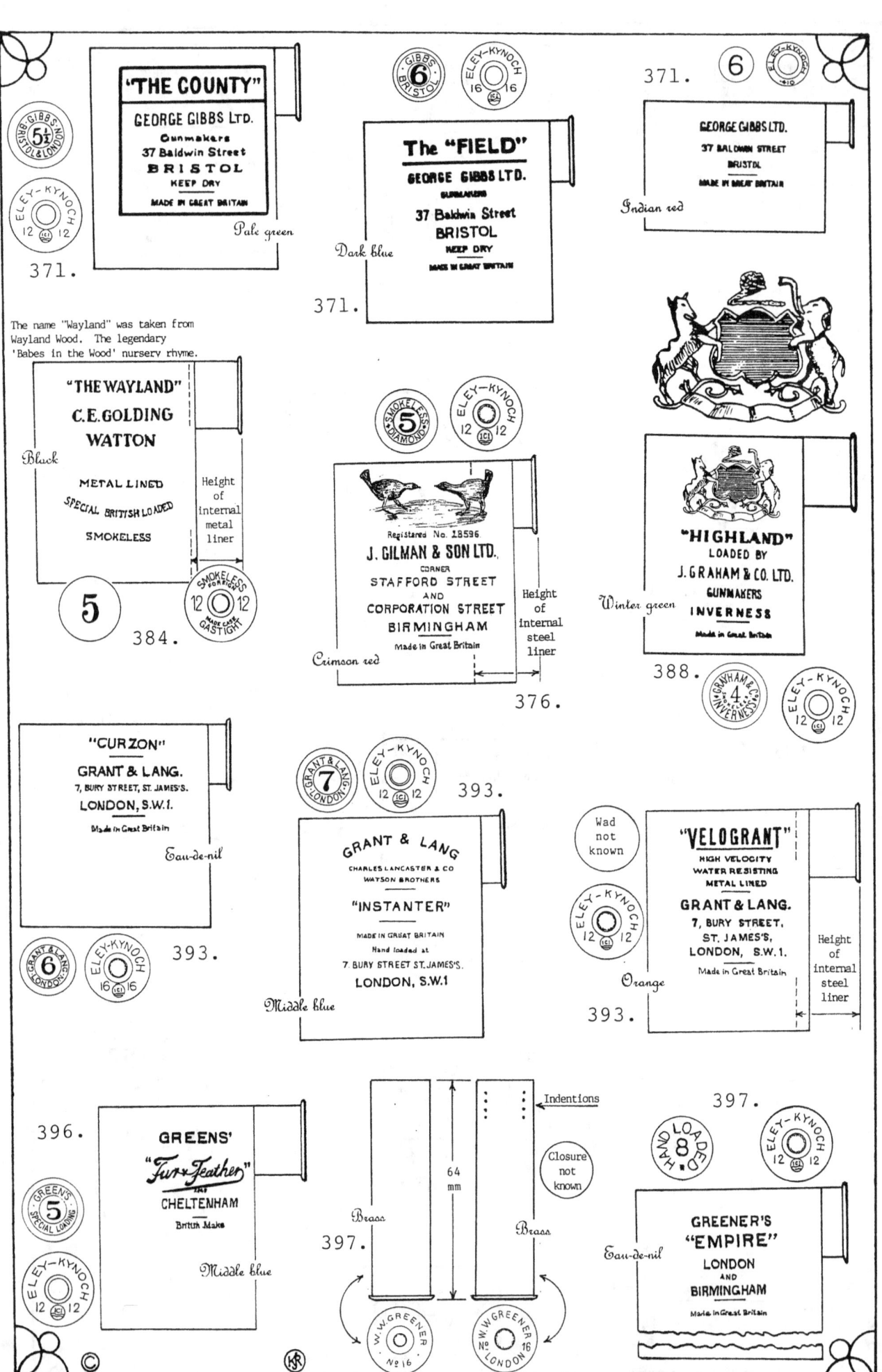

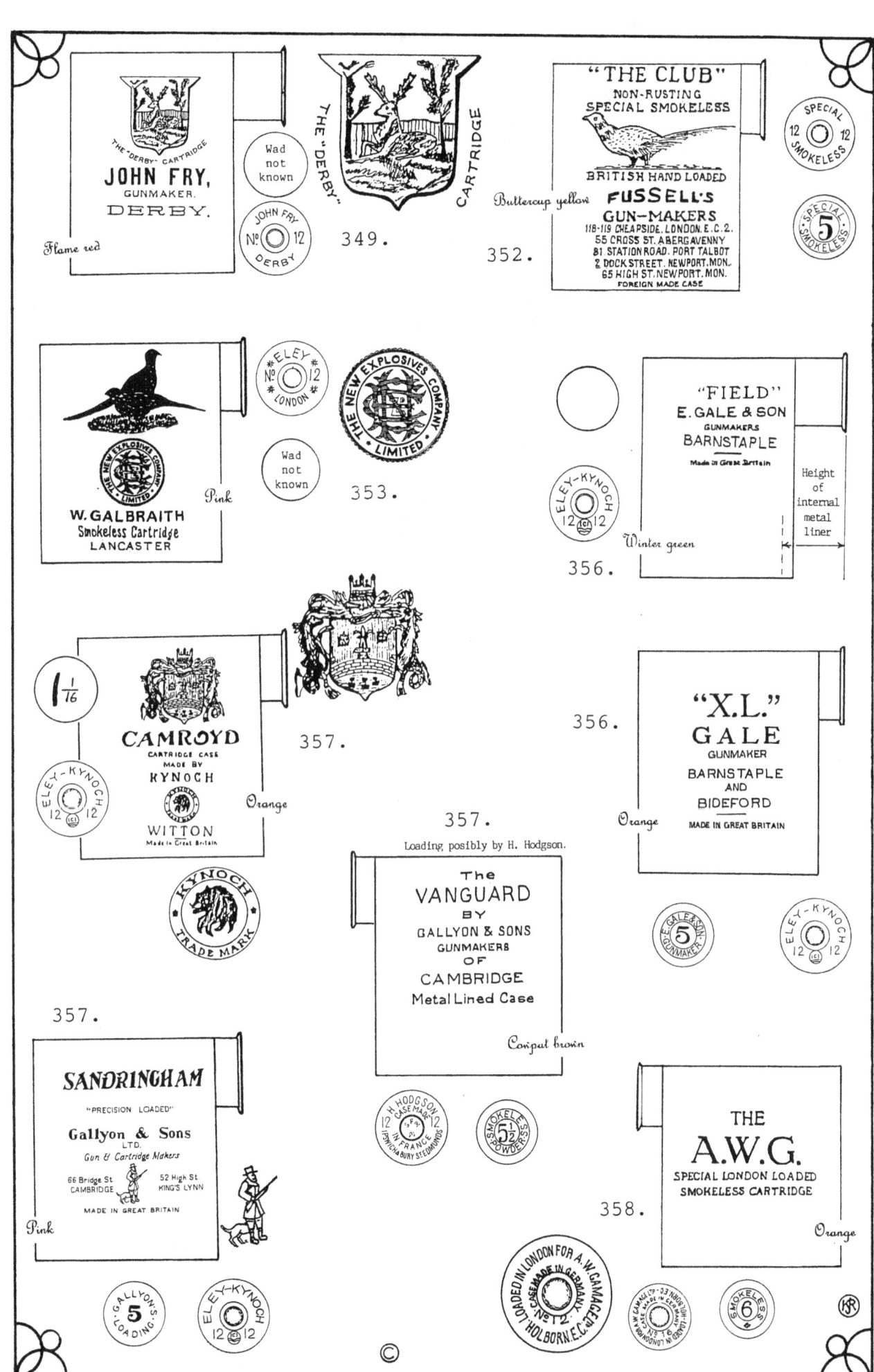

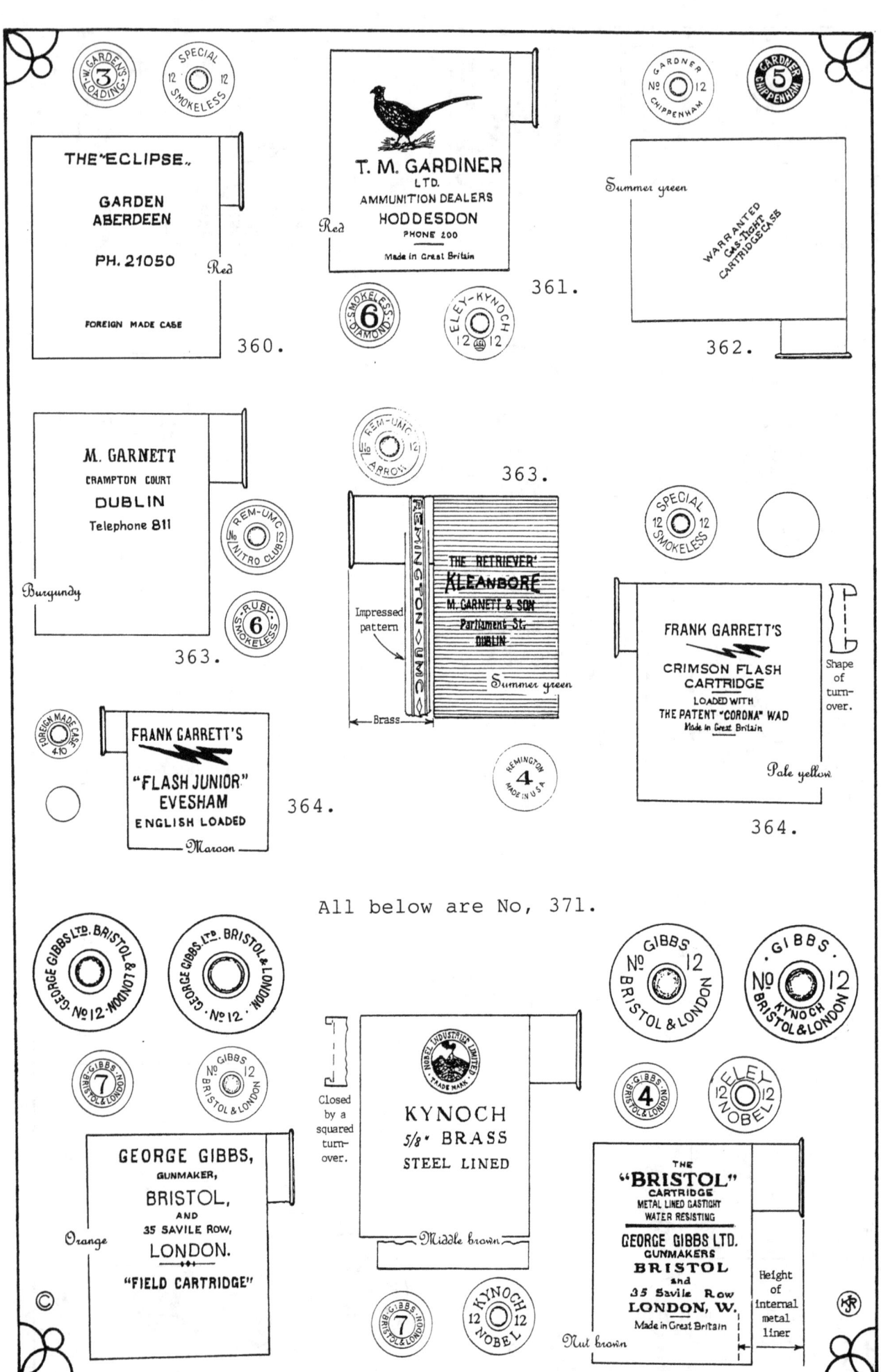

PLATE G2

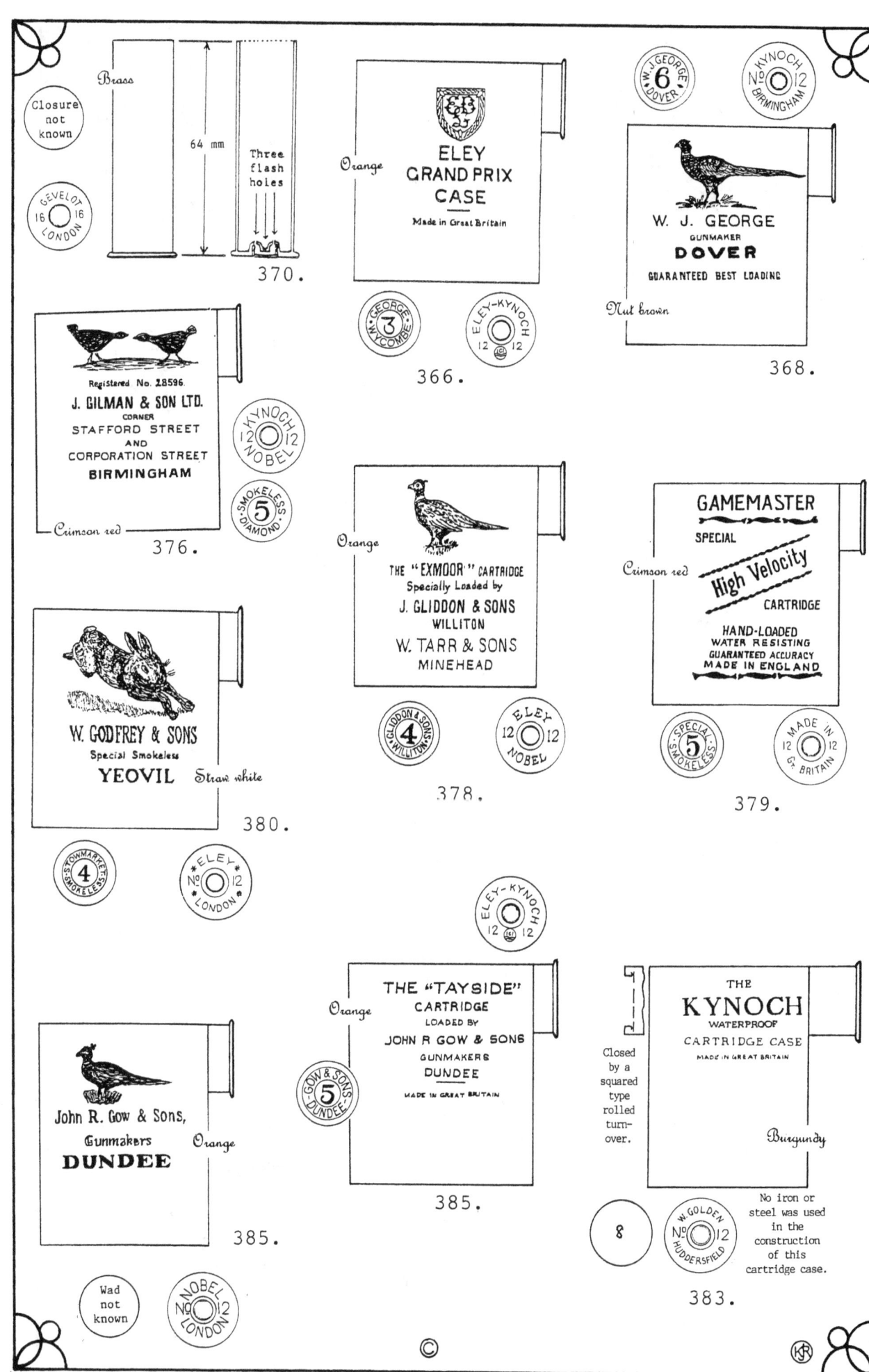

PLATE G3

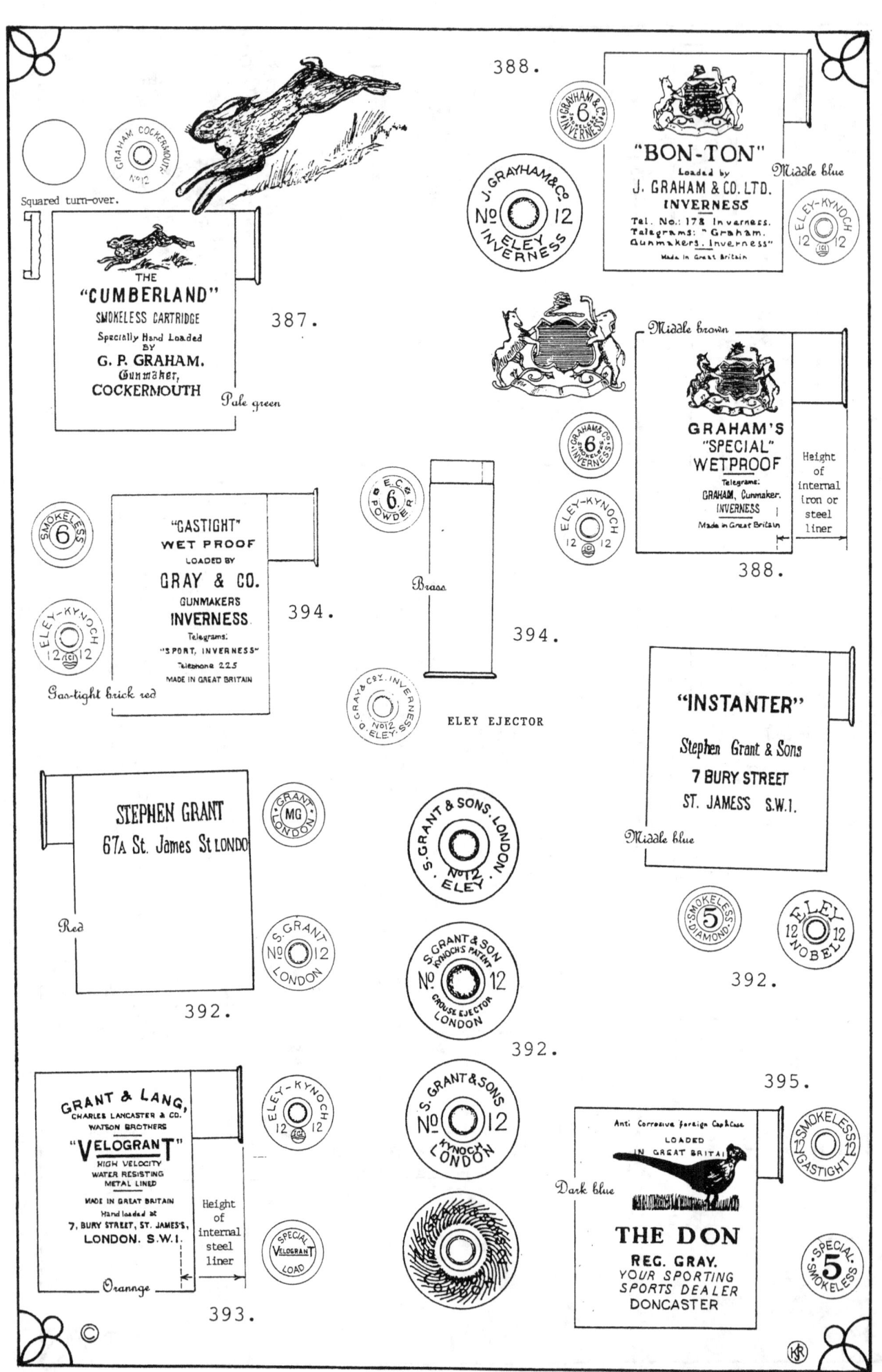

PLATE G4

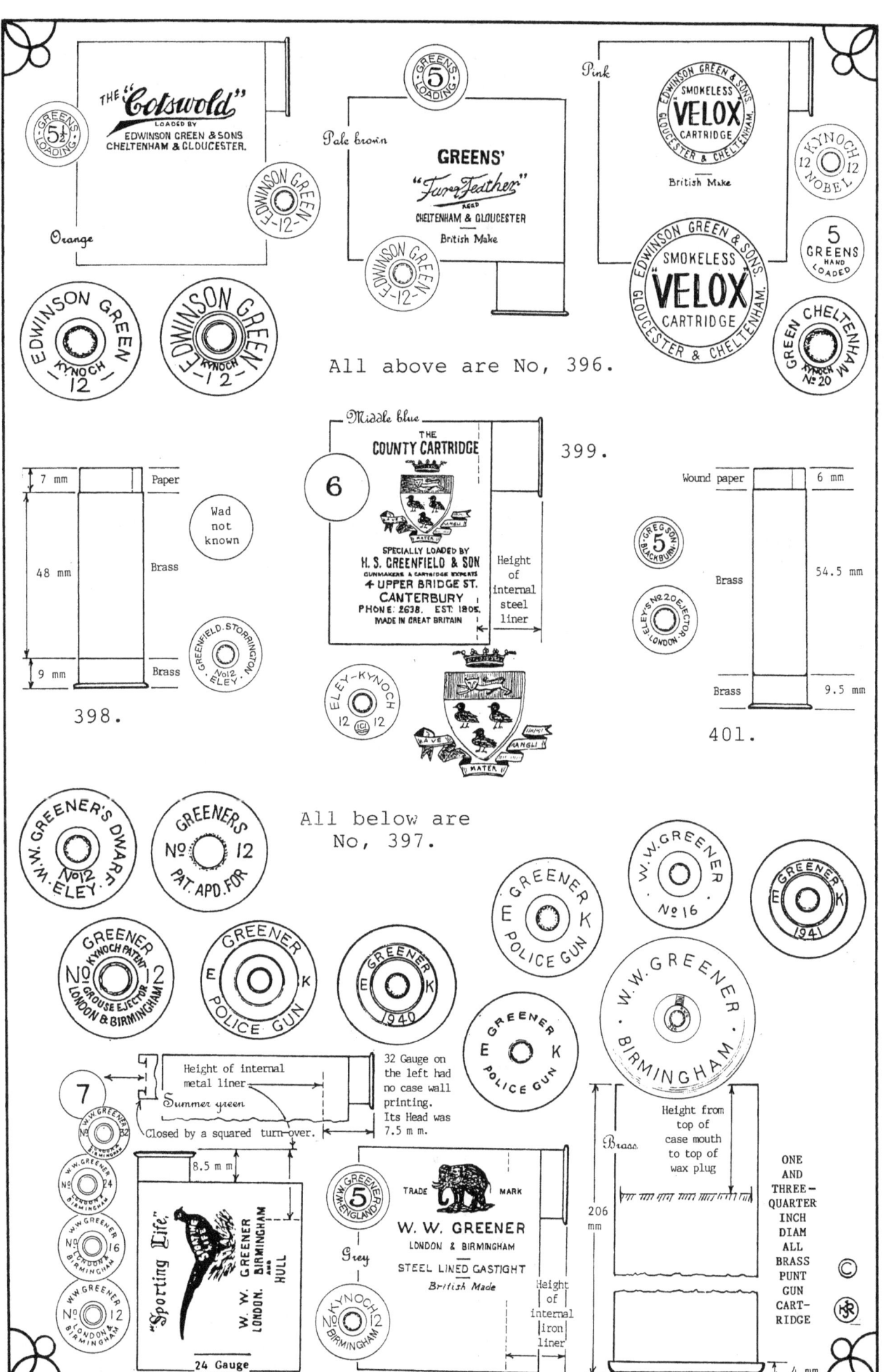

PLATE G5

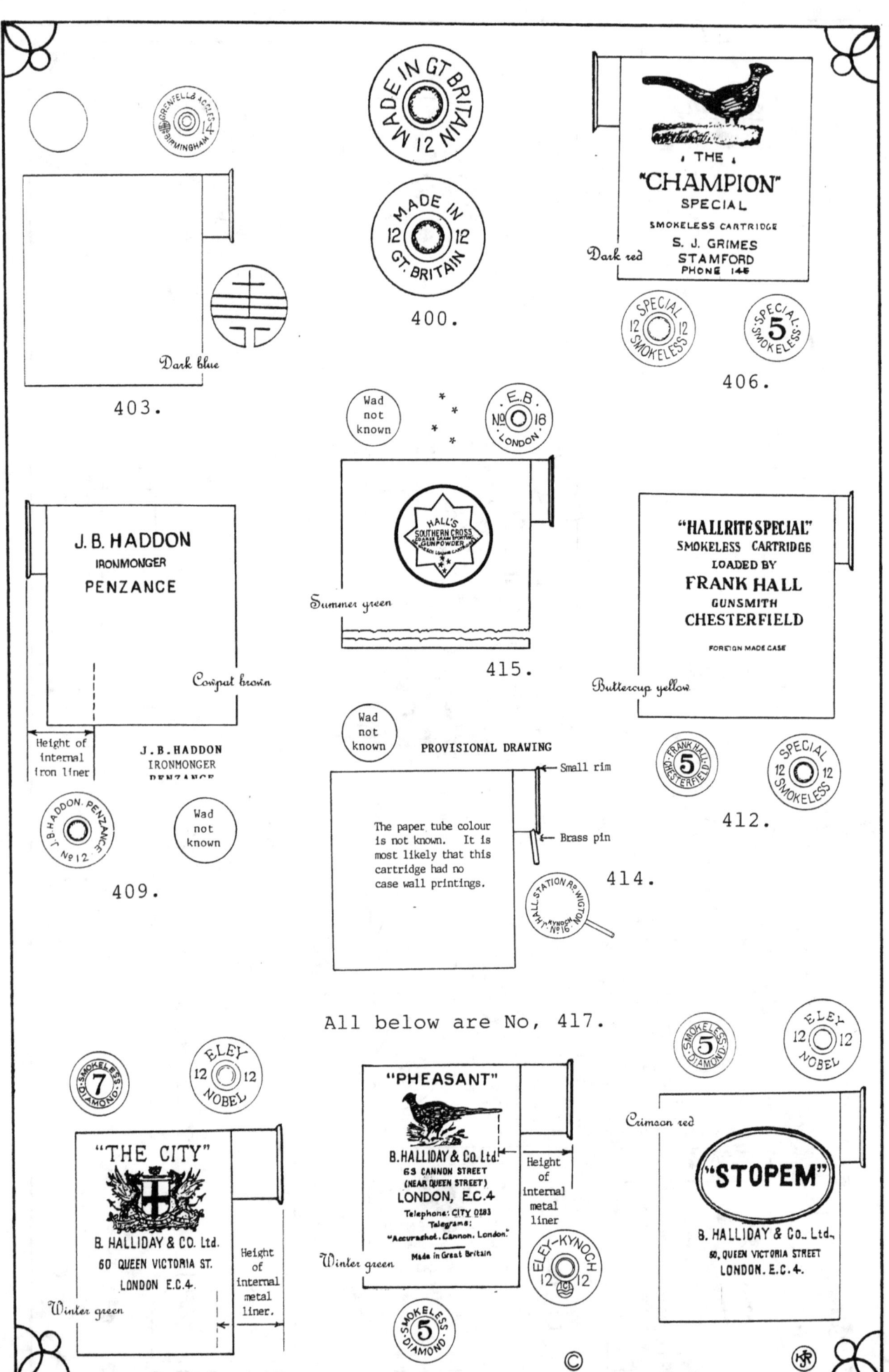

PLATE G6

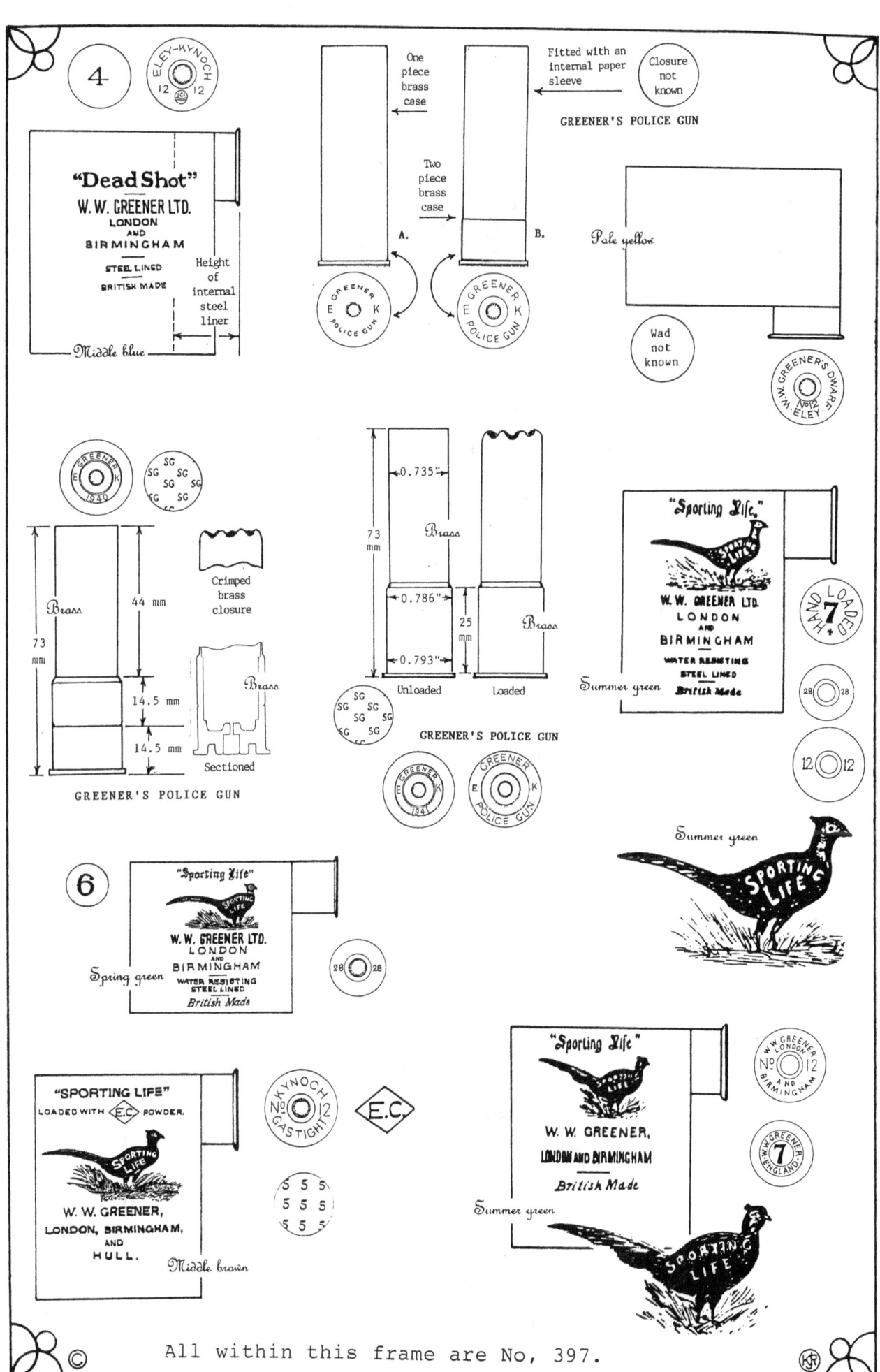

PLATE G7

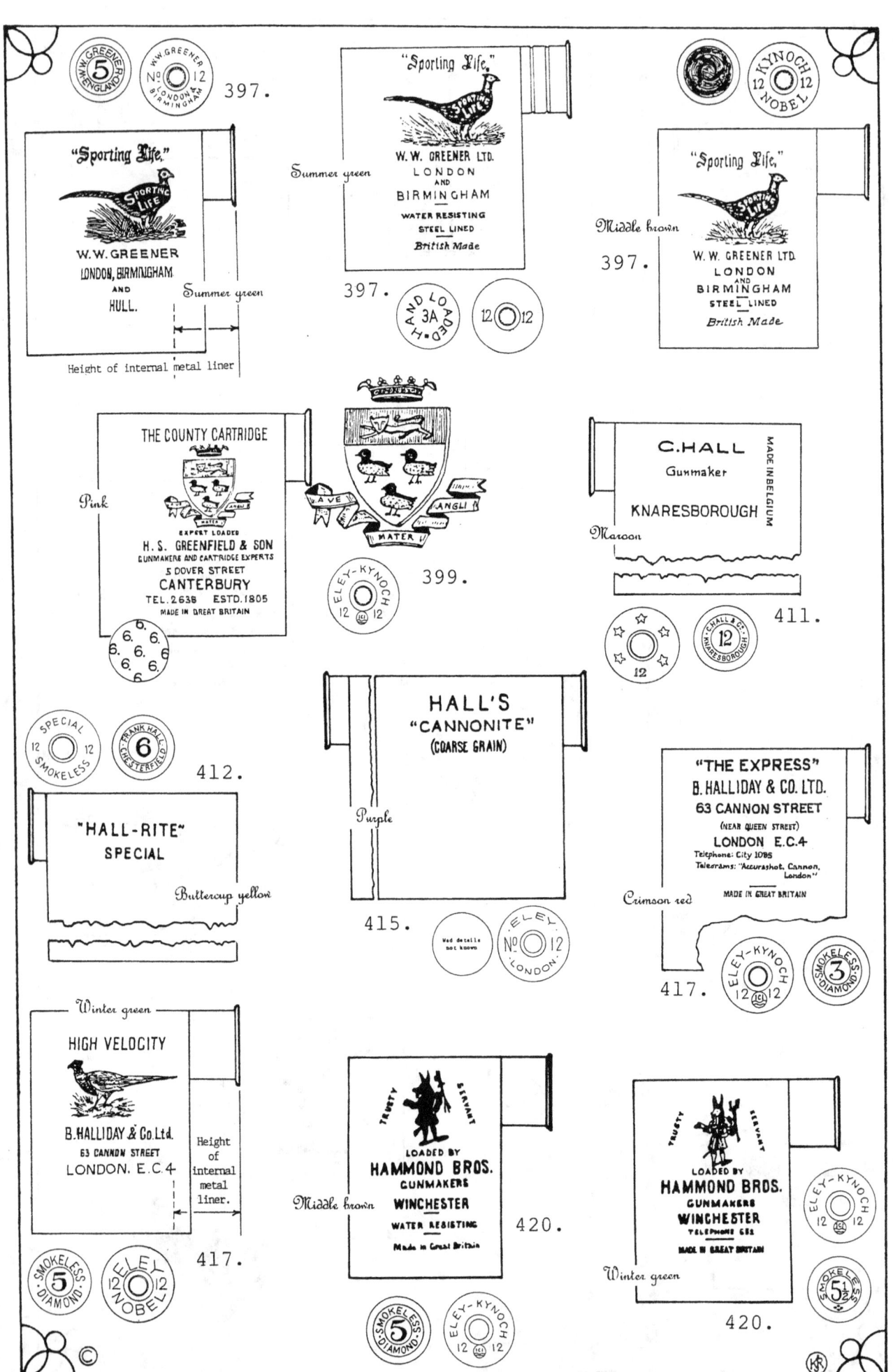

PLATE G8

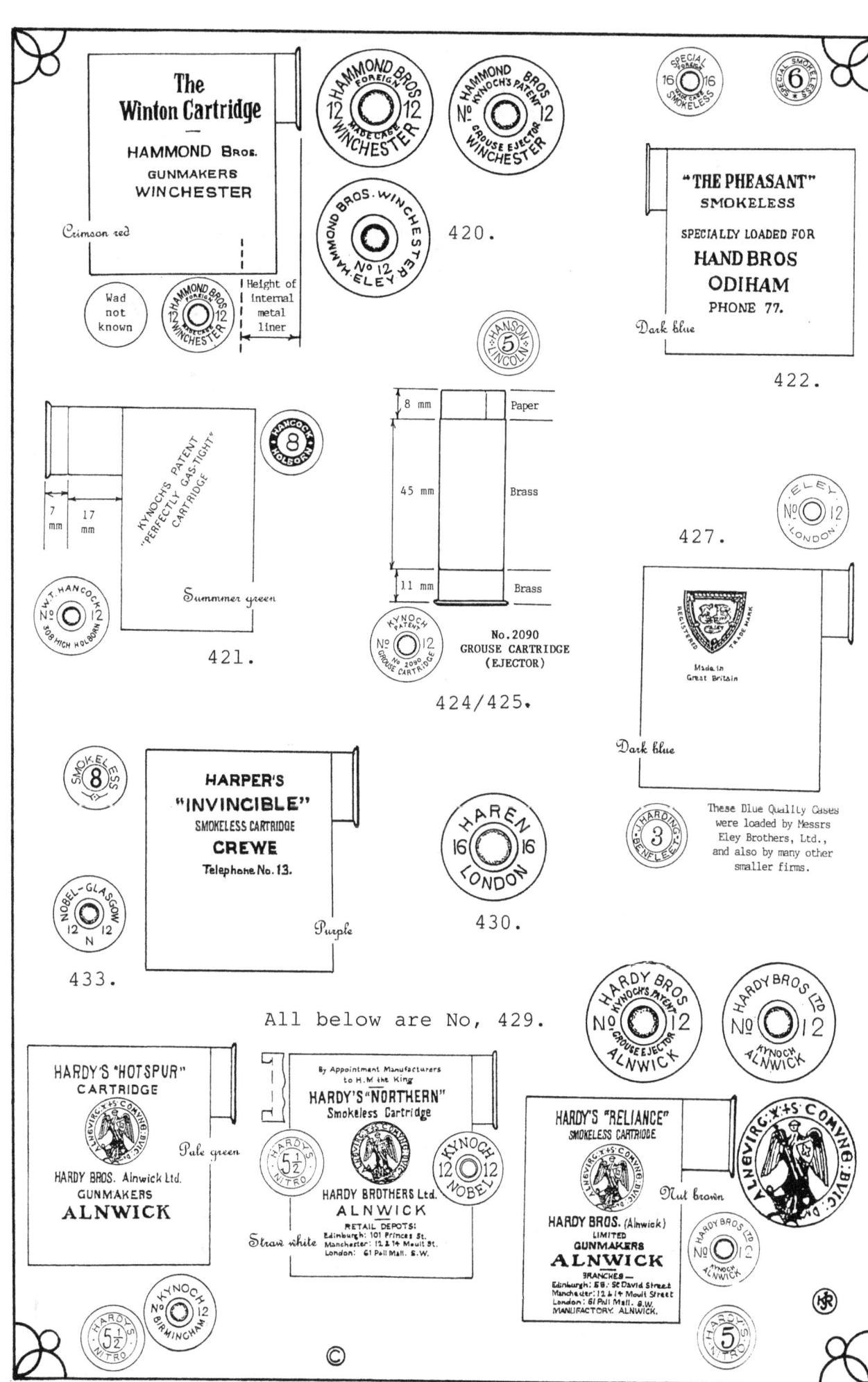

PLATE G9

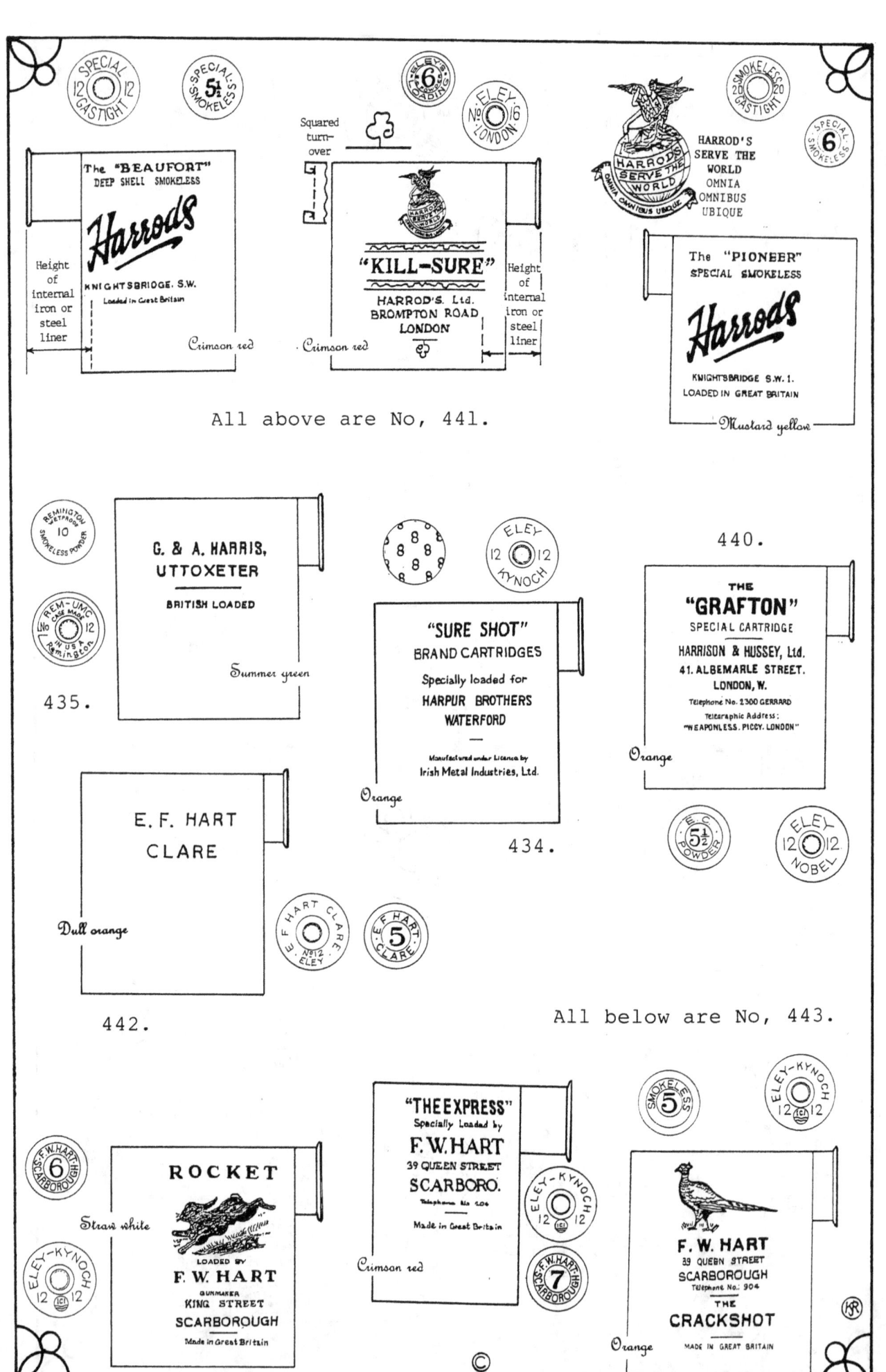

PLATE H1

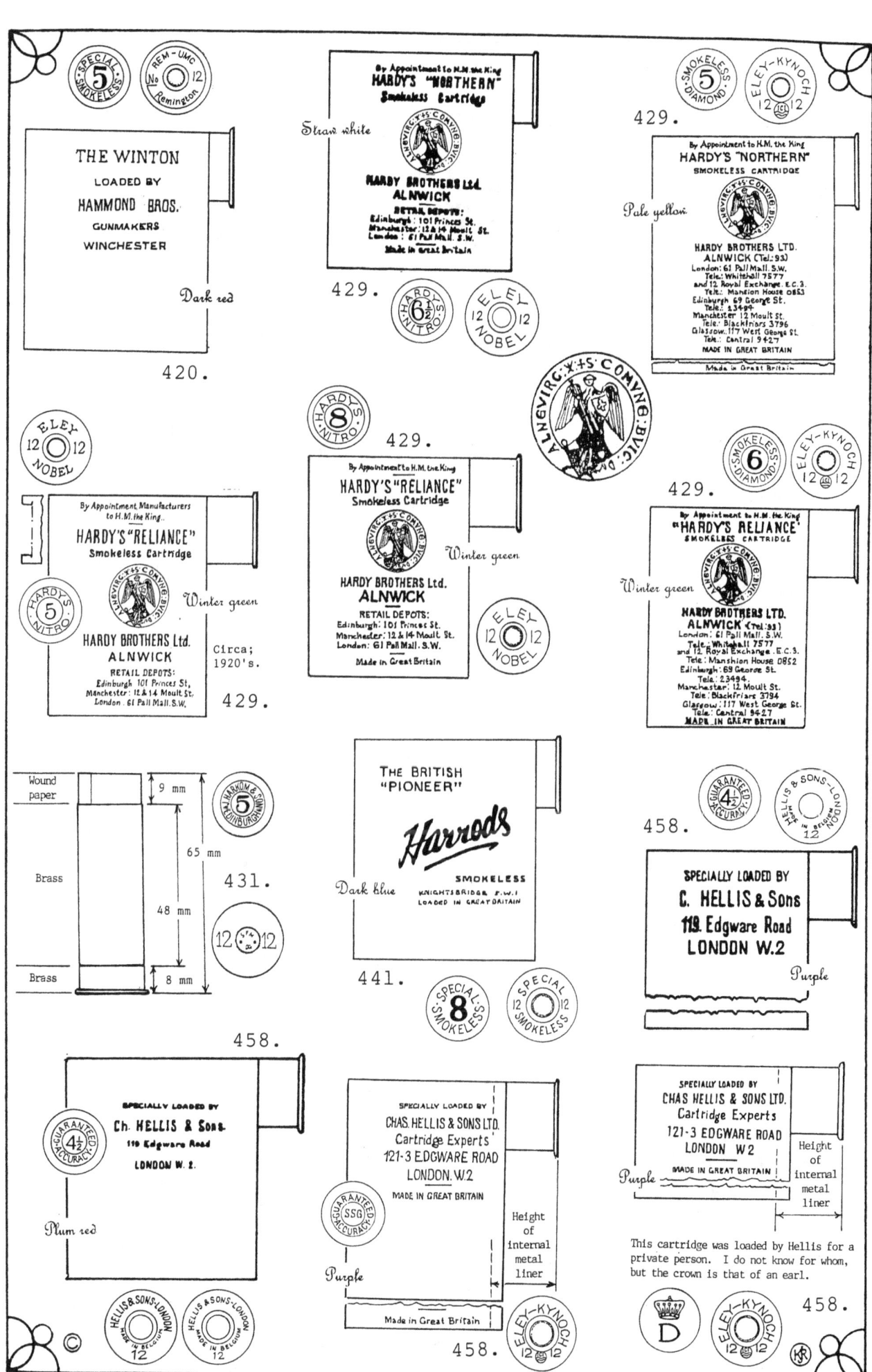

PLATE H2

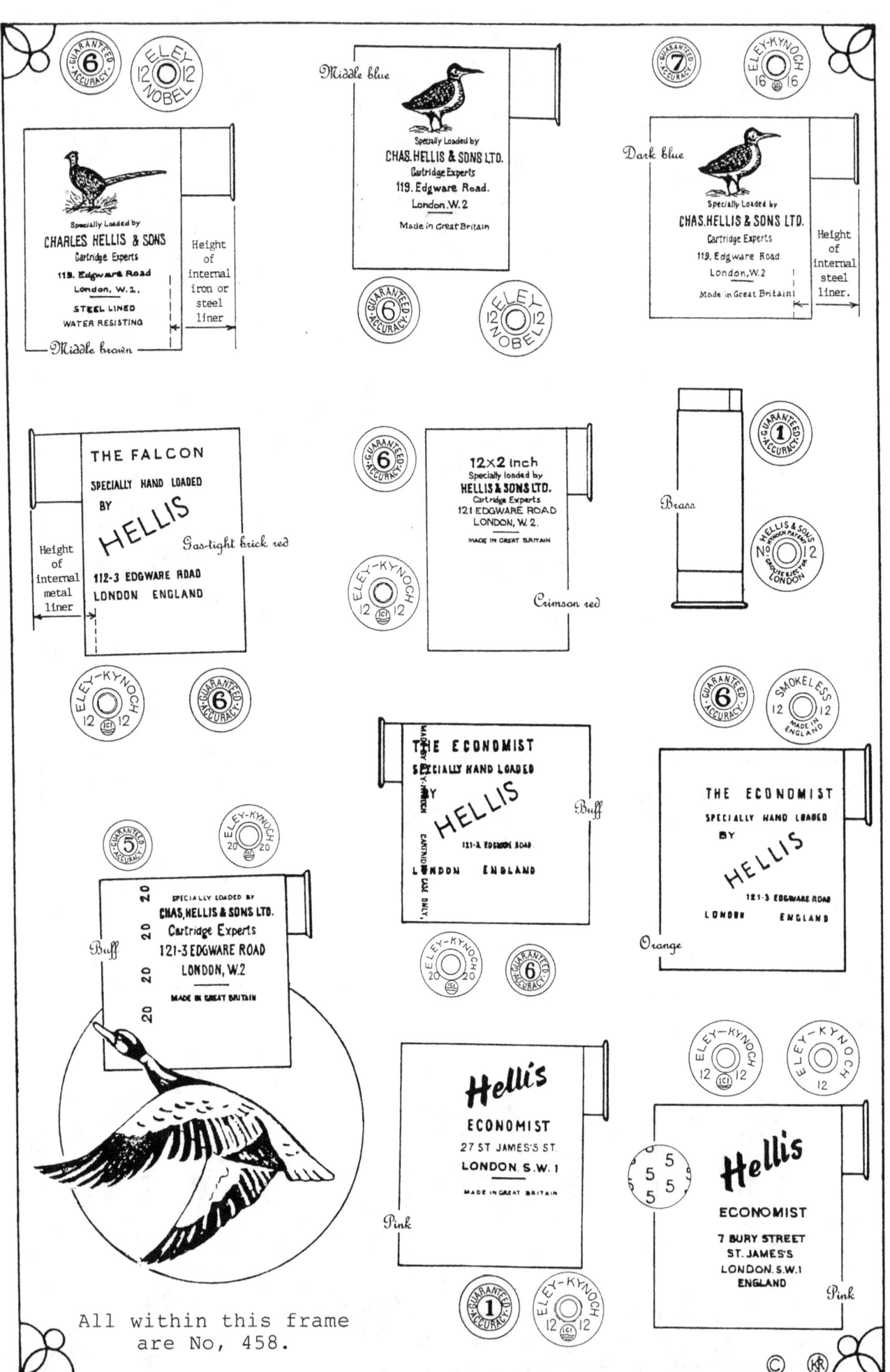

PLATE H3

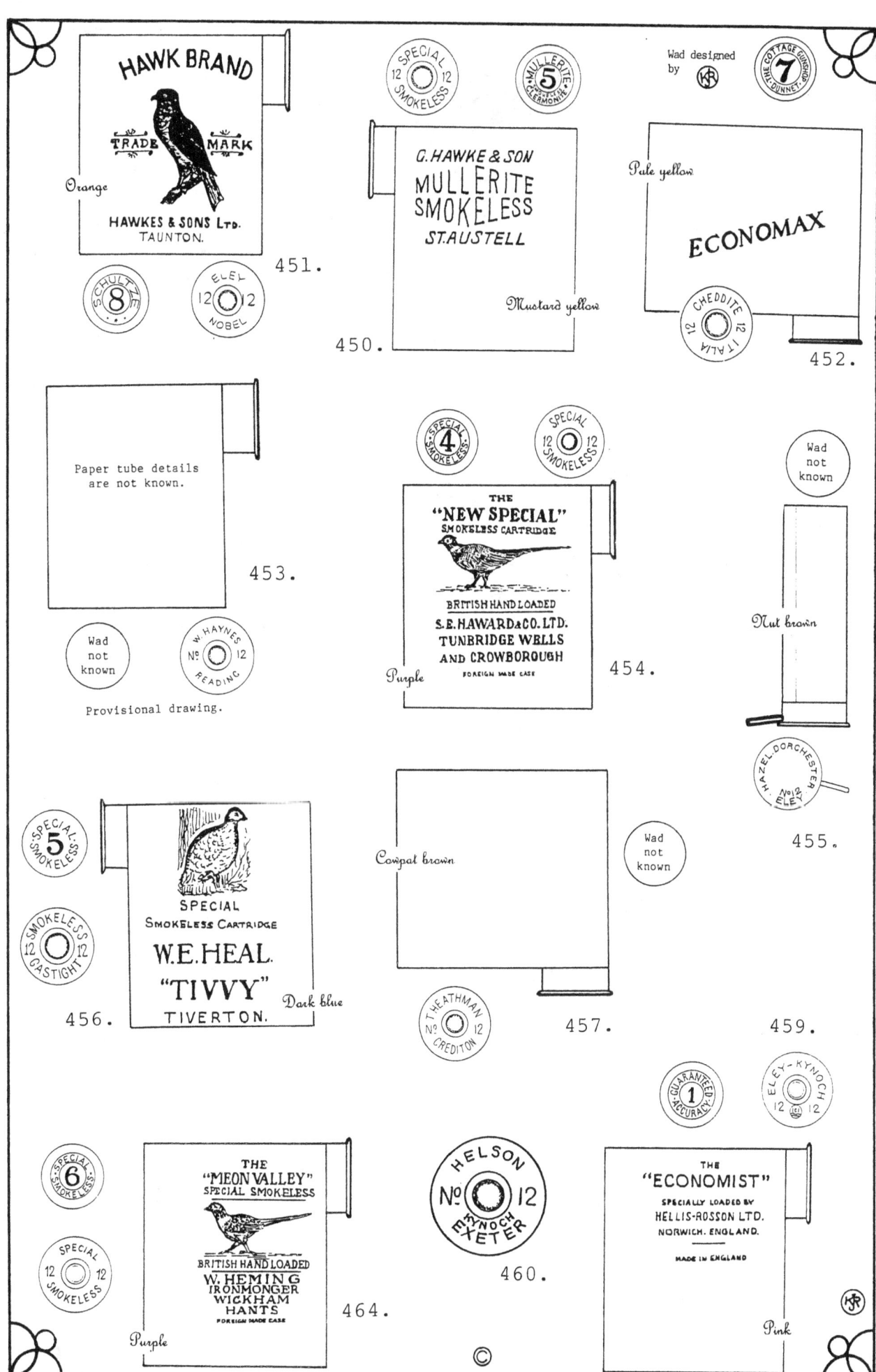

PLATE H4

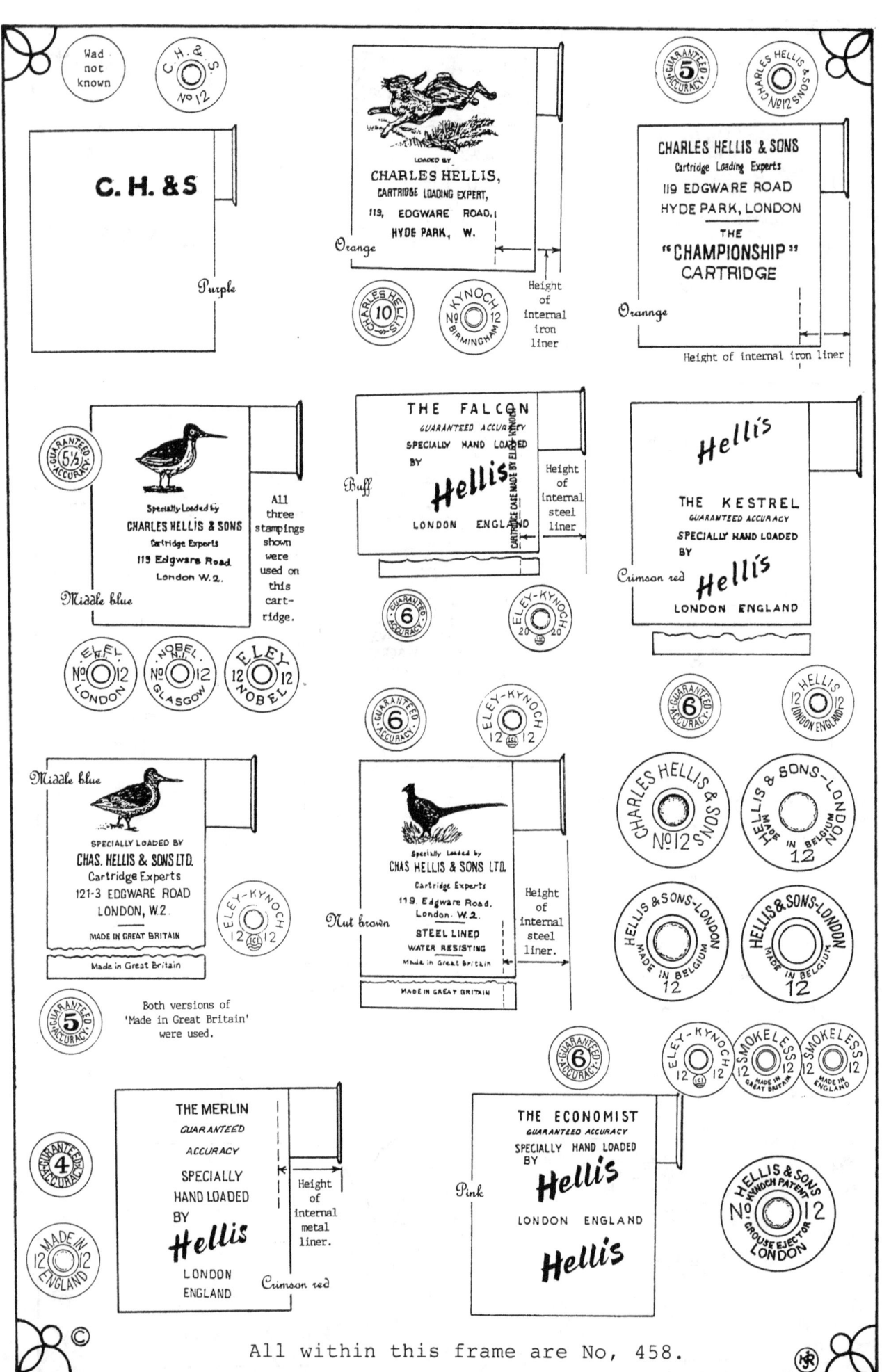

PLATE H5

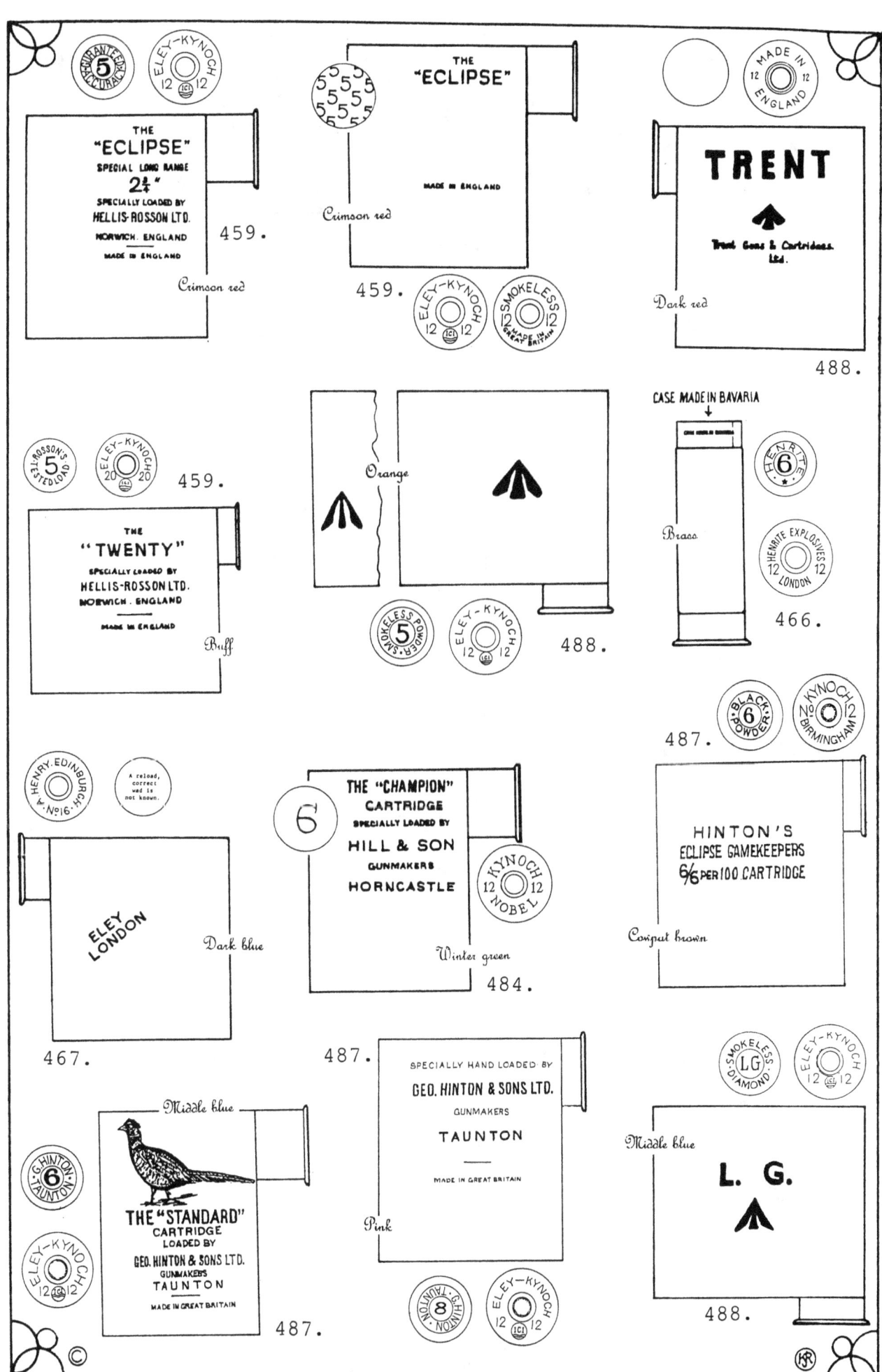

PLATE H6

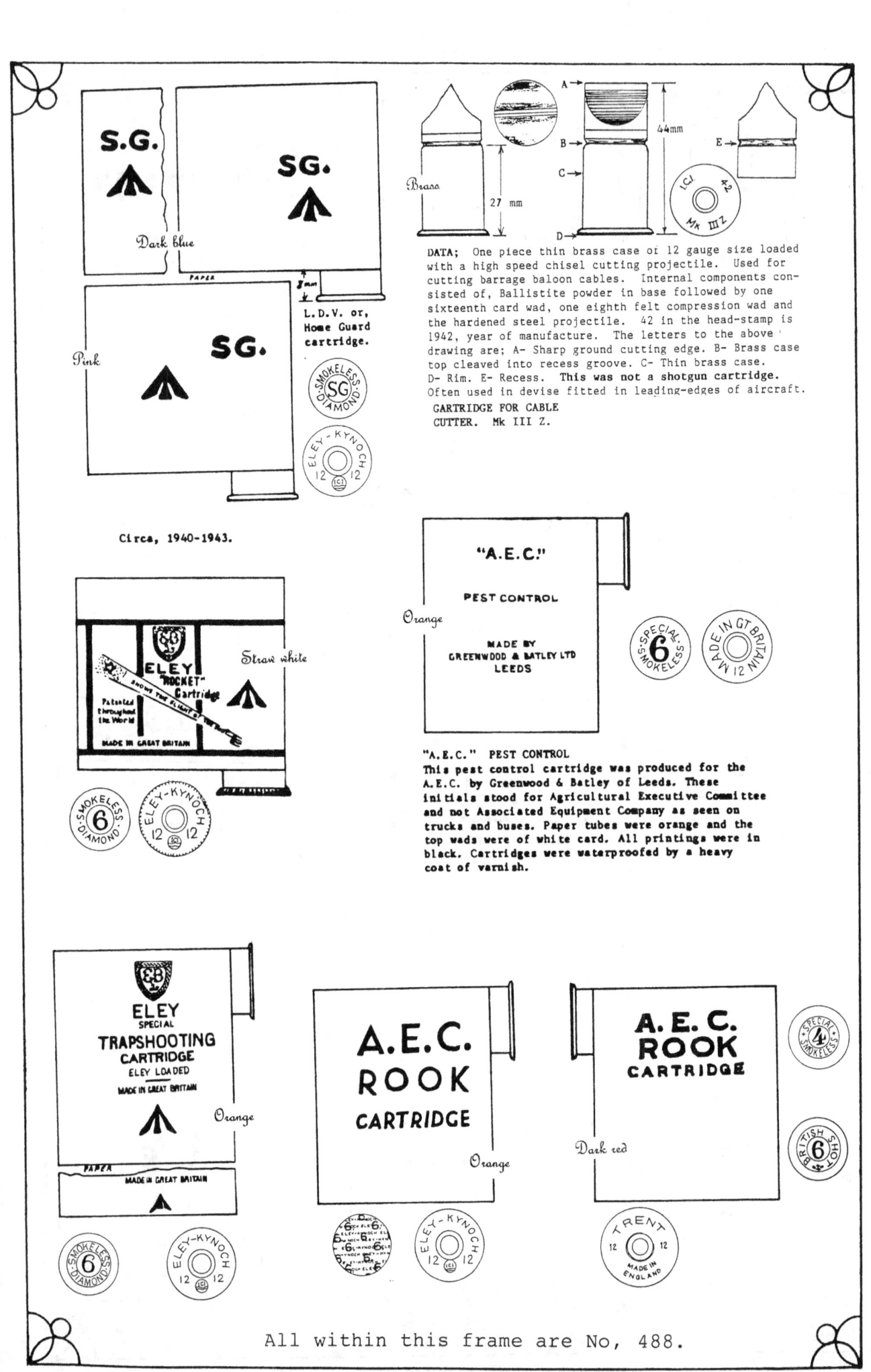

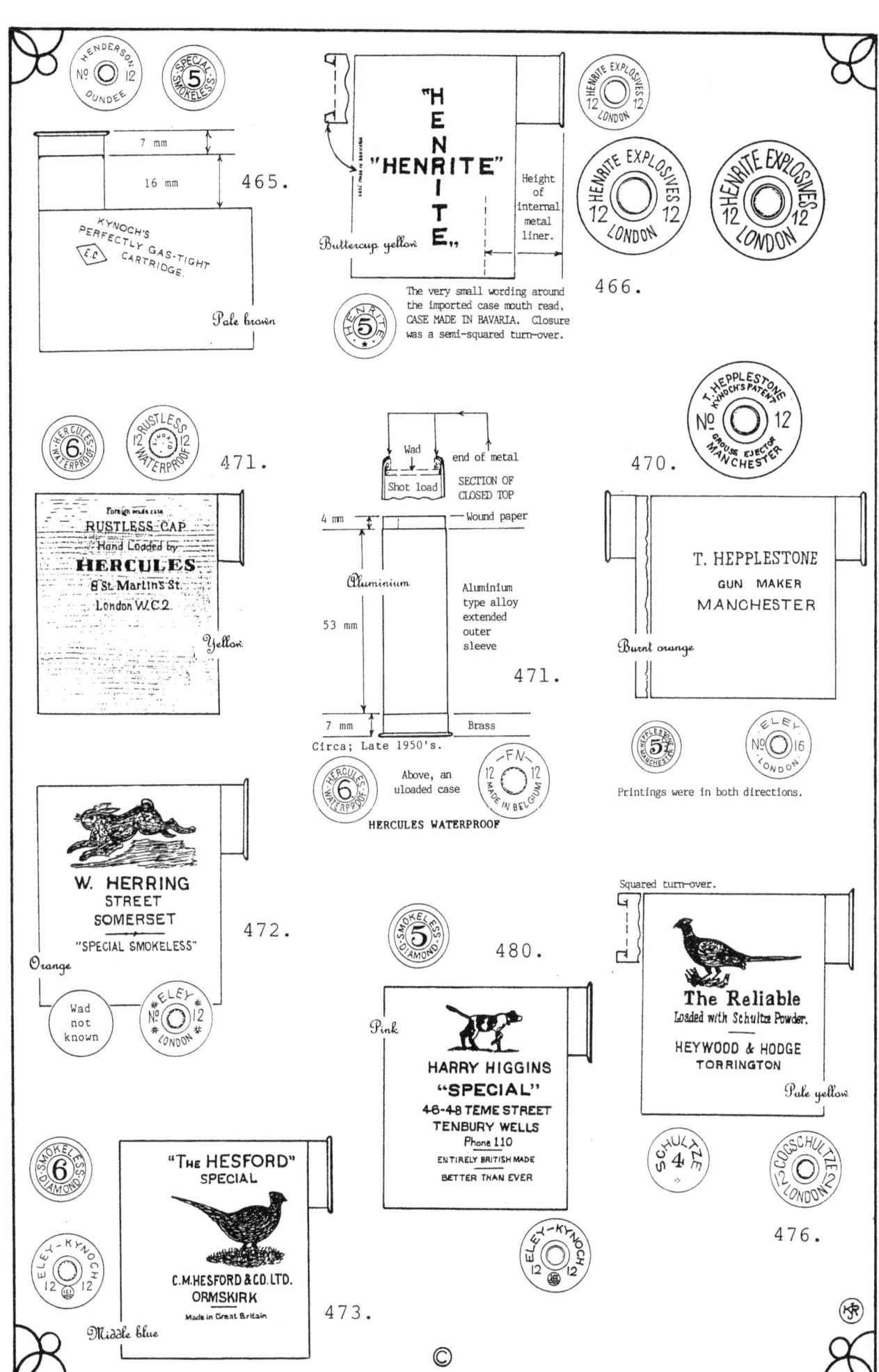

PLATE H8

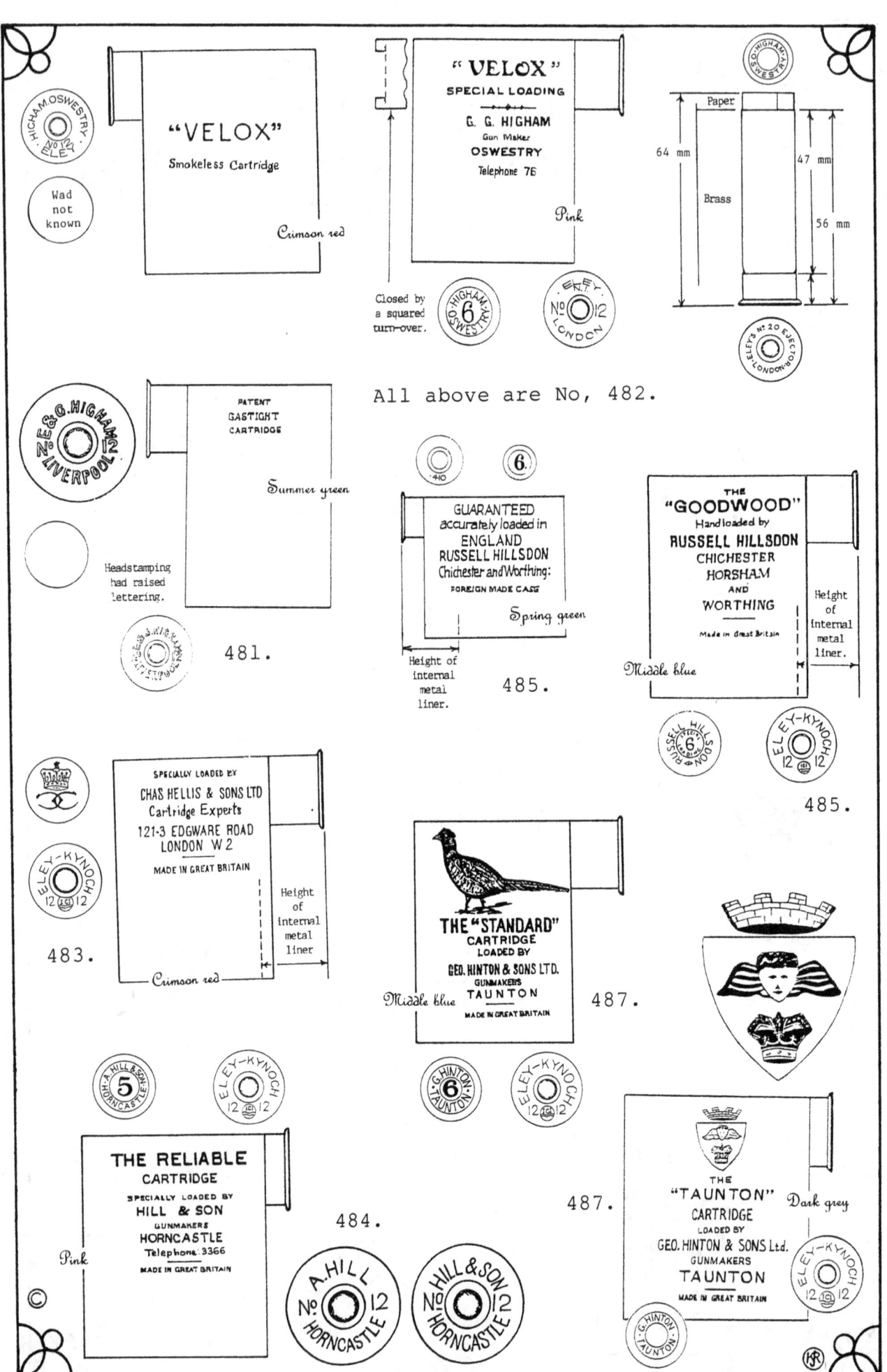

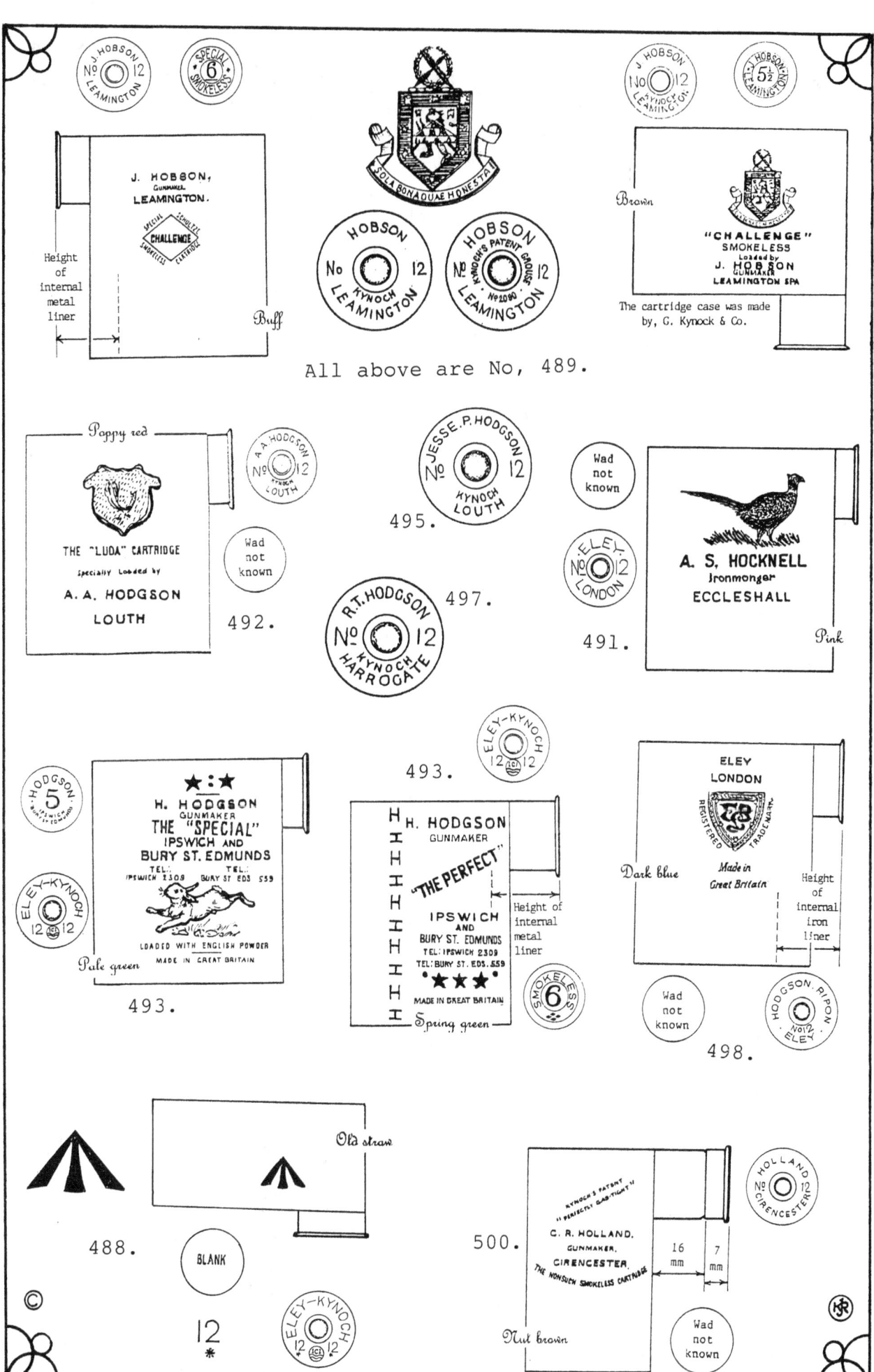

PLATE I1

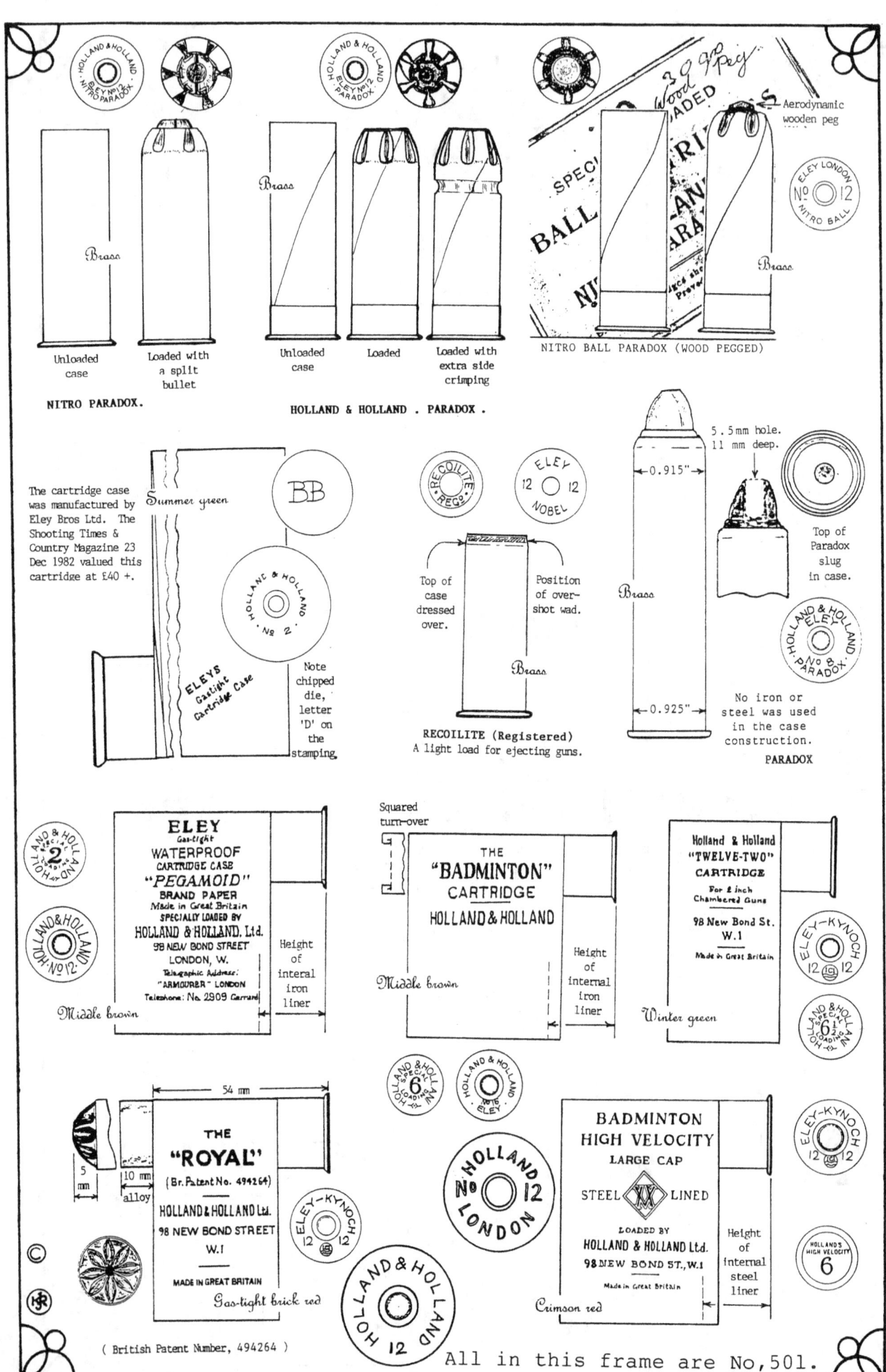

PLATE 12

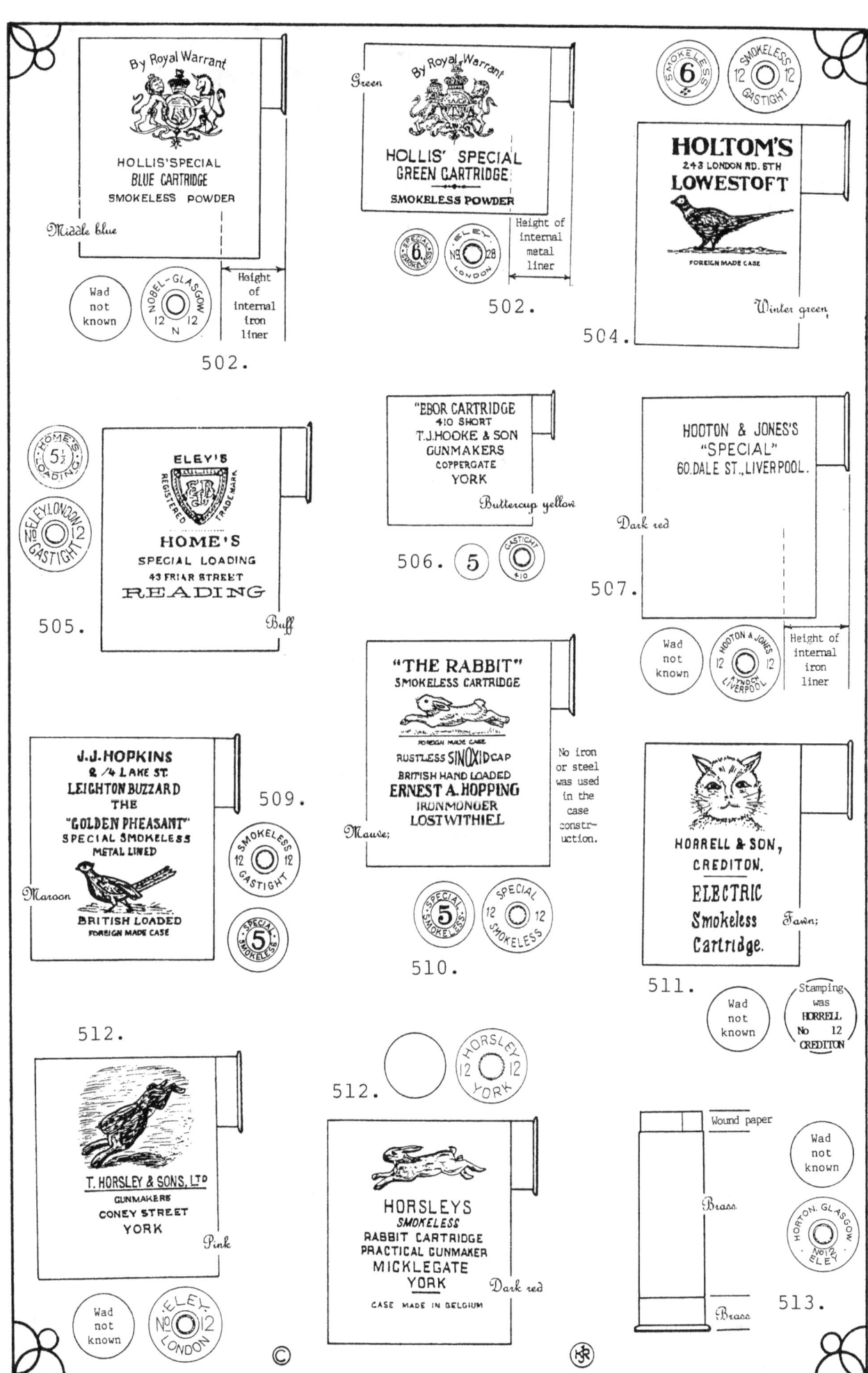

PLATE 13

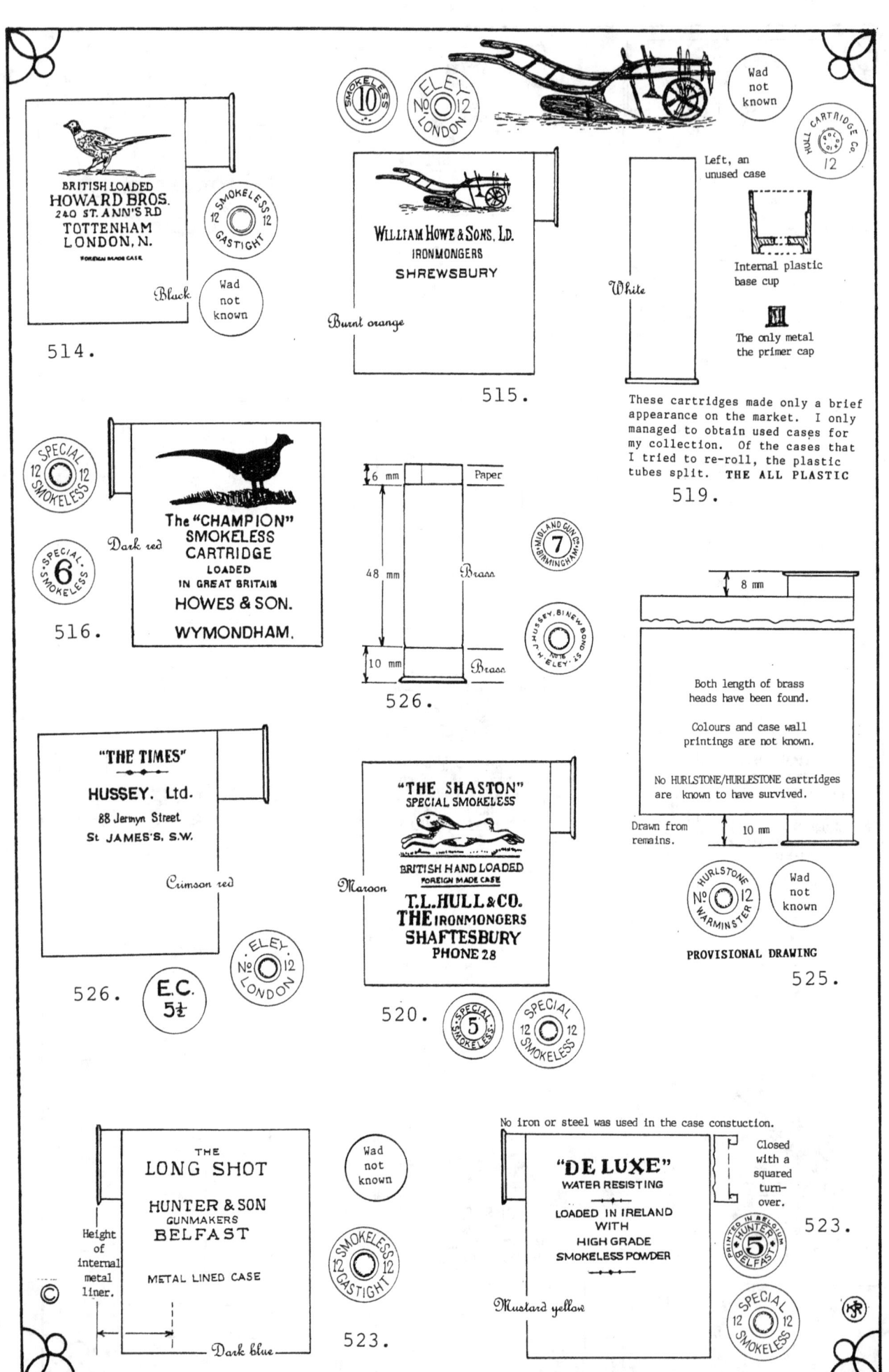

PLATE 14

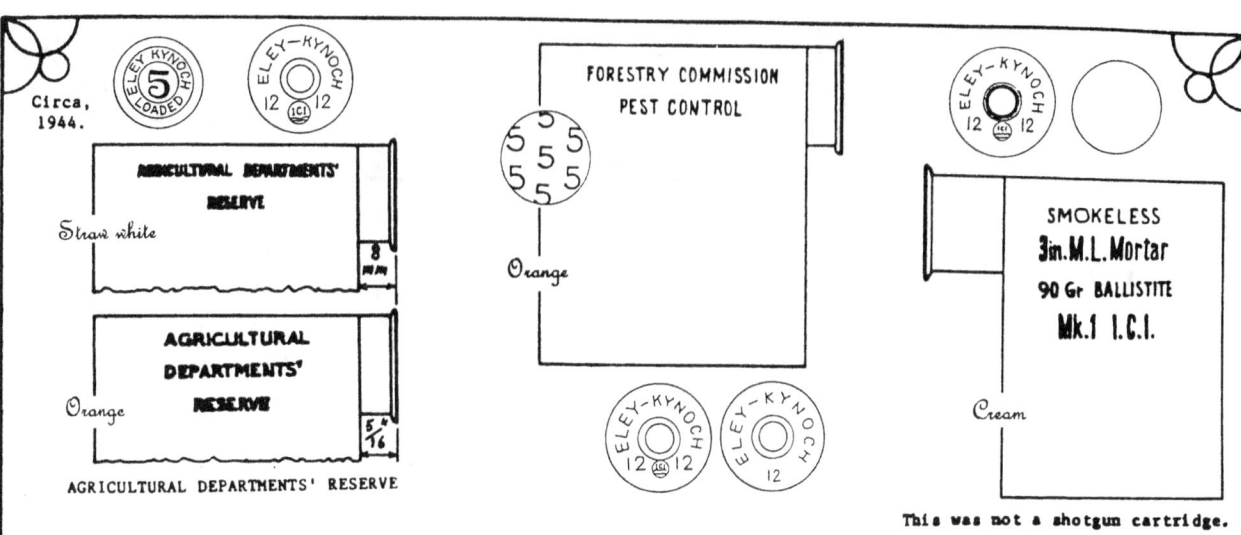
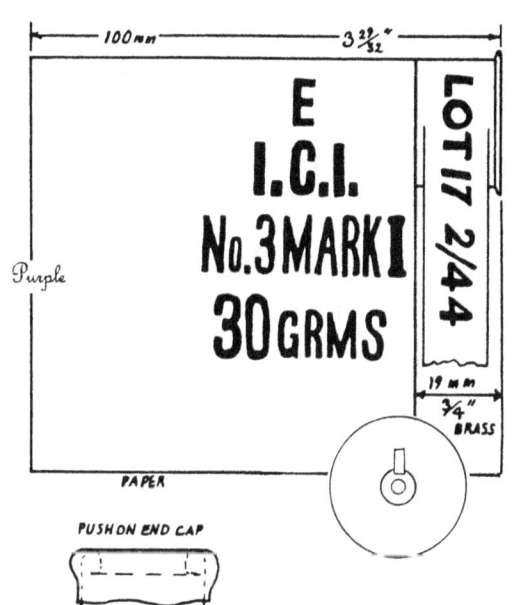
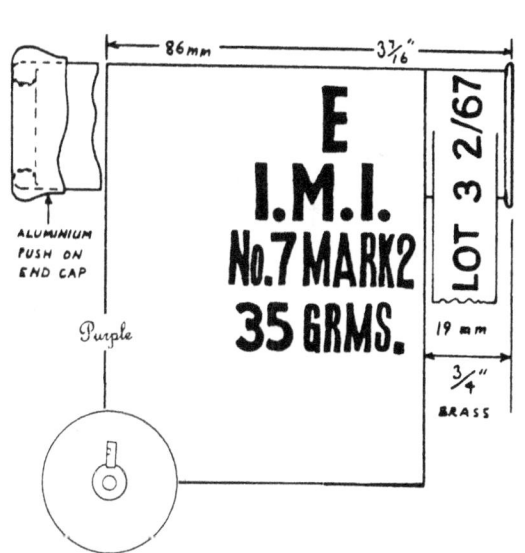

All above are No. 488.

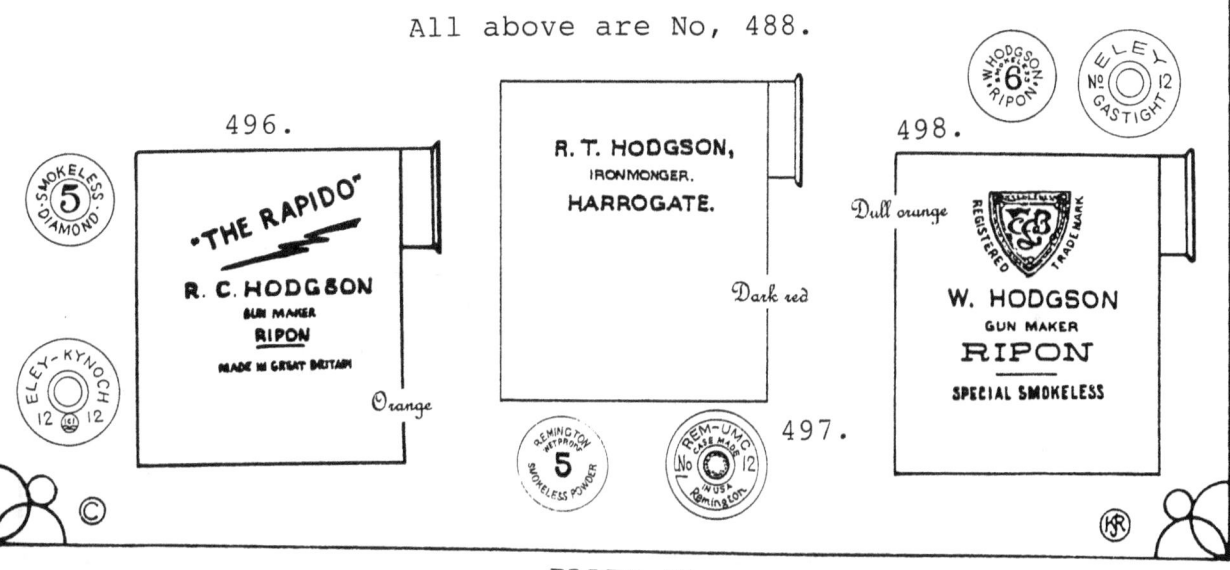

PLATE 15

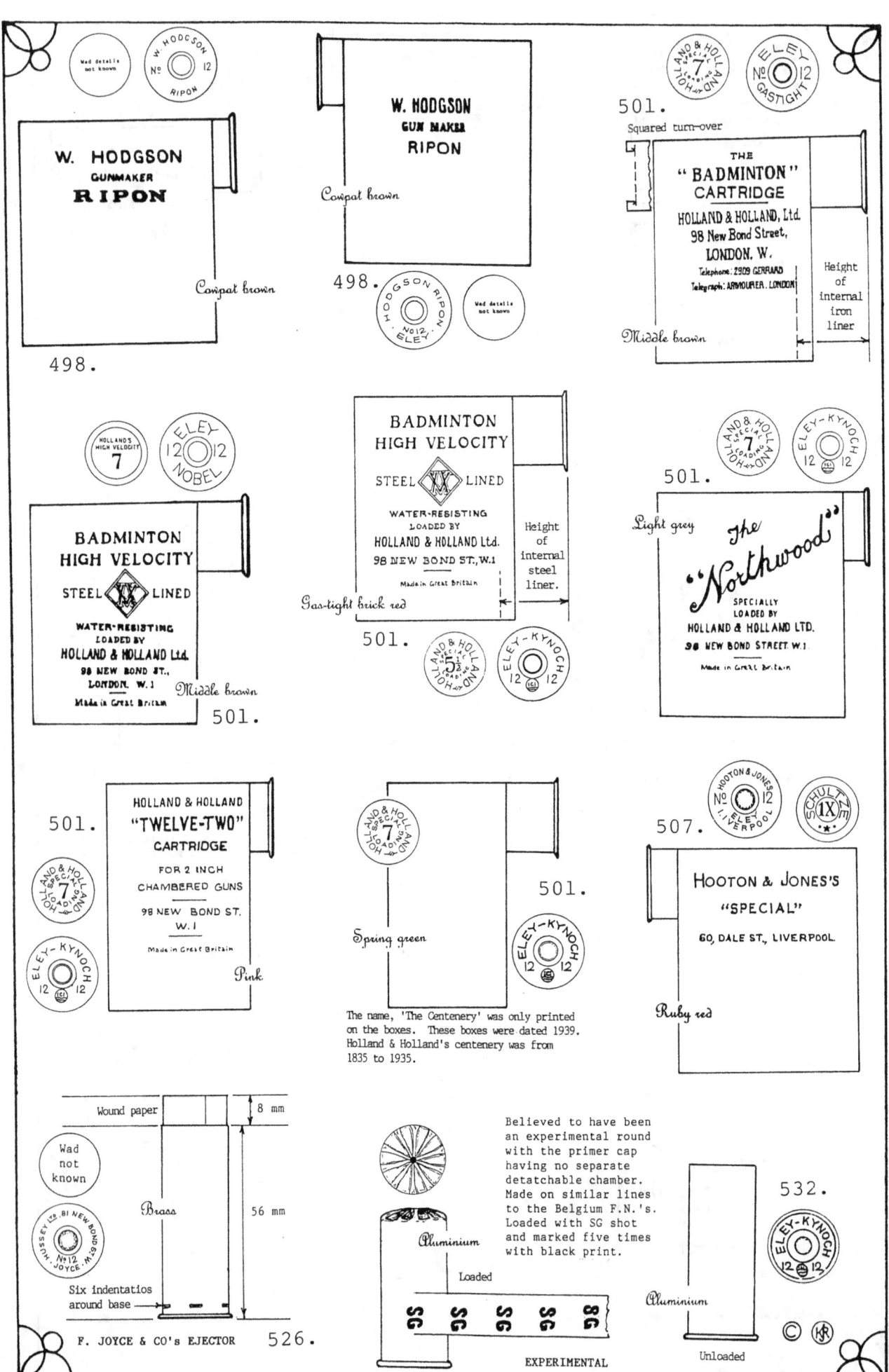

PLATE 16

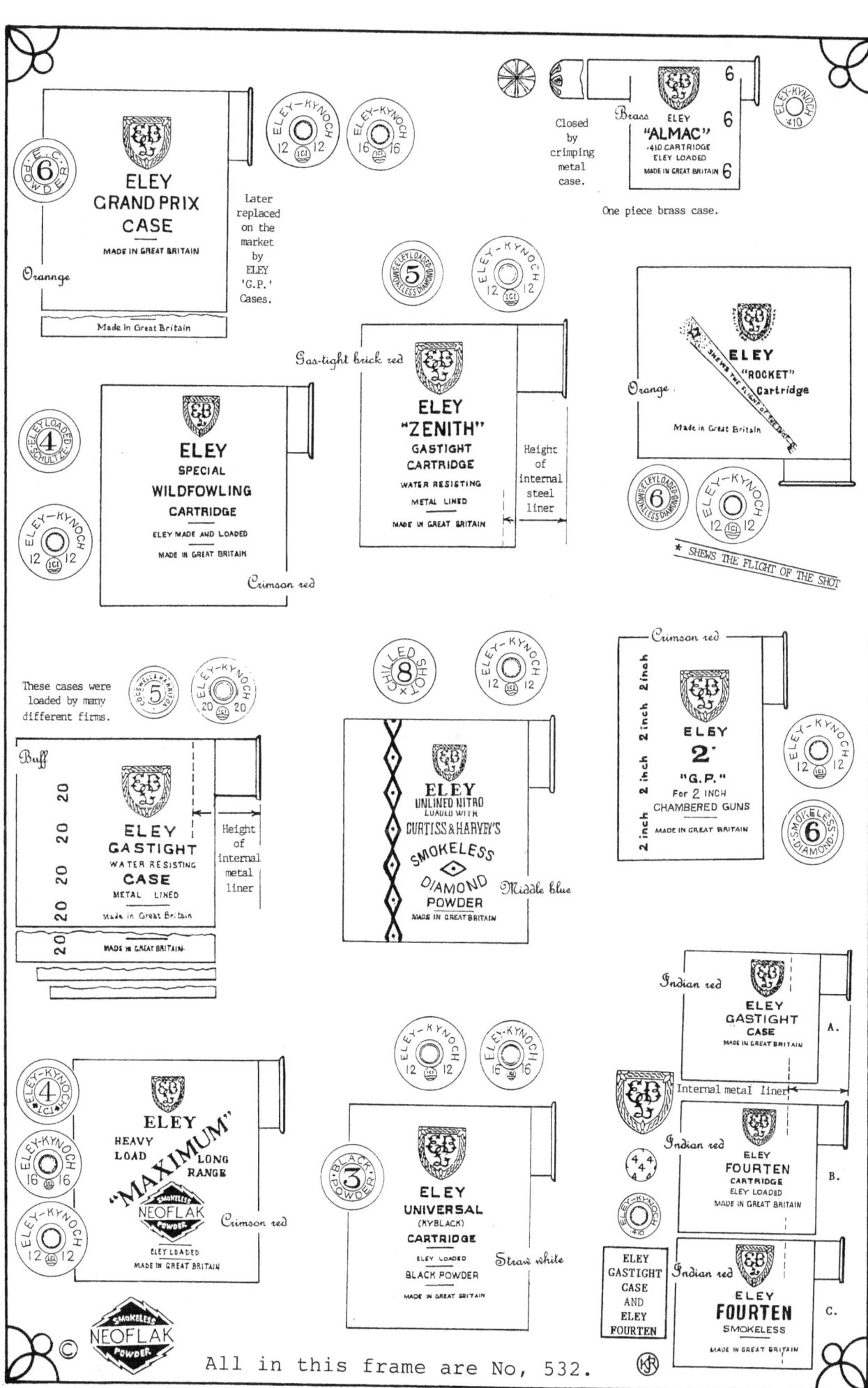

PLATE 17

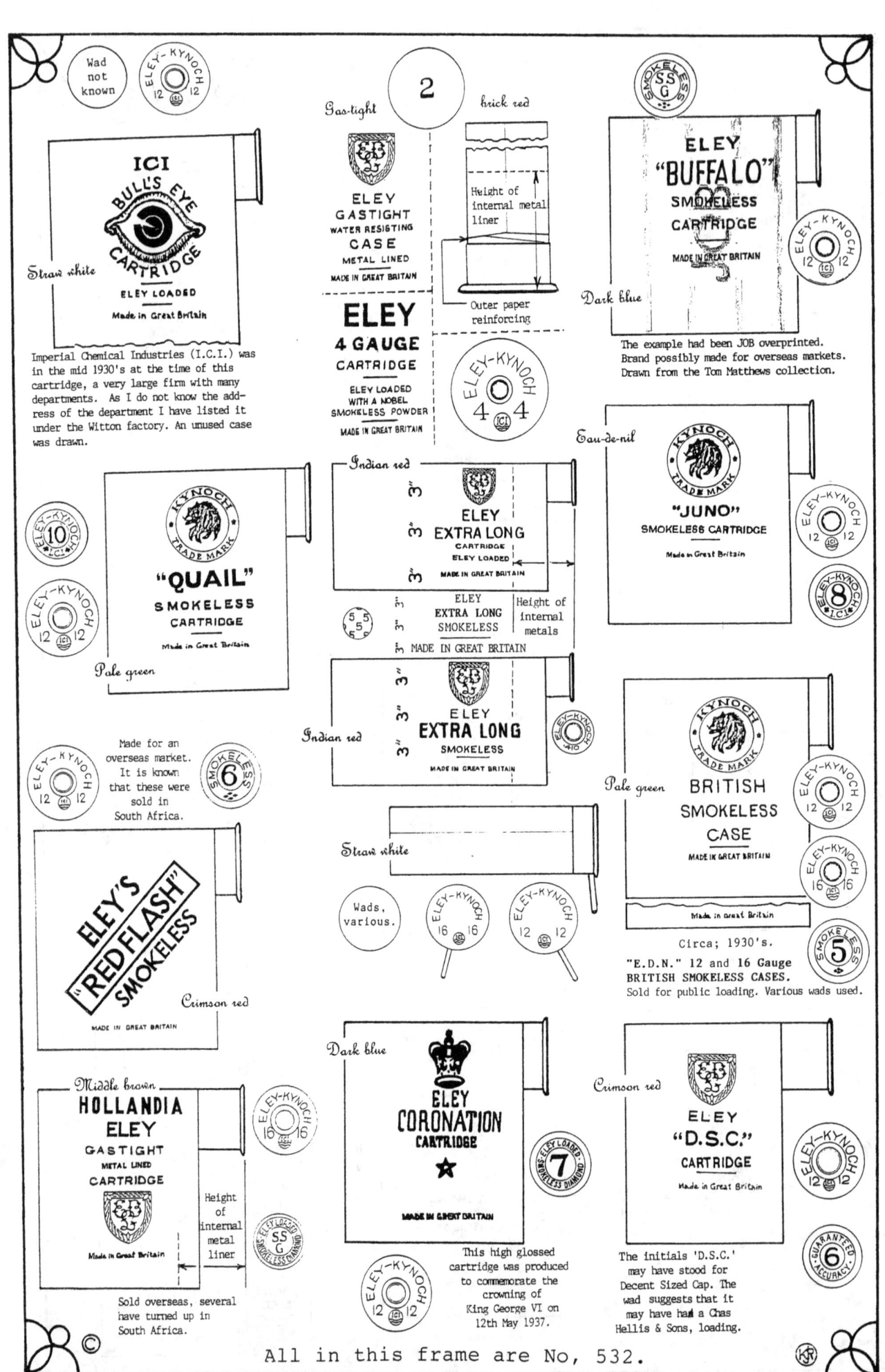

PLATE 18

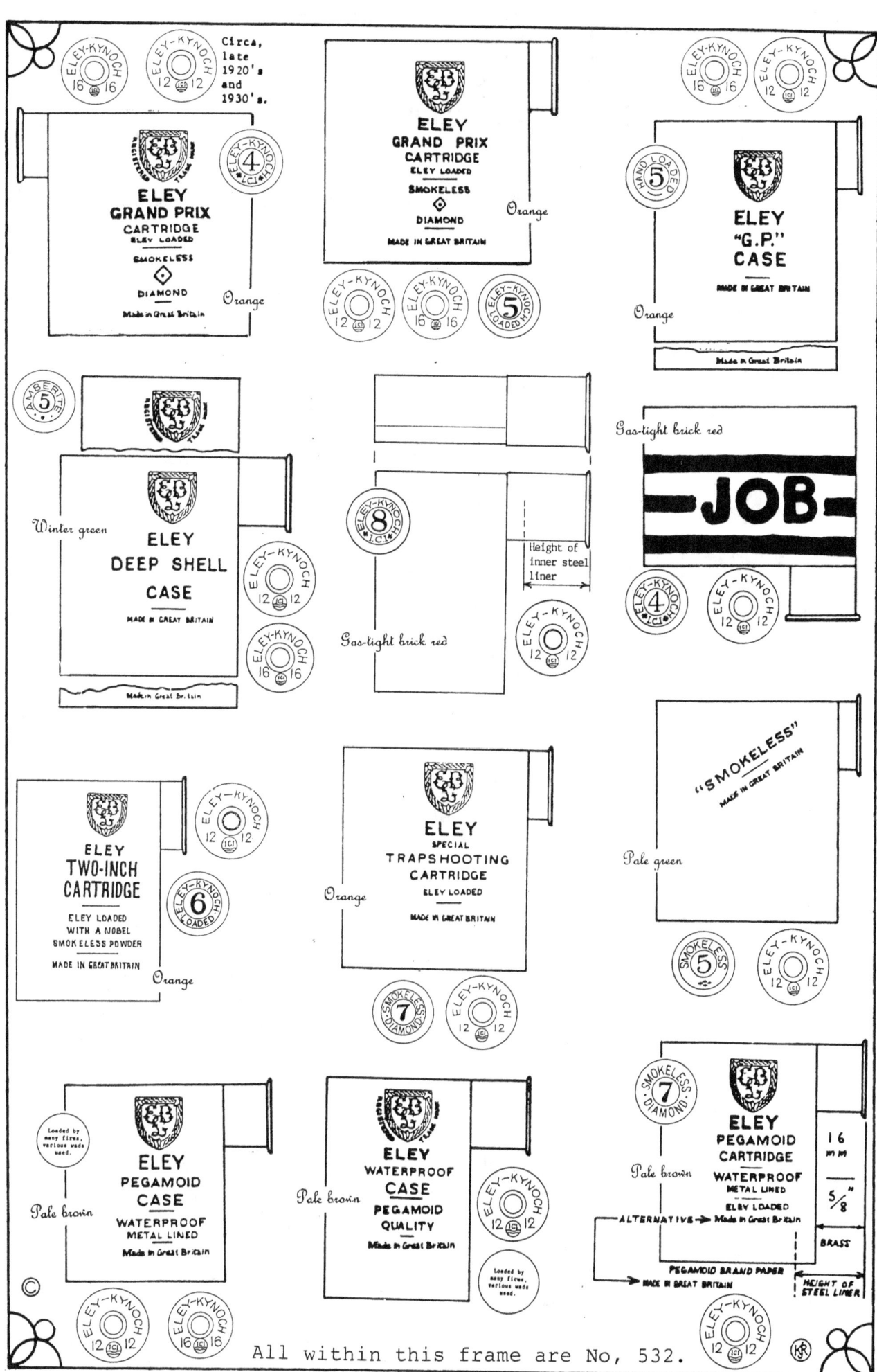

PLATE 19

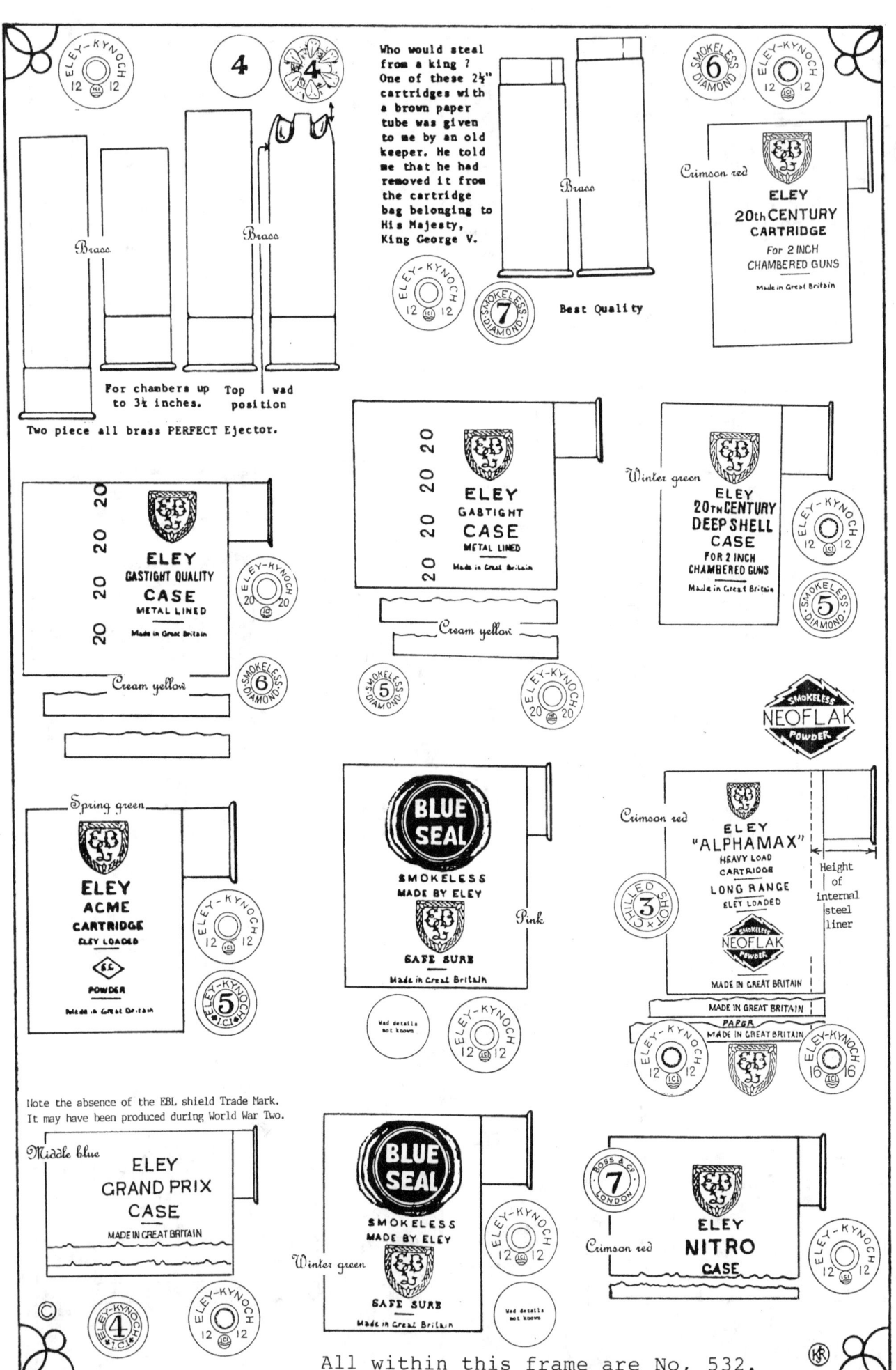

PLATE J1

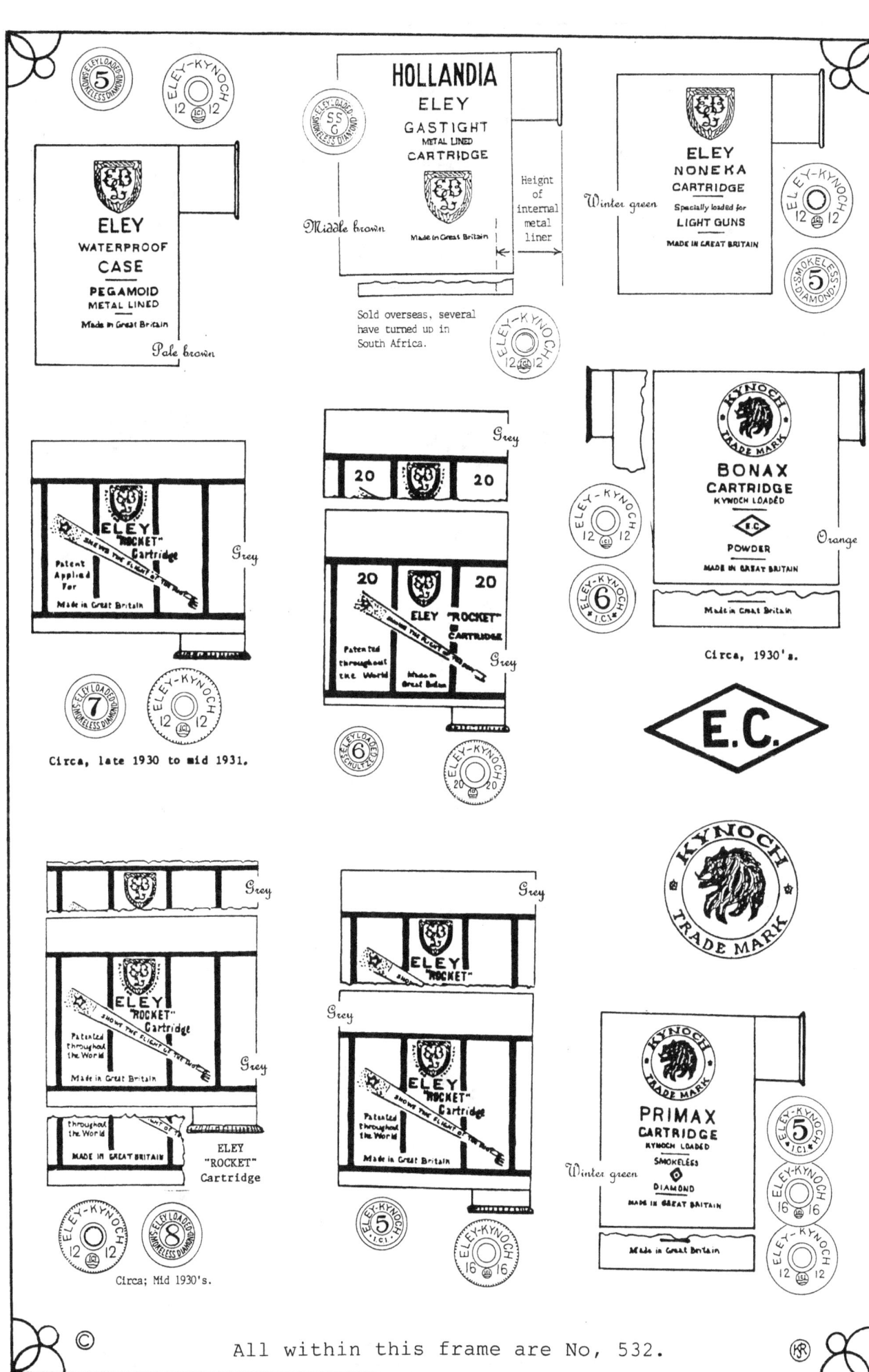

PLATE J2

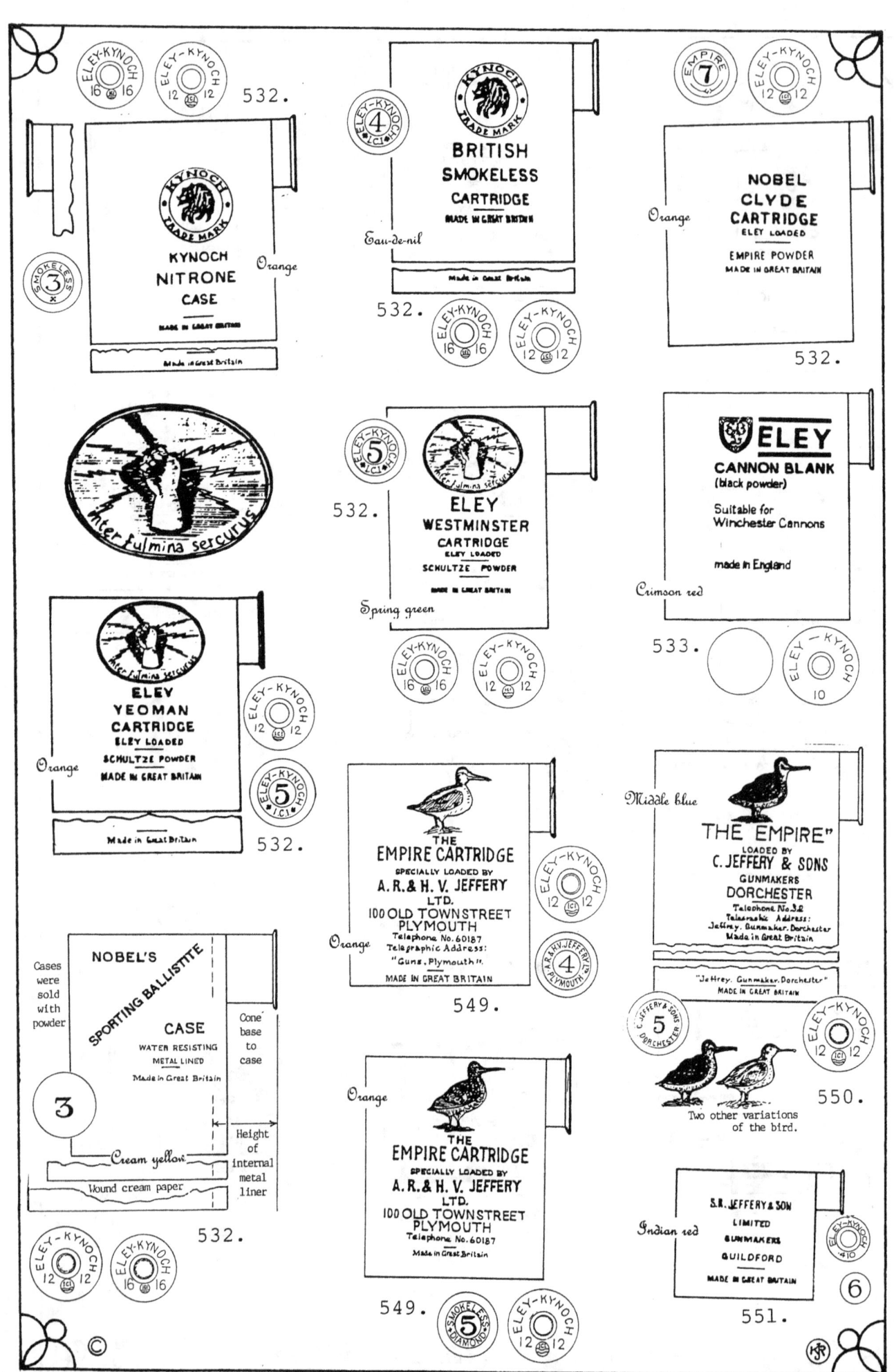

PLATE J3

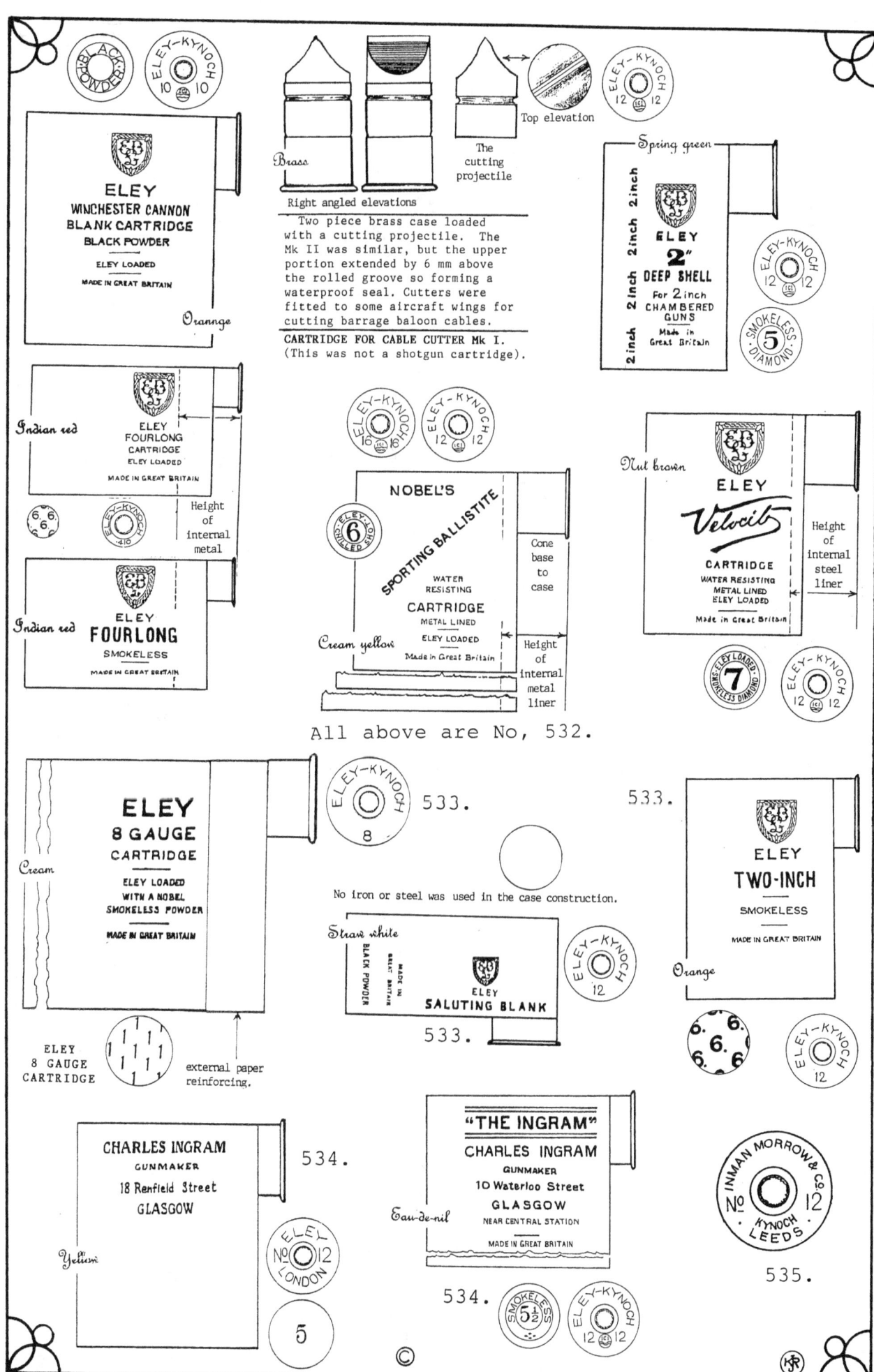

PLATE J4

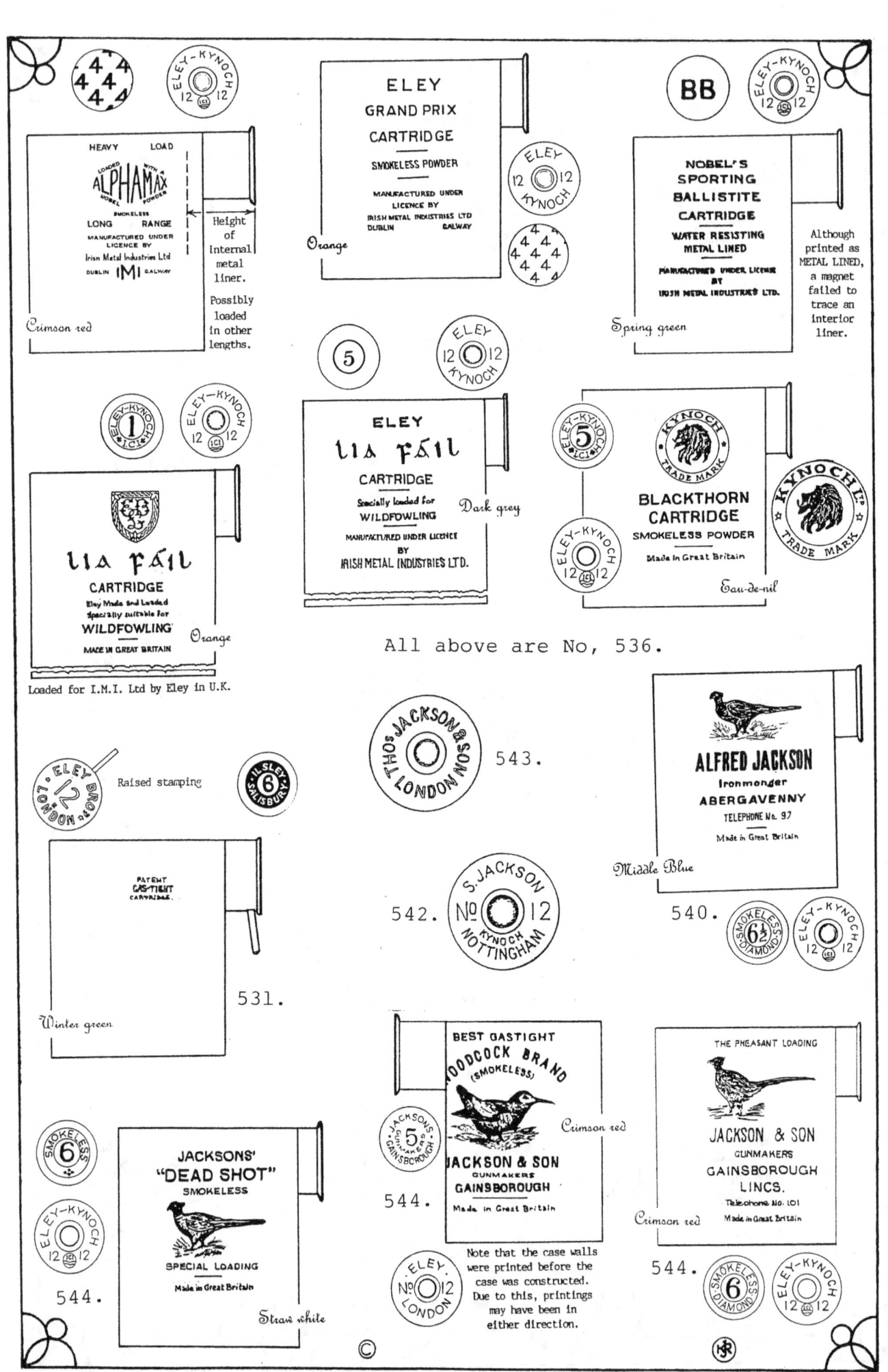

PLATE J5

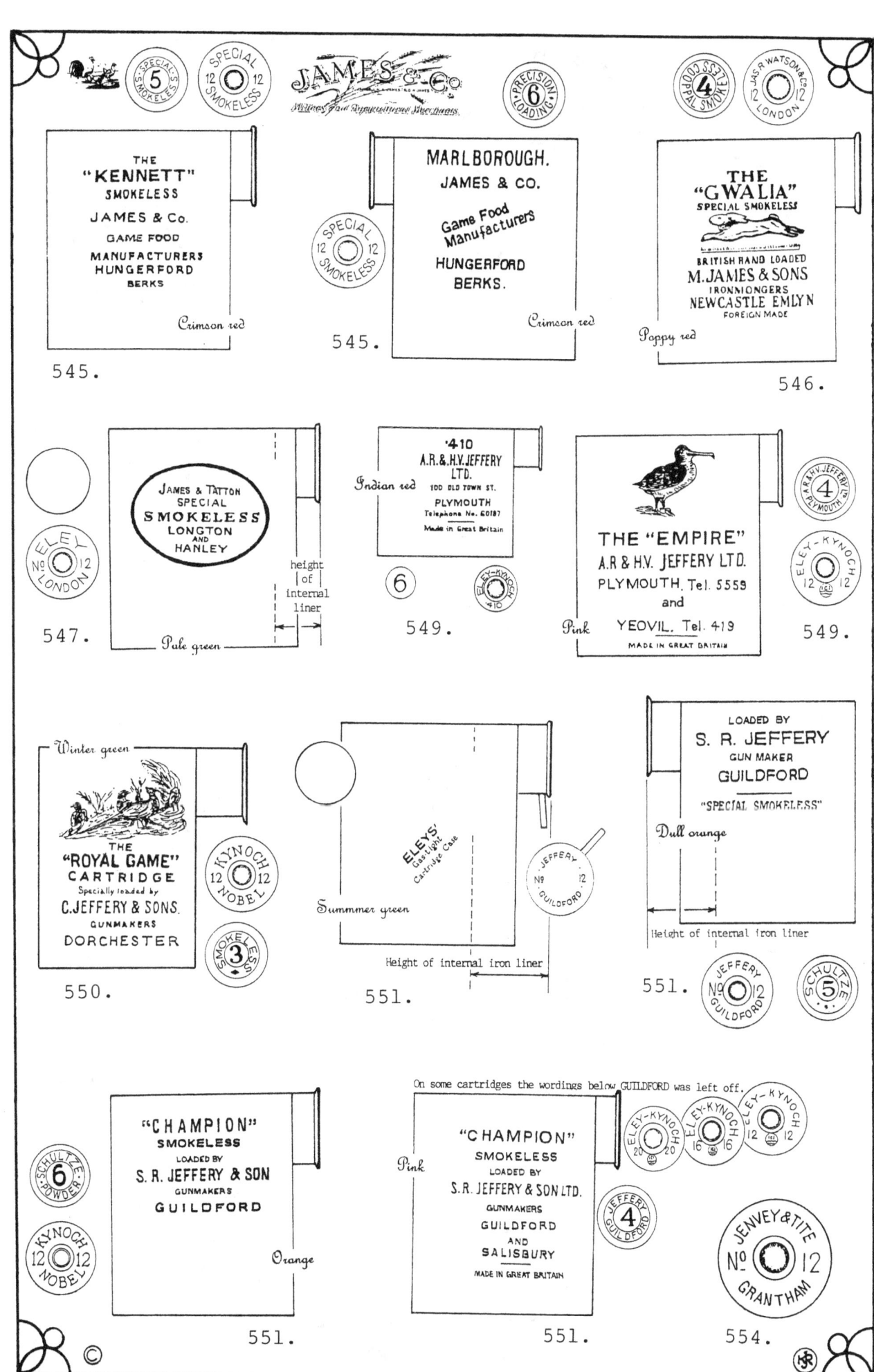

PLATE J6

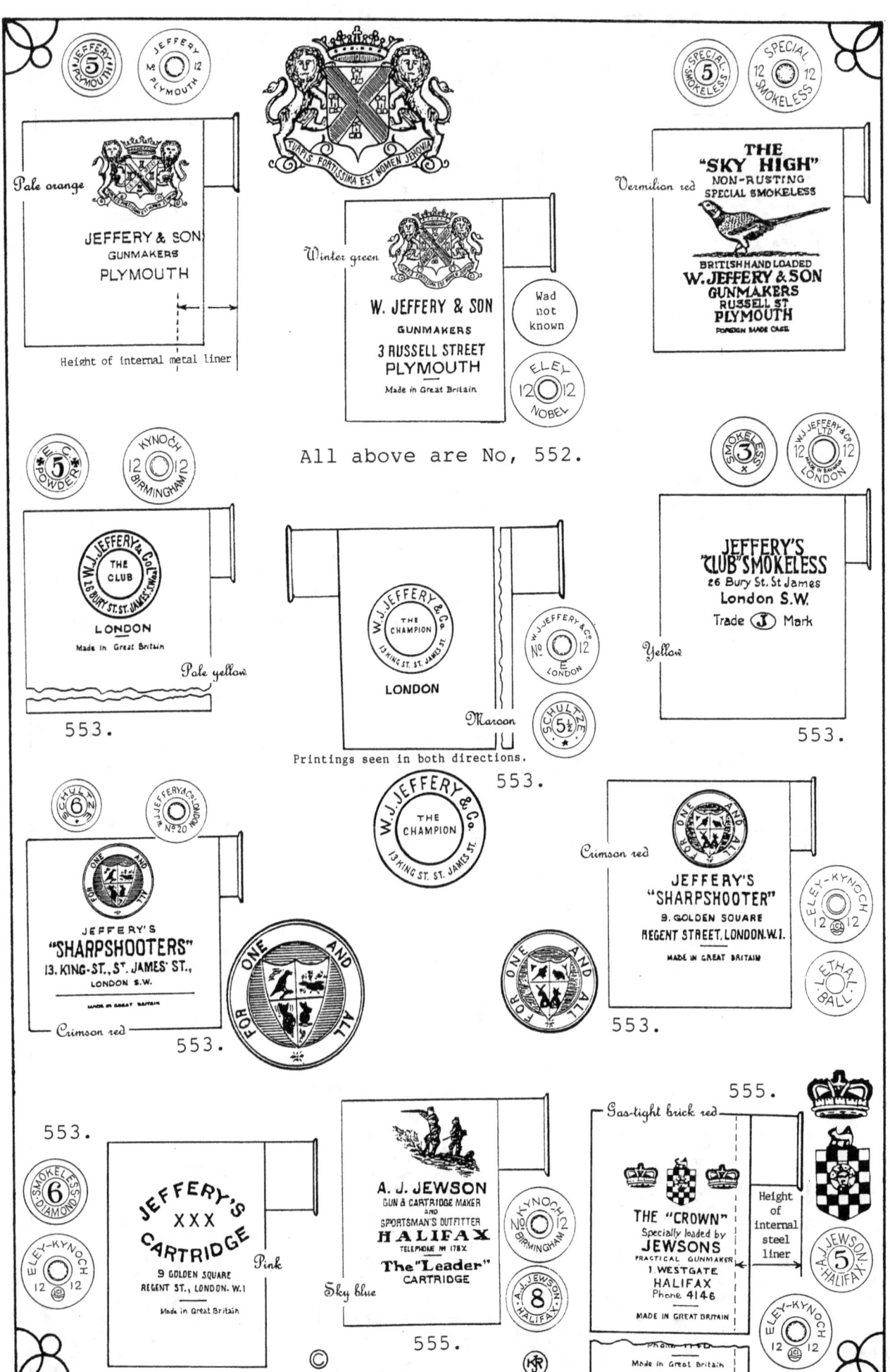

PLATE J7

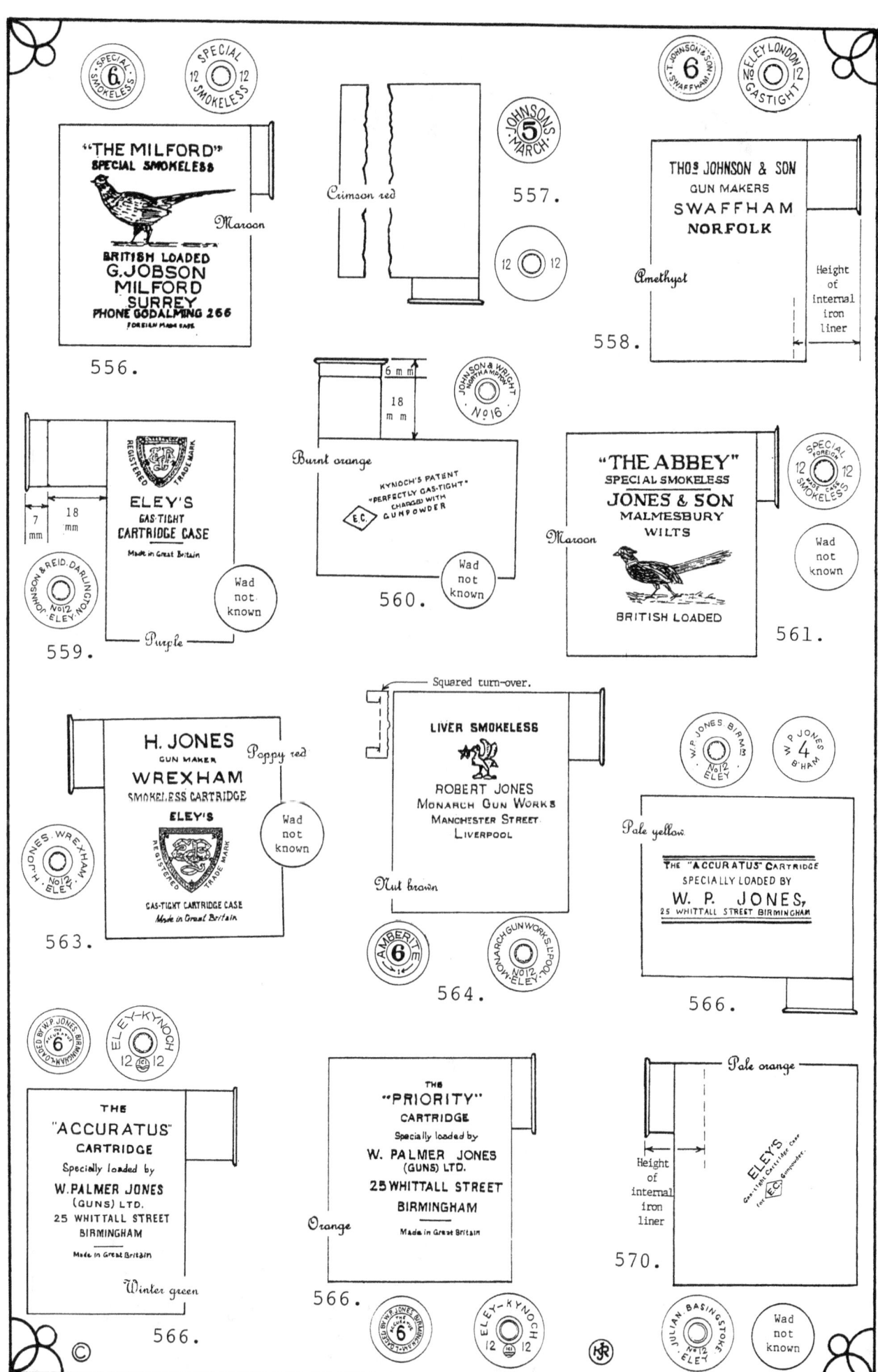

PLATE J8

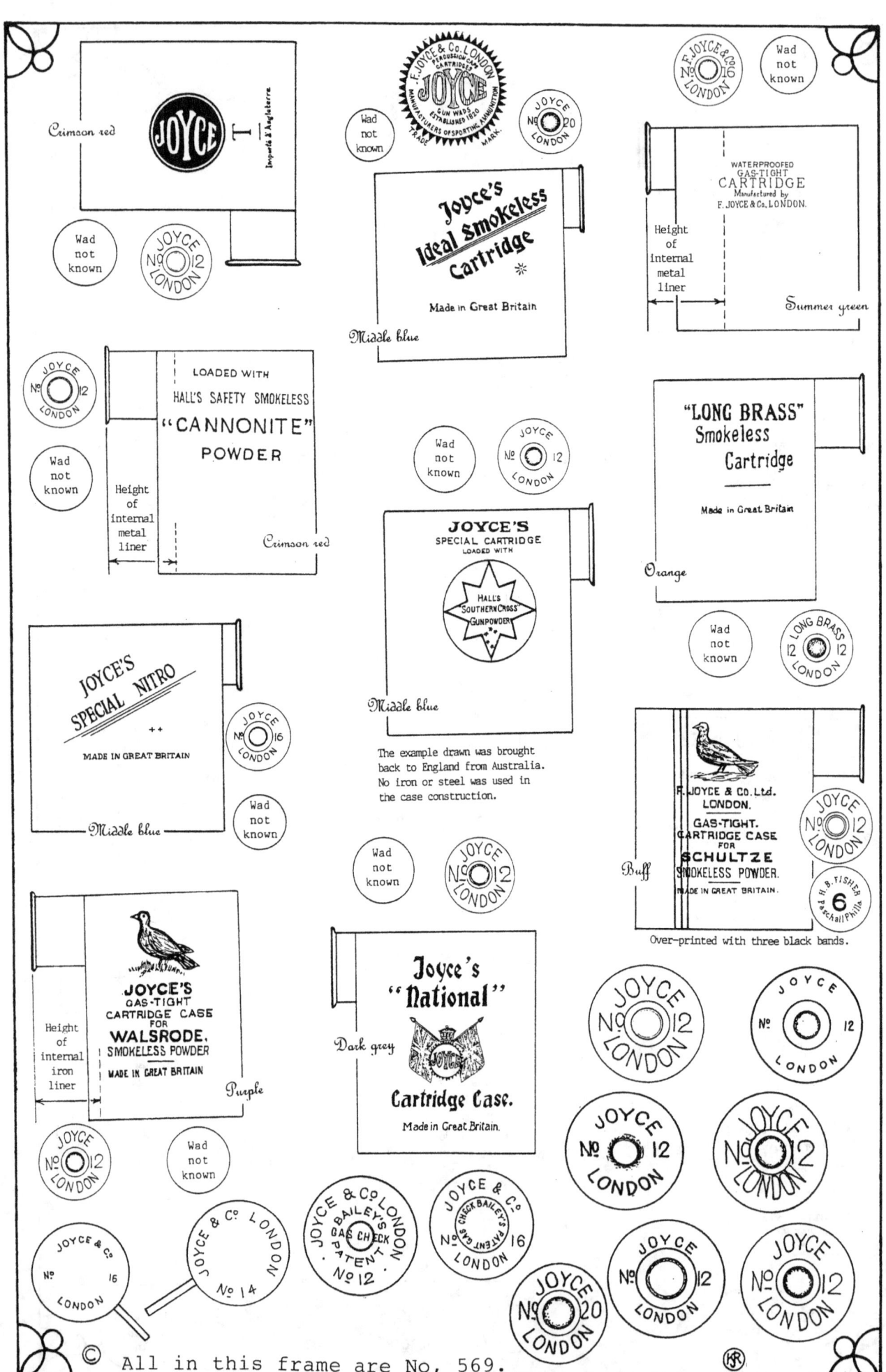

PLATE J9

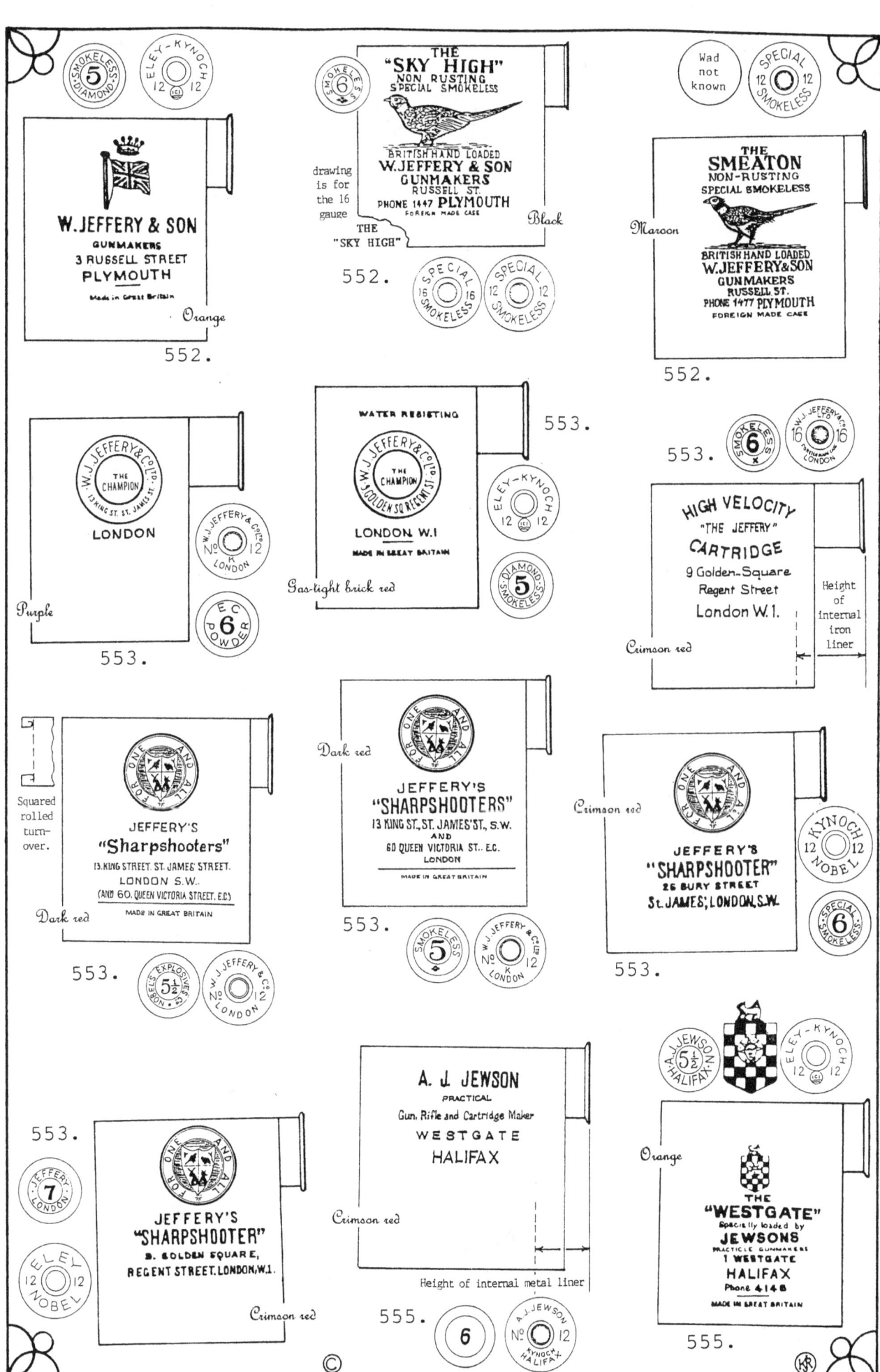

PLATE K1

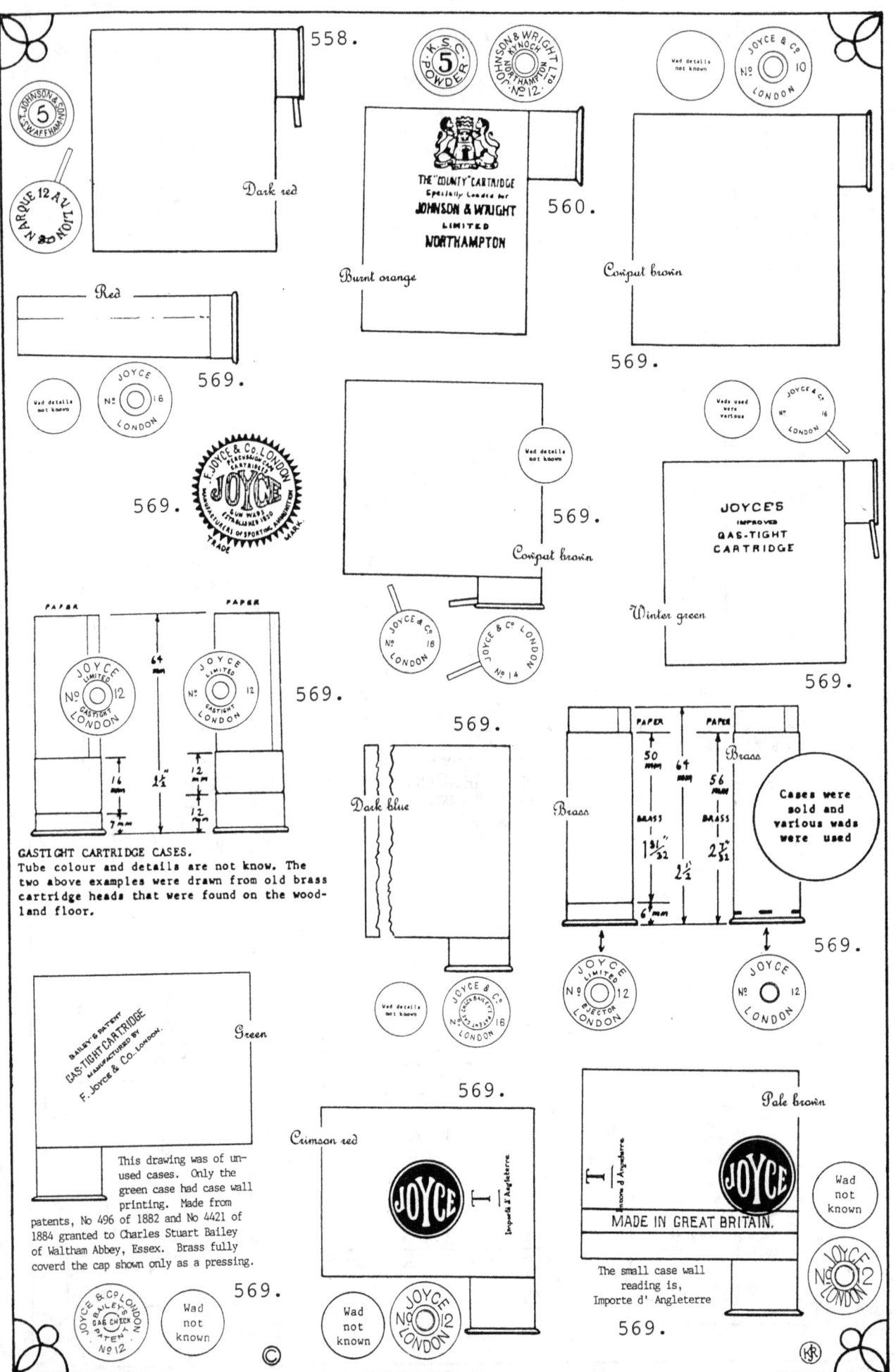

PLATE K2

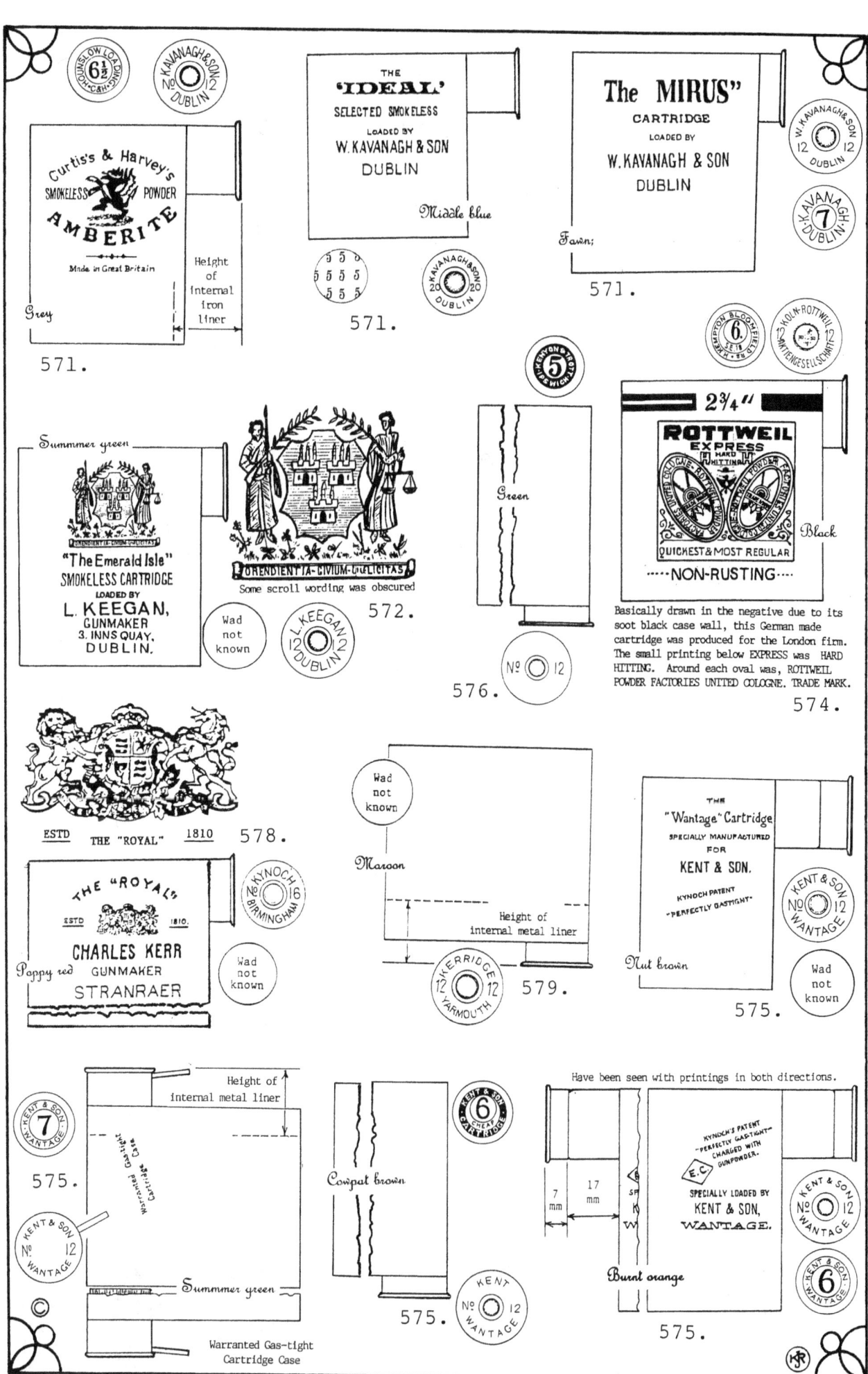

PLATE K3

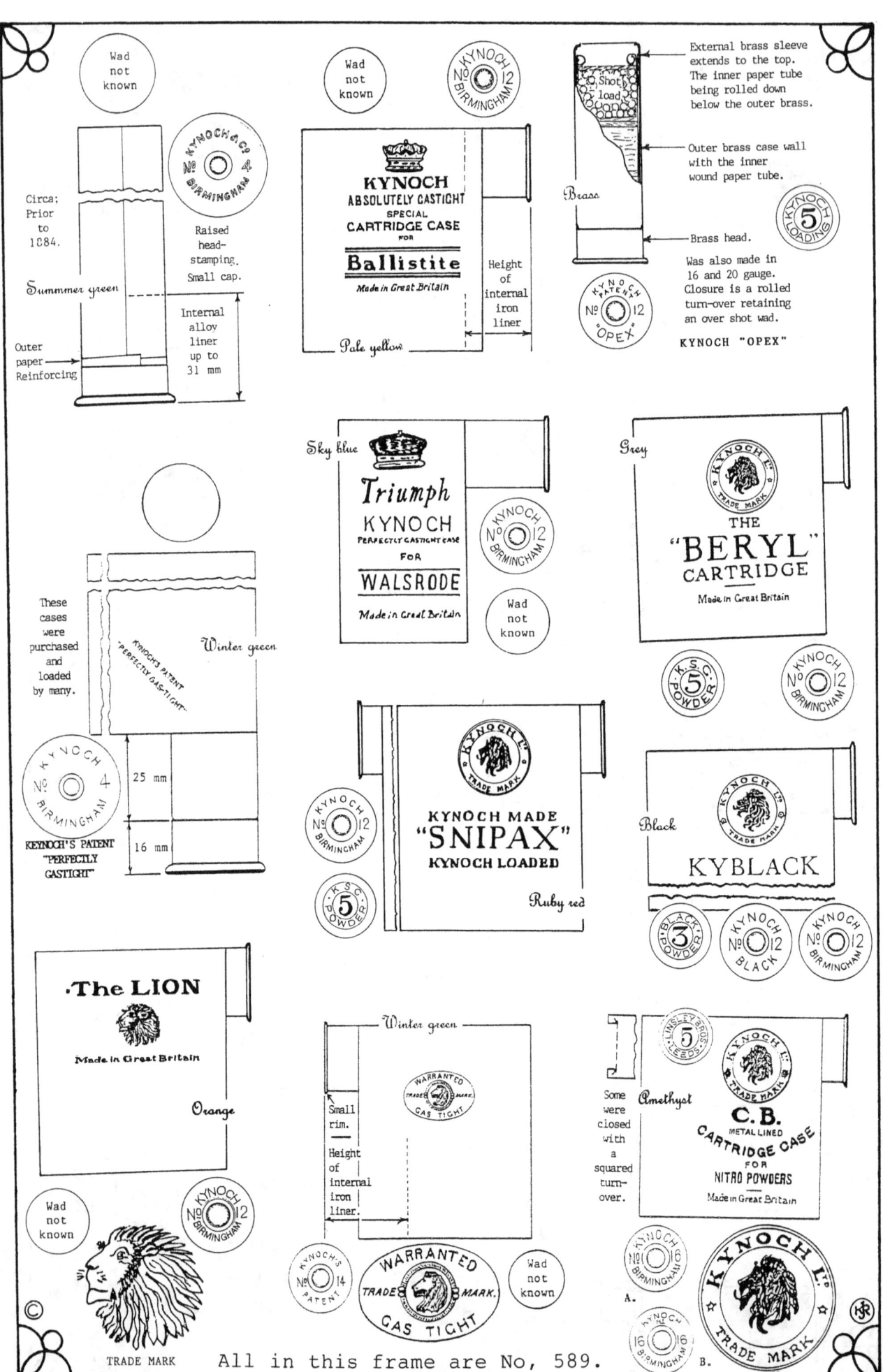

PLATE K4

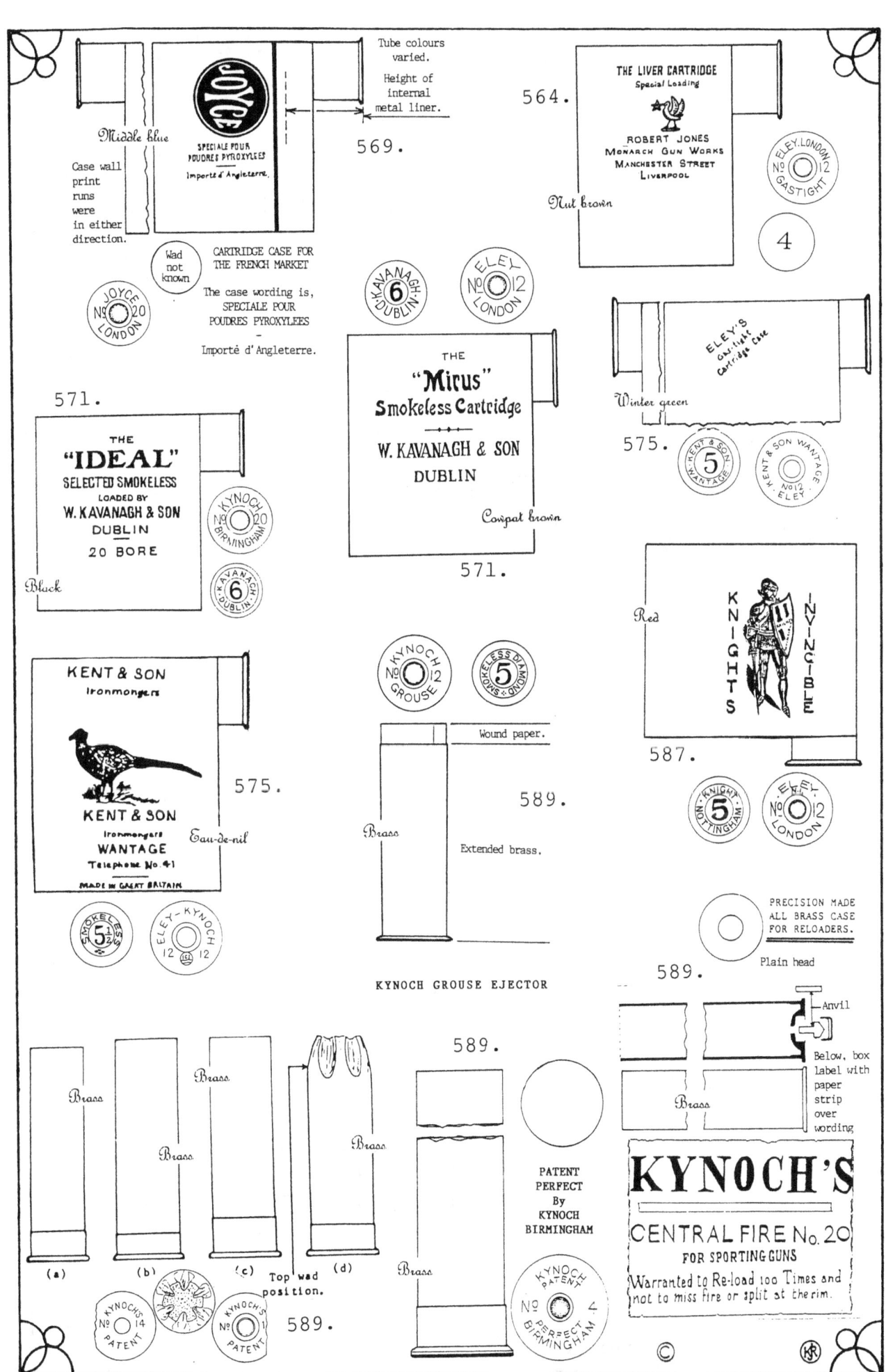

PLATE K5

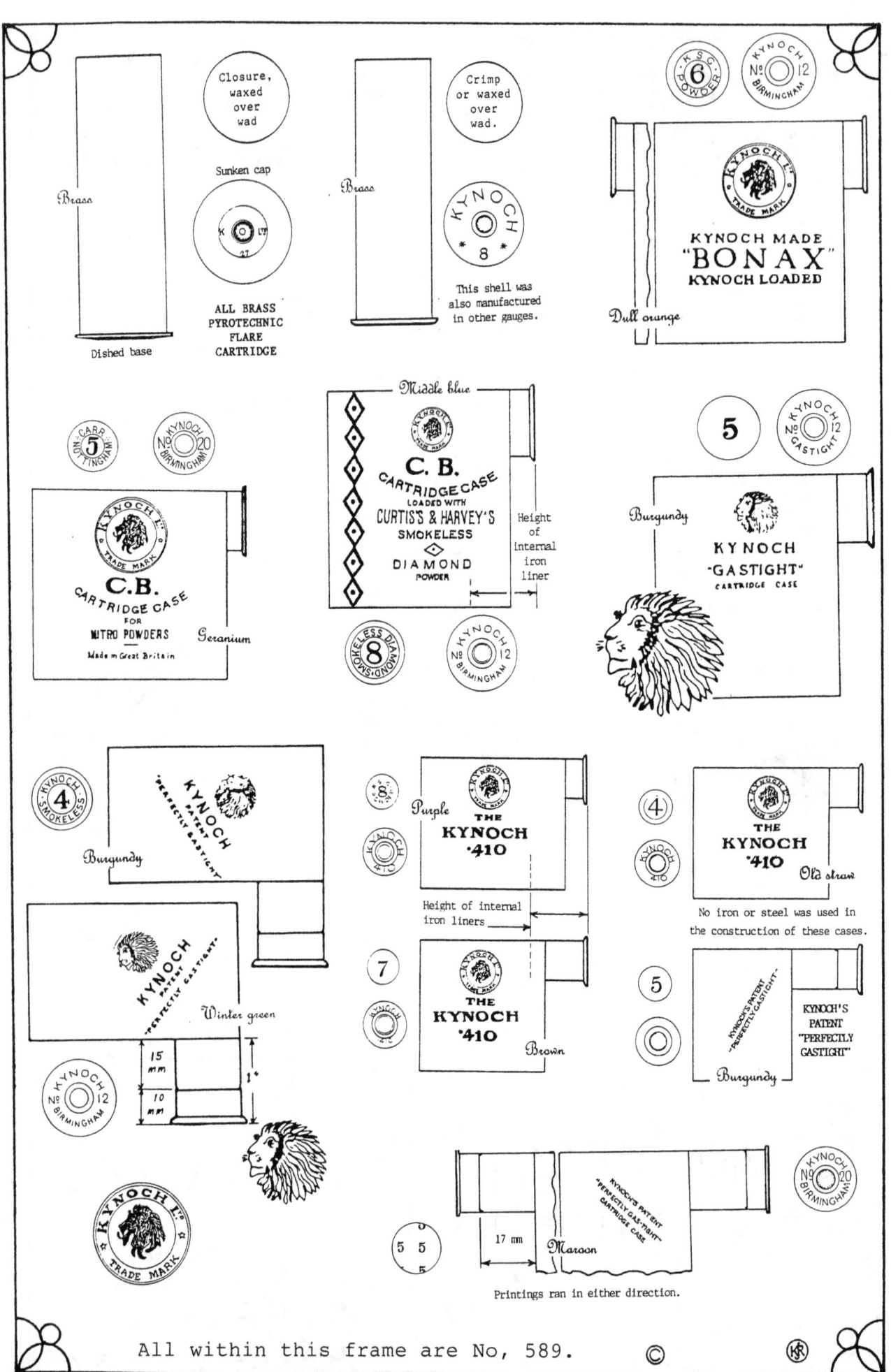

PLATE K6

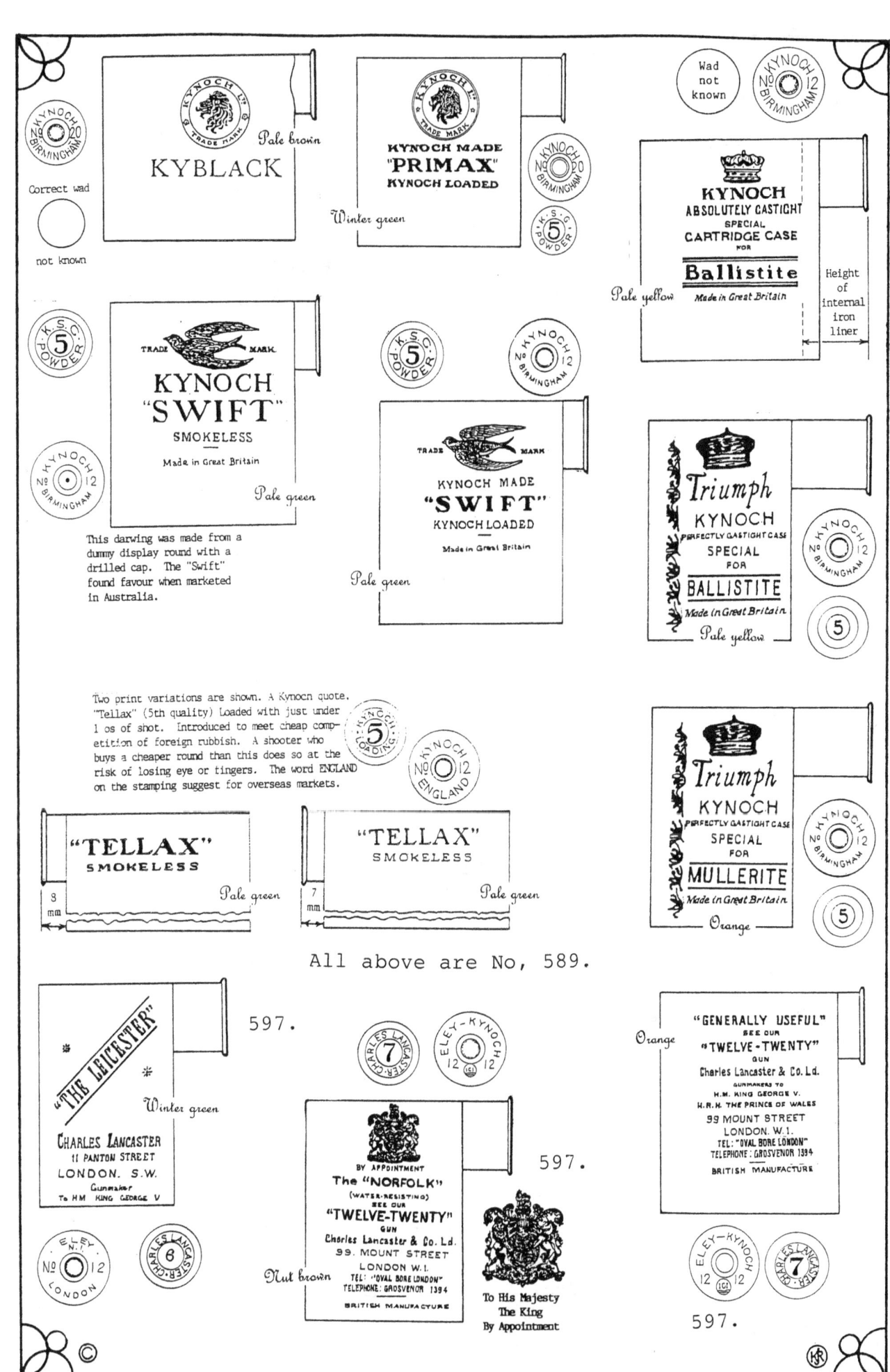

PLATE K7

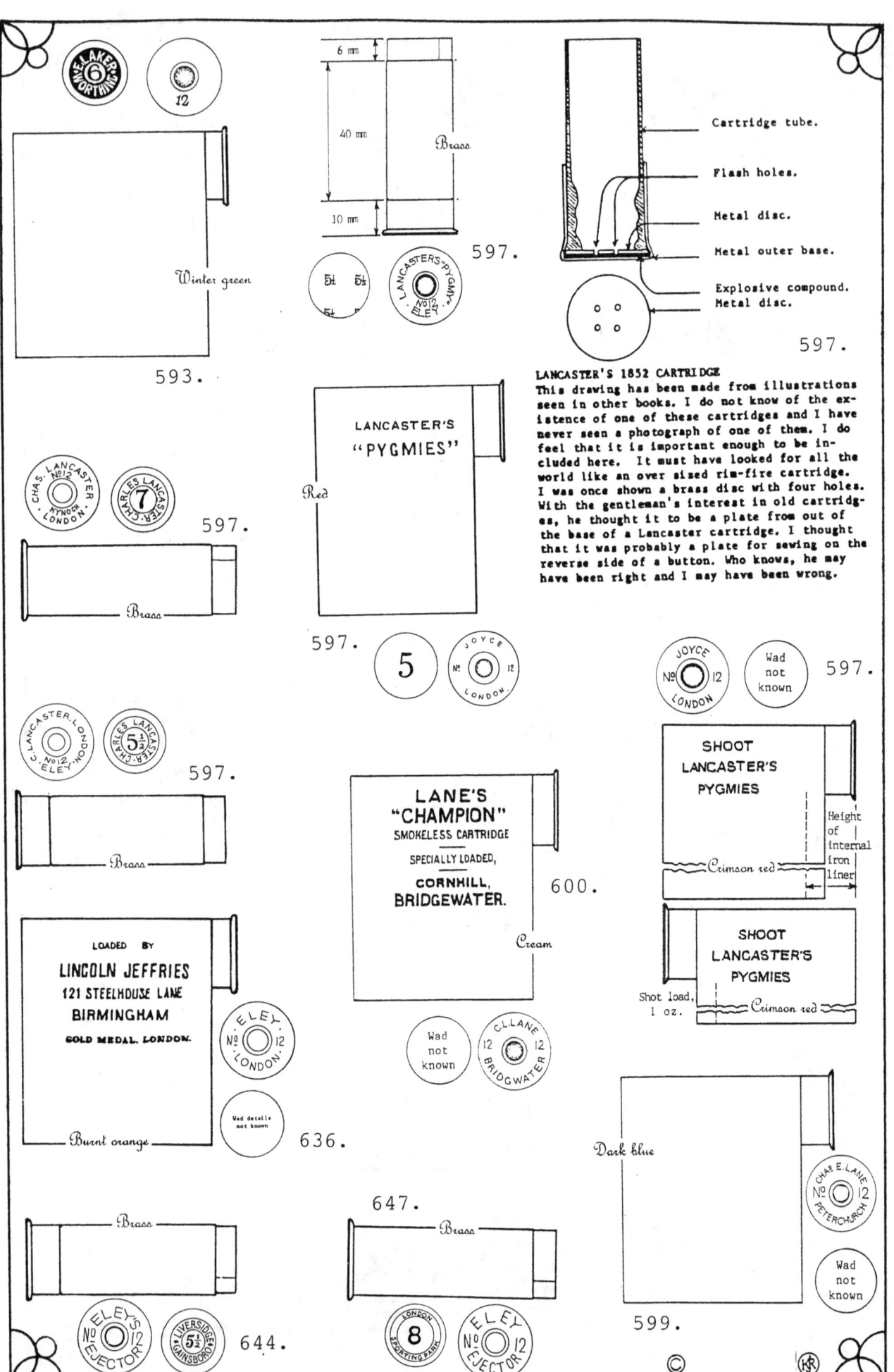

PLATE K8

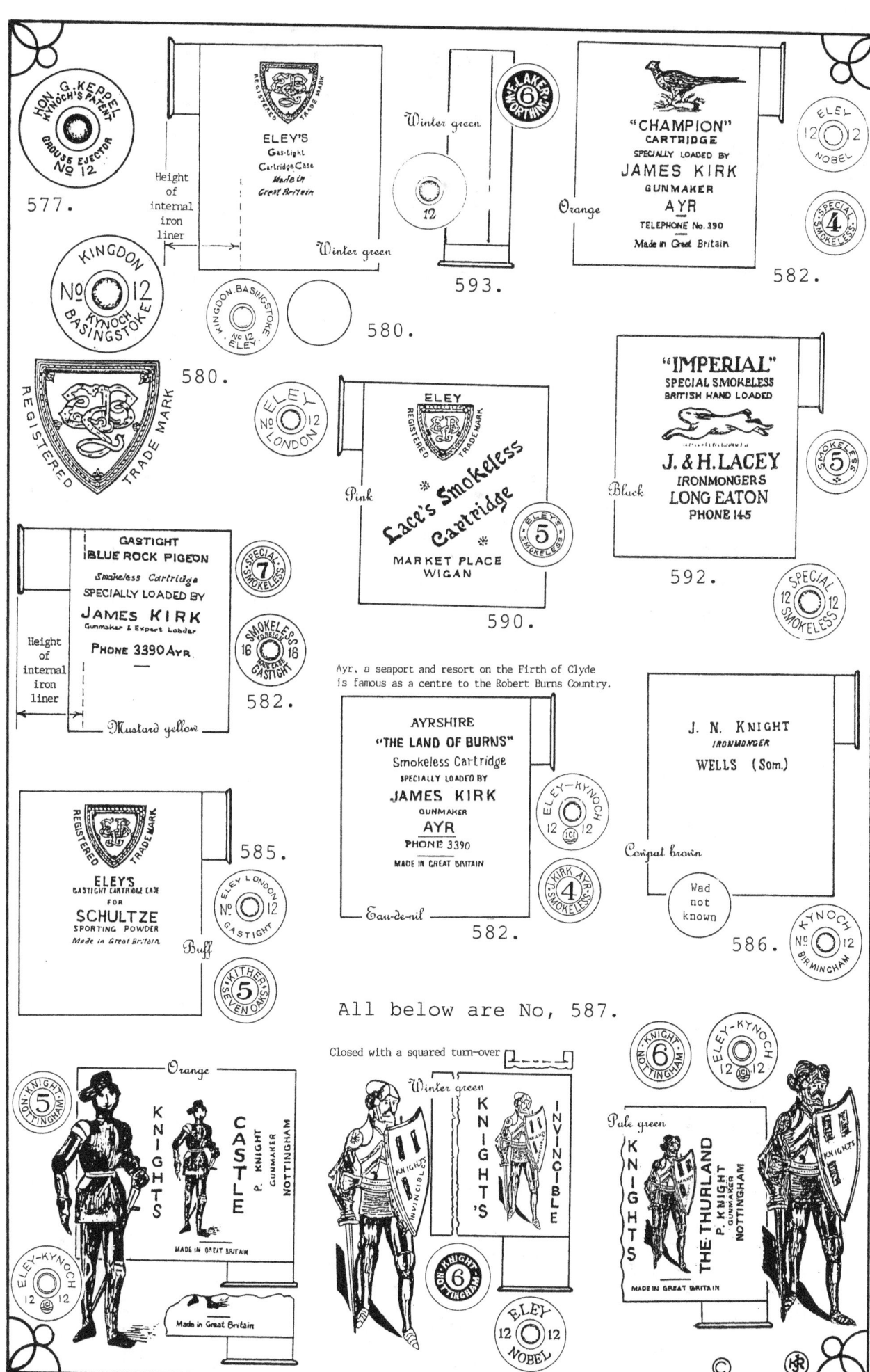

PLATE K9

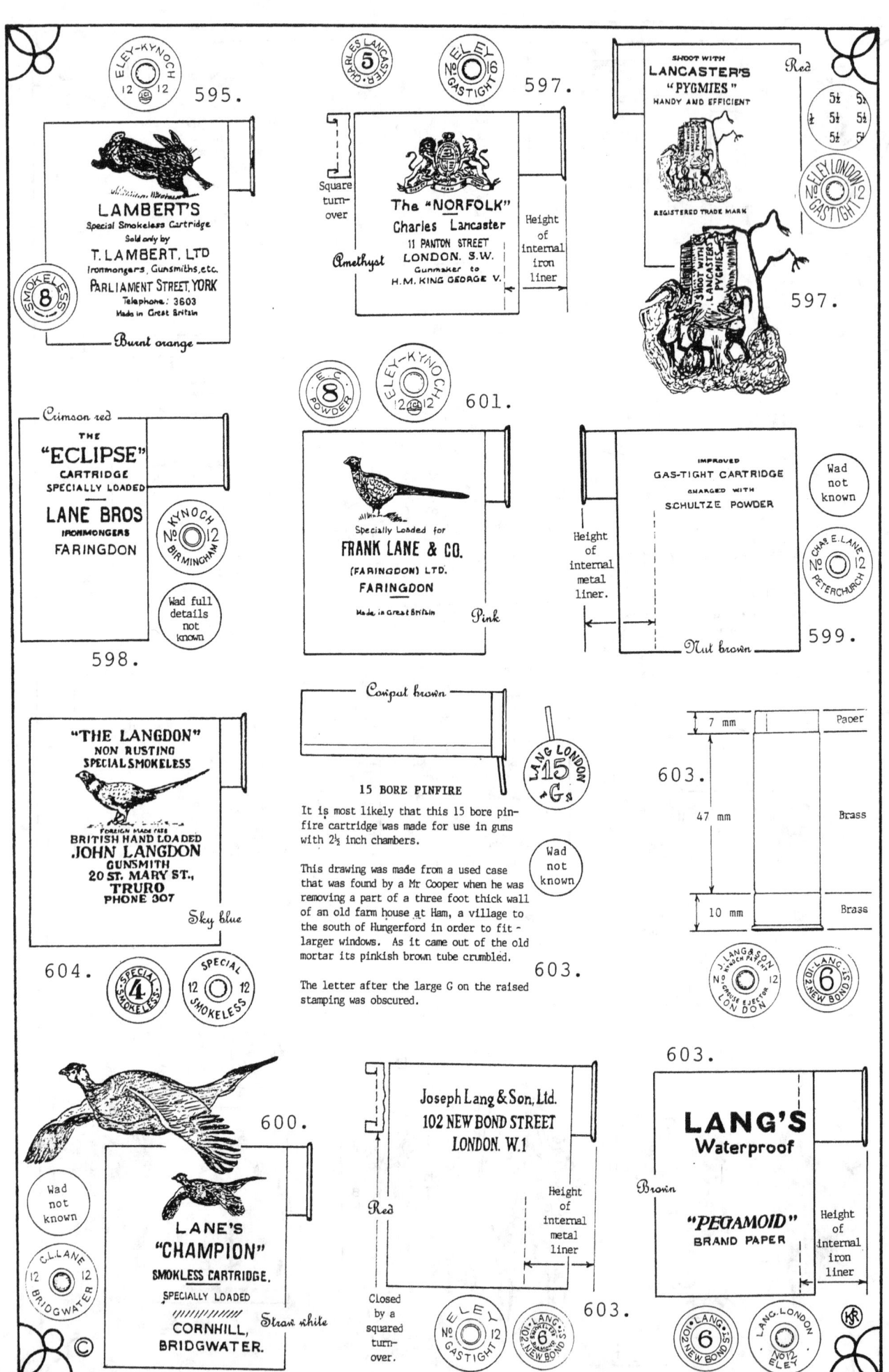

PLATE L1

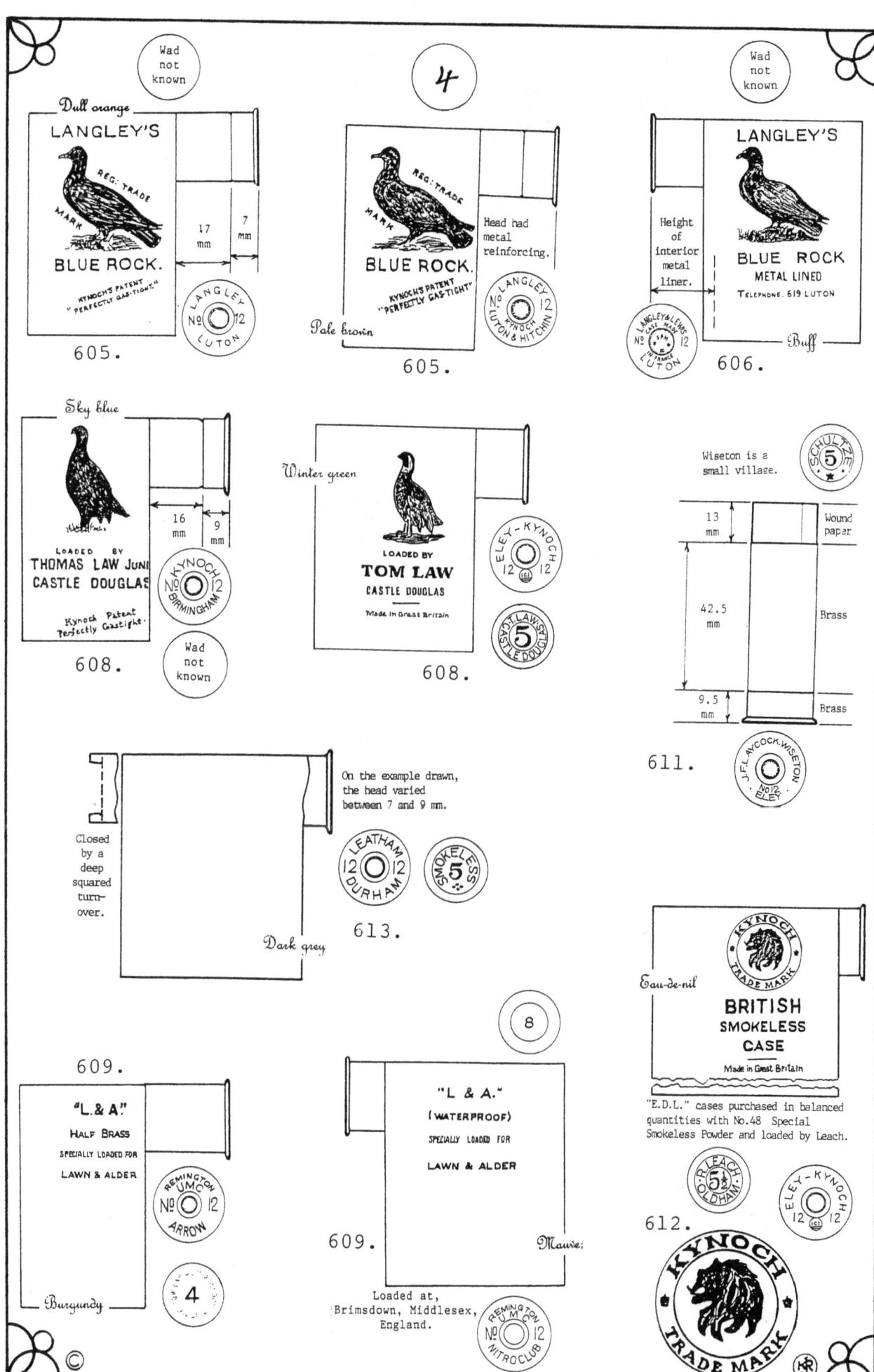

PLATE L2

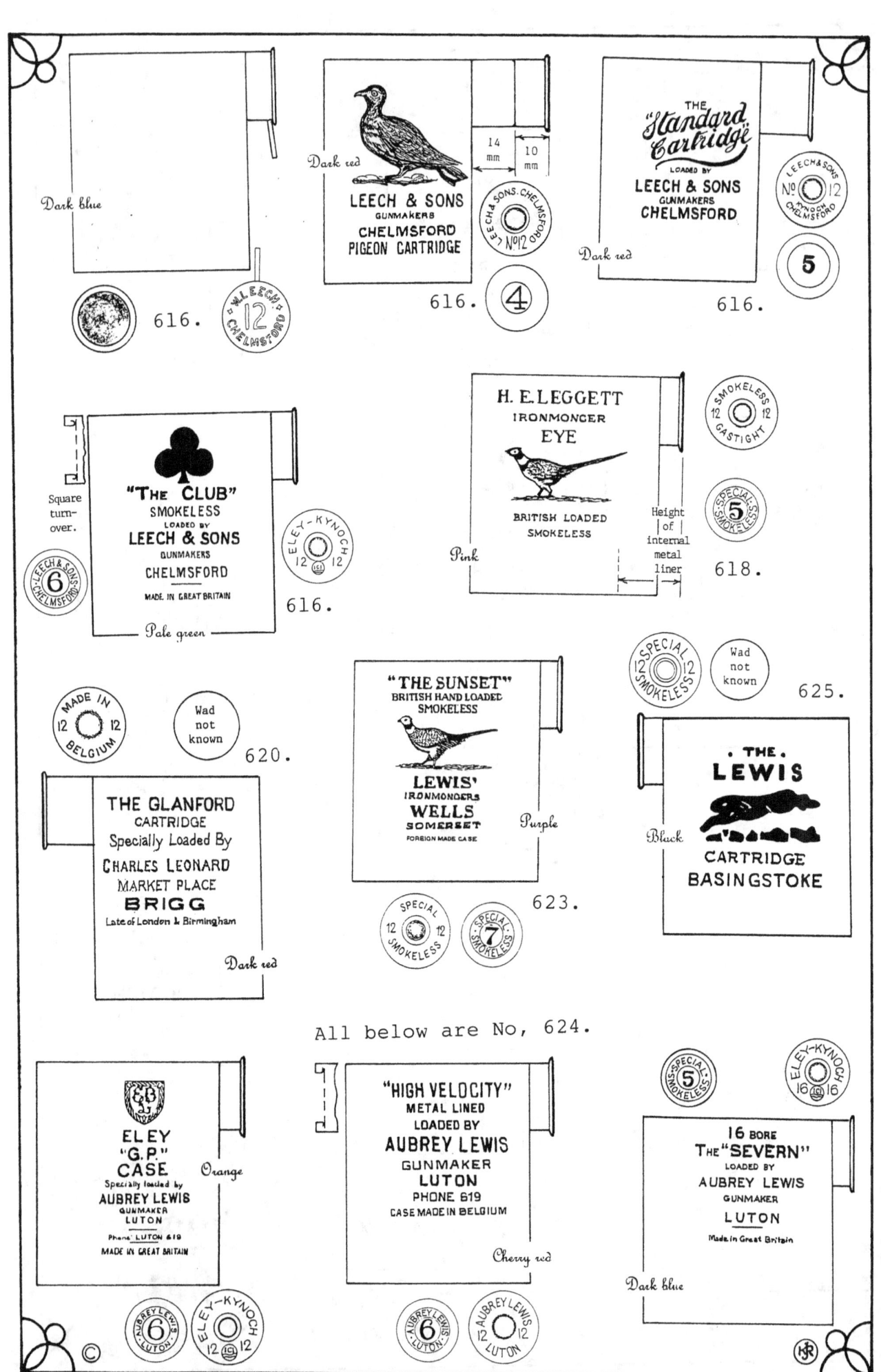

PLATE L3

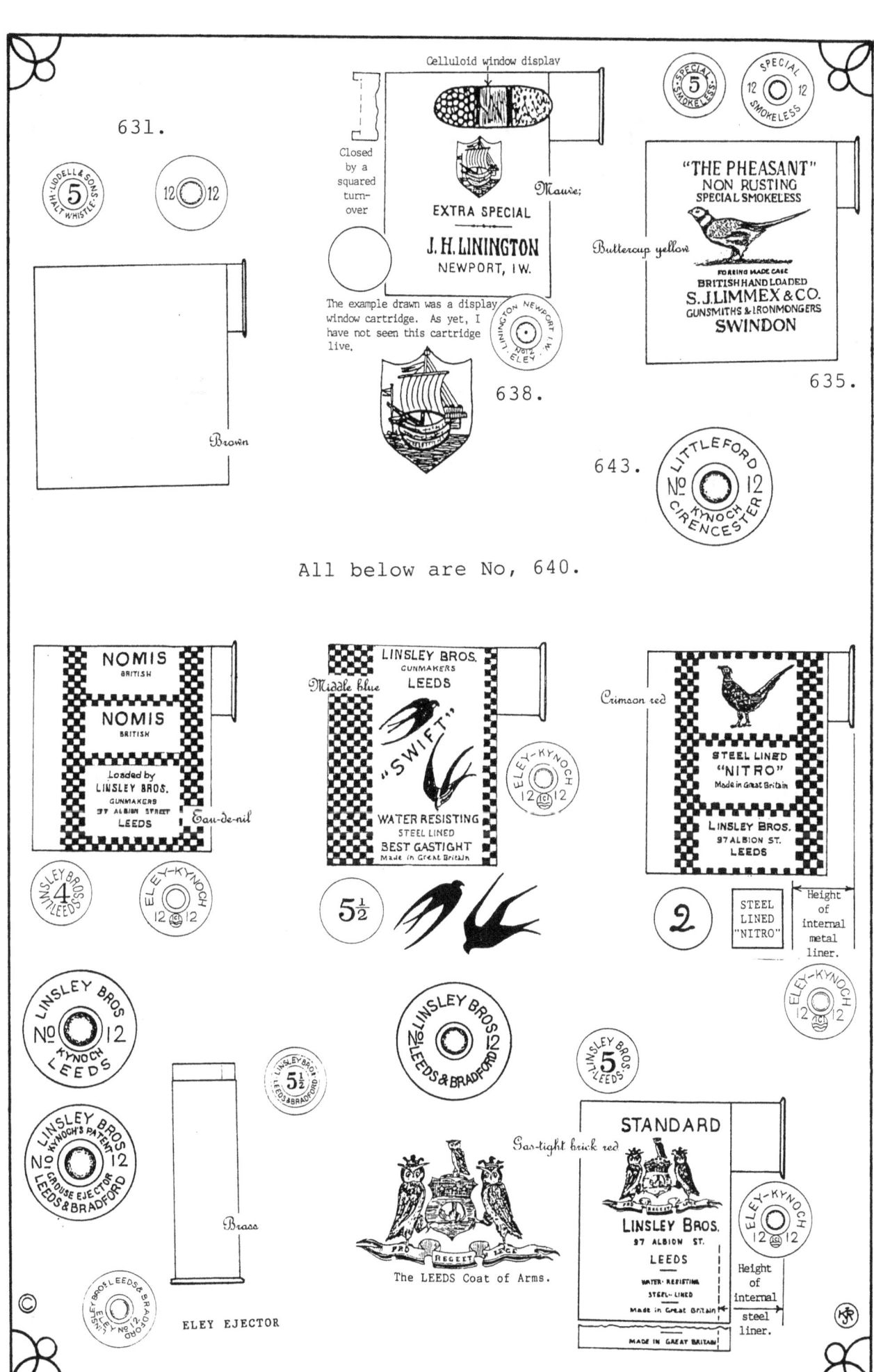

PLATE L4

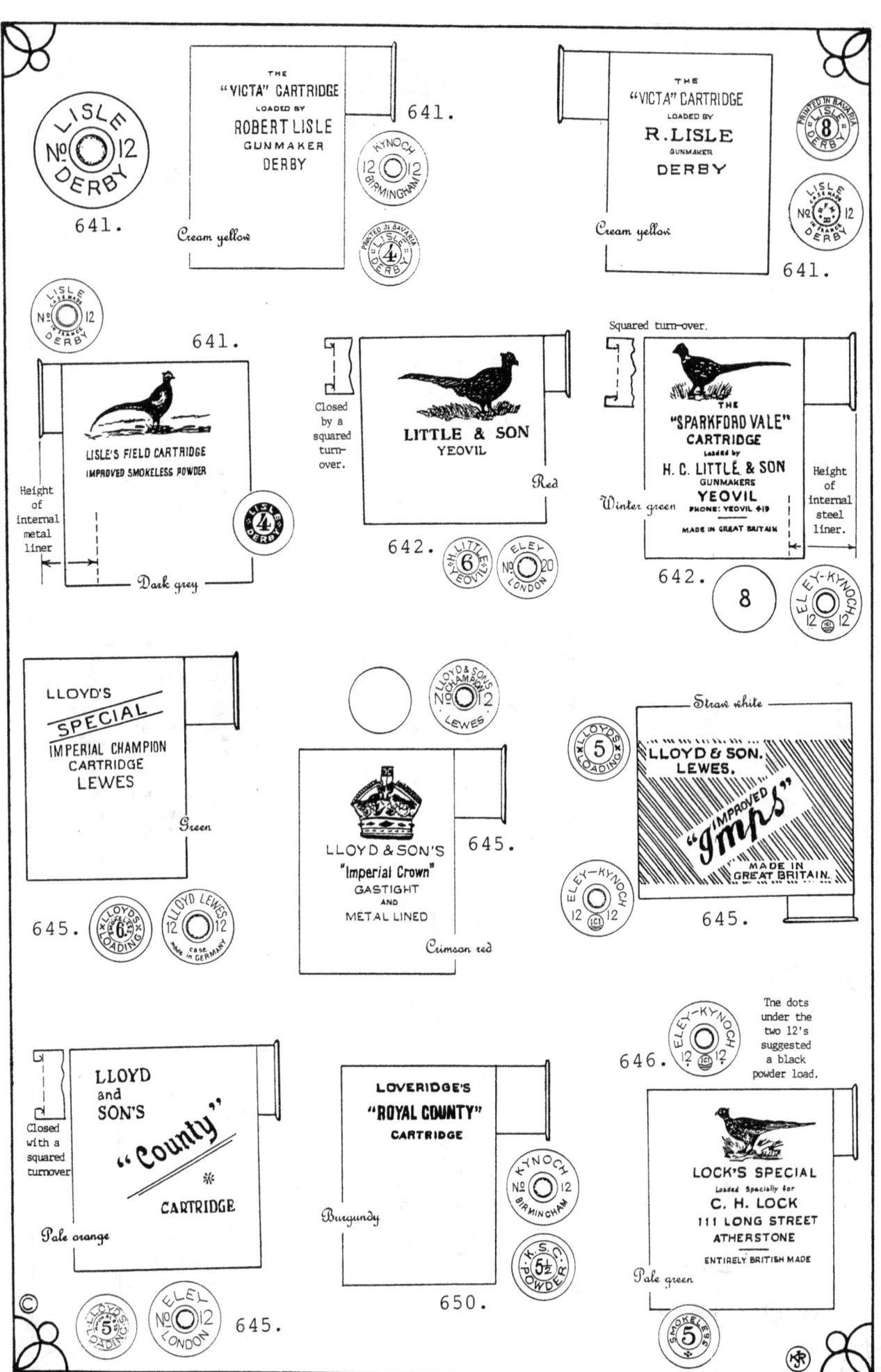

PLATE L5

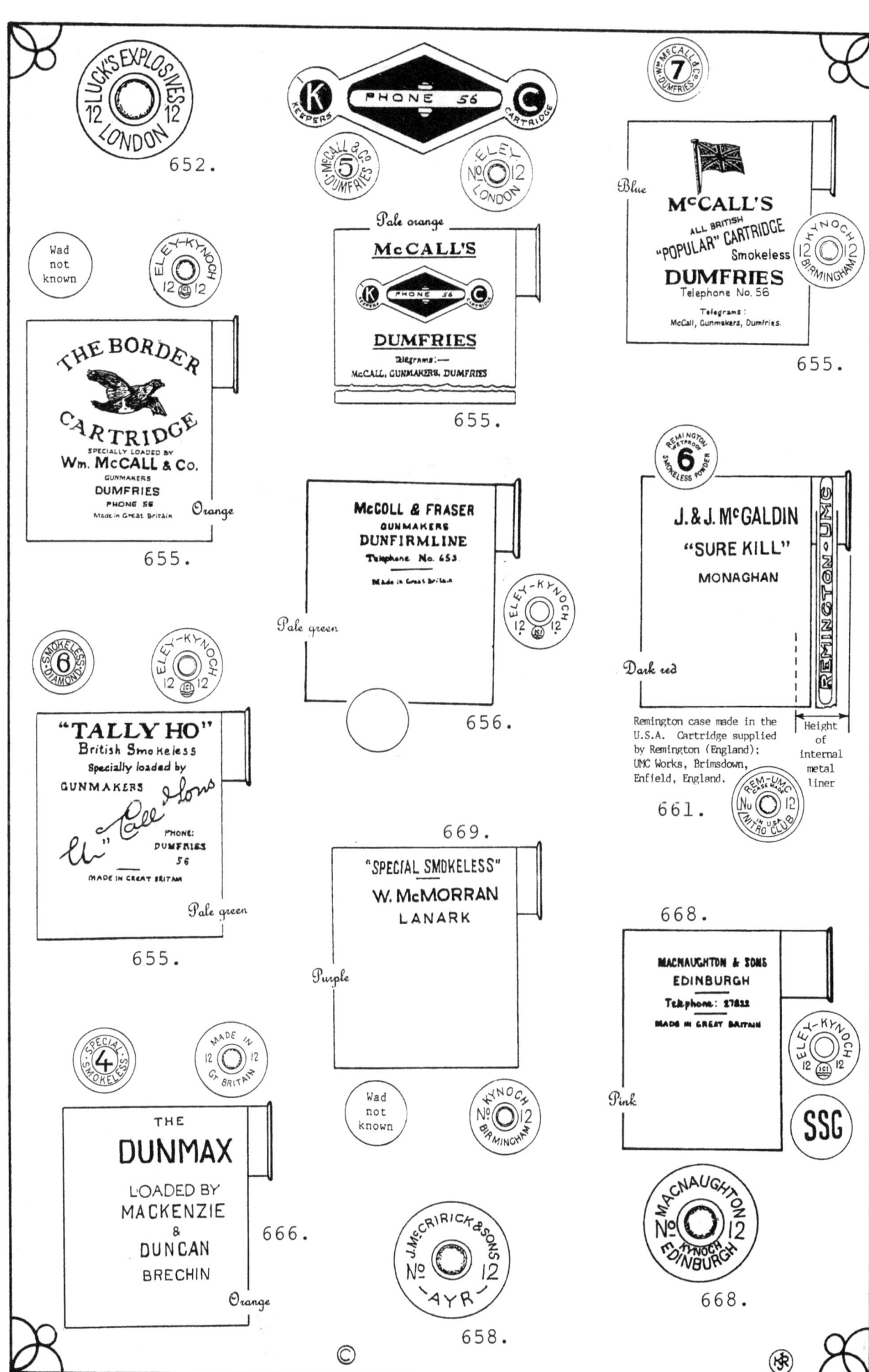

PLATE L6

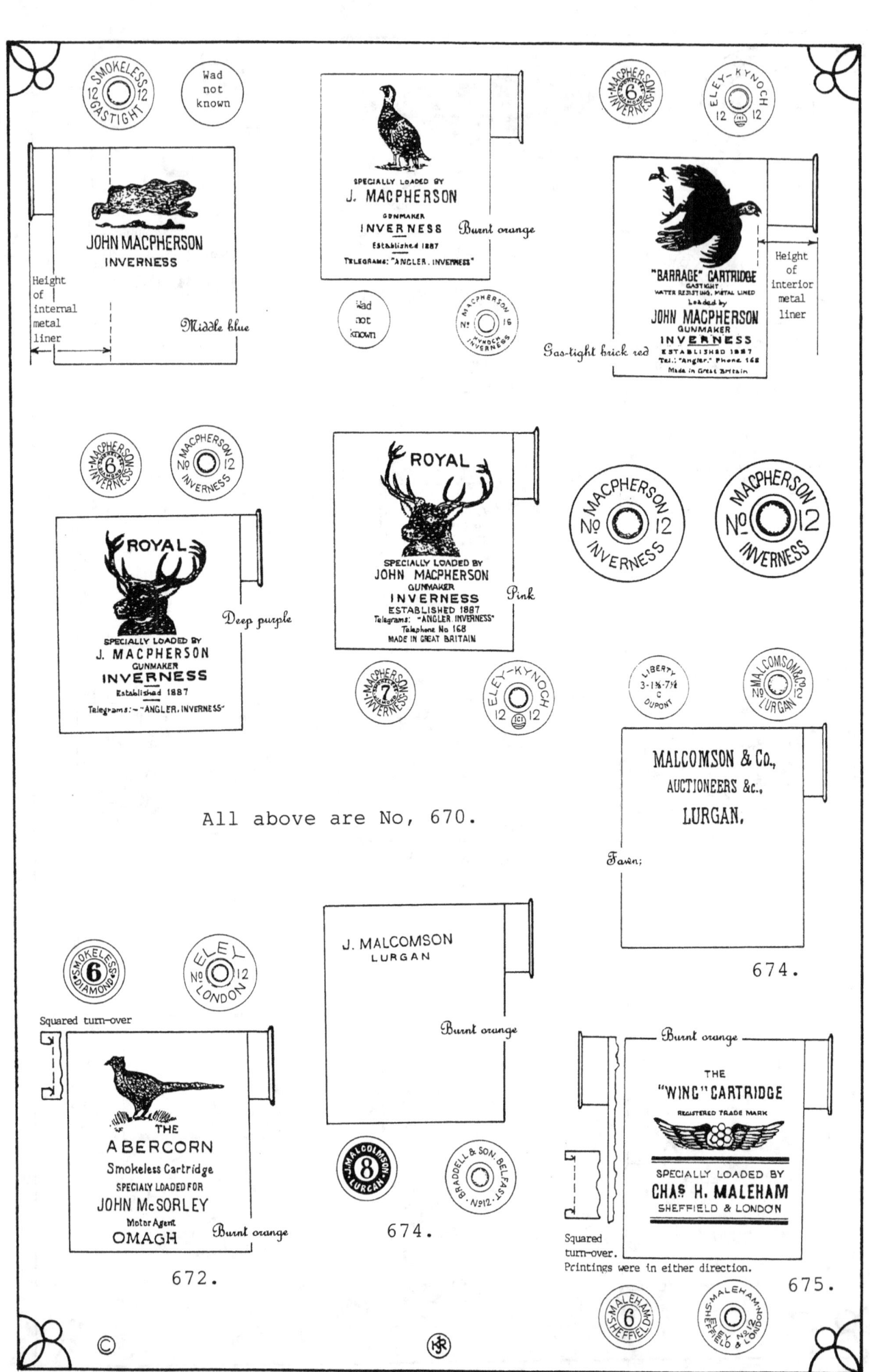

PLATE L7

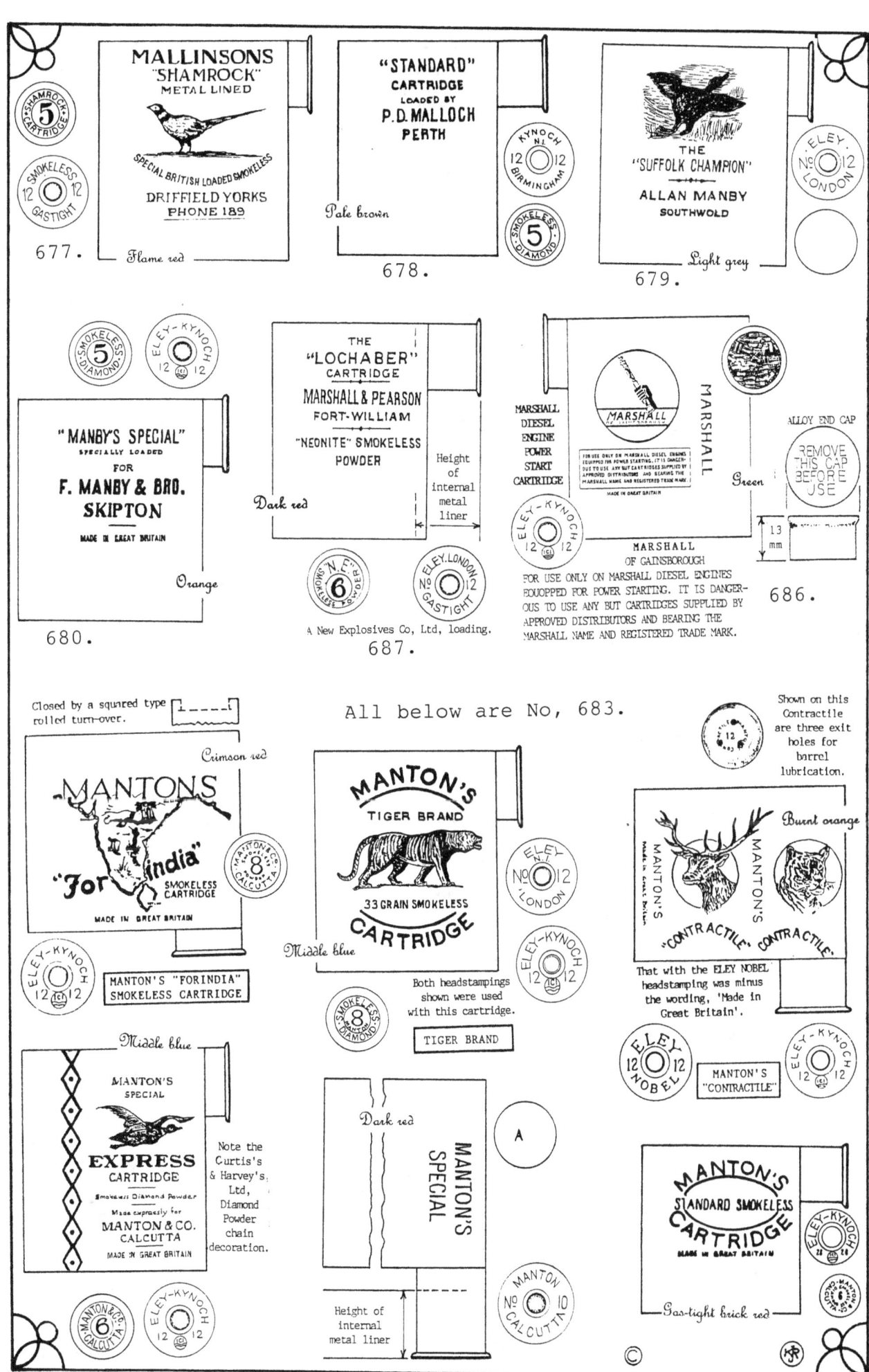

PLATE L8

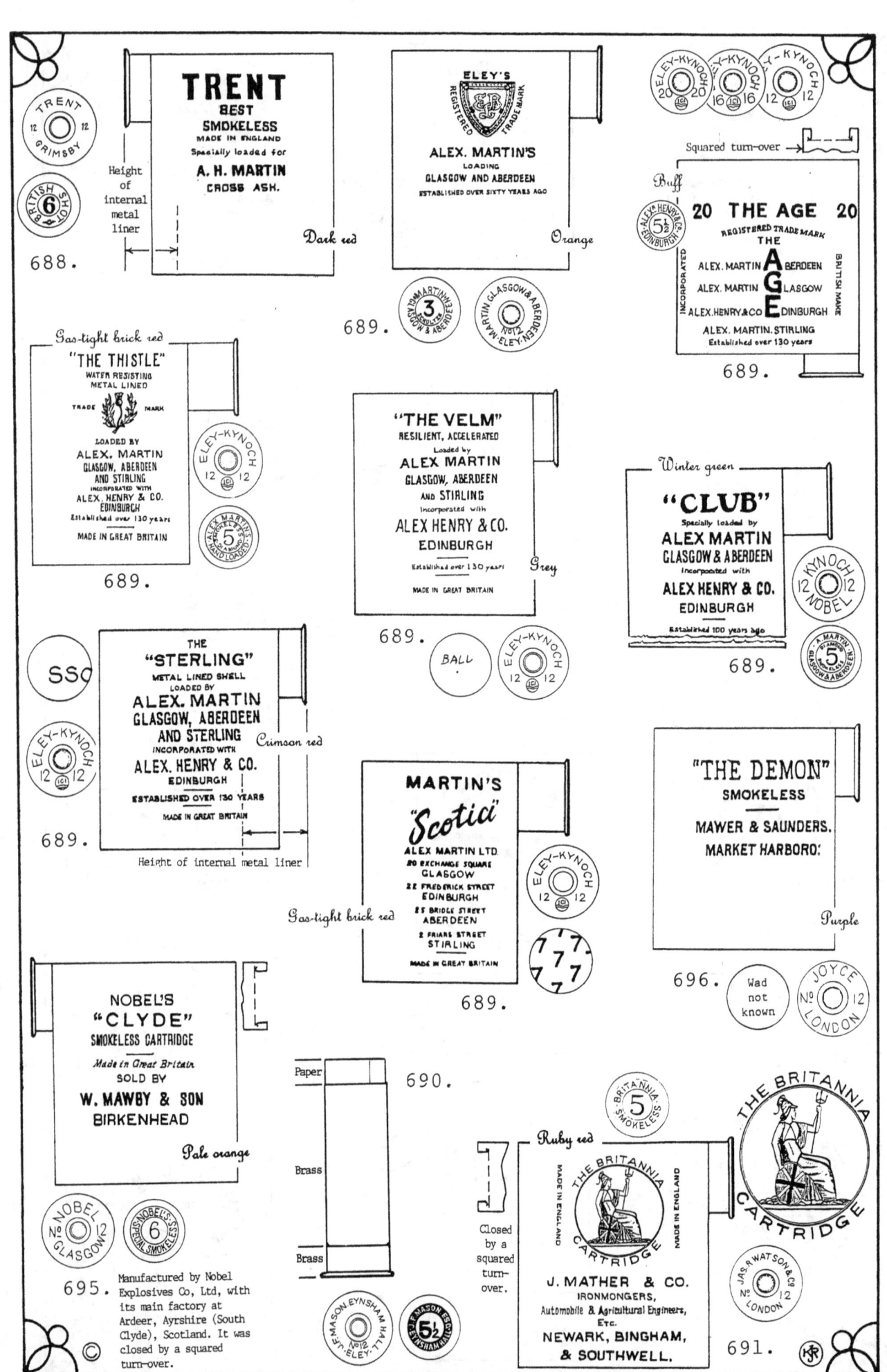

PLATE L9

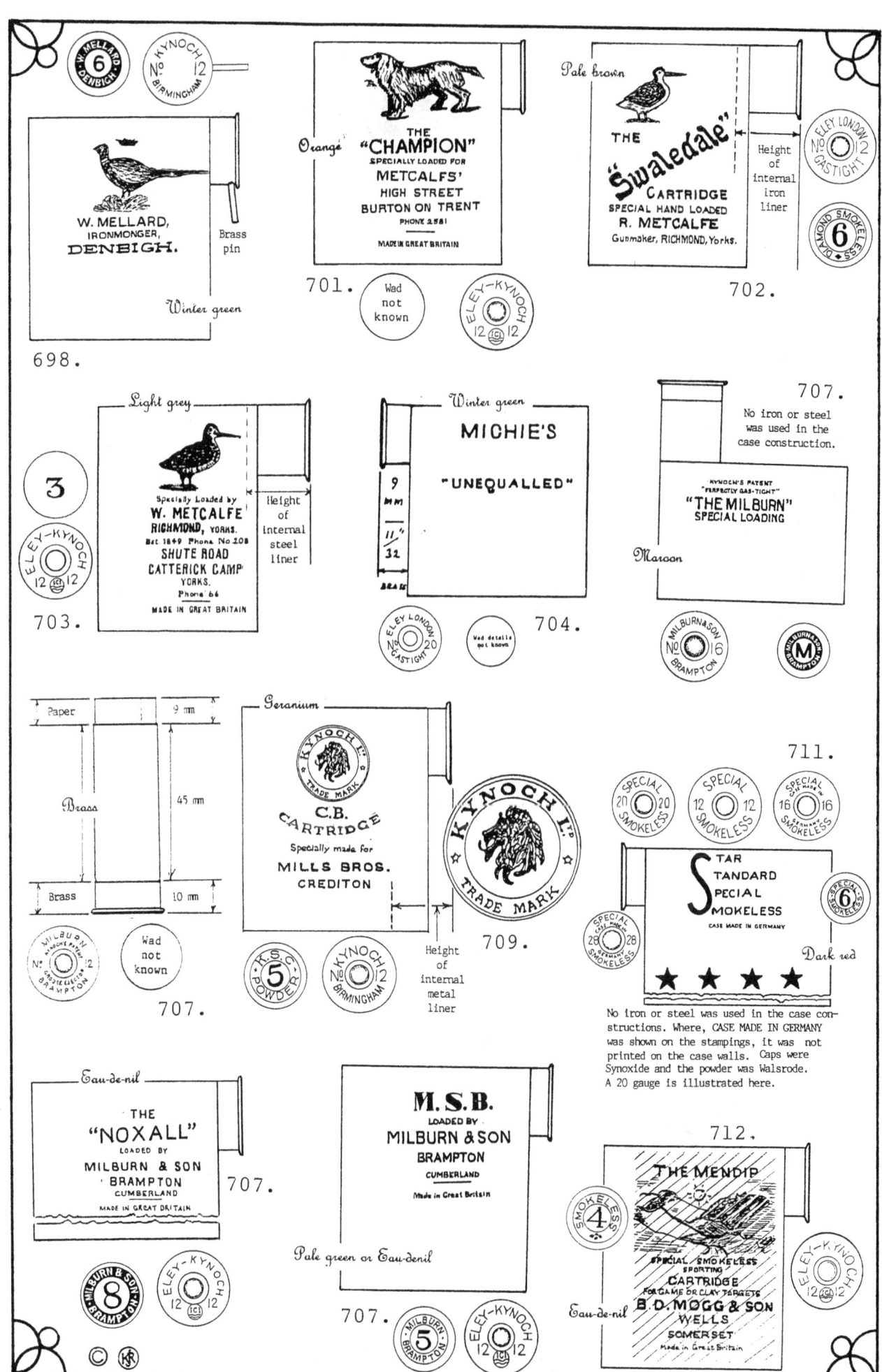

PLATE M1

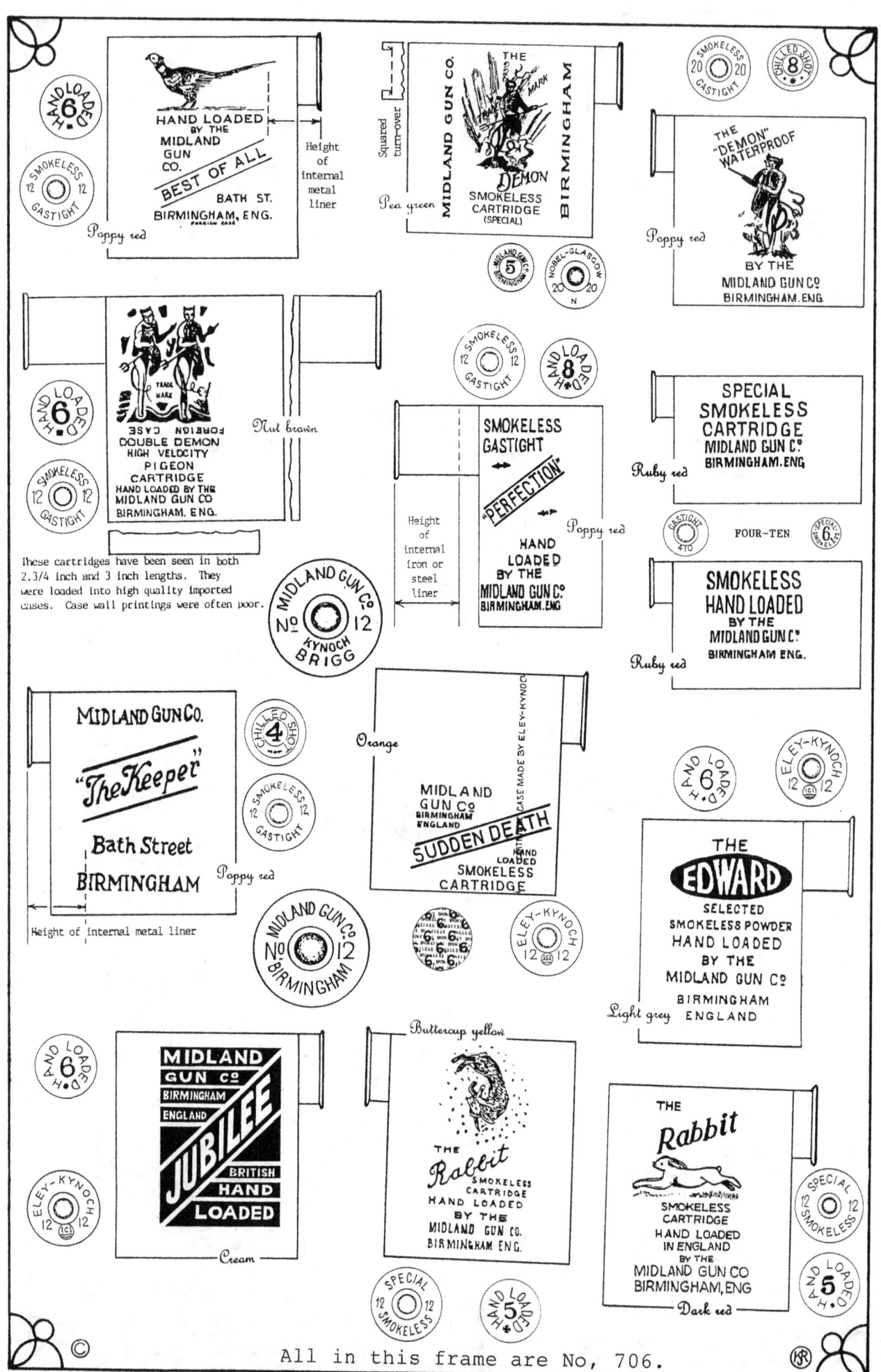

PLATE M2

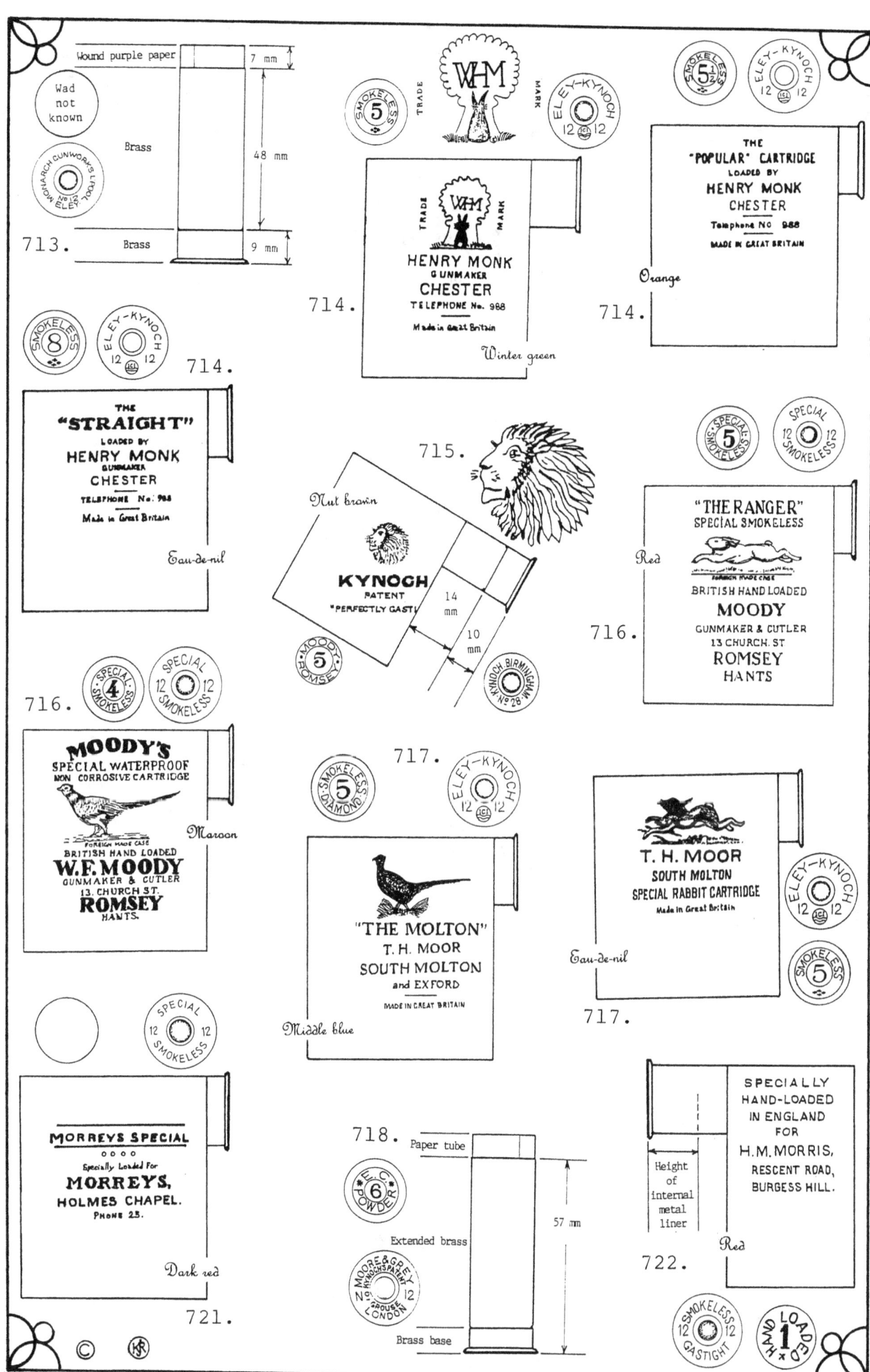

PLATE M3

All in this frame are No, 731.

PLATE M4

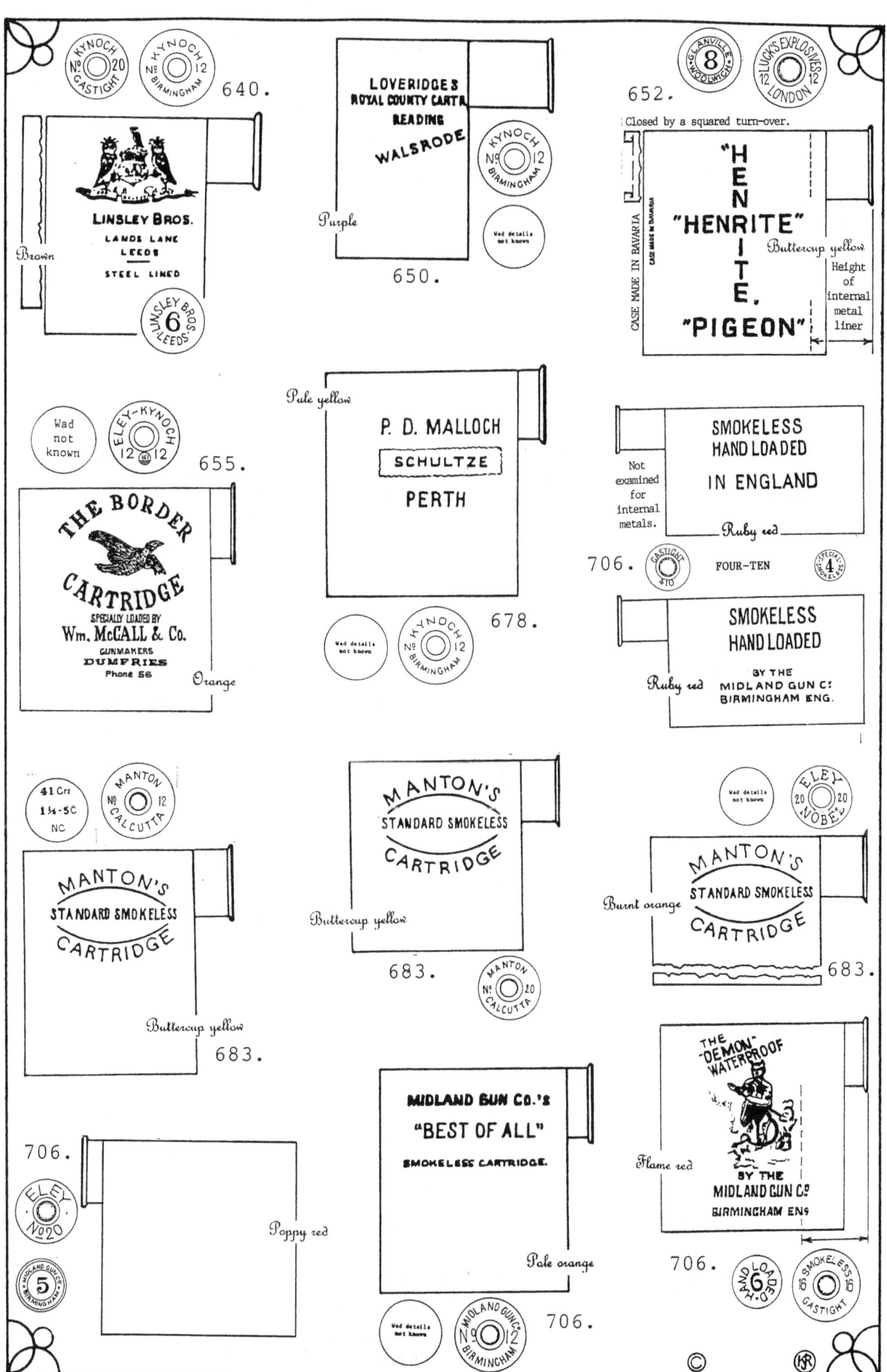

PLATE M5

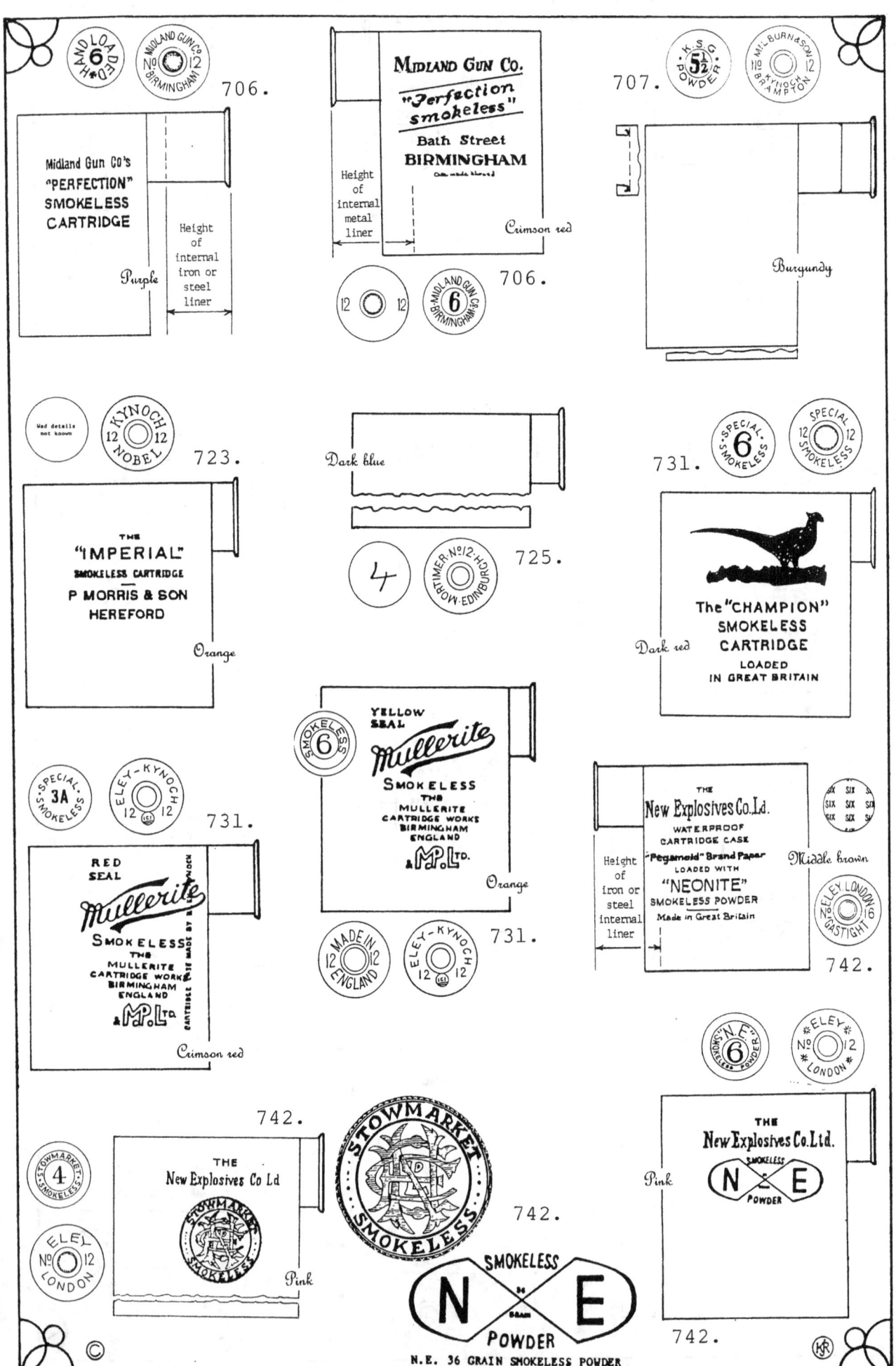

PLATE M6

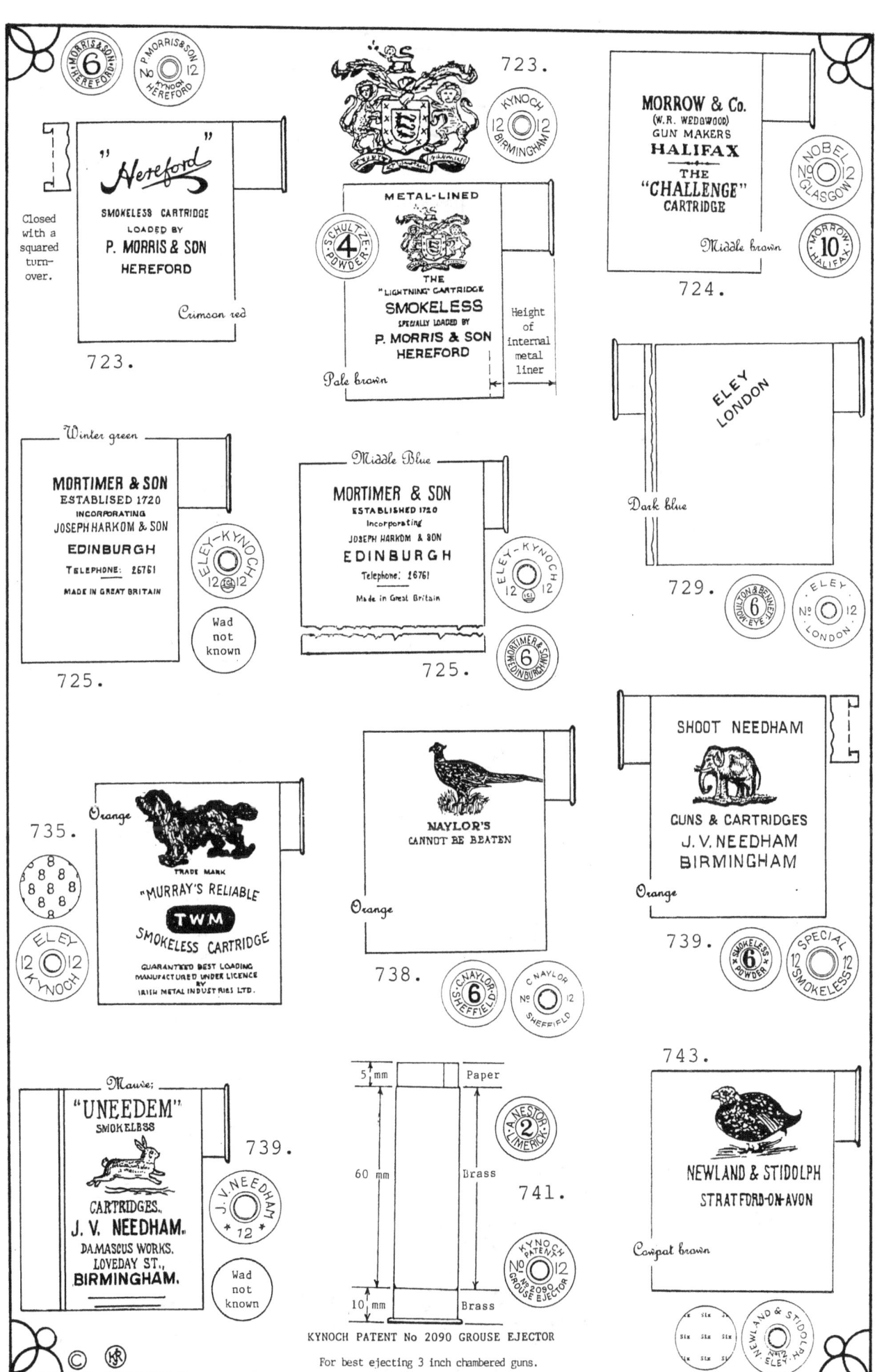

PLATE M7

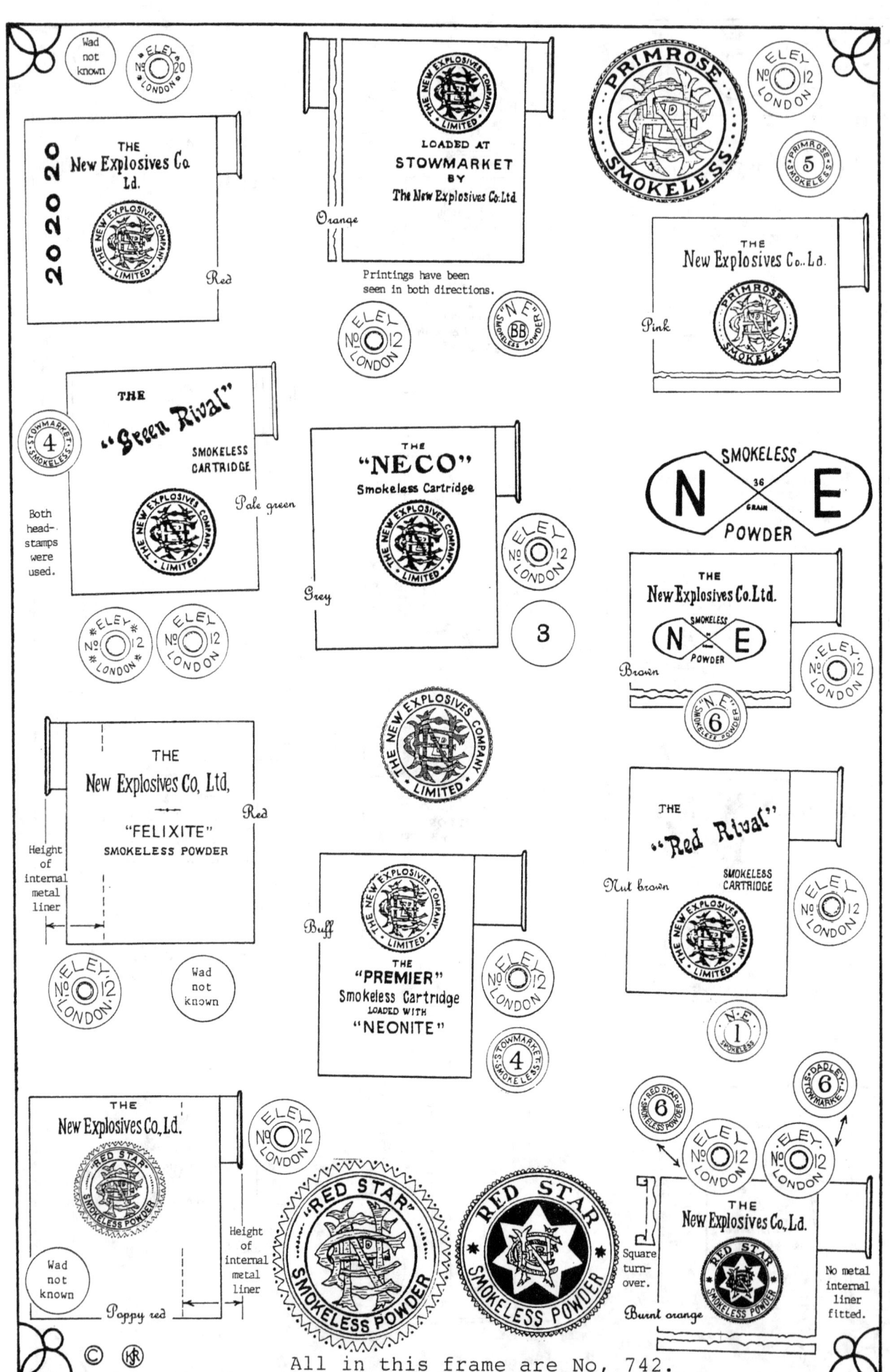

PLATE M8

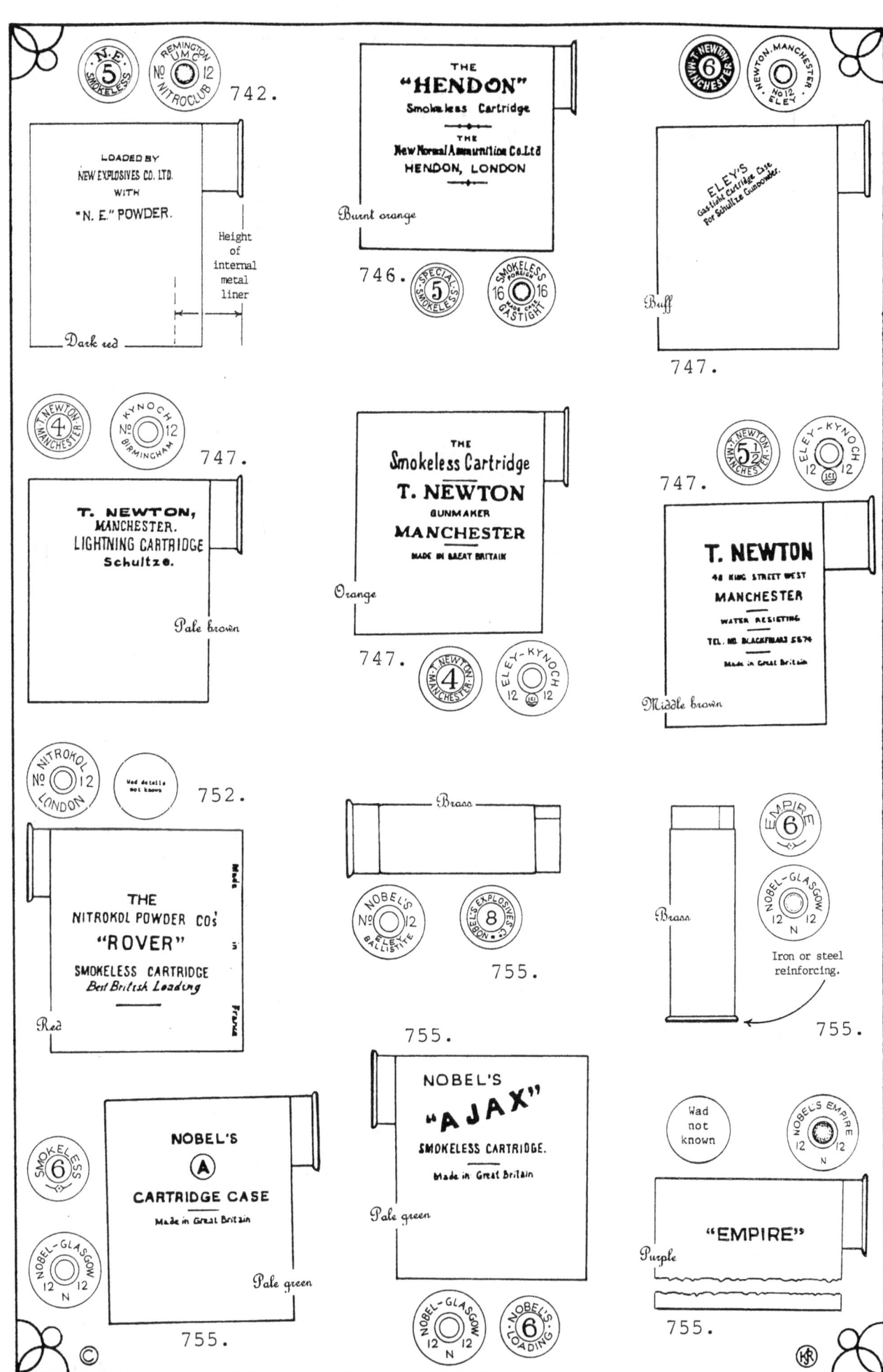

PLATE M9

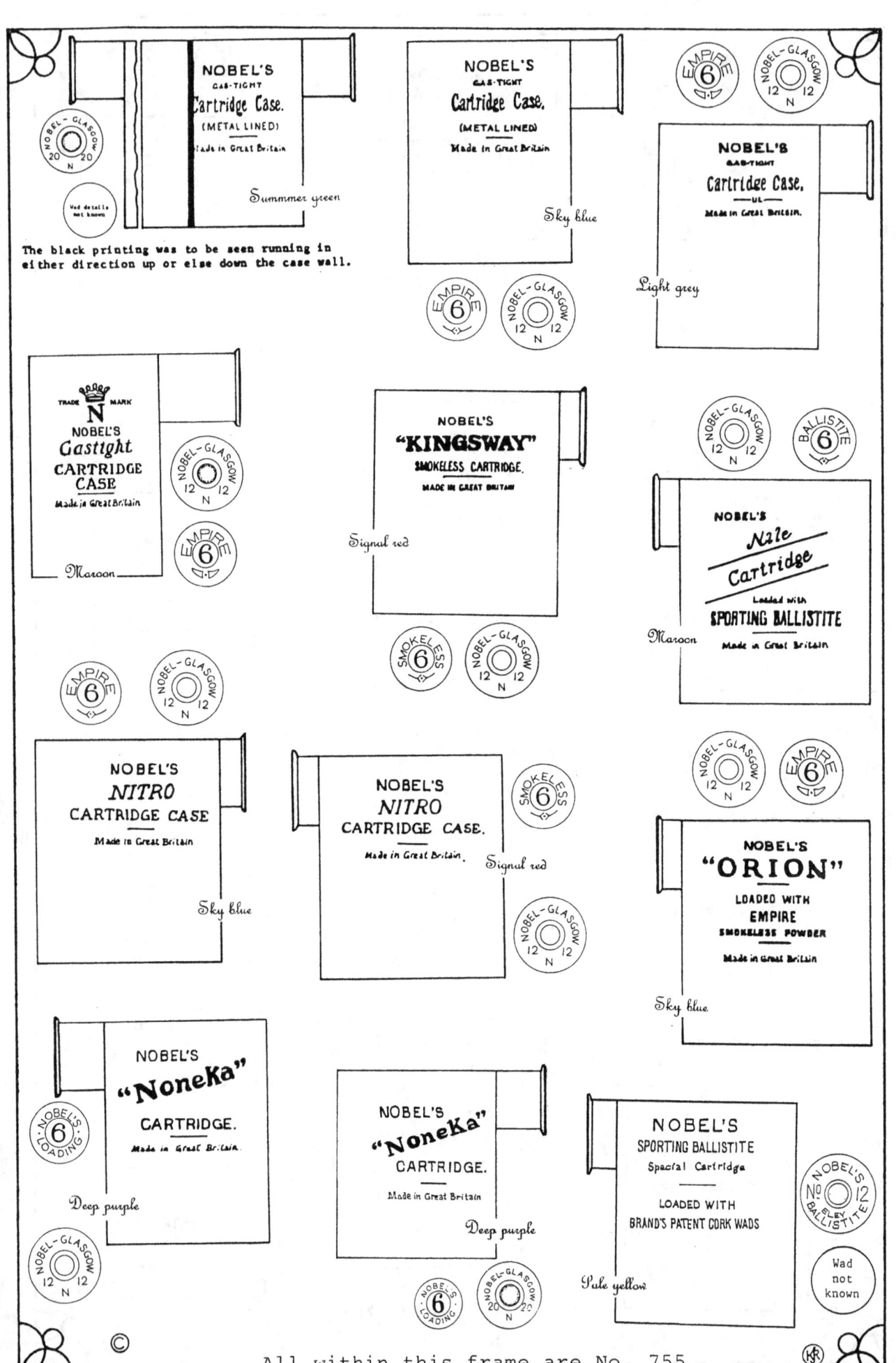

All within this frame are No. 755.

PLATE N1

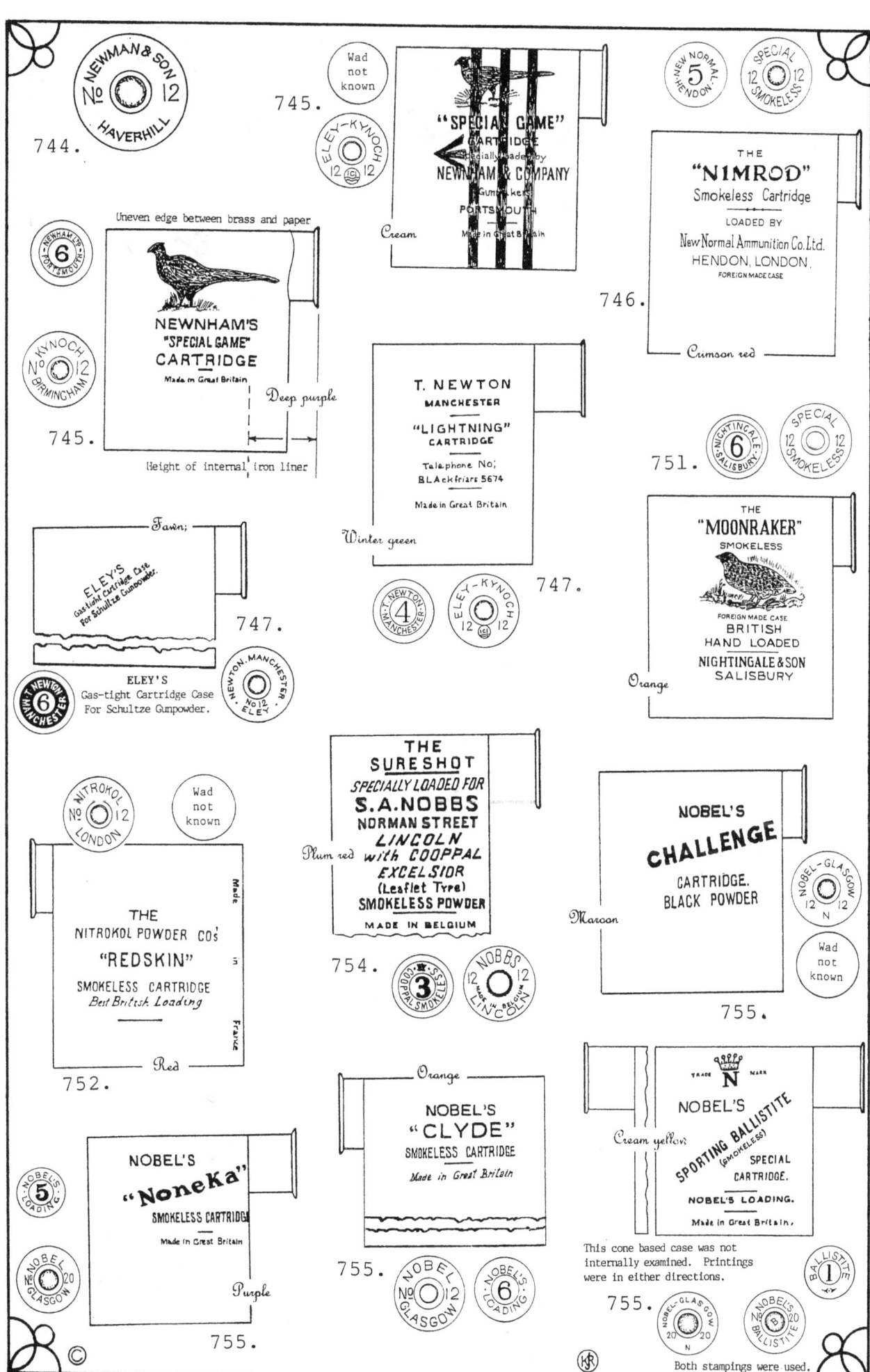

PLATE N2

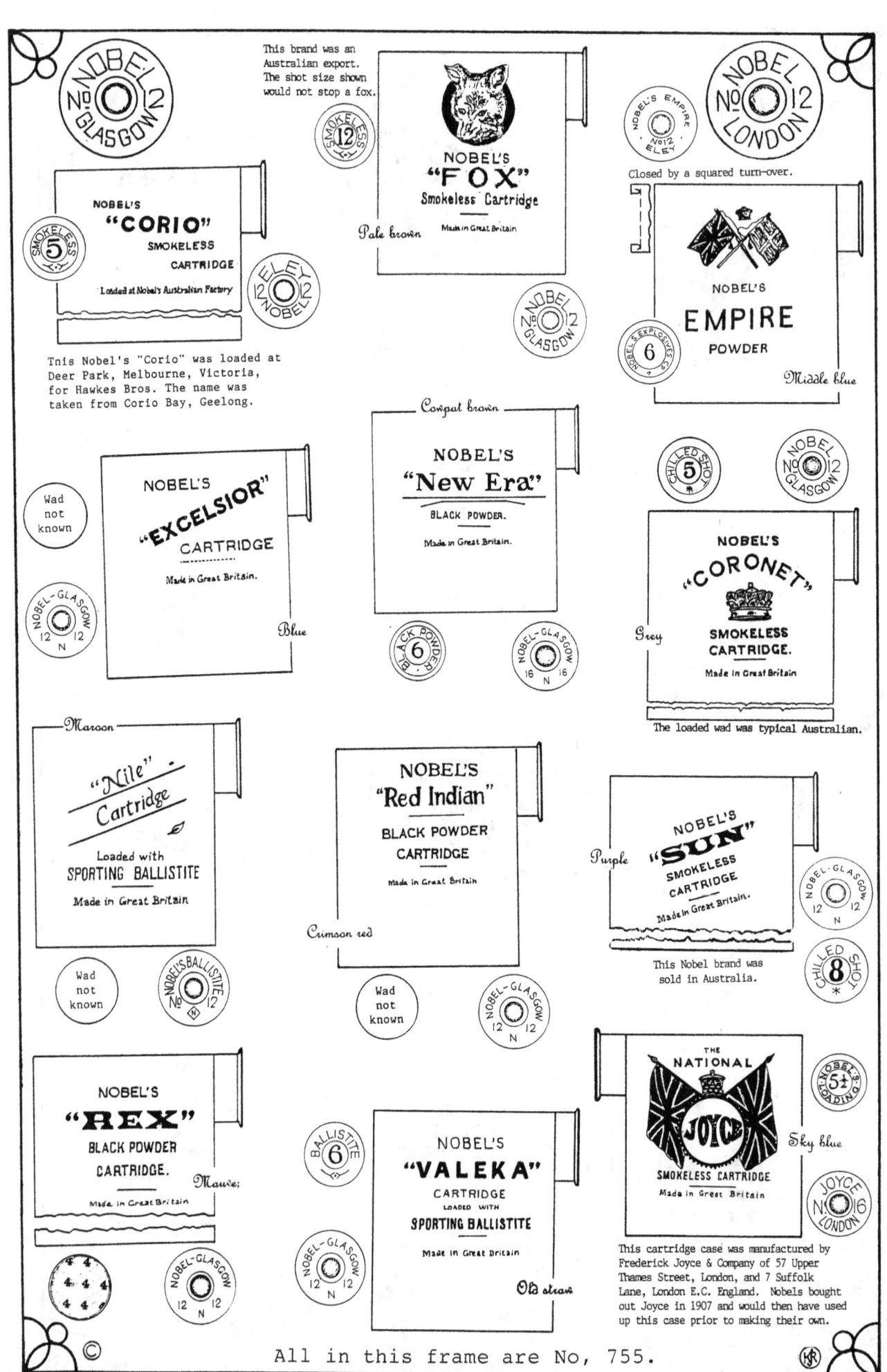

PLATE N3

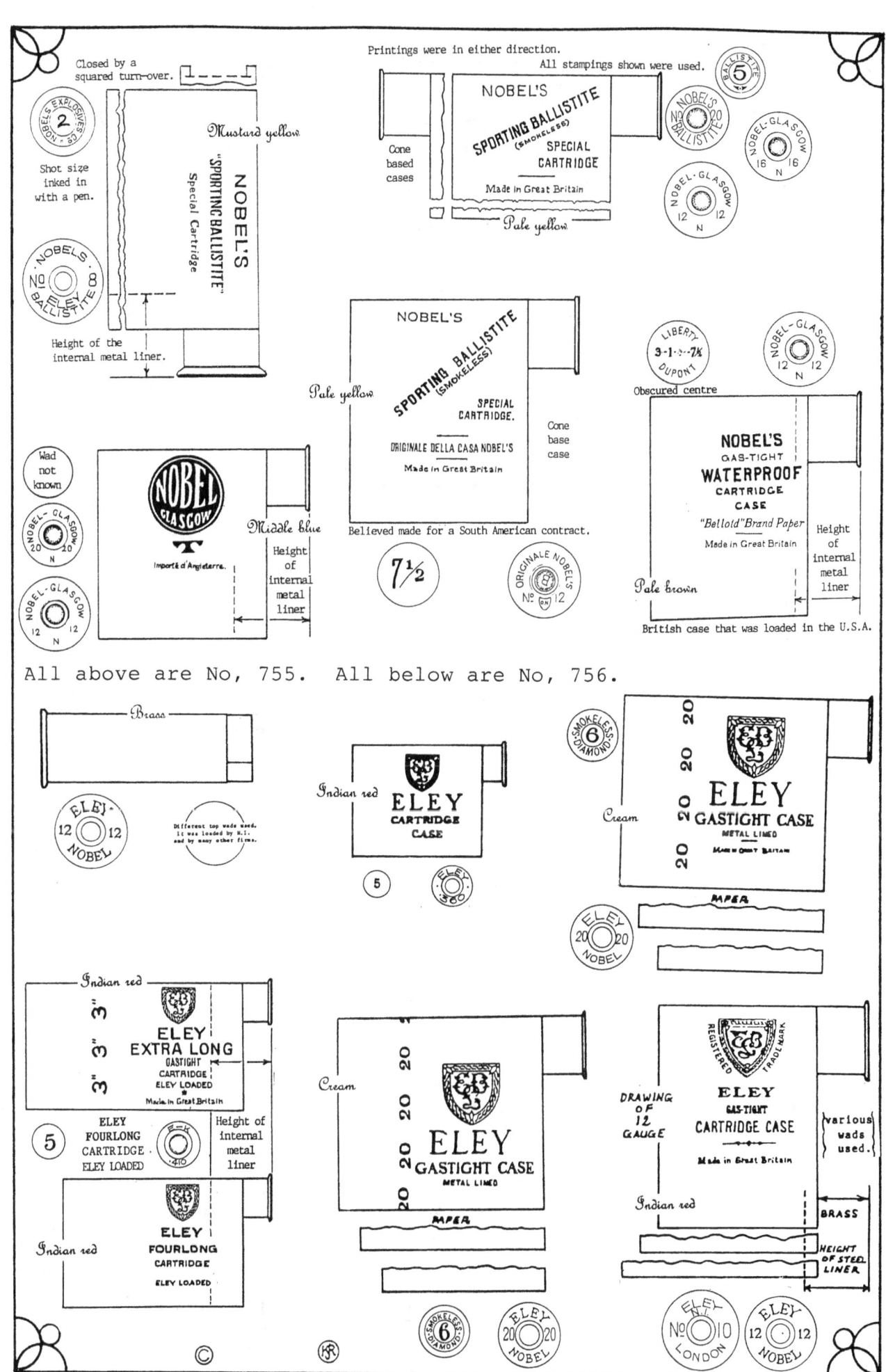

PLATE N4

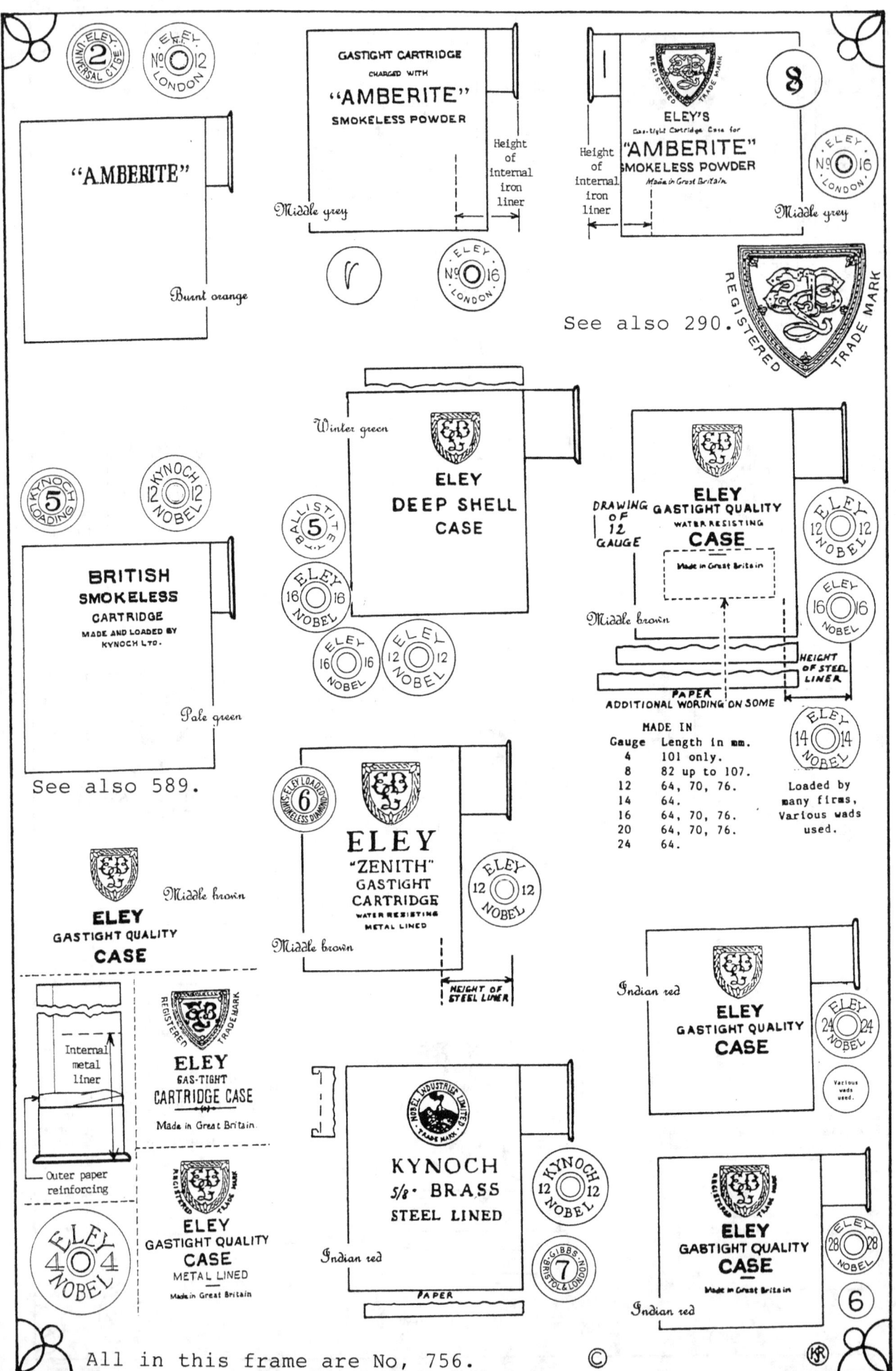

PLATE N5

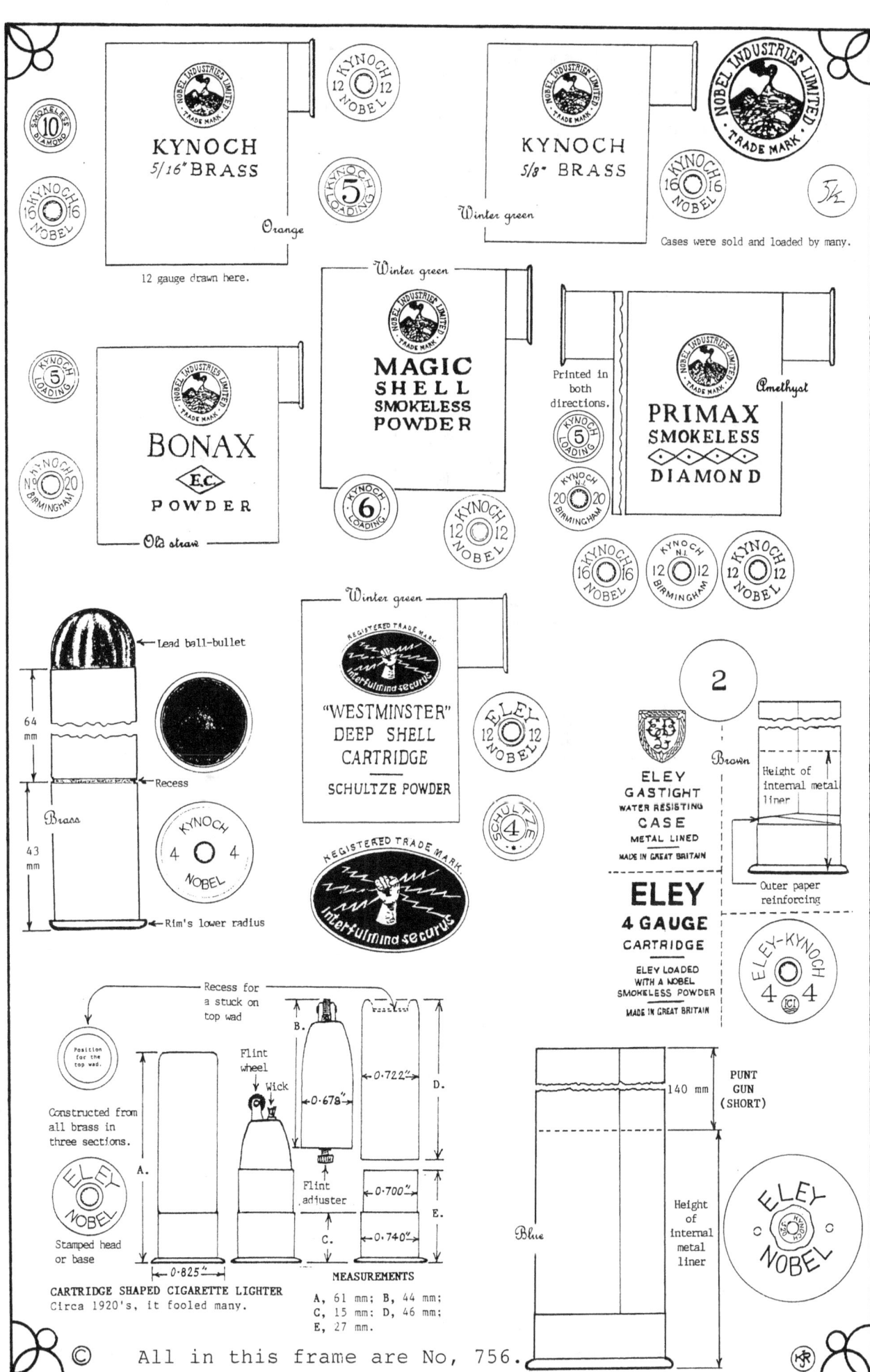

PLATE N6

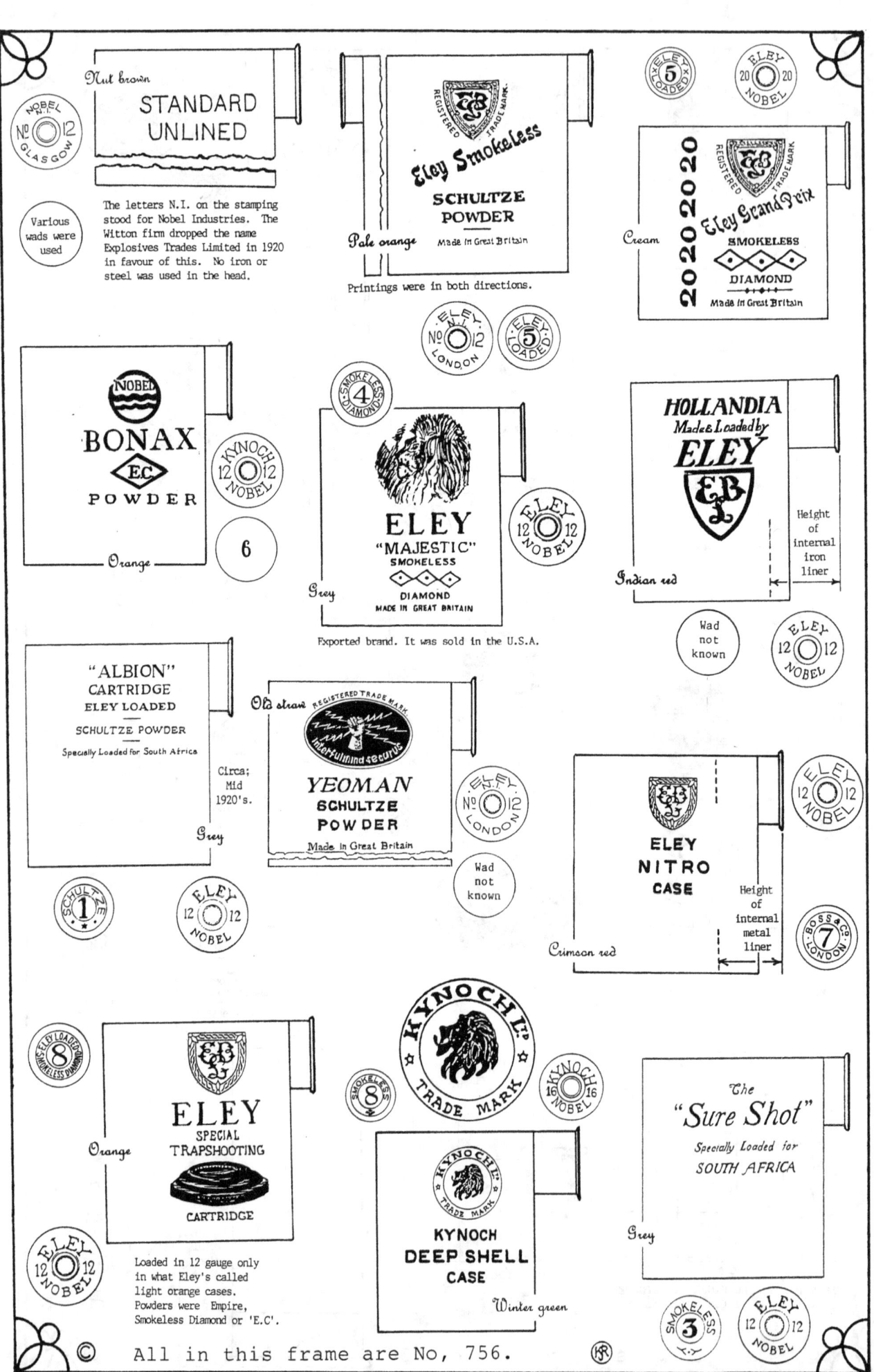

PLATE N7

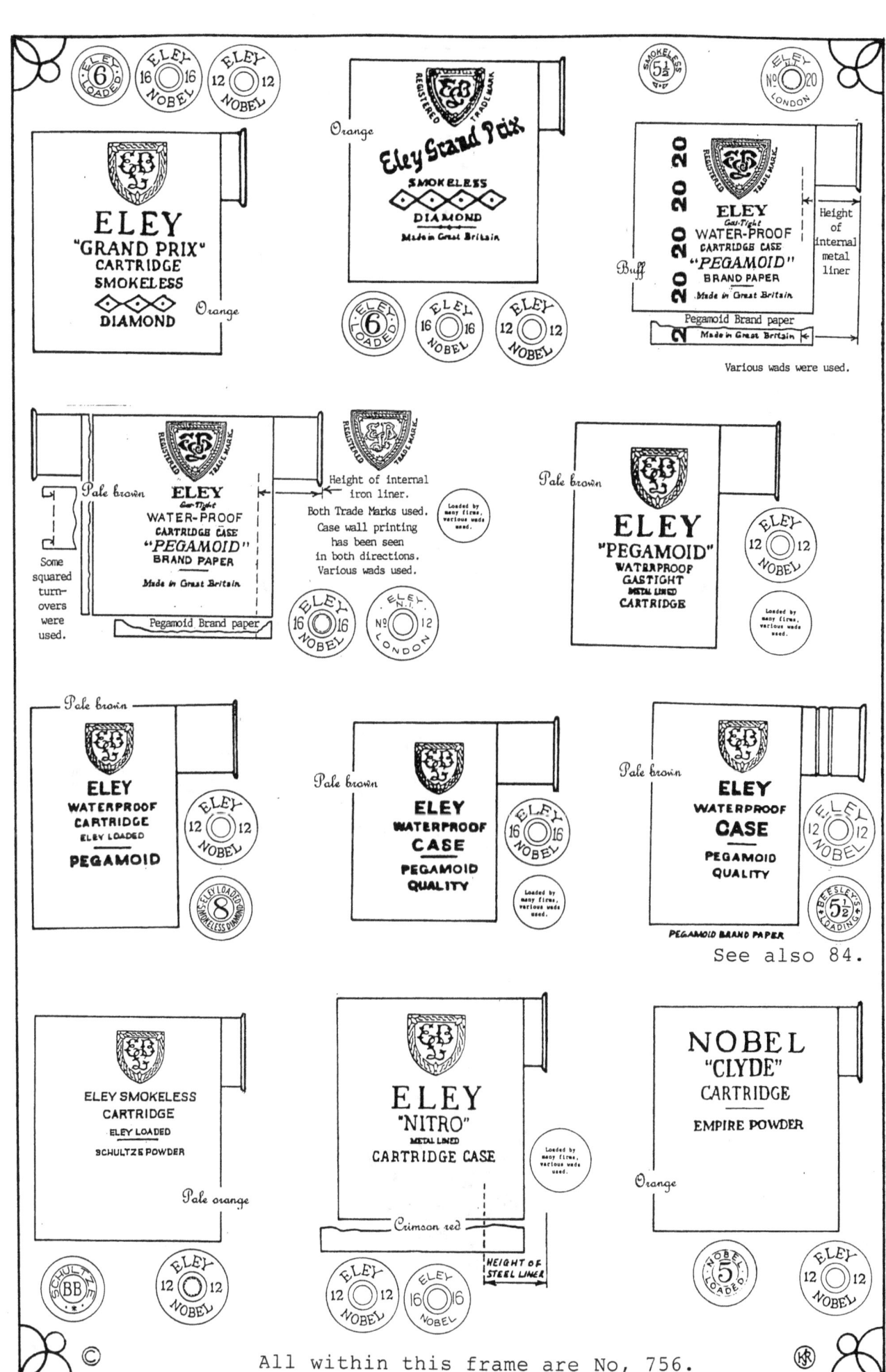

PLATE N8

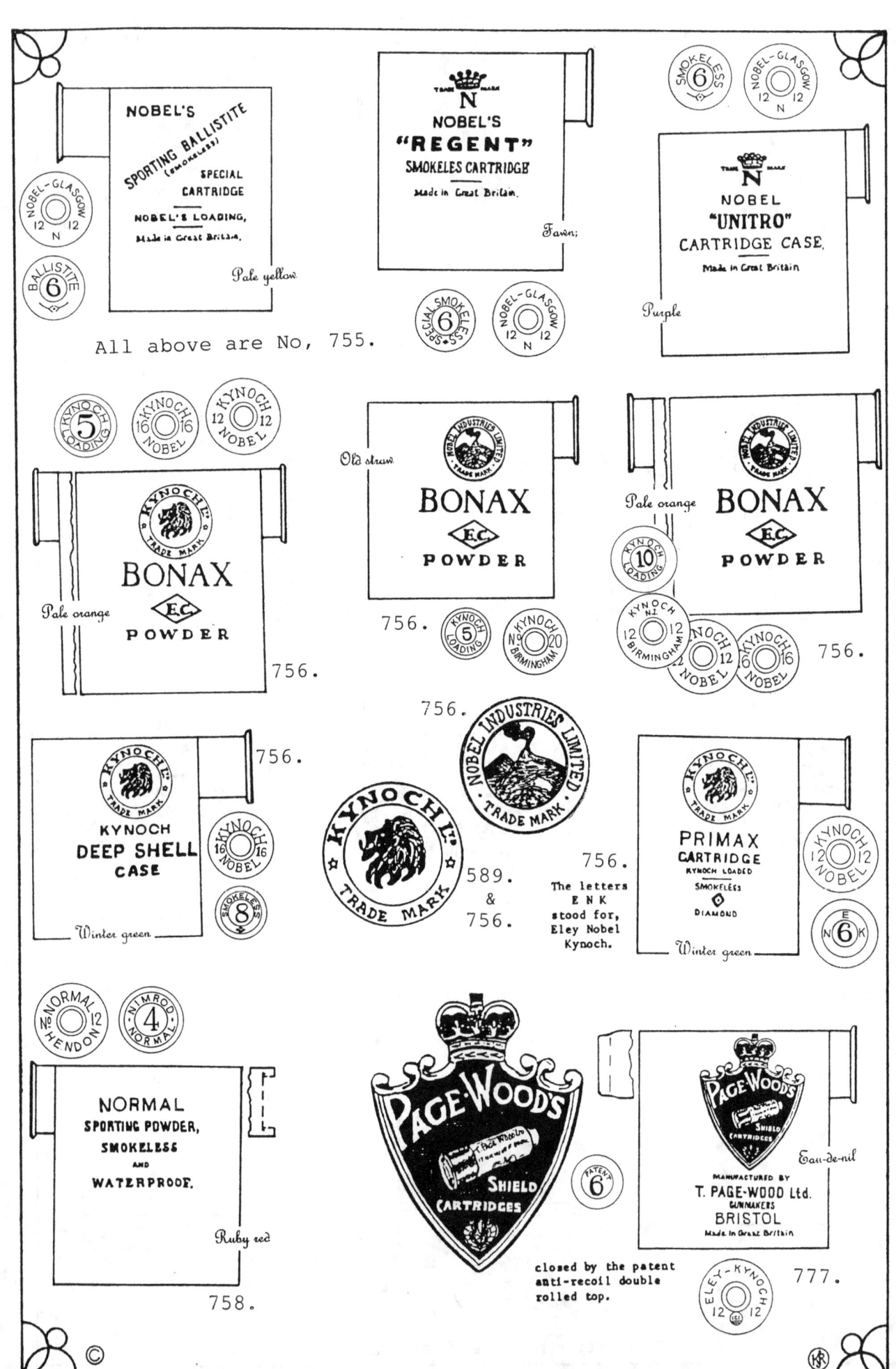

PLATE N9

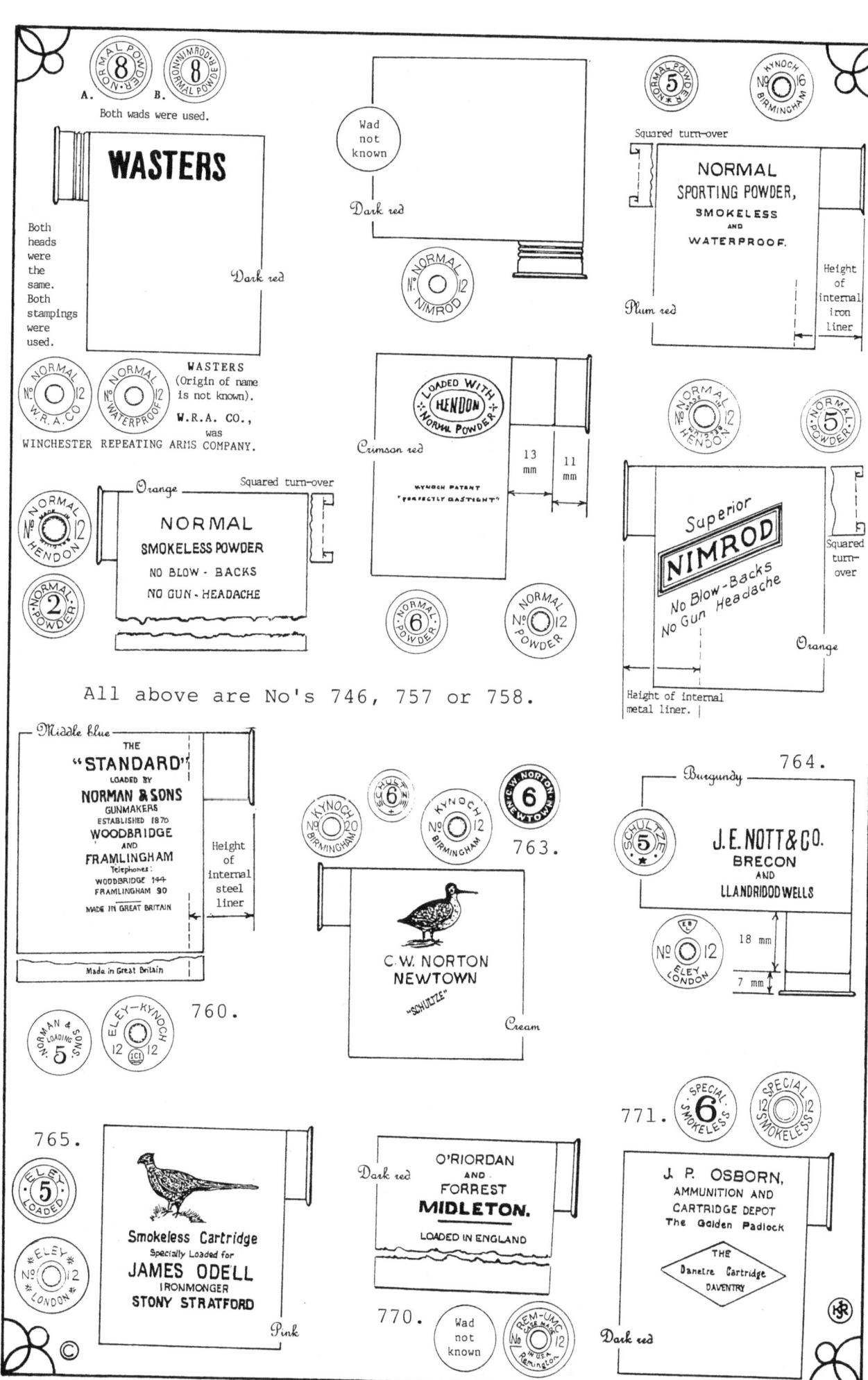

PLATE 01

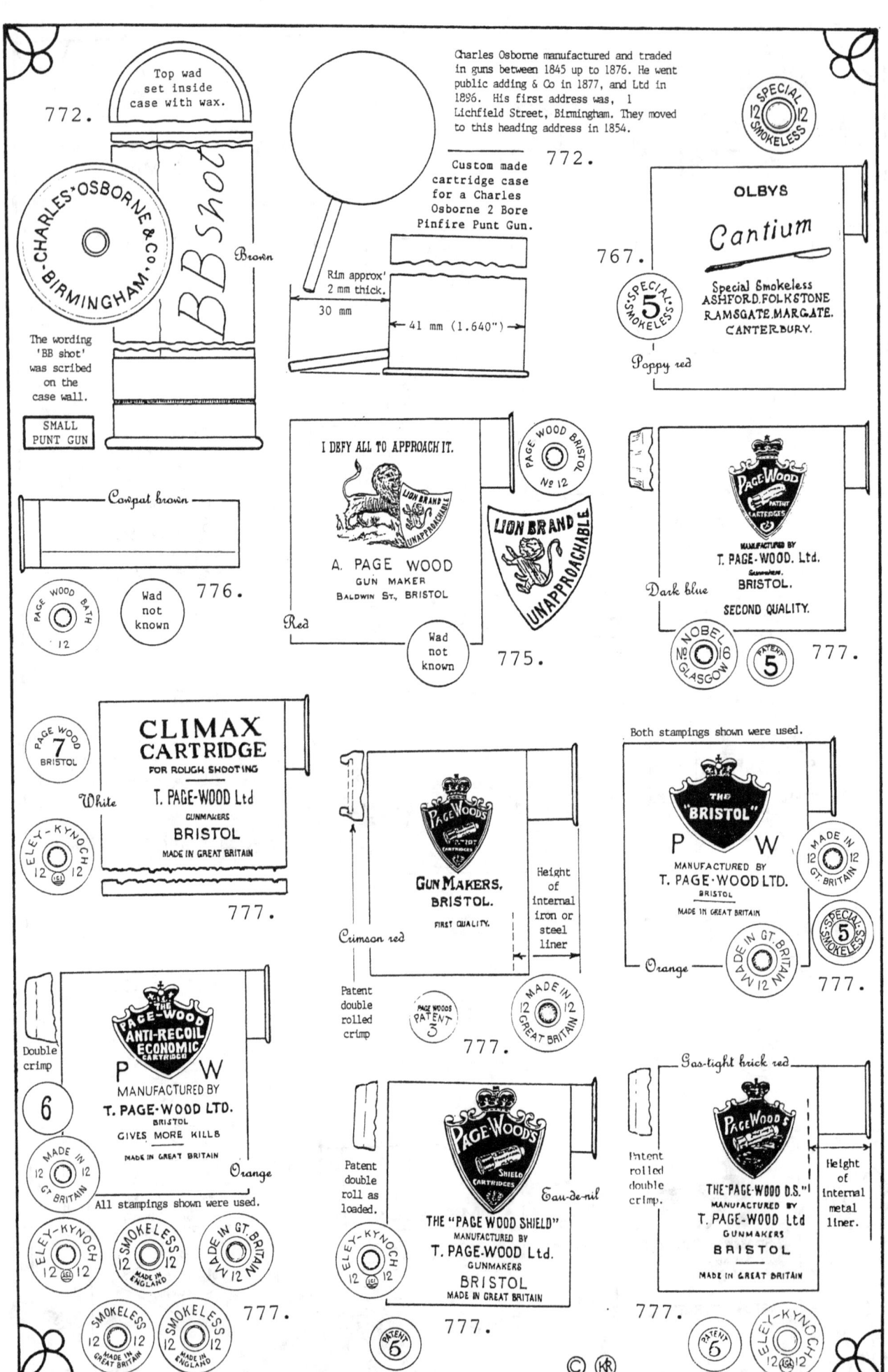

PLATE 02

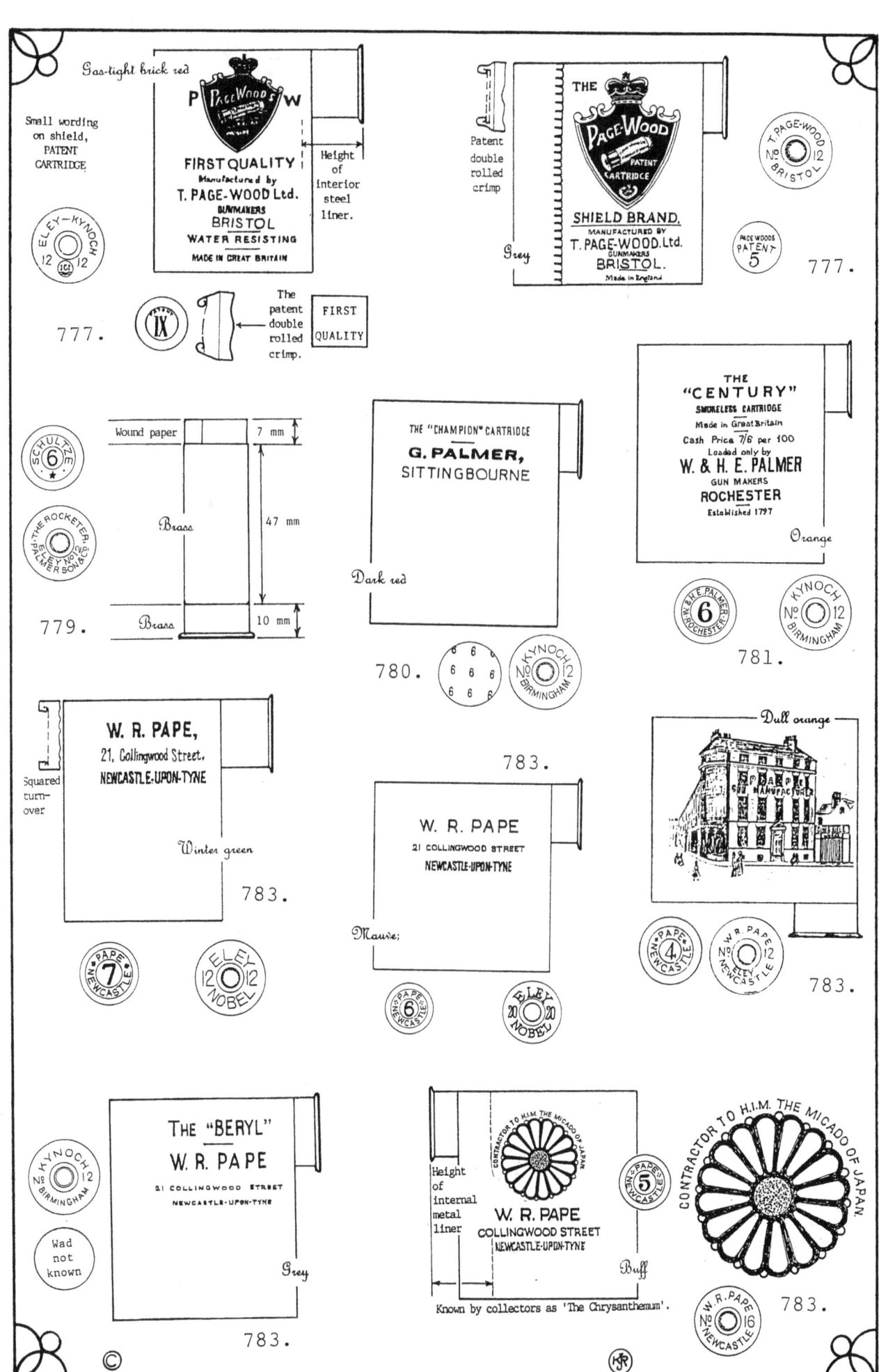

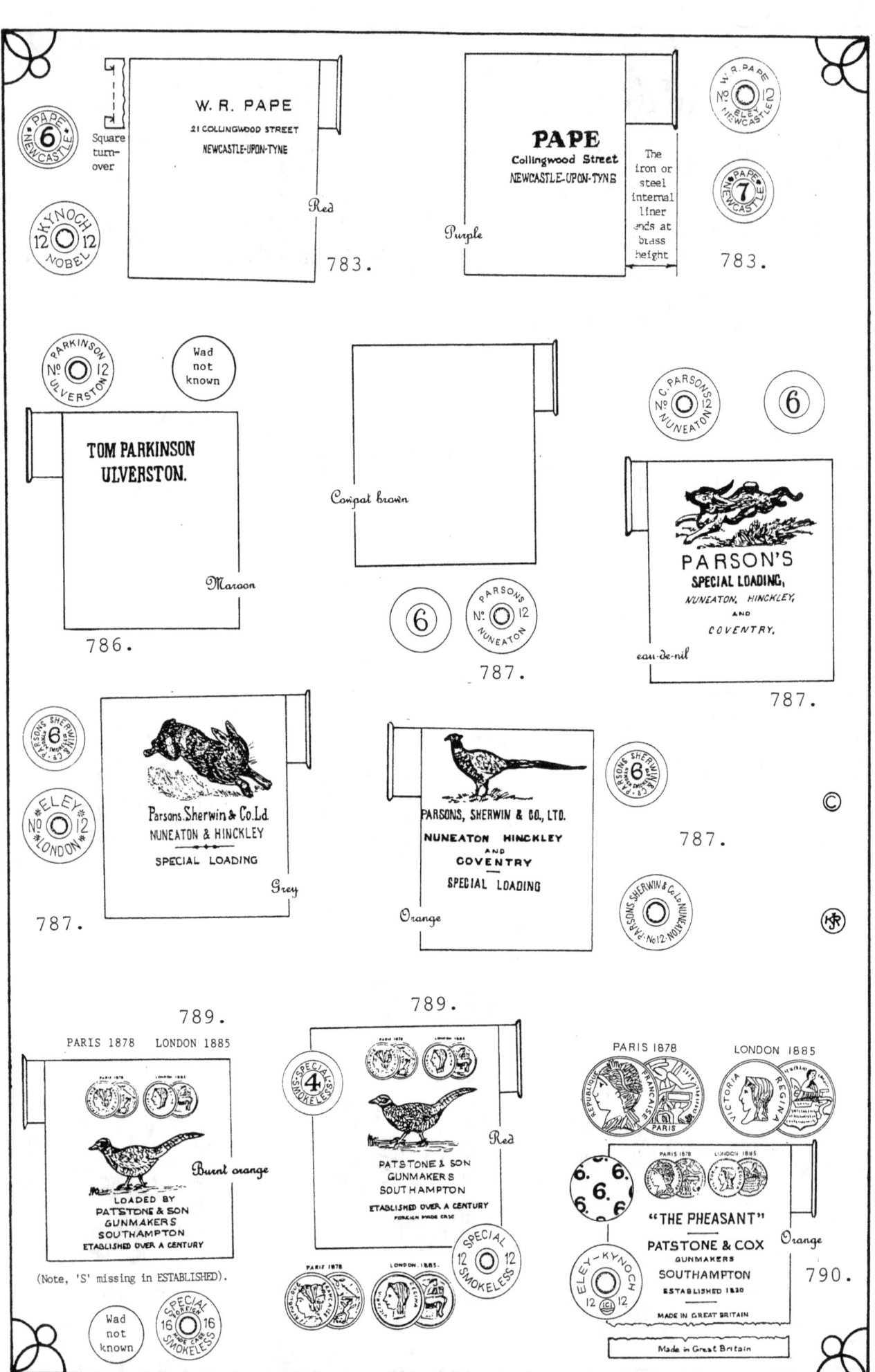

PLATE 04

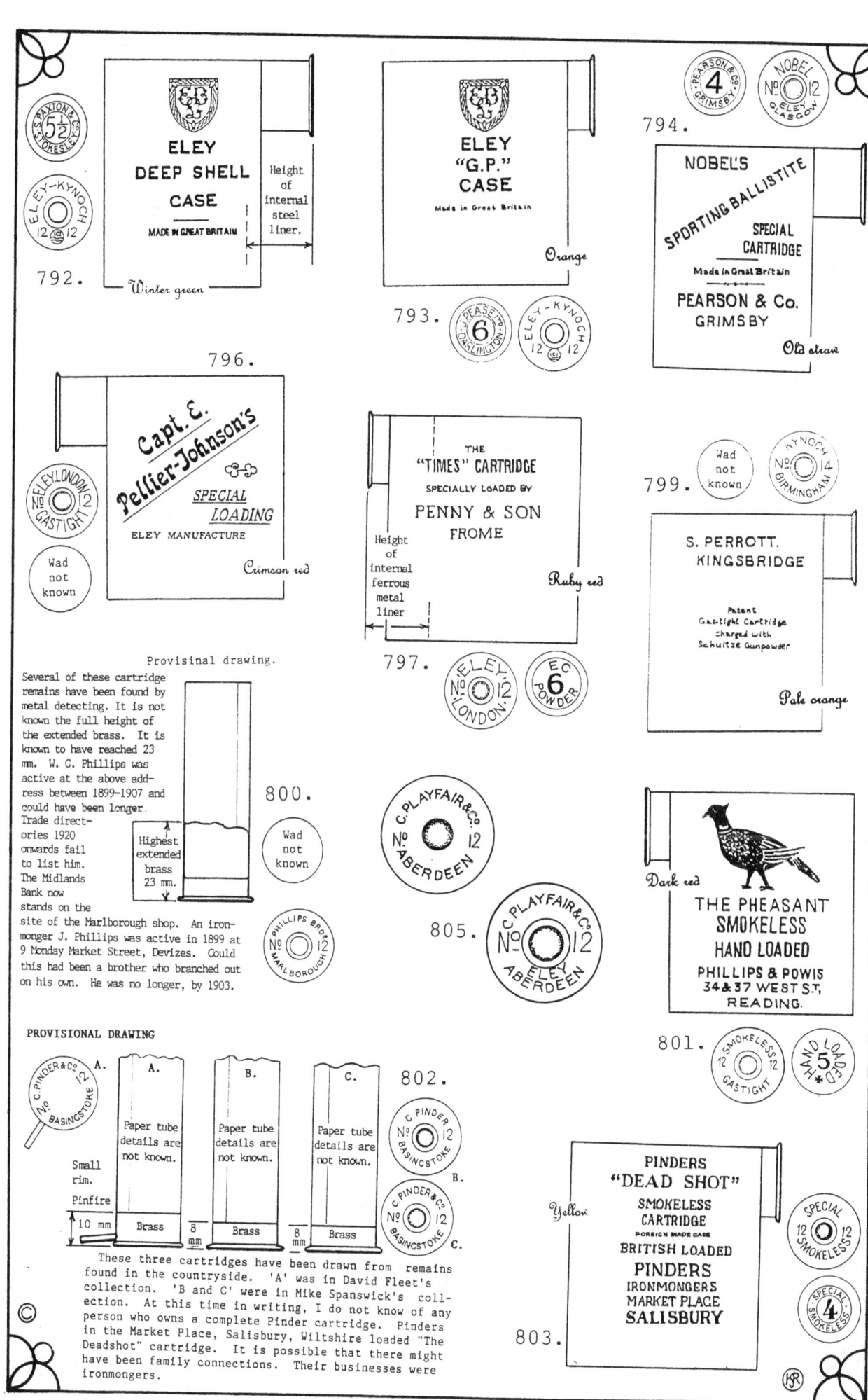

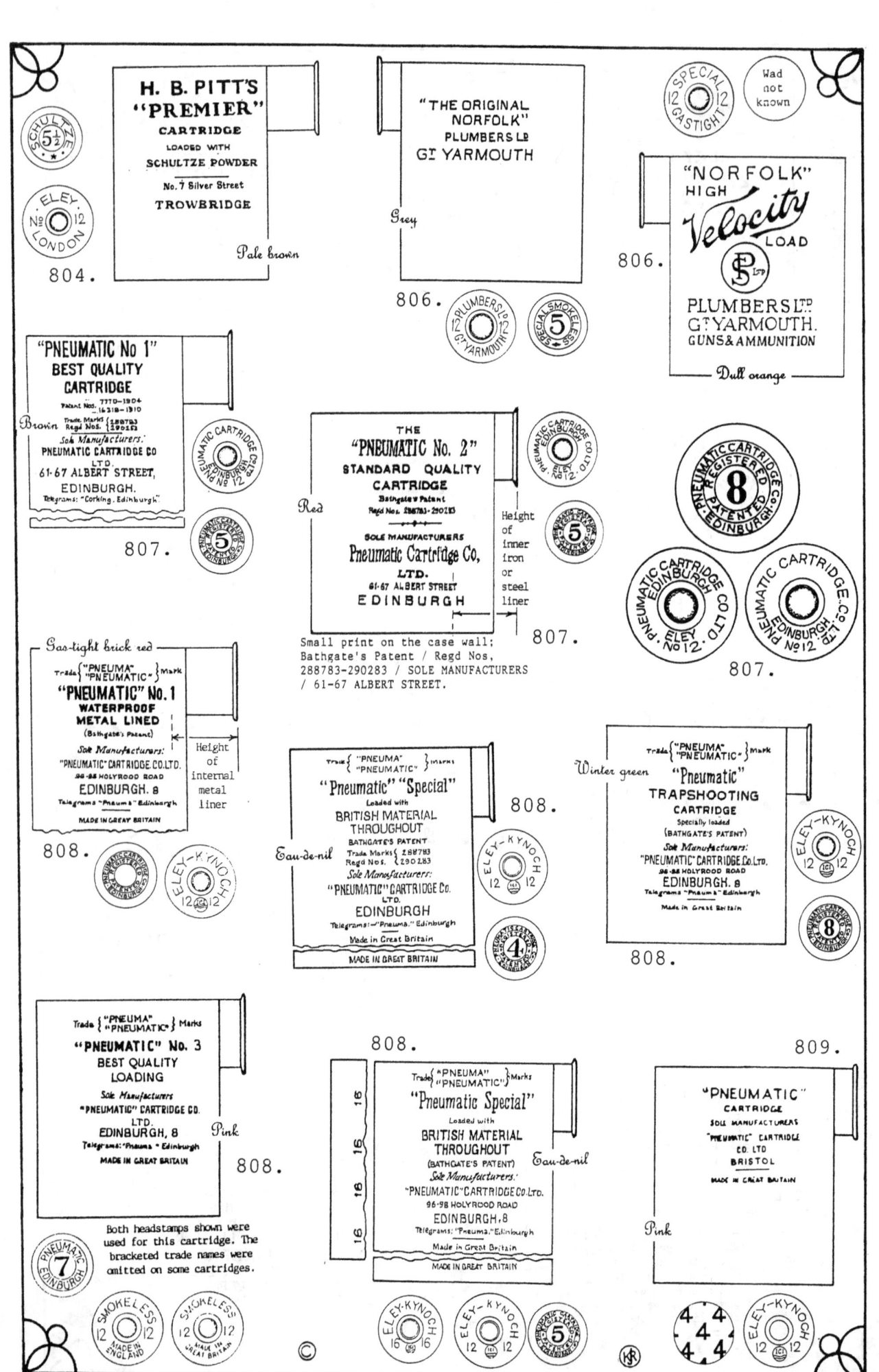

PLATE 06

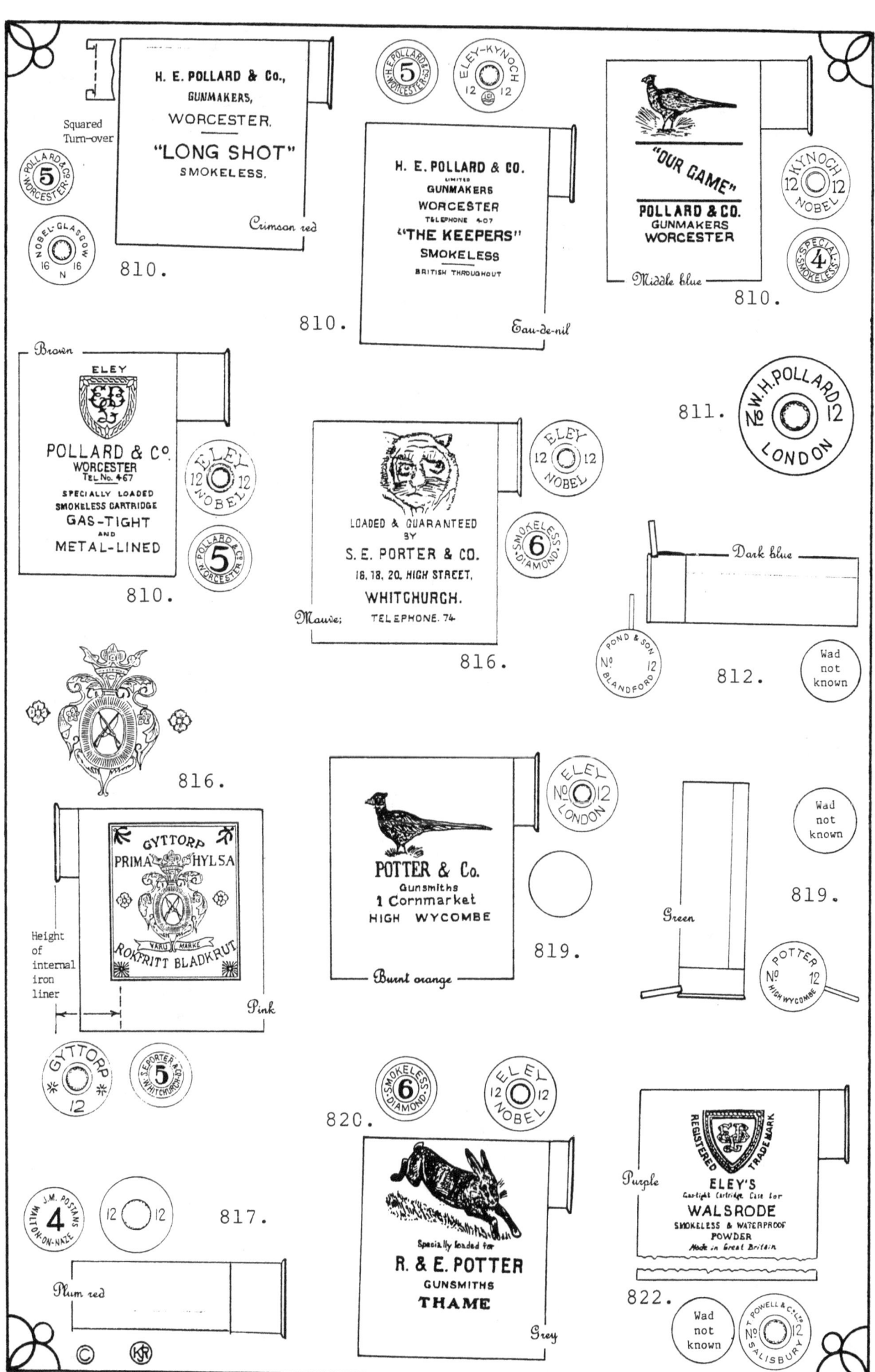

PLATE 07

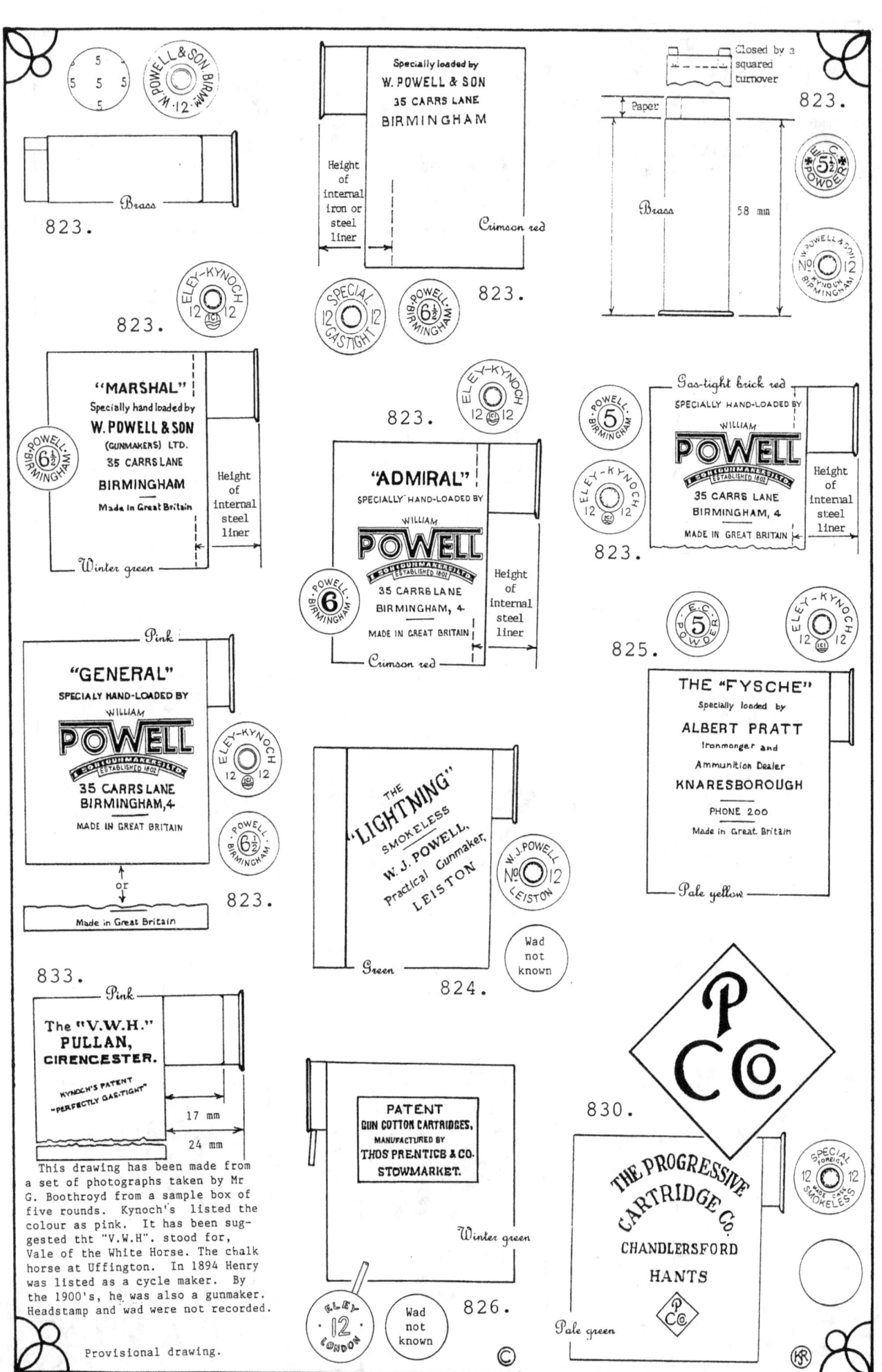

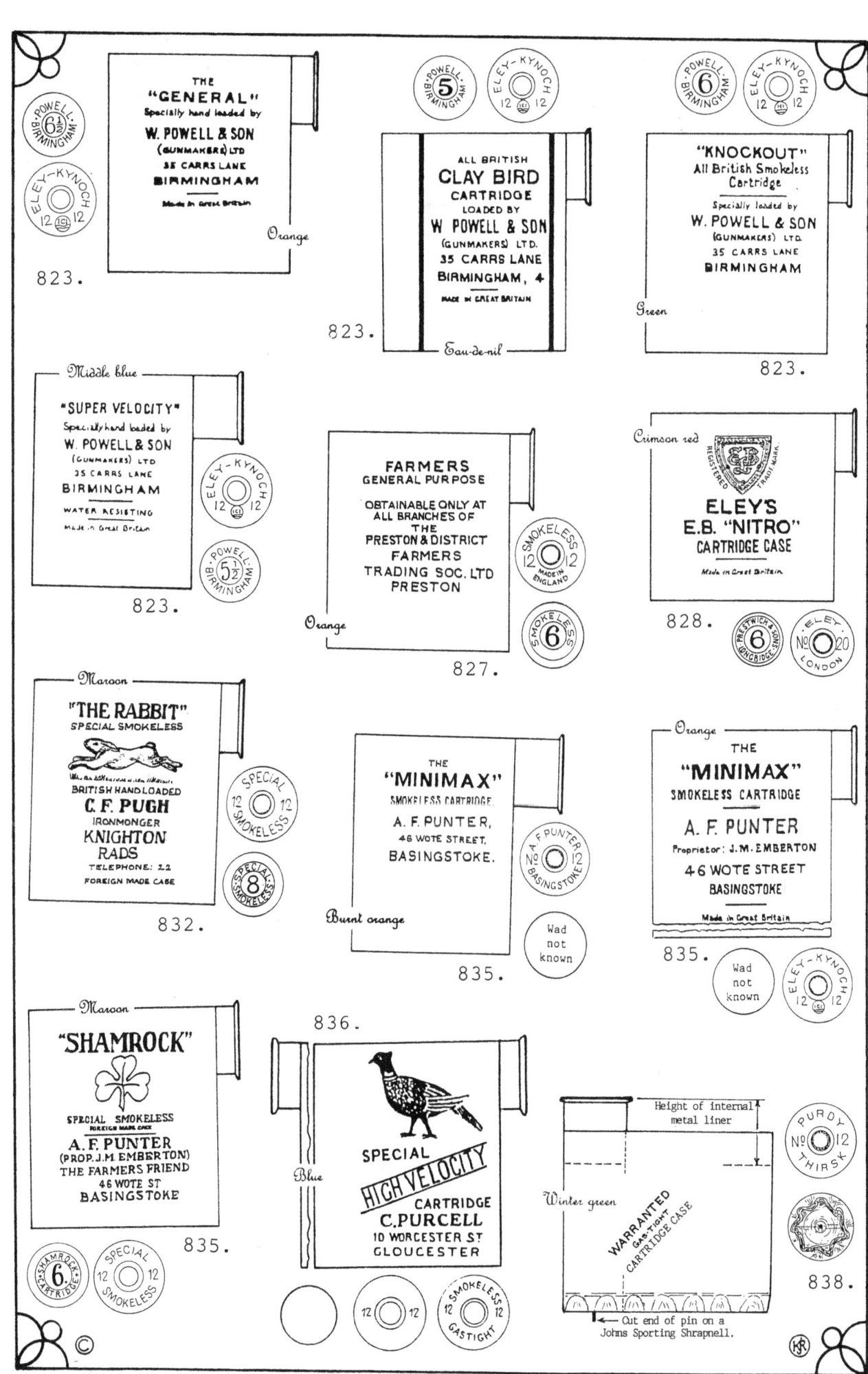

PLATE 09

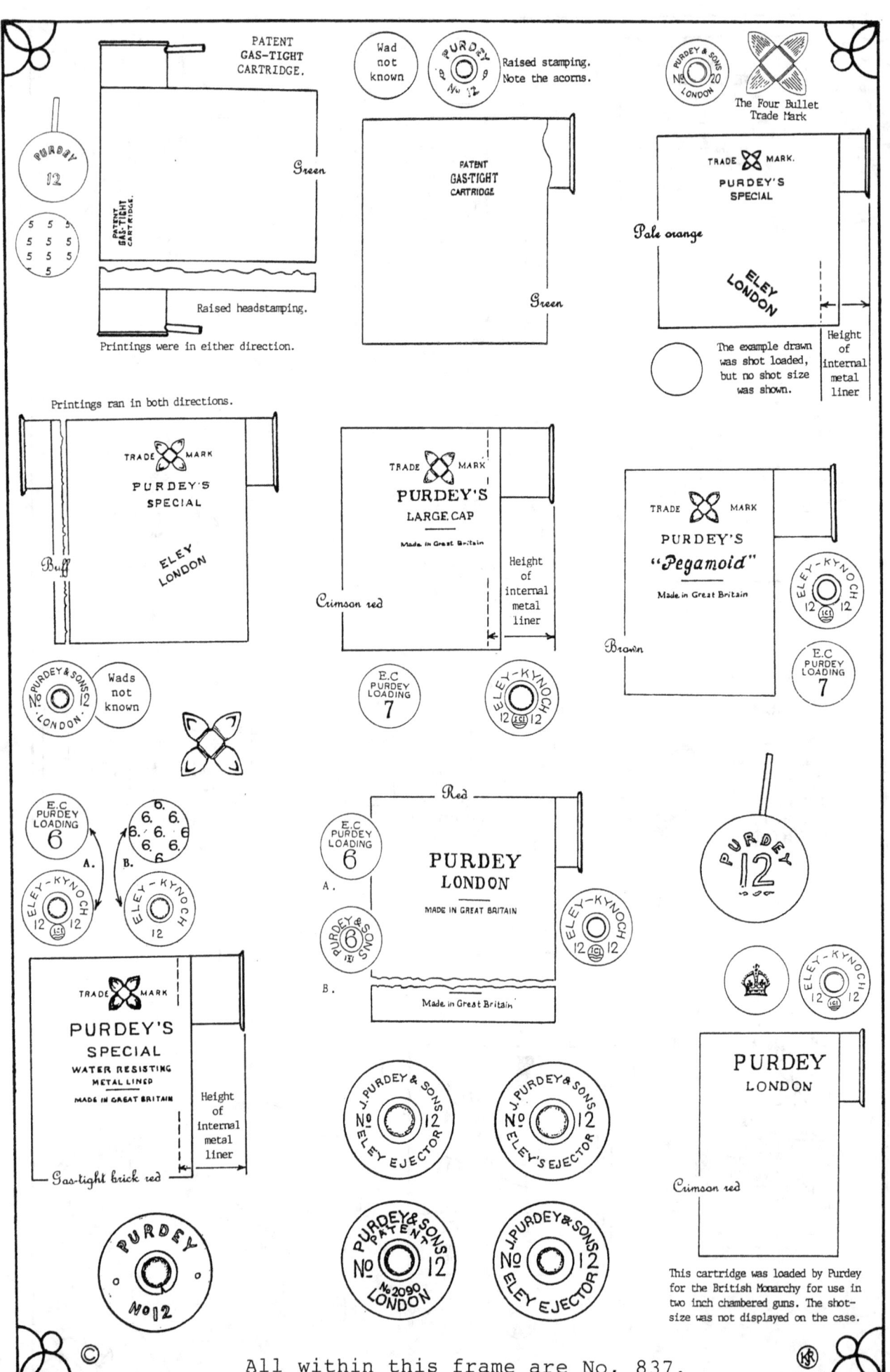

All within this frame are No. 837.

PLATE P1

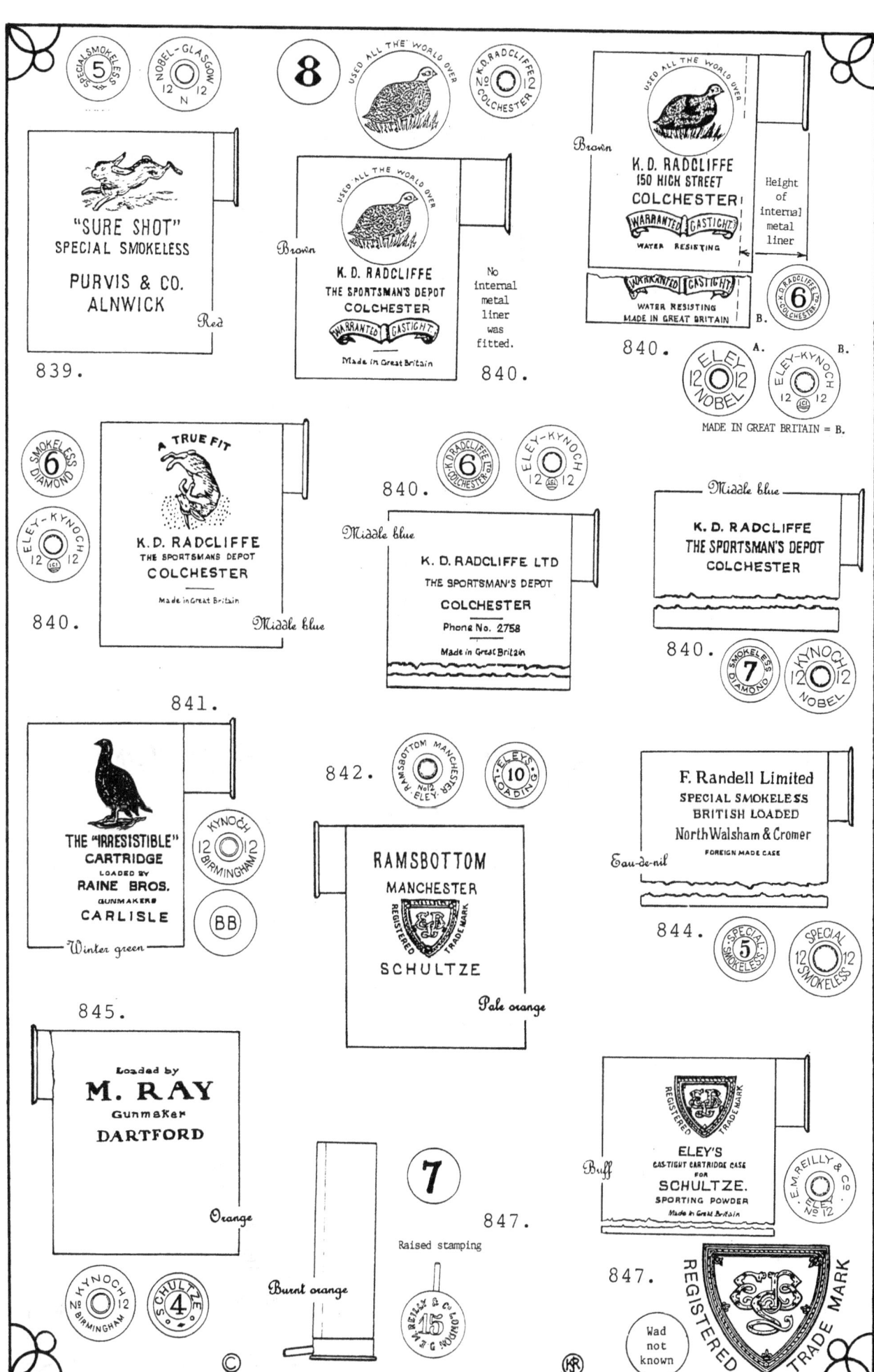

PLATE P2

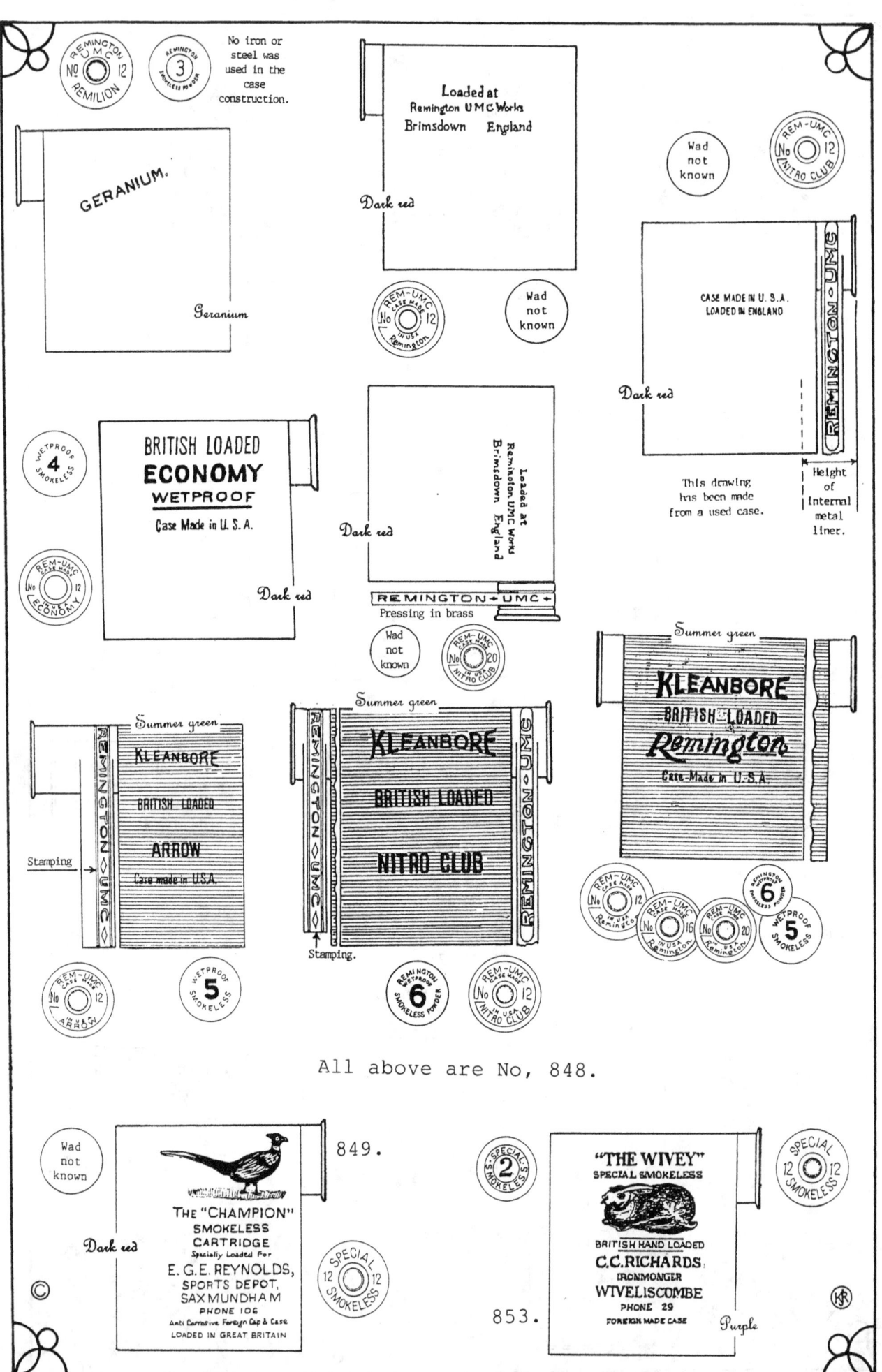

PLATE P3

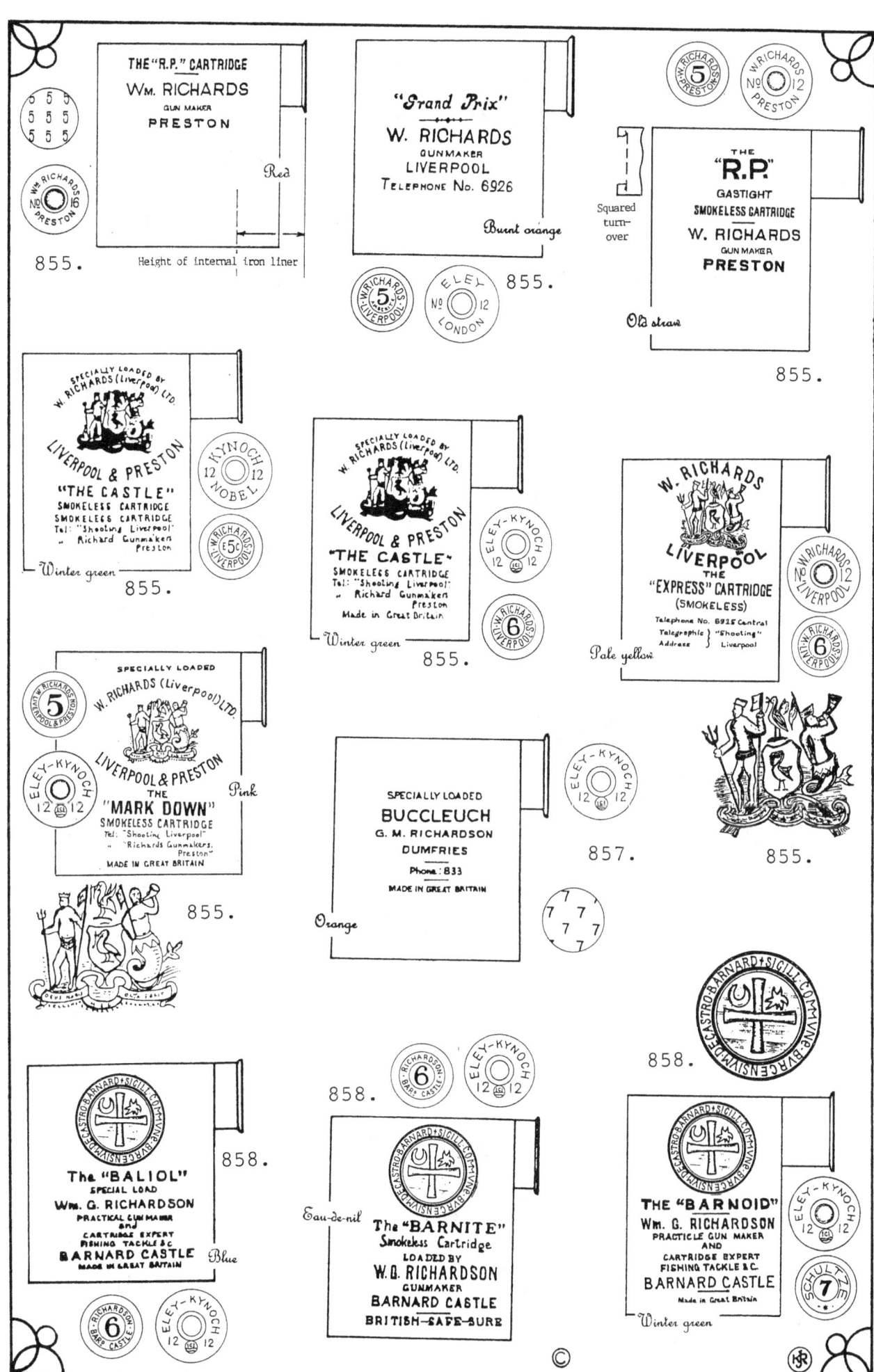

PLATE P4

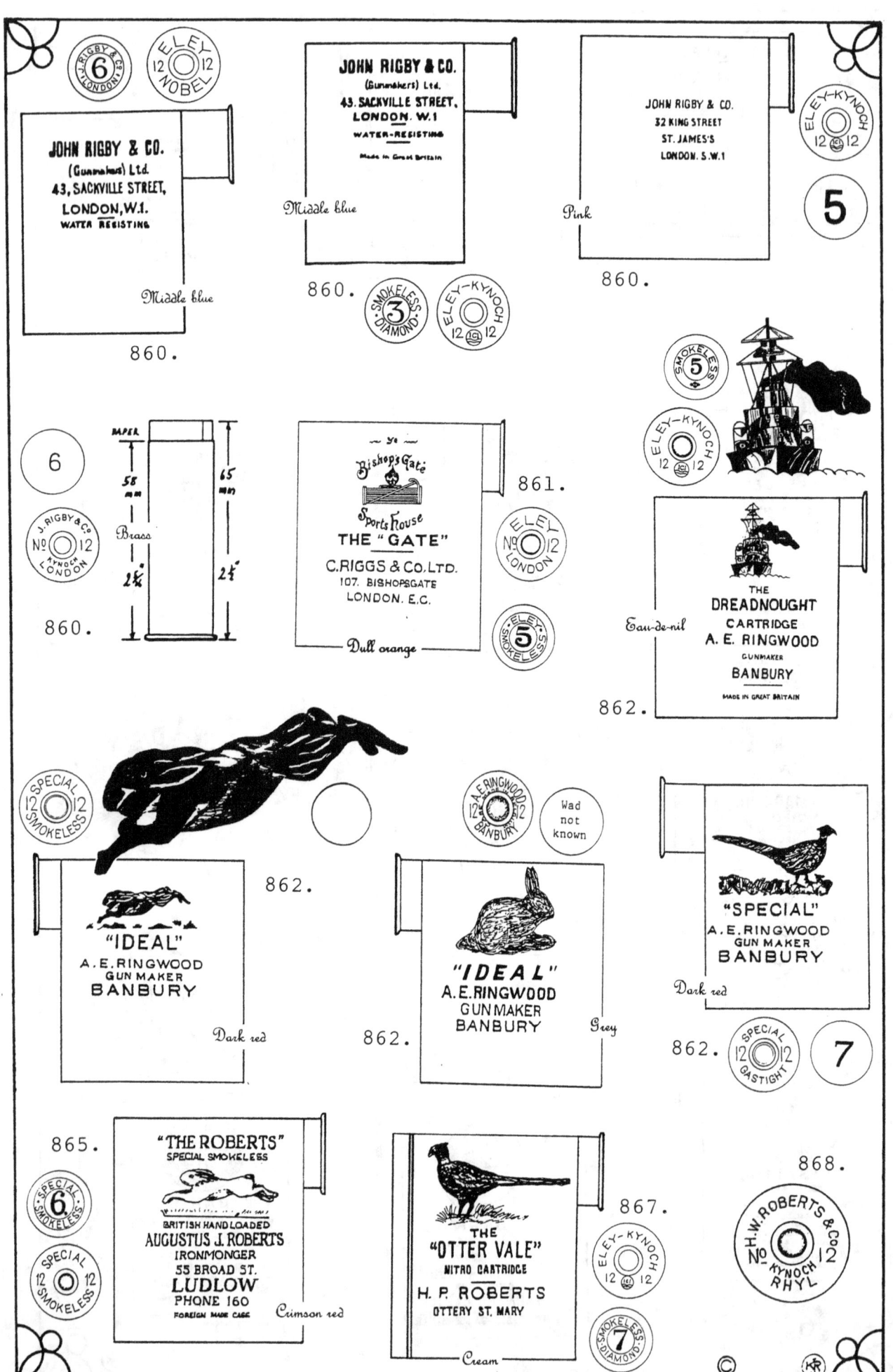

PLATE P5

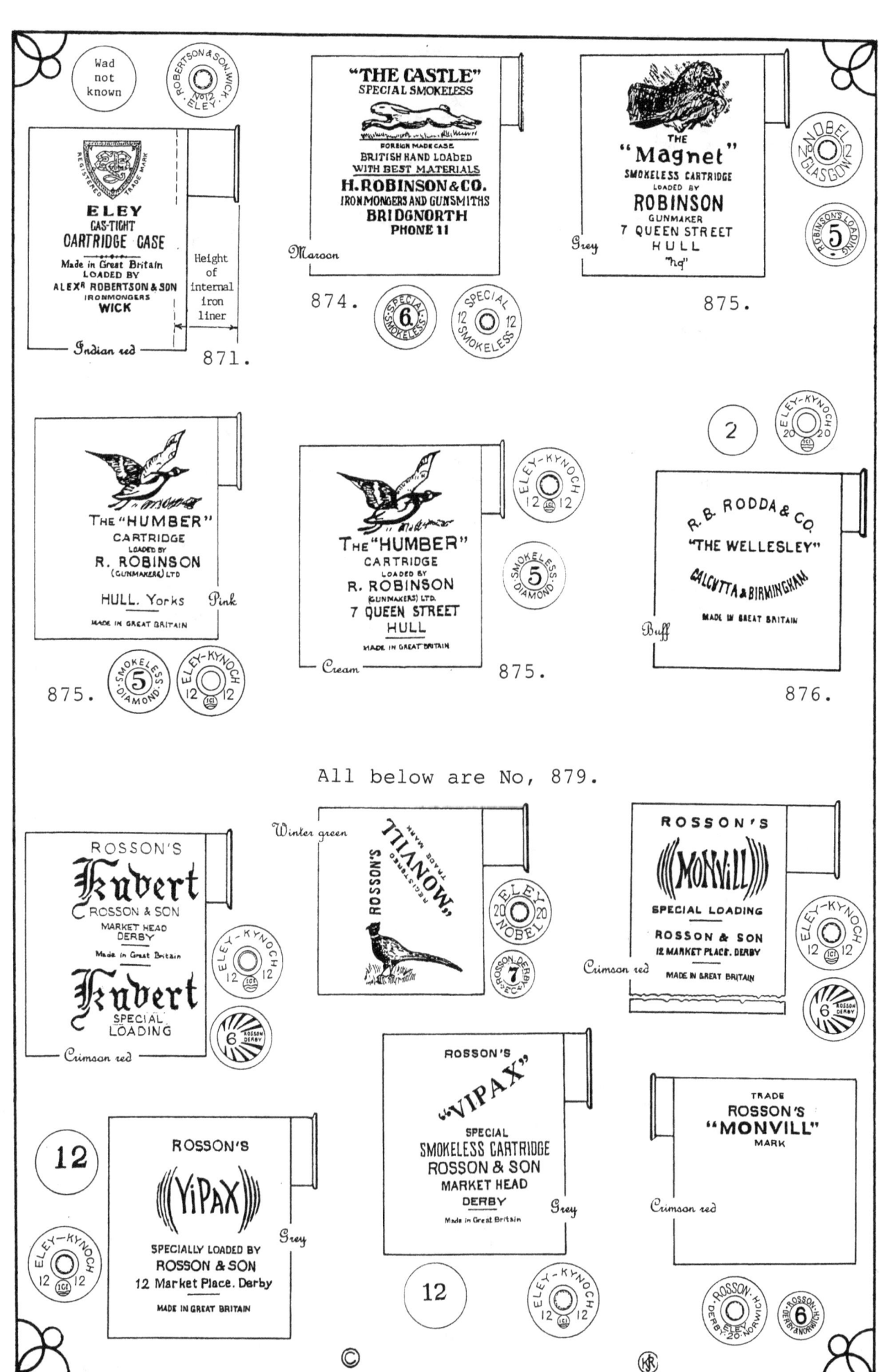

PLATE P6

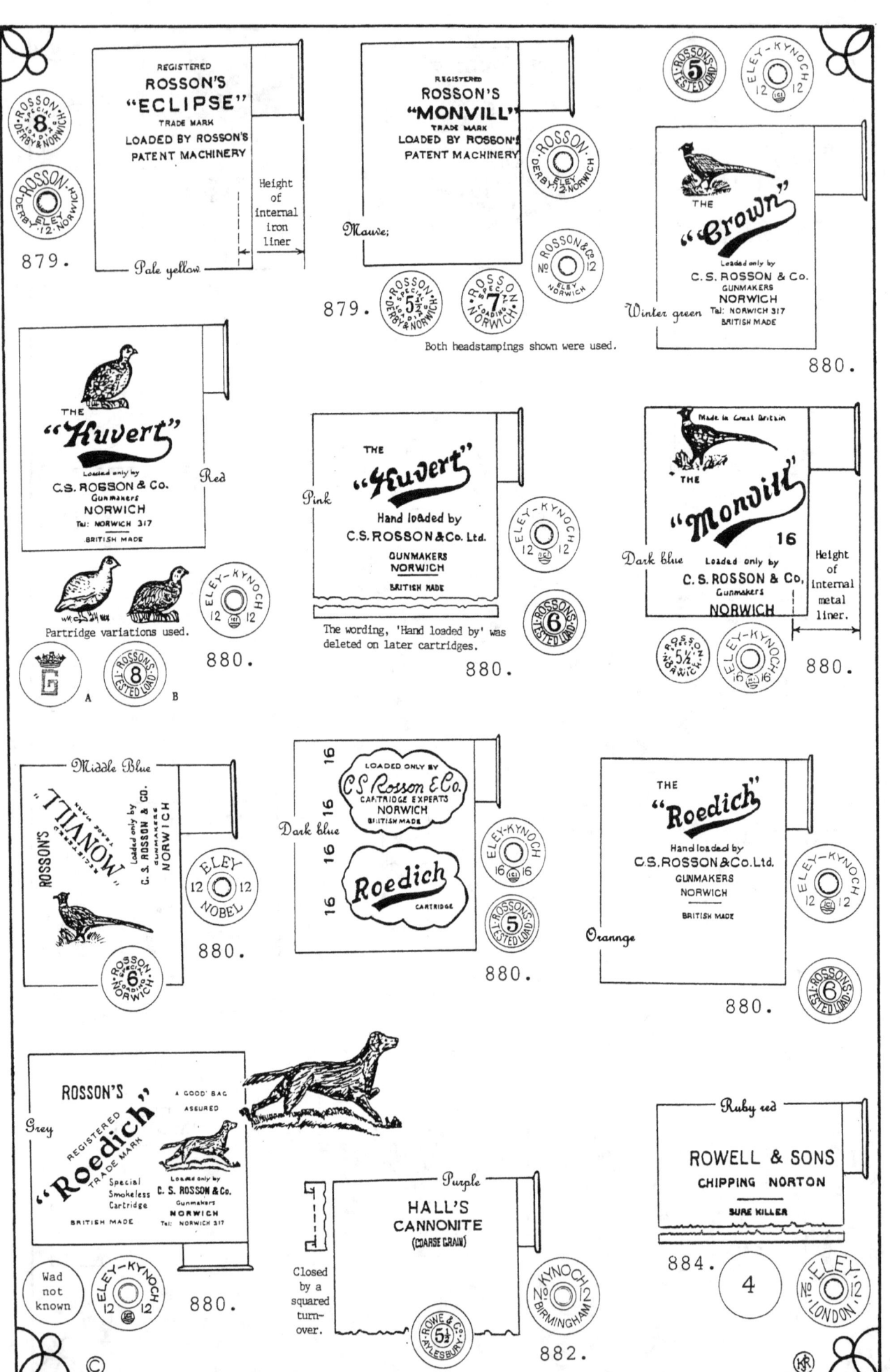

PLATE P7

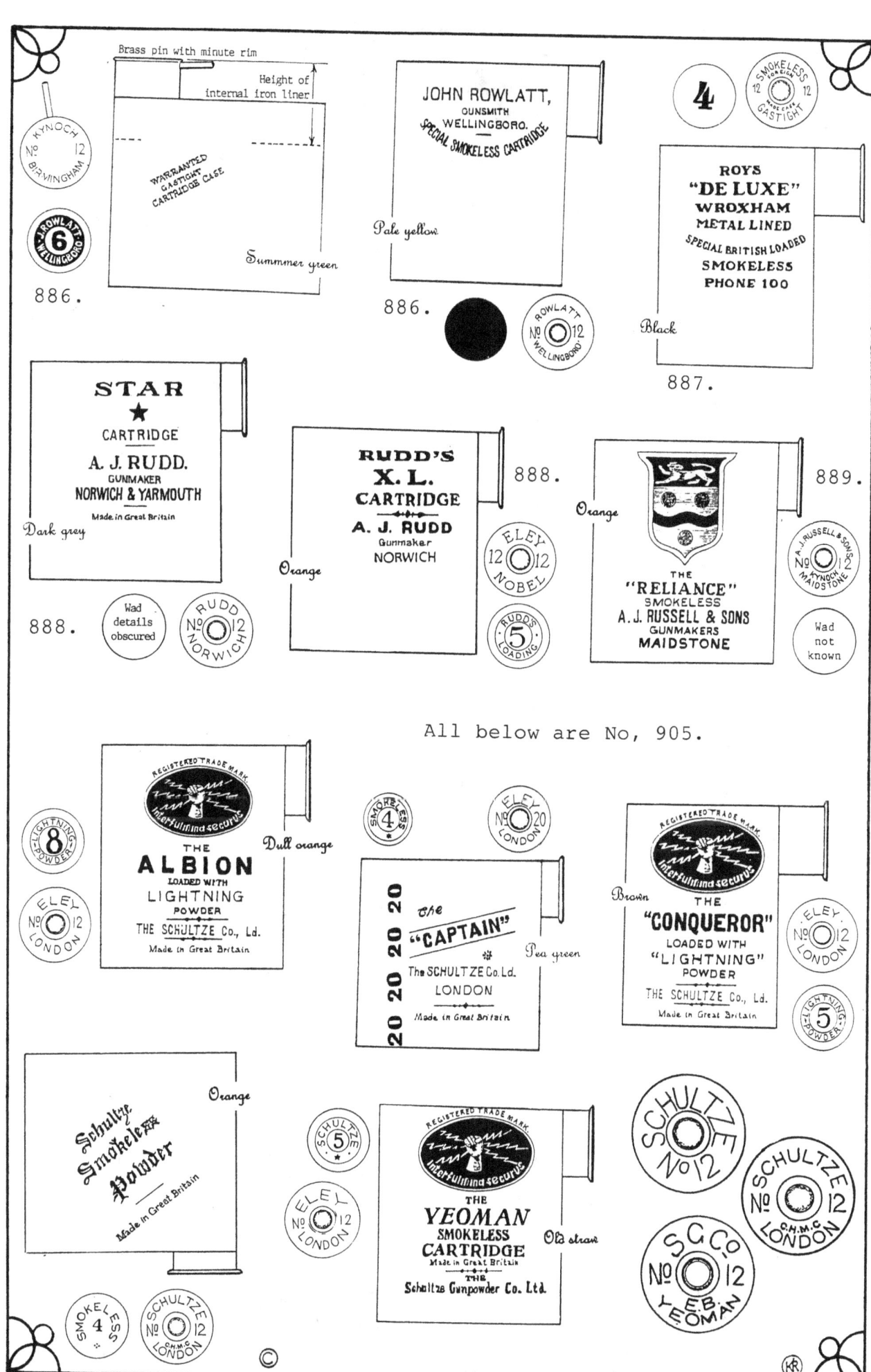

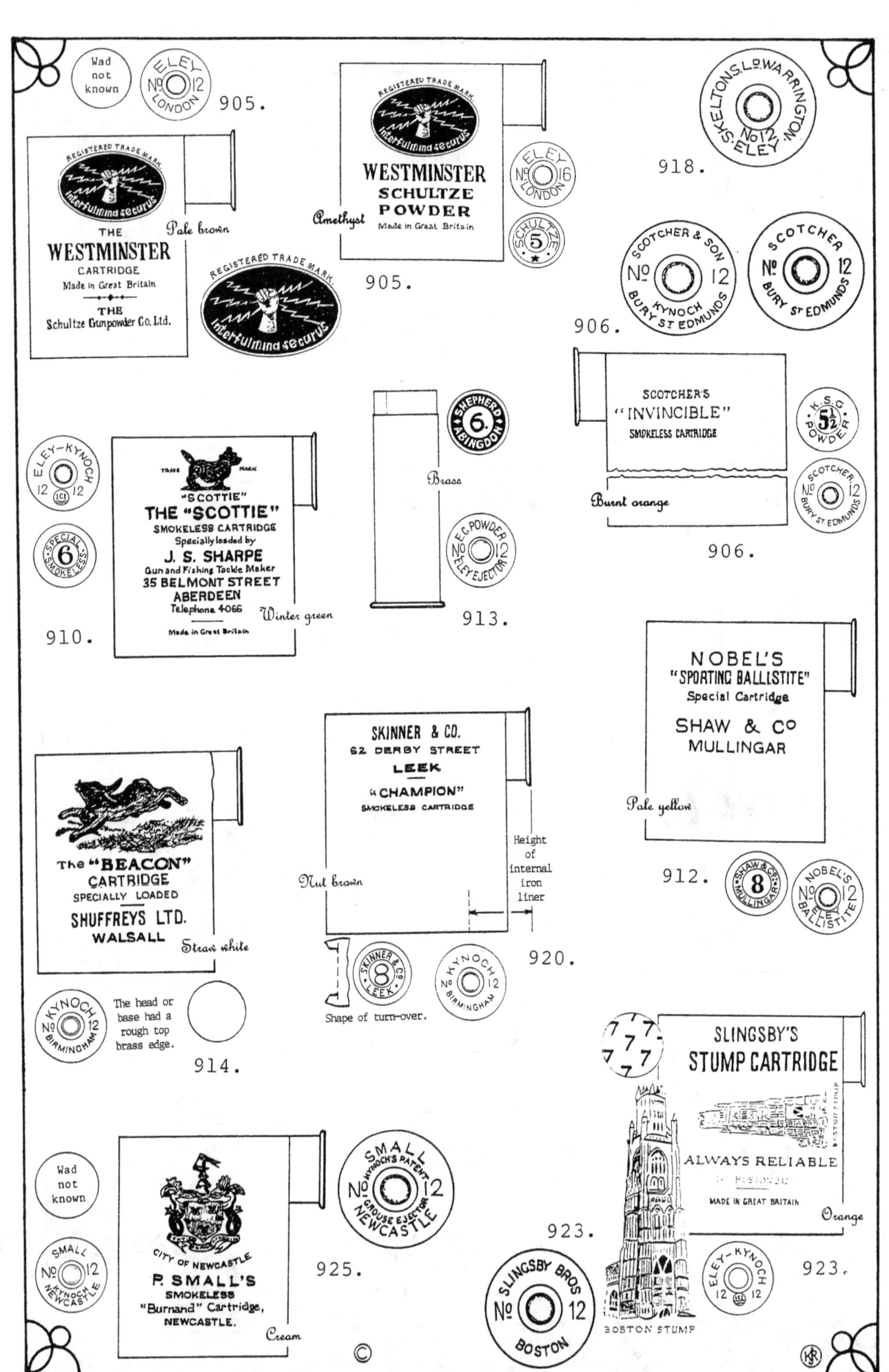

PLATE P9

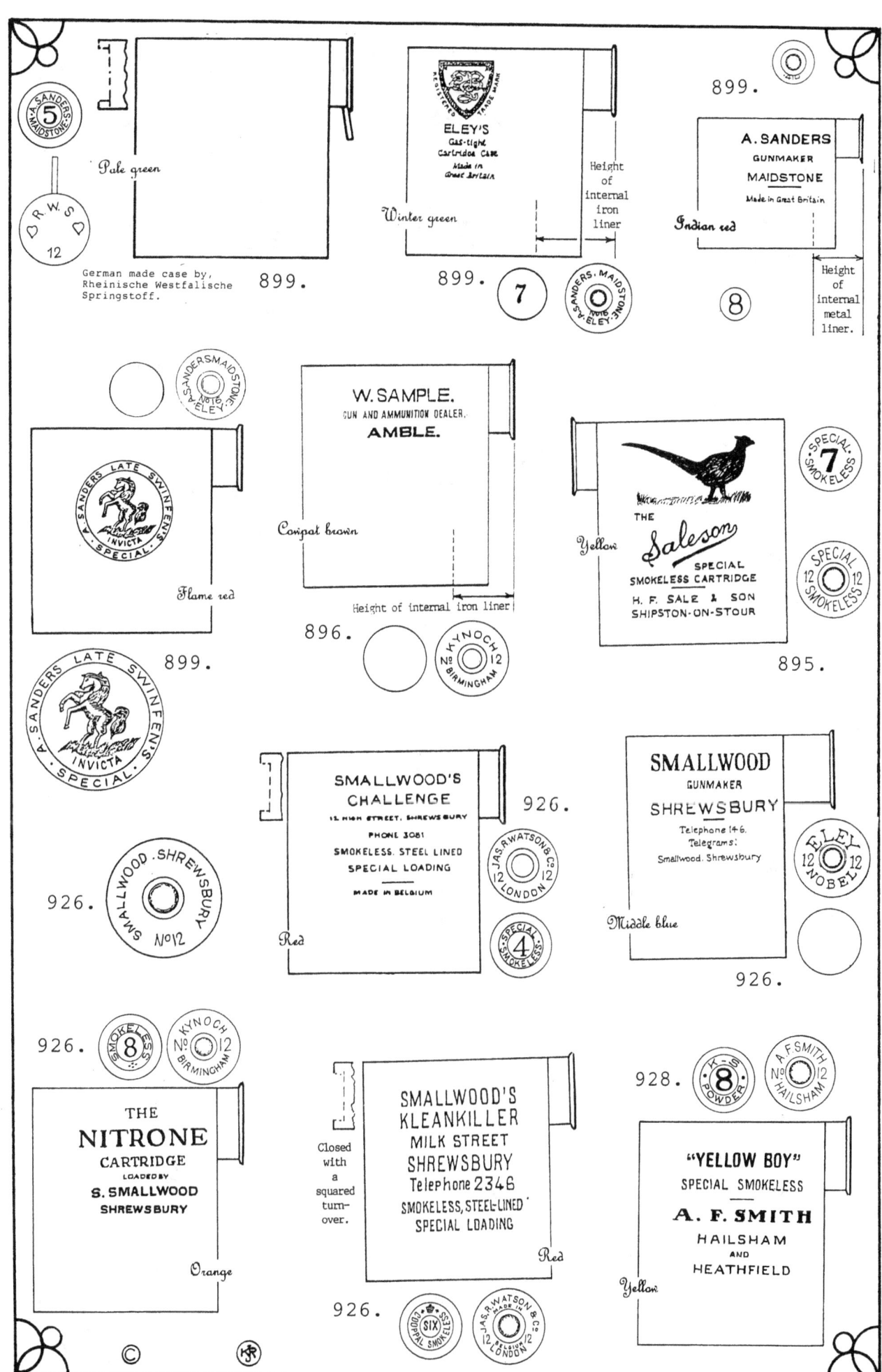

PLATE Q1

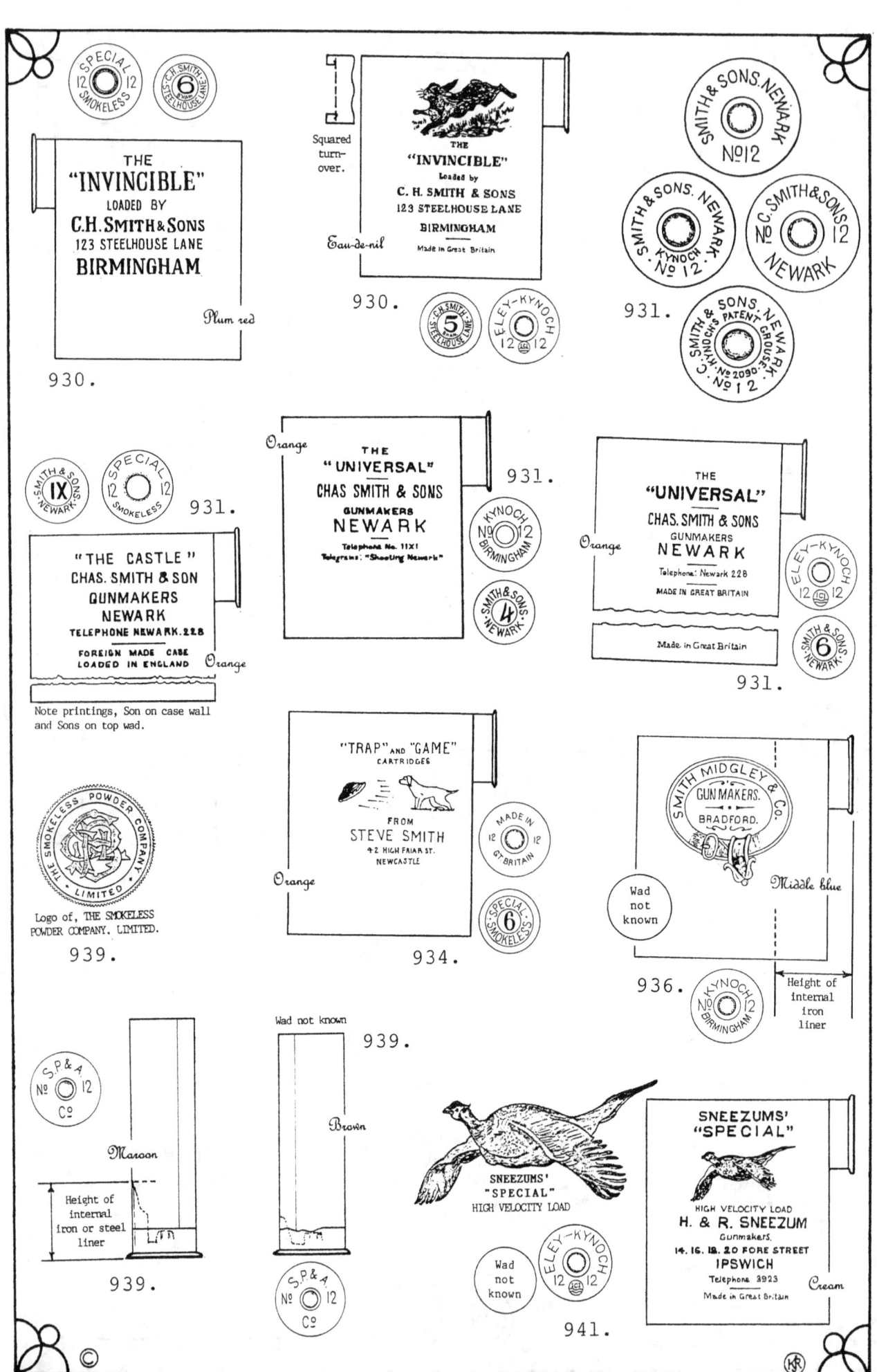

PLATE Q2

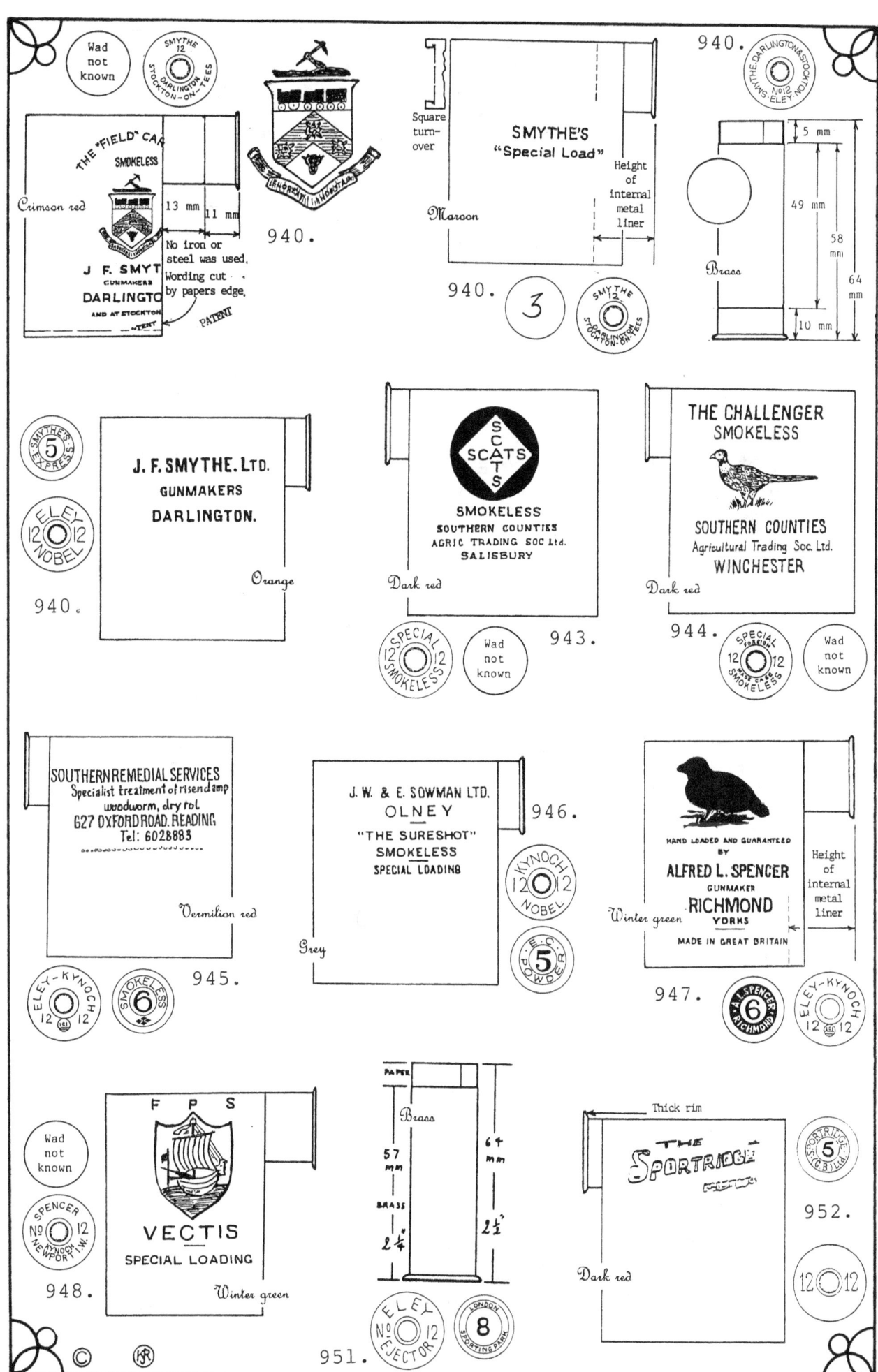

PLATE Q3

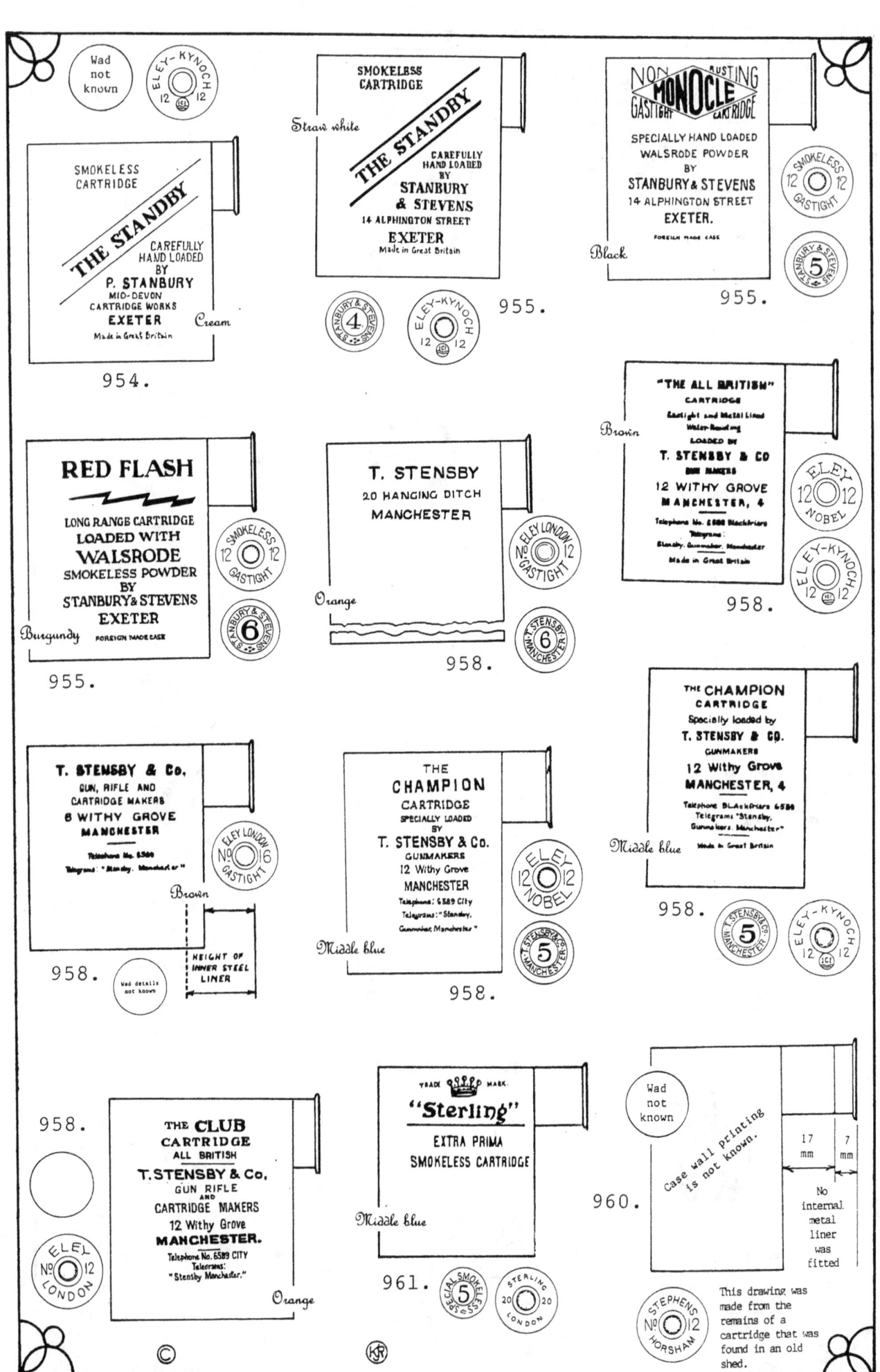

PLATE Q4

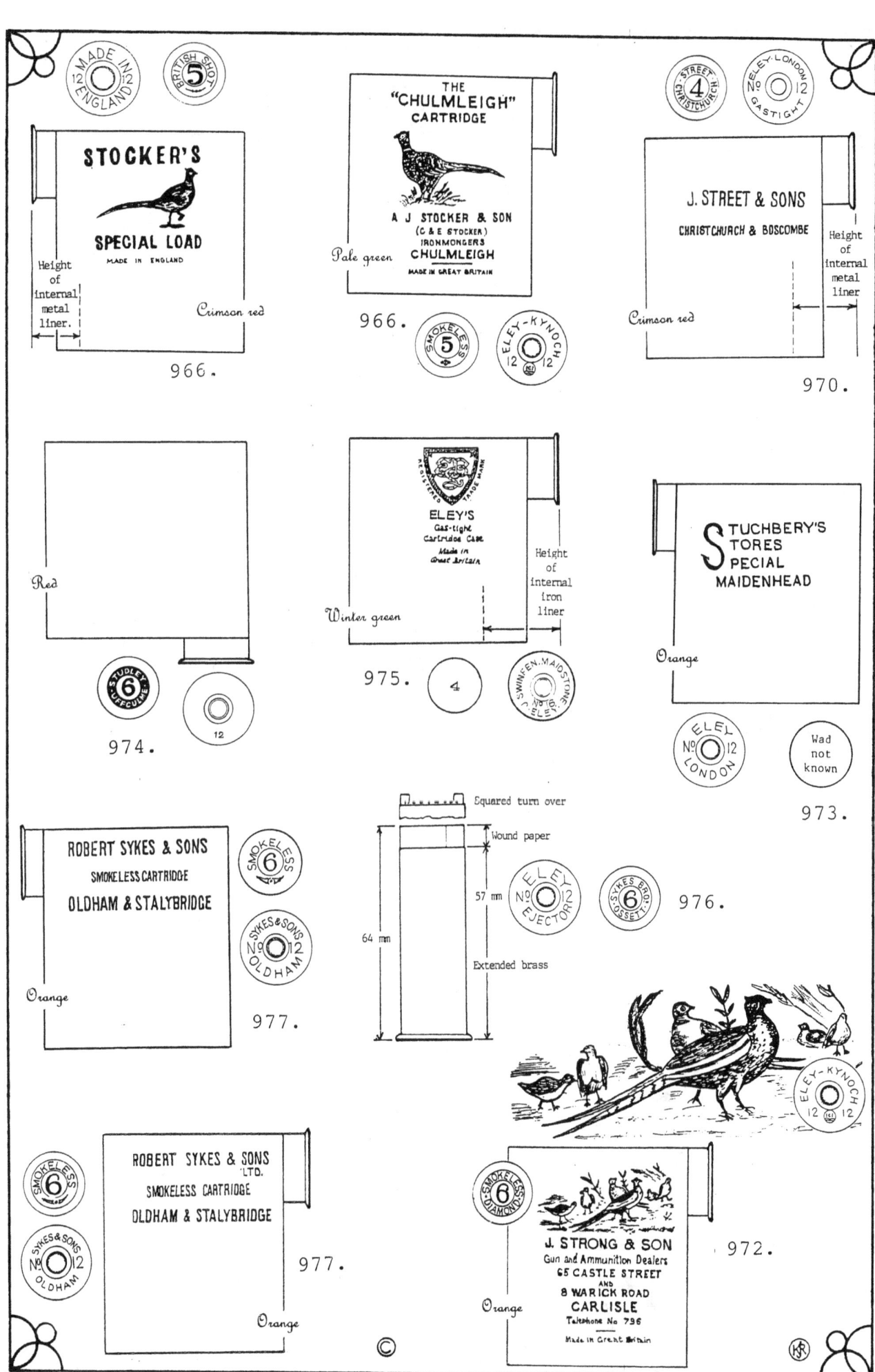

PLATE Q5

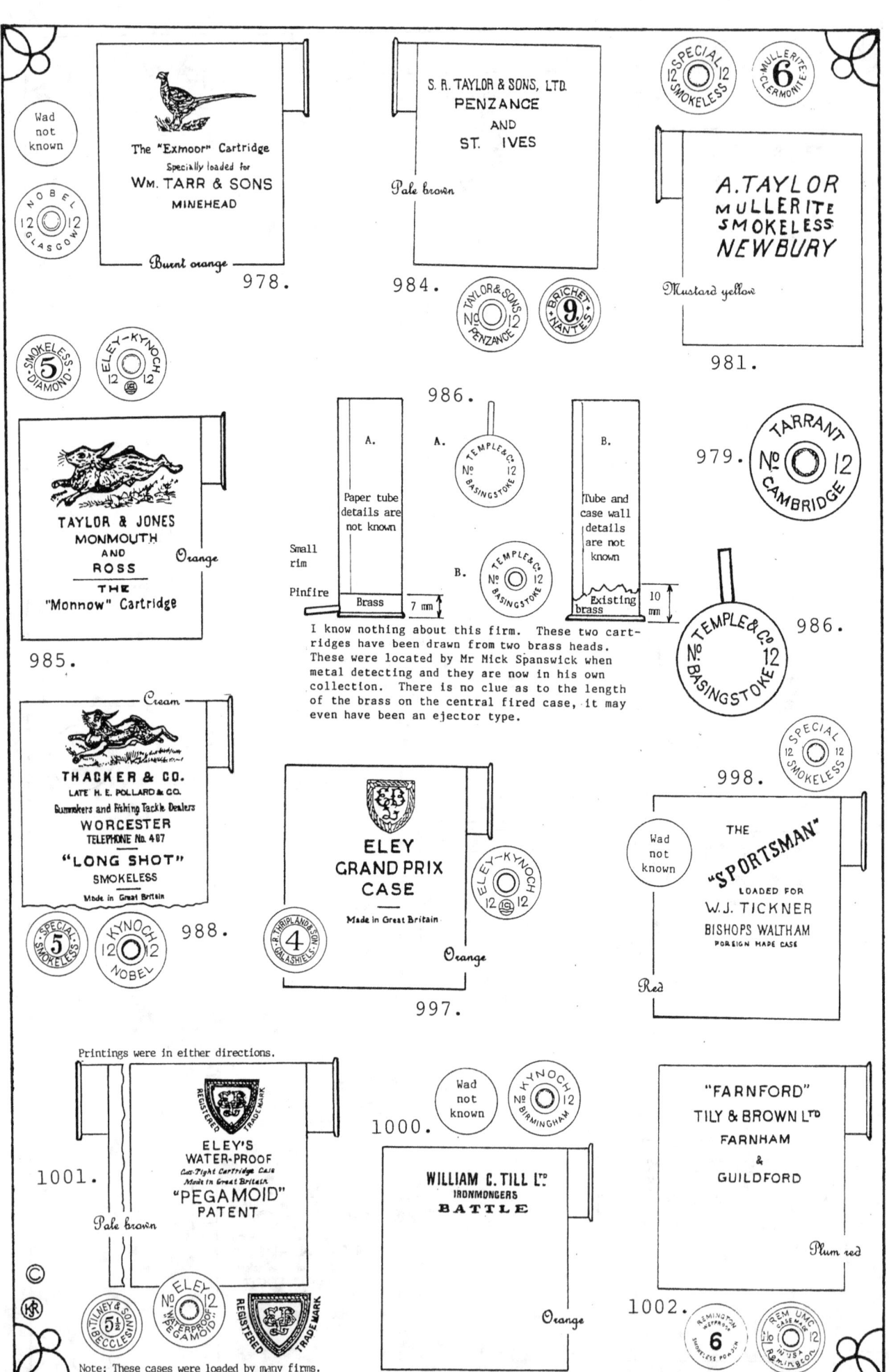

PLATE Q6

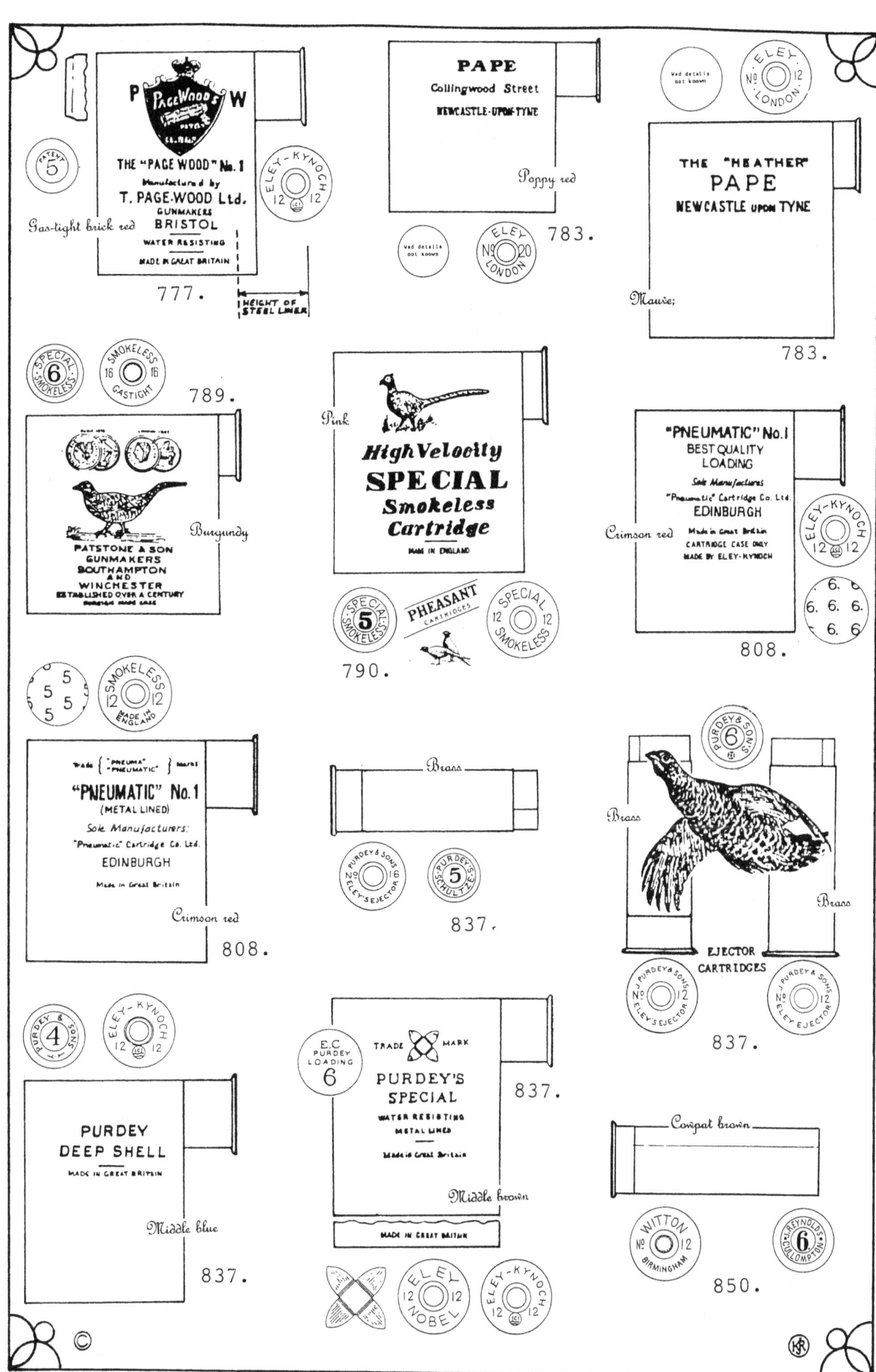

PLATE Q7

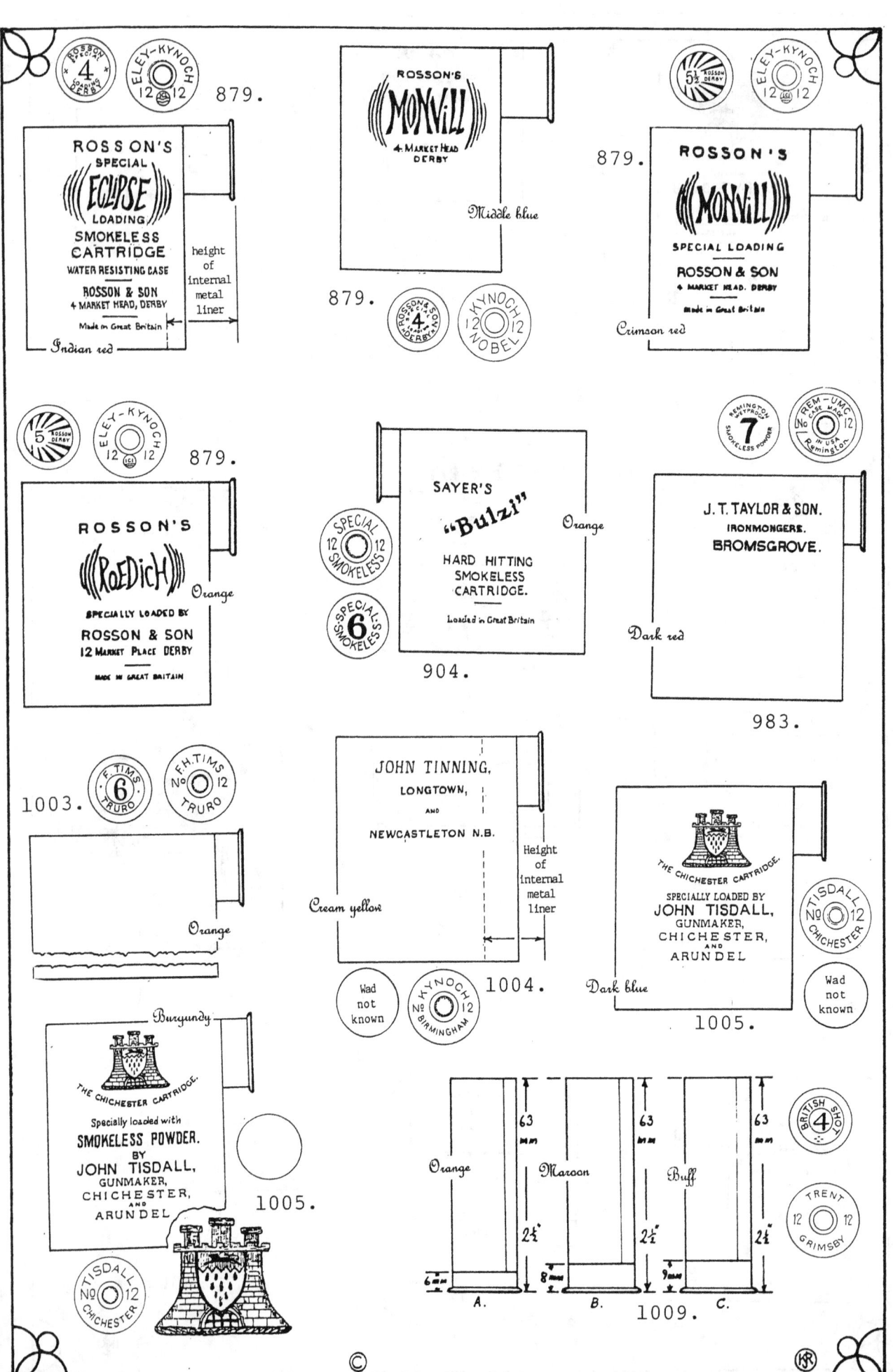

PLATE Q8

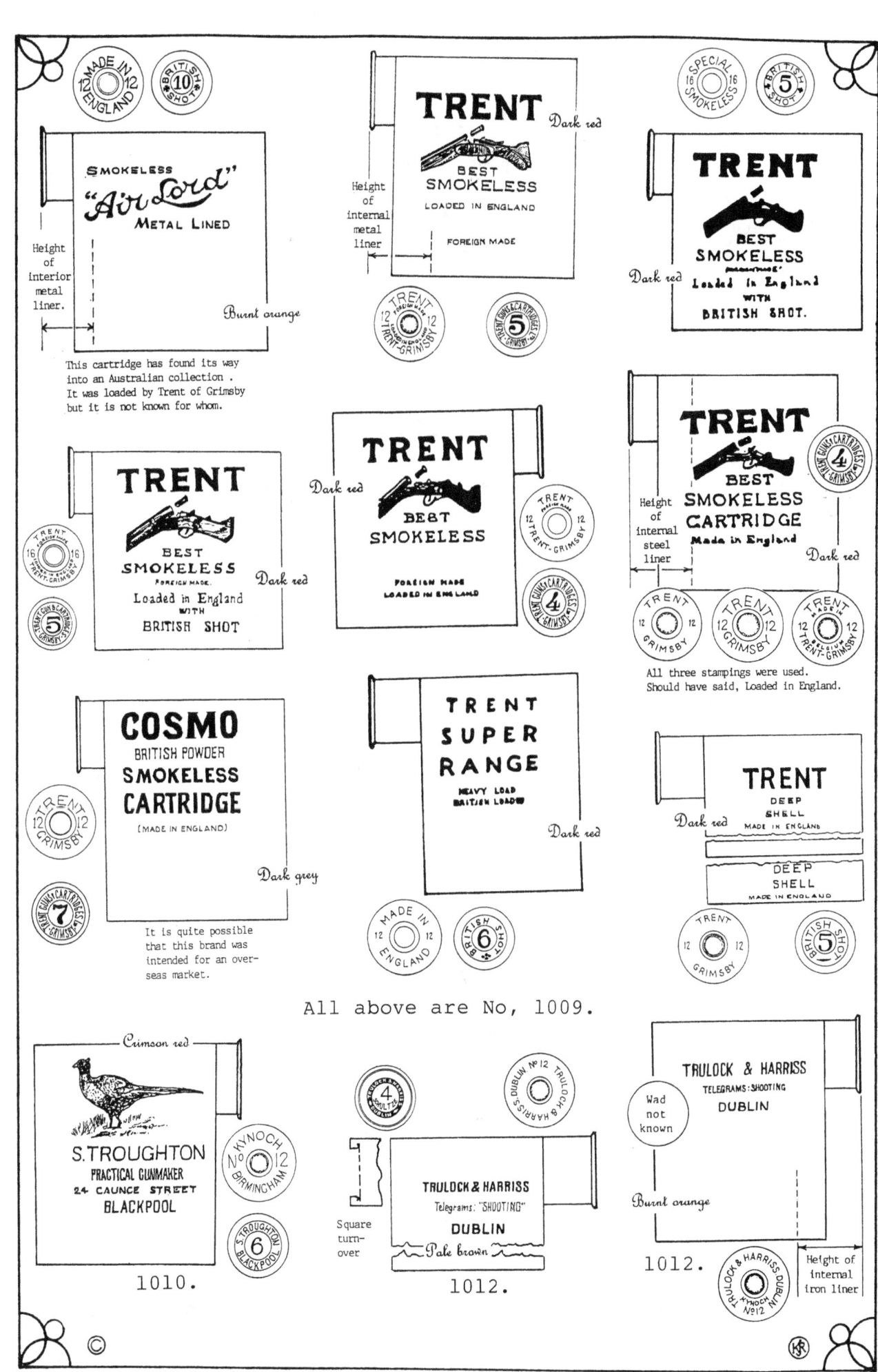

PLATE Q9

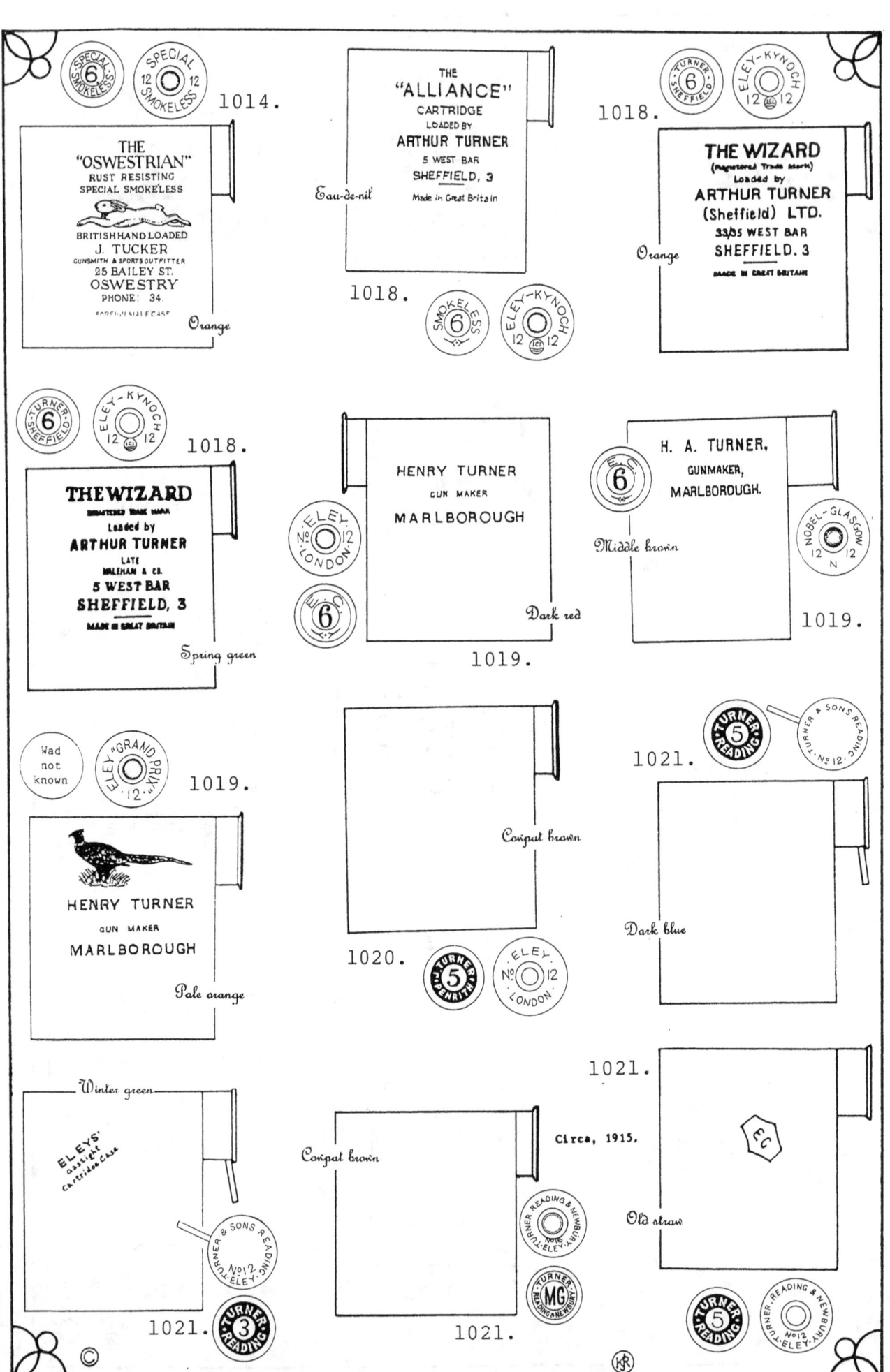

PLATE R1

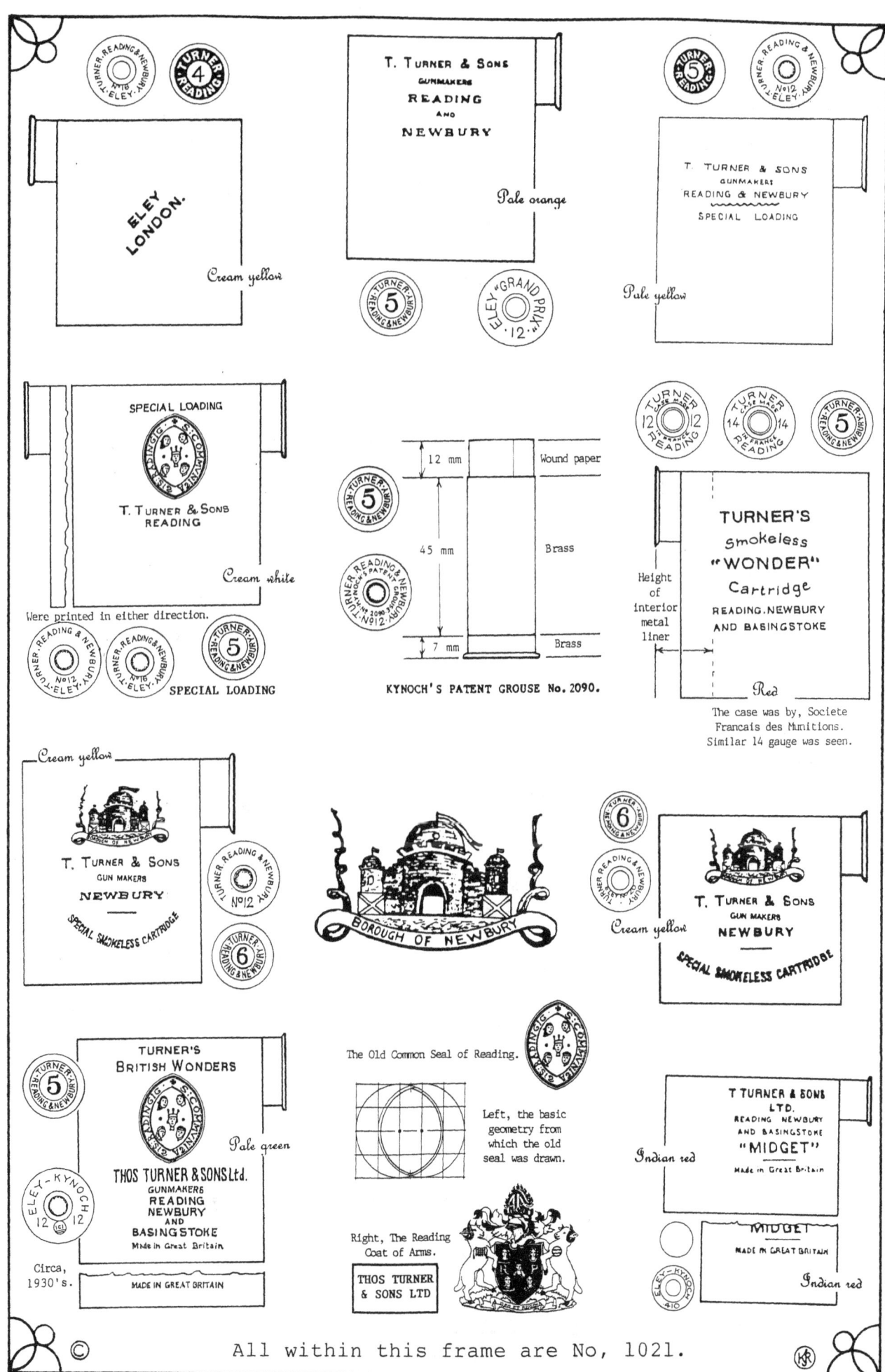

PLATE R2

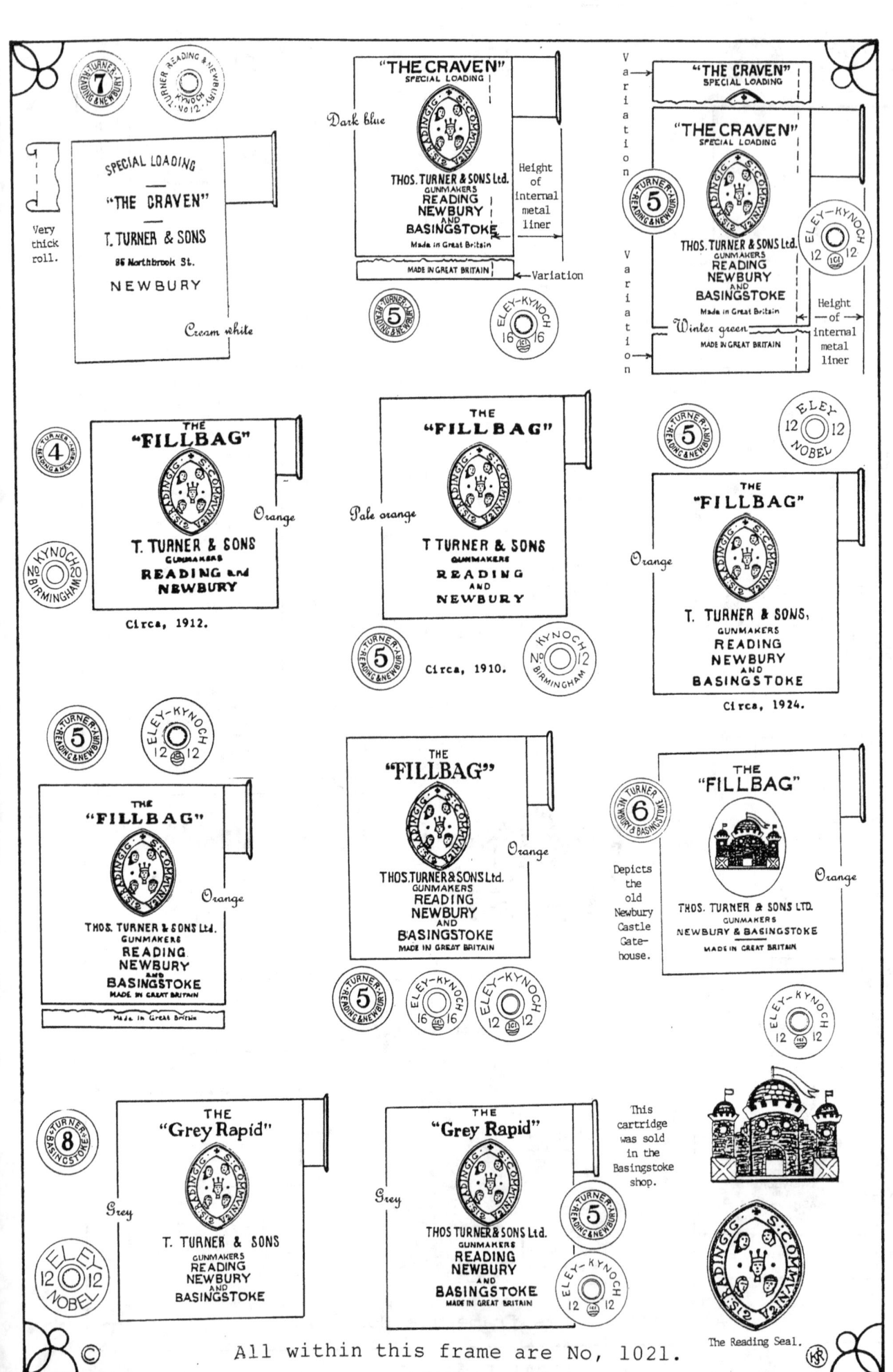

PLATE R3

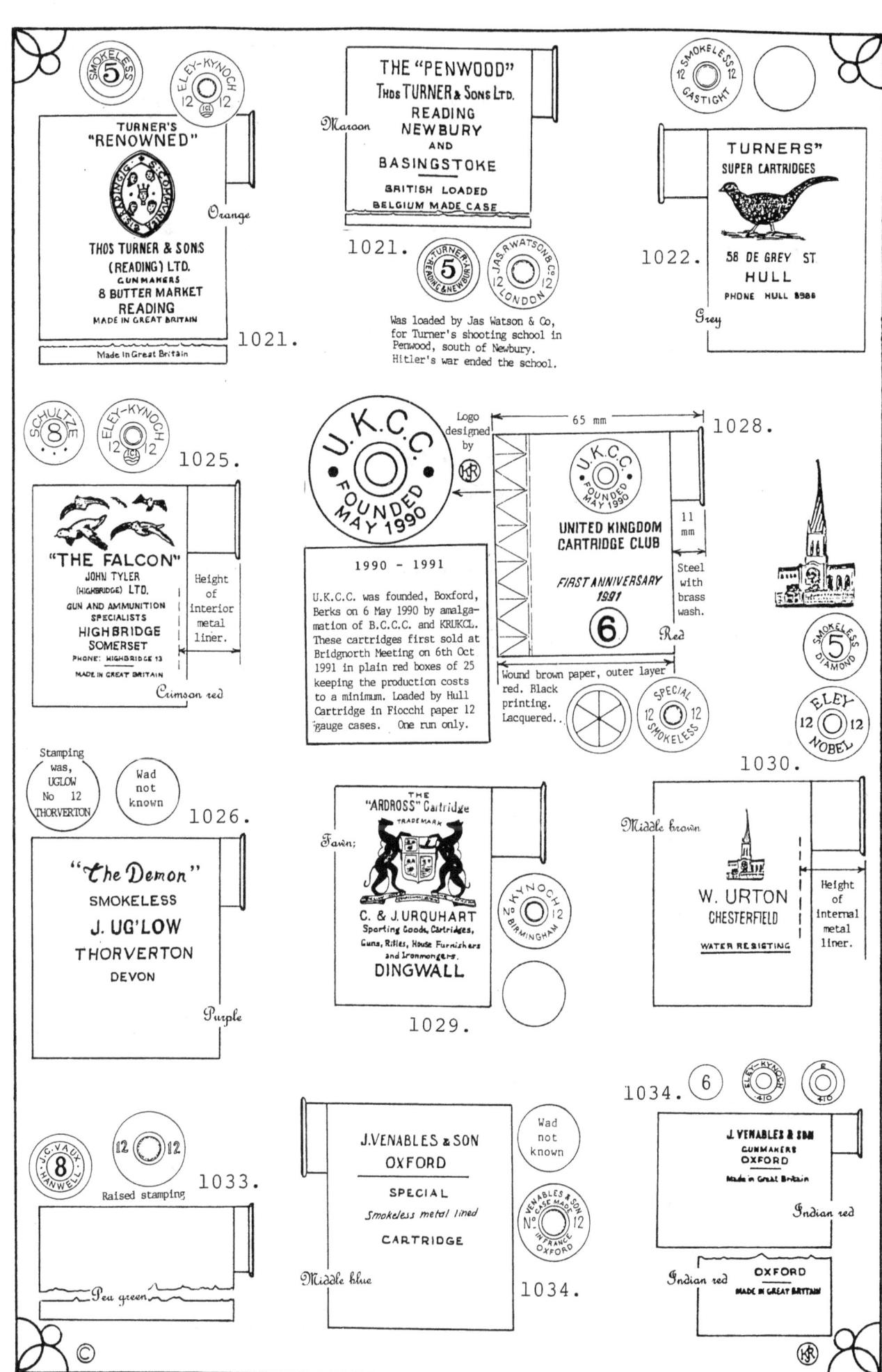

PLATE R4

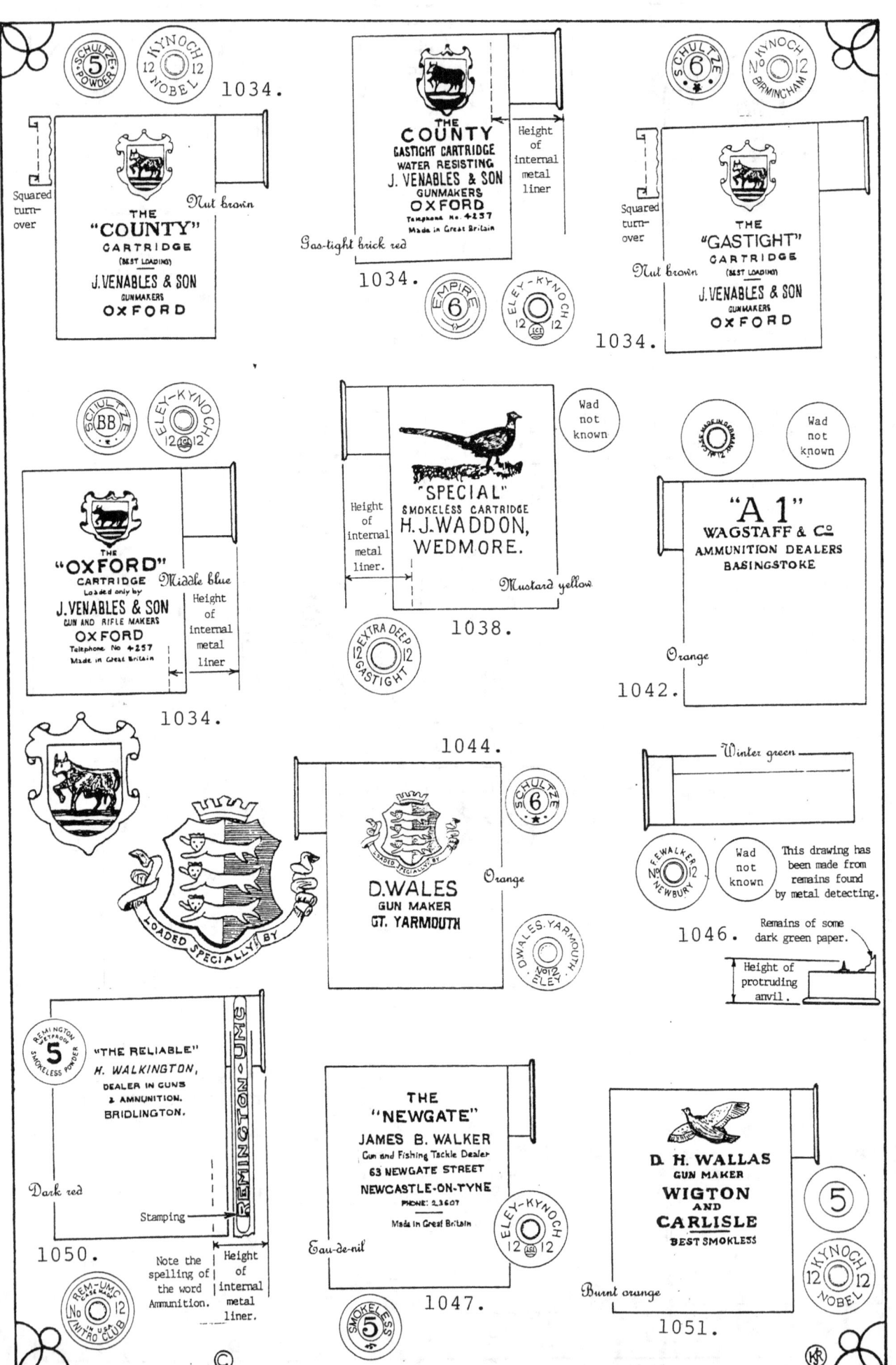

PLATE R5

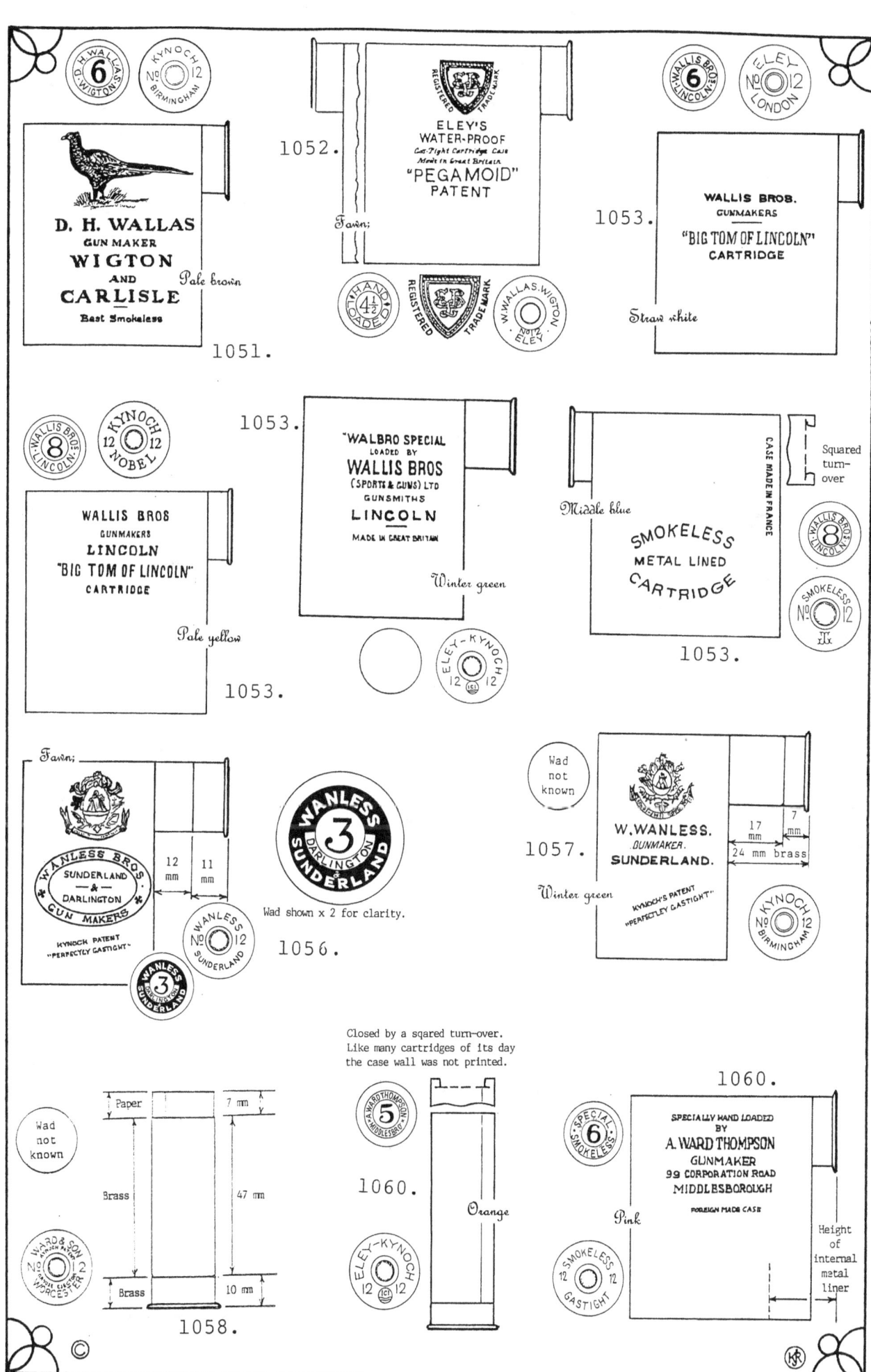

PLATE R6

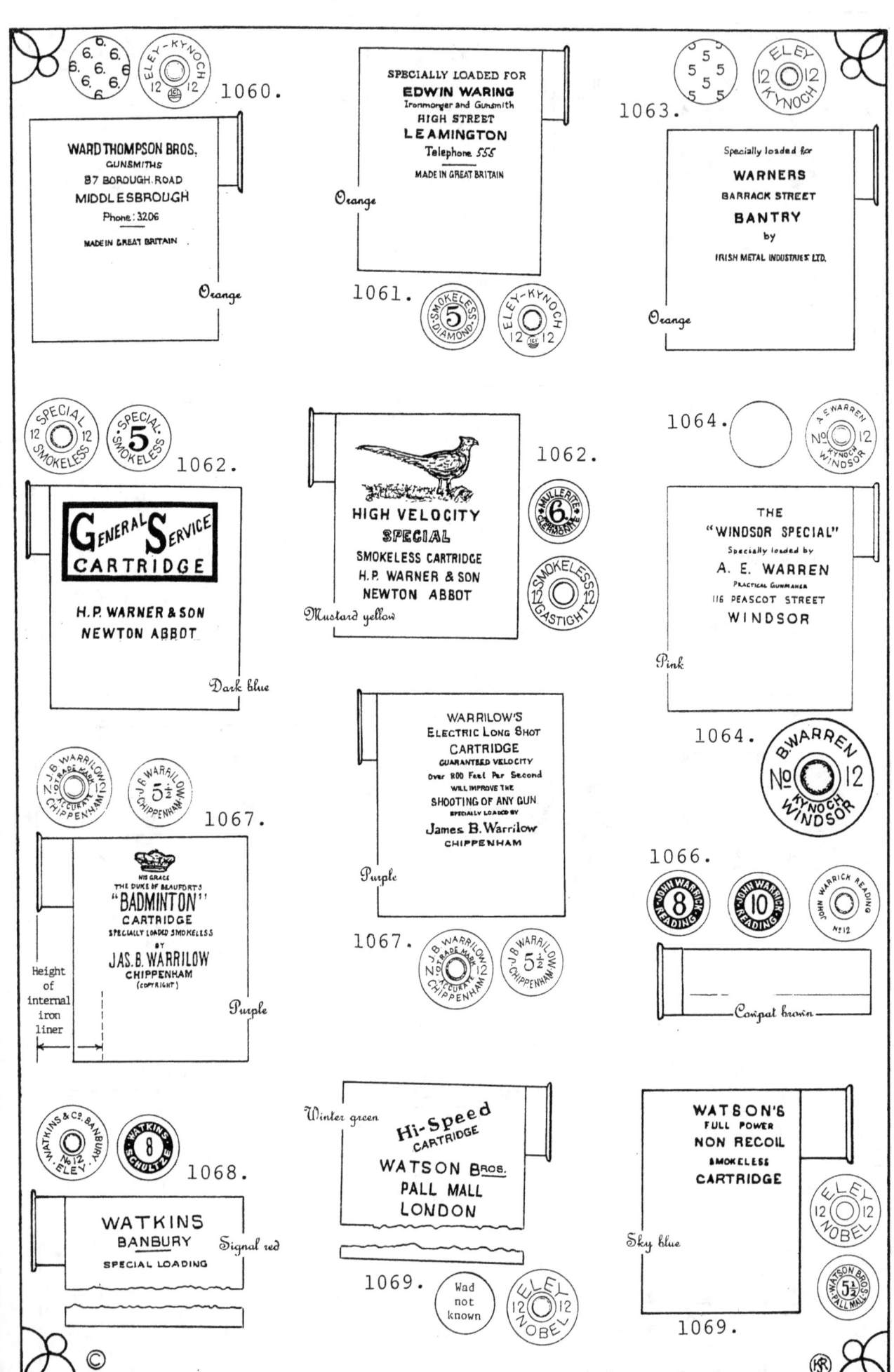

PLATE R7

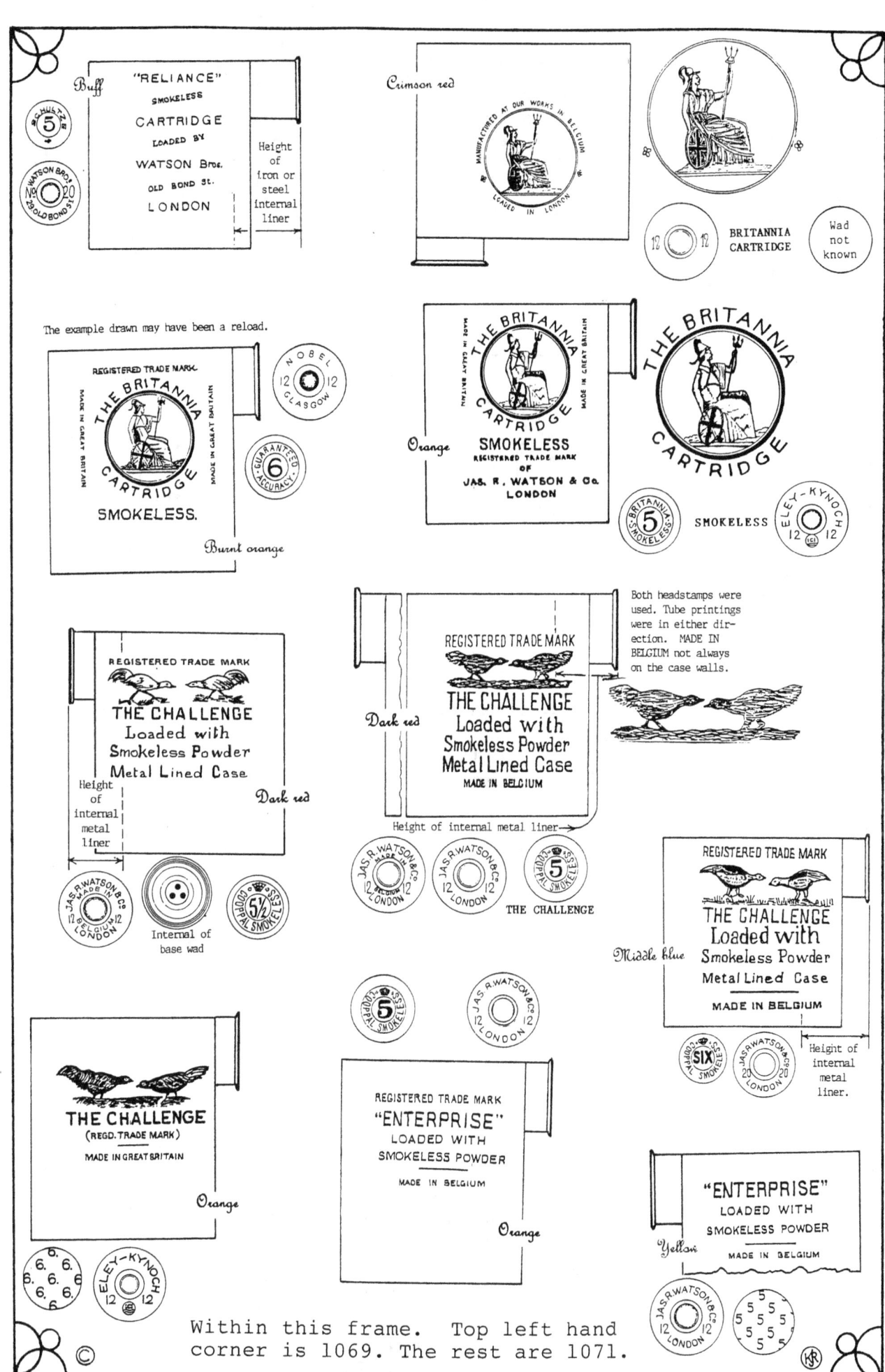

PLATE R8

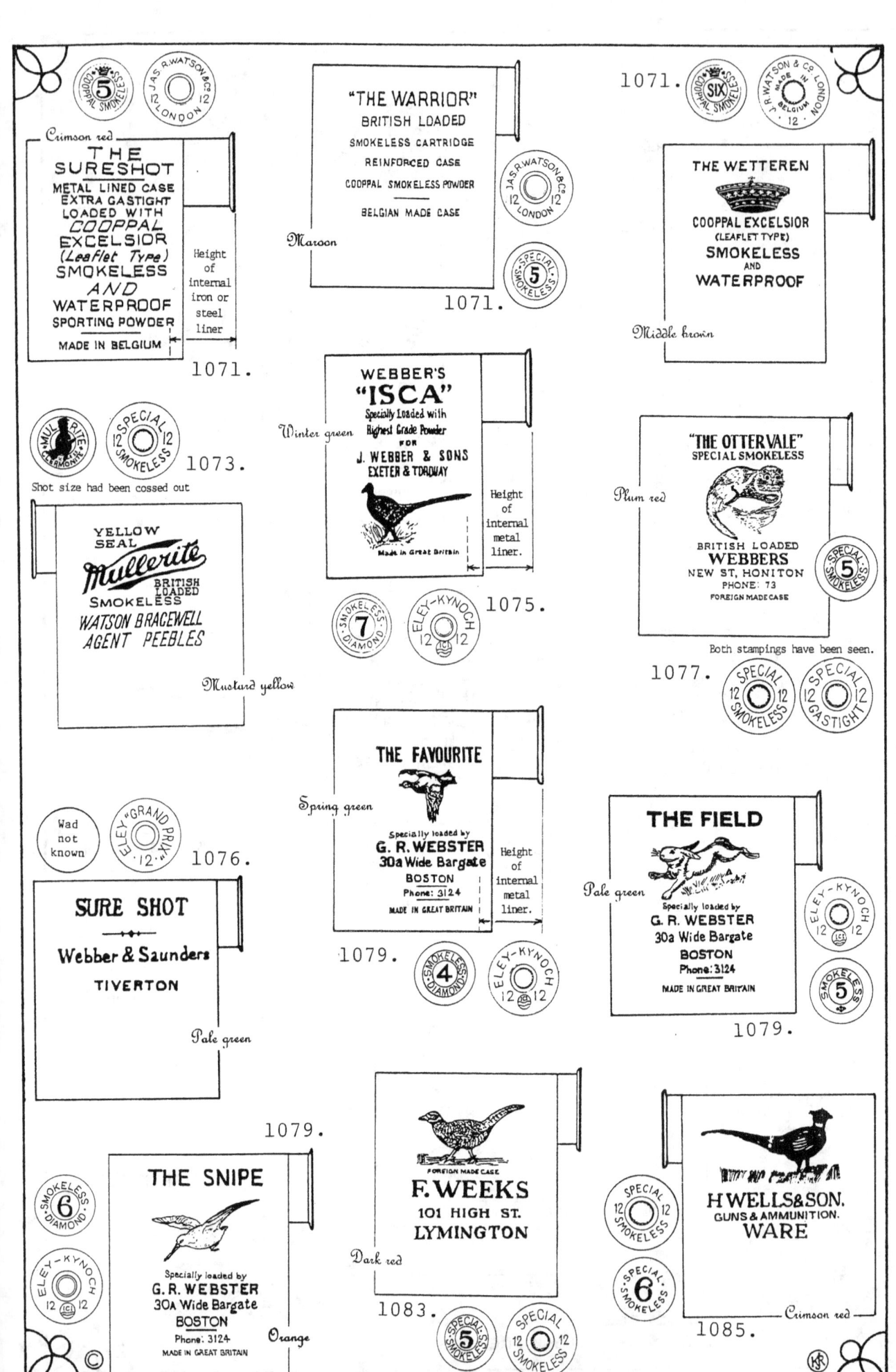

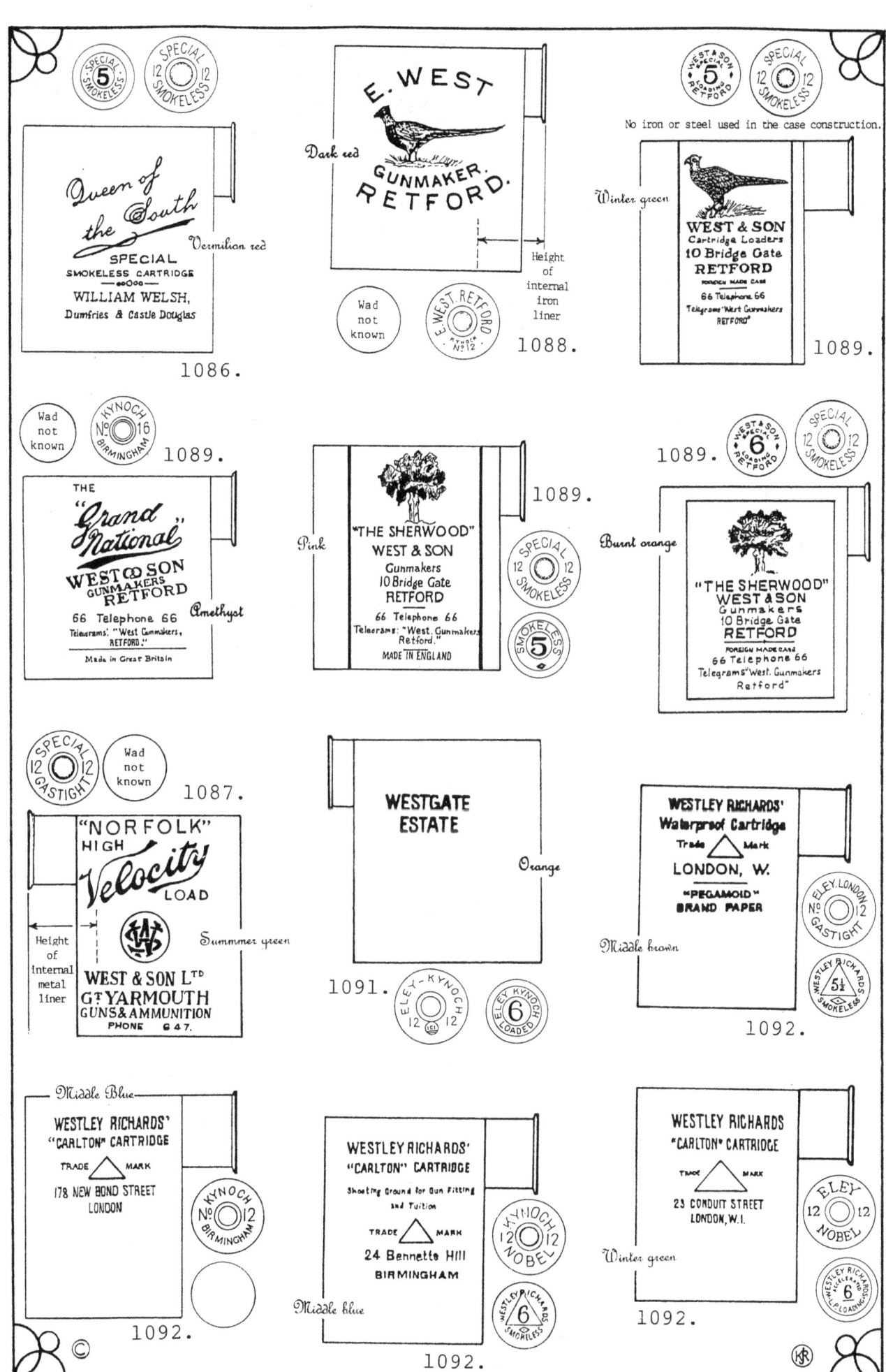

PLATE S1

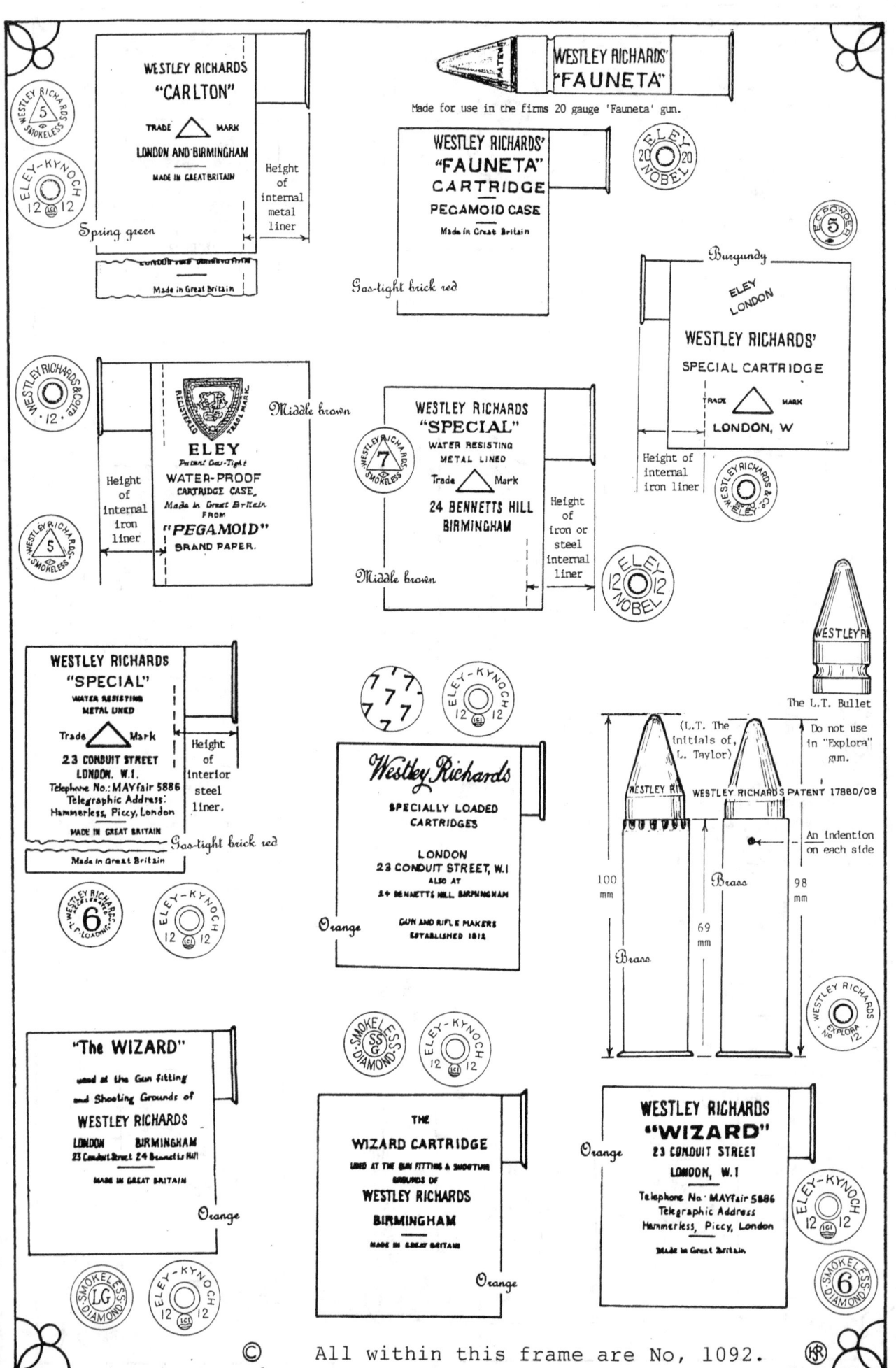

PLATE S2

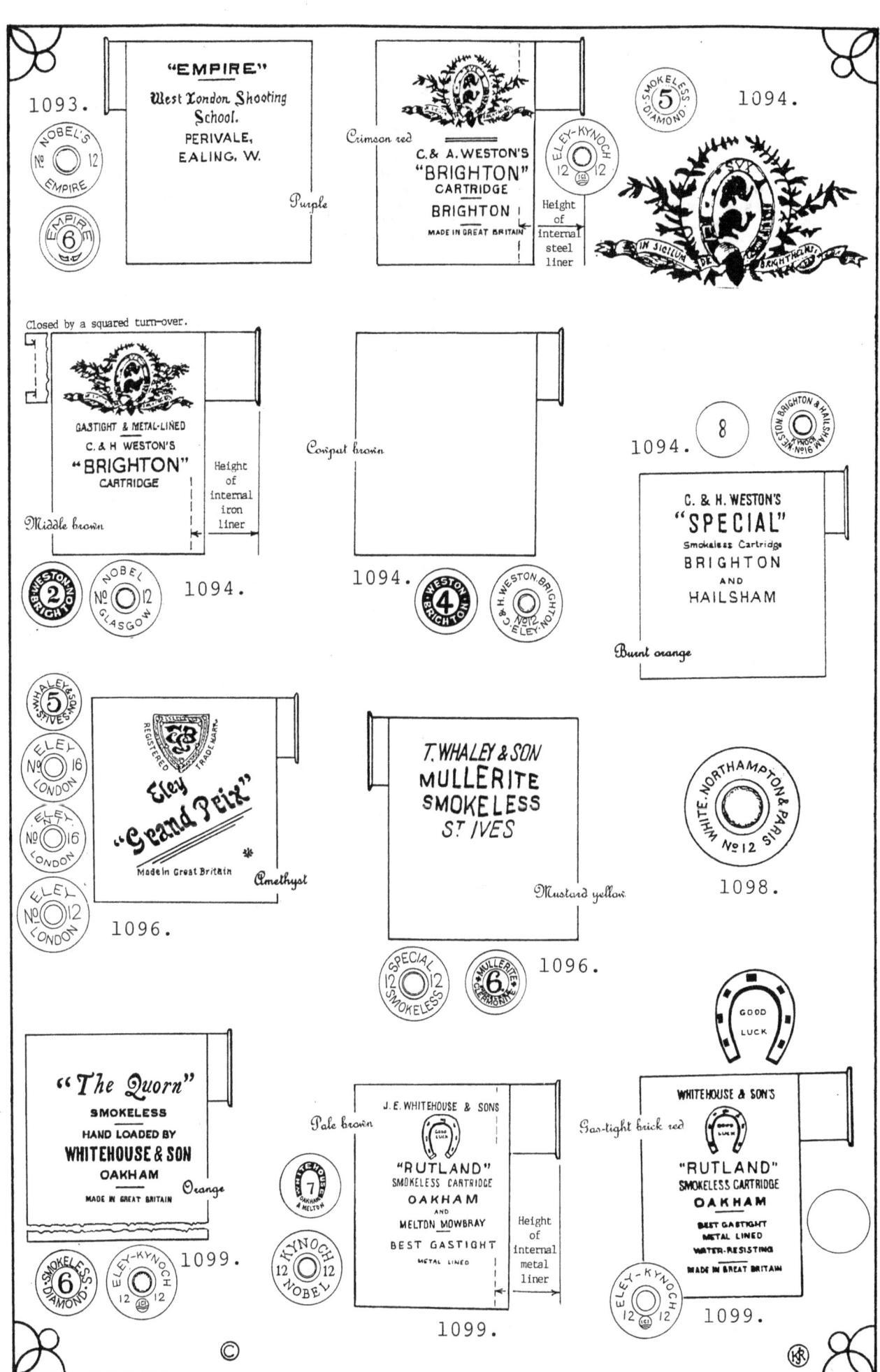

PLATE S3

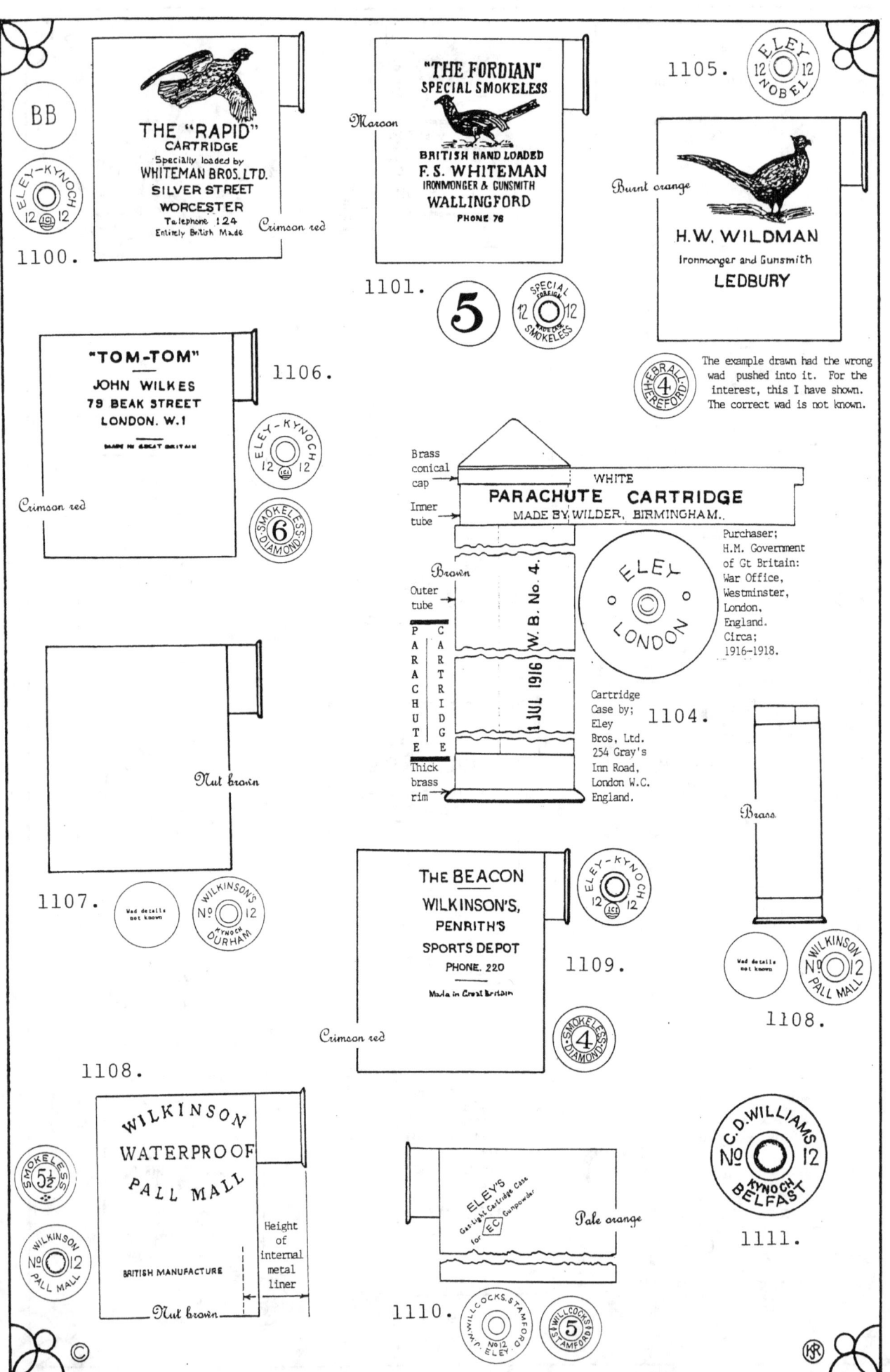

PLATE S4

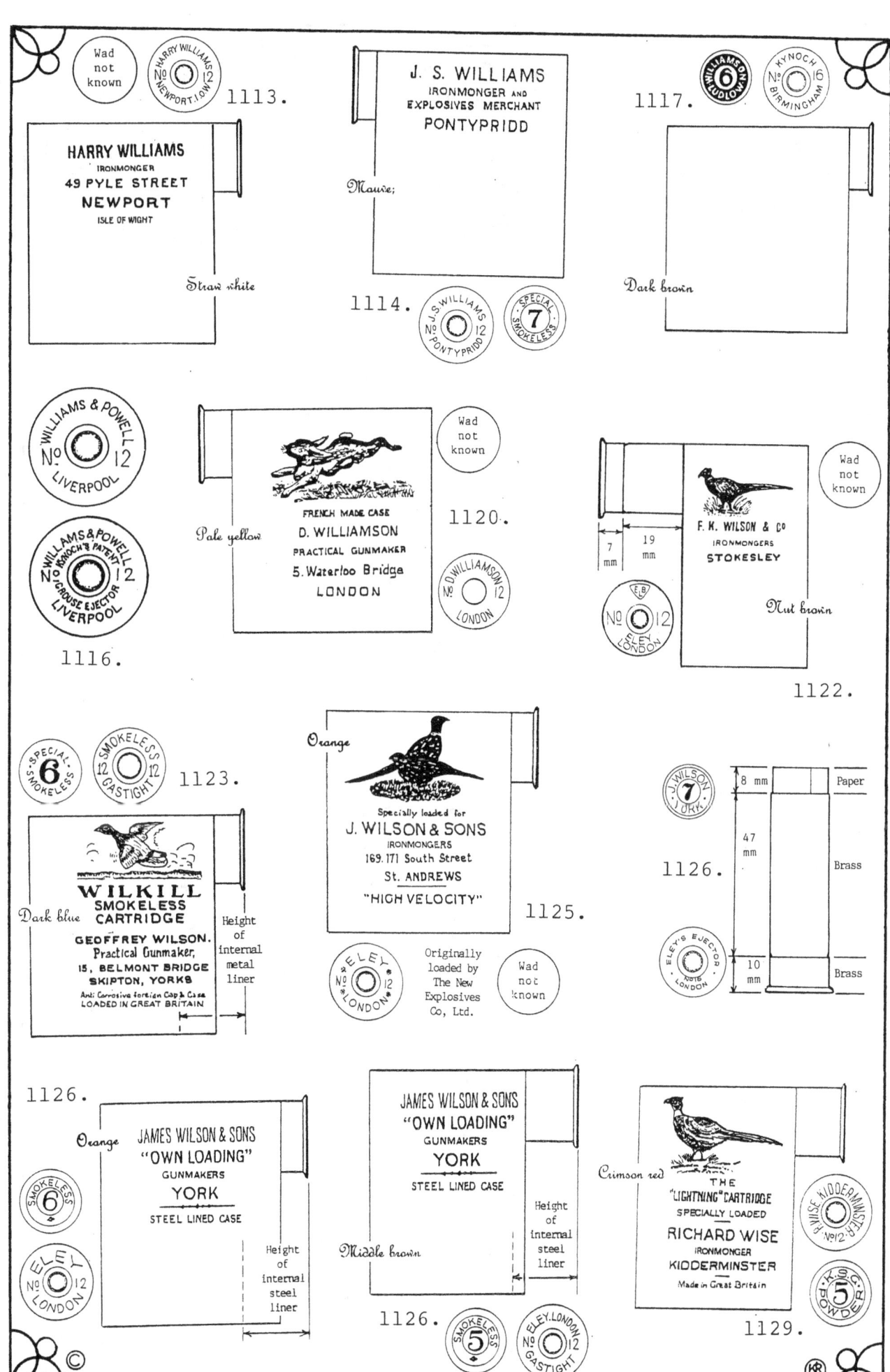

PLATE S5

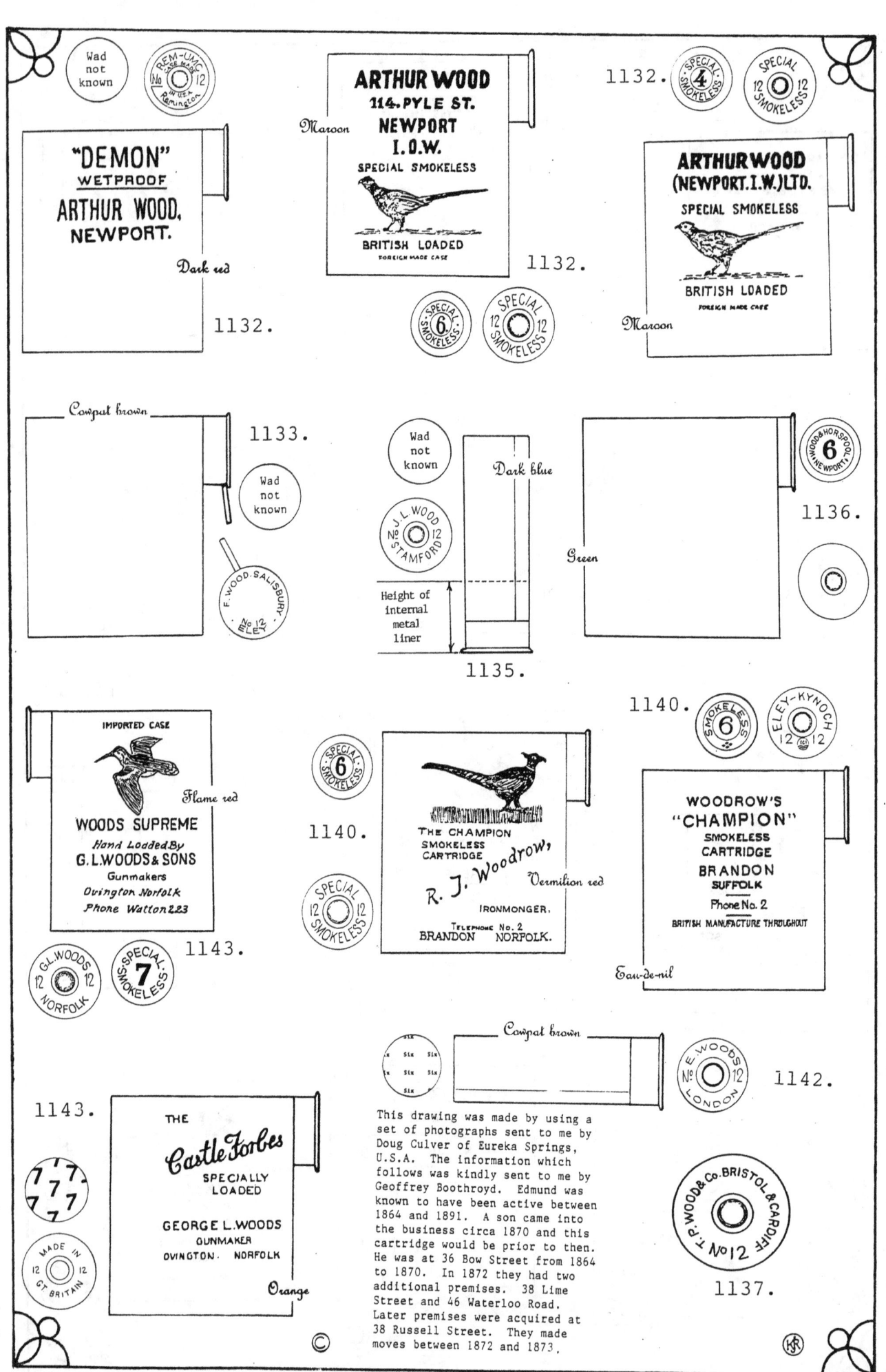

PLATE S6

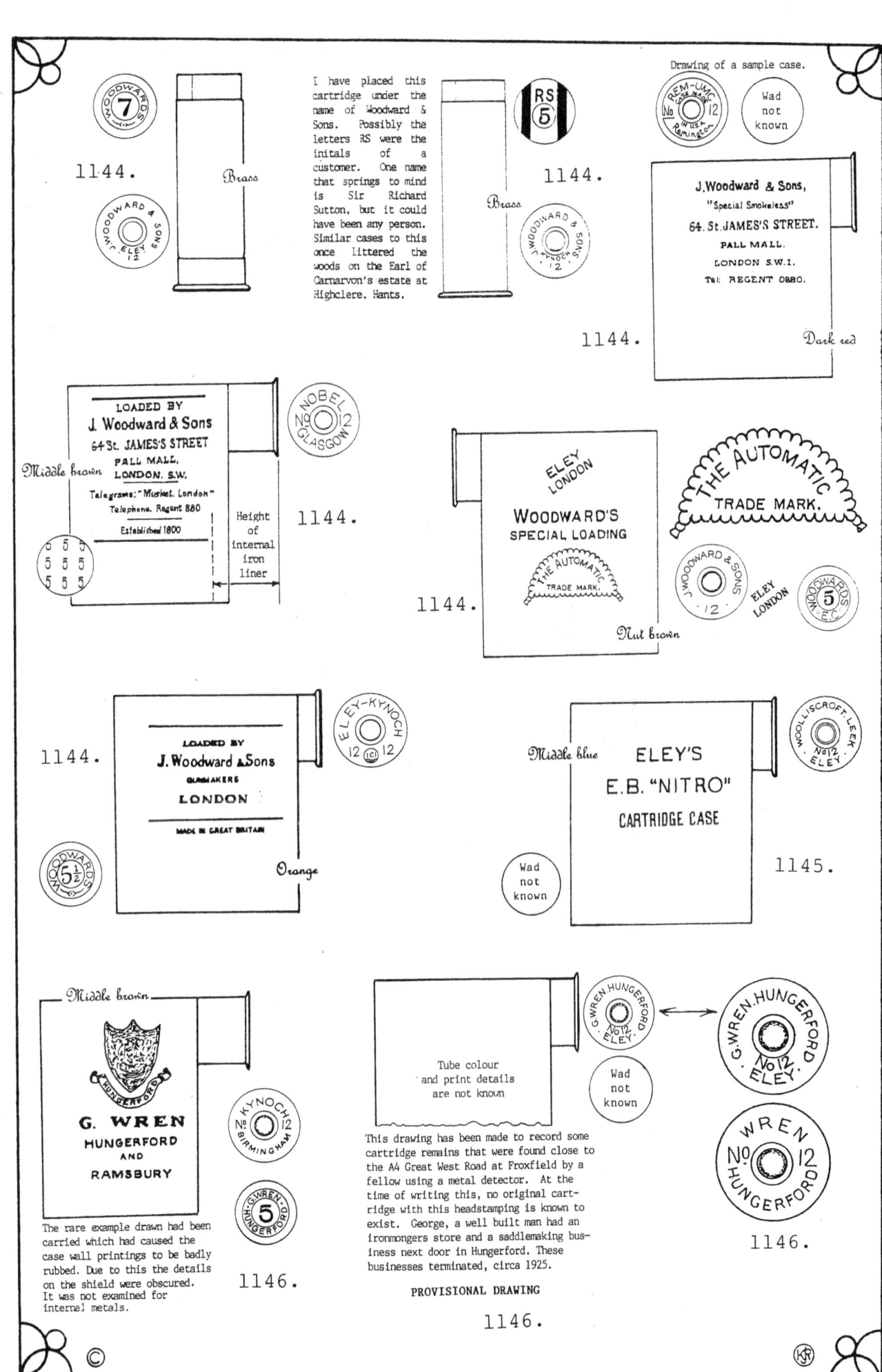

PLATE S7

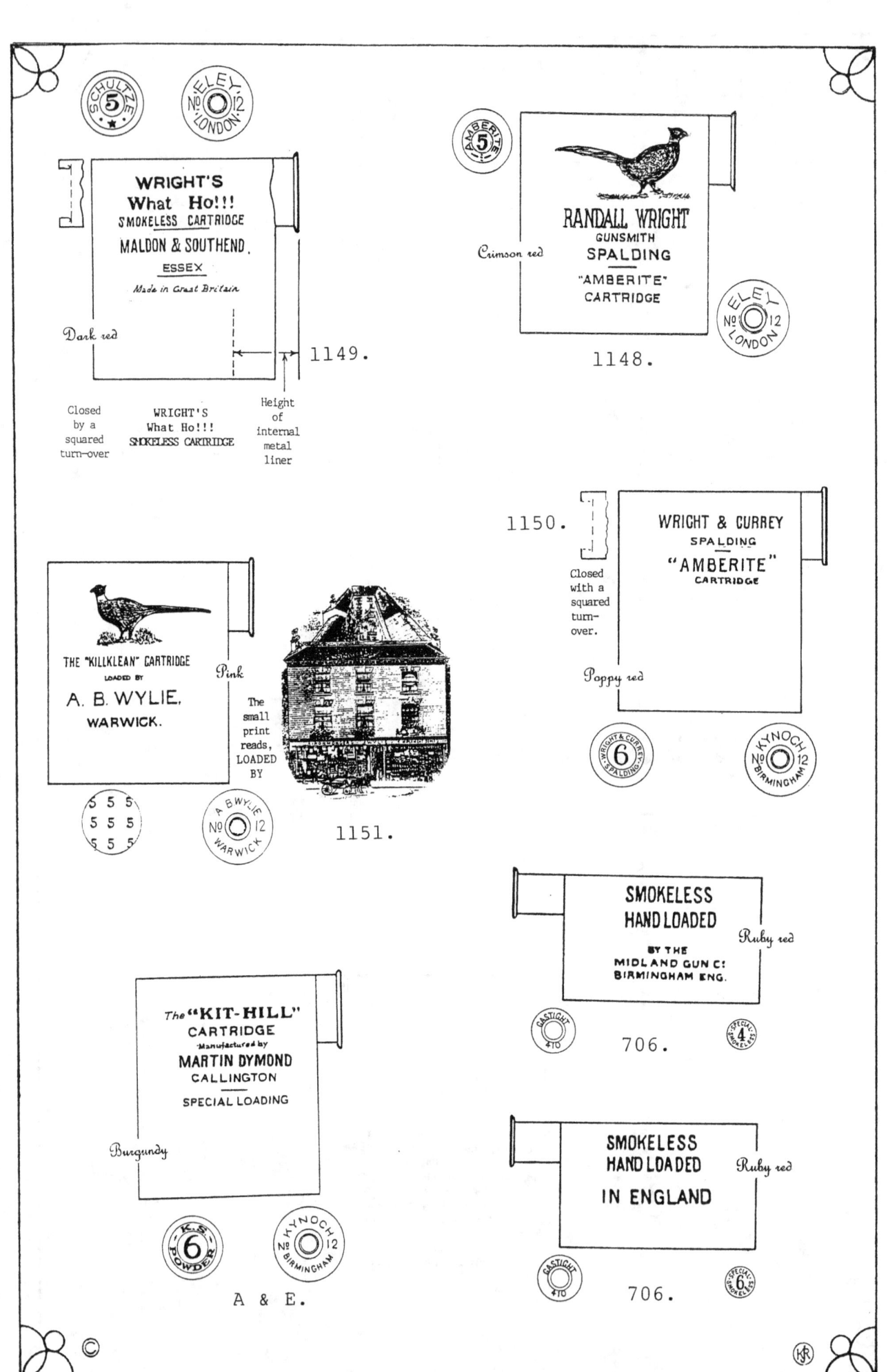

PLATE S8

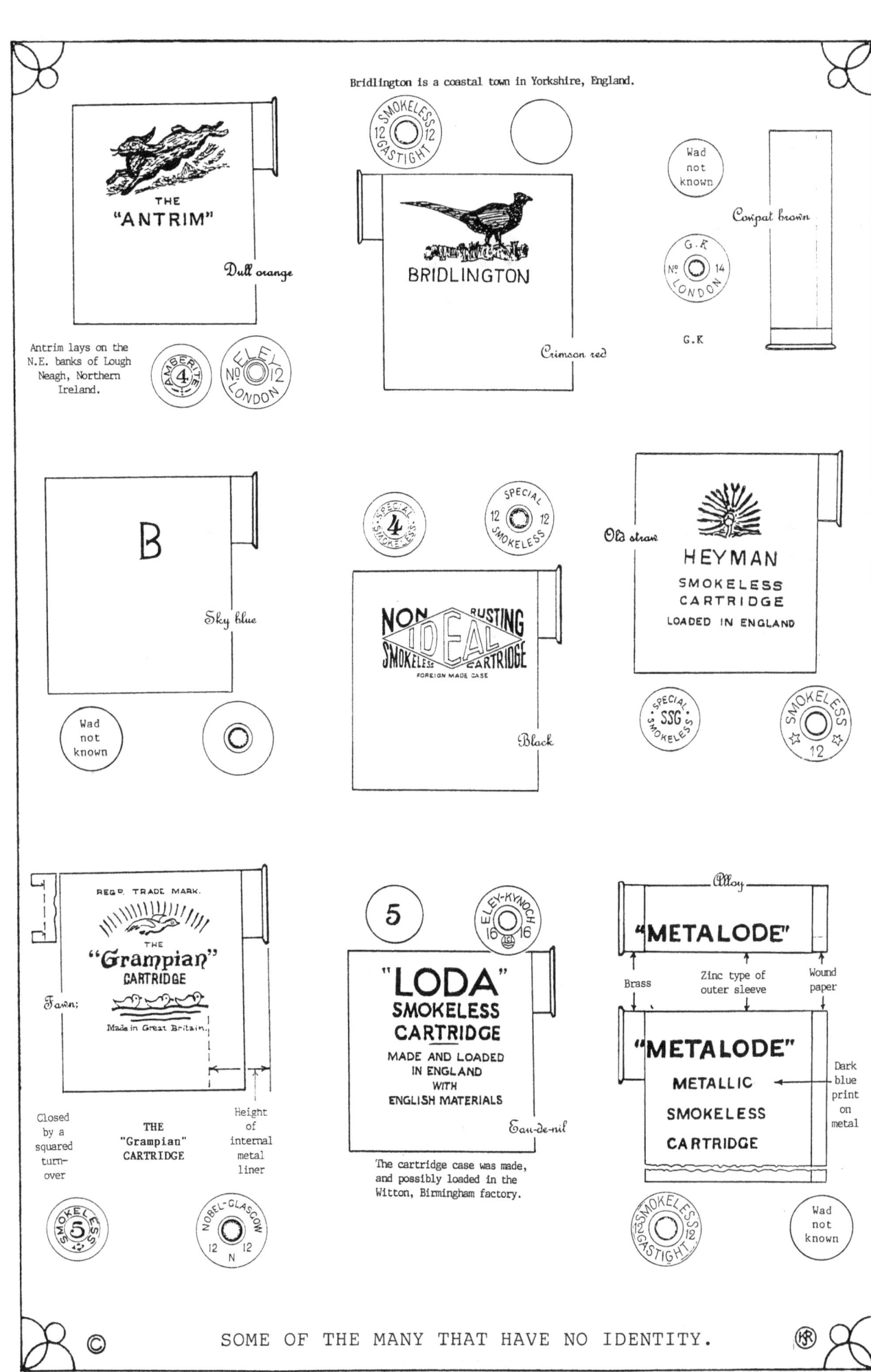

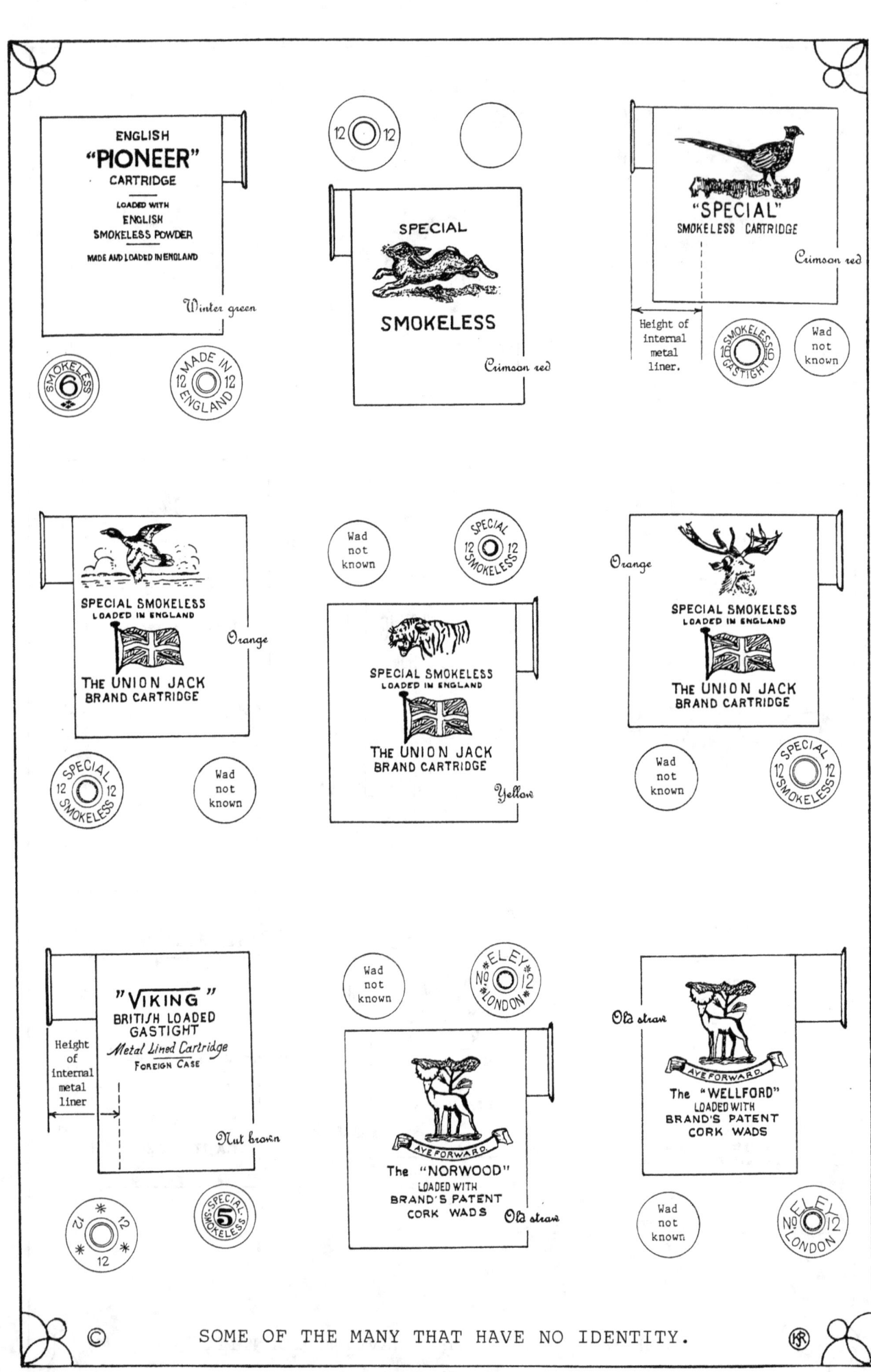

SOME OF THE MANY THAT HAVE NO IDENTITY.

PLATE T1

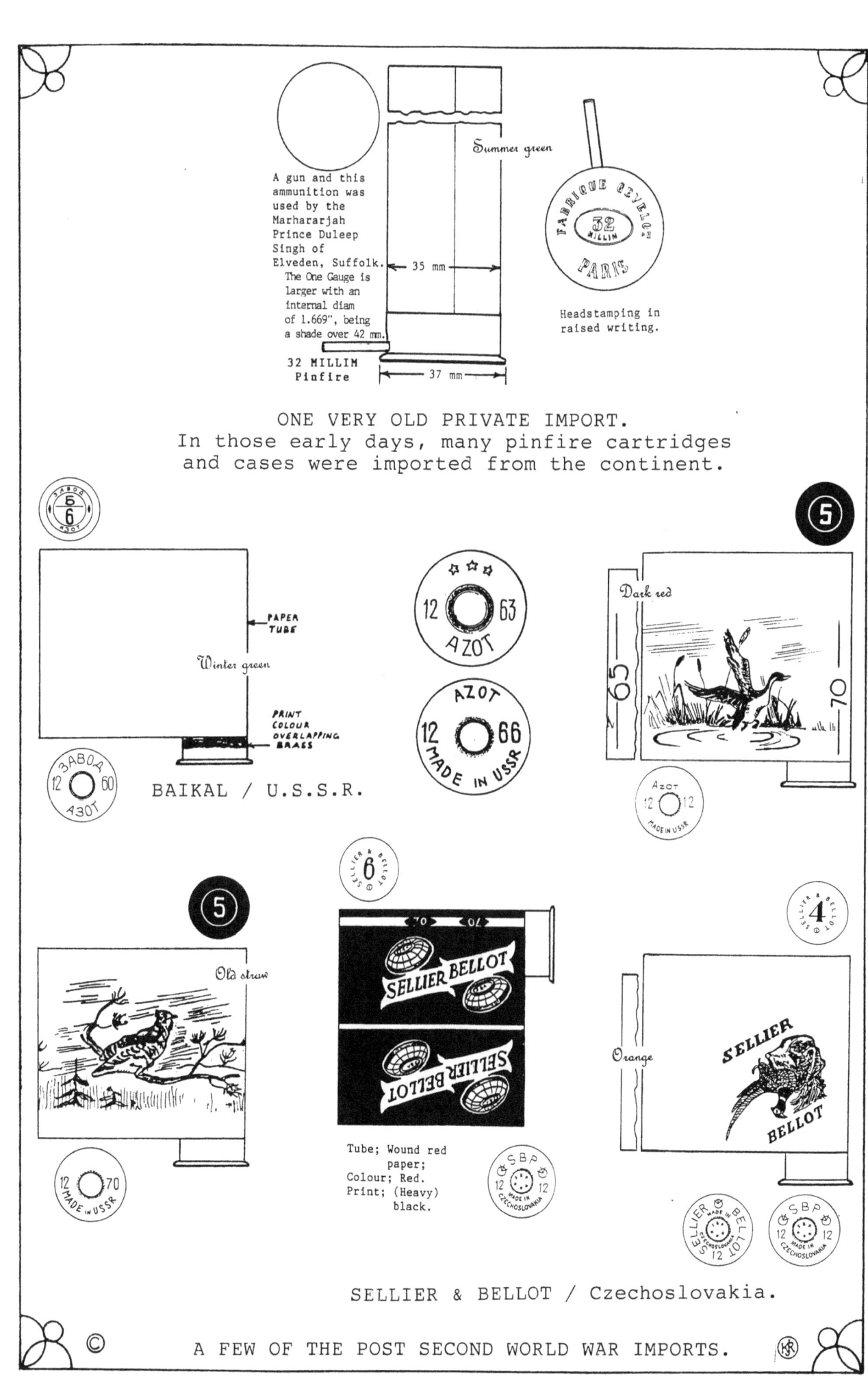

PLATE T2

Index

Index to persons and firms names

DESCRIPTION ON USE OF INDEX. From left to right. The name of a person or a firm. Then in square brackets, the entry number if given in the Cartridge List. Next is the page or pages numbers. Following on from this is the Illustrated Plate letter-numbers when applicable.

EXAMPLE. Army & Navy Stores Ltd: [28]-29,72-A2,A4,A7. The firms name; Cartridge list entry number; Pages 29 and 72; May be found on the illustrated plates to the rear of the book on plates A4 and A7.

Accles Arms, Ammunition & Manufacturing Co: [1]-27,166-A3.
Adams H.R: [2]-27-A2.
Adams J.H. & Sons: [[3]-27-A1.
Adams & Co: [4]-27-A1.
Adgey R.J: [5]-27.
Adgey & Murphy: [6]-27-A1.
Adkin H: [7]-27-A1,A3.
Adkin H. & Sons: [7]-27-A1,A3.
Adsett T. & Son: [8]-27-A1.
Agnew J: [9]-27-A3.
Agnew & Son: [10]-27-A1,A3.
Agricultural Departments Reserve: 80.
Agricultural Executive Committee. (A.E.C.): [11]-27-H7.
Aitken M. & Sons: [12]-27-A1.
Akrill E.H: [13]-28-A3.
Albright J.P: [14]-28.
Aldridge E: [15]-28-A3,A5.
Alexander Bros: [16]-28-A1,A3.
Alexander & Duncan: [17]-28-A3.
Allan A: [18]-28.
Allan A, Ltd: [19]-28-A1,A2,A4.
Alpass & Baker: [20]-28.
Altham & Son: [21]-28-A2,A4.
Anderson J. & Son: [22]-28-A2.
Andrews C.W: [23]-28.
Andrews W: 34.
Anns T.W: [24]-28-A2.
Apps & Son: [25]-28.
Armory Publications: 15.
Arms & Ammunition Manufacturing Co, Ltd: [26]-15,29.
Armstrong & Co: [27]-29-A5,A7.
Armstrongs (Sporting Gun Depot): [27]-29-A5,A7.
Army & Navy Co-operative Soc, Ltd.(A.N.C.S.Ltd): [28]-29,72-A2,A4,A7.
Army & Navy Stores, Ltd: [28]-29,72-A2,A4,A7.
Arnold S.R: [29]-29-A2.
Atkin H: [30]-29,65,71-A5,A7.
Atkin Grant & Lang: [31]-29,65,91.
Atkinson: [32]-29-A5.
Atkinson T: [33]-29-A5,A7.
Atkinson W: [34]-29,30-A8.
Atkinson & Griffin: [35]-30.
Attrill K: [36]-30.
Austin T.C: [37[-30-A6,A8.

I.

Automatic Shrapnell Co: [38]-30-A6.
Averill & Son: [39]-30-A6.
Bacon & Curtis, Ltd: [40]-30-A6.
Bagnall & Kirkwood: [41]-30-A6.
Baildham E. & Son: [42]-30.
Bailey C.S: [43]-30.
Bailey W.R: [44]-30-A6.
Baily's Monthly Magazine: 88.
Baker C.T, Ltd: [45]-31.
Baker F.T: [46]-31-A9.
Baker J.C: [47]-31-A9.
Baker J. & Son: [48]-31-A8,A9.
Baker J.T: [49]-31-A9.
Baker S.W: [50]-31.
Baker W.E: [51]-31-A8,A9.
Baker W.E. & Co: [51]-31-A8,A9.
Baldwin J. & Sons: [52]-31.
Bales F.A: [53]-31-A8,A9.
Bales G.W: [53]-31-A8,A9.
Balls: [54]-31.
Balls Bros: [55]-32-A9.
Balmforth J.J:[56]-32.
Bamford H. & Sons: [57]-32.
Banfield J.G. & Sons: [58]-32-A9.
Bapty & Co, Ltd: [59]-32-A9.
Barford H.W. & Co, Ltd: [60]-32-B1.
Barham H: [61]-32-B1.
Barham C.H: [61-32-B1.
Barkers: [62]-32-B1.
Barker Bros: [63]-32-B1.
Barnard & Levet: [64]-32-B1,B4.
Barnes A: [65]-32-B1.
Barnes G.J: [66]-32-A8,B1.
Barnes G.J. & Son: [66]-32-A8,B1.
Barnes J: [67]-32-A8.
Barnes W: [68]-33-A8.
Barnett T.W: [69]-33.
Barnitt & Co: [70]-33-B1.
Barnwell & Sons, Ltd: [71]-33-B1.
Barratt: [72]-33.
Bartram G.T: [73]-33.
Bassett G.J: [74]-33-B1.
Bate G. (Gunmakers), Ltd: [75]-33-B1.
Bates A: [76]-33-B2,B4.
Bates A.T: [77]-33-B2,B4.
Bates E.R. & Sons: [78]-33.
Bates G: [79]-34-B2.
Bays E. & Co: [80]-34-B2.
Beare H. & S: [81]-34-B2.
Beck: [82]-34.
Beck & Co: [82-34.
Beckwith H: [83-34.
Beesley F: [84]-34-B2,B4.
Belcher A.J: [85-34.
Bellford A.E.L: [86-13,34.
Bellow & Son: [87]-34.
Benigno A: [88]-34-B2.
Bennett G.W: [89]-34.

II.

Bennett G.W. (2): [90]-34-B2.
Bentley J: [91-35-B4.
Berry S.W: [92]-35.
Bevan: [93]-35.
Bevan & Evans: [94]-35.
Bevan & Pritchard: [95]-35.
Bisset G. & G: [96]-35-B4.
Black J: [97]-35-B4.
Blackadder C.G: [98]-35-B4.
Blain J: [99]-35.
Blake Bros: [100]-35.
Blake J: [101]-35-B3,B4.
Blanch J. & Son: [102]-35-49-B3.
Bland T. & Sons: [103]-35-B3,B5.
Blanton R: [104[-36-B3,B5.
Blythe & Wright: [105]-36.
Bole H.W: [106]-36-B3.
Bond E: [107]-36.
Bond G.E & Son: [108]-36,42-B3,B4,B5.
Bontoft Snr: 78.
Boreham J.S: [109]-36,118-B3.
Boss & Co, Ltd: [110]-36-B5,B6,B8.
Boswell C: [111]-36-B6,B8.
Botwell C: [112]-36.
Bowden: [113]-36.
Bowen J: [114]-37.
Bowerbanks: [115]-37-B6.
Boxer Col: 14.
Bozard: [116]-37-B6.
Bozard & Co; [116]-37-B6.
Braddell J. & Son, Ltd: [117]-37-B6,B8.
Brand: [118]-37.
Breakable Wad Co: 29.
Brind Gillingham: [119]-37.
Britt W. & Sons: [120]-37-B9.
Broadhurst R: [121]-37.
Broadway S. & Co: [122]-37.
Brocks Explosives: 123]-37.
Bromley J. & Co: [124]-37.
Brooker: [125]-38-B9.
Brown E.J. & Co: [126]-38-B6.
Brown J: [127]-38-B6,B9.
Brown & Murry: [128]-38.
Buck F: [129]-38-B6.
Buck & Co: [130]-38-B7.
Buckland J: [131]-38-B7.
Buckland J. & Sons: [131]-38-B7.
Buckmaster J: 38.
Buckmaster & Wood: [132]-38-B9.
Budge: [133]-38.
Budgen J. & Co: [134]-38-B7.
Bugler J.U: [135]-38.
Bulcock J: [136]-38.
Bullen Bros: [137]-38.
Bullmore G.G: [138]-38-B7.
Bulpin A.C: [139]-38-B7.
Bunner R.H: [140]-39.
Bunting W: [141]-39-B7,B9.

Burgess F.H, Ltd: [142]-39-B7.
Burgess W: [143]-39.
Burrow J: [144]-39-B9,C1.
Bussems & Parkin, Ltd: [145]-39-C1.
Bussey G.G. & Co: [146-39-B9,C1.
Butcher: [147]-39.
Butler A.R: [148]-39.
Buyers Association: [149]-39.
Calder E: [150]-39.
Calder W: 143.
Calvert J: [151]-39.
Cambridge & Co: [152]-39-S9?.
Cameron W: [153]-40.
Cameron W. & Co: [153]-40.
Campbell & Sons: [154]-40-B9,C1.
Capell R.L: [155]-40-C1.
Carr Bros: [156]-40-C1.
Carr E.P. & Co: [157]-40-C1.
Carswell W.C: [158]-40-B9,C2.
Cartridge Syndicate, Ltd: [159]-40-C2,C3.
Casswell F.G: [160]-40.
Caverhill: [161]-40.
Cawdron H: [162]-40-C2.
Chamberlain A: [163]-41-C2,C3.
Chamberlain E: [164]-8,9,21,41-C2,C3,C4.
Chambers J. & Son: [165]-41-C5.
Chambers R: [166]-41.
Chambers S: [167]-41-B9,C5.
Chaplin B.E: [168]-41,49.
Chappell W: [169]-41.
Charles Mrs S: [170]-41.
Chitty R.S: [171]-41-C5.
Churchill E.J: [172]-42,73-C4,C5,C7.
Clapham: [173]-42-C6.
Clarke C: [174]-42,112-C6.
Clarke F: [175]-42-C6.
Clarke H: [176]-42-C6,C7.
Clarke H. & Sons: [176]-42-C6,C7.
Clarke P.J: [177]-42-C6.
Clarke & Dyke: [178]-42,47,112-C6,C7,C8.
Clatworthy: [179]-42-C6.
Clatworthy Cooke & Co: [179]-42-C6.
Clayton & Son: [180]-42-C6.
Clement: [181]-42.
Clemitson T: [182]-43.
Climie R. & Son: [183]-43-C6.
Clisby F.K: [184]-43.
Clough R.H: [185]-43-C9.
Clough T: [186]-43-C6.
Club Cartridge Co, Ltd: [187]-43-C9.
Clyde B.G: [188]-43.
Cock J.H. & Co: [189]-43-C9.
Cogschultze Ammunition & Powder Co, Ltd: [190]-16,43,125-C9.
Cogswell B: 44.
Cogswell & Harrison, Ltd: [191-14,43,44-C8,C9,D2.
Colby Evans J: [192]-44.
Cole F: [194]-44.

Cole F.J, Ltd: [193]-44-D1.
Cole & Son: [194]-44-B9,D1.
Collins J, Ltd: [195]-44.
Collis J, Ltd; [196]-44-D1.
Coltman: [1153]-152.
Coltman & Co: [197]-44,45-D1,D3.
Coltman & Son: [198]-45.
Conway R: [199]-45-D1.
Conyers A: [200]-45-D2,D4.
Conyers H. & Sons: [201]-45-D4.
Cook C. & Co: [202]-45.
Cook T: [203]-45.
Cooke J.E: [204]-45-D4.
Coombes J: [205]-45.
Coombs W: [206]-45-D4.
Cooney G: [207]-45-D3,D4.
Cooper G. & Sons (Pickering), Ltd: [208]-46.
Cooper T: 129.
Corden S.L: [209]-46-D3,D4.
Cording J.C. & Co: 22.
Cornish J: [210]-46-D4.
Cornwall Cartridge Works: [211]-46-D3,D5.
Cory A.C: [212]-46.
Coster G. & Son: [213]-46.
Coton W: [214]-46-D3,D5.
Cottage Gunshop: [215]-46-H4.
Cottam A: [216]-46.
Cottis & Son: [217]-46.
Coulson: [218]-46-D5.
Coultas B. & J.V: [219]-47.
Coults W: [220]-47.
Country Gentlemens Association: [221]-47-D3,D5.
Cox & Son, Ltd: [222]-47,112-D3,D6.
Cox & Clarke: [223]-47-D6.
Cox & Macpherson: [224]-47,112.
Cozens & Shaw, Ltd: [225]-47-D6.
Craddock T: [226]-47.
Creber A.G: [227]-47.
Creighton G: [228]-47-D5.
Crockart D.B: [229]-48-D5.
Crockart D. & Sons: [230]-48-D6.
Crockart D. & Co: [230]-48-D6.
Crockart J. & Son: [231]-48.
Cross Bros, Ltd: [232]-48-D6.
Cross S.B: [233]-48-D6.
Crudgington C.G: [234]-48.
Curtis's & Harvey, Ltd: [235]-16,48,52,108-D6,E1.
Cutlack H. & J: [236]-48.
Cutts J.H: [237]-48.
Dadley T.A: [238]-48.
Daintith T: [239]-49-D7.
Dall N.S: [240]-49.
Darlow W, Ltd: [241]-49-D7,E1.
Dralow W. & Co: [241]-49-D7,E1.
Date Bros: [242]-49.
Davidson J.A: [243]-49-D7.
Davie F: [244]-49-D7.

```
Davies H.A: [245]-49-D7,E1.
Davies T: [246]-49-D7.
Davis A: [247]-35,49-D8.
Davis H.A: 41.
Davis M.H. & Sons: [248]-49.
Daw G.H: [249]-13,14,49,50-D8.
Dawe A: [250]-50.
Dawson F: [251]-50-D8.
Dawson W: [1154]-152.
Deabill J.G: [252]-50.
Dennis A: [253]-50-D8.
Desborough & Son: [254]-50-D8.
Devon & Somerset Stores: [255]-50-D8.
Dicker P: [256]-50.
Dickins J.T: [257]-50-D8.
Dickson J. & Son, Ltd: [258]-50,99-D9,E2.
Digby S.W: [259]-50.
Dinwoodie & Nicholson: [260]-50-D9.
Diss F.M: [261]-51.
Distin E. & Son: [262]-51-D9.
Dixon & Co: [263]-51-D9.
Dobson & Rosson: [264]-51-D9.
Dodd G: [265]-51-D9.
Donaldson W.G: [266]-51-E1.
Dott Thomson R: [267]-51-E2.
Dougall J.D. & Sons: [268]-51,82,146-E2.
Downing: [269]-51-E3.
Dugdale R.L, Ltd: [270]-51.
Dukes A.J: [271]-51-E3.
Duncalfe A.H: [272]-51-E3.
Duncan S. & Sons: [273]-51-E3.
Duncomb T.S: [274]-52,128.
Dyer & Robson: [275]-52-E2,E3.
Dyke F. & Co, Ltd: [276]-18,52,150-E2,E3.
Dykes A.H: [277]-52.
Dymon M: [278]-52.
Earle G.A: [279]-52-E3.
Eastmond: [280]-52.
Eastmond & Son: [280]-52.
Ebrall: [1155]-152-S4.
E.C. Powder Co, Ltd: [281]-16,52,105-E4.
Edmonds R.E: [282]-53.
Edmonds & Welldon: [283]-53-E4.
Ednie & Kininmonth: [284]-53-E4.
Edwards, Ltd: [285]-53-E4,E5.
Edwards A. & Co, Ltd: [286]-53-E4,E5.
Edwards C.G. & Son: [287]-53-E4.
Edwards & Meluish: [288]-53-E4,E5.
Elderkin & Son: [289]-53-E4.
Eley Bros, Ltd: [290]-13,14,15,16,20,30,50,52,53,54,55,56,57,81,88,
           105,113,125-E5,E6,E7,E8,E9,F1,F2.
Eley C: 55.
Eley W: 15,55.
Ellicott: [291]-57-F4.
Ellicott W: [292]-57-F4.
Elliott H.C: [293]-57-F4.
Ellis J: [294]-57.
Elton Stores, Ltd: [295]-57-F2,F4.
```

Elveden Estate: [296]-57-F4.
Emberton J.M: 22,117.
Entwhistle S: [298]-58-F4.
Erskine: [299]-58,152.
Evans & Son: [300]-58.
Evans B. & Co: [301]-58.
Evans C.A: [302]-58-F4.
Evans D: [303]-58.
Evans T. & Son: [304]-58.
Evans T.J: [305]-58-F4.
Evans W: [306]-58-F2,F5.
Ewen J.W: [307]-58.
Explosives Co. (E.C.): 128.
Explosives Trades, Ltd. (E.T.L.): [308]-16,48,57,58,107,108-F2,F3,F4.
Fabrique Nationale d'Armes de Guerre. (F.N.): 92.
Fairburn: [309]-59.
Farmer R: [310]-59-F3,F5.
Farmiloe G. & Sons, Ltd: [1156]-152.
Farrell G.F. & Sons: [311]-59-F5.
Farrelly B. & Sons: [312]-59-F5.
Fawcett: [314]-59.
Fawcett (2): [314]-59.
Fenwick & Son: [315]-59.
Fernie: [316]-59.
Ferrules: [317]-59.
Fiddian S: [318]-59.
Field C.F: [319]-59.
Finch B. & Sons: [320]-59-F3.
Fischer Bros: [321]-59.
Fisher H.J: [322]-59.
Fitchew A.T: [323]-59-F3,F6.
Fletcher C: [324]-59-F5.
Fletcher Mrs E: [325]-59,60-F3,F5.
Fletcher E. & Son: [325]-59,60-F3,F5.
Fletcher Mrs R: [325]-60-F3,F5.
Fletchers (Sports): [325]-59,60-F3,F5.
Flint: [326]-60.
Flint H. & A: [327]-60-F5.
Foden G: [328]-60-F6.
Follett: [329]-60.
Foort R: [330]-60.
Foort R. & Son: [330]-60.
Ford W: [331]-60-F6.
Forestry Commission: 80.
Forrest & Sons: [332]-60-F3.
Forsyth Rev J: 12.
Foster A.J: [333]-60-F3,F6.
Foster Bros: [334]-60-F6.
Foster Lott & Co: [335]-60.
Fox C: [336]-60,61-F7.
Fox I: [336]-60,61,66-F7.
Foy E.J: [337]-61.
Foys: [338]-61.
Francis C: [339]-61-F3,F7,F8.
Francis C. & Son: [339]-61-F3,F7,F8.
Francis C. & Sons: [339]-61-F3,F7,F8.
Francis & Dean: [340]-61-F6.

Franks J.W: [341]-61.
Fraser D. & Co: [342.
Fraser J: [343]-61-F7.
Fraser N: [344]-61-F7.
Freeney: [345]-61.
French W.H: [346]-61-F7.
French & Son[346]-61-F7.
Frost E: [347]-61-F7.
Frost E. (2): [348]-61-F7.
Fry J: [349]-62-G1.
Fuller S.C: [350-62.
Furlong: [351]-62.
Fussell's, Ltd: [352]-62-G1.
Galbraith W: [353]-62-G1.
Galding J. & J.M: [354]-62.
Gale A: [355]-62.
Gale E: [356]-62-F8,G1.
Gale E. & Sons, Ltd: [356]-62-F8,G1.
Gallyon & Sons, Ltd: [357]-62-F8,G1.
Gamage A.W, Ltd: [358]-62-F8,G1.
Gamble J.G: [359]-62.
Garden W: [360]-62-G2.
Gardiner T.M, Ltd: [361]-63-G2.
Gardner W: [362]-63-G2.
Garnett M: [363]-63-G2.
Garnett M. & Son: [363]-63-G2.
Garnett & Keegan: 63.
Garrett F: [364]-63-F8,G2.
Garrick A: [365]-63.
George F.W: [366]-63-G3.
George W: [367]-63.
George W.J: [368]-19,63-G3.
Germans: [369]-63.
Gevelot & Co (London): [370]-63-G3.
Gibbs E: [1157]-152.
Gibbs G, Ltd: [371]-63-F8,F9,G2.
Gill & Co: [372]-63.
Gill J.H: [373]-64.
Gill J.H. & Sons: [374]-64.
Gillman C. & Sons: [375]-64.
Gilman J. & Sons, Ltd: [376]-64-F9,G3.
Glanville R.W: [377]-64.
Gliddon J. & Sons: [378]-64,111,132-G3.
Globemaster Arms & Ammunition: [379]-64-G3.
Godfrey W. & Sons: [380]-64-G3.
Gold G.E: [381]-64.
Golden C: [382]-64.
Golden W: [383]-64-G3.
Golding C.E: [384]-64-F9.
Gow J.R. & Sons: [385]-65-G3.
Grace G. & Son: [386]-65.
Graham G.P: [387]-65-G4.
Graham J. & Co, Ltd: [388]-65-F9,G4.
Graham J.J: [389]-65.
Graham J. & J: [390]-65.
Grandisons: [391]-65.
Grant S: [392]-65,,91-G4.
Grant S. & Sons: [392]-65-G4.

Grant & Lang: [393]-29,65,90,91,143-F9,G4.
Gray D. & Co: [394]-65-G4.
Gray R: [395]-65-G4.
Green E.C: [396]-66-F9,G5.
Green E. & Sons: [396]-66-F9,G5.
Greener W.W: [397]-66-F9,G5,G7,G8.
Greener W.W, Ltd: [397]-66-F9,G5,G7,G8.
Greenfield: [398]-66-G5.
Greenfield H.S. & Son: [399]-61,66-G5,G8.
Greenwood & Batley: [400]-35,66,128-G6.
Gregson: [401]-66.
Greighton G: [402]-66.
Grenfell & Accles: [403]-27,66-G6.
Griffiths W: [404]-67.
Griffiths W. (2): [405]-67.
Grimes S.J: [406]-67-G6.
Gun Shop: [407]-67.
Gye & Moncrieff: [408]-67.
Haddon J.B: [409]-67-G6.
Hagens: [410]-67.
Hall C: [67-G8.
Hall F: [412]-67-G6,G8.
Hall H: [413]-67.
Hall J: [414]-67-G6.
Hall J. & Son: [415]-16,48,67-G6,G8.
Hall T: [416]-67.
Halliday B. & Co, Ltd: [417]-68-G6,G8.
Ham & Huddy: [418]-68.
Hameyer & Co: [419]-68.
Hammond Bros: [420]-41,68-G8,G9,H2.
Hancock W.T: [421]-68-G9.
Hand Bros: [422]-68-G9.
Handscombe F.G: [423]-68.
Hanson J.R: [424]-68-G9.
Hanson L: [425]-68-G9.
Harding Bros, Ltd: [426]-68.
Harding J: [427]-68-G9.
Harding T: [428]-69.
Hardy Bros, Ltd: [429]-69-G9,H2.
Haren: [430]-69-G9.
Harkom J. & Son: [431]-69-H2.
Harkom J. & Sons, Ltd: [431]-69,102-H2.
Harper J: [432]-69.
Harper P.J: [433]-69-G9.
Harpur Bros: [434]-69-H1.
Harris G. & A: [435]-69-H1.
Harris H: [436]-69.
Harris W.H. & Son: [437]-69.
Harrison Bros: [438]-69.
Harrison E: 44.
Harrison T. & W: [439]-69.
Harrison & Hussey, Ltd: [440]-69-H1.
Harrods, Ltd: [441]-11,70-H1,H2.
Hart E.F: [442]-70-H1.
Hart F.W: [443]-70-H1.
Hartforth: [444]-70.
Hartwell J.T: [445]-70.

Harvey A.B: [446]-70.
Harvey Guns: [447]-70.
Harwood J.T: [448]-70.
Haste: [449]-70.
Hawke & Sons, Ltd: [450]-70-H4.
Hawkes & Sons, Ltd: [451]-70-H4.
Haygarth C: [452]-70-H4.
Haynes W: [453]-71-H4.
Hayward S.E. & Co, Ltd: [454]-71-H4.
Hazel R: [455]-71-H4.
Heal W.E: [456]-71-H4.
Heal W.E, Ltd: [456]-71-H4.
Heathman T, Ltd: [457]-71-H4.
Hedlund D.J: 15.
Hellis C: [458]-18,71,74,122-H2,H3,H5.
Hellis C. & Sons, Ltd: [458]-18,71,72,74,122-H2,H3,H5.
Helson J: [460]-72-H4.
Hely: [461]-72.
Helyar: [462]-72.
Helyer: [463]-72.
Heming W: [464]-72-H4.
Henderson: [465]-72-H8.
Henrite Explosives: [466]-72-H4,H8.
Henry A: [467]-72-H4.
Henry A. & Co: [467]-50,72,99-H4.
Henry L: 95.
Hensman W: [468]-72.
Henton W.G: [469]-73.
Hepplestone T: [470]-73-H8.
Hercules Arms Co, Ltd: [471]-42,73-H8.
Herring W: [472]-73-H8.
Hesford C.M. & Co, Ltd: [473]-73-H8.
Hewen Mrs E: [474]-73.
Hewett & Son: [475]-73.
Heywood & Hodge: [476]-73-H8.
Hick Ferns & Co: [477]-73.
Hickley: [478]-73.
Hicks F: [479]-73.
Higgins H: [480]-73-H8.
Higham E. & G: [481]-73-H9.
Higham G.G: [482]-74-H9.
Highclere Castle Estate: [483]-71,74-H9.
Hill A: [484]-74,148-H6,H9.
Hillsdon R: [485]-74-H9.
Hinde W.R: [486]-74.
Hinton G. & Sons, Ltd: [487]-74-H6,H9.
H.M. Government of Great Britain: [488]-27,66,74,80,135-H6,H7,I1,
                I5.
Hobson J: [489]-75-I1.
Hockey: [491]-75-I1.
Hocknell A.S: [491]-75-I1.
Hodgson A.A: [492]-75-I1.
Hodgson H: [493]-75,125-I1.
Hodgson J: [494]-75.
Hodgson J.P: [495]-75-I1.
Hodgson R.C: [496]-75-I5.
Hodgson R.T: [497]-75-I1,I5.
Hodgson W: [498]-75-I1,I5,I6.

Holdron J: [499]-75.
Holland C.R: [500]-75,76-I1.
Holland D: 76.
Holland & Holland, Ltd: [501]-76-I1,I6.
Hollis I: [502]-76-I3.
Holme & Ash: [503]-76.
Holtom's: [504]-76-I3.
Home's: [505]-76-I3.
Hooke J.A: 76.
Hooke T.J: [506]-76-I3.
Hooton & Jones: [507]-76-I3,I6.
Hooton W.M: [508]-77.
Hopkins J.J, Ltd: [509]-77-I3.
Hopping E.A: [510]-77-I3.
Horne: [1158]-152.
Horrell & Son: [511]-77-I3.
Horsley T: [512]-77-I3.
Horsley T. & Sons, Ltd: [512]-77-I3.
Horton W: [513]-77-I3.
Howard Bros: [514]-77-I4.
Howe W. & Sons, Ltd: [515]-77-I4.
Howes & Son: [516]-77-I4.
Hudson C.S: [517]-77.
Huish: [518]-78.
Hull Cartridge Co, Ltd: [519]-70,78,91,121,138-I4.
Hull T.L. & Co: [520]-79-I4.
Hume G: [521]-79.
Hunt G: [1159]-152.
Hunter & Maddil: [522]-79.
Hunter & Son: [523]-79-I4.
Hunter & Vaughan: [524]-79.
Hurlstone W: [525]-79-I4.
Hussey H.J: [526]-79-I4,I6.
Hussey H.J, Ltd: [526]-79-I4,I6.
Hutchings J: [527]-79.
Hutchinson: [528]-79.
Icke W.H: [530]-79.
Imperial Chemical Industries (I.C.I) Metals Division (Eley-Kynoch),
   Ltd: [532]-17,24,80,81,82,107,154-I6,I7,I8,I9,J1,J2,J3,J4.
Imperial Metal Industries (I.M.I.) (Kynoch), Ltd. Eley Ammunition
   Division: [533]-17,81-J3,J4.
Ingram C: [534]-82-J4.
Inman Morrow & Co: [535]-82-J4.
Irish Metal Industries, Ltd: [536]-82,104-J5.
Irons D. & Sons: [537]-82.
Irvin G: [538]-82.
Isley: [531]-79-J5.
Jackson & Sons: [539]-82.
Jackson A: [540]-82-J3,J5.
Jackson H.G: [541]-82.
Jackson S: [542]-82-J5.
Jackson T. & Son: [543]-82-J5.
Jackson W: [544]-83-J5.
Jackson W. & Son: [544]-83-J5.
James & Co: [545]-17,83-J6.
James M. & Sons: [546]-83-J6.
James & Tatton: [547]-83-J6.
Jane W.H: [548]-83.

Jeffery A.R. & H.V, Ltd: [549]-83-J3,J6.
Jeffery C: [550]-83-J3,J6.
Jeffery C. & Sons: [550]-83-J3,J6.
Jeffery S.R: [551]-83-J3,J6.
Jeffery S.R. & Son, Ltd: [551]-83-J3,J6.
Jeffery W. & Son: [552]-83-J7,K1.
Jeffery W.J. & Co: [553]-84-J7,K1.
Jeffery W.J. & Co, Ltd: [553]-84-J7,K1.
Jennvey & Co: [554]-84-J6.
Jenvey & Tite: [554]-84-J6.
Jewson A.J: [555]-84-J7,K1.
Jobson G: [556]-84-J8.
Johnson R.B: [557]-84-J8.
Johnson T. & Son: [558]-84-J8,K2.
Johnson & Reid: [559]-84-J8.
Johnson & Wright: [560]-84-J8,K2.
Jones & Son: [561]-85-J8.
Jones F: [562]-85.
Jones H: [563]-85-J8.
Jones R: [564]-85-J8,K5.
Jones T: [565]-85.
Jones W.P: [566]-85-J8.
Jowett W: [567]-85.
Joyce F. & Co, Ltd: [569]-15,30,81,85,86,106,108-J9,K2,K5.
Julian H. & Sons, Ltd: [570]-21,86-J8.
Kavanagh W. & Son: [571]-86-K3,K5.
Keegan L: [572]-86-K3.
Kelly & Son: [573]-86.
Kempton H: [574]-86-K3.
Kent A: [575]-11,86-K3,K5.
Kent & Son: [575]-11,86-K3,K5.
Kent J: 86.
Kenyon & Trott: [576]-87-K3.
KeppelHon G: [577]-87-K9.
Kerr C: [578]-87-K3.
Kerridge H.E: [579]-87-K3.
Kingdon T.M. & Co, Ltd: [580]-22,87-K9.
King's Norton Metal Co: [581]-87.
Kirk J: [582]-87-K9.
Kirker T: [583]-87.
Kirman H: [584]-87.
Kither: [585]-87-K9.
Knight J.N: [586]-87-K9.
Knight P: [587]-87,88-K5,K9.
Kynaston Bros: [588]-88.
Kynoch G: [589]-7,15,16,18,57,67,88,89,108-K4,K5,K6,K7,N9.
Kynoch G. & Co: [589]-7,15,16,18,57,67,88,89,108-K4,K5,K6,K7,N9.
Kynoch, Ltd: [589]-7,15,16,18,57,67,88,89,108-K4,K5,K6,K7,N9.
Lace: [590]-89-K9.
Lacey A: [591]-89.
Lacey & Son: [591]-89.
Lacey J. & H: [592]-89-K9.
Laker E: [593]-89-K8,K9.
Laker H. & Son: [594]-89.
Lambert T, Ltd: [595]-89-L1.
Lanaway R.S: [596]-89.
Lancaster C: [597]-13.
Lancaster C. & Co, Ltd: [597]-13,65,90-K7,K8,L1.

Lane Bros: [598]-90-L1.
Lane C.E: [599]-90-K8,L1.
Lane C.L: [600]-90-K8,L1.
Lane F. & Co: [601]-90,91-L1.
Lanes: [602]-91.
Lang J.H: [603]-65,91-L1.
Lang J. & Son: [603]-65,91-L1.
Lang J. & Son, Ltd: [603]-65,91-L1.
Lang & Hussey, Ltd: [526]-79-I4,I6.
Langdon J: [604]-91-L1.
Langley J.J: [605]-91,93-L2.
Langley & Lewis: [606]-91-L2.
Lanning W: 93.
Last R.G.F: [607]-91.
Law T: [608]-91-L2.
Law T. Jnr: [608]-91-L2.
Lawn & Alder: [609]-91-L2.
Lawrence: [610]-92.
Laycock J.F: [611]-92-L2.
Leach R: [612]-92-L2.
Leatham: [613]-92-L2.
Leaver: [614]-92.
Lee: [615]-92.
Leech W: [616]-92-L3.
Leech W. & Sons: [616]-92-L3.
Leeson W.R: [617]-92.
Lefaucheux Mr: 12.
Leggett H.E: [618]-92-L3.
Leigh & Jackson: [619]-92.
Leonard C: [620]-92-L3.
Lepco Cartridges: 92.
LePersonne L. & Co: [621]-92.
Lever Bros: [622]-92.
Lewis: [623]-93-L3.
Lewis A: [624]-91,93-L3.
Lewis E.G: [625]-22,93-L3.
Lewis F. & Sons: [626]-93.
Lewis G.E. & Sons: [627]-93.
Lewis J.D: [628]-93.
Lewis R: [629]-93.
Lewis & Moss: 93.
Lichfield Agricultural Co: [630]-93.
Liddell & Sons: [631]-93-L4.
Lightwood: [632]-93.
Lightwood & Son: [633]-93.
Lightwood F.W: [634]-94.
Limmex S.J. & Co: [635]-94-L4.
Lincoln Jefferies: [636]-94-K8.
Lincoln Jefferies & Co: [636]-94-K8.
Lindsay: [1160]-153.
Lines G: [637]-94.
Linnington J.H: [638]-94-L4.
Linscott: [639]-94.
Linsley Bros: [640]-94-L4,M5.
Lisle R: [641]-94-L5.
Little H.C. & Son: [642]-94-L5.
Littleford A.T: [643]-95-L4.
Liversidge C.F: [644]-95-K8.

Lloyd & Sons: [645]-95-L5.
Lock C.H: [646]-95-L5.
London Sporting Park, Ltd: [647]-95-K8.
Long H. & Sons: [648]-95.
Look C.T: [649]-95.
Loveridge & Co: [650]-95-L5,M5.
Luckes S: [651]-95.
Luck's Explosives, Ltd: [652]-64,72,95-L6,M5.
Lynscott: [653]-96. (Also listed as Linscott [639[. An error?

Mac-Mc. These are both treated here as Mac. The next letter in the name determines the entry position.

McBean R: [654]-96.
McCall W. & Co: [655]-96-L6,M5.
McColl & Fraser: [656]-96-L6.
McCririck & Sons: [657]-96.
McCririck J. & Sons: [658]-96-L6.
MacDougall & Co: [659]-96.
McDougall D: [660]-96.
McGalding J. & J: [661]-96-L6.
MacGregor C: [662]-96.
McIlwraith & Co: [663]-96.
Macintosh A. & Sons, Ltd: [664]-96.
MacKay A. & Son: [665]-96.
MacKenzie & Duncan: [666]-97-L6.
MacLeod J.M: 96.
McLoughlin C: [667]-97.
MacNaughton & Sons: [668]-97-L6.
McMorran W: [669]-97-L6.
MacPherson J: [670]-97-L7.
MacPherson J. & Sons: [670]-97-L7.
MacPherson R: [671]-97.
McSorley J: [672]-97-L7.
McVery Bros: [673]-97.
Malcomson J: [674]-97-L7.
Malcomson J. & Co: [674]-97-L7.
Maleham C.H: [675]-97,136-L7.
Maleham C.H. & Co: [675]-97,136-L7.
Mallett & Son: [676]-97,98.
Mallinsons: [677]-98-L8.
Malloch P.D: [678]-98-L8,M5.
Manby A: [679]-98-L8.
Manby F. & Brother: [680]-98-L8.
Manning: [681]-98.
Manning T.G: [682]-98.
Manton & Co: [683]-98-L8,M5.
Marfell G: [684]-98.
Mark J.S: [685]-98.
Marshall, Sons & Co: [686]-98-L8.
Marshall & Pearson: [687]-98-L8.
Martin A.H: [688]-98-L9.
Martin A, Ltd: [689]-50,72,99-L9.
Mason J.F: [690]-99-L9.
Mather J. & Co: [691]-99-L9.
Matterson, Huxley & Watson: [692]-99.
Matthews Bros: [693]-99.
Matthews J: [694]-99.

Mawby W. & Son: [695]-99-L9.
Mawer & Saunders: [696]-100-L9.
Mayes Bros: [697]-100.
Mellard W: [698]-100-M1.
Melville A. & Sons: [699]-100.
Meredith H.L: [700]-100.
Metcalf G.F: [701]-100-M1.
Metcalfe R: [702]-100-M1.
Metcalfe W: [703]-100-M1.
Michie G.M. & Co: [704]-100-M1.
Midgley G.A: [705]-100.
Midland Gun Co: [706]-18,100,101-M2,M5,M6,S8.
Milburn W: [707]-101-M1,M6.
Milburn & Son: [707]-101-M1,M6.
Miles Aircraft, Ltd: 113.
Millett R: [708]-101.
Mills Bros: [709]-101-M1.
Minto: [710]-101.
Modern Arms Co, Ltd: [711]-101-M1.
Mogg B.D. & Son: [712]-101-M1.
Monarch Gun Works: [713]-101-M3.
Monk H: [714]-101-M3.
Monk W,H: [714]-101-M3.
Moody C: [715]-101-M3.
Moody W.F: [716]-102-M3.
Moor T.H: [717]-102-M3.
Moore W: [718]-102-M3.
Moore & Grey: [718]-102.
Moreland S: [719]-102.
Morgan: [720]-102.
Morreys: [721]-102-M3.
Morris H.M: [722]-102-M3.
Morris P. & Son: [723]-102-M6,M7.
Morrow & Co (W.R. Wedgwood): [724]-102-M7.
Mortimer: [725]-50,102-M6,M7.
Mortimer & Son: [725]-50,102-M6,M7.
Mortimer H: [726]-102.
Morton G.P. & Son: [727]-103.
Motterm C: [728]-103.
Moulton & Bennett: [729]-103-M7.
Muller & Co: [730]-103.
Mullerite Cartridge Works: [731]-18,34,39,43,69,70,92,103,115,117,
    132-M4,M6,S9.
Mumford R.C: [732]-104.
Murch W.H: [733]-104.
Murray D. & Son: [734]-104.
Murray T.W. & Co, Ltd: [735]-104-M7.
National Arms & Ammunition Co (N.A. & A.Co): [736]-104.
Naughton T. & Sons, Ltd: [737]-104.
Naylor C, Ltd: [738]-104-M7.
Needham J.V: [739]-104-M7.
Nelson F: [740]-104.
Nelson F. & Sons, Ltd: [740]-104.
Nestor A: [741]-104-M7.
New Explosives Co, Ltd: [742]-16,105,128-M6,M8,M9.
Newland & Stidolph: [743]-105-M7.
Newman W. & Son: [744]-105-N2.
Newnham G: [745]-105-N2.

Newnham & Co: [745]-105-N2.
New Normal Ammunition Co, Ltd: [746]-105-M9,N2,O1.
Newton T: [747]-105-M9,N2.
Nicholas J.H: [748]-105.
Nichols: [749]-105.
Nicoll J.O. & R.W: [750]-105,106.
Nitingale A.P. & Son, Ltd: [751]-106-N2.
Nitrokol Powder Co: [752]-106-M9,N2.
Nixon & Naughton: [753]-106.
Nobbs S.A: [754]-106-N2.
Nobel Explosives Co, Ltd: [755]-15,16,85,86,106,107,108-M9,N1,N2, N3,N4,N9.
Nobel Industries, Ltd: [756]-16,58,81,107,108,125-N4,N5,N6,N7,N8, N9.
Normal Improved Ammunition Co: [757]-108-O1.
Normal Powder Co: [758]-108,109-N9,O1.
Normal Powder & Ammunition Co, Ltd: [758]-108,109-N9,O1.
Normal Powder Syndicate, Ltd: [759]-109.
Norman B: [760]-109-O1.
Norman & Sons: [760]-109-O1.
Norrington: [761]-109.
Norris: 131.
North J.H.B. & Son: [762]-109.
Norton C.W: [763]-109-O1.
Nott J.E. & Co: [764]-109-O1.
Odell J (1): [765]-109-O1.
Odell J (2): [766]-109.
Odell Bros: [766]-109.
Olbys, Ltd: [767]-110-O2.
O'Lee H: [768]-110.
Oliver & Co: [769]-110.
O'Riordan & Forrest: [770]-110-O1.
Osborn J.P: [771]-110-O1.
Osborne C. & Co, Ltd: [772]-110-O2.
Otton W: [773]-110.
Overseas Buying Agency: [774]-110.
Page Wood A: [775]-110-O2.
Page Wood & Co: [776]-64,110,111-O2.
Page Wood T: [777]-111-N9,O2,O3,Q7.
Pain J. & Sons: [778]-111.
Palmer Son & Co: [779]-111-O3.
Palmer W.G: [780]-111-O3.
Palmer W. & H.E: [781]-111-O3.
Palmer W.J. (Guns): [566]-111-J8.
Palmer & Tarr: [782]-111.
Pape W.R: [783]-111-O3,O4,Q7.
Paragon Gun Specialists: [784]-111.
Parker Hale, Ltd: 101.
Parkinson J: [785]-112.
Parkinson T: [786]-112-O4.
Parsons C: [787]-112-O4.
Parsons Sherwin & Co, Ltd: [787]-112-O4.
Parsons F: [788]-112.
Patstone J. & Son: [789]-47,112,144-O4,Q7.
Patstone & Cox: [790]-47,112-O4,Q7.
Patterson J.C: [791]-113.
Paxton S. & Co: [792]-113-O5.

Peace J, Ltd: [793]-113-05.
Pearson & Co: [794]-113-05.
Peck G. & J, Ltd: [795]-113.
Pellier-Johnson Captain E: [796]-113-05.
Penny & Son: [797]-113-05.
Perrins & Son: [798]-113.
Perrott S: [799]-113-05.
Personne L.E: 31.
Phillips Bros: [800]-113-05.
Phillips & Powis: [801]-113-05.
Pinder C: [802]-22,114-05.
Pinder C. & Co: [802]-114-05.
Pinder J.E:[803]-114-05.
Pitt H.B: [804]-114-06.
Playfair C. & Co: [805]-114-05.
Plumbers S, Ltd: [806]-114-06.
Pneumatic Cartridge Co, Ltd (1): [807]-114-06.
Pneumatic Cartridge Co, Ltd (2); [808]-114-06,Q7.
Pneumatic Cartridge Co, Ltd (3): [809]-114,115-06.
Pollard H.E. & Co: [810]-115-07.
Pollard W.H: [811]-115-07.
Pond & Son: [812]-115-07.
Ponting J.E: [813]-115.
Poole Bros: [814]-115.
Poole W: [815]-115.
Porter S.E. & Co: [816]-115-07.
Postans J.M: [817]-115-07.
Potter J.Y: [818]-115.
Potter R.C: [819]-115-07.
Potter & Co: [819]-115-07.
Potter R. & E: [820]-116-07.
Pottet Mr: 13.
Powell: [821]-116.
Powell T. & Co, Ltd: [822]-116-07.
Powell W. & Son (Gunmakers), Ltd: [823]-116-08,09.
Powell W.J: [824]-116-08.
Pratt A: [825]-116-08.
Prentice T. & Co: [826]-116-08.
Preston & District Farmers Trading Soc, Ltd: [827]-116-09.
Prestwich & Sons: [828]-116-09.
Price W.H: [829]-116.
Progressive Cartridge Co: [830]-116-08.
Prout W: [831]-116.
Pugh C.F: [832]-116-09.
Pullan H: [833]-117-08.
Pulvermann M. & Co, Ltd: [834]-103,117.
Punter A.F: [835]-20,22,117-09.
Punter A.F. (Proprietor, Emberton J.M.): [835]-20,22,117-09.
Purcell C: [836]-117-09.
Purdey J: [837]-117-P1,Q7.
Purdey J. & Son, Ltd: [837]-117-P1,Q7.
Purdey J. & Sons, Ltd: [837]-117-P1,Q7.
Purdey R.S: [838]-117-09.
Pursall & Phillips: 15.
Purvis & co: [839]-117-P2.
Radcliffe K.D: [840]-36,117,118-P2.
Raine R: [841]-118-P2.
Raine Bros: [841]-118-P2.

Ramsbottom R: [842]-118-P2.
Randall Wright: [843]-118.
Randell F, Ltd: [844]-118-P2.
Ray M: [845]-118-P2.
Redmayne & Todd: [846]-118.
Reilly E.M. & Co: [847]-118-P2.
Remington Arms, Union Metalic Cartridge Co, Ltd: [848]-70,78,118--P3.
Remington U.M.C. (England): [848]-70,78 118,119-P3.
Reynolds E.G.E: [849]-119-P3.
Reynolds J: [850]-119-Q7.
Rheinische Westfalische Springstoff (R.W.S.): 124.
Rhodes: [851]-119.
Rhodes & Paget: [852]-119.
Richards C.C: [853]-119-P3.
Richards F.J: [854]-119.
Richards W: [855]-119-P4.
Richards W. (Liverpool), Ltd: [855]-119-P4.
Richardson G.B: [856]-119.
Richardson G.M: [857]-119-P4.
Richardson W.G, Ltd: [858]-119-P4.
Rickarby & Partner (A.G. Rickarby: [859]-120.
Rigby J: [860]-120-P5.
Rigby J. & Co (Gunmakers), Ltd: [860]-120-P5.
Riggs C. & Co, Ltd: [861]-120-P5.
Ringwood A.E: [862]-120-P5.
R.L. Ammunition Co: [863]-120.
Roberson H.E: [864]-120.
Roberts A.J: [865]-120-P5.
Roberts E: [866]-120.
Roberts H.P: [867]-120-P5.
Roberts H.W. & Co: [868]-120,136-P5.
Roberts T.H. & Son: [869]-120.
Robertson: [870]-121.
Robertson A. & Son: [871]-121-P6.
Robinson Bros: [872]-121.
Robinson H: [873]-121.
Robinson H. & Co: [874]-121-P6.
Robinson R: [875]-78,121,145-P6.
Robinson R. (Gunmakers), Ltd: [875]-78,121,145-P6.
Rodda R.B. & Co: [876]-121-P6.
Roper R. Son & Co: [877]-121.
Roskelley B.L: [878]-121.
Rosson C: [879]-51,72,122-P6,P7,Q8.
Rosson & Son: [879]-122-P6,P7,Q8.
Rosson C.S. & Co, Ltd: [880-122-P7.
Rottweil Powder Factories: 86-K3.
Rous R: [881]-122.
Rowe & Co: [882]-122-P7.
Rowe W.W: [883]-122.
Rowell R. & Son: [884]-122-P7.
Rowland R.H: [885-122.
Rowlatt J: [886]-122-P8.
Roys: [887]-122-P8.
Rudd A.J: [888]-123-P8.
Russell A.J: [889]-123-P8.
Russell A.J. & Sons: [889-P8.
Rutherford A, Ltd: [890]-123.

Rutherford W.M.E.E: [891]-123.
Rutt & Co: [892]-123.
Rutt A.H: [893]-123.
Ryder R.D: [894]-123.
Sale H.F. & Son: [895]-123-Q1.
Sample W: [896]-123-Q1.
Sandbrook & Dawe: [897]-123.
Sanders: [898]-123.
Sanders A: [899]-123,124-Q1.
Sanders J.H: [900]-124.
Sandleford Priory Estate: [901]-124.
Saul G.E: [902]-124.
Saunders E.F: [903]-124.
Sayer: [904]-124-Q8.
Schultze Captain E: 124.
Schultze Co: [905]-16,43,81,108,124,125,128-P8,P9.
Schultze Gunpowder Co, Ltd: [905]-16,43,81,108,124,125,128-P8,P9.
Scotcher J.A: [906]-125-P9.
Scott & Sargeant: [907]-126.
Sercombe: [908]-126.
Sharp F.A. & Son: [909]-126.
Sharpe J.S: [910]-126-P9.
Sharpland Bros: [911]-126.
Shaw & Co: [912]-126-P9.
Shepherd E.L: [913]-126-P9.
Shuffery F.B: [914]-126-P9.
Shufferys, Ltd: [914]-126-P9.
Silver S.W. & Co: [915]-126.
Simpson: [916]-126.
S. & J. Pipework, Ltd: [917]-126.
Skeltons, Ltd: [918]-126-P9.
Skempton: [919]-126.
Skinner & Co: [920]-126-P9.
Slater: [921]-127.
Slingsby: [922]-127.
Slingsby Bros: [923]-127-P9.
Slingsby Guns: [923]-127-P9.
Smail J. & Sons: [924]-127.
Small P: [925]-127-P9.
Smallwood S: [926]-127-Q1.
Smart R.B: [927]-127.
Smith A.F: [928]-127-Q1.
Smith B: [929]-127.
Smith C.H. & Sons: [930]-127-Q2.
Smith C: [931]-127-Q2.
Smith C. & Sons: [931]-127-Q2.
Smith E.H: [932]-128.
Smith E.H. & Sons: [933]-128.
Smith S: [934]-128-Q2.
Smith Duncomb: [935]-128.
Smith Midgley: [936]-128-Q2.
Smithson G.J: [937]-128.
Smokeless Powder Co, Ltd: [938]-128.
Smokeless Powder & Ammunition Co (S.P. & A. Co): [939]-128-Q2.
Smyth J.F, Ltd: [940]-128-Q3.
Sneezum H. & R: [941]-129-Q2.
Snelling: [942]-129.

Southern Counties Agricultural Trading Soc (S.C.A.T.S.): [943]-129-Q3.
Southern Counties Agricultural Trading Soc (S.C.A.T.S.): [944]-129-Q3.
Southern Remedial Services: [945]-129-Q3.
Sowman J.W. & E, Ltd: [946]-129-Q3.
Spencer A.A: 129.
Spencer A.L: [947]-129-Q3.
Spencer F.P: [948]-129-Q3.
Spiller G: [949]-129.
Sporting Gun & Cartridge Co: [950]-130.
Sporting Park: [951]-130-Q3.
Sportridge (G.B.), Ltd: [952]-130-Q3.
Stacey: [953]-130.
Stanbury P: [954]-130-Q4.
Stanbury & Stevens: [955]-130-Q4.
Stanger: [956]-130.
Starsmore: [1161]-153.
Stebbings & Son: [957]-130.
Stensby T: [958]-130-Q4.
Stensby T. & Co: [958]-130-Q4.
Stephens C: [959]-130.
Stephens H: [960]-130-Q4.
Sterling: [961]-130-Q4.
Stewart M.J: [962]-131.
Stiles Bros: [963]-131.
Stoakes A: [964]-131.
Stoakes K. & Co: 131.
Stockdale: [965]-131.
Stocker A.J. & Son: [966]-131-Q5.
Stocker C. & E: [966]-131-Q5.
Stocker F.E: [967]-131.
Stovin W: [968]-131.
Stowie: [969]-131.
Street J. & Sons: [970]-131-Q5.
Street R: [971]-132.
Strong J. & Son: [972]-132-Q5.
Stubbs W.A: 117.
Stuchbery's Stores (Thompson P. & S, Ltd): [973]-132-Q5.
Studley: [974]-132-Q5.
Suggs H.B: 148.
Swinfen J: [975]-124,132-Q5.
Sykes Bros: [976]-132-Q5.
Sykes R. & Sons, Ltd: [977]-132-Q5.
Tarr W: [978]-132-Q6.
Tarr W. & Son: [978]-64,132-Q6.
Tarrant E: [979]-132-Q6.
Taylor: [980]-132.
Taylor A.V: [981]-132,133-Q6.
Taylor C.H. & Son, Ltd: [982]-133.
Taylor J.T: [983]-133-Q8.
Taylor J.T. & Son: [983]-133-Q8.
Taylor S.R. & Sons, Ltd: [984]-133-Q6.
Taylor & Jones: [985]-133-Q6.
Temple & Co: [986]-133-Q6.
Temple & Portsmouth: 133.
Tett H.G: [987]-133.

Thacker & Co: [988]-133-Q8.
Thain E.W. & R: [989]-133.
Thompson Bros: [990]-133.
Thompson H: [991]-133.
Thompson P. & S, Ltd: 132.
Thorn & Son: [992]-133.
Thorne Bros: [993]-134.
Thorne W: [994]-134.
Thornley S, Ltd: [995]-134.
Thornycroft J.I. & Co: 21.
Thornycroft Steam Wagon Co: 21.
Thrasher F: [996]-134.
Thripland R. & Son: [997]-134-Q6.
Tickner W.J: [998]-134-Q6.
Tilbury G.S. & Jeffries F.A: [999]-134.
Till W.C, Ltd: [1000]-134-Q6.
Tilney R. & Son: [1001]-134-Q6.
Tily & Brown, Ltd: [1002]-134-Q6.
Tims F.H: [1003]-134-Q8.
Tinning J: [1004]-134-Q8.
Tisdall J: [1005]-134-Q8.
Tovey P: [1006]-135.
Towt-Tivy-Farmers: [1007]-135.
Tozer E: [1008]-135.
Trent Gun & Cartridge Works: [1009]-18,40,135-Q8,Q9.
Troughton S: [1010]-135-Q9.
Trulock Bros: [1011]-136.
Trulock & Harris (1): [1012]-136-Q9.
Trulock & Harris (2): [1013]-136.
Tucker J: [1014]-136-R1.
Tudge S: [1015]-136.
Tulloch W. & Co: [1016]-136.
Turnbull: [1017]-136.
Turner A: [1018]-136-R1.
Turner A. (Sheffield), Ltd: [1018]-97,136-R1.
Turner H.A: [1019]-136-R1.
Turner H.A, Ltd: [1019]-136-R1.
Turner J: [1020]-136-R1.
Turner T: [1021]-22,41.
Turner T. & Sons: [1021]-22,41,136,137,138,140,154-R1,R2,R3,R4.
Turner T. & Sons, Ltd: 22,41,136,137,138,140,154-R1,R2,R3,R4.
Turners Carbides, Ltd: [1022]-138]-78,138-R4.
Turvey F: [1023]-138.
Turvey F. & Sons: [1023]-138.
Twyble J.A: [1024]-138.
Tyler J: [1025]-138-R4.
Tyler J. (Highbridge), Ltd: [1025]-138-R4.
Uglow J: [1026]-138-R4.
Underhill: [1027]-138.
United Kingdom Cartridge Club (U.K.C.C.): [1028]-138,139-R4.
United States Cartridge Co (U.S.): 119,120.
Urquhart C. & J: [1029]-139-R4.
Urton W, Ltd: [1030]-139-R4.
Utting & Buckenham: [1031]-139.
Vale Agricultural: 91.
Vale Ironmongers: 91.
Varley W: [1032]-139.
Vaux J.C: [1033]-139-R4.

Venables J. & Son: [1034]-139-R4,R5.
Versey: [1035]-139.
Vickery F: [1036]-139.
Vincent Bros: [1037]-139.
Waddon J.H: [1038]-139-R5.
Waddon J. & Sons: [1039]-140.
Waddon & Sons (2): [1040]-140.
Wager & Sons: [1041]-140.
Wagstaff R.H. & Co: [1042]-22,140-R5.
Wakefield: [1043]-140.
Wales D: [1044]-140-R5.
Walker A.E. & A: [1045]-140.
Walker F.E: [1046]-140-R5.
Walker G.E: 140.
Walker J.B: [1047]-140-R5.
Walker R: [1048]-140.
Walker & Cooke: [1049]-140.
Walkington H: [1050]-141-R5.
Wallas D.H: [1051]-141-R5,R6.
Wallas W: [1052]-141-R6.
Wallis Bros: [1053]-141-R6.
Wallis Bros & Skemptons: [1054]-141.
Wallis & Steevens: 21.
Wanless & Co; [1055]-141.
Wanless Bros: [1056]-141-R6.
Wanless W: [1057]-141-R6.
War Agricultural Executive Committee (W.A.E.C.): 80.
Ward J. & Son: [1058]-141-R6.
Ward & Taylor: [1059]-142.
Ward Thompson A: [1060]-142-R6,R7.
Ward Thompson Bros: [1060]-142-R6,R7.
Waring E: [1061]-142-R7.
Warner H.P. & Son: [1062]-142-R7.
Warners: [1063]-142-R7.
Warren A.E: [1064]-142-R7.
Warren G.A: [1065]-142.
Warrick J: [1066]-142-R7.
Warrilow J.B: [1067]-142-R7.
Watkins & co: [1068]-142-R7.
Watkins T.J: [1068]-142-R7.
Watson Bros: [1069]-65,91,142,143-R7,R8.
Watson J. & Son: [1070]-143.
Watson J.R. & Co: [1071]-18,29,99,101,143-R8,R9.
Watson R: [1072]-143.
Watson Bracewell: [1073]-143-R9.
Webb: [1074]-143.
Webber J. & Sons: [1075]-143-R9.
Webber & Saunders: [1076]-143-R9.
Webbers: [1077]-143-R9.
Webley & Scott, Ltd: [1078]-143.
Webster G.R: [1079]-144-R9.
Websters: [1080]-144.
Wedgwood W.R: [1081]-144.
Weekes C. & Co: [1082]-144.
Weeks F: [1083]-144-R9.
Welch W.A: [1084]-144.
Wells H. & Son: [1085]-144-R9.
Welsh W: [1086]-144-S1.

West & Son (1): [1087]-144-S1.
West & Son (2): [1089]-144-S1.
West Mrs E: [1088]-144-S1.
West E: [1090]-145.
Westgate Estate: [1091]-145-S1.
Westley Richards & Co, Ltd: [1092]-145-S1,S2.
West London Shooting School: [1093]-145-S3.
Weston C. & A: [1094]-145-S3.
Weston C. & H: [1094]-145-S3.
Weston J: [1095]-145.
Whaley T. & Son: [1096]-145-S3.
Wheater J: [1097]-121,145.
White: [1098]-146-S3.
Whitehouse J.E: [1099]-146-S4.
Whitehouse J.E. & Sons: [1099]-146-S4.
Whiteman F.S: [1101]-146-S4.
Whitney H.H: [1102]-146.
Wholesale Arms & Ammunition Trading Co: [1103]-146.
Wilder: [1104]-146-S4.
Wildman H.W: [1105]-146-S4.
Wilkes J: [1106]-146-S4.
Wilkinson: [1107]-146-S4.
Wilkinson J. & Son: [1108]-146-S4.
Wilkinsons: [1109]-146-S4.
Willcocks J.W: [1110]-147-S4.
Williams C.D: [1111]-147-S4.
Williams E: [1112]-147.
Williams H: [1113]-147-S5.
Williams J.S: [1114]-147-S5.
Williams T.M: [1115]-147.
Williams & Powell: [1116]-147-S5.
Williamson: [1117]-147-S5.
Williamson & Son: [1117]-147-S5.
Williamson C: [1118]-147.
Williamson D (1): [1119]-147.
Williamson D (2): [1120]-147-S5.
Wilson E: [1121]-147.
Wilson F.K. & Co: [1122]-147-S5.
Wilson G: [1123]-148-S5.
Wilson G.H: [1124]-74,148.
Wilson J: [1126]-148-S5.
Wilson J. & Sons (1): [1125]-148-S5.
Wilson J. & Sons (2): [1126]-148-S5.
Wilson T. & Sons, Ltd: [1127]-148.
Wilton & Nicholls: [1128]-148.
Winchester Repeating Arms Co (W.R.A.Co.): 108,109.
Wise R: [1129]-148-S5.
Witchell W: [1130]-148.
Wood: [1131]-148.
Wood A: [1132]-148,149-S6.
Wood A. (Newport I.W.): [1132]-148,149-S6.
Wood F: [1133]-148-S6.
Wood G. & Co: [1134]-148.
Wood J.L: [1135]-149-S6.
Wood T.P. & Co: [1137]-149-S6.
Wood W.F: 149.
Wood & Horspool: [1136]-149-S6.
Wood Page & Co: [1138]-110,149.

Wooddisse & Desborough: [1139]-149.
Woodrow R.J: [1140]-149-S6.
Woodrow & Co, Ltd: [1141]-149.
Woods E: [1142]-149-S6.
Woods G.L: [1143]-109,149-S6.
Woods G.L. & Sons: [1143]-149-S6.
Woodward J. & Sons: [1144]-150-S7.
Wooliscroft R: [1145]-150-S7.
Wren G: [1146]-150-S7.
Wright J (1): [1147]-150.
Wright J (2): 150.
Wright R: [1148]-150-S7.
Wright & Currey: [1150]-150-S7.
Wrights: [1149]-150-S7.
Wylie A.B: [1151]-150-S7.
Young S. & Sons: [1152]-150.